Lecture Notes in Computer Science   11665

Commenced Publication in 1973
Founding and Former Series Editors:
Gerhard Goos, Juris Hartmanis, and Jan van Leeuwen

More information about this series at http://www.springer.com/series/7407

Michele Boreale · Flavio Corradini ·
Michele Loreti · Rosario Pugliese (Eds.)

Models, Languages, and Tools for Concurrent and Distributed Programming

Essays Dedicated to Rocco De Nicola
on the Occasion of His 65th Birthday

 Springer

Editors
Michele Boreale ⓘ
Department of Statistics, Computer Science,
Applications
University of Florence
Florence, Italy

Michele Loreti ⓘ
School of Science and Technology
University of Camerino
Camerino, Italy

Flavio Corradini
School of Science and Technology
University of Camerino
Camerino, Italy

Rosario Pugliese ⓘ
Department of Statistics, Computer Science,
Applications
University of Florence
Florence, Italy

ISSN 0302-9743   ISSN 1611-3349   (electronic)
Lecture Notes in Computer Science
ISBN 978-3-030-21484-5   ISBN 978-3-030-21485-2   (eBook)
https://doi.org/10.1007/978-3-030-21485-2

LNCS Sublibrary: SL1 – Theoretical Computer Science and General Issues

This Springer imprint is published by the registered company Springer Nature Switzerland AG
The registered company address is: Gewerbestrasse 11, 6330 Cham, Switzerland

Rocco De Nicola

Preface

This Festschrift volume contains the 27 papers written by close collaborators and friends of Rocco De Nicola to celebrate him on the occasion of his 65th birthday.

Rocco De Nicola has made seminal contributions to concurrency theory, semantics of programming languages, distributed systems, and logic in computer science. He is also contributing to a wide variety of other emerging topics in which theoretical foundations can have a tremendous effect on the practice of computing. His many scientific achievements are documented by more than 180 papers he published in international journals, proceedings of high-quality conferences and workshops, and refereed chapters in books with international editors.

The papers gathered in this book present many research ideas that have been influenced by Rocco's work. They testify to his intellectual curiosity, versatility, and tireless research activity, and provide an overview of further developments to come.

The volume consists of six sections. The first one contains a laudatio illustrating the distinguished career and the main scientific contributions by Rocco and a witness of working experiences with Rocco. The remaining five sections comprise scientific papers related to specific research interests of Rocco:

- Observational Semantics
- Coordination Models and Languages
- Logics and Types
- Distributed Systems Modelling
- Security

Each scientific contribution has undergone the scrutiny of two anonymous reviewers. We would like to thank all of them for their assistance.

This volume was presented to Rocco on July 1, 2019, during a two-day symposium held in Lucca at the IMT School for Advanced Studies. During the symposium all papers were presented by one of the authors. The symposium was attended by many other colleagues and friends of Rocco. We thank all of them for having accepted our invitation.

We are grateful to Mirco Tribastone and the System Modelling and Analysis group at IMT for the local organization of the symposium and to the IMT School for Advanced Studies for financial support. We would also like to thank Alfred Hofmann and the Springer LNCS team for their support during the publication of this volume, and the providers of the conference management system EasyChair, which was used to run the submission and review process and to facilitate the preparation of the proceedings.

People who have contributed to the present volume in honour of Rocco have had the opportunity to know him professionally over the years. Many have collaborated with him and in doing so have been fortunate to spend time with him. Each of us has taken something significant from this personal contact. Rocco was, and is, a true "scientific dad" for several of us and a loyal scientific collaborator for all of us. Passionate about research, curious about the new, never stinting with his knowledge or with his contacts, he has always stimulated new collaborations, both within and without his group. He has always encouraged the dignity and self confidence that any collaborator must have to work well. He made you feel you were a researcher 'at the same level' — part of a team, a real 'school for researchers' for younger colleagues. He could joke when he had to control excessive enthusiasm, be serious and rigorous when he had to arrive at the 'qed'. We have always appreciated his ability to transform competition within the group into a stimulus to do better, to grow faster. Thanks for everything, Rocco!

July 2019

Michele Boreale
Flavio Corradini
Michele Loreti
Rosario Pugliese

Organization

Reviewers

Abd Alrahman, Yehia
Aceto, Luca
Bernardi, Giovanni
Bettini, Lorenzo
Bodei, Chiara
Bruni, Roberto
Cacciagrano, Diletta Romana
Ciancia, Vincenzo
Corradini, Andrea
De Liguoro, Ugo
Dezani, Mariangiola
Fantechi, Alessandro
Ferrari, Gian-Luigi
Gadducci, Fabio
Galletta, Letterio
Giannini, Paola
Gorla, Daniele
Hennessy, Matthew
Inverso, Omar
Labella, Anna
Lanese, Ivan
Lluch Lafuente, Alberto

Massink, Mieke
Melgratti, Hernan
Mezzina, Claudio Antares
Miculan, Marino
Montanari, Ugo
Najm, Elie
Nenzi, Laura
Neykova, Rumyana
Palamidessi, Catuscia
Pérez, Jorge A.
Re, Barbara
Sangiorgi, Davide
Tesei, Luca
Tiezzi, Francesco
Torres Vieira, Hugo
Tribastone, Mirco
Trubiani, Catia
Tuosto, Emilio
Venneri, Betti
Viroli, Mirko
Zavattaro, Gianluigi

Contents

Security

Homage from Friends

From Tuscany to Scotland and Back

A Homage to Rocco de Nicola for His 65th Birthday

Ugo Montanari[✉]

Dipartimento di Informatica, University of Pisa, Pisa, Italy
ugo@di.unipi.it

1 Pisa and Milan

Rocco De Nicola graduated at the University of Pisa in *Scienze dell'Informazione* on December 1978 *summa cum laude*.

At the time there were few curricula in Italy with a substantial content of computer science, and Pisa 4-year *Scienze dell'Informazione* bachelor of science/master of science was among the first available ones (curricula in computer engineering started later). It was an exciting period: a special effort was going on about structuring the syllabi of the courses with respect: to foundational content; to rapidly growing research in proper computer science; and to professional abilities required for the degree holders.

PhD courses did not exist yet in Italy, in any discipline: they started for math, physics etc. *and* computer science ten years later.

The theoretical material about models of computation, including computability, automata and formal languages, program and programming language semantics, was taught in *Metodi per il Trattamento dell'Informazione*, a course with a peculiar name due to historical reasons. The organisation of the course was due mainly to Giuseppe Longo and myself.

Rocco was theoretically minded, and thus it was natural for him to ask me for a thesis. The results were eventually published in the paper *Communication Through Message Passing or Shared Memory: A Formal Comparison* presented at the *International Conference on Distributed Computing Systems* (ICDCS), Paris, 1981. The paper already discusses, quite informally, relevant issues about communicating processes, namely the subject of most of Rocco future work. Among the authors of the conference, there were names well known in a broad computer science context, like Manfred Broy, Michael J. Fischer, Matthew Hennessy, Tony Hoare, Leonard Kleinrock, Jeff Kramer, Nancy Lynch, Jeff Magee, Gordon Plotkin.

After a period spent in Pisa at IEI, the main CNR institute in computer science, where I also worked until 1976, Rocco was hired by ITALTEL, the main Italian company for telephones and telephone exchanges. He worked in Milan in a special group applying formal methods to telecommunication applications. While very appealing from a research point of view in an industrial context, the work he was carrying on in Milan was not matching Rocco's ambitions. Thus I encouraged him to apply for a PhD program abroad (remember that there were no PhD programs in Italy). Edinburgh proved actually to be a very good choice.

© Springer Nature Switzerland AG 2019
M. Boreale et al. (Eds.): De Nicola-Festschrift, LNCS 11665, pp. 3–6, 2019.
https://doi.org/10.1007/978-3-030-21485-2_1

2 Edinburgh

At the time, the University of Edinburgh was a leading research center in computer science and related areas. The worldwide IFIP Congress 1968, which took place at Edinburgh, was a showcase of already well developed *Mathematics* and *Software* research areas. In particular Edinburgh activity was especially strong in Artificial Intelligence: I had visited there for a period in 1974, for a collaboration with Bob Kowalski, Robert Boyer and J. Strother Moore about logic programming (*Algorithm = Logic + Control*).

When Rocco was there, the center of gravity of research had moved to the semantic aspects of theoretical computer science. In particular, Robin Milner and Gordon Plotkin had introduced in Edinburgh a *Calculus for Communicating Systems* (CCS) defined by a style called *Structural Operational Semantics* (SOS) and equipped with a congruence relation called *bisimilarity*.

More or less at the same time, also Tony Hoare had introduced at Oxford a specification language called *Communicating Sequential Processes* (CSP) equipped with a denotational semantics, and Jan Bergstra and Willem Klop had developed at Amsterdam a theory of processes (a *process algebra*) equipped with an equational theory of process cooperation. This line of development was very promising, and in fact a variety of process description languages with different definition styles were developed in the following decades, with an important impact on the design of specification and programming languages for concurrent distributed systems, of program verification via model checking and theorem proving, and of metamodels able to capture the essential semantic structure of process behavior, e.g. coalgebras and bialgebras.

Rocco studied the various proposals and eventually developed, with the collaboration of his PhD thesis advisor Matthew Hennessy, a different approach to process equivalence based on *testing*: given a set of processes and a set of tests, two processes are equivalent if they pass exactly the same set of tests. Nondeterminism and nontermination actually require two distinct notions of *may* and *must* test passing. For CCS, it is convenient to define a test on a process just as its parallel composition with a given process. These notions are very general and flexible, they have good properties as they originate fully abstract models and they were applied in the following years to a variety of process description languages.

3 True Concurrency

When back from Edinburgh, Rocco worked again at IEI and then in 1990 he obtained a full professor position in Rome. In this period I had the strongest collaboration with him. The subject was again about process description languages, but now the issue was *true concurrency*. Ordinary CCS does not distinguish between concurrency and nondeterminism, e.g. $a\,nil \mid b\,nil$ is equivalent to $ab\,nil + ba\,nil$. The issue was to equip languages with a more expressive semantics, assigning to events notions of causal dependency or mutual concurrency: in the latter case they can be executed in any order. Adequate notions of concurrency had been developed in the literature in the context of Petri nets, with prime algebraic semantic domains and prime event structures. Rocco, in collaboration with Pierpaolo Degano and myself (DDM!), defined a translation decomposing a CCS term p into a net marking $dec(p)$ and equipping it with firing sequences corresponding to transitions of p. Thus the final result was to obtain a concurrent semantics of CCS in terms of a prime algebraic domain. A further contribution of DDM was to equip CCS with an *abstract, concurrent* semantics, via bisimulation. The idea was to extend observations to partial ordering of events. However the resulting construction was not fully satisfactory in the presence of isomorphisms of the partial orderings. These can be avoided by adding a total ordering observation, obtaining a *mixed* ordering version. Equivalent constructions were proposed by Pierpaolo Degano and Philippe Darondeau (*causal trees*), and by Boris Trakhtenbrot and Alexander Rabinovich (*history preserving bisimilarity*).

The research on concurrency was supported by European Union with several ESPRIT projects. The project *Compositional DIStributed SYStems* (CEDISYS), 1988-91 was dedicated to true concurrency. It included four sites: Aarhus, INRIA Sophia Antipolis, Pisa, and Sussex. I was the project leader. Rocco contributed remarkably to project organization: for instance he took care of the *2nd Workshop on Concurrency and Compositionality* in San Miniato, where the results of the project were presented and evaluated by the ESPRIT-appointed reviewers.

In 1995 Rocco was offered a chair in Florence, where he started to build up his research group. Thus he was able to carry on more ambitious projects, which included the definition of original models of computation together with their type systems, their implementation, logics for proving their properties and model checking tools. I will mention only a few of them, those more relevant in my view, and closer to the main themes of his work.

4   KLAIM, CASPIS and AbC

One of Rocco's main achievements was the *Kernel Language for Agents Interaction and Mobility*, KLAIM. It consists of a core *Linda* with multiple tuple spaces and operators for building processes. Linda is a very simple coordination language developed at Yale by David Gelernter and colleagues, where processes cannot interact between them, but they can only read and write on an associative memory of tuples. In KLAIM, tuples and operations over them are located at specific sites of a net. Processes have higher-order capabilities, in that tuples may contain processes. KLAIM was supported by many projects, in particular by European project *Architectures for Mobility* (AGILE, 2002–2004), which also Pisa collaborated to.

Another important European project with contribution by Firenze and Pisa (actually the site leaders were Rocco and myself) was *Software ENgineering for Service-ORIented overlay computers*, SENSORIA, 2006–2010, which provided a novel software engineering approach to service-oriented computing. Again Rocco contribution, together with colleagues in Florence and Pisa, was to define a specialized language for services. It was called *Service Centered Calculus*, SCC, later renamed *CAlculus of Services with PIpelines and Sessions*, CASPIS. It is dataflow oriented and makes use of a pipelining operator to model the exchange of information between sessions (sequences of structured communications between two peers). Services are seen as passive objects that can be invoked by clients, and service definitions can be seen as specific instances of input prefixed processes. Pipelining permits orchestrating the flow of data produced by different sessions.

A more recent project was *Autonomic Service-Component ENSembles*. ASCENS, 2010–2014. Here service oriented programming has to cope with *Collective Adaptive Systems*, CAS. They consist of a large number of heterogeneous entities, with no centralized control and with the ability to adapt to changes in their coordination structure and in the environment. The main contribution has been to define the software life cycle of these mutable systems. As in the previous projects, Rocco contributed defining a calculus for attribute-based communication: *Attribute-based Communication*, AbC. It is a communication paradigm that permits a group of partners to communicate by considering the predicates over the attributes they expose. Communication takes place anonymously in an implicit multicast fashion, without a prior agreement between the communicating partners. A number of case studies show the generality and the flexibility of such an approach.

5   IMT, Lucca

Rocco contributed to several other research areas, both theoretical and practical. His scientific production is impressive in its quality and considering the number of citations: he is member of Gruppo 2003, which includes the Italian scientists appearing in the lists of the most cited scientific authors according to the Institute for Scientific Information (ISI). But what I want to emphasize the most, looking at his activity, is the rigorous methodology he adopted in his approach to distributed systems: (i) focus on a few key features of the class of applications of interest; (ii) define a process description language embedding basic primitives for programming such features; (iii) program by hand a few case studies; (iv) implement a prototypical version; (v) define a logic for expressing the interesting properties of the applications under scrutiny. As shown by the results, this approach is very effective.

Starting from 2011, Rocco moved to IMT School for Advanced Studies, Lucca, a recently established public research institution and a selective graduate school, where, starting from 2005, I had helped to organize the PhD school in computer science. IMT and University of Pisa are now collaborating in a number of initiatives, with Rocco playing often a leading role.

My last remark is about Rocco's activity as a nurturer: from the beginning of his career he taught a number of young students and associates how to progress in research. Several of them have now important responsabilities in the Italian and European teaching and research community, e.g. Director of the Executive Board of a professional institution or even University Rector.

Building International Doctoral Schools in Computer Science in Italy, De Nicola's Way

Luca Aceto[1,2], Gianlorenzo D'Angelo[1], Michele Flammini[1],
Omar Inverso[1], Ludovico Iovino[1], and Catia Trubiani[2(✉)]

[1] Gran Sasso Science Institute, L'Aquila, Italy
{gianlorenzo.dangelo,michele.flammini,
omar.inverso,ludovico.iovino}@gssi.it
[2] School of Computer Science, Reykjavik University, Reykjavik, Iceland
luca@ru.is, catia.trubiani@gssi.it

Abstract. Rocco De Nicola has played a key role in establishing two international PhD schools in computer science in Italy, one at IMT Lucca and the other at the GSSI in L'Aquila. This short article describes some of the principles that have guided the establishment of the doctoral programmes at those institutions and the lessons the authors have learnt by working with Rocco De Nicola at the GSSI.

Keywords: Research education · PhD in computer science · Mentoring

1 Introduction

The work of an academic has many facets and involves an increasing number of tasks. However, most academics would agree that the 'core business' in academia is centred on research, teaching and service. Rocco De Nicola's research impact is covered abundantly in the other articles in this celebrative volume and his research is well known to everyone working on topics related to concurrency theory, programming-language semantics and distributed computing. His teaching impact, broadly construed, is witnessed amongst other things by the courses at Italian universities, covering the denotational and operational semantics of programming languages, that are based on, or use, the textbook he co-authored with Adolfo Piperno [2], and by the number of his master and doctoral students who have had successful careers in academia and industry.

Rocco De Nicola has also served his research community in many ways over the years, both nationally and internationally, and has received many recognitions for his tireless service. To wit, we limit ourselves to mentioning that he has been one of the prime movers in raising public awareness of the importance of cybersecurity in Italy—see, for instance, the book [1].

In this short article, we will describe Rocco De Nicola's key role in the establishment of two international doctoral programmes in computer science in Italy

© Springer Nature Switzerland AG 2019
M. Boreale et al. (Eds.): De Nicola-Festschrift, LNCS 11665, pp. 7–12, 2019.
https://doi.org/10.1007/978-3-030-21485-2_2

at two separate centres for advanced studies, discuss the importance of those enterprises for Italian computer science, and academia in general, and reflect on the main principles underlying the design of those PhD programmes and on the lessons we think we have learnt by working with Rocco De Nicola on laying their foundations and on developing them.

Our tenet is that the establishment of international doctoral schools in computer science is one of the most important contributions by Rocco De Nicola to Italian academia and we hope that this article will convince our readers of that claim.

1.1 The Cultural Context

Before discussing Rocco De Nicola's contributions to the GSSI and IMT Lucca, we find it appropriate to provide a brief description of the context within which those two international doctoral schools operate.

Italy is home to six centres for advanced studies and international PhD schools, namely the Gran Sasso Science Institute (GSSI) in L'Aquila[1], IMT Lucca[2], IUSS in Pavia[3], Sant'Anna[4] and the Scuola Normale Superiore[5] in Pisa, and SISSA in Trieste[6]. One of the roles of those centres for graduate education is to entice talented students from all over the world to carry out their research in Italy, a country that, for many reasons, has found it difficult to attract and retain foreign academics and students. To our mind, this is one of the main reasons why graduate schools that must admit a good number of non-Italian students and that have English as their working language have an important role to play in the Italian academic ecosystem. By attracting talented students and researchers from outside Italy, as well as Italian academics whose career has been largely spent abroad, these schools contribute to bringing fresh ideas and approaches into a research community that has often been perceived as inward-looking, and are a first step towards a brain-gain strategy for a country that has so far mostly been known for exporting well-educated workforce without a matching incoming flow of talent.

Amongst the aforementioned schools, the GSSI and IMT Lucca are the only ones that offer PhD programmes in computer science (in the case of IMT Lucca in computer science and system engineering), whereas the Sant'Anna and the Scuola Normale Superiore in Pisa have specific PhD lines in data science. Both the computer science PhD programmes at the GSSI and at IMT have been shaped by Rocco De Nicola and bear witness to his far-sighted approach and his international experience. In what follows, we will focus on describing Rocco De Nicola's vision for the PhD programme in computer science at the GSSI,

---

[1] http://www.gssi.it/.

[2] https://www.imtlucca.it/.

[3] http://www.iusspavia.it/home.

[4] https://www.santannapisa.it/en.

[5] https://en.sns.it/.

[6] https://www.sissa.it/.

which is the one we know best, and how his style of leadership has influenced the development of that programme and the academic growth of the faculty at the institute.

2   Structuring an International PhD Programme in Computer Science at the GSSI

The Gran Sasso Science Institute (GSSI) is an international research centre and PhD school, which was founded in 2013 with the objective of revitalising the city of L'Aquila after the strong earthquake it experienced in 2009. The GSSI was initially established on a trial basis as an international postgraduate teaching and research institute with a special statute, and became a permanent university in 2016 after receiving a positive assessment by the Italian National Agency of the University System Evaluation and Research (ANVUR).

Rocco De Nicola was appointed as coordinator of the International PhD Programme in Computer Science at the GSSI for the first three years and, in this role, he paved the way for the current research and teaching activities. The PhD programme offers courses that, on the one hand, provide incoming students with the necessary formal background and, on the other, offer specialised courses to introduce students to the newest developments in the areas of reactive systems, software systems and complex networks. During the first year, students are exposed to courses that are organised around three main pillars: (i) Foundations of (Modern) Networks; (ii) Specification and Analysis of Concurrent Reactive Systems; (iii) Software Systems and Services. Apart from internal GSSI courses, students are encouraged to take classes also at summer schools or at other institutions in Italy or abroad. Each student has to prepare, together with the coordinator of the PhD programme, a study plan to be approved by the Scientific Board. Performance in the course exams and the quality of the thesis proposal (submitted at the end of the first year) are the main criteria for deciding admission to the second year. The remaining years of the PhD programme are mainly dedicated to research. Students are assisted by a supervisor and their progress is assessed by an advisory board consisting of experts in the relevant area of their scientific interests. Students are also strongly encouraged to spend part of their research studies at external research laboratories in Italy or abroad.

The GSSI offers three types of courses. First, so-called *immigration* courses aim at providing basic knowledge on each of the three pillars mentioned above. Such courses target the acquisition of fundamental techniques, methods and skills needed to conduct research in computer science in later years. Second, the *core* courses offer in-depth accounts of topics that are of central interest to the PhD programme at the GSSI, and expose doctoral students to the main research areas within the specific pillars. Third, the *advanced* courses focus on specific, cutting-edge research topics and are of shorter duration than the core courses. Immigration and core courses are mainly delivered by GSSI faculty members, while advanced courses are typically given by top-notch external researchers coming from well-respected universities or research institutes. Guest lecturers and seminar speakers from outside the GSSI and the many foreign visitors allow students enrolled in the PhD programme in computer science at the GSSI to network with, and to learn from, high-class academics; these frequent guests help to create a vibrant research environment at the institute that benefits both its students and faculty members.

3   The De Nicola Lessons on Establishing a Graduate School and a Centre for Advanced Studies

We are now at a stage in our article at which we are ready to step back and reflect on the underlying principles on which the design of the PhD programme in computer science at the GSSI is based. (To our mind, the one at IMT Lucca follows similar principles.) We will try to distill them in the form of 'lessons' we have learnt from Rocco De Nicola, hoping he will not strongly disagree with any of them.

Lesson 1: It is All About the Students. This might seem a platitude, but the success of a PhD school is measured by the achievements of its students during their PhD programme and, most importantly, after they graduate. Attending a PhD school like the GSSI should turn students into independent researchers, providing a solid foundation that will allow them to achieve their goals for the future and to pursue the challenging careers for which they trained. To our mind, this means that a PhD school should offer each committed student the chance to carry out the best research work of which they are capable on some topic that has a reasonable connection with both the interests of some faculty member and those of the student. There is very little point in considering a student as a resource to carry out some research task within one's own project if he/she is not interested in that specific research topic. We all know by experience that doing research is hard work, which requires motivation, dedication and stamina amongst many other things. Those are difficult to muster if one's heart is somewhere else, research-wise at least.

In the daily practice of supervising students, one should try to understand what makes them tick, getting them interested in one's own research topics, providing them with the 'big picture view' of the field they lack as budding academics and finding a suitable middle ground when possible. Rocco De Nicola has been an example for us in the difficult art of student supervision. His broad array of interests has allowed him to supervise successful theses in a variety of topics in computer science. To wit, the list of his published papers in 2018 includes work related to evaluating the efficiency of Linda implementations, blockchain, models and languages for verified multi-robot systems, attribute-based communication in a variety of languages, scheduling in edge computing, formal methods for engineering domain-specific distributed systems, models and analysis techniques for collective adaptive systems, and the analysis of social networks such as Twitter, amongst others. He has often gone out of his way to find suitable external supervisors when he did not think he was sufficiently qualified to follow the work of some student on a specific topic of great interest to her/him.

Lesson 2: Level the Playing Field. An international PhD school, such as the one at the GSSI, admits students from all over the world. These students are all talented and motivated. However, one cannot assume that their computer science background is uniform and covers the basic material that is needed to undertake research work in the areas covered by the faculty at the GSSI. To create a shared computer science culture, Rocco De Nicola decided to devote roughly the first two months of the PhD programme in computer science at the GSSI to three so-called *immigration courses.* The goal of those courses is 'to level the playing field' by introducing fundamental topics in algorithmics, formal methods and software engineering that provide the foundations for the material covered in core and advanced courses.

Lesson 3: Give Early Independence to Young Researchers. A centre for advanced studies and international PhD school like the GSSI should be a training ground for future generations of research leaders. As an experienced academic with an international outlook, Rocco De Nicola realised early on that junior academics at the GSSI need to become independent in their research, set themselves research goals that are both ambitious and reachable, and basically act as principal investigators. He has involved them in joint supervision of doctoral theses, encouraged them to build an international network of collaborators, taking advantage of the freedom to invite potential collaborators they have at the GSSI, and given them the responsibility of the day-to-day management of the PhD programme. He provided advice and guidance as needed, and was always ready to take action at short notice, but the junior researchers in L'Aquila were empowered by the responsibility they were given and grew into mature academics in the process.

Lesson 4: Build a Cooperative Research Environment. Rocco De Nicola firmly believes that research advances through cooperation, not through competition. His pragmatism, open-mindedness and unique ability to connect with people has enabled a large number of scientific collaborations. According to his DBLP page[7], Rocco De Nicola has had over 135 co-authors, but he has collaborated with many more researchers both through funded joint research projects and in the course of informal research interactions. As mentioned above, his mentoring and collaboration style is characterised by entrusting and empowerment.

Lesson 5: The Human Side Matters. One of the things that stands out the most when interacting with Rocco De Nicola is his care for human relationships in the management of a research group. He works very hard at building a collegial spirit and at human resource management. He is always ready to crack a joke to put the ups and downs of research life into perspective, and treats everyone on an equal footing, be they first-year students or Turing Award recipients. He gives young researchers the feeling that their opinions matter when discussing research and invites them to present their work to distinguished guests and to participate in social activities. To our mind, this is an important skill for a research leader

---

[7] https://dblp.uni-trier.de/pers/hd/n/Nicola:Rocco_De.

and we hope that we have learnt to practise it a little by watching a master like Rocco De Nicola at work.

4   Conclusions

Rocco De Nicola's impact on the career development of many researchers in computer science has been huge, both in Italy and elsewhere. However, as described in this short essay, we believe that the establishment of the international PhD schools in computer science at the GSSI and at IMT Lucca will be one of his lasting legacies to Italian academia. The success of those postgraduate schools has been possible because of Rocco De Nicola's human, leadership and scientific qualities, some of which we have highlighted here. There is, of course, much more that we have learnt from him; we have no doubt that he will continue to lead the community by example and to inspire future generations of researchers.

Acknowledgments. We have all worked with Rocco De Nicola in the establishment of the PhD school in computer science at the GSSI and thank him for his guidance, and inspirational and friendly leadership. Luca Aceto was one of the first two students who graduated under Rocco De Nicola's supervision and still greatly appreciates his advice on all matters. Omar Inverso and Catia Trubiani thank Rocco De Nicola for joint research work and joint supervision of doctoral students.

References

1. Baldoni, R., De Nicola, R., Prinetto, P.: The Future of Cybersecurity in Italy: strategic focus areas. CINI Cybersecurity National Lab, May 2018. https://www.consorzio-cini.it/images/Libro-Bianco-2018-en.pdf
2. De Nicola, R., Piperno, A.: Semantica Operazionale e Denotazione dei Linguaggi di Programmazione. CittàStudi (1999). (in Italian)

Observational Semantics

An Equational Characterisation
of the Must Testing Pre-order
for Regular Processes

Matthew Hennessy$^{(\boxtimes)}$

Trinity College Dublin, Dublin, Ireland
matthew.hennessy@cs.tcd.ie

Abstract. In his PhD thesis of 1985 Rocco De Nicola showed how the
*must testing **pre-order*** over the process calculus *CCS* can be captured
using a set of *in-equations* and an infinitary proof rule. We show how, at
least for regular processes, this infinitary rule is unnecessary. We present
a standard proof system, which uses a simple co-inductive rule, which is
both sound and complete for regular processes.

1   Introduction

In his PhD thesis, *Testing Equivalences and Fully Abstract Models for Communicating Processes* [4], Rocco gave a systematic account of certain behavioural
pre-orders over processes. I am quite familiar with the contents of this thesis,
as I had the great pleasure of being Rocco's PhD supervisor. The main focus
there, and in some joint papers we wrote around the same time, was judgements
of the form

$$p \sqsubseteq_{\text{must}} q \tag{1}$$

where p, q are recursive process descriptions from a Turing-complete abstract
process language CCS. This pre-order is meant to capture the idea that any
external *test* guaranteed by p is also guaranteed by q; intuitively q is at least as
reliable as p. In his thesis Rocco gave three characterisations of this pre-order[1]:
(i) behavioural: using intensional behavioural properties of the processes; (ii)
denotational: using fully-abstract mathematical models; and (iii) in-equational:
using a collection of in-equational axioms satisfied by the pre-order (1) above.
In this short note we reconsider this last characterisation.

  For convenience and simplicity we use a variation on CCS which contains an
explicit operator for internal choice $\oplus$ and one for external choice $+$, [3,5,8]. Thus
for example $\text{REC}x.a.x + b.(c.x \oplus d.x)$ is a recursive process which continually
offers an (external) choice between the two actions a and b. If the latter is chosen

---

[1] and some variations.

This work was supported with the financial support of the Science Foundation Ireland
grant 13/RC/2094, funding Lero – the Irish Software Research Centre.

© Springer Nature Switzerland AG 2019
M. Boreale et al. (Eds.): De Nicola-Festschrift, LNCS 11665, pp. 15–27, 2019.
https://doi.org/10.1007/978-3-030-21485-2_3

then it chooses internally whether to subsequently offer a c or a d. There is a well-known collection of in-equations which capture precisely the pre-order (1) for recursion-free processes; Rocco's thesis contains a corresponding collection for recursion-free CCS. The core collection for our language is reproduced in Fig. 3, with typical examples including

$$X \oplus Y \leq X \qquad\qquad X \oplus Y \leq X + Y \qquad\qquad a.X \oplus a.Y \leq a.(X + Y)$$

The question we address here is how this in-equational characterisation can be extended to recursive processes.

In Rocco's thesis [4], and in [2,5], in-equational reasoning has been augmented with rules for unwinding recursive processes, and an **infinitary** proof rule to obtain a sound and (ground) complete system for arbitrary recursive processes. This latter takes the form

$$\frac{d \leq q, \ \forall d \in \mathsf{Fin}(p)}{p \leq q} \quad \text{(General Recursion)}$$

where $\mathsf{Fin}(p)$ is the set, usually infinite, of *finite approximations* to p.[2] Intuitively these finite approximations are recursion-free processes obtained by unwinding all occurrences of recursive definitions in p; see page 82 of [4]. Thus to prove $p \leq q$ in this proof system, it is necessary to prove an infinite set of judgements, $d \leq q$ for each d in $\mathsf{Fin}(p)$, using in-equational reasoning; q may have occurrences of recursion, which can be handled by suitable unwinding rules.

For CCS, the process language used in [4], a non-effective proof rule such as (General Recusion) is necessary to obtain completeness, since CCS is Turing-complete. However suppose we consider the more restrictive sub-language, of *regular* processes; this corresponds essentially to a language for describing finite automata. For such a language we should be able to forgo such non-effective rules.

Effective characterisations for various behavioural **equivalences** have long been known, using sets of equations augmented by a rule called *Unique fixpoint induction*:[3]

$$\frac{t\{x \mapsto q\} = q}{\mathsf{REC}x.t = q} \quad (\text{U}_{\text{FI}})$$

For classical examples see [9–12]. However the corresponding rule for **pre-orders**, *Fixpoint induction*,

$$\frac{t\{x \mapsto q\} \leq q}{\mathsf{REC}x.t \leq q} \quad (\text{F}_{\text{I}})$$

appears to be substantially weaker; see [6] for a discussion.

Instead in this paper we show that it is sufficient to augment standard in-equational reasoning with a single proof rule, co-inductive in nature, to obtain a

---

[2] Because of space considerations we omit the formal definition.

[3] For soundness the variable x in body t should be *guarded*.

$$\frac{}{a.p \xrightarrow{a} p} \text{(A-Pre)} \qquad\qquad \frac{}{\text{REC}x.t \xrightarrow{\tau} t\{x \mapsto \text{REC}x.t\}} \text{(Rec)}$$

$$\frac{p \xrightarrow{\mu} p'}{p + q \xrightarrow{\mu} p'} \text{(Ext-L)} \qquad\qquad \frac{q \xrightarrow{\mu} q'}{p + q \xrightarrow{\mu} q'} \text{(Ext-R)}$$

$$\frac{}{p \oplus q \xrightarrow{\tau} p} \text{(Int-L)} \qquad\qquad \frac{}{p \oplus q \xrightarrow{\tau} q} \text{(Int-R)}$$

Fig. 1. Operational semantics

sound and complete proof system for the **pre-order** judgements $p \precsim_{\text{must}} q$ over regular processes. The rule was originally introduced in [6], which in turn was heavily influenced by [1].

In the next section we define our language for regular processes, rCCS; we recall its semantics, review the notion of testing pre-orders, and give the well-known alternative characterisation of $\precsim_{\text{must}}$. In Sect. 3 we explain our proof system, and give two examples of it's use. This is followed by two sections, one devoted to *soundness* of the system and the other to *completeness*.

2   Regular Processes and Testing

2.1   The Language

The language of recursive terms we use is a cut down version of TCCS from [3], and is given by the following grammar:

$$\text{rCCS}: \qquad t ::= 0 \mid a.t, a \in \text{Act} \mid t_1 + t_2 \mid t_1 \oplus t_2$$
$$\mid x \in \text{Var} \mid \text{REC}x.t$$

where Act is a pre-defined set of actions. Thus rCCS essentially consists of recursive definitions over the alphabet $\Sigma = \{0, a.-, -+-, -\oplus-\}$. We assume all occurrences of the variable x in t are *bound* in the term $\text{REC}x.t$, and this leads to the standard notion of *free* and *bound* variables. We are only interested in *closed terms*, those not containing any free variables, which we refer to as *processes*. For the sake of simplicity we will also assume that all terms of the form $\text{REC}x.t$ are *guarded*; that is every occurence of x in the body of the recursion t appears underneath an external prefix $a.-$.

The (standard) operational semantics of processes is given in Fig. 1, with judgements for transitions of the form $p \xrightarrow{\mu} q$, where μ ranges over $\text{Act}_\tau = \text{Act} \uplus \{\tau\}$. The rule (Rec) uses the standard notion of substitution: in general $t\{x \mapsto p\}$ represents the result of substituting all free occurrences of the variable x in the term t by the *closed* term p. This may be defined by structural induction on t.

$$\frac{p \xrightarrow{\tau} p'}{p \parallel q \longrightarrow p' \parallel q} \ \text{(L-TAU)} \qquad\qquad \frac{q \xrightarrow{\tau} q'}{p \parallel q \longrightarrow p \parallel q'} \ \text{(R-TAU)}$$

$$\frac{p \xrightarrow{a} p', \ q \xrightarrow{\bar{a}} q'}{p \parallel q \longrightarrow p' \parallel q'} \ \text{(COM)}$$

Fig. 2. Interaction

2.2   Testing

To facilitate the definition of testing we assume that the set of actions Act has an idempotent operation, mapping the action a to it's complement $\bar{a}$. Then communication is the simultaneous occurrence of an action and it's complement.

Interaction between processes p and q is defined as a transition of the form $p \parallel q \longrightarrow p' \parallel q'$, with the rules given in Fig. 2. A *test* is a process which in addition to the standard actions Act_τ is allowed to perform the special action $\checkmark$, signifying that the application of the test has succeeded.

Definition 1 (Passing tests). *We write p must t whenever, for every maximal sequence of transitions*

$$p \parallel t \, (= p_0 \parallel t_0) \longrightarrow p_1 \parallel t_1 \longrightarrow \ldots \longrightarrow p_k \parallel t_k \longrightarrow \ldots$$

there exists some $n \geq 0$ such that $t_n \xrightarrow{\checkmark}$[4]. Then we write $p \sqsubseteq_{must} p'$ if p must t implies p' must t, for every test t.

2.3   Characterisation

This requires some notation. The transitions in Fig. 1 are generalised to *weak transitions* of the form $p \xRightarrow{s} q$, where s ranges over Act^* as follows:

- $p \xRightarrow{\varepsilon} p$
- $p \xrightarrow{a} p', \ p' \xRightarrow{s} q$ imply $p \xRightarrow{as} q$
- $p \xrightarrow{\tau} p', \ p' \xRightarrow{s} q$ imply $p \xRightarrow{s} q$

Definition 2 (Acceptance sets). *First for any process p let $S(p) = \{ a \in \text{Act} \mid p \xrightarrow{a} \}$. Then we define $\mathcal{A}(p, s)$, the acceptance sets of p after $s \in \text{Act}^*$, by*

$$\mathcal{A}(p, s) = \{ S(p') \mid p \xRightarrow{s} p' \xrightarrow{\tau} \!\!\!\!\! / \ \}$$

Because p is a process from the regular language rCCS we are assured that $\mathcal{A}(p, s)$ is a finite set of finite sets of actions.

Then we write $p \ll q$ if, for every $s \in \text{Act}^*$, for every $A \in \mathcal{A}(q, s)$, there exists some $B \in \mathcal{A}(p, s)$ such that $B \subseteq A$.   □

---

[4] A maximal sequence may be finite or infinite.

$$
\begin{array}{lll}
X + X = X & X + Y = Y + X & X + (Y + Z) = (X + Y) + Z \\
X \oplus X = X & X \oplus Y = Y \oplus X & X \oplus (Y \oplus Z) = (X \oplus Y) \oplus Z \\
a.(X + Y) = a.X \oplus a.Y & X + (Y \oplus Z) = (X + Y) \oplus (X + Z) & \\
a.(X \oplus Y) = a.X \oplus a.Y & X \oplus (Y + Z) = (X \oplus Y) + (X \oplus Z) & \\
X + 0 = X & X \oplus Y \leq X &
\end{array}
$$

Fig. 3. Axioms for must testing, **MA**

Theorem 1. *For all $p, q \in$ rCCS, $p \precsim_{must} q$ if and only if $p \ll q$.*

Proof. A slight simplification of the corresponding standard results in papers such as [2,3,5].

3   The Proof System for the Testing Prorder

Consider the well-known set of in-equations in Fig. 3; formally the equations, such as $X + X = X$, are abbreviations for two in-equations, such as $X + X \leq X$ and $X \leq X + X$. These, or slight variations due to difference in syntax, have been used in publications such as [2–5,7]; it is well-known that they provide a sound and (ground) complete set of in-equations for finite rCCS, that is processes which do not use recursion; see for example [3,5].

Our proof system uses in-equational reasoning with this set of in-equations. It has judgements of the form

$$
A \vdash p \leq p'
$$

where p, p' are processes and A is a *finite set* of assumptions, each of which takes the form $a.p_1 \leq a.p_2$, for some $a \in$ Act. The rules for forming proof trees are given in Fig. 4. We have (INEQ) for instantiating in-equations, (SUB) for substitution into contexts, together with (ID), (TR); in short standard in-equational reasoning over processes. We also have two standard rules (UFD) and (FLD) for unfolding and folding recursive definitions, and two obvious rules for managing assumptions, (HYP) and (W). The novel rule is (COREC); We call this a *coinductive* rule because the conclusion of the rule is one of assumptions in the hypothesis. This of course makes it's soundness problematic; see the discussion in the next section.

Let us write $\vdash_{mst} A \vdash p \leq p'$ to mean that there is a valid proof tree with conclusion $A \vdash p \leq p'$; that is a proof tree constructed using the rules in Fig. 4, using the set of in-equations just outlined. We abbreviate $\vdash_{mst} \emptyset \vdash p \leq p'$ to $\vdash_{mst} p \leq p'$. We also use $p \leq_{ineq} p'$ to mean that p may be rewritten to p' using this set of in-equations. More specifically, in the rewriting all the rules in Fig. 4 may be used, except (HYP),(W) and (COREC).

Example 1. Let r_1, r_2 denote REC$x.a.x \oplus b.x$, REC$x.a.x + b.x$ respectively. Our aim is to prove $\vdash_{mst} r_1 \leq r_2$ by showing how to construct a valid proof tree for the judgement $\vdash r_1 \leq r_2$. First note that $X \oplus Y \leq X + Y$ is a derived axiom from

$$\frac{}{\vdash p \leq p} \; (\text{ID}) \qquad\qquad \frac{A \vdash p_1 \leq p_2, \; A \vdash p_2 \leq p_3}{A \vdash p_1 \leq p_3} \; (\text{TR})$$

$$\frac{A \vdash p_i \leq p_i', \; 0 \leq i \leq n}{A \vdash f(p_0, \dots, p_n)} \; (\text{SUB}) \qquad\qquad \frac{\langle p, p' \rangle \in \mathsf{Ins}(\mathbf{InEq})}{A \vdash p \leq p'} \; (\text{INEQ})$$

$$\frac{}{\vdash \text{REC}x.t \leq t\{x \mapsto \text{REC}x.t\}} \; (\text{UFD}) \qquad\qquad \frac{}{\vdash t\{x \mapsto \text{REC}x.t\} \leq \text{REC}x.t} \; (\text{FLD})$$

$$\frac{}{p \leq p' \vdash p \leq p'} \; (\text{HYP}) \qquad\qquad \frac{B \vdash p \leq p', \; A \supseteq B}{A \vdash p \leq p'} \; (\text{W})$$

$$\boxed{\frac{A, a.p \leq a.p' \vdash p \leq p'}{A \vdash a.p \leq a.p'} \; (\text{CoREC})}$$

Fig. 4. The proof system

those in Fig. 3. So if we were allowed to apply axioms to open terms, and had substitutivity under $\text{REC}x.-$, then the derivation would be trivial. Unfortunately the proof system in Fig. 4 only manipulates processes, that is closed terms.

As a first step let us show how the judgement

$$a.r_1 \leq a.r_2 \vdash b.r_1 \leq b.r_2 \tag{2}$$

can be derived. Using the new rule (CoREC) this will follow from the judgement $a.r_1 \leq a.r_2, b.r_1 \leq b.r_2 \vdash r_1 \leq r_2$. By unwinding the recursive definitions this amounts to deriving $a.r_1 \leq a.r_2, b.r_1 \leq b.r_2 \vdash a.r_1 \oplus b.r_1 \leq a.r_2 + b.r_2$. However this is straightforward, using two instances of (HYP), substitutivity and the derived axiom mentioned above.

Armed with a derivation of (2) above we can now construct, using (HYP), substitutivity and the derived axiom, a derivation for $a.r_1 \leq a.r_2 \vdash a.r_1 \oplus b.r_1 \leq a.r_2 + b.r_2$; then, using (UFD), (FLD), this gives a derivation of $a.r_1 \leq a.r_2 \vdash r_1 \leq r_2$. By (CoREC) this leads to a derivation of

$$\vdash a.r_1 \leq a.r_2$$

Similar reasoning can be used to show that the judgement $\vdash b.r_1 \leq b.r_2$ can be derived. From these two derivations we can now easily construct a derivation of $\vdash r_1 \leq r_2$, using (UFD), (FLD), the derived axiom and substitutivity. In other words $\vdash_{\mathsf{mst}} r_1 \leq r_2$. $\qquad\square$

Example 2. Let r_3, r_4 denote $\text{REC}x.a.x + b.(c.x \oplus d.x)$, $\text{REC}x.a.(a.x + b.d.x) + b.c.x$ respectively. The process r_3 repeatedly offers the actions a and b, and after the latter internally decides whether to offer c or d. On the other hand r_4 also repeatedly offers a and b, but after the latter alternatively offers either c or d.

We prove $\vdash_{\mathsf{mst}} r_3 \leq r_4$ by showing how to construct a valid proof tree for the judgement $\vdash r_3 \leq r_4$. For convenience we use B_3, B_4 denote the initial unwindings $a.r_3 + b.(c.r_3 \oplus d.r_3)$, $a.(a.r_4 + b.d.r_4) + b.c.r_4$ respectively. It will be sufficient to show how to construct a valid proof tree for

$$\vdash B_3 \leq B_4 \tag{3}$$

First let us consider the hypothesis $a.r_3 \leq a.(a.r_4 + b.d.r_4)$, which for convenience we denote by H. This turns out to be quite strong. For example,

$$H \vdash c.r_3 \leq c.r_4 \tag{4}$$

because by an application of (COREC) this reduces to $H, c.r_3 \leq c.r_4 \vdash r_3 \leq r_4$. This in turn follows from an application of (HYP), the unwinding of recursive definitions, together with some elementary in-equational reasoning; an application here of the in-equation $X \oplus Y \leq X$ is essential.

With an application of (4) we can now derive $H \vdash r_3 \leq r_4$ as can be seen by again unwinding the recursive definitions. Applying substitutivity, and the in-equation $X \oplus Y \leq X$, this leads to (a derivation of) $H \vdash r_3 \leq a.r_4 + b.d.r_4$, again by unwinding r_3. Finally an application of (COREC) gives

$$\vdash a.r_3 \leq a.(a.r_4 + b.d.r_4) \tag{5}$$

Now let us turn our attention to constructing a valid proof tree for (3) above, as required. By substitutivity, and an application of (5) this is reduced to finding a valid proof tree for $\vdash b.(c.r_3 \oplus d.r_3) \leq b.c.r_4$. In turn, using substitutivity and elementary in-equational reasoning this amounts to considering $\vdash c.r_3 \leq c.r_4$.

Because of (COREC) we need to derive $c.r_3 \leq c.r_4 \vdash r_3 \leq r_4$, which by unwinding reduces to $c.r_3 \leq c.r_4 \vdash a.r_3 + b.(c.r_3 \oplus d.r_4) \leq a.(a.r_4 + b.d.r_4) + b.c.r_4$. However this will follow because of (5), using (HYP) and substitutivity. $\square$

4   Soundness

To prove soundness of the proof system we need a semantic interpretation of the judgements $A \vdash p \leq p'$ which is preserved by all instances of the proof rules. As explained in [6] the obvious choice is unsound. For completeness we re-iterate the counter-example.

Example 3. Let us write

$$p_1 \leq p'_1, \ldots p_k \leq p'_k \vDash^w p \leq p', \text{ for } k \geq 0,$$

if $p_1 \lesssim_{\text{must}} p'_1, \ldots, p_k \lesssim_{\text{must}} p'_k$ implies $p \lesssim_{\text{must}} p'$.

Unfortunately this is not preserved by the rule (COREC). An instance of this rule is

$$\frac{a.b.0 \leq a.0 \vdash b.0 \leq 0}{\vdash a.b.0 \leq a.0}$$

Note that the premise is (vacuously) semantically valid, $a.b.\,0 \leq a.\,0 \vDash^w b.\,0 \leq 0$, because $a.b.\,0 \not\lesssim_{\text{must}} a.\,0$. However the conclusion is not semantically valid, $\not\vDash^w a.b.\,0 \leq a.\,0$, because $a.b.\,0$ must t while $a.\,0$ must t, where t is the test $\overline{a}.\overline{b}.\checkmark$ $\qquad\qquad$ □

Instead, as in [1,6], we base our semantic interpretation on a *stratified* characterisation of testing pre-order, using Theorem 1.

Definition 3 (Semantic interpretation). *For $k \geq 0$ let $p \ll^n q$ if for every $s \in \mathsf{Act}^\star$ of length at most n, for every $A \in \mathcal{A}(q,s)$ there exists some $B \in \mathcal{A}(p,s)$ such that $B \subseteq A$.*

Then, for $n \geq 0$, write

$$p_1 \leq p_1', \ldots, p_k \leq p_k' \vDash_n p \leq p'$$

if $p_1 \ll^n p_1' \ldots \ldots p_k \ll^n p_k'$ implies $p \ll^n p'$.

We use $A \vDash p \leq p'$ to mean that $A \vDash_n p \leq p'$ for every $n \geq 0$. $\qquad$ □

The counterexample given above no longer works for this stratified semantic interpretation. This is because

$$a.b.\,0 \leq a.\,0 \not\vDash b.\,0 \leq 0$$

In particular $a.b.\,0 \leq a.\,0 \not\vDash_1 b.\,0 \leq 0$. To see this first note that

- $\mathcal{A}(a.b.\,0, \varepsilon) = \mathcal{A}(a.\,0, \varepsilon) = \{\,\{\,a\,\}\,\}$
- $\mathcal{A}(a.b.\,0, a) = \{\,\{\,b\,\}\,\}, \mathcal{A}(a.\,0, a) = \{\,\{\,\}\,\}$
- $\mathcal{A}(a.b.\,0, s) = \mathcal{A}(a.\,0, s) = \{\,\}$ whenever s is different from ε, a.

Therefore $a.b.\,0 \ll^1 a.\,0$. However $\mathcal{A}(b.\,0, b) = \{\,\{\,\}\,\}$ and $\mathcal{A}(0, b) = \{\,\}$, and therefore $b.\,0 \not\ll^1 0$.

A very useful property of these stratified behavioural relations is given in the following lemma.

Lemma 1. *For $m \geq 0$, $p \ll^m q$ implies $a.p \ll^{(m+1)} a.q$*

Proof. For a given m suppose $p \ll^m q$. To establish $a.p \ll^{(m+1)} a.q$, suppose $A \in \mathcal{A}(a.p, s)$ where the length of s is at most $m + 1$. We have to find some $B \in \mathcal{A}(a.q, s)$ such that $B \subseteq A$. There are two cases. If s is the empty sequence ε then A is $\{\,a\,\}$ and the required B is the same set $\{\,a\,\}$. Otherwise s has the form $a.t$ and the required B can be found using $p \ll^m q$, since $A \in \mathcal{A}(p,t)$. $\qquad$ □

Theorem 2 (Soundness). $\vdash_{\text{mst}} A \vdash p \leq p'$ *implies* $A \vDash p \leq p'$.

Proof. It suffices to show that each of the proof rules in Fig. 4 preserves the semantics, and the only non-trivial case is the rule (COREC). Here the proof is very similar in style and structure to the corresponding proof in [6], that of Theorem 2.

So suppose $A, a.p \leq a.p' \vDash p \leq p'$; that is

$$A, a.p \leq a.p' \vDash_k p \leq p' \qquad \text{for all } k \geq 0 \tag{6}$$

We have to show that from this hypothesis, which we refer to as the *outer hypothesis*, the conclusion $A \vDash a.p \leq a.p'$ follows. In particular we show that $A \vDash_n a.p \leq a.p'$, for every $n \geq 0$, by induction on n.

The base case, when $n = 0$, is straightforward, as $\mathcal{A}(a.p, \varepsilon) = \mathcal{A}(a.p', \varepsilon) = \{\{a\}\}$.

In the inductive case we let $n = (m + 1)$, and we can assume

$$A \vDash_m a.p \leq a.p' \tag{7}$$

which we refer to as the *inner hypothesis*. We have to deduce $A \vDash_{(m+1)} a.p \leq a.p'$.

To this end suppose $q \ll^{(m+1)} q'$ for every $q \leq q' \in A$. We have to show $a.p \ll^{(m+1)} a.p'$.

First we apply the inner hypothesis (7): this is possible since $q \ll^{(m+1)} q'$ implies $q \ll^m q'$ So we obtain $a.p \ll^m a.p'$.

With this we can apply the outer hypothesis (6) with $k = m$. We obtain $p \ll^m p'$, from which the required $a.p \ll^{(m+1)} a.p'$ now follows using Lemma 1.

$\square$

In particular this soundness result means that if we can construct a valid proof tree for the judgement $\vdash p \leq q$ then $p \precsim_{must} q$:

Corollary 1 (Soundness). $\vdash_{mst} p \leq q$ *implies* $p \precsim_{must} q$.

Proof. Suppose $\vdash_{mst} p \leq q$, that is $\emptyset \vdash p \leq q$. By Theorem 2 we have that $p \ll^m q$ for every $m \geq 0$, that is $p \ll q$. So by Theorem 1 it follows that $p \precsim_{must} q$. $\square$

5   Completeness

The proof of completeness has the same structure as the corresponding result in [6], with some variations in some definitions and proofs. It relies on the concept of *head normal forms*.

First some notation. A non-empty finite collection of finite sets of actions $\mathcal{A}$ is said to be *saturated* if

- $A, B \in \mathcal{A}$ implies $A \cup B \in \mathcal{A}$
- $A, B \in \mathcal{A}, A \subseteq C \subseteq B$, implies $C \in \mathcal{A}$

$\sum_{i \in I} p_i$ is a standard abbreviation for $p_1 + \ldots\ldots + p_n$, where I is the finite index set $\{1, \ldots n\}$; when I is empty this is taken to represent 0. In a similar manner we use $\sum_{i \in I} p_i$ as an abbreviation for $p_1 \oplus \ldots\ldots \oplus p_n$, but here the index set I must be non-empty.

Definition 4 (Head normal forms). *A process of the form* $\sum_{A \in \mathcal{A}} (\sum_{a \in A} a.p_a)$, *where* $\mathcal{A}$ *is saturated, is said to be a* head normal form, *abbreviated to hnf.* $\square$

```
 1 C(p,q)  Input:    p, q
 2               Output:    (YES),  if  p ⊑_must q
 3                          (NO),   otherwise
 4
 5 Let  Σ_{A∈𝒜}(Σ_{a∈A} a.p_a)  =  hnf(p)
 6 Let  Σ_{B∈ℬ}(Σ_{b∈B} b.q_b)  =  hnf(q)
 7 If  ℬ ⊄ 𝒜  return  (NO)
 8     otherwise
 9     for  each  b ∈ ∪{ B ∈ ℬ}
10              if    C(p_b,q_b)  returns   (NO)
11              then return   (NO)
12     otherwise return  (YES)
```

Fig. 5. An informal procedure

Note that 0 is a *hnf* since it can be written as $\sum_{A∈\{∅\}}(\sum_{a∈A} a.p_a)$, and $\{∅\}$ is saturated.

Proposition 1. *For every process p there exists some head normal form,* $\mathrm{HNF}(p)$, *such that $p =_{ineq} \mathrm{HNF}(p)$.*

Proof. The proof relies on the fact that all processes are *guarded*. First consider all processes r given by the grammar

$$r ::= 0 \mid a.p, a ∈ \mathsf{Act} \mid r_1 + r_2 \mid r_1 ⊕ r_2$$

where p ranges over arbitrary regular processes. Using the standard techniques from [5] one can construct a process $\mathrm{HNF}(r)$ such that $p =_{ineq} \mathrm{HNF}(p)$.

The only other possible structure for a regular process is $\mathrm{REC}x.t$. But

$$\mathrm{REC}x.t =_{ineq} t\{x ↦ \mathrm{REC}x.t\}$$

and since we only allow guarded processes $t\{x ↦ \mathrm{REC}x.t\}$ is included in the grammar above. So it already has a head normal form, and therefore so does $\mathrm{REC}x.t$. □

The attraction of *hnfs* is that using the alternative characterisation in Theorem 1 it is in principle straightforward to check whether

$$\sum_{A∈𝒜}\left(\sum_{a∈A} a.p_a\right) ⊑_{must} \sum_{B∈ℬ}\left(\sum_{b∈B} b.p_b\right)$$

If $ℬ ⊄ 𝒜$ then they are not related; otherwise it is sufficient to check whether $p_b ⊑_{must} q_b$ for each $b ∈ ∪\{ B ∈ ℬ\}$. An informal recursive procedure $C(p,q)$ based on these ideas is given in Fig. 5.

As currently constituted calls to $C(p,q)$ may never terminate; the recursive calls on line 10 may go on forever. To remedy this the procedure could have an extra parameter, a set of pairs of processes which have already been tested,

```
1  M(A,p,q) ⇒ if (p or q not in hnf)
2                 then
3                     let T = M(A,hnf(p),hnf(q))
4                     in return   (T;(HNF))
5
6  M(A,∑_{A∈𝒜}(∑_{a∈A} a.p_a),∑_{B∈ℬ}(∑_{b∈B} b.p_b)) ⇒
7                 if ℬ ⊄ 𝒜 return  (FAIL)
8                 else
9                     let T_i = Mp(A,b.p_{b_i},b.q_{b_i}),  for each  b_i ∈ ∪{ B | B ∈ ℬ }
10                    in (T_1;......;T_n);TA(𝒜,ℬ)
11
12 Mp(A,a.p,a.q) ⇒ if a.p ≤a.q in A then return  (HYP)
13                 else let B = {A,  a.p<a.q}
14                      let T = M(B,p,q)
15                      in
16                      T;(coRec)
```

Fig. 6. The algorithm

similar to the set A used in our proof system in Fig. 4. As a further enhancement, instead of simply returning (YES) it could return an actual valid proof tree for the judgement $p \leq q$.

Such a procedure is outlined in Fig. 6 where, as with the proof system, the extra parameter A is a finite set of hypotheses each of the form $a.p \leq a.q$; intuitively these are pairs of processes which have already been visited. On line 4 we use (HNF) to refer to a tactical which transforms the two processes under consideration into *hnfs*; this is possible within the proof systems because of Proposition 1. On line 12 we use $TA(\mathcal{A}, \mathcal{B})$ to refer to a slightly more complicated tactical which takes a set of valid proof trees T_i for the judgements $A \vdash b_i.p_{b_i} \leq b_i.q_{b_i}$, one for each $b_i \in \cup\{ B \mid B \in \mathcal{B} \}$, and constructs a valid proof tree for the judgement

$$A \vdash \sum_{A \in \mathcal{A}}(\sum_{a \in A} a.p_a), \leq \sum_{B \in \mathcal{B}}(\sum_{b \in B} b.p_b)$$

assuming that $\mathcal{B} \subseteq \mathcal{A}$; this tactical can easily be constructed using in-equational reasoning, and the substitution rules.

On line 12–14 we have recursive calls for derivative processes. But these calls only take place if the derivatives are not already in the already visited set A, which is then increased appropriately.

Proposition 2.

(a) **[Algorithmic correctness]** *Suppose* $M(A, p, q)$ *terminates.*
   (i) *If it returns* **FAIL** *then* $p \not\sqsubseteq_{must} q$.
   (ii) *If it returns a proof tree, then this is a valid proof tree for the judgement* $A \vdash p \leq q$.

*(b) [**Termination**] The recursive procedure $M(A, p, q)$ terminates for all parameters A, p, q.*

Proof. (Outline)

(a) In each case the proof is by induction on the number of recursive calls to $M(-, -, -)$.
(b) By examining the code, particularly line 12, one can see that in any sequence of calls to $Mp(A_i, a_i.p_i, a_i.q_i)$ an arbitrary pair of processes $(a_i.p, a_i.q)$ can appear at most once. Moreover each action name a_i must appear textually in one of the original processes p, q; there are thus a finite number of possible action names a_i which can appear in the sequence. Finally it can also be shown that the set of possible p_i, q_i is also finite. Technically, for example, each p_i is *reachable* from the initial process p. In [6] this set of reachable terms is called Reach(p) and can be shown to be finite.[5]
Termination now follows because now any sequence of calls $Mp(A_i, a_i.p_i, a_i.q_i)$ must be finite.

The finiteness result used here (that Reach(p) is finite) is non-trivial to prove. But a detailed account for a language very similar to rCCS may be found in Sect. 7 of [6]. □

Corollary 2 (Completeness). $p \sqsubseteq_{must} q$ *implies* $\vdash_{mst} p \leq q$.

Proof. Suppose $p \sqsubseteq_{must} q$. We know from Proposition 2(b) that $M(\emptyset, p, q)$ terminates. By design this algorithm either returns **FAIL** or a valid proof tree. The former is not possible since $p \sqsubseteq_{must} q$. The same proposition ensures that the returned proof tree is a valid proof tree for $\emptyset \vdash p \leq q$. That is $\vdash_{mst} p \leq q$. □

Acknowledgements. The author would like to thank the referees for their careful reading of the first version of this paper.

References

1. Brandt, M., Henglein, F.: Coinductive axiomatization of recursive type equality and subtyping. Fundam. Inform. **33**(4), 309–338 (1998)
2. De Nicola, R., Hennessy, M.: Testing equivalences for processes. Theor. Comput. Sci. **34**, 83–133 (1984)
3. De Nicola, R., Hennessy, M.: CCS without τ's. In: Ehrig, H., Kowalski, R., Levi, G., Montanari, U. (eds.) CAAP 1987. LNCS, vol. 249, pp. 138–152. Springer, Heidelberg (1987). https://doi.org/10.1007/3-540-17660-8_53
4. De Nicola, R.: Testing equivalences and fully abstract models for communicating processes. Ph.D. thesis, University of Edinburgh (1985)
5. Hennessy, M.: Algebraic Theory of Processes. MIT Press, Cambridge (1988)

---

[5] Technically here we need to work up to the idempotency of both binary operators $(- + -)$ and $(- \oplus -)$.

6. Hennessy, M.: A coinductive equational characterisation of trace inclusion for regular processes. In: Aceto, L., Bacci, G., Bacci, G., Ingólfsdóttir, A., Legay, A., Mardare, R. (eds.) Models, Algorithms, Logics and Tools. LNCS, vol. 10460, pp. 449–465. Springer, Cham (2017). https://doi.org/10.1007/978-3-319-63121-9_22

7. Hoare, C.A.R.: Communicating sequential processes. Commun. ACM **26**(1), 100–106 (1983). (reprint)

8. Hoare, C.A.R.: Communicating Sequential Processes. Prentice-Hall Inc., Upper Saddle River (1985)

9. Kozen, D.: A completeness theorem for Kleene algebras and the algebra of regular events. Inf. Comput. **110**(2), 366–390 (1994)

10. Milner, R.: A complete inference system for a class of regular behaviours. J. Comput. Syst. Sci. **28**(3), 439–466 (1984)

11. Rabinovich, A.: A complete axiomatisation for trace congruence of finite state behaviors. In: Brookes, S., Main, M., Melton, A., Mislove, M., Schmidt, D. (eds.) MFPS 1993. LNCS, vol. 802, pp. 530–543. Springer, Heidelberg (1994). https://doi.org/10.1007/3-540-58027-1_25

12. Salomaa, A.: Two complete axiom systems for the algebra of regular events. J. ACM **13**(1), 158–169 (1966)

Testing Equivalence vs. Runtime Monitoring

Luca Aceto[1,2]([⊠])[iD], Antonis Achilleos[2][iD], Adrian Francalanza[3][iD],
Anna Ingólfsdóttir[2][iD], and Karoliina Lehtinen[4][iD]

[1] Gran Sasso Science Institute, L'Aquila, Italy
luca.aceto@gssi.it
[2] School of Computer Science, Reykjavik University, Reykjavik, Iceland
{luca,antonios,annai}@ru.is
[3] Department of Computer Science, ICT, University of Malta, Msida, Malta
adrian.francalanza@um.edu.mt
[4] Department of Computer Science, University of Liverpool, Liverpool, UK
karoliina.lehtinen@liverpool.ac.uk

Abstract. Rocco De Nicola's most cited paper, which was coauthored
with his PhD supervisor Matthew Hennessy, introduced three seminal
testing equivalences over processes represented as states in labelled transition systems. This article relates those classic process semantics with
the framework for runtime monitoring developed by the authors in the
context of the project 'TheoFoMon: Theoretical Foundations for Monitorability'. It shows that may-testing semantics is closely related to the
basic monitoring set-up within that framework, whereas, over strongly-
convergent processes, must-testing semantics is induced by a collection
of monitors that can detect when processes are unable to perform certain
actions.

Keywords: Testing equivalence · Runtime monitoring ·
Trace equivalence · Failure equivalence ·
Hennessy-Milner logic with recursion

1 Introduction

Rocco De Nicola is probably best known for the introduction of the notions of
testing equivalence over concurrent processes, in joint work with his PhD supervisor Matthew Hennessy that was reported in the conference paper [14] and the
subsequent journal paper [15]. These testing equivalences embody in a natural

This research was partially supported by the projects 'TheoFoMon: Theoretical Foundations for Monitorability' (grant number: 163406-051; http://icetcs.ru.is/theofomon/)
and 'Epistemic Logic for Distributed Runtime Monitoring' (grant number: 184940-051)
of the Icelandic Research Fund, by the BMBF project 'Aramis II' (project number:
01IS160253) and the EPSRC project 'Solving parity games in theory and practice'
(project number: EP/P020909/1).

© Springer Nature Switzerland AG 2019
M. Boreale et al. (Eds.): De Nicola-Festschrift, LNCS 11665, pp. 28–44, 2019.
https://doi.org/10.1007/978-3-030-21485-2_4

and mathematically elegant way the intuitive idea that two processes should be equated unless they behave differently when subjected to some 'experiment' or 'test'. The origin of this notion of equivalence can be traced back to Gottfried Wilhelm Leibniz (1646–1716), whose Identity of Indiscernibles principle states that two (mathematical) objects are equal if there is no property that distinguishes them [24, 'Discourse on Metaphysics', Section 9]. In the semantics of programming languages, its earliest precursor is, to the best of our knowledge, the notion of contextual equivalence proposed by Morris in his doctoral dissertation [26].

In general, given a set of processes, a set of tests and a relation between processes and tests that describes when a process passes a test, one can apply Leibniz's motto and declare two processes to be equivalent if they pass exactly the same set of tests. In the work of De Nicola and Hennessy, processes are states in some labelled transition system [22]. A test is itself a process, which interacts with a concurrent system under observation by hand-shake synchronisation and uses a distinguished action to report success in its observation. Since both processes and tests may be nondeterministic, the interaction between a process and a test may lead to different outcomes depending on how the two systems resolve their nondeterministic choices in the course of a computation. This led De Nicola and Hennessy to define three notions of testing semantics, which are naturally expressed in terms of preorders over processes. In the so-called *may semantics*, a process q is at least as good as some process p if the set of tests that p may pass is included in the set of tests that q may pass. In may semantics, possible failure under a test is immaterial and therefore nondeterminism is *angelic*. On the other hand, one may take the view that failure in the testing effort is *catastrophic*, in the sense that a process that may fail some test is just as bad as one that always fails it. The notion of testing semantics that captures this viewpoint is the so-called *must semantics*, according to which a process q is at least as good as some process p if the set of tests that p must pass is included in the set of tests that q must pass. Finally, a third testing preorder over processes is obtained as the intersection of the may and must preorders described above. According to this more refined view of process behaviour, a process that always fails a test is worse than one that may pass that test, which in turn is worse than one that always passes it.

De Nicola and Hennessy explored the rich theory of the testing semantics in [15] (see [19] for a book-length treatment), where each of these semantics is given operational, denotational and axiomatic accounts that are in agreement one with the other. Their ideas and the accompanying technical results have had an enormous impact on further research, as witnessed, among other things, by the over $1,650$ citations to [15][1].

Our goal in this article is to provide some evidence supporting our view that De Nicola and Hennessy's work may also be seen as providing the theoretical foundations for runtime verification [9], a line of research that is becoming

---

[1] Source: https://scholar.google.com/citations?user=Meb6JFkAAAAJ&hl=en, last accessed on the 24th of March 2019.

increasingly important in the field of computer-aided verification. Runtime verification is a lightweight verification technique that checks whether the system under scrutiny satisfies a correctness property by analysing its current execution. In this approach, a computational entity called a *monitor*, which is synthesised from a given correctness property, is used to observe the current system execution and to report whether the observed computation satisfies the given property.

The high-level description of runtime verification given above hints at conceptual similarities between that approach to computer-aided verification and testing equivalences à la De Nicola and Hennessy. Indeed, the monitors used in runtime verification seem to play a role akin to that of the tests in the work of De Nicola and Hennessy. In this paper, we will see that the connection between runtime verification and testing semantics can be made precise within the operational framework for runtime monitoring developed in [1,3,16,17]. More precisely, we will show that may-testing semantics is closely related to the basic monitoring set-up presented in [16,17] (Sect. 3), whereas must-testing semantics over strongly-convergent, finitely-branching processes is induced by a collection of monitors that can detect refusals and that stem from the framework for parameterised monitorability developed in [1] (Sect. 4). Together with the results presented in [7,12], we feel that Theorems 2 and 7 in this study substantiate our tenet that runtime verification owes much to the work of De Nicola and Hennessy on testing equivalences for processes.

2 Preliminaries

We begin by briefly reviewing the model of labelled transition systems used in this study (Sect. 2.1) and by presenting an informal account of De Nicola-Hennessy testing equivalences (Sect. 2.2).

2.1 Labelled Transition Systems

We assume a finite set of *external* actions ACT and, following Milner [25], a distinguished *silent* action τ. We let α, a, b, c range over ACT and μ over ACT $\cup$ $\{\tau\}$. A *labelled transition system* (LTS) over ACT is a triple

$$L = \langle P, \text{ACT}, \rightarrow_L \rangle,$$

where P is a nonempty set of system states referred to as *processes* $(p, q, \ldots \in P)$, and $\rightarrow_L \subseteq P \times (\text{ACT} \cup \{\tau\}) \times P$ is a transition relation. We write $p \xrightarrow{\mu}_L q$ instead of $(p, \mu, q) \in \rightarrow_L$. We use $p \xRightarrow{\alpha}_L q$ to mean that, in L, p can reach q using a single α action and any number of silent actions, i.e., $p(\xrightarrow{\tau}_L)^* \xrightarrow{\alpha}_L (\xrightarrow{\tau}_L)^* q$. By $p \xrightarrow{\mu}_L$ (respectively, $p \xRightarrow{\alpha}_L$) we mean that there is some q such that $p \xrightarrow{\mu}_L q$ (respectively, $p \xRightarrow{\alpha}_L q$) and $p \not\xrightarrow{\mu}_L$ (respectively, $p \not\xRightarrow{\alpha}_L$) means that no such q exists. For a trace $s = \alpha_1 \alpha_2 \ldots \alpha_\ell \in \text{ACT}^*$, $p \xRightarrow{s}_L q$ means $p \xRightarrow{\alpha_1}_L \xRightarrow{\alpha_2}_L \ldots \xRightarrow{\alpha_\ell}_L q$ when $\ell \geq 1$ and $p(\xrightarrow{\tau}_L)^* q$ when $s = \varepsilon$ is the empty trace. We say that s is a trace of p when $p \xRightarrow{s}_L q$ for some q, and write traces(p) for the set of all the traces of p.

From now on we will omit the subscript L as the LTS will be always clear from the context.

In the rest of the paper, processes will be specified using expressions in the fragment of Milner's CCS [25] containing the operators for describing finite synchronisation trees over $\text{ACT} \cup \{\tau\}$ [29].

2.2   Testing Equivalences à la De Nicola and Hennessy

We will now informally recall the testing semantics from [15,19]. We will not present the full details of the formal definitions of the testing semantics, since our technical results will rely on the alternative, test-free characterisations of the may- and must-testing preorders, which we will state in Sects. 3.3 and 4.2 where they are used.

The testing equivalences over processes introduced in [15] embody in a natural and mathematically elegant way the intuitive idea that two programs should be equated unless they behave differently when subjected to some 'experiment'. In the setting of the above-mentioned paper, an experiment is itself a process, called *test*, that interacts with the observed system by communicating with it and that uses a distinguished action ω to report a successful outcome resulting from its observations.

We say that

- process p *may pass* a test t if there is *some* maximal computation resulting from the interaction between p and t in which t reports success;
- process p *must pass* a test t if t reports success in *every* maximal computation resulting from the interaction between p and t.

The classification of the possible outcomes resulting from process-test interactions leads to three different notions of semantic equivalence over processes: one in which nondeterminism is angelic (the may-testing preorder), another in which the possibility of failure is catastrophic (the must-testing preorder) and a third in which a process that may both fail and pass a test is distinguished from one that always fails it or always passes it (the intersection of the may- and must-testing preorders). Each of these semantics is given operational, denotational and axiomatic accounts that are in agreement one with the other in [15,19].

Definition 1 (Testing preorders). *For all $p, q \in P$,*

- *$p \sqsubseteq_{may} q$ iff, for each test t, p may pass t implies q may pass t;*
- *$p \sqsubseteq_{must} q$ iff, for each test t, p must pass t implies q must pass t;*
- *$p \sqsubseteq_T q$ iff $p \sqsubseteq_{may} q$ and $p \sqsubseteq_{must} q$.*

Example 1. It is well known that nil $\sqsubseteq_{may}$ a.nil and that $a.(b.\text{nil} + c.\text{nil}) \sqsubseteq_{may}$ $a.b.\text{nil} + a.c.\text{nil}$. On the other hand, nil $\not\sqsubseteq_{must}$ a.nil and $a.(b.\text{nil} + c.\text{nil}) \not\sqsubseteq_{must}$ $a.b.\text{nil} + a.c.\text{nil}$. Indeed, unlike nil, the process a.nil may fail the test $a.\text{nil} + \tau.\omega.\text{nil}$ (read 'ask the process under observation to do a and terminate unsuccessfully, or internally decide to succeed') and, unlike $a.(b.\text{nil} + c.\text{nil})$, the process $a.b.\text{nil} +$ $a.c.\text{nil}$ may fail the test $a.b.\omega.\text{nil}$ (read 'ask the process under observation to do a followed by b and then succeed').

3   Monitoring May Testing

We now characterise the may-testing preorder in terms of the basic framework for runtime monitoring presented in [16,17]. We first recall the needed definitions and results from those references in Sects. 3.1–3.2 and then we use them to give a monitor-based version of the may-testing preorder in Sect. 3.3.

3.1   A Framework for Runtime Monitoring

We now review the operational framework proposed in [16,17] for runtime monitoring of properties expressed in Hennessy-Milner Logic with recursion [8,23]. In this framework, a monitor is a computational entity that observes the current system execution and uses the information so acquired to try to ascertain whether the system satisfies a given property.

Monitors. We first define the notion of a monitor given in [16,17]. Monitors are states of an LTS, much like processes and tests. Syntactically, monitors are specified using expressions in a variation on the regular fragment of CCS, where the nil process is replaced by verdicts. A verdict can be one of yes, no and end, which represent acceptance, rejection and inconclusive termination, respectively.

Definition 1. *The set* MON *of monitors is defined by the following grammar:*

$$m, n \in \text{MON} ::= v \quad | \quad \alpha.m \quad | \quad m + n \quad | \quad \textbf{rec } x.m \quad | \quad x$$
$$v ::= end \quad | \quad no \quad | \quad yes$$

where x ranges over a countably infinite set of monitor variables.

An acceptance monitor *is one without occurrences of the verdict* no *and a* rejection monitor *is one that does not contain occurrences of the verdict* yes.

The behaviour of a monitor is defined by the derivation rules of Table 1, so monitors are states of an LTS whose transitions are those that are provable using those rules. Intuitively, a transition $m \xrightarrow{\alpha} m'$ indicates that a monitor in state m can analyse action α and become the monitor described by m' in doing so. We highlight the transition rule for verdicts in Table 1, describing the fact that, from a verdict state, any action can be analysed by transitioning to the same state; verdicts are thus irrevocable.

Monitored System. Monitors are intended to run in conjunction with the system (process) they are analysing. While monitoring a process $p \in P$, a monitor $m \in$ MON tries to mirror every visible action p performs. If m cannot match an action performed by p and it cannot perform an internal action, then p performs that action and continues executing, while m becomes the inconclusive end verdict. We are only looking at the visible actions and so we allow m and p to perform silent τ actions independently of each other.

Table 1. Monitor dynamics

$$\text{MACT} \frac{}{\alpha.m \xrightarrow{\alpha} m} \qquad\qquad \text{MREC} \frac{}{\mathbf{rec}\, x.m \xrightarrow{\tau} m[\mathbf{rec}\, x.m/x]}$$

$$\text{MSELL} \frac{m \xrightarrow{\mu} m'}{m + n \xrightarrow{\mu} m'} \qquad\qquad \text{MSELR} \frac{n \xrightarrow{\mu} n'}{m + n \xrightarrow{\mu} n'}$$

$$\text{MVERD} \frac{}{v \xrightarrow{\alpha} v}$$

where $\alpha \in \text{ACT}$ and $\mu \in \text{ACT} \cup \{\tau\}$.

Definition 2. *A monitored system consists of a monitor $m \in \text{MON}$ and a process $p \in P$ that run side-by-side, denoted $m \vartriangleleft p$. The behaviour of a monitored system is defined by the derivation rules in Table 2.*

The following lemmata describe how the monitor and system LTSs can be composed and decomposed according to instrumentation [17].

Table 2. Monitored systems

$$\text{IMON} \frac{p \xrightarrow{\alpha} p' \quad m \xrightarrow{\alpha} m'}{m \vartriangleleft p \xrightarrow{\alpha} m' \vartriangleleft p'} \qquad\qquad \text{ITER} \frac{p \xrightarrow{\alpha} p' \quad m \xrightarrow{\alpha}\!\!\!\!\!/\;\; \quad m \xrightarrow{\tau}\!\!\!\!\!/}{m \vartriangleleft p \xrightarrow{\alpha} \mathsf{end} \vartriangleleft p'}$$

$$\text{IASYP} \frac{p \xrightarrow{\tau} p'}{m \vartriangleleft p \xrightarrow{\tau} m \vartriangleleft p'} \qquad\qquad \text{IASYM} \frac{m \xrightarrow{\tau} m'}{m \vartriangleleft p \xrightarrow{\tau} m' \vartriangleleft p}$$

Lemma 1 (General Unzipping). $m \vartriangleleft p \xRightarrow{s} n \vartriangleleft q$ *implies*

- $p \xRightarrow{s} q$ *and*
- $m \xRightarrow{s} n$ *or* $(\exists s_1, s_2, \alpha\, \exists m'.\ s = s_1 \alpha s_2,\ m \xRightarrow{s_1} m' \xrightarrow{\tau}\!\!\!\!\!/\,,\ m' \xrightarrow{\alpha}\!\!\!\!\!/\ and\ n = \mathsf{end})$.

Lemma 2 (Zipping). $(p \xRightarrow{s} q\ and\ m \xRightarrow{s} n)$ *implies* $m \vartriangleleft p \xRightarrow{s} n \vartriangleleft q$.

If a monitored system $m \vartriangleleft p$ can reach a configuration where the monitor component is the yes verdict, we say that m *accepts* p, and similarly m *rejects* p if the monitored system can reach a configuration where the monitor component is no.

Definition 3 (Acceptance/Rejection). *We define*

$$\boldsymbol{acc}(m, p) \stackrel{def}{=} \exists s, p'.\ m \vartriangleleft p \xRightarrow{s} \mathsf{yes} \vartriangleleft p' \quad and$$

$$\boldsymbol{rej}(m, p) \stackrel{def}{=} \exists s, p'.\ m \vartriangleleft p \xRightarrow{s} \mathsf{no} \vartriangleleft p'.$$

The Logic. We use μHML, the Hennessy-Milner logic with recursion, to describe properties of processes.

Definition 4. *The formulae of μHML are constructed using the following grammar:*

$$\varphi, \psi \in \mu\text{HML}:: = tt \qquad\qquad\qquad | \ \ ff$$
$$| \ \ \varphi \wedge \psi \qquad\qquad\qquad | \ \ \varphi \vee \psi$$
$$| \ \ \langle \alpha \rangle \varphi \qquad\qquad\qquad | \ \ [\alpha]\varphi$$
$$| \ \ \min X.\varphi \qquad\qquad\qquad | \ \ \max X.\varphi$$
$$| \ \ X$$

where X ranges over a countably infinite set of logical variables LVAR.

Formulae are evaluated in the context of a labelled transition system and an environment, $\rho : \text{LVAR} \to 2^P$, which gives values to the logical variables in the formula. For an environment ρ, variable X, and set $S \subseteq P$, we write $\rho[X \mapsto S]$ for the environment which maps X to S and all $Y \neq X$ to $\rho(Y)$. The semantics for μHML formulae is given through a function $[\![\cdot]\!]$, which, given an environment ρ, maps each formula to a set of processes — namely the processes that satisfy the formula under the assumption that each $X \in \text{LVAR}$ is satisfied by the processes in $\rho(X)$. The function $[\![\cdot]\!]$ is defined as follows:

$$[\![tt, \rho]\!] \stackrel{def}{=} P \quad \text{and} \quad [\![ff, \rho]\!] \stackrel{def}{=} \emptyset$$

$$[\![\varphi_1 \wedge \varphi_2, \rho]\!] \stackrel{def}{=} [\![\varphi_1, \rho]\!] \cap [\![\varphi_2, \rho]\!]$$

$$[\![\varphi_1 \vee \varphi_2, \rho]\!] \stackrel{def}{=} [\![\varphi_1, \rho]\!] \cup [\![\varphi_2, \rho]\!]$$

$$[\![[\alpha]\varphi, \rho]\!] \stackrel{def}{=} \left\{ p \mid \forall q.\ p \stackrel{\alpha}{\Rightarrow} q \text{ implies } q \in [\![\varphi, \rho]\!] \right\}$$

$$[\![\langle \alpha \rangle \varphi, \rho]\!] \stackrel{def}{=} \left\{ p \mid \exists q.\ p \stackrel{\alpha}{\Rightarrow} q \text{ and } q \in [\![\varphi, \rho]\!] \right\}$$

$$[\![\max X.\varphi, \rho]\!] \stackrel{def}{=} \bigcup \{S \mid S \subseteq [\![\varphi, \rho[X \mapsto S]]\!]\}$$

$$[\![\min X.\varphi, \rho]\!] \stackrel{def}{=} \bigcap \{S \mid S \supseteq [\![\varphi, \rho[X \mapsto S]]\!]\}$$

$$[\![X, \rho]\!] \stackrel{def}{=} \rho(X).$$

A formula is closed when every occurrence of a variable X is in the scope of recursive operator $\max X$ or $\min X$. Note that the environment ρ has no effect on the semantics of a closed formula. Thus, for a closed formula φ, we often drop the environment from the notation for $[\![\cdot]\!]$ and write $[\![\varphi]\!]$ instead of $[\![\varphi, \rho]\!]$.

The safety fragment of μHML, denoted by sHML, and its dual co-safety fragment, cHML, are defined by the grammar:

| $\varphi, \psi \in$ sHML | ::=tt | $\mid ff$ | $\mid [\alpha]\varphi$ | $\mid \varphi \wedge \psi$ | $\mid \max X.\varphi$ | $\mid X$ |
| $\varphi, \psi \in$ cHML | ::=tt | $\mid ff$ | $\mid \langle \alpha \rangle \varphi$ | $\mid \varphi \vee \psi$ | $\mid \min X.\varphi$ | $\mid X.$ |

Definition 5 (Monitorable Formulae). *We say that a rejection monitor m monitors a formula $\varphi \in \mu$HML for violation when, for each process p, $\mathbf{rej}(m,p)$ if and only if $p \notin [\![\varphi]\!]$. Similarly, an acceptance monitor m monitors a formula $\varphi \in \mu$HML for satisfaction when, for each process p, $\mathbf{acc}(m,p)$ if and only if $p \in [\![\varphi]\!]$. A formula $\varphi \in \mu$HML is* monitorable *if there is a monitor that monitors it for satisfaction or violation.*

3.2 Previous Results

The main result from [16,17] is to define a monitorable subset of μHML and show that it is maximally expressive. This subset is called MHML and consists of the safety and co-safety syntactic fragments of μHML: MHML $\stackrel{def}{=}$ SHML $\cup$ CHML. From now on, we focus on SHML, but the case of CHML is dual. The interested reader can see [16,17] for more details.

In order to prove that SHML is monitorable, in [16,17] Francalanza, Aceto, and Ingólfsdóttir define a monitor synthesis function, $(\!|\cdot|\!)$, which maps formulae to monitors, and show that for each $\varphi \in$ SHML, $(\!|\varphi|\!)$ monitors φ for violation, in that $\mathbf{rej}((\!|\varphi|\!),p)$ holds exactly for those processes p for which $p \notin [\![\varphi]\!]$.

Definition 6 (Monitor Synthesis).

$$(\!|t t|\!) \stackrel{def}{=} \textit{yes} \qquad\qquad (\!|f f|\!) \stackrel{def}{=} \textit{no} \qquad\qquad (\!|X|\!) \stackrel{def}{=} x$$

$$(\!|[\alpha]\psi|\!) \stackrel{def}{=} \begin{cases} \alpha.(\!|\psi|\!) & \textit{if } (\!|\psi|\!) \neq \textit{yes} \\ \textit{yes} & \textit{otherwise} \end{cases}$$

$$(\!|\psi_1 \wedge \psi_2|\!) \stackrel{def}{=} \begin{cases} (\!|\psi_1|\!) & \textit{if } (\!|\psi_2|\!) = \textit{yes} \\ (\!|\psi_2|\!) & \textit{if } (\!|\psi_1|\!) = \textit{yes} \\ (\!|\psi_1|\!) + (\!|\psi_2|\!) & \textit{otherwise} \end{cases}$$

$$(\!|\max X.\psi|\!) \stackrel{def}{=} \begin{cases} \mathbf{rec}\, x.(\!|\psi|\!) & \textit{if } (\!|\psi|\!) \neq \textit{yes} \\ \textit{yes} & \textit{otherwise} \end{cases}$$

Lemma 3. *For every formula $\varphi \in$ SHML, $(\!|\varphi|\!)$ monitors φ for violation.*

Definition 7 (Formula Synthesis). *We define a formula synthesis function $\|\cdot\|$ from rejection monitors to SHML.*

$$\|end\| = tt \qquad\qquad \|no\| = ff \qquad\qquad \|x\| = X$$
$$\|\alpha.m\| = [\alpha]\|m\| \qquad \|m + n\| = \|m\| \wedge \|n\| \qquad \|rec\ x.m\| = \max X.\|m\|.$$

Lemma 4. *Every monitor m monitors $\|m\|$ for violation.*

As previously mentioned, dual results hold for CHML, whose formulae can be monitored for satisfaction using acceptance monitors.

3.3 May Testing via Monitors

The goal of this section is to show how the monitoring framework we just reviewed can be used to give an alternative characterisation of classic may-testing semantics à la De Nicola and Hennessy. As a first step, we define three natural preorders over states of LTSs that are induced by monitors. We will then show that these three preorders coincide with the may-testing preorder. In what follows, we assume a fixed LTS $L = \langle P, \text{ACT}, \rightarrow \rangle$. All the results we present in this section hold for arbitrary LTSs.

Definition 2 (Monitoring preorders). *For all $p, q \in P$,*

- $p \sqsubseteq_M^A q$ *iff, for each acceptance monitor m, $\mathbf{acc}(m, p)$ implies $\mathbf{acc}(m, q)$;*
- $p \sqsubseteq_M^R q$ *iff, for each rejection monitor m, $\mathbf{rej}(m, p)$ implies $\mathbf{rej}(m, q)$;*
- $p \sqsubseteq q$ *iff $p \sqsubseteq_M^A q$ and $p \sqsubseteq_M^R q$.*

The following alternative characterization of the may testing preorder is well known—see [15,19].

Theorem 1. *For all $p, q \in P$, $p \sqsubseteq_{may} q$ iff $traces(p) \subseteq traces(q)$.*

One of the consequences of the above result is that tests of the form

$$a_1.\ldots.a_n.\omega.\mathsf{nil},$$

with $n \geq 0$ and $a_1, \ldots, a_n \in \text{ACT}$, suffice to characterize the may-testing preorder. Another one is that deciding the may-testing preorder and its induced equivalence over states in finite LTSs is PSPACE-complete [28].

Theorem 2. *For all $p, q \in P$, the following are equivalent:*

1. *$p \sqsubseteq_{may} q$,*
2. *$p \sqsubseteq_M^A q$,*
3. *$p \sqsubseteq_M^R q$ and*
4. *$p \sqsubseteq q$.*

To show the above result, we first prove that the preorder over processes induced by trace inclusion, which coincides with the may-testing preorder by Theorem 1, is included in both $\sqsubseteq_M^A$ and $\sqsubseteq_M^R$.

Lemma 3. *For all $p, q \in P$, if $traces(p) \subseteq traces(q)$ then $p \sqsubseteq_M^A q$ and $p \sqsubseteq_M^R q$.*

Proof. Assume that $traces(p) \subseteq traces(q)$. We first show that $p \sqsubseteq_M^A q$ holds.

To this end, let m be an acceptance monitor such that $\mathbf{acc}(m, p)$. By definition, this means that $m \lhd p \overset{s}{\Rightarrow} \mathsf{yes} \lhd p'$ for some $s \in \text{ACT}^*$ and process p'. Using the 'unzipping lemma' (Lemma 1), this yields that $m \overset{s}{\Rightarrow} \mathsf{yes}$ and $p \overset{s}{\Rightarrow} p'$. So s is a trace of p and, by the proviso of the lemma, also of q. Thus, $q \overset{s}{\Rightarrow} q'$ for some q'. Using the 'zipping lemma' (Lemma 2), we obtain that $m \lhd q \overset{s}{\Rightarrow} \mathsf{yes} \lhd q'$, which means that $\mathbf{acc}(m, q)$. Since m was an arbitrary acceptance monitor, we conclude that $p \sqsubseteq_M^A q$, and we are done.

The argument proving $p \sqsubseteq_M^R q$ is similar. Simply replace acceptance monitors with rejection monitors, $\mathbf{acc}$ with $\mathbf{rej}$ and yes with no in the above proof. $\square$

Next, we establish that the converse inclusions also hold.

Lemma 4. *For all $p, q \in P$, if $p \sqsubseteq_M^A q$ or $p \sqsubseteq_M^R q$ then $traces(p) \subseteq traces(q)$.*

Proof. We limit ourselves to proving that if $p \sqsubseteq_M^A q$ then $traces(p) \subseteq traces(q)$, as the proof of the other implication is similar. To this end, assume that $p \sqsubseteq_M^A q$ and that $p \overset{s}{\Rightarrow} p'$ for some p'. We will show that $s \in traces(q)$.

First of all, observe that, for each $t \in \text{ACT}^*$, we can construct an acceptance monitor $m(t)$ thus:

$$m(\varepsilon) = \mathsf{yes}$$
$$m(at') = a.m(t').$$

Note that, for each $t \in \text{ACT}^*$, by construction,

$$m(t) \overset{t'}{\Rightarrow} \mathsf{yes} \text{ iff } t = t'.$$

Since $p \overset{s}{\Rightarrow} p'$, the 'zipping lemma' (Lemma 2) yields that $m(s) \triangleleft p \overset{s}{\Rightarrow} \mathsf{yes} \triangleleft p'$. Thus $\mathbf{acc}(m(s), p)$ and, from the assumption that $p \sqsubseteq_M^A q$, we may infer that $\mathbf{acc}(m(s), q)$. By definition and the observation above, this means that $m(s) \triangleleft q \overset{s}{\Rightarrow} \mathsf{yes} \triangleleft q'$ for some q'. The 'unzipping lemma' (Lemma 1) now yields that $q \overset{s}{\Rightarrow} q'$, which was to be shown.   □

Theorem 2 and the monitorability results presented in [1,17] can now be combined to obtain logical characterization results for the may-testing preorder. Even though these results are folklore, we believe that recasting them in terms of monitorability builds a pleasing connection between a classic testing preorder and runtime monitoring for μHML.

In the statement of the following result, for each process p, we define

$$\text{cHML}(p) = \{\varphi \mid \varphi \in \text{cHML and } p \models \varphi\} \text{ and}$$
$$\text{sHML}(p) = \{\varphi \mid \varphi \in \text{sHML and } p \models \varphi\}.$$

Theorem 5. *For all $p, q \in P$, the following statements hold:*

1. $p \sqsubseteq_{may} q$ *iff* $\text{cHML}(p) \subseteq \text{cHML}(q)$.
2. $p \sqsubseteq_{may} q$ *iff* $\text{sHML}(q) \subseteq \text{sHML}(p)$.

Proof. We limit ourselves to presenting the proof of the second statement. The proof of the first statement is similar.

In order to establish the 'only if' implication, assume that $p \sqsubseteq_{may} q$ and $p \not\models \varphi$, for some $\varphi \in \text{sHML}$. We claim that $q \not\models \varphi$. To this end, observe that, as $p \not\models \varphi$ by assumption, Lemma 3 yields that $\mathbf{rej}((\!|\varphi|\!), p)$. By Theorem 2 and $p \sqsubseteq_{may} q$, we have that $p \sqsubseteq_M^R q$. Hence, $\mathbf{rej}((\!|\varphi|\!), q)$ and, using Lemma 3 again, we may conclude that $q \not\models \varphi$, as claimed.

To prove the 'if' implication, we assume that $\text{sHML}(q) \subseteq \text{sHML}(p)$ and show that $p \sqsubseteq_{may} q$. By Theorem 2, this suffices to establish that claim. Suppose that $\mathbf{rej}(m, p)$ for some rejection monitor m. By Lemma 4, we have that $p \not\models \|m\| \in \text{sHML}$. By assumption, this means that $q \not\models \|m\|$ either. Hence, again using Lemma 4, we conclude that $\mathbf{rej}(m, q)$, and we are done.   □

4   Monitoring Must Testing

As Theorem 2 indicates, the monitoring framework presented in [16,17] is not expressive enough to characterise the must-testing preorder, as monitor acceptance and rejection are only determined by the traces processes can perform. This means that monitors from the basic framework reviewed in Sect. 3.1 cannot distinguish, for instance, the processes described by the CCS expressions $a.(b.\mathsf{nil} + c.\mathsf{nil})$ and $a.b.\mathsf{nil} + a.c.\mathsf{nil}$, which are not must-testing equivalent because $a.(b.\mathsf{nil} + c.\mathsf{nil}) \not\sqsubseteq_{\mathsf{must}} a.b.\mathsf{nil} + a.c.\mathsf{nil}$.

The first four authors presented a framework for parameterised monitorability in [1] and studied several of its instantiations. In what follows, we will first present one such instantiation (Sect. 4.1) and then show how a natural restriction of that specific monitoring framework offers a characterisation of must-testing semantics in terms of monitors (Sect. 4.2).

4.1   A Framework for Runtime Monitoring with Refusals

The instance of the monitoring framework from [1] we consider here is the one obtained by extending the syntax for rejection monitors given in Definition 1 with 'conditions' of the form $\mathrm{ref}(a)$, where $a \in \mathrm{ACT}$. (In the terminology of [1], 'conditions' are predicates over processes.)

Formally, following [1, Sections 4.1 and 5.2], we extend the formation rules for monitors given in Definition 1 with those of the form $\mathrm{ref}(a).m$, for each $a \in \mathrm{ACT}$. In the rest of this paper, we use the term *refusal monitors* for the monitors generated by that augmented grammar. In the behaviour of monitors, $\mathrm{ref}(a)$ is treated as an ordinary action prefixing operator and thus the rules in Table 1 are extended with the following ones:

$$\frac{}{\mathrm{ref}(a).m \xrightarrow{\mathrm{ref}(a)} m}, \ a \in \mathrm{ACT}.$$

Intuitively, in the spirit of Phillips' refusal testing [27], a monitor of the form $\mathrm{ref}(a).m$ checks whether the system it observes can *refuse* action a and, if so, continues monitoring as m. This is expressed by the following instrumentation rules for such conditions, which are added to the rules in Table 2:

$$\frac{m \xrightarrow{\mathrm{ref}(a)} m' \quad p \not\xrightarrow{\tau} \quad p \not\xrightarrow{a}}{m \triangleleft p \xrightarrow{\tau} m' \triangleleft p} \ a \in \mathrm{ACT}. \tag{1}$$

In what follows, we say that p *refuses* a when $p \not\xrightarrow{\tau}$ and $p \not\xrightarrow{a}$.

The syntax for refusal monitors allows one to write monitors such as

$$a.\mathrm{ref}(b).c.\mathrm{ref}(d).\mathsf{no}.$$

Since our goal is to define a monitor-based characterisation of must-testing semantics, monitors that alternate the observation of action occurrences with that of refusals arbitrarily are too powerful. Indeed, they would characterise *failure-trace semantics*, which coincides with Phillips' refusal testing over image-finite processes [18]. Therefore, in what follows, we only consider the sub-language MON_F of refusal monitors that consists of the monitors m that are generated by the following grammar:

$$m, n \in \mathrm{MON}_F :: = v \quad | \quad a.m \quad | \quad \mathrm{ref}(a).r \quad | \quad m + n \quad | \quad \mathbf{rec}\, x.m \quad | \quad x$$

$$r :: = \mathsf{no} \quad | \quad \mathrm{ref}(a).r$$

$$v :: = \mathsf{end} \quad | \quad \mathsf{no},$$

where x comes from a countably infinite set of monitor variables. We refer to those monitors as *failure monitors* and use them to define a preorder over processes as follows.

Definition 3 (Failure monitoring preorder). *For all $p, q \in P$,*

$$p \sqsubseteq_M^{Ref} q \text{ iff, for each failure monitor } m \in \mathrm{MON}_F, \ \mathbf{rej}(m, q) \text{ implies } \mathbf{rej}(m, p).$$

Intuitively, as in must-testing semantics, $p \sqsubseteq_M^{\mathrm{Ref}} q$ means that q is 'at least as well behaved as' p when its executions are observed by a failure monitor, in the sense that each failure monitor that rejects q will also reject p, and being rejected by a monitor is considered harmful. However, there might be some monitor that rejects p, but not q. For example, it is not too hard to see that $a.b.\mathsf{nil} + a.c.\mathsf{nil} \sqsubseteq_M^{\mathrm{Ref}} a.(b.\mathsf{nil} + c.\mathsf{nil})$, as each failure monitor that rejects $a.(b.\mathsf{nil} + c.\mathsf{nil})$ will also reject $a.b.\mathsf{nil} + a.c.\mathsf{nil}$. On the other hand, the monitor $a.\mathrm{ref}(b).\mathsf{no}$ rejects $a.b.\mathsf{nil} + a.c.\mathsf{nil}$, but not $a.(b.\mathsf{nil} + c.\mathsf{nil})$.

The following lemma describes how failure-monitor and system LTSs can be composed and decomposed according to instrumentation (cf. Lemmas 1 and 2).

Lemma 5 (Unzipping and zipping for failure monitors). *Let m be a failure monitor and let $p \in P$.*

1. *Assume that $m \lhd p \overset{s}{\Rightarrow} \mathsf{no} \lhd q$. Then*
   - *$p \overset{s}{\Rightarrow} q$ and*
   - *$m \xrightarrow{s\mathrm{ref}(a_1)\cdots\mathrm{ref}(a_\ell)} \mathsf{no}$ for some $\ell \geq 0$ and $a_1 \ldots a_\ell \in \mathrm{ACT}^*$ such that q refuses a_i for each $i \in \{1, \ldots, \ell\}$.*
2. *Assume that $p \overset{s}{\Rightarrow} q$ and $m \xrightarrow{s\mathrm{ref}(a_1)\cdots\mathrm{ref}(a_\ell)} \mathsf{no}$, for some $\ell \geq 0$ and $a_1 \ldots a_\ell \in \mathrm{ACT}^*$ such that q refuses a_i for each $i \in \{1, \ldots, \ell\}$. Then $m \lhd p \overset{s}{\Rightarrow} \mathsf{no} \lhd q$.*

4.2 Must Testing via Monitors

The goal of this section is to show how the monitoring framework we just reviewed can be used to give an alternative characterisation of classic must-testing semantics à la De Nicola and Hennessy over strongly-convergent, finitely-branching processes, which we now proceed to define.

Definition 4 (Strongly convergent and stable processes). *A process $p \in P$ is convergent iff it cannot perform an infinite sequence of τ transitions, that is, there is no infinite sequence $p_0, p_1, p_2, \ldots$ of processes in P such that $p_0 = p$ and $p_i \xrightarrow{\tau} p_{i+1}$ for each $i \geq 0$. We say that $p \in P$ is strongly convergent iff each of the processes that can be reached from it via a sequence of transitions is convergent.*

A process $p \in P$ is stable iff it cannot perform a τ transition, that is, $p \not\xrightarrow{\tau}$.

Definition 5 (Finitely branching processes). *A process $p \in P$ is finitely branching iff each of the processes that can be reached from it via a sequence of transitions has only finitely many outgoing transitions, that is, the set*

$$\{(\mu, q') \mid q \xrightarrow{\mu} q'\}$$

is finite for each q such that $p \xRightarrow{s} q$ for some $s \in \text{Act}^*$.

The alternative characterisation of the must-testing preorder in terms of failures, which we will present in Theorem 6 to follow, is by now folklore in concurrency theory. To the best of our knowledge, it was first proved by Rocco De Nicola in [13] and offers a connection between must-testing semantics and failures semantics [11] that, at the time, was considered rather unexpected. As a corollary of that result and a classic one by Kanellakis and Smolka [21, Theorem 5.1], deciding the must-testing preorder and equivalence is PSPACE-complete.

Definition 6 (Initials and failures of a process). *Let $p \in P$.*

- *The set $I(p)$ of initials of p is $\{a \mid p \xRightarrow{a}\}$.*
- *A pair (s, A) is a failure of a process $p \in P$ iff $s \in \text{Act}^*$, $A \subseteq \text{Act}$ and $I(p') \cap A = \emptyset$ for some stable p' such that $p \xRightarrow{s} p'$. We write failures(p) for the set of failures of process p.*

Theorem 6 (De Nicola [13]). *For all strongly convergent, finitely branching $p, q \in P$, $p \sqsubseteq_{must} q$ iff failures$(q) \subseteq$ failures(p).*

Remark 1. In the classic treatment of must-testing semantics over CCS and other process description languages, strongly convergent processes are guaranteed to be finitely branching. In this paper, for the sake of clarity, we have chosen to make the requirement that processes be finitely branching explicit.

Using the above theorem, we will now show the following result, to the effect that the must testing preorder coincides with the failure monitoring preorder from Definition 3.

Theorem 7. *For all strongly convergent, finitely branching $p, q \in P$, $p \sqsubseteq_{must} q$ iff $p \sqsubseteq_M^{Ref} q$.*

Proof. Let $p, q \in P$ be strongly convergent and finitely branching. By Theorem 6, it suffices only to prove that

$$\text{failures}(q) \subseteq \text{failures}(p) \text{ iff } p \sqsubseteq_M^{\text{Ref}} q.$$

We show the two implication separately.

To prove the 'only if' implication, assume that $\text{failures}(q) \subseteq \text{failures}(p)$ and that $\mathbf{rej}(m, q)$ for some failure monitor m. We claim that $\mathbf{rej}(m, p)$ also holds. To see this, observe that, since $\mathbf{rej}(m, q)$, there are some $s \in \text{ACT}^*$ and some $q' \in P$ such that $m \vartriangleleft q \overset{s}{\Rightarrow} \text{no} \vartriangleleft q'$. By the unzipping lemma for failure monitors (Lemma 5(1)), we have that

- $q \overset{s}{\Rightarrow} q'$ and
- $m \xrightarrow{\text{sref}(a_1)\cdots\text{ref}(a_\ell)} \text{no}$ for some $\ell \geq 0$ and $a_1 \ldots a_\ell \in \text{ACT}^*$ such that q' refuses a_i for each $i \in \{1, \ldots, \ell\}$.

It follows that $(s, \{a_1, \ldots, a_\ell\})$ is a failure of q and, by our assumption, also of p. This means that $p \overset{s}{\Rightarrow} p'$ for some p' that refuses a_i for each $i \in \{1, \ldots, \ell\}$. Using the zipping lemma for failure monitors (Lemma 5(2), we conclude that $m \vartriangleleft p \overset{s}{\Rightarrow} \text{no} \vartriangleleft p'$ and thus $\mathbf{rej}(m, p)$, as claimed.

To prove the 'if' implication, assume that $p \sqsubseteq_M^{\text{Ref}} q$. We claim that $\text{failures}(q)$ is included in $\text{failures}(p)$. This follows from the observation that rejection monitors can be used to encode the failures of a process. More precisely, consider a failure pair $(s, \{a_1, \ldots, a_\ell\})$. We can associate with it a rejection monitor $m(s, \{a_1, \ldots, a_\ell\})$ by induction on s thus:

$$m(\varepsilon, \{a_1, \ldots, a_\ell\}) = \text{ref}(a_1).\ldots.\text{ref}(a_\ell).\text{no} \quad \text{and}$$
$$m(as', \{a_1, \ldots, a_\ell\}) = a.m(s', \{a_1, \ldots, a_\ell\}).$$

By induction on s, it is easy to prove that $(s, \{a_1, \ldots, a_\ell\})$ is a failure of some process p iff $\mathbf{rej}(m(s, \{a_1, \ldots, a_\ell\}), p)$. We can now complete the proof of the claim thus:

$$
\begin{aligned}
(s, \{a_1, \ldots, a_\ell\}) \in \text{failures}(q) &\Leftrightarrow \mathbf{rej}(m(s, \{a_1, \ldots, a_\ell\}), q) \\
&\Rightarrow \mathbf{rej}(m(s, \{a_1, \ldots, a_\ell\}), p) \quad (\text{as } p \sqsubseteq_M^{\text{Ref}} q) \\
&\Leftrightarrow (s, \{a_1, \ldots, a_\ell\}) \in \text{failures}(p),
\end{aligned}
$$

and we are done. $\qquad\square$

5   Conclusions

In this celebratory article, we have provided a formal connection between the theory of testing equivalence, developed by De Nicola and Hennessy during De Nicola's PhD studies in Edinburgh, and the increasingly important field of run-time verification. The results in this study are not deep, but we hope that they highlight the pervasive nature of the ideas that underlie the definition of the testing equivalences from [15] and will convince our readers that the field of runtime monitoring owes much to the seminal work by De Nicola and Hennessy. Some of us were influenced by that work at the start of their careers [5,6,20] and are still working on testing-based approaches to the analysis of concurrent processes after about thirty years.

An interesting avenue for future research is to investigate whether the must-testing-like preorders over clients studied by Bernardi and Francalanza in [10] capture some interesting properties of monitors. So far, our work on monitorability has used the trace-based notions of *verdict equivalence* and *ω-verdict equivalence* over monitors—see, for instance, the papers [2–4].

Acknowledgments. We are grateful to the anonymous reviewers for their suggestions, which helped us to improve the paper. Luca Aceto thanks Ugo Montanari, who asked him a question that led to the work presented in this article during a talk he gave at IMT Lucca in July 2018. Luca Aceto and Anna Ingólfsdóttir have been lucky to count Rocco De Nicola as one of their friends and mentors for many years. Luca Aceto's 'tesi di laurea' was jointly supervised by Rocco De Nicola and Alessandro Fantechi, and he was one of the first two students to graduate under Rocco De Nicola's supervision in 1986.

References

1. Aceto, L., Achilleos, A., Francalanza, A., Ingólfsdóttir, A.: A framework for parameterized monitorability. In: Baier, C., Dal Lago, U. (eds.) FoSSaCS 2018. LNCS, vol. 10803, pp. 203–220. Springer, Cham (2018). https://doi.org/10.1007/978-3-319-89366-2_11
2. Aceto, L., Achilleos, A., Francalanza, A., Ingólfsdóttir, A., Kjartansson, S.Ö.: On the complexity of determinizing monitors. In: Carayol, A., Nicaud, C. (eds.) CIAA 2017. LNCS, vol. 10329, pp. 1–13. Springer, Cham (2017). https://doi.org/10.1007/978-3-319-60134-2_1
3. Aceto, L., Achilleos, A., Francalanza, A., Ingólfsdóttir, A., Lehtinen, K.: Adventures in monitorability: from branching to linear time and back again. In: Proceedings of the ACM on Programming Languages (POPL), vol. 3, pp. 52:1–52:29 (2019). https://dl.acm.org/citation.cfm?id=3290365
4. Aceto, L., Achilleos, A., Francalanza, A., Ingólfsdóttir, A., Lehtinen, K.: The cost of monitoring alone. CoRR abs/1902.05152 (2019). http://arxiv.org/abs/1902.05152
5. Aceto, L., De Nicola, R., Fantechi, A.: Testing equivalences for event structures. In: Zilli, M.V. (ed.) Mathematical Models for the Semantics of Parallelism. LNCS, vol. 280, pp. 1–20. Springer, Heidelberg (1987). https://doi.org/10.1007/3-540-18419-8_9
6. Aceto, L., Ingólfsdóttir, A.: A theory of testing for ACP. In: Baeten, J.C.M., Groote, J.F. (eds.) CONCUR 1991. LNCS, vol. 527, pp. 78–95. Springer, Heidelberg (1991). https://doi.org/10.1007/3-540-54430-5_82
7. Aceto, L., Ingólfsdóttir, A.: Testing Hennessy-Milner logic with recursion. In: Thomas, W. (ed.) FoSSaCS 1999. LNCS, vol. 1578, pp. 41–55. Springer, Heidelberg (1999). https://doi.org/10.1007/3-540-49019-1_4
8. Aceto, L., Ingólfsdóttir, A., Larsen, K.G., Srba, J.: Reactive Systems: Modelling, Specification and Verification. Cambridge University Press, New York (2007). https://doi.org/10.1017/cbo9780511814105

9. Bartocci, E., Falcone, Y. (eds.): Lectures on Runtime Verification - Introductory and Advanced Topics. LNCS, vol. 10457. Springer, Cham (2018). https://doi.org/10.1007/978-3-319-75632-5

10. Bernardi, G.T., Francalanza, A.: Full-abstraction for client testing preorders. Sci. Comput. Program. **168**, 94–117 (2018). https://doi.org/10.1016/j.scico.2018.08.004

11. Brookes, S.D., Hoare, C.A.R., Roscoe, A.W.: A theory of communicating sequential processes. J. ACM **31**(3), 560–599 (1984). https://doi.org/10.1145/828.833

12. Cerone, A., Hennessy, M.: Process behaviour: formulae vs. tests (extended abstract). In: Fröschle, S.B., Valencia, F.D. (eds.) Proceedings 17th International Workshop on Expressiveness in Concurrency, EXPRESS 2010. Electronic Proceedings in Theoretical Computer Science, vol. 41, pp. 31–45 (2010). https://doi.org/10.4204/EPTCS.41.3

13. De Nicola, R.: Extensional equivalences for transition systems. Acta Informatica **24**(2), 211–237 (1987). https://doi.org/10.1007/BF00264365

14. de Nicola, R., Hennessy, M.C.B.: Testing equivalences for processes. In: Diaz, Josep (ed.) ICALP 1983. LNCS, vol. 154, pp. 548–560. Springer, Heidelberg (1983). https://doi.org/10.1007/BFb0036936

15. De Nicola, R., Hennessy, M.: Testing equivalences for processes. Theor. Comput. Sci. **34**, 83–133 (1984). https://doi.org/10.1016/0304-3975(84)90113-0

16. Francalanza, A., Aceto, L., Ingolfsdottir, A.: On verifying Hennessy-Milner logic with recursion at runtime. In: Bartocci, E., Majumdar, R. (eds.) RV 2015. LNCS, vol. 9333, pp. 71–86. Springer, Cham (2015). https://doi.org/10.1007/978-3-319-23820-3_5

17. Francalanza, A., Aceto, L., Ingolfsdottir, A.: Monitorability for the Hennessy-Milner logic with recursion. Form. Methods Syst. Des. **51**(1), 87–116 (2017). https://doi.org/10.1007/s10703-017-0273-z

18. van Glabbeek, R.J.: The linear time - branching time spectrum I: the semantics of concrete, sequential processes (Chap. 1). In: Bergstra, J.A., Ponse, A., Smolka, S.A. (eds.) Handbook of Process Algebra, pp. 3–99. Elsevier, Amsterdam (2001)

19. Hennessy, M.: Algebraic Theory of Processes. Foundations of Computing, MIT Press, Cambridge (1988)

20. Hennessy, M., Ingolfsdottir, A.: A theory of communicating processes with value passing. Inf. Comput. **107**(2), 202–236 (1993). https://doi.org/10.1006/inco.1993.1067

21. Kanellakis, P.C., Smolka, S.A.: CCS expressions, finite state processes, and three problems of equivalence. Inf. Comput. **86**(1), 43–68 (1990). https://doi.org/10.1016/0890-5401(90)90025-D

22. Keller, R.M.: Formal verification of parallel programs. Commun. ACM **19**(7), 371–384 (1976). https://doi.org/10.1145/360248.360251

23. Larsen, K.G.: Proof systems for satisfiability in Hennessy-Milner logic with recursion. Theor. Comput. Sci. **72**(2), 265–288 (1990). https://doi.org/10.1016/0304-3975(90)90038-J. http://www.sciencedirect.com/science/article/pii/030439759090038J

24. Loemker, L.E. (ed.): G. W. Leibniz: Philosophical Papers and Letters, 2nd edn. D. Reidel, Dordrecht (1969)

25. Milner, R.: A Calculus of Communicating Systems. Springer, Heidelberg (1980). https://doi.org/10.1007/3-540-10235-3

26. Morris, J.H.: Lambda-calculus models of programming languages. Ph.D. thesis, Massachusetts Institute of Technology (1968)

27. Phillips, I.: Refusal testing. Theor. Comput. Sci. **50**(3),241–284 (1987). https://doi.org/10.1016/0304-3975(87)90117-4. http://www.sciencedirect.com/science/article/pii/0304397587901174
28. Stockmeyer, L.J., Meyer, A.R.: Word problems requiring exponential time: preliminary report. In: Aho, A.V., et al. (eds.) Proceedings of the 5th Annual ACM Symposium on Theory of Computing, pp. 1–9. ACM (1973). https://doi.org/10.1145/800125.804029
29. Winskel, G.: Synchronization trees. Theor. Comput. Sci. **34**, 33–82 (1984). https://doi.org/10.1016/0304-3975(84)90112-9

Reward Testing Equivalences
for Processes

Rob van Glabbeek[1,2]([✉])

[1] Data61, CSIRO, Sydney, Australia
[2] Computer Science and Engineering, University of New South Wales,
Sydney, Australia
rvg@cs.stanford.edu

Abstract. May and must testing were introduced by De Nicola and Hennessy to define semantic equivalences on processes. May-testing equivalence exactly captures safety properties, and must-testing equivalence liveness properties. This paper proposes *reward testing* and shows that the resulting semantic equivalence also captures conditional liveness properties. It is strictly finer than both the may- and must-testing equivalence.

Keywords: Reward testing · Semantic equivalences ·
Conditional liveness properties · Labelled transition systems ·
Process algebra · CCS · Axiomatisations · Recursion · Congruence ·
Divergence

1 Introduction

The idea behind semantic equivalences $\equiv$ and refinement preorders $\sqsubseteq$ on processes is that $P \equiv Q$ says, essentially, that for practical purposes processes P and Q are equally suitable, i.e. one can be replaced for by the other without untoward side effects. Likewise, $P \sqsubseteq Q$ says that for all practical purposes under consideration, Q is at least as suitable as P, i.e. it will never harm to replace P by Q. To this end, Q must have all relevant good properties that P enjoys. Among the properties that ought to be so *preserved*, are *safety properties*, saying that nothing bad will even happen, and *liveness properties*, saying that something good will happen eventually.

In the setting of the process algebra CCS, refinement preorders $\sqsubseteq_{may}$ and $\sqsubseteq_{must}$, and associated semantic equivalences $\equiv_{may}$ and $\equiv_{must}$, were proposed by De Nicola & Hennessy in [6]. In [12] I argue that $\equiv_{may}$ and $\equiv_{must}$ are the

---

This paper is dedicated to Rocco De Nicola, on the occasion of his 60th birthday. Rocco's work has been a source of inspiration to my own.

M. Boreale et al. (Eds.): De Nicola-Festschrift, LNCS 11665, pp. 45–70, 2019.
https://doi.org/10.1007/978-3-030-21485-2_5

Fig. 1. Processes identified by may and must testing, but with different conditional liveness properties

coarsest equivalences that enjoy some basic compositionality requirements[1] and preserve safety and liveness properties, respectively. Yet neither preserves so-called *conditional liveness properties*. This is illustrated in Fig. 1, showing two processes that are identified under both may and must testing. From a practical point of view, the difference between these two processes may be enormous. It could be that the action c comes with a huge cost, that is only worth making when the good action g happens afterwards. Only the right-hand side process is able to incur the cost without any benefits, and for this reason it lacks an important property that the left-hand process has. I call such properties *conditional liveness properties*. A conditional liveness property says that

under certain conditions something good will eventually happen.

This paper introduces a stronger form of testing that preserves conditional liveness properties.

2   General Setting

It is natural to view the semantics of processes as being determined by their ability to pass tests [6,17]; processes P_1 and P_2 are deemed to be semantically equivalent unless there is a test which can distinguish them. The actual tests used typically represent the ways in which users, or indeed other processes, can interact with P_i. This idea can be formulated in the following general testing scenario [9], of which the testing scenarios of [6,17] are instances. It assumes

- a set of processes $\mathbb{P}$,
- a set of tests $\mathbb{T}$, which can be applied to processes,
- a set of outcomes $\mathbb{O}$, the possible results from applying a test to a process,
- and a function $\mathcal{A}pply : \mathbb{T} \times \mathbb{P} \to \mathscr{P}^+(\mathbb{O})$, representing the possible results of applying a specific test to a specific process.

Here $\mathscr{P}^+(\mathbb{O})$ denotes the collection of non-empty subsets of $\mathbb{O}$; so the result of applying a test T to a process P, $\mathcal{A}pply(T, P)$, is in general a *set* of outcomes, representing the fact that the behaviour of processes, and indeed tests, may be nondeterministic.

---

[1] Namely being congruences for injective renaming and partially synchronous interleaving operators, or equivalently all operators of CSP, or equivalently the CCS operators parallel composition, restriction and relabelling.

Moreover, some outcomes are considered better then others; for example the application of a test may simply succeed, or it may fail, with success being better than failure. So one can assume that $\mathbb{O}$ is endowed with a partial order, in which $o_1 \leq o_2$ means that o_2 is a better outcome than o_1.

When comparing the result of applying tests to processes one needs to compare subsets of $\mathbb{O}$. There are two standard approaches to make this comparison, based on viewing these sets as elements of either the Hoare or Smyth powerdomain [1,16] of $\mathbb{O}$. For $O_1, O_2 \in \mathscr{P}^+(\mathbb{O})$ let

(i) $O_1 \sqsubseteq_{\mathrm{Ho}} O_2$ if for every $o_1 \in O_1$ there exists some $o_2 \in O_2$ such that $o_1 \leq o_2$
(ii) $O_1 \sqsubseteq_{\mathrm{Sm}} O_2$ if for every $o_2 \in O_2$ there exists some $o_1 \in O_1$ such that $o_1 \leq o_2$.

Using these two comparison methods one obtains two different semantic preorders for processes:

(i) For $P, Q \in \mathbb{P}$ let $P \sqsubseteq_{\mathrm{may}} Q$ if $\mathcal{A}pply(T, P) \sqsubseteq_{\mathrm{Ho}} \mathcal{A}pply(T, Q)$ for each test T
(ii) Similarly, let $P \sqsubseteq_{\mathrm{must}} Q$ if $\mathcal{A}pply(T, P) \sqsubseteq_{\mathrm{Sm}} \mathcal{A}pply(T, Q)$ for each test T.

Note that $\sqsubseteq_{\mathrm{may}}$ and $\sqsubseteq_{\mathrm{must}}$ are reflexive and transitive, and hence preorders. I use $P \equiv_{\mathrm{may}} Q$ and $P \equiv_{\mathrm{must}} Q$ to denote the associated equivalences.

The terminology *may* and *must* refers to the following reformulation of the same idea. Let $Pass \subseteq \mathbb{O}$ be an upwards-closed subset of $\mathbb{O}$, i.e. satisfying $o' \geq o \in Pass \Rightarrow o' \in Pass$, thought of as the set of outcomes that can be regarded as *passing* a test. Then one says that a process P *may* pass a test T with an outcome in $Pass$, notation "P **may** $Pass\ T$", if there is an outcome $o \in \mathcal{A}pply(P, T)$ with $o \in Pass$, and likewise P *must* pass a test T with an outcome in $Pass$, notation "P **must** $Pass\ T$", if for all $o \in \mathcal{A}pply(P, T)$ one has $o \in Pass$. Now

$$P \sqsubseteq_{\mathrm{may}} Q \text{ iff } \forall T \in \mathbb{T}\ \forall Pass \in \mathrm{P}^\uparrow(\mathbb{O})\ (P \textbf{ may } Pass\ T \ \Rightarrow\ Q \textbf{ may } Pass\ T)$$

$$P \sqsubseteq_{\mathrm{must}} Q \text{ iff } \forall T \in \mathbb{T}\ \forall Pass \in \mathrm{P}^\uparrow(\mathbb{O})\ (P \textbf{ must } Pass\ T \ \Rightarrow\ Q \textbf{ must } Pass\ T)$$

where $\mathrm{P}^\uparrow(\mathbb{O})$ is the set of upwards-closed subsets of $\mathbb{O}$.

The original theory of testing [6,17] is obtained by using as the set of outcomes $\mathbb{O}$ the two-point lattice

with $\top$ representing the success of a test application, and $\bot$ failure.

3   CCS: The Calculus of Communicating Systems

CCS [24] is parametrised with a set $\mathscr{C}$ of *names*; $Act := \mathscr{C} \,\dot{\cup}\, \bar{\mathscr{C}} \,\dot{\cup}\, \{\tau\}$ is the set of *actions*, where τ is a special *internal action* and $\bar{\mathscr{C}} := \{\bar{c} \mid c \in \mathscr{C}\}$ is the

Table 1. Structural operational semantics of CCS

$$\alpha.E \xrightarrow{\alpha} E \qquad \frac{E_j \xrightarrow{\alpha} E_j'}{\sum_{i \in I} E_i \xrightarrow{\alpha} E_j'} \quad (j \in I)$$

$$\frac{E \xrightarrow{\alpha} E'}{E|F \xrightarrow{\alpha} E'|F} \qquad \frac{E \xrightarrow{a} E', \ F \xrightarrow{\bar{a}} F'}{E|F \xrightarrow{\tau} E'|F'} \qquad \frac{F \xrightarrow{\alpha} F'}{E|F \xrightarrow{\alpha} E|F'}$$

$$\frac{E \xrightarrow{\alpha} E'}{E\backslash L \xrightarrow{\alpha} E'\backslash L} \ (\alpha, \bar{\alpha} \notin L) \qquad \frac{E \xrightarrow{\alpha} E'}{E[f] \xrightarrow{f(\alpha)} E'[f]} \qquad \frac{\mathbf{fix}(\!|S_X{:}S|\!) \xrightarrow{\alpha} E}{\mathbf{fix}(\!|X{:}S|\!) \xrightarrow{\alpha} E}$$

set of *co-names*. Complementation is extended to $\bar{\mathscr{C}}$ by setting $\bar{\bar{c}} = c$. Below, a ranges over $\mathscr{A} := \mathscr{C} \cup \bar{\mathscr{C}}$ and α over *Act*. A *relabelling* is a function $f : \mathscr{C} \to \mathscr{C}$; it extends to *Act* by $f(\bar{c}) = \overline{f(c)}$ and $f(\tau) := \tau$. Let $\mathscr{X}$ be a set $X, Y, \ldots$ of *process variables*. The set $\mathbb{E}_{\text{CCS}}$ of CCS expressions is the smallest set including:

$\alpha.E$	for $\alpha \in Act$ and $E \in \mathbb{E}_{\text{CCS}}$	*action prefixing*
$\sum_{i \in I} E_i$	for I an index set and $E_i \in \mathbb{E}_{\text{CCS}}$	*choice*
$E|F$	for $E, F \in \mathbb{E}_{\text{CCS}}$	*parallel composition*
$E\backslash L$	for $L \subseteq \mathscr{C}$ and $E \in \mathbb{E}_{\text{CCS}}$	*restriction*
$E[f]$	for f a relabelling and $E \in \mathbb{E}_{\text{CCS}}$	*relabelling*
X	for $X \in \mathscr{X}$	*process variable*
$\mathbf{fix}(\!|X{:}S|\!)$	for $S: \mathscr{X} \rightharpoonup \mathbb{E}_{\text{CCS}}$ and $X \in dom(S)$	*recursion*

The expression $\sum_{i \in \{1,2\}} \alpha_i.E_i$ is often written as $\alpha_1.E_1 + \alpha_2.E_2$, $\sum_{i \in \{1\}} \alpha_i.E_i$ as $\alpha_1.E_1$, and $\sum_{i \in \emptyset} \alpha_i.E_i$ as $\mathbf{0}$. Moreover, one abbreviates $\alpha.\mathbf{0}$ by α, and $P\backslash\{c\}$ by $P\backslash c$. A partial function $S : \mathscr{X} \rightharpoonup \mathbb{E}_{\text{CCS}}$ is called a *recursive specification*, and traditionally written as $\{Y \stackrel{def}{=} S(Y) \mid Y \in dom(S)\}$. A CCS expression E is *closed* if each occurrence of a process variable Y in E lays within a subexpression $\mathbf{fix}(\!|X{:}S|\!)$ of E with $Y \in dom(S)$; $\mathbb{P}_{\text{CCS}}$, ranged over by $P, Q, \ldots$, denotes the set of closed CCS expressions, or *processes*.

The semantics of CCS is given by the labelled transition relation $\rightarrow \subseteq \mathbb{P}_{\text{CCS}} \times Act \times \mathbb{P}_{\text{CCS}}$, where transitions $P \xrightarrow{\alpha} Q$ are derived from the rules of Table 1. Here $\mathbf{fix}(\!|S_X{:}S|\!)$ denotes the expression $S(X)$ (written S_X) with $\mathbf{fix}(\!|Y{:}S|\!)$ substituted for each free occurrence of Y, for all $Y \in dom(S)$, while renaming bound variables in S_X as necessary to avoid name-clashes.

The process $\alpha.P$ performs the action α first and subsequently acts as P. The choice operator $\sum_{i \in I} P_i$ may act as any of its arguments P_i, depending on which of these processes is able to act at all. The parallel composition $P|Q$ executes an action from P, an action from Q, or in the case where P and Q can perform complementary actions a and $\bar{a}$, the process can perform a synchronisation, resulting in an internal action τ. The restriction operator $P \backslash L$ inhibits execution of the actions from L and their complements. The relabelling $P[f]$ acts like process P with all labels α replaced by $f(\alpha)$. Finally, the rule for recursion says that a recursively defined process $\mathbf{fix}(\!|X{:}S|\!)$ behaves exactly as the body S_X of the recursive equation $X \stackrel{def}{=} S_X$, but with recursive calls $\mathbf{fix}(\!|Y{:}S|\!)$ substituted for the variables $Y \in dom(S)$.

4   Classical May and Must Testing for CCS

Let $Act^\omega := Act \cup \{\omega\}$, where $\omega \notin Act$ is a special action reporting success. A CCS test $T \in \mathbb{T}_{\text{CCS}}$ is defined just like a CCS process, but with α ranging over Act^ω. So a CCS process is a special kind of CCS test, namely one that never performs the action ω. To apply the test T to the process P one runs them in parallel; that is, one runs the combined process $T|P$—which is itself a CCS test.

Definition 1. A *computation* π is a finite or infinite sequence $T_0, T_1, T_2, \ldots$ of tests, such that (i) if T_n is the final element in the sequence, then $T_n \stackrel{\tau}{\longrightarrow} T$ for no T, and (ii) otherwise $T_n \stackrel{\tau}{\longrightarrow} T_{n+1}$.

A computation is *successful* if it has a state T with $T \stackrel{\omega}{\longrightarrow} T'$ for some T'.

For $T \in \mathbb{T}_{\text{CCS}}$, $P \in \mathbb{P}_{\text{CCS}}$, let $Comp(T, P)$ be the set of computations whose initial element is $T|P$.

Let $\mathcal{Apply}(T, P) := \{\top \mid \exists \text{ successful } \pi \in Comp(T, P)\} \cup$
$\qquad\qquad\qquad\quad \{\bot \mid \exists \text{ unsuccessful } \pi \in Comp(T, P)\}.$

Using this definition of $\mathcal{Apply}$ it follows that $P \sqsubseteq_{\text{may}} Q$ holds unless there is a test T such that $T|P$ has (that is, is the initial state of) a successful computation but Q has not. Likewise $P \sqsubseteq_{\text{must}} Q$ holds unless there is a test T such that $T|P$ has only successful computations but Q has not.

5   Dual May and Must Testing

A *liveness property* [20] is a property that says that *something good will eventually happen*. In the context of CCS, any test T can be regarded to specify a liveness property; a process P is defined to have this property iff all computations of $T|P$ are successful. Now $P \sqsubseteq_{\text{must}} Q$ holds iff all liveness properties $T \in \mathbb{T}_{\text{CCS}}$ that are enjoyed by P also hold for Q.

A *safety property* [20] is a property that says that *something bad will never happen*. When thinking of the special action ω as reporting that something bad has occurred, rather than something good, any test T can also be regarded to specify a safety property; a process P is defined to have this property iff none of the computations of $T|P$ are catastrophic; here *catastrophic* is simply another word for "successful", when reversing the connotation of ω. Now $Q \sqsubseteq_{\text{may}} P$ holds iff all safety properties $T \in \mathbb{T}_{\text{CCS}}$ that are enjoyed by P also hold for Q.

A *labelled transition system* (LTS) over a set Act is a pair $(\mathbb{P}, \rightarrow)$ where $\mathbb{P}$ is a set of *processes* or *states* and $\rightarrow \subseteq \mathbb{P} \times Act \times \mathbb{P}$ a set of *transitions*. In

[12] preorders $\sqsubseteq_{liveness}$ and $\sqsubseteq_{safety}$ are defined on LTSs. Specialised to the LTS $(\mathbb{P}_{CCS}, \rightarrow)$ induced by CCS, $\sqsubseteq_{liveness}$ coincides with $\sqsubseteq_{must}$, and $\sqsubseteq_{safety}$ is exactly the reverse of $\sqsubseteq_{may}$, in accordance with the reasoning above.

To explain the reversal of $\sqsubseteq_{may}$ when dealing with safety properties, I propose a variant of CCS testing where in Definition 1 the word "catastrophic" is used for "successful" and $\mathcal{A}pply$ is redefined by

$$\mathcal{A}pply(T, P) := \{\bot \mid \exists \text{ catastrophic } \pi \in Comp(T, P)\} \cup$$
$$\{\top \mid \exists \text{ uncatastrophic } \pi \in Comp(T, P)\}.$$

An equivalent alternative to redefining $\mathcal{A}pply$ is to simply invert the order between $\bot$ and $\top$. Let $\sqsubseteq_{may}^{dual}$ and $\sqsubseteq_{must}^{dual}$ be the versions of the may- and must-testing preorders obtained from this alternative definition. It follows immediately from the definitions that $P \sqsubseteq_{may}^{dual} Q$ iff $Q \sqsubseteq_{must} P$ and that $P \sqsubseteq_{must}^{dual} Q$ iff $Q \sqsubseteq_{may} P$. Based on this, it may be more accurate to say that $\sqsubseteq_{safety}$ coincides with $\sqsubseteq_{must}^{dual}$.

A *possibility property* [21] is a property that says that *something good might eventually happen*. A test T can be regarded to specify a possibility property; a process P is defined to have this property iff some computation of $T|P$ is successful. Now $P \sqsubseteq_{may} Q$ holds iff all possibility properties $T \in \mathbb{T}_{CCS}$ that are enjoyed by P also hold for Q. Lamport argues that "verifying possibility properties tells you nothing interesting about a system" [21]. As an example, consider the following models of coffee machines:

$$C_1 := \tau \qquad C_2 := \tau.c + \tau \qquad C_3 := \tau.c$$

where c is the act of dispensing coffee. The machine C_1 surely will not make coffee, C_2 makes a nondeterministic choice between making coffee or not, and C_3 surely makes coffee. Under may testing, systems $C2$ and C_3 are equivalent—both have the possibility of making coffee—and each of them is better than C_1: $C_1 \sqsubseteq_{may} C_2 \equiv_{may} C_3$. The relevance of this indeed is questionable. It takes must testing to formalise that C_3 is better than C_2: only C_3 guarantees that coffee will eventually be dispensed.

When employing dual testing, the same example applies, but with c denoting a catastrophe. Now C_1 is safe, whereas C_2 and C_3 are not: $C_1 \sqsupseteq_{must}^{dual} C_2 \equiv_{must}^{dual} C_3$. Dual may testing would argue that C_2 is better than C_3 because a catastrophe might be avoided. This however, can be deemed a weak argument.

In view of these considerations, I will focus on the preorders $\sqsubseteq_{must}$ and $\sqsubseteq_{must}^{dual}$ (or $\sqsubseteq_{safety}$). The (dual) may preorders simply arise as their inverses, and hence do not require explicit treatment.

6   Reward Testing for CCS

A CCS *reward test* is defined just like a CCS process, but with α ranging over $Act \times \mathbb{R}$, the *valued actions*. A valued action is an action tagged with a real number, the *reward* for executing this action. A negative reward can be seen as a penalty. Let $\mathbb{T}_{CCS}^{R}$ be the set of CCS reward tests. The structural operational semantics for CCS reward tests has the following modified rules:

$$\frac{P \xrightarrow{a,r} P', \ Q \xrightarrow{\bar{a},r'} Q'}{P|Q \xrightarrow{\tau,r+r'} P'|Q'} \qquad \frac{P \xrightarrow{\alpha,r} P'}{P\backslash L \xrightarrow{\alpha,r} P'\backslash L} \ (\alpha, \bar{\alpha} \notin L) \qquad \frac{P \xrightarrow{\alpha,r} P'}{P[f] \xrightarrow{f(\alpha),r} P'[f]}$$

Thus, in synchronising two actions one reaps the rewards of both. In all other rules of Table 1, α is simply replaced by α, r, with $r \in \mathbb{R}$. A valued action $\alpha, 0$ is simply denoted α, so that a CCS process can be seen as a special CCS reward test, namely one in which all rewards are 0. To apply a reward test T to a process P one again runs them in parallel.

Definition 2. A *reward computation* π is a finite or infinite sequence $T_0, r_1, T_1, r_2, T_2 \ldots$ of reward tests, such that (i) if T_n is the final element in π, then $T_n \xrightarrow{\tau,r} T$ for no r and T, and (ii) otherwise $T_n \xrightarrow{\tau,r_{n+1}} T_{n+1}$.

The *reward* of a finite computation π ending in T_n is $\sum_{i=1}^{n} r_i$. The *reward* of an infinite computation $T_0, r_1, T_1, r_2, T_2 \ldots$ is

$$\inf_{n \to \infty} \sum_{i=1}^{n} r_i \quad \in \mathbb{R} \cup \{-\infty, \infty\}.$$

For $T \in \mathbb{T}_{\text{CCS}}^R$, $P \in \mathbb{P}_{\text{CCS}}$, let $Comp^R(T, P)$ be the set of reward computations with initial element $T|P$.
Let $\mathcal{A}pply(T, P) := \{reward(\pi) \mid \pi \in Comp^R(T, P)\}$.

This defines reward preorders $\sqsubseteq_{\text{reward}}^{\text{may}}$ and $\sqsubseteq_{\text{reward}}^{\text{must}}$ on $\mathbb{P}_{\text{CCS}}$. It will turn out that $P \sqsubseteq_{\text{reward}}^{\text{may}} Q$ iff $Q \sqsubseteq_{\text{reward}}^{\text{must}} P$. As a consequence I will focus on $\sqsubseteq_{\text{reward}}^{\text{must}}$, and simply call it $\sqsubseteq_{\text{reward}}$.

7   Characterising Reward Testing

Assuming a fixed LTS $(\mathbb{P}, \to)$, labelled over a set $Act = \mathscr{A} \ \dot{\cup} \ \{\tau\}$, the ternary relation $\Longrightarrow \subseteq \mathbb{P} \times \mathscr{A}^* \times \mathbb{P}$ is the least relation satisfying

$$P \xRightarrow{\epsilon} P \ , \qquad \frac{P \xrightarrow{\tau} Q}{P \xRightarrow{\epsilon} Q} \ , \qquad \frac{P \xrightarrow{a} Q, \ a \neq \tau}{P \xRightarrow{a} Q} \quad \text{and} \quad \frac{P \xRightarrow{\sigma} Q \xRightarrow{\rho} r}{P \xRightarrow{\sigma\rho} r} \ .$$

For $\sigma \in \mathscr{A}^*$ and $\nu \in \mathscr{A}^* \cup \mathscr{A}^\infty$ write $\sigma \leq \nu$ for "σ is a prefix of ρ", i.e. "$\exists \rho . \sigma \rho = \nu$".

Definition 3. Let $P \in \mathbb{P}$.

- $a_1 a_2 a_3 \cdots \in \mathscr{A}^\infty$ is an *infinite trace* of P if $\exists P_i$ such that $P \xRightarrow{a_1} P_1 \xRightarrow{a_2} \cdots$.
- $inf(P)$ denotes the set of infinite traces of P.
- P *diverges*, notation $P{\Uparrow}$, if $\exists P_i \in \mathbb{P}$ such that $P \xrightarrow{\tau} P_1 \xrightarrow{\tau} P_2 \xrightarrow{\tau} \cdots$.
- $divergences(P) := \{\sigma \in \mathscr{A}^* \mid \exists Q. P \xRightarrow{\sigma} Q{\Uparrow}\}$, the *divergence traces* of P.
- $initials(P) := \{a \in \mathscr{A} \mid \exists Q. P \xrightarrow{\alpha} Q\}$.
- $deadlocks(P) := \{\sigma \in \mathscr{A}^* \mid \exists Q. P \xRightarrow{\sigma} Q \wedge initials(Q) = \emptyset\}$.
- $CT(P) := inf(P) \cup divergences(P) \cup deadlocks(P)$, the *complete traces* of P.

- $ptraces(P) := \{\sigma \in \mathscr{A}^* \mid \exists Q.\ P \overset{\sigma}{\Rightarrow} Q\}$, the set of *partial traces* of P.
- $failures(P) := \left\{ \langle \sigma, X \rangle \in \mathscr{A}^* \times \mathscr{P}(\mathscr{A}) \ \middle|\ \begin{array}{l} \exists Q.\ P \overset{\sigma}{\Rightarrow} Q\ \wedge \\ initials(Q) \cap (X \cup \{\tau\}) = \emptyset \end{array} \right\}$.
- $failures_d(P) := failures(P) \cup \{\langle \sigma, X \rangle \mid \sigma \in divergences(P) \wedge X \subseteq \mathscr{A}\}$.
- $inf_d(P) := inf(P) \cup \{\nu \in \mathscr{A}^\infty \mid \forall \sigma < \nu\ \exists \rho \in divergences(P).\ \sigma \le \rho < \nu\}$.
- $divergences_\perp(P) := \{\sigma \rho \mid \sigma \in divergences(P) \wedge \rho \in \mathscr{A}^*\}$.
- $inf_\perp(P) := inf(P) \cup \{\sigma \nu \mid \sigma \in divergences(P) \wedge \nu \in \mathscr{A}^\infty\}$.
- $failures_\perp(P) := failures(P) \cup \{\langle \sigma \rho, X \rangle \mid \sigma \in divergences(P) \wedge \rho \in \mathscr{A}^* \wedge X \subseteq \mathscr{A}\}$.

Note that $\quad ptraces(R) = \{\sigma \mid \langle \sigma, \emptyset \rangle \in failures_d(R)\} \quad$ for any $R \in \mathbb{P}$. $\quad$ (*)
A *path* of a process $P \in \mathbb{P}$ is an alternating sequence $P_0\ \alpha_1\ P_1\ \alpha_2\ P_2 \cdots$ of processes/states and actions, starting with a state and either being infinite or ending with a state, such that $P_i \overset{\alpha_{i+1}}{\longrightarrow} P_{i+1}$ for all relevant i. Let $l(\pi) := \alpha_1 \alpha_2 \cdots$ be the sequence of actions in π, and $\ell(\pi)$ the same sequence after all τs are removed. Now $\sigma \in inf(P) \cup divergences(P)$ iff P has an infinite path π with $\ell(\pi) = \sigma$. Likewise, $\sigma \in ptraces(P)$ iff P has a finite path π with $\ell(\pi) = \sigma$. Finally, $\sigma \in inf(P) \cup ptraces(P)$ iff P has an path π with $\ell(\pi) = \sigma$.

Any transition $P|Q \overset{\alpha}{\longrightarrow} R$ derives, through the rules of Table 1, from

- a transition $P \overset{\alpha}{\longrightarrow} P'$ and a state Q, where $R = P'|Q$,
- two transitions $P \overset{a_1}{\longrightarrow} P'$ and $Q \overset{\bar{a}_2}{\longrightarrow} Q'$, where $R = P'|Q'$,
- or from a state P and a transition $Q \overset{\alpha}{\longrightarrow} Q'$, where $R = P|Q'$.

This transition/state, transition/transition or state/transition pair is called a *decomposition* of $P|Q \overset{\alpha}{\longrightarrow} R$; it need not be unique. Now a *decomposition* of a path π of $P|Q$ into paths π_1 and π_2 of P and Q, respectively, is obtained by decomposing each transition in the path, and concatenating all left-projections into a path of P and all right-projections into a path of Q—notation $\pi \in \pi_1|\pi_2$ [15]. Here it could be that π is infinite, yet either π_1 or π_2 (but not both) are finite. Again, decomposition of paths need not be unique.

Theorem 1. Let $P, Q \in \mathbb{P}_{CCS}$.
Then $P \sqsubseteq_{reward} Q \quad \Leftrightarrow \quad divergences(P) \supseteq divergences(Q)\ \wedge$
$$inf(P) \supseteq inf(Q)\ \wedge$$
$$failures_d(P) \supseteq failures_d(Q).$$

Proof: Let $\sqsubseteq_{NDFD}$ be the preorder defined by: $P \sqsubseteq_{NDFD} Q$ iff the right-hand side of Theorem 1 holds.

For $\sigma = a_1 a_2 \cdots a_n \in \mathscr{A}^*$, let $\bar{\sigma}.T$ with $T \in \mathbb{T}^R_{CCS}$ be the CCS reward test $\bar{a}_1.\bar{a}_2.\cdots\bar{a}_1.T$. It starts with performing the complements of the actions in σ, where each of these actions is given a reward 0.

Write α^r for $(\alpha, r) \in Act \times \mathbb{R}$. For $\nu = a_1 a_2 a_3 \cdots \in \mathscr{A}^\infty$, let $\bar{\nu}^r$ be the CCS reward test $\mathbf{fix}(\!|X_0{:}S|\!)$ where $S = \{X_i \overset{def}{=} \bar{a}^r_{i+1}.X_{i+1} \mid i \ge 0\}$. This test simply performs the infinite sequence of complements of the actions in ν, where each of these actions is given a reward r.

"$\Rightarrow$": Suppose $P \not\sqsubseteq_{NDFD} Q$.

Case 1: Let $\sigma \in divergences(Q) \setminus divergences(P)$. Take $T := \bar{\sigma}.\tau^{-1}.\tau^1 \in \mathbb{T}^R_{CCS}$. Then $T|Q$ has a computation π with $reward(\pi) < 0$, whereas $T|P$ has no such computation. Hence $P \not\sqsubseteq_{reward} Q$.

Case 2: Let $\nu \in inf(Q) \setminus inf(P)$. Take $T := \bar{\nu}^{-1} \in \mathbb{T}^R_{CCS}$. Then $T|Q$ has a computation π with $reward(\pi) = -\infty$, whereas $T|P$ has no such computation. Hence $P \not\sqsubseteq_{reward} Q$.

Case 3: Let $\langle \sigma, X \rangle \in failures_d(Q) \setminus failures_d(P)$. Take $T := \bar{\sigma}.\tau^{-1}.\sum_{a \in X} a^1 \in \mathbb{T}^R_{CCS}$. Then $T|Q$ has a computation π with $reward(\pi) < 0$, whereas $T|P$ has no such computation. Hence $P \not\sqsubseteq_{reward} Q$.

"$\Leftarrow$": Suppose $P \sqsubseteq_{NDFD} Q$. Let $T \in \mathbb{T}^R_{CCS}$ and $r \in \mathbb{R}$ be such that $\exists \pi \in Comp(T|Q)$ with $reward(\pi) = r$. It suffices to find a $\pi' \in Comp(T|P)$ with $reward(\pi') \leq r$. The computation π can be seen as a path of $T|Q$ in which all actions are τ. Decompose this path into paths π_1 of T and π_2 of Q. Note that $reward(\pi) = reward(\pi_1)$.

Case 1: Let π_2 be infinite. Then $\ell(\pi_2) \in inf(Q) \cup divergences(Q) \subseteq inf(P) \cup divergences(P)$. Thus P has an infinite path π'_2 with $\ell(\pi'_2) = \ell(\pi_2)$. Consequently, $T|P$ has an infinite path $\pi' \in \pi_1|\pi'_2$ that is a computation with $reward(\pi') = r$.

Case 2: Let π_2 be finite and π_1 be infinite. Then $\ell(\pi_1) \in divergences(T)$ and $\ell(\pi_2) \in ptraces(Q) \subseteq ptraces(P)$. The latter inclusion follows by (*). Thus P has a finite path π'_2 with $\ell(\pi'_2) = \ell(\pi_2)$. Consequently, $T|P$ has an infinite path $\pi' \in \pi_1|\pi'_2$ that is a computation with $reward(\pi') = r$.

Case 3: Let π_1 and π_2 be finite. Let T' and Q' be the last states of π_1 and π_2, respectively. Let $X := \{a \in Act \mid a^r \in initials(T')\}$. Then $\tau \notin X$, $\tau \notin initials(Q')$ and $initials(Q') \cap X = \emptyset$. So $\langle \ell(\pi_2), X \rangle \in failures(Q) \subseteq failures_d(Q) \subseteq failures_d(P)$. Thus P has either an infinite path π'_2 with $\ell(\pi'_2) = \ell(\pi_2)$ or a finite path π'_2 with $\ell(\pi'_2) = \ell(\pi_2)$ and whose last state P' satisfies $initials(P') \cap (X \cup \{\tau\}) = \emptyset$. Consequently, $T|P$ has a finite or infinite path $\pi' \in \pi_1|\pi'_2$ that is a computation with $reward(\pi') = r$.   □

8   Weaker Notions of Reward Testing

Finite-penalty reward testing doesn't allow computations that incur infinitely many penalties. A test $T \in \mathbb{T}^R_{CCS}$ has *finite penalties* if each infinite path $T\alpha_1^{r_1}T_1\alpha_2^{r_2}T_2 \cdots$ has only finitely many transitions i with $r_i < 0$. Let $P \sqsubseteq_{\text{fp-reward}} Q$ iff $Apply(T, P) \sqsubseteq_{Sm} Apply(T, Q)$ for every finite-penalty reward test T.

Theorem 2. Let $P, Q \in \mathbb{P}_{CCS}$.
Then $P \sqsubseteq_{\text{fp-reward}} Q \Leftrightarrow divergences(P) \supseteq divergences(Q) \wedge$
$$inf_d(P) \supseteq inf_d(Q) \wedge$$
$$failures_d(P) \supseteq failures_d(Q).$$

Proof: Let $\sqsubseteq^d_{FDI}$ be the preorder defined by: $P \sqsubseteq^d_{FDI} Q$ iff the right-hand side of Theorem 2 holds.

"$\Rightarrow$": Suppose $P \not\sqsubseteq^d_{FDI} Q$. Case 1 and 3 proceed exactly as in the proof of Theorem 1, but the proof of Case 2 needs to be revised, as its proof uses a test with infinitely many penalties. So assume

$$divergences(P) \supseteq divergences(Q) \quad \wedge \quad failures_d(P) \supseteq failures_d(Q)$$

and let $\nu \in inf_d(Q) \setminus inf_d(P)$. I can rule out the case $\forall \sigma < \nu \ \exists \rho \in divergences(q).\sigma \leq \rho < \nu$ because then $\nu \in inf_d(P)$, using that $divergences(Q) \subseteq divergences(P)$. So $\nu \in inf(Q)$. Let $\nu := \nu_1 \nu_2$, where each $\rho \in divergences(Q)$ with $\rho < \nu$ satisfies $\rho < \nu_1$. Let $\nu_2 = b_1 b_2 \cdots \in \mathscr{A}^\infty$. Take $T := \bar{\nu}_1.\tau^{-1}.\mathbf{fix}(\!(Y_0{:}S)\!)$, where $S = \{Y_i \overset{def}{=} \tau^1 + \bar{b}_{i+1}.Y_{i+1} \mid i \geq 0\}$. Then $T|Q$ has a computation π with $reward(\pi) < 0$, whereas $T|P$ has no such computation. Hence $P \not\sqsubseteq_{\text{fp-reward}} Q$.

"$\Leftarrow$": Suppose $P \sqsubseteq^d_{FDI} Q$. The proof proceeds just as the one of Theorem 1, except for Case 1.

Case 1: Let π_2 be infinite. Then $\ell(\pi_2) \in inf(Q) \cup divergences(Q) \subseteq inf_d(P) \cup divergences(P)$. In case $\ell(\pi_2) \in inf(P) \cup divergences(P)$ the proof concludes as for Theorem 1. So assume that $\ell(\pi_2) \in \mathscr{A}^\infty$ and $\forall \sigma < \ell(\pi_2) \ \exists \rho \in divergences(P).\sigma \leq \rho < \ell(\pi_2)$. Then there are prefixes $\pi^\dagger$, $\pi_1^\dagger$ and $\pi_2^\dagger$ of π, π_1 and π_2 such that (i) $\pi^\dagger \in \pi_1^\dagger|\pi_2^\dagger$, (ii) there are no negative rewards allocated in the suffix of π_1 past $\pi_1^\dagger$, and (iii) $\ell(\pi_2^\dagger) \in divergences(P)$. Let π_2' be an infinite path of P with $\ell(\pi_2') = \ell(\pi_2^\dagger)$. Then there is a computation $\pi' \in \pi_1^\dagger|\pi_2'$ of $T|P$ with $reward(\pi') = reward(\pi_1^\dagger) \leq reward(\pi_1) = r$. □

Single penalty reward testing doesn't allow computations that incur multiple penalties. A test $T \in \mathbb{T}^R_{\text{CCS}}$ has the *single penalty* property if each path $T\alpha_1^{r_1}T_1\alpha_2^{r_2}T_2\cdots$ has at most one transition i with $r_i < 0$. Let $P \sqsubseteq_{\text{sp-reward}} Q$ iff $Apply(T,P) \sqsubseteq_{\text{Sm}} Apply(T,Q)$ for every single penalty reward test T. Obviously, $\sqsubseteq_{\text{sp-reward}}$ coincides with $\sqsubseteq_{\text{fp-reward}}$. This follows because all test used in the proof of Theorem 2 have the single penalty property.

Analogously one might weaken reward testing and/or single penalty reward testing by requiring that in each computation only finitely many, or at most one, positive reward can be reaped. This does not constitute a real weakening, as the tests used in Theorems 1 and 2 already allot at most a single positive reward per computation only.

Nonnegative reward testing requires all rewards to be nonnegative. Let $P \sqsubseteq_{+\text{reward}} Q$ iff $Apply(T,P) \sqsubseteq_{\text{Sm}} Apply(T,Q)$ for every nonnegative reward test T. Likewise $\sqsubseteq_{-\text{reward}}$ requires all rewards to be 0 or negative.

Theorem 3. $P \sqsubseteq_{+\text{reward}} Q \ \Leftrightarrow \ divergences_\perp(P) \supseteq divergences_\perp(Q) \wedge$
$$inf_\perp(P) \supseteq inf_\perp(Q) \wedge$$
$$failures_\perp(P) \supseteq failures_\perp(Q).$$

Proof: Let $\sqsubseteq^\perp_{FDI}$ be the preorder defined by: $P \sqsubseteq^\perp_{FDI} Q$ iff the right-hand side of Theorem 3 holds.

"$\Rightarrow$": Suppose $P \not\sqsubseteq^\perp_{FDI} Q$.

Case 1: Let $\sigma = a_1 a_2 \cdots a_n \in divergences_\perp(Q) \setminus divergences_\perp(P)$. Take $T := \mathbf{fix}(\!(X_0{:}S)\!)$ in which

$$S = \{X_i \overset{def}{=} \tau^1 + a_{i+1}.X_{i+1} \mid 0 \leq i < n\} \cup \{X_n \overset{def}{=} \tau^1\}.$$

Then $T|Q$ has a computation π with $reward(\pi) < 1$, which $T|P$ has not. Hence $P \not\sqsubseteq_{+\text{reward}} Q$.

Case 2: Let $\nu = a_1 a_2 \cdots \in inf_{\perp}(Q) \setminus inf_{\perp}(P)$. Let $T := \mathbf{fix}(\!|X_0{:}S|\!)$ with $S = \{X_{i-1} \stackrel{def}{=} \tau^1 + a_i.X_i \mid i \geq 1\}$. Then $T|Q$ has a computation π such that $reward(\pi) < 1$, which $T|P$ has not. Hence $P \not\sqsubseteq_{+\text{reward}} Q$.

Case 3: Let $\langle a_1 a_2 \cdots a_n, X \rangle \in failures_{\perp}(Q) \setminus failures_{\perp}(P)$. Take $T := \mathbf{fix}(\!|X_0{:}S|\!)$ in which

$$S = \{X_i \stackrel{def}{=} \tau^1 + a_{i+1}.X_{i+1} \mid 0 \leq i < n\} \cup \{X_n \stackrel{def}{=} \sum_{a \in X} a^1\}.$$

Then $T|Q$ has a computation π with $reward(\pi) < 1$, which $T|P$ has not. Hence $P \not\sqsubseteq_{+\text{reward}} Q$.

"$\Leftarrow$": Suppose $P \sqsubseteq^{\perp}_{FDI} Q$. Let $T \in \mathbb{T}^R_{\text{CCS}}$ be a nonnegative rewards test and $r \in \mathbb{R}$ be such that there is a $\pi \in Comp(T|Q)$ with $reward(\pi) = r$. It suffices to find a $\pi' \in Comp(T|P)$ with $reward(\pi') \leq r$. The computation π can be seen as a path of $T|Q$ in which all actions are τ. Decompose this path into paths π_1 of T and π_2 of Q. Note that $reward(\pi) = reward(\pi_1)$.

Case 1: Let π_2 be infinite. Then $\ell(\pi_2) \in inf(Q) \cup divergences(Q) \subseteq inf_{\perp}(P) \cup divergences_{\perp}(P)$. If $\ell(\pi_2) \in inf(P) \cup divergences(P)$ then P has an infinite path π'_2 with $\ell(\pi'_2) = \ell(\pi_2)$. Consequently, $T|P$ has an infinite path $\pi' \in \pi_1|\pi'_2$ that is a computation with $reward(\pi') = r$. The alternative is that $\ell(\pi_2)$ has a prefix in $divergences(P)$. In that case there are prefixes $\pi^{\dagger}$, $\pi^{\dagger}_1$ and $\pi^{\dagger}_2$ of π, π_1 and π_2 such that $\pi^{\dagger} \in \pi^{\dagger}_1|\pi^{\dagger}_2$ and $\ell(\pi^{\dagger}_2) \in divergences(P)$. Let π'_2 be an infinite path of P with $\ell(\pi'_2) = \ell(\pi^{\dagger}_2)$. Then there is a computation $\pi' \in \pi^{\dagger}_1|\pi'_2$ of $T|P$ with $reward(\pi') = reward(\pi^{\dagger}_1) \leq reward(\pi_1) = r$.

Case 2: Let π_2 be finite and π_1 be infinite. Then $\ell(\pi_1) \in divergences(T)$ and $\ell(\pi_2) \in ptraces(Q) \subseteq ptraces(P) \cup divergences_{\perp}(P)$. The latter inclusion follows since

$$ptraces(R) \cup divergences_{\perp}(R) = \{\sigma \mid \langle \sigma, \emptyset \rangle \in failures_{\perp}(R)\}$$

for any $R \in \mathbb{P}$. If $\ell(\pi_2) \in ptraces(P)$ then P has a finite path π'_2 with $\ell(\pi'_2) = \ell(\pi_2)$. Consequently, $T|P$ has an infinite path $\pi' \in \pi_1|\pi'_2$ that is a computation with $reward(\pi') = r$. The alternative is handled just as for Case 1 above.

Case 3: Let π_1 and π_2 be finite. Let T' and Q' be the last states of π_1 and π_2, respectively. Let $X := \{a \in Act \mid a^r \in initials(T')\}$. Then $\tau \notin X$, $\tau \notin initials(Q')$ and $initials(Q') \cap X = \emptyset$. So $\langle \ell(\pi_2), X \rangle \in failures(Q) \subseteq failures_{\perp}(Q) \subseteq failures_{\perp}(P)$. If $\langle \ell(\pi_2) \in failures(P)$ then P has a finite path π'_2 with $\ell(\pi'_2) = \ell(\pi_2)$ and whose last state P' satisfies $initials(P') \cap (X \cup \{\tau\}) = \emptyset$. Consequently, $T|P$ has a finite or infinite path $\pi' \in \pi_1|\pi'_2$ that is a computation with $reward(\pi') = r$. The alternative is handled just as for Case 1 above. $\square$

One might weaken nonnegative reward testing by requiring that in each computation only finitely many, or at most one, reward can be reaped. This does not constitute a real weakening, as the tests used in Theorem 3 already allot at most a single reward per computation only.

Theorem 4. $P \sqsubseteq_{-\text{reward}} Q \iff ptraces(P) \supseteq ptraces(Q) \wedge$
$$inf(P) \supseteq inf(Q)$$

Proof: Let $\sqsubseteq_T^\infty$ be the preorder defined by: $P \sqsubseteq_T^\infty Q$ iff the right-hand side of Theorem 4 holds.

"$\Rightarrow$": Suppose $P \not\sqsubseteq_T^\infty Q$.

Case 1: Let $\sigma \in ptraces(Q) \setminus ptraces(P)$. Take $T := \bar{\sigma}.\tau^{-1}$. Then $T|Q$ has a computation π with $reward(\pi) < 1$, which $T|P$ has not. Hence $P \not\sqsubseteq_{-\text{reward}} Q$.

Case 2 proceeds exactly as in the proof of Theorem 1.

"$\Leftarrow$": Suppose $P \sqsubseteq_T^\infty Q$. Let $T \in \mathbb{T}_{\text{CCS}}^R$ be a nonpositive rewards test and $r \in \mathbb{R}$ be such that there is a $\pi \in Comp(T|Q)$ with $reward(\pi) = r$. It suffices to find a $\pi' \in Comp(T|P)$ with $reward(\pi') \leq r$. The computation π can be seen as a path of $T|Q$ in which all actions are τ. Decompose this path into paths π_1 of T and π_2 of Q. Note that $reward(\pi) = reward(\pi_1)$.

Moreover, $\ell(\pi_2) \in inf(Q) \cup ptraces(Q) \subseteq inf(P) \cup ptraces(P)$. So P has a path π_2' with $\ell(\pi_2') = \ell(\pi_2)$. Consequently, $T|P$ has an path $\pi' \in \pi_1|\pi_2'$ that is either a computation, or a prefix of a computation, with $reward(\pi') = r$. In case it is a prefix of a computation π'' then $reward(\pi'') \leq reward(\pi') = r$. □

Finite-penalty nonpositive reward testing only allows computations that incur no positive rewards and merely finitely many penalties. Let $P \sqsubseteq_{\text{fp--reward}} Q$ iff $Apply(T,P) \sqsubseteq_{\text{Sm}} Apply(T,Q)$ for each finite-penalty nonpositive reward test T.

Theorem 5. $P \sqsubseteq_{\text{fp--reward}} Q \iff ptraces(P) \supseteq ptraces(Q)$

Proof: Let $\sqsubseteq_T$ be the preorder defined by: $P \sqsubseteq_T Q$ iff the right-hand side of Theorem 5 holds.

"$\Rightarrow$": Suppose $P \not\sqsubseteq_T Q$. Let $\sigma \in ptraces(Q) \setminus ptraces(P)$. Take $T := \bar{\sigma}.\tau^{-1}$. Then $T|Q$ has a computation π with $reward(\pi) < 1$, which $T|P$ has not. Hence $P \not\sqsubseteq_{-\text{reward}} Q$.

"$\Leftarrow$": Suppose $P \sqsubseteq_T Q$. Let $T \in \mathbb{T}_{\text{CCS}}^R$ be a finite-penalty nonpositive rewards test and $r \in \mathbb{R}$ be such that there is a $\pi \in Comp(T|Q)$ with $reward(\pi) = r$. Then π has a finite prefix $\pi^\dagger$ (not necessarily a computation) with $reward(\pi) = r$. It suffices to find a prefix π' of a computation of $T|P$ with $reward(\pi') = r$. The finite prefix $\pi^\dagger$ can be seen as a path of $T|Q$ in which all actions are τ. Decompose this path into finite paths π_1 of T and π_2 of Q. Now $\ell(\pi_2) \in ptraces(Q) \subseteq ptraces(P)$. So P has a path π_2' with $\ell(\pi_2') = \ell(\pi_2)$. Consequently, $T|P$ has a path $\pi' \in \pi_1|\pi_2'$ that is a prefix of a computation, with $reward(\pi') = r$. □

Single penalty nonpositive reward testing only allows computations that incur no positive rewards and at most one penalty. Let $P \sqsubseteq_{\text{sp--reward}} Q$ iff $Apply(T, P) \sqsubseteq_{\text{Sm}} Apply(T, Q)$ for every single penalty nonpositive reward test T. Obviously, $\sqsubseteq_{\text{sp--reward}}$ coincides with $\sqsubseteq_{\text{fp--reward}}$. This follows because all test used in the proof of Theorem 5 have the single penalty property.

9   Reward May Testing

Call a test $T \in \mathbb{T}^R_{\mathrm{CCS}}$ *well-behaved* if for each infinite path $T\alpha_1^{r_1}T_1\alpha_2^{r_2}T_2\cdots$ the limit $\lim_{n\to\infty}\sum_{i=1}^{n} r_i \in \mathbb{R} \cup \{-\infty, \infty\}$ exists. If the sequence $(r_i)_{i=1}^{\infty}$ alternates between 1 and -1 for instance, the test is not well-behaved. Since all tests used in the proof of Theorem 1 are well-behaved, the reward testing preorder $\sqsubseteq_{\mathrm{reward}}$ would not change if one restricts the collection of available test to the well-behaved ones only. When restricting to well-behaved tests, the infimum $\inf_{n\to\infty}$ in Definition 2 may be read as $\lim_{n\to\infty}$.

Theorem 6. $P \sqsubseteq^{\mathrm{may}}_{\mathrm{reward}} Q$ iff $Q \sqsubseteq^{\mathrm{must}}_{\mathrm{reward}} P$.

Proof: For any well-behaved test T, let $-T$ be obtained by changing all occurrences of actions (α, r) into $(\alpha, -r)$. Now $\mathcal{A}pply(-T, P) = \{-r \mid r \in \mathcal{A}pply(T, P)\}$. This immediately yields the claimed result.   □

All weaker notions of testing contemplated in Sect. 8 employ well-behaved tests only. The same reasoning as above yields (besides $\sqsubseteq^{\mathrm{may}}_{\mathrm{reward}} = \sqsubseteq^{-1}_{\mathrm{reward}}$)

$$\sqsubseteq^{\mathrm{may}}_{\mathrm{fp\text{-}reward}} = \sqsubseteq^{-1}_{\mathrm{reward}} \qquad , \qquad \sqsubseteq^{\mathrm{may}}_{+\mathrm{reward}} = \sqsubseteq^{-1}_{-\mathrm{reward}} \qquad ,$$
$$\sqsubseteq^{\mathrm{may}}_{-\mathrm{reward}} = \sqsubseteq^{-1}_{+\mathrm{reward}} \qquad \text{and} \qquad \sqsubseteq^{\mathrm{may}}_{\mathrm{fp\text{-}-reward}} = \sqsubseteq^{-1}_{-\mathrm{reward}} \qquad .$$

10   A Hierarchy of Testing Preorders

Theorem 7. $P \sqsubseteq_{\mathrm{must}} Q$ iff $P \sqsubseteq_{+\mathrm{reward}} Q$. Likewise, $P \sqsubseteq^{\mathrm{dual}}_{\mathrm{must}} Q$ iff $P \sqsubseteq_{\mathrm{fp\text{-}-reward}} Q$.

Proof: "If": Without affecting $\sqsubseteq_{\mathrm{must}}$ one may restrict attention to tests $T \in \mathbb{T}_{\mathrm{CCS}}$ with the property that each path of T contains at most one success state—one with an outgoing transition labelled ω. Namely, any outgoing transition of a success state may safely be omitted. Now each such test T can be converted into a nonnegative reward test T', namely by assigning a reward 1 to any action leading into a success state, keeping the rewards of all other actions 0. The success action itself may then be renamed into τ, or omitted. Now trivially, a computation of $T|P$ is successful iff the matching computation of T' yields a reward 1; a computation of $T|P$ is unsuccessful iff the matching computation of T' yields a reward 0. It follows that must-testing can be emulated by nonnegative reward testing.

"Only if": As remarked in Sect. 8, nonnegative reward testing looses no power when allowing only one reward per computation. For the same reasons it looses no power if each positive reward is 1. Now any reward test $T' \in \mathbb{T}^R_{\mathrm{CCS}}$ with these restrictions can be converted to a test $T \in \mathbb{T}_{\mathrm{CCS}}$ by making any target state of a reward-1 transition into a success state. It follows that nonnegative reward testing can be emulated by must-testing.

The second statement follows in the same way, but using a reward -1.   □

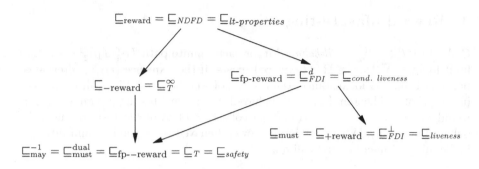

Fig. 2. A spectrum of testing preorders

A preorder $\sqsubseteq_X$ is said to be *finer* than or equal to a preorder $\sqsubseteq_Y$ iff $P \sqsubseteq_X Q \Rightarrow P \sqsubseteq_Y Q$ for all P and Q; in that case $\sqsubseteq_Y$ is *coarser* than or equal to $\sqsubseteq_X$.

Theorem 8. The preorders occurring in this paper are related as indicated in Fig. 2, where the arrows point in the coarser direction.

Proof: The relations between $\sqsubseteq_{\text{reward}}$, $\sqsubseteq_{\text{fp-reward}}$, $\sqsubseteq_{+\text{reward}}$, $\sqsubseteq_{-\text{reward}}$ and $\sqsubseteq_{\text{fp--reward}}$ follow immediately from the definitions, as the coarser variant uses only a subset of the tests available to the finer variant. The strictness of all these relations is obtained by the examples below.

The connections with $\sqsubseteq_{\text{must}}$, $\sqsubseteq_{\text{must}}^{\text{dual}}$ and the inverse of $\sqsubseteq_{\text{may}}$ are provided by Theorem 7 and Sect. 5. The characterisations in terms of $\sqsubseteq_{NDFD}$, $\sqsubseteq_{FDI}^{d}$, $\sqsubseteq_{FDI}^{\perp}$, $\sqsubseteq_{F}^{\infty}$ and $\sqsubseteq_{T}$ are provided by Theorems 1–5. The connections with $\sqsubseteq_{\text{lt-properties}}$, $\sqsubseteq_{\text{cond. liveness}}$, $\sqsubseteq_{\text{liveness}}$ and $\sqsubseteq_{\text{safety}}$ will be established in Sect. 11.   □

Let $a^n.P$ be defined by $a^0.P := P$ and $a^{i+1}.P = a.a^i.P$. Furthermore, let $a^\infty := \mathbf{fix}(\!|X: X \overset{def}{=} a.X|\!)$ be a process that performs infinitely many as. Let Δ be the unary operator given by $\Delta P := \mathbf{fix}(\!|X: X \overset{def}{=} \tau.X + P|\!)$. It first performs 0 or more τ-actions, and if this number is finite subsequently behaves as its argument P. So $\Delta 0 = \tau^\infty$ just performs an infinite sequence of τ-moves.

Example 1. $\sum_{n\geq 1} a^n.\Delta 0 \equiv_{\text{fp-reward}} a^\infty + \sum_{n\geq 1} a^n.\Delta 0$, but

$\sum_{n\geq 1} a^n.\Delta 0 \not\sqsubseteq_{-\text{reward}} a^\infty + \sum_{n\geq 1} a^n.\Delta 0$ (and thus $\not\sqsubseteq_{\text{reward}}$).

Example 2. $\Delta(c.g) \equiv_{\text{must}} \Delta(c + c.g)$ and $\Delta(c.g) \equiv_{-\text{reward}} \Delta(c + c.g)$, yet $\Delta(c.g) \not\sqsubseteq_{\text{fp-reward}} \Delta(c + c.g)$. These are the processes displayed in Fig. 1. A test showing the latter is $c^{-1}.g^1$.

Example 3. $c.g \equiv_{\text{fp--reward}} c + c.g$, yet $c.g \not\sqsubseteq_{+\text{reward}} c + c.g$. A test showing the latter is $c.g^1$.

Example 4. $\Delta a \equiv_{+\text{reward}} \Delta 0$, yet $\Delta a \not\sqsubseteq_{\text{fp--reward}} \Delta 0$. A test showing the latter is a^{-1}.

A process P is *divergence-free* if $divergences(P) = \emptyset$. It is *regular*, or *finite-state*, if there only finitely many processes Q such that $\exists \sigma \in \mathscr{A}^*. P \stackrel{\sigma}{\Longrightarrow} Q$. It is $\Longrightarrow$-*image-finite* if for each $\sigma \in A^*$ there are only finitely many Q such that $P \stackrel{\sigma}{\Longrightarrow} Q$. Note that the class of $\Longrightarrow$-image-finite processes is not closed under parallel composition, or under renaming transition labels $a \in \mathscr{A}$ into τ. Regular processes are $\Longrightarrow$-image-finite. Any $P \in \mathbb{P}_{\mathrm{CCS}}$ without parallel composition, relabelling or restriction is regular. Any $P \in \mathbb{P}_{\mathrm{CCS}}$ without recursion is both divergence-free and regular.

Proposition 1. If $P \in \mathbb{P}_{\mathrm{CCS}}$ is divergence-free, then $P \sqsubseteq_{+\mathrm{reward}} Q$ iff $P \sqsubseteq_{\mathrm{reward}} Q$.

Proof: This follows from Theorems 1 and 3, using that $divergences(P) = \emptyset$, $inf_\perp(P) = inf_d(P) = inf(P)$ and $failures_\perp(P) = failures_d(P) = failures(P)$. (In case Q is not divergence-free one has neither $P \sqsubseteq_{+\mathrm{reward}} Q$ nor $P \sqsubseteq_{\mathrm{reward}} Q$.) $\square$

Proposition 2. If P is $\Longrightarrow$-image-finite then (a) $P \sqsubseteq_{\mathrm{fp-}-\mathrm{reward}} Q$ iff $P \sqsubseteq_{-\mathrm{reward}} Q$ and (b) $P \sqsubseteq_{\mathrm{fp-reward}} Q$ iff $P \sqsubseteq_{\mathrm{reward}} Q$.

Proof: By Königs lemma $\nu \in \mathscr{A}^\infty$ is an infinite trace of P iff only if each finite prefix of ν is a partial trace of P. Now (a) follows immediately from Theorems 4 and 5: Suppose $P \sqsubseteq_{-\mathrm{reward}} Q$ and $\nu \in inf(Q)$. Then each finite prefix of ν is in $ptraces(Q)$ and thus in $ptraces(P)$. Thus $\nu \in inf(P)$.

(b) follows in the same way from Theorems 1 and 2, using (*). $\square$

11   Conditional Liveness Properties

To obtain a general liveness property for labelled transition systems, assume that some notion of *good* is defined. Now, to judge whether a process P satisfies this liveness property, one should judge whether P can reach a state in which one would say that something good had happened. But all observable behaviour of P that is recorded in a labelled transition system until one comes to such a verdict, is the sequence of visible actions performed until that point. Thus the liveness property is completely determined by the set sequences of visible actions that, when performed by P, lead to such a judgement. Therefore one can just as well define a liveness property in terms of such a set.

Definition 4. A *liveness property* of processes in an LTS is given by a set $G \subseteq \mathscr{A}^*$. A process P *satisfies* this liveness property, notation $P \models liveness(G)$, when each complete trace of P has a prefix in G.

This formalisation of liveness properties stems from [12] and is essentially different from the one in [2] and most subsequent work on liveness properties; this point is discussed in [12, Sect. 6].

A preorder $\sqsubseteq$ *preserves* liveness properties if $P \sqsubseteq Q$ implies that Q enjoys any liveness property that P has. It is a *precongruence* for an n-ary operator op if $P_i \sqsubseteq Q_i$ for $i = 1, \ldots, n$ implies $op(P_1, \ldots, P_n) \sqsubseteq op(Q_1, \ldots, Q_n)$. Now let $\sqsubseteq_{liveness}$ be the coarsest preorder that is a precongruence for the operators of CSP and preserves liveness properties. In [12] it is shown that this preorder exists, and equals $\sqsubseteq_{FDI}^{\perp}$, as defined in the proof of Theorem 3. The proof of this result does not require that $\sqsubseteq_{liveness}$ be a preorder for all operators of CSP; it goes through already when merely requiring it to be precongruence for injective renaming and partially synchronous interleaving operators. Looking at this proof, the same can also be obtained requiring $\sqsubseteq_{liveness}$ to be a precongruence for the CCS operators $|$, $\backslash L$ and injective relabelling.

It follows that $\sqsubseteq_{liveness}$ coincides with $\sqsubseteq_{+reward}$ (cf. Theorem 8). This connection can be illustrated by a translation from liveness properties $G \subseteq \mathscr{A}^*$ (w.l.o.g. assumed to have the property that if $\sigma \in G$ then $\sigma\rho \notin G$ for any $\rho \neq \epsilon$) to nonnegative reward tests T_G. Here T_G can be rendered as a deterministic tree in which all transitions completing a trace from $\bar{G}$ yield a reward 1, so that all computations of $T|P$ earn a positive reward iff $P \models liveness(G)$.

One obtains a general concept of safety property by means of the same argument as for liveness properties above, but using "bad" instead of "good".

Definition 5. A *safety property* of processes in an LTS is given by a set $B \subseteq \mathscr{A}^*$. A process P *satisfies* this safety property, notation $P \models safety(B)$, when $ptraces(p) \cap B = \emptyset$.

This formalisation of safety properties stems from [12] and is in line with the one in [2]. Now let $\sqsubseteq_{safety}$ be the coarsest precongruence (for the same choice of operators as above) that preserves safety properties. In [12] it is shown that this preorder exists, and equals $\sqsubseteq_T$, as defined in the proof of Theorem 5.

It follows that $\sqsubseteq_{safety}$ coincides with $\sqsubseteq_{fp--reward}$ (cf. Theorem 8). This connection can be illustrated by a translation from safety properties $B \subseteq \mathscr{A}^*$ (w.l.o.g. assumed to have the property that if $\sigma \in B$ then $\sigma\rho \notin B$ for any $\rho \neq \epsilon$) to nonnegative reward tests T_B. Here T_B can be rendered as a deterministic tree in which all transitions completing a trace from $\bar{B}$ yield a reward -1, so that all computations of $T|P$ earn a nonnegative reward iff $P \models safety(B)$.

A conditional liveness property says that *under certain conditions something good will eventually happen*. To obtain a general conditional liveness property for LTSs, assume that some condition, and some notion of *good* is defined. Now, to judge whether a process P satisfies this conditional liveness property, one should judge first of all in which states the condition is fulfilled. All observable behaviour of P that is recorded in an LTS until one comes to such a verdict, is the sequence of visible actions performed until that point. Thus the condition is completely determined by the set of sequences of visible actions that, when performed by P, lead to such a judgement. Next one should judge whether P can reach a state in which one would say that something good had happened. Again, this judgement can be expressed in terms of the sequences of visible actions that lead to such a state.

Definition 6. ([12]) A *conditional liveness property* of processes in an LTS is given by two sets $C, G \subseteq \mathscr{A}^*$. A process P *satisfies* this conditional liveness property, notation $P \models liveness_C(G)$, when each complete trace of P that has a prefix in C, also has a prefix in G.

Now let $\sqsubseteq_{cond.\ liveness}$ be the coarsest precongruence (for the same choice of operators as above) that preserves conditional liveness properties. In [12] it is shown that this preorder exists, and equals $\sqsubseteq^d_{FDI}$, as defined in the proof of Theorem 2. So $\sqsubseteq_{safety}$ coincides with $\sqsubseteq_{\text{fp-reward}}$ (cf. Theorem 8). Similar to the above cases, this connection can be illustrated by a translation from conditional liveness properties $C, G \subseteq \mathscr{A}^*$ to reward tests in which each computation has at most one negative and one positive reward, which are always -1 and $+1$.

Definition 7. A *linear time property* of processes in an LTS is given by a set $\Phi \subseteq \mathscr{A}^* \cup \mathscr{A}^\infty$ of finite and infinite sequences of actions. A process P *satisfies* this property, notation $P \models \Phi$, when $CT(P) \subseteq \Phi$.

A liveness property is a special kind of linear time property:
$$liveness(G) = \{\sigma \in \mathscr{A}^* \cup \mathscr{A}^\infty \mid \exists \rho \in G.\ \rho \leq \sigma\}.$$
Likewise, $safety(B) = \{\sigma \in \mathscr{A}^* \cup \mathscr{A}^\infty \mid \neg \exists \rho \in B.\ \rho \leq \sigma\}$, and
$$liveness_C(G) = \{\sigma \in \mathscr{A}^* \cup \mathscr{A}^\infty \mid (\exists \rho \in C.\ \rho \leq \sigma) \Rightarrow (\exists \nu \in G.\ \nu \leq \sigma)\}.$$
Now let $\sqsubseteq_{lt.\ properties}$ be the coarsest precongruence (for the same choice of operators as above) that preserves linear time properties. In [12,19] it is shown that this preorder exists, and equals $\sqsubseteq_{NDFD}$, as defined in the proof of Theorem 1. It follows that $\sqsubseteq_{lt.\ properties}$ coincides with $\sqsubseteq_{reward}$ (cf. Theorem 8).

12 Congruence Properties

Theorem 9. The preorders of this paper are precongruences for $|$, $\backslash L$ and $[f]$.

Proof: Note that $Apply(T, R|P) = Apply(T|R, P)$, using the associativity (up to strong bisimilarity) of $|$. Therefore $P \sqsubseteq_{reward} Q$ implies $R|P \sqsubseteq_{reward} R|Q$, showing that $\sqsubseteq_{reward}$ is a precongruence for parallel composition. The same holds for $\sqsubseteq_{\text{fp-reward}}$, $\sqsubseteq_{\text{+reward}}$, $\sqsubseteq_{\text{-reward}}$ and $\sqsubseteq_{\text{fp--reward}}$.

Likewise $Apply(T, P\backslash L) = Apply(T\backslash L, P)$. This yields precongruence results for restriction.

Finally, $Apply(T, P[f]) = Apply(T[f^{-1}], P)$, yielding precongruence results for relabelling. Here $[f^{-1}]$ is an operator with rule

$$\frac{E \xrightarrow{\alpha, r} E'}{E[f^{-1}] \xrightarrow{\beta, r} E'[f^{-1}]} \quad (f(\beta) = \alpha).$$

Although this is not a CCS operator, for any test T the test $T[f^{-1}]$ is expressible in CCS, on grounds that each process in an LTS is expressible in CCS.   □

Theorem 10. The preorders of this paper are precongruences for action prefix.

Proof: This follows from the characterisations of the preorders in Sects. 7 and 8. For instance, $failures_d(a.P) = \{\langle a\sigma, X\rangle \mid \langle \sigma, X\rangle \in failures_d(a.P)\}$.   □

In the same way it follows that $\sqsubseteq_{\text{fp--reward}}$ and $\sqsubseteq_{\text{--reward}}$ are precongruences for the CCS operator $+$. However, the preorders $\sqsubseteq_{\text{reward}}$, $\sqsubseteq_{\text{fp-reward}}$ and $\sqsubseteq_{\text{+reward}}$ fail to be congruences for choice:

Example 5. One has $\mathbf{0} \equiv_{\text{reward}} \tau$, yet $\mathbf{0} + a \not\sqsubseteq_{\text{+reward}} \tau + a$, using that $\langle \epsilon, \mathscr{A} \rangle \in$ $failures_\perp (\tau + a) \setminus failures_\perp (\mathbf{0} + a)$.

This issue occurs for almost all semantic equivalences and preorders that abstract from internal actions. The standard solution is to replace each such preorder $\sqsubseteq_X$ by the coarsest precongruence for the operators of CCS that is finer than $\sqsubseteq_X$. Let $stable$ be the predicate that holds for a process P iff there is no P' with $P \xrightarrow{\tau} P'$. Write $P \sqsubseteq_X^\tau Q$ iff $P \sqsubseteq_X Q \wedge (stable(P) \Rightarrow stable(Q))$.

Theorem 11. Let $X \in \{\text{reward, fp-reward, +reward}\}$. Then $\sqsubseteq_X^\tau$ is the coarsest precongruence for the operators of CCS that is contained in $\sqsubseteq_X$.

Proof: That $\sqsubseteq_{\text{+reward}}^\tau$ is a precongruence for $+$ follows with Theorem 3 since

$$stable(P + Q) \iff stable(P) \wedge stable(Q)$$

$$\begin{aligned} failures_\perp (P + Q) = \{&\langle \sigma, X \rangle \in failures_\perp (P) \mid \sigma \neq \epsilon \vee \neg stable(P)\} \cup \\ \{&\langle \sigma, X \rangle \in failures_\perp (Q) \mid \sigma \neq \epsilon \vee \neg stable(Q)\} \cup \\ \{&\langle \epsilon, X \rangle \mid \langle \epsilon, X \rangle \in failures_\perp (P) \cap failures_\perp (Q)\}, \end{aligned}$$

$$inf_\perp (P + Q) = inf_\perp (P) \cup inf_\perp (Q)$$
$$divergences_\perp (P + Q) = divergences_\perp (P) \cup divergences_\perp (Q) \, .$$

That it is a congruence for action prefixing, $|$, $\setminus L$ and $[f]$ follows since

$$\begin{aligned} stable(\alpha.P) \;&\text{iff}\; \alpha \neq \tau \\ stable(P|Q) \;&\text{iff}\; stable(P) \wedge stable(Q) \wedge \\ &\quad \neg \exists a \in \mathscr{A}. \, (\langle a, \emptyset \rangle \in failures_\perp (P) \wedge \langle \bar{a}, \emptyset \rangle \in failures_\perp (P)) \\ stable(P \setminus L) \;&\text{iff}\; stable(P) \quad\; and \quad\; stable(P[f]) \;\text{iff}\; stable(P). \end{aligned}$$

By definition, $\sqsubseteq_{\text{+reward}}^\tau$ is contained in $\sqsubseteq_{\text{+reward}}$. To see that it is the coarsest precongruence contained in $\sqsubseteq_{\text{+reward}}$, suppose $P \not\sqsubseteq_{\text{+reward}}^\tau Q$. It suffices to build a context $C[\_\_]$ from CCS operators such that $C[P] \not\sqsubseteq_{\text{+reward}} C[Q]$. The case $P \not\sqsubseteq_{\text{+reward}} Q$ is immediate—take the trivial context with $C[P] := P$. So assume $P \sqsubseteq_{\text{+reward}} Q$. Then $stable(P)$ and $\neg stable(Q)$. Hence $\epsilon \notin divergences_\perp (P) \supseteq divergences_\perp (Q)$. Choose $a \notin ptraces(Q)$—in case no such a exists, one first applies an injective relabelling to P and Q such that $a \notin range(f)$.

Now $\langle \epsilon, \{a\} \rangle \in failures(Q) \subseteq failures_\perp (Q) \subseteq failures_\perp (P)$. However, whereas $\langle \epsilon, \{a\} \rangle \in failures_\perp (Q + a)$ one has $\langle \epsilon, \{a\} \rangle \notin failures_\perp (P + a)$. It follows that $P + a \not\sqsubseteq_{\text{+reward}} Q + a$.

The arguments for $X \in \{\text{reward, fp-reward}\}$ are very similar. $\square$

13   Axiomatisations

The following axioms are easily seen to be sound for $\sqsubseteq_{\text{reward}}^\tau$. Here an equality $P \equiv Q$ can be seen as a shorthand for the two axioms $P \sqsubseteq Q$ and $Q \sqsubseteq P$. Action prefixing and Δ bind stronger than $+$.

$$\left\{ \begin{array}{llr}
\text{(R1)} & \tau.X + Y \equiv \tau.X + \tau.(X + Y) & \\
\text{(R2)} & \alpha.X + \tau.(\alpha.Y + Z) \equiv \tau(\alpha.X + \alpha.Y + Z) & \\
\text{(R3)} & \alpha.(\tau.X + \tau.Y) \equiv \alpha.X + \alpha.Y & \\
\text{(RP1)} & \tau.X + Y \sqsubseteq \tau.(X + Y) & \\
\text{(RP2)} & \tau.X + Y \sqsubseteq X & \\
\text{(R4)} & \tau.\Delta X + Y \equiv \Delta(X + Y) &
\end{array} \right\}$$

For recursion-free processes, and dropping the infinite choice operator in favour of $+$ and $\mathbf{0}$, $\sqsubseteq^\tau_{\text{must}}$ coincides with $\sqsubseteq^\tau_{\text{reward}}$ and $\sqsubseteq^\tau_{\text{fp-reward}}$. Together with the standard axioms for strong bisimilarity [24], the three axioms (R1)–(R3) constitute a sound and complete axiomatisation of $\equiv^\tau_{\text{must}}$ [5, Theorem 4.2], and thus for $\equiv^\tau_{\text{reward}}$. Likewise, axioms (RP1), (RP2) and (R3) constitute a sound and complete axiomatisation of $\sqsubseteq^\tau_{\text{must}}$ [5, Theorem 4.1], and thus for $\sqsubseteq^\tau_{\text{reward}}$; the axioms (R1) and (R2) are derivable from them. The first sound and complete axiomatisation of $\sqsubseteq^\tau_{\text{must}}$ appears in [6]; their axioms are derivable from the ones above (and vise versa).

A sound and complete axiomatisation of $\equiv_{\text{may}}$ (and hence of $\equiv_{-\text{reward}}$) is obtained by adding the axioms $\tau.X \equiv X$ and $\alpha(X + Y) \equiv \alpha.X + \alpha.Y$ to the standard axioms for strong bisimilarity [5, Theorem 4.5]. The axioms (R1)–(R3) are derivable from them. Adding the axiom $X + Y \sqsubseteq X$ yields a sound and complete axiomatisation of $\sqsubseteq^{-1}_{\text{may}}$ (and hence of $\sqsubseteq_{-\text{reward}}$) [5, Theorem 4.6]. The axioms (RP1) and (RP2) are then also derivable. The first sound and complete axiomatisation of $\sqsubseteq_{\text{may}}$ appears in [6]; their axioms are derivable from the ones above (and vise versa).

To illustrate the difference between $\equiv^\tau_{\text{must}}$ and $\equiv^\tau_{\text{reward}}$, without having to deal with recursion, I consider recursion-free CCS with finite choice (as done above), but upgraded with the *delay operator* Δ introduced in [3] and in Sect. 10. Clearly all preorders of this paper are precongruences for Δ. With (R4), sound for $\equiv^\tau_{\text{reward}}$, one can derive $\tau.\Delta X \equiv \Delta X$ and $\Delta X + Y \equiv \Delta(X + Y)$. Writing Ω for $\Delta\mathbf{0}$, the latter implies $\Delta Y \equiv \Omega + Y$ so one can equally well take Ω as Δ as primitive. It also follows that $\Delta\Delta X \equiv \Delta X$.

The above sound and complete axiomatisations of $\equiv_{\text{may}}$ and $\sqsubseteq^{-1}_{\text{may}}$ (and hence of $\equiv_{-\text{reward}}$ and $\sqsubseteq_{-\text{reward}}$) are extended with Δ by adding the trivial axiom $\Delta X = X$; (R4) is then derivable. This illustrates that these preorders abstract from divergence. The axiom

$$\text{(R5)} \qquad \Delta X \equiv \Delta Y$$

is sound for $\equiv^\tau_{\text{must}}$. It expresses that must testing does not record any information past a divergence. Axioms (RP2), (R4) and (R5) imply $\Omega \sqsubseteq X$, an axiom featured in [6]. Neither $\Delta X = X$ nor (R5) is sound for $\equiv^\tau_{\text{reward}}$.

14   Failure of Congruence Property for Recursion

Each preorder $\sqsubseteq$ on CCS processes ($=$ closed CCS expressions) can be extended to one on all CCS expressions by defining $E \sqsubseteq F$ iff all closed substitution instances of this inequality hold.

Definition 8. A preorder $\sqsubseteq$ on $\mathbb{E}_{\mathrm{CCS}}$ is a (full) precongruence for recursion if $S_Y \sqsubseteq T_Y$ for each $Y \in dom(S) = dom(T)$ implies $\mathbf{fix}(\!|X{:}S|\!) \sqsubseteq \mathbf{fix}(\!|X{:}T|\!)$.

The following counterexample shows that the must-testing preorder $\sqsubseteq^\tau_{\mathrm{must}}$ fails to be a precongruence for recursion, implying that the must-testing equivalence $\equiv^\tau_{\mathrm{must}}$ fails to be a congruence for recursion.

Example 6. Let $P{\in}\mathbb{T}_{\mathrm{CCS}}$ be such that $\epsilon \notin divergences(P)$—for instance $P = \mathbf{0}$. Then by (R1) one has $\tau.P + X \equiv^\tau_{\mathrm{must}} \tau.P + \tau.(X + P)$. Yet

$$\mathbf{fix}(\!|X{:} X \stackrel{def}{=} \tau.P + X|\!) \not\sqsubseteq^\tau_{\mathrm{must}} \mathbf{fix}(\!|X{:} X \stackrel{def}{=} \tau.P + \tau.(X + P)|\!),$$

because only the latter process has a divergence ϵ.

The same example shows that also $\sqsubseteq^\tau_{\mathrm{reward}}$, $\sqsubseteq^\tau_{\mathrm{fp\text{-}reward}}$, $\sqsubseteq_{\mathrm{reward}}$, $\sqsubseteq_{\mathrm{fp\text{-}reward}}$ and $\sqsubseteq_{\mathrm{must}}$ fail to be precongruences for recursion. However, I conjecture that all these preorders are *lean* precongruences for recursion as defined in [14].

15   Unguarded Recursion

The must-testing preorder $\sqsubseteq_{\mathrm{must}}$ on CCS presented in this paper is not quite the same as the original one $\sqsubseteq^{\mathrm{org}}_{\mathrm{must}}$ from [6]. The following example shows the difference.

Example 7. $\mathbf{0} \quad \begin{matrix} \equiv_{\mathrm{must}} \\ \not\sqsubseteq^{\mathrm{org}}_{\mathrm{must}} \end{matrix} \quad \mathbf{fix}(\!|X{:} X \stackrel{def}{=} X|\!) \quad \begin{matrix} \not\equiv_{\mathrm{must}} \\ \equiv^{\mathrm{org}}_{\mathrm{must}} \end{matrix} \quad \mathbf{fix}(\!|X{:} X \stackrel{def}{=} \tau.X|\!).$

The $\equiv_{\mathrm{must}}$-statement follows since neither process has a single outgoing transition; the processes are even *strongly bisimilar* [24]. The $\not\equiv_{\mathrm{must}}$-statement follows since $\epsilon \in divergences(\mathbf{fix}(\!|X{:} X \stackrel{def}{=} \tau.X|\!))$, yet $\epsilon \notin divergences(\mathbf{fix}(\!|X{:} X \stackrel{def}{=} X|\!))$. A test showing the difference is $\tau.\omega$.

The reason that in the original must-testing approach $\mathbf{fix}(\!|X{:} X \stackrel{def}{=} X|\!)$ sides with $\mathbf{fix}(\!|X{:} X \stackrel{def}{=} \tau.X|\!)$ rather than with $\mathbf{0}$, is that [6] treats a process featuring unguarded recursion (cf. [24]), such as $\mathbf{fix}(\!|X{:} X \stackrel{def}{=} X|\!)$, as if it diverges, regardless whether it can do any internal actions τ. This leads to a must-testing equivalence that is incomparable with strong bisimilarity.

In my view, the decision whether $\mathbf{fix}(\!|X{:} X \stackrel{def}{=} X|\!)$ diverges or not is part of the definition of the process algebra CCS, and entirely orthogonal to the development of testing equivalences. Below I define a process algebra $\mathrm{CCS}_\perp$ that resembles CCS in all aspects, expect that any process with unguarded recursion is declared to diverge. I see the work of [6] not so much as defining a must-testing equivalence on CCS that is incomparable with strong bisimilarity, but rather as defining a must-testing equivalence on $CCS_\perp$, a languages that is almost, but not quite, the same as CCS.[2] This is a matter of opinion, as there is no technical difference between these approaches.

I now proceed to define $CCS_\perp$, and apply the reward testing preorders of this paper to that language.

Definition 9. Let $\downarrow$ be the least predicate on $\mathbb{P}_{CCS}$ which satisfies

- $\alpha.P \downarrow$ for any $\alpha \in Act$,
- if $P_i \downarrow$ for all $i \in I$ then $\sum_{i \in I} P_i \downarrow$,
- if $P \downarrow$ and $Q \downarrow$ then $P|Q \downarrow$, $P \backslash L \downarrow$ and $P[f] \downarrow$,
- if $\mathbf{fix}(\!|S_X{:}S|\!) \downarrow$ then $\mathbf{fix}(\!|X{:}S|\!) \downarrow$.

Let $P \uparrow$ if not $P \downarrow$. If $P \uparrow$ then P features *strongly unguarded recursion*.[3]

Note that $\mathbf{0} \downarrow$, $\mathbf{fix}(\!|X{:}X \overset{def}{=} X|\!) \uparrow$ and $\mathbf{fix}(\!|X{:}X \overset{def}{=} \tau.X|\!) \downarrow$, the latter because in Definition 9 τ is allowed as a *guard*. The definitions of this paper are adapted to $CCS_\perp$ by redefining P *diverges*, notation $P \Uparrow$, if either there is a P' with $P \Longrightarrow P' \uparrow$ or there are $P_i \in \mathbb{P}$ for all $i > 0$ such that $P \overset{\tau}{\longrightarrow} P_1 \overset{\tau}{\longrightarrow} P_2 \overset{\tau}{\longrightarrow} \cdots$. In Definition 2, and similarly for Definition 1, clause (i) is replaced by (i') "if T_n is the final element in π, then either $T_n \uparrow$ or $T_n \overset{\tau,r}{\longrightarrow} T$ for no r and T". Now all results for CCS from Sects. 4–13 remain valid for $CCS_\perp$ as well. The only change in the proofs of Theorems 1–3, direction "$\Leftarrow$", is that finite paths ending in $\downarrow$ are treated like infinite paths.

My definition of $\sqsubseteq_{must}$ on $CCS_\perp$ differs on two points from the definition of $\sqsubseteq_{must}$ on $CCS_\perp$ from [6]. But both differences are inessential, and the resulting notion of $\sqsubseteq_{must}$ is the same. The first difference is that in [6] the notion of computation is exactly as in Definition 1, rather than the amended form above. However, in [6] a computation $\pi = T_0, T_1, T_2, \cdots \in Comp(T|P)$ counts as successful only if (a) it contains a state T with $T \overset{\omega}{\longrightarrow} T'$ for some T', and (b) if $T_k \uparrow$ then $T_{k'} \overset{\omega}{\longrightarrow} T'$ for some T' and some $k' \leq k$. It is straightforward to check that $\mathcal{A}pply(T|P)$ remains the same upon dropping (b) and changing (i) into (i'). The other difference is that in [6] τ does not count as a guard—their version of Definition 9 requires $\alpha \in \mathcal{A}$. So in [6] one has $\mathbf{fix}(\!|X{:}X \overset{def}{=} \tau.X|\!) \uparrow$. The notion of $\downarrow$ from [6] is therefore closer to unguarded recursion rather than strongly unguarded recursion. However, in the treatment of [6] one would have $\mathbf{fix}(\!|X{:}X \overset{def}{=} a.X|\bar{a}|\!) \downarrow$, showing that the resulting notion of guardedness is not very robust. Since the essential difference between CCS and $CCS_\perp$ is that in $CCS_\perp$ a strongly unguarded recursion is treated as a divergence, it does not matter whether $\downarrow$ also includes all or some not-strongly unguarded recursions,

---

[2] All processes of Example 7 are *weakly bisimilar* [24]. In my view this does not mean that weak bisimulation semantics uses a variant of CCS in which none of these processes diverges. Instead it tells that weak bisimilarity abstracts from divergence.

[3] Un(strongly unguarded) recursion should not be called "strongly guarded" recursion; it is weaker than guarded recursion.

such as $\mathbf{fix}(\!(X\!:\!X \stackrel{def}{=} \tau.X)\!)$. For any such not-strongly unguarded recursion is already divergent, and hence it does not make difference whether it is declared syntactically divergent as well.

An alternative to moving from CCS to CCS$_\perp$ is to restrict either language to processes P satisfying $P \!\downarrow$. This restriction rules out the process $\mathbf{fix}(\!(X\!:\!X \stackrel{def}{=} X)\!)$, but includes $\mathbf{fix}(\!(X\!:\!X \stackrel{def}{=} \tau.X)\!)$. On this restricted set of processes their is no difference between CCS and CCS$_\perp$.

Another approach to making unguarded recursions divergent is to change the rule for recursion from Table 1 into $\mathbf{fix}(\!(X\!:\!S)\!) \stackrel{\tau}{\longrightarrow} \mathbf{fix}(\!(S_X\!:\!S)\!)$; this is done in the setting of CSP [26]. This would not have the same result, however, as here and in [6] one has $a + \mathbf{fix}(\!(X\!:\!X \stackrel{def}{=} b)\!) \equiv_{\mathrm{must}} a + b$.

The great advantage of moving from CCS to CCS$_\perp$ is that Counterexample 6, against testing preorders being congruences for recursion, disappears.

Question: Are $\sqsubseteq^\tau_{\mathrm{reward}}$, $\sqsubseteq^\tau_{\mathrm{fp\text{-}reward}}$ and $\sqsubseteq^\tau_{\mathrm{must}}$ precongruences for recursion on CCS$_\perp$?

In [6] it is shown that, in the absence of infinite choice, $\sqsubseteq^\tau_{\mathrm{must}}$ is a precongruences for recursion. Central in the proof is that on CCS$_\perp$ with finite choice, the clause on infinite traces $(inf_\perp(P) \supseteq inf_\perp(Q))$ may be dropped from Theorem 3, since the infinite traces $inf_\perp(P)$ of a CCS$_\perp$ process P with finite choice are completely determined by $divergences_\perp(P)$ and $failures_\perp(P)$. This proof does not generalise to $\sqsubseteq^\tau_{\mathrm{reward}}$ or $\sqsubseteq^\tau_{\mathrm{fp\text{-}reward}}$, since here, on CCS$_\perp$ with finite choice, the infinite traces are not redundant. The proof also does not generalise to $\sqsubseteq^\tau_{\mathrm{must}}$ on CCS with infinite choice.

In [28] it is shown that $\sqsubseteq^\perp_{FDI}$ (cf. Theorem 3), which coincides with $\sqsubseteq_{\mathrm{must}}$, is a congruence for recursion on the language CSP. I expect that similar reasoning can show that $\sqsubseteq^\tau_{\mathrm{reward}}$ is a congruence for recursion on CCS$_\perp$. In [29] it is shown that $\sqsubseteq^d_{FDI}$ (cf. Theorem 2), which coincides with $\sqsubseteq_{\mathrm{fp\text{-}reward}}$, is a congruence for recursion on CSP. I expect that similar reasoning can show that $\sqsubseteq^\tau_{\mathrm{fp\text{-}reward}}$ is a congruence for recursion on CCS$_\perp$. Roscoe [29] also presents an example, independently discovered by Levy [23], showing that $\equiv_{NDFD}$ (cf. Theorem 1), which coincides with $\sqsubseteq_{\mathrm{reward}}$, fails to be a congruence for recursion:[4] Let FA be a process that has *all* conceivable failures, divergences and infinite traces, except for the infinite trace a^∞. Then $FA + \tau.X \equiv_{NDFD} FA + a.X$, for both sides have all conceivable failures, divergences and infinite traces, with the possible exception of a^∞, and both side have the infinite trace a^∞ iff X has it. However,

$$\mathbf{fix}(\!(X\!:\!FA + \tau.X)\!) \not\equiv_{NDFD} \mathbf{fix}(\!(X\!:\!FA + a.X)\!)$$

since only the latter process has the infinite trace a^∞.

It could be argued that this example shows that the definition of being a congruence for recursion ought to be sharpened, for instance by requiring that $E \sqsubseteq F$ holds only if all closed substitutions of $E \sqsubseteq F$ employing an extended

---

[4] The example was formulated for another equivalence, but actually applies to a range of equivalences, including $\equiv_{NDFD}$.

alphabet of actions hold. This would invalidate $FA + \tau.X \equiv_{NDFD} FA + a.X$, namely by substituting b for X, with b a fresh action, not alluded to in FA. With such a sharpening, the question whether $\sqsubseteq^\tau_{\text{reward}}$ is a congruence for recursion on $\text{CCS}_\perp$ is open.

16   Related Work

The concept of reward testing stems from [18], in the setting of nondeterministic probabilistic processes. In the terminology of Sect. 8, they employ single reward nonnegative reward testing. In [10] it was shown, again in a probabilistic setting, that nonnegative reward testing is no more powerful then classical testing. This result is a probabilistic analogue of Theorem 7. Negative rewards were first proposed in [11], a predecessor of the present paper. In [8], reward testing with also negative rewards, called *real-reward* testing, was applied to nondeterministic probabilistic processes. Although technically no rewards can be gathered after a first reward has been encountered, thanks to probabilistic branching rewards can be distributed over multiple actions in a computation. This makes the approach a probabilistic generalisation of the reward testing proposed here. The main result of [8] is that for finitary (= finite-state and finitely many transitions) nondeterministic probabilistic processes without divergence, real-reward testing coincides with nonnegative reward testing. This is a generalisation (to probabilistic processes) of a specialisation (to finitary processes) of Proposition 1. An explicit characterisation (as in Theorem 1) of real-reward testing for processes with divergence was not attempted in [8].

The *nondivergent failures divergences* equivalence, $\equiv_{NDFD}$, defined in the proof of Theorem 1, stems from [19]. There it was shown to be the coarsest congruence (for a collection of operators equivalent to the ones used in Sect. 11) that preserves those linear-time properties (cf. Definition 7) that can be expressed in linear-time temporal logic without the nexttime operator. If follows directly from their proof that it is also the coarsest congruence that preserves *all* linear-time properties as defined in Definition 7; so $\equiv_{NDFD}$ coincides with $\equiv_{lt. \; properties}$, as remarked at the end of Sect. 11. It is this result that inspired Theorem 1 in the current paper.

The paper [22] argues that $\equiv_{NDFD}$ can be seen as a testing equivalence, but does not offer a testing scenario in the same style as [6] or the current paper.

The semantic equivalence $\equiv^d_{FDI}$, whose associated preorder occurs in the proof of Theorem 2, stems from [27]. There it was shown to be the coarsest congruence (for the same operators) that preserves $deadlocks(P) \cup divergences(P)$, the combined deadlock and divergence traces of a process (cf. Definition 3). It is this result that directly led (via [12, Theorem 9]) to Theorem 2 in the current paper.

In [6] the action ω is used merely to mark certain states as success states, namely the states were an ω-transition is enabled; a computation is successful iff it passes through such a success state. In [30], on the other hand, it is the *actual execution* of ω that constitutes success. In [7,10], this is called *action-based testing*; [7, Proposition 5.1 and Example 5.3] shows that action-based must testing is strictly less discriminating than state-based must-besting:

$$\tau.a.\Omega \equiv_{\text{must}}^{\text{action-based}} \tau.a.\Omega + \tau.\mathbf{0}, \qquad \text{whereas} \qquad \tau.a.\Omega \not\sqsubseteq_{\text{must}} \tau.a.\Omega + \tau.\mathbf{0}.$$

The preorders in the current paper are generalisations of state-based testing; an action-based form of reward testing could be obtained by only allowing τ-actions to carry non-0 rewards. The same counterexample as above would show the difference between state- and action-based reward testing.

The reward testing contributed here constitutes a strengthening of the testing machinery of De Nicola & Hennessy. As such it differs from testing-based approaches that lead to incomparable preorders, such as the *efficiency testing* of [31], or the *fair testing* independently proposed in [4] and [25].

In [13] I advocate an overhaul of concurrency theory to ensure liveness properties when making the reasonable assumption of *justness*. The current work is prior to any such overhaul. It is consistent with the principles of [13] when pretending that the parallel composition | of CCS is in fact not a parallel composition of independent processes, but an interleaving operator, scheduling two parallel treads by means of arbitrary interleaving.

17 Conclusion

In this paper I contributed a concept of reward testing, strengthening the may and must testing of De Nicola & Hennessy. Inspired by [19,27], I provided an explicit characterisation of the reward-testing preorder, as well as of a slight weakening, called finite-penalty reward testing. Must testing can be recovered by only considering positive rewards, and may testing by only considering negative rewards. While the must-testing preorder preserves liveness properties, and the inverse of the may-testing preorder (which can also be seen as a must-testing preorder dealing with catastrophes rather than successes) preserves safety properties, the (finite-penalty) reward testing preorder, which is finer than both, additionally preserves conditional liveness properties. I illustrated the difference between may testing, must testing and (finite-penalty) reward testing in terms of their equational axiomatisations. When applied to CCS as intended by Milner, must-testing equivalence fails to be a congruence for recursion, and the same problem exists for reward testing. The counterexample is eliminated by applying it to a small variant of CCS that, following [6], treats a process with unguarded recursion as if it is diverging, even if it cannot make any internal moves. In this setting, by analogy with Roscoe's work on CSP [28,29], I expect must-testing and finite-penalty reward testing to be congruences for recursion; for reward testing this question remains open.

References

1. Abramsky, S., Jung, A.: Domain theory. In: Handbook of Logic and Computer Science, vol. 3, pp. 1–168. Clarendon Press (1994)
2. Alpern, B., Schneider, F.B.: Defining liveness. Inf. Process. Lett. **21**(4), 181–185 (1985). https://doi.org/10.1016/0020-0190(85)90056-0
3. Bergstra, J.A., Klop, J.W., Olderog, E.-R.: Failures without chaos: a new process semantics for fair abstraction. In: Wirsing, M. (ed.) Formal Description of Programming Concepts - III, Proceedings of the 3th IFIP WG 2.2 Working Conference, Ebberup 1986, North-Holland, Amsterdam, pp. 77–103 (1987)
4. Brinksma, E., Rensink, A., Vogler, W.: Fair testing. In: Lee, I., Smolka, S. (eds.) CONCUR 1995. LNCS, vol. 962, pp. 313–327. Springer, Berlin (1995). https://doi.org/10.1007/3-540-60218-6_23
5. Chen, T., Fokkink, W.J., van Glabbeek, R.J.: On the axiomatizability of impossible futures. Logical Methods Comput. Sci. **11**(3), 17 (2015). https://doi.org/10.2168/LMCS-11(3:17)2015
6. De Nicola, R., Hennessy, M.: Testing equivalences for processes. Theor. Comput. Sci. **34**, 83–133 (1984). https://doi.org/10.1016/0304-3975(84)90113-0
7. Deng, Y., van Glabbeek, R.J., Hennessy, M., Morgan, C.C.: Characterising testing preorders for finite probabilistic processes. Logical Methods Comput. Sci. **4**(4), 4 (2008). https://doi.org/10.2168/LMCS-4(4:4)2008
8. Deng, Y., van Glabbeek, R.J., Hennessy, M., Morgan, C.C.: Real-reward testing for probabilistic processes. Theor. Comput. Sci. **538**, 16–36 (2014). https://doi.org/10.1016/j.tcs.2013.07.016
9. Deng, Y., van Glabbeek, R.J., Hennessy, M., Morgan, C.C., Zhang, C.: Remarks on testing probabilistic processes. In: Cardelli, L., Fiore, M., Winskel, G. (eds.) Computation, Meaning, and Logic: Articles Dedicated to Gordon Plotkin, ENTCS, vol. 172, pp. 359–397. Elsevier (2007). https://doi.org/10.1016/j.entcs.2007.02.013
10. Deng, Y., van Glabbeek, R., Morgan, C., Zhang, C.: Scalar outcomes suffice for finitary probabilistic testing. In: De Nicola, R. (ed.) ESOP 2007. LNCS, vol. 4421, pp. 363–378. Springer, Berlin (2007). https://doi.org/10.1007/978-3-540-71316-6_25
11. van Glabbeek, R.J.: The Linear Time – Branching time spectrum after 20 years, or full abstraction for safety and liveness properties. Copies of slides. Invited talk for IFIP WG 1.8 at CONCUR 2009 in Bologna (2009). http://theory.stanford.edu/~rvg/abstracts.html#20years
12. van Glabbeek, R.J.: The coarsest precongruences respecting safety and liveness properties. In: Calude, C.S., Sassone, V. (eds.) TCS 2010. IFIPAICT, vol. 323, pp. 32–52. Springer, Berlin (2010). https://doi.org/10.1007/978-3-642-15240-5_3
13. van Glabbeek, R.J.: Ensuring liveness properties of distributed systems (a research agenda). Position paper (2016). https://arxiv.org/abs/1711.04240
14. van Glabbeek, R.J.: Lean and full congruence formats for recursion. In: Proceedings 32nd Annual ACM/IEEE Symposium on Logic in Computer Science, LICS 2017, Reykjavik, Iceland, June 2017. IEEE Computer Society Press (2017). https://doi.org/10.1109/LICS.2017.8005142
15. van Glabbeek, R.J., Höfner, P.: Progress, fairness and justness in process algebra. Technical Report 8501, NICTA, Sydney, Australia (2015). http://arxiv.org/abs/1501.03268
16. Hennessy, M.C.B.: Powerdomains and nondeterministic recursive definitions. In: Dezani-Ciancaglini, M., Montanari, U. (eds.) Programming 1982. LNCS, vol. 137, pp. 178–193. Springer, Heidelberg (1982). https://doi.org/10.1007/3-540-11494-7_13

17. Hennessy, M.: An Algebraic Theory of Processes. MIT Press, Cambridge (1988)
18. Jonsson, B., Ho-Stuart, C., Yi, W.: Testing and refinement for nondeterministic and probabilistic processes. In: Langmaack, H., de Roever, W.P., Vytopil, J. (eds.) FTRTFT 1994, ProCoS 1994. Lecture Notes in Computer Science, vol. 863, pp. 418–430. Springer, Berlin (1994). https://doi.org/10.1007/3-540-58468-4_176
19. Kaivola, R., Valmari, A.: The weakest compositional semantic equivalence preserving nexttime-less linear temporal logic. In: Cleaveland, W.R. (ed.) CONCUR 1992. LNCS, vol. 630, pp. 207–221. Springer, Heidelberg (1992). https://doi.org/10.1007/BFb0084793
20. Lamport, L.: Proving the correctness of multiprocess programs. IEEE Trans. Softw. Eng. **3**(2), 125–143 (1977). https://doi.org/10.1109/TSE.1977.229904
21. Lamport, L.: Proving possibility properties. Theor. Comput. Sci. **206**(1–2), 341–352 (1998). https://doi.org/10.1016/S0304-3975(98)00129-7. http://research.microsoft.com/en-us/um/people/lamport/pubs/pubs.html#lamport-possibility
22. Leduc, G.: Failure-based congruences, unfair divergences and new testing theory. In: Vuong, S.T., Chanson, S.T. (eds.) 1994 Proceedings Fourteenth IFIP WG6.1 International Symposium on Protocol Specification, Testing and Verification, Vancouver, BC, Canada, IFIP Conference Proceedings, vol. 1, pp. 252–267. Chapman & Hall (1994)
23. Levy, P.B.: Infinite trace equivalence. Ann. Pure Appl. Logic **151**(2–3), 170–198 (2008). https://doi.org/10.1016/j.apal.2007.10.007
24. Milner, R.: Operational and algebraic semantics of concurrent processes. In: van Leeuwen, J. (ed.) Handbook of Theoretical Computer Science. Elsevier Science Publishers B.V. (North-Holland), pp. 1201–1242 (1990). (Chap. 19) Communication and Concurrency, Prentice-Hall, Englewood Cliffs, 1989
25. Natarajan, V., Cleaveland, R.: Divergence and fair testing. In: Fülöp, Z., Gécseg, F. (eds.) ICALP 1995. LNCS, vol. 944, pp. 648–659. Springer, Heidelberg (1995). https://doi.org/10.1007/3-540-60084-1_112
26. Olderog, E.-R., Hoare, C.A.R.: Specification-oriented semantics for communicating processes. Acta Informatica **23**, 9–66 (1986). https://doi.org/10.1007/BF00268075
27. Puhakka, A.: Weakest congruence results concerning "any-lock". In: Kobayashi, N., Pierce, B.C. (eds.) TACS 2001. LNCS, vol. 2215, pp. 400–419. Springer, Berlin (2001). https://doi.org/10.1007/3-540-45500-0_20
28. Roscoe, A.W.: The Theory and Practice of Concurrency. Prentice-Hall, Upper Saddle River (1997). http://www.comlab.ox.ac.uk/bill.roscoe/publications/68b.pdf
29. Roscoe, A.W.: Seeing beyond divergence. In: Abdallah, A.E., Jones, C.B., Sanders, J.W. (eds.) Communicating Sequential Processes. The First 25 Years. Lecture Notes in Computer Science, vol. 3525, pp. 15–35. Springer, Berlin (2005). https://doi.org/10.1007/11423348_2
30. Segala, R.: Testing probabilistic automata. In: Montanari, U., Sassone, V. (eds.) CONCUR 1996. LNCS, vol. 1119, pp. 299–314. Springer, Heidelberg (1996). https://doi.org/10.1007/3-540-61604-7_62
31. Vogler, W.: Efficiency of asynchronous systems, read arcs, and the MUTEX-problem. Theor. Comput. Sci. **275**(1–2), 589–631 (2002). https://doi.org/10.1016/S0304-3975(01)00300-0

Playing with Bisimulation in Erlang

Ivan Lanese, Davide Sangiorgi, and Gianluigi Zavattaro[✉]

Focus Team, University of Bologna/Inria, Bologna, Italy
ivan.lanese@gmail.com, davide.sangiorgi@gmail.com,
gianluigi.zavattaro@unibo.it

Abstract. Erlang is a functional and concurrent programming language. The aim of this paper is to investigate basic properties of the Erlang concurrency model, which is based on asynchronous communication through mailboxes accessed via pattern matching. To achieve this goal, we consider Core Erlang (which is an intermediate step in Erlang compilation) and we define, on top of its operational semantics, an observational semantics following the approach used to define asynchronous bisimulation for the π-calculus. Our work allows us to shed some light on the management of process identifiers in Erlang, different from the various forms of name mobility already studied in the literature. In fact, we need to modify standard definitions to cope with such specific features of Erlang.

1 Introduction

Erlang is a message passing concurrent and functional programming language [3]. Erlang was originally a proprietary language within Ericsson, developed in 1986 to ensure high availability and fault-tolerance in distributed and massively concurrent telephony applications, but was released as open source in 1998 [2]. Along the years, it has been used not only in telephony, but also in many other high-visibility concurrent and distributed projects such as some versions of the Facebook chat [22].

Formal methods research on Erlang concentrated on defining its semantics, e.g., to precisely formalise the behaviour of Erlang implementations [15,29] and to drive future development [30]. Erlang semantics has been used also as a basis to develop tools, such as model checkers [16], static analysers [31], theorem provers for modal logics [17], declarative debuggers [9] and reversible debuggers [20,21].

Despite the remarkable interest in Erlang and its concurrency model, to the best of our knowledge, there is no research dealing with observational semantics for such language. Observational semantics represents one of the main fields of interest of Rocco De Nicola, with several pioneering contributions to which this paper (as well as many others from the authors) is strongly indebted.

This work has been partially supported by the French National Research Agency (ANR), project DCore n. ANR-18-CE25-0007.

M. Boreale et al. (Eds.): De Nicola-Festschrift, LNCS 11665, pp. 71–91, 2019.
https://doi.org/10.1007/978-3-030-21485-2_6

The aim of this paper is to initiate the investigation of the applicability to Erlang of observational semantics already available in the literature. Instead of considering full Erlang that, e.g., includes rather expressive mechanisms for fault handling, in this work we focus on a simpler language corresponding to the functional and concurrent fragment of *Core Erlang* [10], which is an intermediate step in the compilation of Erlang.

Erlang is based on asynchronous communication, hence we have started by considering observational theories tailored to asynchrony. One of the first papers dealing with asynchronous communication in process algebra is by de Boer et al. [5], where different observation criteria are studied (bisimulation, traces and abstract traces) following the axiomatic approach typical of the process algebra ACP [4]. An alternative approach has been followed by Amadio et al. [1] who defined asynchronous bisimulation for the π-calculus [26]. They started from operational semantics (expressed as a standard labelled transition system), and then considered the largest bisimulation defined on internal steps that equates processes only when they have the same observables, and which is closed under contexts. The equivalence obtained in this way is called *barbed congruence* [24]. Notably, when asynchronous communication is considered, barbed congruence is defined assuming as observables the messages that are ready to be delivered to a potential external observer.

Merro and Sangiorgi [23] have subsequently studied barbed congruence in the context of the *Asynchronous Localised π-calculus* (ALπ), which is a fragment of the asynchronous π-calculus in which only output capabilities can be transmitted, i.e., when a process receives the name of a channel, it can only send messages along this channel (and not receive on it). Another line of research deals with the application of the testing approach to asynchronous communication; this has been investigated by Castellani and Hennessy [11] and by Boreale et al. [7,8]. These papers consider an asynchronous variant of CCS [25], and the proposed semantics turns out to be incomparable with barbed congruence for two main reasons. As usual, testing discriminates less as far as non deterministic choices are concerned, while it is able to observe divergent behaviours (while barbed congruence is not).

In Erlang, process identifiers can be passed around; this mechanism is similar to name passing in the π-calculus. Moreover, when a process receives a process identifier, it receives the capability to send messages to that process; this corresponds to the specific form of name mobility (transmission of output capability) of ALπ. For these reasons, we have adopted the approach by Merro and Sangiorgi defined for ALπ as our starting point. Differently from ALπ, in Erlang there is a unique receiver for each name, namely the process with that name.

Technically speaking, we consider the syntax of Core Erlang, and we investigate the applicability of the usual definition of barbed congruence. The direct application of standard definitions does not equate Erlang systems that are intuitively equivalent. Namely, consider an Erlang system A composed of a process that sends messages to a. Such system is expected to be equivalent to a system B in which the same process sends its messages to b instead of a, composed in parallel with a *wire* from b to a, i.e. a process with identifier b that simply forwards to a the messages that it receives.

If we apply to Erlang standard barbed congruence (denoted, as usual, with $\approx$) we have that $A \not\approx B$. The expected equivalence fails for two main reasons. First, if we put A and B in a context in which there is a process with identifier b, in the first case the obtained system is correct while in the second one it is not, because there are two distinct processes having the same identifier. The second problem is that if we put A and B in a context in which there is a message to b ready to be delivered, in the first case such message is observable while in the second one it is not because the unique receiver for such message (i.e., the wire) is already in the observed system.

We discuss a new definition of barbed congruence that solves the two above problems; we denote this new equivalence by $\approx_V^U$, where U and V are two sets of process identifiers. Both sets are used to impose limitations to the possible contexts considered in the barbed congruence definition. The set U contains names that cannot be used as identifiers for processes in the context; this can be used to solve the first of the two problems above by assuming $b \in U$, hence disallowing contexts that contain a process with identifier b. The set V contains identifiers that cannot be present in the context; this can be used to solve the second of the two problems above by assuming $b \in V$, hence disallowing contexts that contain messages to be delivered to b. Our novel bisimulation $\approx_V^U$ allows us to prove that the two above systems are equivalent.

Besides presenting the definition of this novel barbed congruence for Erlang, we use it to investigate basic properties of the concurrency model underlying such language. More precisely, we discuss the conditions under which we can rephrase in Core Erlang some typical equivalences of asynchronous name passing calculi. We also point out that some specific features of the Erlang language, like casting process identifiers to other data types or pattern matching operations on process identifiers, can break most of such equivalences.

The paper is structured as follows. In Sects. 2 and 3 we present the syntax and semantics of Core Erlang. In Sect. 4 we present the definition of our novel barbed congruence and discuss some of its basic features, while in Sect. 5 we apply it to formalise some properties of Erlang. Finally, in Sect. 6 we discuss some possible extensions for our work, and we conclude in Sect. 7.

2   Erlang Syntax

In this section, we present the syntax of a first-order concurrent functional language that follows the actor model. Our language is essentially a subset of Core Erlang [10]. This material is mostly taken from [21].

The syntax of the language can be found in Fig. 1. Here, a module is a sequence of function definitions, where each function name f/n (atom/arity) has an associated definition fun $(X_1, \ldots, X_n) \rightarrow e$. We consider that a program consists of a single module for simplicity. The body of a function is an *expression*, which can include variables, literals, function names, lists, tuples,

$$
\begin{aligned}
module &::= \text{module } Atom = fun_1 \ \ldots \ fun_n \\
fun &::= fname = \text{fun } (Var_1, \ldots, Var_n) \to expr \\
fname &::= Atom/Integer \\
lit &::= Atom \mid Integer \mid Float \mid Pid \mid [\,] \\
expr &::= Var \mid lit \mid fname \mid [expr_1|expr_2] \mid \{expr_1, \ldots, expr_n\} \\
&\mid \text{ call } Op \ (expr_1, \ldots, expr_n) \mid \text{apply } fname \ (expr_1, \ldots, expr_n) \\
&\mid \text{ case } expr \text{ of } clause_1; \ldots; clause_m \text{ end} \\
&\mid \text{ let } Var = expr_1 \text{ in } expr_2 \mid \text{receive } clause_1; \ldots; clause_n \text{ end} \\
&\mid \text{ spawn}(fname, [expr_1, \ldots, expr_n]) \mid expr \,!\, expr \mid \text{self}() \\
clause &::= pat \text{ when } expr_1 \to expr_2 \\
pat &::= Var \mid lit \mid [pat_1|pat_2] \mid \{pat_1, \ldots, pat_n\}
\end{aligned}
$$

Fig. 1. Language syntax rules

calls to built-in functions—mainly arithmetic and relational operators—, function applications, case expressions, let bindings, and receive expressions; furthermore, we also include the functions spawn, "!" (for sending a message), and self() that are usually considered built-ins in the Erlang language. As is common practice, we assume that X is a fresh variable in a let binding of the form let $X = expr_1$ in $expr_2$.

As shown by the syntax in Fig. 1, we only consider first-order expressions. Therefore, the first argument in applications and spawns is a function name. Analogously, the first argument in calls is a built-in operation Op.

In this language, we distinguish expressions, patterns, and values. Here, *patterns* are built from variables, literals, lists, and tuples, while *values* are built from literals, lists, and tuples, i.e., they are *ground*—without variables—patterns. Expressions are denoted by $e, e', e_1, e_2, \ldots$, patterns by pat, pat', pat_1, $pat_2, \ldots$ and values by $v, v', v_1, v_2, \ldots$ Atoms are typically denoted with roman letters, while variables start with an uppercase letter. As it is common practice, a *substitution* θ is a mapping from variables to expressions, and $\mathcal{D}om(\theta) = \{X \in Var \mid X \neq \theta(X)\}$ is its domain. Substitutions are usually denoted by sets of bindings like, e.g., $\{X_1 \mapsto v_1, \ldots, X_n \mapsto v_n\}$. Substitutions are extended to morphisms from expressions to expressions in the natural way. The identity substitution is denoted by id. Composition of substitutions is denoted by juxtaposition. Also, we denote by $\theta[X_1 \mapsto v_1, \ldots, X_n \mapsto v_n]$ the *update* of θ with the mapping $\{X_1 \mapsto v_1, \ldots, X_n \mapsto v_n\}$.

In a case expression "case e of pat_1 when $e_1 \to e'_1$; $\ldots$; pat_n when $e_n \to e'_n$ end", we first evaluate e to a value, say v; then, we should find (if any) the first clause pat_i when $e_i \to e'_i$ such that v matches pat_i (i.e., there exists a substitution σ for the variables of pat_i such that $v = pat_i\sigma$) and $e_i\sigma$—the *guard*—reduces to *true*; then, the case expression reduces to $e'_i\sigma$.

As for the concurrent features of the language, we consider that a *system* is a pool of processes that can only interact through message passing. Each process has an associated *pid* (process identifier). We consider a specific domain Pid for pids. Furthermore, in this work, we assume that pids can only be introduced in a computation from the evaluation of functions spawn and self (see below), and

$$\text{main}/0 = \text{fun } () \rightarrow \text{let } Pid2 = \text{spawn}(\text{target}/0, [\,])$$
$$\text{in let } Pid3 = \text{spawn}(\text{echo}/1, [Pid2])$$
$$\text{in let } \_ = Pid2 \,!\, \text{hello}$$
$$\text{in } Pid3 \,!\, \text{world}$$

$$\text{target}/0 = \text{fun } () \rightarrow \text{receive}$$
$$M1 \rightarrow \text{receive}$$
$$M2 \rightarrow \{M1, M2\}$$
$$\text{end}$$
$$\text{end}$$

$$\text{echo}/1 = \text{fun } (PidT) \rightarrow \text{receive}$$
$$M \rightarrow PidT \,!\, M$$
$$\text{end}$$

Fig. 2. A simple concurrent program

that there is no pid literal and no built-in function taking pids as arguments, apart for message sending. Pids however are valid values at runtime. The previous assumption forbids, e.g., casting from pids to strings and testing pids for equality. We further discuss this assumption in Sect. 6. By abuse of notation, when no confusion can arise, we refer to a process with its pid.

An expression of the form $\text{spawn}(f/n, [e_1, \ldots, e_n])$ has, as a *side effect*, the creation of a new process, with a fresh pid a, initialised with the expression $\text{apply } f/n \ (v_1, \ldots, v_n)$, where $v_1, \ldots, v_n$ are the evaluations of $e_1, \ldots, e_n$, respectively; the expression $\text{spawn}(f/n, [e_1, \ldots, e_n])$ itself evaluates to the new pid a. The function $\text{self}()$ just returns the pid of the current process. An expression of the form $e_1 \,!\, e_2$, where e_1 evaluates to a pid a and e_2 to a value v, also evaluates to the value v and, as a side effect, the value v—the *message*—will be stored in the queue or *mailbox* of process a at some point in the future.

Finally, an expression "receive pat_1 when $e_1 \rightarrow e'_1; \ldots; pat_n$ when $e_n \rightarrow e'_n$ end" traverses the messages in the process' queue until one of them matches a branch in the receive statement; i.e., it should find the *first* message v in the process' queue (if any) such that case v of pat_1 when $e_1 \rightarrow e'_1; \ldots; pat_n$ when $e_n \rightarrow e'_n$ end can be reduced to some expression e; then, the receive expression evaluates to the expression e, with the side effect of deleting the message v from the process' queue. If there is no matching message in the queue, the process suspends its execution until a matching message arrives.

Example 1. Consider the program shown in Fig. 2, where the symbol "_" is used to denote an *anonymous* variable, i.e., a variable whose name is not relevant. The computation starts with "apply main/0 ()". This creates a process, say a1. Then, a1 spawns two new processes, say a2 and a3, and then sends the message hello to process a2 and the message world to process a3, which then resends world to a2. Note that we consider that variables $Pid2$ and $Pid3$ are bound to pids a2 and a3, respectively.

Given that there is no guarantee regarding which message arrives first to a3, function target/0 may return either $\{\text{hello}, \text{world}\}$ or $\{\text{world}, \text{hello}\}$. This is coherent with the semantics of Erlang, where it is not possible to make any assumption on the order in which two messages, sent by two distinct senders, will be delivered to the same target process. In Erlang, the only expected assumption on message ordering is that if two messages are sent from a process to the same target, and both are delivered, then the order of these messages is kept. Nevertheless, current implementations only guarantee this property within the same node.

3 Erlang Semantics

In this section we formalise the semantics of the considered language. The semantics we present is equivalent to the one in [21], but allows for a simpler technical treatment.

Definition 1 (Process). *A process is denoted by a tuple $\langle a, (\theta, e), q \rangle$ where a is the pid of the process, (θ, e) is the control—which consists of an environment (a substitution) and an expression to be evaluated—and q is the process' mailbox, a queue with the sequence of messages that have reached the process.*

Given a message v and a mailbox q, we let $v : q$ denote a new mailbox with message v on top of it (i.e., v is the newer message). We also denote with $q \backslash\backslash v$ a new queue that results from q by removing the oldest occurrence of message v.

A running *system* is a pool of processes and floating messages, which we define as follows:

Definition 2 (System). *Systems, ranged over by $A, B, \ldots$, are generated by the following grammar:*

$$A := \langle a, (\theta, e), q \rangle \; \big| \; (a, v) \; \big| \; A_1 \,|\, A_2$$

that is, they are parallel compositions of processes and floating messages, where (a, v) is a floating message with content v targeting process a.

We only allow well-formed systems, in that the pids of the processes in a system are pairwise distinct. Moreover, we consider systems up-to associativity and commutativity of the parallel composition operator $|$. We therefore write $A = B$ to mean that the systems A and B are the same up-to associativity and commutativity of $|$.

In the definition above, floating messages represent messages in the system after they are sent, and before they are inserted in the target mailbox, in other terms, when they are in the network. Floating messages correspond to messages in the global mailbox of [21] or in the ether of [30].

The system representation above abstracts away from the distribution of processes over computing nodes. As a result, the only guarantee on message ordering offered by current Erlang implementations (i.e., order preserved among messages exchanged between the same pair of processes only if hosted in the same

$$(Var) \ \frac{}{\theta, X \overset{\tau}{\hookrightarrow} \theta, \theta(X)} \qquad (Tuple) \ \frac{\theta, e_i \overset{\ell}{\hookrightarrow} \theta', e_i' \quad i \in \{1, \ldots, n\}}{\theta, \{\overline{v_{1,i-1}}, e_i, \overline{e_{i+1,n}}\} \overset{\ell}{\hookrightarrow} \theta', \{\overline{v_{1,i-1}}, e_i', \overline{e_{i+1,n}}\}}$$

$$(List1) \ \frac{\theta, e_1 \overset{\ell}{\hookrightarrow} \theta', e_1'}{\theta, [e_1|e_2] \overset{\ell}{\hookrightarrow} \theta', [e_1'|e_2]} \qquad (List2) \ \frac{\theta, e_2 \overset{\ell}{\hookrightarrow} \theta', e_2'}{\theta, [v_1|e_2] \overset{\ell}{\hookrightarrow} \theta', [v_1|e_2']}$$

$$(Let1) \ \frac{\theta, e_1 \overset{\ell}{\hookrightarrow} \theta', e_1'}{\theta, \mathsf{let}\ X = e_1\ \mathsf{in}\ e_2 \overset{\ell}{\hookrightarrow} \theta', \mathsf{let}\ X = e_1'\ \mathsf{in}\ e_2} \qquad (Let2) \ \frac{}{\theta, \mathsf{let}\ X = v\ \mathsf{in}\ e \overset{\tau}{\hookrightarrow} \theta[X \mapsto v], e}$$

$$(Case1) \ \frac{\theta, e \overset{\ell}{\hookrightarrow} \theta', e'}{\theta, \mathsf{case}\ e\ \mathsf{of}\ cl_1; \ldots; cl_n\ \mathsf{end} \overset{\ell}{\hookrightarrow} \theta', \mathsf{case}\ e'\ \mathsf{of}\ cl_1; \ldots; cl_n\ \mathsf{end}}$$

$$(Case2) \ \frac{\mathsf{match}(\theta, v, cl_1, \ldots, cl_n) = \langle \theta_i, e_i \rangle}{\theta, \mathsf{case}\ v\ \mathsf{of}\ cl_1; \ldots; cl_n\ \mathsf{end} \overset{\tau}{\hookrightarrow} \theta\theta_i, e_i}$$

$$(Call1) \ \frac{\theta, e_i \overset{\ell}{\hookrightarrow} \theta', e_i' \quad i \in \{1, \ldots, n\}}{\theta, \mathsf{call}\ op\ (\overline{v_{1,i-1}}, e_i, \overline{e_{i+1,n}}) \overset{\ell}{\hookrightarrow} \theta', \mathsf{call}\ op\ (\overline{v_{1,i-1}}, e_i', \overline{e_{i+1,n}})}$$

$$(Call2) \ \frac{\mathsf{eval}(op, v_1, \ldots, v_n) = v}{\theta, \mathsf{call}\ op\ (v_1, \ldots, v_n) \overset{\tau}{\hookrightarrow} \theta, v}$$

$$(Apply1) \ \frac{\theta, e_i \overset{\ell}{\hookrightarrow} \theta', e_i' \quad i \in \{1, \ldots, n\}}{\theta, \mathsf{apply}\ f/n\ (\overline{v_{1,i-1}}, e_i, \overline{e_{i+1,n}}) \overset{\ell}{\hookrightarrow} \theta', \mathsf{apply}\ f/n\ (\overline{v_{1,i-1}}, e_i', \overline{e_{i+1,n}})}$$

$$(Apply2) \ \frac{\mu(f/n) = \mathsf{fun}\ (X_1, \ldots, X_n) \to e}{\theta, \mathsf{apply}\ f/n\ (v_1, \ldots, v_n) \overset{\tau}{\hookrightarrow} \theta \cup \{X_1 \mapsto v_1, \ldots, X_n \mapsto v_n\}, e}$$

Fig. 3. Standard semantics: evaluation of sequential expressions

node) does not apply. Thus, we drop any assumption on the order of delivery of messages.

We write $\mathsf{ppid}(P)$ (for process' pid) for the pid of the process P, and $\mathsf{ppid}(A)$ for the set of the pids of the processes in A. A pid a is *fresh for* B, if a does not appear in B.

In the following, we denote by $\overline{o_n}$ a sequence of syntactic objects $o_1, \ldots, o_n$ for some n. We also write $\overline{o_{i,j}}$ for the sequence $o_i, \ldots, o_j$ when $i \leq j$ (and the empty sequence otherwise, i.e., when $i > j$). We write $\overline{o}$ when the number of elements is not relevant.

The semantics is defined by means of two relations: $\hookrightarrow$ for expressions and $\longrightarrow$ for systems. We start by considering the relation $\hookrightarrow$ for expressions, which is a labelled transition relation

$$\hookrightarrow : (Env, Exp) \times Label \times (Env, Exp)$$

$$(Send1) \quad \frac{\theta, e_1 \overset{\ell}{\hookrightarrow} \theta', e_1'}{\theta, e_1\,!\,e_2 \overset{\ell}{\hookrightarrow} \theta', e_1'\,!\,e_2} \qquad (Send2) \quad \frac{\theta, e_2 \overset{\ell}{\hookrightarrow} \theta', e_2'}{\theta, v_1\,!\,e_2 \overset{\ell}{\hookrightarrow} \theta', v_1\,!\,e_2'}$$

$$(Send3) \quad \frac{}{\theta, v_1\,!\,v_2 \xrightarrow{\mathsf{send}(v_1, v_2)} \theta, v_2}$$

$$(Recv) \quad \frac{}{\theta, \mathsf{receive}\ cl_1; \ldots; cl_n\ \mathsf{end} \xrightarrow{\mathsf{rec}(\kappa, \overline{cl_n})} \theta, \kappa}$$

$$(Spawn1) \quad \frac{\theta, e_i \overset{\ell}{\hookrightarrow} \theta', e_i' \quad i \in \{1, \ldots, n\}}{\theta, \mathsf{spawn}(f/n, [\overline{v_{1, i-1}}, e_i, \overline{e_{i+1, n}}]) \overset{\ell}{\hookrightarrow} \theta', \mathsf{spawn}(f/n, [\overline{v_{1, i-1}}, e_i', \overline{e_{i+1, n}}])}$$

$$(Spawn2) \quad \frac{}{\theta, \mathsf{spawn}(f/n, [\overline{v_n}]) \xrightarrow{\mathsf{spawn}(\kappa, f/n, [\overline{v_n}])} \theta, \kappa} \qquad (Slf) \quad \frac{}{\theta, \mathsf{self}() \xrightarrow{\mathsf{self}(\kappa)} \theta, \kappa}$$

Fig. 4. Standard semantics: evaluation of concurrent expressions

where *Env* and *Exp* are the domains of environments (i.e., substitutions) and expressions, respectively, and *Label* denotes an element of the set

$$\{\tau, \mathsf{send}(v_1, v_2), \mathsf{rec}(\kappa, \overline{cl_n}), \mathsf{spawn}(\kappa, a/n, [\overline{v_n}]), \mathsf{self}(\kappa)\}$$

whose meaning will be explained below. We use ℓ to range over labels. For clarity, we divide the transition rules of the semantics for expressions in two sets: rules for sequential expressions are depicted in Fig. 3, while rules for concurrent ones are in Fig. 4. Note, however, that concurrent expressions can occur inside sequential expressions.

Most of the rules are self-explanatory. In the following, we only discuss some subtle or complex issues. In principle, the transitions are labelled either with τ (a reduction without side effects) or with a label that identifies the reduction of an action with some side-effects. Labels are used in the system rules (Fig. 5) to determine the associated side effects and/or the information to be retrieved.

We consider that the order of evaluation of the arguments in a tuple, list, etc., is fixed from left to right.

For case evaluation, we assume an auxiliary function match which selects the first clause, $cl_i = (pat_i\ \mathsf{when}\ e_i' \to e_i)$, such that v matches pat_i, i.e., $v = \theta_i(pat_i)$, and the guard holds, i.e., $\theta\theta_i, e_i' \hookrightarrow^* \theta', true$ (here $\hookrightarrow^*$ is the reflexive and transitive closure of $\hookrightarrow$). We assume that the patterns can only contain fresh variables. For simplicity, we assume here that if the argument v matches no clause then the evaluation is blocked.

Functions can either be defined in the program (in this case they are invoked by apply) or be a built-in (invoked by call). In the latter case, they are evaluated using the auxiliary function eval. In rule *Apply2*, we consider that the mapping μ stores all function definitions in the program, i.e., it maps every function name f/n to a copy of its definition fun $(X_1, \ldots, X_n) \to e$, where $X_1, \ldots, X_n$ are (distinct) fresh variables and are the only variables that may occur free in

$$(Seq) \quad \frac{\theta, e \xrightarrow{\tau} \theta', e'}{\langle a, (\theta, e), q \rangle \xrightarrow{\emptyset} \langle a, (\theta', e'), q \rangle} \qquad (Send) \quad \frac{\theta, e \xrightarrow{\mathsf{send}(a', v)} \theta', e'}{\langle a, (\theta, e), q \rangle \xrightarrow{\emptyset} \langle a, (\theta', e'), q \rangle \mid (a', v)}$$

$$(Receive) \quad \frac{\theta, e \xrightarrow{\mathsf{rec}(\kappa, \overline{cl_n})} \theta', e' \quad \mathsf{matchrec}(\theta, \overline{cl_n}, q) = (\theta_i, e_i, v)}{\langle a, (\theta, e), q \rangle \xrightarrow{\emptyset} \langle a, (\theta'\theta_i, e'\{\kappa \mapsto e_i\}), q \backslash\!\backslash v \rangle}$$

$$(Spawn) \quad \frac{\theta, e \xrightarrow{\mathsf{spawn}(\kappa, f/n, [\overline{v_n}])} \theta', e' \quad a' \text{ is a fresh pid for } \langle a, (\theta, e), q \rangle}{\langle a, (\theta, e), q \rangle \xrightarrow{\{a'\}} \langle a, (\theta', e'\{\kappa \mapsto a'\}), q \rangle \mid \langle a', (id, \mathsf{apply}\ f/n\ (\overline{v_n})), [\,] \rangle}$$

$$(Self) \quad \frac{\theta, e \xrightarrow{\mathsf{self}(\kappa)} \theta', e'}{\langle a, (\theta, e), q \rangle \xrightarrow{\emptyset} \langle a, (\theta', e'\{\kappa \mapsto a\}), q \rangle}$$

$$(Sched) \quad \frac{}{(a, v) \mid \langle a, (\theta, e), q \rangle \xrightarrow{\emptyset} \langle a, (\theta, e), v{:}q \rangle} \qquad (Par) \quad \frac{A \xrightarrow{U} A' \quad U \cap \mathsf{ppid}(B) = \emptyset}{A \mid B \xrightarrow{U} A' \mid B}$$

Fig. 5. Standard semantics: system rules

e. Note that we only consider first-order functions. In order to also consider higher-order functions, one should reduce the function name to a *closure* of the form $(\theta', \mathsf{fun}\ (X_1, \ldots, X_n) \to e)$. We leave this extension for future work.

Let us now consider the evaluation of expressions with side effects (Fig. 4). Here, we can distinguish two kinds of rules. On the one hand, we have rules *Send1*, *Send2* and *Send3* for "!". In this case, we know *locally* what the expression should be reduced to (i.e., v_2 in rule *Send3*). For the remaining rules, this is not known locally and, thus, we return a fresh distinguished symbol, κ—by abuse, κ is dealt with as a variable—so that the system rules of Fig. 5 will eventually bind κ to its correct value: the selected expression in rule *Recv* and a pid in rules *Spawn* and *Slf*. In these cases, the label of the transition contains all the information needed by system rules to perform the evaluation at the system level, including the symbol κ. This trick allows us to keep the rules for expressions and systems separated (i.e., the semantics shown in Figs. 3 and 4 is mostly independent from the rules in Fig. 5).

Finally, we consider the system rules, depicted in Fig. 5. Reductions are of the form $A \xrightarrow{U} A'$ where U is the set of pids of processes spawned by the reduction. Also, $A \xRightarrow{U} A'$ means that A evolves into A' via a finite number of reductions in which the processes with pids in U have been spawned.

Rule *Seq* just updates the control (θ, e) of the considered process when a sequential expression is reduced using the expression rules.

Rule *Send* adds a new floating message (a', v) to the system. Adding it directly to the mailbox of the target process would not allow one to model all possible message interleavings (as discussed in Example 1). Observe that e' is usually different from v since e may have nested operators.

In rule *Receive*, we use the auxiliary function matchrec to evaluate a receive expression. The main difference w.r.t. match is that matchrec also takes a queue q and returns the selected message v. More precisely, function matchrec scans the queue q looking for the *first* message v matching a pattern of the receive statement. Then, κ is bound to the expression in the selected clause, e_i, and the environment is extended with the matching substitution. If no message in the queue q matches any clause, then the rule is not applicable and the selected process cannot be reduced (i.e., it suspends). As in case expressions, we assume that the patterns can only contain fresh variables.

Rule *Spawn* creates a new process with a fresh pid a', initialized with the application of function f/n. Its environment and queue are initially empty. The pid a' replaces κ in the process performing the spawn.

Rule *Self* simply replaces κ with the pid of the process.

Rule *Sched* delivers the message v in a pair (a, v) to the target process a. As discussed above, here we deliberately ignore the restriction mentioned in Example 1 that the messages sent –directly– between two given processes arrive in the same order they were sent, since current implementations only guarantee it within the same node. In practice, this amounts to consider that each process is potentially run in a different node. An alternative definition ensuring this restriction can be found in [27].

Rule *Par* allows one to lift a reduction to a larger system.

4   Behavioural Equivalence

In this section we initiate the study of behavioural equivalence for Erlang. Observational equivalences have been studied in the context of process calculi following the intuition that two systems should be considered equivalent only when they cannot be distinguished by any external observer. In our case—as in concurrent process calculi—an external observer is an additional pool of processes composed in parallel with the system to be observed. As discussed in the Introduction, to the best of our knowledge, the process calculus (equipped with an appropriate observational equivalence) which is closest to Erlang is the Asynchronous Localised π-calculus (ALπ) [23].

4.1   Barbed Congruence

We now start the investigation of barbed congruence for the Erlang language. In ALπ, communication is based on channels identified by names: a process sends messages on a channel by indicating its name, and consumes messages by specifying the channel from which they are expected to be consumed. In Erlang, on the other hand, messages are sent to processes, and pids take the role of names. We introduce some terminology on pids.

Definition 3. *The pid a is taken by A if $a \in \mathsf{ppid}(A)$. The pid a occurs untaken in A if a appears in A (i.e., it is used in A) but is not taken by A.*

In the equivalence that we are going to define, we will equate only systems that are *pid-compatible*. The intuition is that two pid-compatible systems have the same expectations on the pids that should be taken by the environment, i.e. the context in which they will be observed. Thus a name that is taken by a system cannot occur untaken in the other one (as the latter is expecting the pid to be taken by the environment).

Definition 4. *A pair A, B of systems is* pid-compatible *if any pid that occurs untaken in A may not be taken by B, and conversely. Similarly, a relation $\mathcal{R}$ on systems is* pid-compatible *if all pairs of systems in $\mathcal{R}$ are pid-compatible.*

Only pid-compatible systems should be related. Below we implicitly assume that relations are pid-compatible. The notion of pid-compatibility is extended to reductions.

Definition 5. *Two reductions $A \overset{U}{\Longrightarrow} A'$ and $B \overset{V}{\Longrightarrow} B'$ are* pid-compatible *if A and B are pid-compatible and moreover the pids in U do not occur untaken in B, and conversely.*

As $\overset{U}{\longrightarrow}$ implies $\overset{U}{\Longrightarrow}$, the above terminology extends to one-step reductions.

Lemma 1. *If reductions $A \overset{U}{\Longrightarrow} A'$ and $B \overset{V}{\Longrightarrow} B'$ are pid-compatible, then also the derivatives A', B' are pid-compatible.*

Sometimes we write $A \longrightarrow A'$ and $A \Longrightarrow A'$ omitting the set of pids above the arrow if not important.

We are now ready to define *barbed congruence*. Such an equivalence can be defined in any calculus possessing: (i) a *reduction relation* (i.e., the 'internal steps' of process calculi), modelling the evolution of a system; and (ii) an *observability predicate* $\downarrow_a$ for each name a (pid in Erlang), which detects the possibility of a system of being observed from the outside by means of communication on a.

In Erlang, as in other calculi with asynchronous communication [1], only output messages are considered observable; this because an observer has no direct way of knowing when a message is actually received by the observed system. More precisely, we write $A \downarrow_a$ if A contains a floating message targeting a process with pid a expected to be in the context (i.e. not taken in A). Formally, $A \downarrow_a$ iff $A = A' \,|\, (a, v)$ with $a \notin \mathrm{ppid}(A')$, for some v. Also, $A \Downarrow_a$ iff there exists B and U such that $A \overset{U}{\Longrightarrow} B$ and $B \downarrow_a$.

We first introduce the barbed bisimulation equivalence, and then we close it by parallel contexts. The main novelty is that we need definitions that are compliant with the notion of pid-compatibility introduced above.

Definition 6 (Barbed bisimulation and congruence). *A relation $\mathcal{S}$ on systems is a U-barbed bisimulation if $A \,\mathcal{S}\, B$ implies:*

1. *if $A \overset{V}{\longrightarrow} A'$ then there exists a pid-compatible reduction $B \overset{W}{\Longrightarrow} B'$ with $A' \,\mathcal{S}\, B'$;*

2. *the converse of the above clause, on the reductions from B;*
3. *if $A \downarrow_a$ with $a \notin U$, then $B \Downarrow_a$;*
4. *the converse of the above clause, on the observables from B.*

Two systems A and B are U-barbed bisimilar, written $A \overset{.}{\sim}^U B$, if $A \mathcal{S} B$ for some U-barbed bisimulation $\mathcal{S}$.

Let A and B be systems with $\mathbf{ppid}(A) \cup \mathbf{ppid}(B) \subseteq U$, and $V \subseteq U$. We say that A and B are barbed congruent at $U; V$, written $A \approx^U_V B$, if, for each system C without occurrences of the pids in V and with $\mathbf{ppid}(C) \cap U = \emptyset$, we have $A \mid C \overset{.}{\sim}^U B \mid C$.

In barbed bisimulation, the parameter U contains pids that cannot be taken by the context, hence the pids in U are considered not observable. Barbed congruence has an additional parameter V; this is a set of special pids that the environment is not even allowed to know. This additional parameter compensates the absence, in Erlang, of explicit restriction operators denoting pid scopes; the scope of the pids in V is expected to be within the observed system. We preferred this approach instead of adding a restriction operator to stay closer to the semantics in [21] that we used as starting point for our development. Intuitively, it is reasonable to assume to have in V the pids of those processes that have been created within the observed system, whose name is never communicated outside.

We omit V when empty simply writing $A \approx^U B$. We also omit U both in barbed bisimulation and in barbed congruence, when not important.

4.2   A Proof Technique

We introduce a useful proof technique for barbed bisimilarity, based on the notion of expansion [28]. Intuitively expansion expresses the possibility for a system to match the reduction of another system using fewer reductions, i.e., more efficiently. Expansion is often used as an auxiliary relation in proof techniques for bisimulation.

We write: $A \longrightarrow_? A'$ if $A \longrightarrow A'$ or $A = A'$ (that is, A evolves into A' by means of one or zero reductions); and $A \Longrightarrow_1 A'$ to mean that A evolves into A' by means of at least one reduction. As announced, we omit below the requirements on compatibility between matching reductions, and therefore also the pid-labels decorating the reductions.

Definition 7 (barbed expansion). *A relation $\mathcal{S}$ on systems is a U-barbed expansion if $A \mathcal{S} B$ implies:*

1. *if $A \longrightarrow A'$ then $B \longrightarrow_? B'$ with $A' \mathcal{S} B'$;*
2. *if $B \longrightarrow B'$ then $A \Longrightarrow_1 A'$ with $A' \mathcal{S} B'$;*
3. *if $A \downarrow_a$ with $a \notin U$, then $B \downarrow_a$;*
4. *if $B \downarrow_a$ with $a \notin U$, then $A \Downarrow_a$.*

Two systems A and B are in the U-barbed expansion, written $A \succeq^U B$, if $A \mathcal{S} B$ for some U-barbed expansion $\mathcal{S}$.

As usual, we often omit the index U when empty (or not important) and simply write $A \succeq B$.

Definition 8. *A relation $\mathcal{S}$ on systems is a U-barbed bisimulation up-to expansion if $A \mathcal{S} B$ implies:*

1. *if $A \longrightarrow A'$ then there are B', A'', B'' such that $B \Longrightarrow B'$, $A' \succeq^U A''$, $B'' \succeq^U B'$ and $A'' \mathcal{S} B''$;*
2. *the converse of the above clause, on the reductions from B;*
3. *if $A \downarrow_a$ with $a \notin U$, then $B \Downarrow_a$;*
4. *the converse of the above clause, on the observables from B.*

Lemma 2. *If $\mathcal{S}$ is a U-barbed bisimulation up-to expansion then $\mathcal{S} \subseteq \overset{\cdot}{\sim}^U$.*

Proof. A standard diagram-chasing argument [28]. $\qquad\qquad\qquad\qquad\square$

The lemma above would become unsound if, in Definition 8, expansion were replaced by barbed bisimulation [28].

We conclude this section by showing a monotonicity property.

Lemma 3. *If $U \subseteq U'$ then $\overset{\cdot}{\sim}^U \subseteq \overset{\cdot}{\sim}^{U'}$ and $\succeq^U \subseteq \succeq^{U'}$.*

5 Properties

We now exploit the barbed congruence relation defined in the previous section to prove some properties of Erlang terms. The first property will be discussed in Theorem 1, where we prove that renaming a local pid a into b, is the same as adding in parallel a *wire* process that receives the messages on a and forwards them to b. In order to prove this first property, we need several preliminary results on pid renaming and system normalisation. The latter (which relies as usual on our restrictions on pid management) means that while proving two systems barbed equivalent, it is possible to focus only on those states of the system in which processes have completed their internal steps, where we assume internal all process transitions excluding the arrival of a new message in the process queue. Intuitively, normalisation holds because processes have a deterministic internal behaviour; the unique source of nondeterminism is in the order of arrival of messages.

5.1 Renaming

The first preliminary results deal with the correspondence between the transitions of the system A and that of $A\{a/b\}$. In the formalisation of these results, we use $A[a \triangleleft v]$ to mean the system obtained from A by adding the message v as the newer message in the queue of the process a of A.

Lemma 4. *Suppose $b \notin \mathrm{ppid}(A)$. We have:*

1. *if $A \xrightarrow{U} A'$ and $a \notin U$, then $A\{a/b\} \xrightarrow{U} A'\{a/b\}$;*

2. if $A\{a/b\} \xrightarrow{U} A''$, with $b \notin U$, is a reduction derived without applying rule
   Sched to process a, then there is A' such that $A \xrightarrow{U} A'$ and $A'' = A'\{a/b\}$;
3. if $A\{a/b\} \longrightarrow A''$ is a reduction derived by applying rule Sched to process a
   and floating message (a, v), then either
   (a) there is A' such that $A \longrightarrow A'$ and $A'' = A'\{a/b\}$; or
   (b) $A = (b, v') \mid B$, with $(b, v')\{a/b\} = (a, v)$ and $A'' = B\{a/b\}[a \lhd v]$.

Lemma 4(1) can be refined if a is fresh. We write $A[a \leftrightarrow b]$ for the system
obtained from A by exchanging a and b (i.e., a simultaneous substitution).

Lemma 5. *Suppose $b \notin$ ppid(A) and a is fresh for A. We have:*

1. if $A \xrightarrow{U} A'$ and $a \notin U$, then $A\{a/b\} \xrightarrow{U} A'\{a/b\}$;
2. if $A \xrightarrow{\{a\}} A'$ then $A\{a/b\} \xrightarrow{\{b\}} A'[a \leftrightarrow b]$.

Concerning the simultaneous renaming $[a \leftrightarrow b]$, we have a stronger correspondence between the transitions of A and $A[a \leftrightarrow b]$, when names a and b are
already taken in A.

Lemma 6. *Suppose $\{a, b\} \subseteq$ ppid(A). If $A \xrightarrow{U} A'$ then $A[a \leftrightarrow b] \xrightarrow{U} A'[a \leftrightarrow b]$.*

Corollary 1. *Suppose $\{a, b\} \subseteq$ ppid(A). Then $A \succeq A[a \leftrightarrow b]$.*

We now move towards a result (Lemma 8) which is the Erlang analogous of
the α-conversion renaming of name-passing calculi such as the π-calculus. We
first need to introduce a new notation (Definition 9) and a preliminary lemma
(Lemma 7).

Definition 9. *Two systems A and B are a/b-convertible, for pids a, b with a
fresh for B, if $A = B\{a/b\}$.*

Lemma 7. *Suppose A and B are a/b-convertible, then $A \succeq^{\{a,b\}} B$. Moreover if
$\{a, b\} \subseteq ($ppid$(A) \cup$ ppid$(B))$ then also $A \succeq B$.*

Proof. If $\mathcal{S}$ is the set of all pairs (A, B) as in the assertion of the lemma, then
$\mathcal{S} \cup \succeq$ is an expansion. This holds because: the reductions from two systems
(A, B) as in the lemma are the same, either (Lemma 5(1)) modulo a renaming
between a and b, or (Lemma 5(2)) producing derivatives that, by Corollary 1,
are in the expansion relation; their observables different from a, b are the same
too.   □

When a, b are pids in A, B then they are not in the observables and therefore
the assertion can be strengthened.

Lemma 8 (Erlang analogous of α-conversion). *Suppose A and B are a/b-
convertible and $\{a, b\} \subseteq U$. Then $A \approx^U_{\{a,b\}} B$.*

Proof. Let C be a system in which a, b do not occur, and with $U \cap$ ppid$(C) = \emptyset$.
We have to show that $A \mid C \overset{.}{\sim}^U B\{a/b\} \mid C$. This follows from Lemma 7 and the
inclusion $\succeq^U \subseteq \overset{.}{\sim}^U$.   □

5.2   Normalisation

In conjunction with the proof technique above, a crucial result that will be used afterwards is Lemma 10 below. For its proof we need Lemma 9 stating that the addition of a new message at the end of a process queue does not forbid the process from executing previously executable reductions.

Lemma 9. *Suppose* $P \xrightarrow{\emptyset} A$; *then, for any* a, v, *also* $P[a \triangleleft v] \xrightarrow{\emptyset} A[a \triangleleft v]$.

Proof. A case analysis on the possible rules that caused the reduction $P \longrightarrow A$. $\qquad\square$

Essentially Lemma 10 below says that we can *normalise* any system, by letting the processes composing it evolve as long as there are messages in their queues that can be consumed (the only reduction of the system that we cannot perform in the normalisation are those that move a floating message into a queue). This includes the fetching of a message from its queue and the spawn of a new process. In Lemma 10, the reduction $P \xrightarrow{U} A$ has not been derived using rule *Sched* as it emanates from a process.

Lemma 10. *For any reduction* $P \xrightarrow{U} A$ *and system* C, *it holds that* $P \mid C \succeq A \mid C$.

Proof. We show that

$$\mathcal{R} \overset{\text{def}}{=} \{(P \mid C, A \mid C) \text{ s.t. } P \longrightarrow A\} \cup \succeq$$

is a barbed expansion. The interesting case is that of a challenge from $P \mid C$ in which P is involved (the case when only C is involved is trivial).

- If the reduction involving P is precisely $P \xrightarrow{U} A$ then $A \mid C$ need not move, as $\succeq$ includes the identity relation.
  If however the reduction is a spawn with, say $U = \{b\}$, then in its challenge P could choose to make a spawn on a different pid, say a. Thus the reduction is $P \mid C \xrightarrow{\{a\}} A\{a/b\}\mid C$. In this case we exploit Lemma 7, to derive $A\{a/b\}\mid C \succeq A\mid C$.
- Suppose the reduction involving P is a *Sched*, and let $P[a \triangleleft v]$ be the derivative of P, and C' the derivative of C. That is, the challenge is $P \mid C \longrightarrow P[a \triangleleft v] \mid C'$. We have $A \mid C \longrightarrow A[a \triangleleft v] \mid C'$. Moreover, by Lemma 9, $P[a \triangleleft v] \longrightarrow A[a \triangleleft v]$ (the reduction is not a *Sched* since $P[a \triangleleft v]$ is a process, hence does not contain floating messages). Hence $P[a \triangleleft v] \mid C' \mathcal{R} A[a \triangleleft v] \mid C'$. $\qquad\square$

5.3   Wires

We prove a number of results concerning wires, which bring out fundamental properties of asynchrony for Erlang systems.

A *wire from a to b* is a process with pid a that sends at b all messages received at a, without modifying their content. We write $(q, a \triangleright b)$ for a wire from a to b whose queue is q.

Definition 10 (Wire). *We define* $(q, a \triangleright b)$ *as follows:*

$$(q, a \triangleright b) \stackrel{def}{=} \langle a, (\theta, \text{apply } wire \ (b)), q \rangle$$

for any θ. *Furthermore, we assume to have the definition:*

$$wire/1 = \text{fun } (Y) \rightarrow \text{receive } X \rightarrow \text{let } \_ = Y \,! \, X \text{ in apply } wire \ (Y) \text{ end}$$

The first result that we prove on wires is that adding a wire from a into b is barbed bisimilar to renaming a into b, under the assumption that a is not already taken (hence it can be safely taken by the wire itself).

Lemma 11. *For all* C *with* $a \notin \text{ppid}(C)$, *we have*

$$C \mid (\emptyset, a \triangleright b) \; \dot{\sim} \; C\{b\!/a\}$$

Proof. We show that the set of all such pairs is a barbed bisimulation up to expansion. The observables in the two related systems are the same: the only non-trivial case is an observable at b in $C\{b\!/a\}$, which corresponds to a floating message targeting a in C; this becomes an observable at b via the wire. Hence we only have to look at reductions. There are a few cases to consider. We exploit Lemma 4.

1. A reduction within C, say $C \longrightarrow C'$. By Lemma 4, we also have $C\{b\!/a\} \longrightarrow C'\{b\!/a\}$.
2. A floating message is moved into the queue of the wire, thus the reduction is $C \mid (\emptyset, a \triangleright b) \longrightarrow C' \mid (v : \emptyset, a \triangleright b)$, and $C = C' \mid (a, v)$. By Lemma 10, $C' \mid (v : \emptyset, a \triangleright b) \succeq C' \mid (b, v) \mid (\emptyset, a \triangleright b)$. Thus $C\{b\!/a\}$ need not move (up-to expansion), since $(C' \mid (b, v))\{b\!/a\} = C\{b\!/a\}$.
3. The case of reductions within $C\{b\!/a\}$ in which Lemma 4(2) or Lemma 4(3.a) can be applied is handled in a way similar to case (1) above.
   We consider the case in which Lemma 4(3.b) applies. Thus there is a floating message (b, v) in $C\{b\!/a\}$ that is moved into the queue of process b, with derivative C''. Let (a, v') be the corresponding floating message in C. Thus $C = C' \mid (a, v')$, and $C'' = C'\{b\!/a\}[b \triangleleft v]$. We also have the reductions

$$\begin{aligned} C \mid (\emptyset, a \triangleright b) &\longrightarrow C' \mid (v' : \emptyset, a \triangleright b) \\ &\Longrightarrow C' \mid (b, v') \mid (\emptyset, a \triangleright b) \\ &\longrightarrow C''' \mid (\emptyset, a \triangleright b) \end{aligned}$$

where $C''' = C'[b \triangleleft v']$. This is sufficient, since $C'''\{b\!/a\} = C''$.   □

We are now ready to prove our first example of barbed congruent systems, by extending to barbed congruence the previous result about barbed bisimilarity.

Theorem 1. *Suppose* $a \subseteq U$. *We have:*

$$A \mid (\emptyset, a \triangleright b) \approx^U_{\{a\}} A\{b\!/a\}$$

Proof. We have to show that for all B that does not contain a, we have

$$A \mid (\emptyset, a \triangleright b) \mid B \stackrel{\cdot}{\sim} A\{b\!/\!a\} \mid B$$

We have $A \mid (\emptyset, a \triangleright b) \mid B = (A \mid B) \mid (\emptyset, a \triangleright b)$, and $(A \mid B)\{b\!/\!a\} = A\{b\!/\!a\} \mid B$, hence we can apply Lemma 11. □

The above theorem indicates under which conditions adding a wire from a to b is barbed congruent w.r.t. applying directly a renaming of a into b: this holds only under the assumption that pid a is a restricted name that is not known by the environment. Nevertheless, under the assumption that a is known (but not taken) by the environment, we have the following result.

Theorem 2. *Suppose* $a \subseteq U$. *We have:*

$$A \mid (\emptyset, a \triangleright b) \approx_\emptyset^U A\{b\!/\!a\} \mid (\emptyset, a \triangleright b)$$

Proof. We have to show that for any C with $a \notin \mathrm{ppid}(C)$, we have

$$A \mid C \mid (\emptyset, a \triangleright b) \stackrel{\cdot}{\sim} A\{b\!/\!a\} \mid C \mid (\emptyset, a \triangleright b)$$

Using Lemma 11, we have $A \mid C \mid (\emptyset, a \triangleright b) \stackrel{\cdot}{\sim} (A \mid C)\{b\!/\!a\} \mid (\emptyset, a \triangleright b) \stackrel{\mathrm{def}}{=} B_1$. Similarly, $A\{b\!/\!a\} \mid C \mid (\emptyset, a \triangleright b) \stackrel{\cdot}{\sim} (A\{b\!/\!a\} \mid C)\{b\!/\!a\} \mid (\emptyset, a \triangleright b) \stackrel{\mathrm{def}}{=} B_2$. This completes the proof, since $B_1 = B_2$. □

As a corollary of Theorem 1 we have an additional equivalence result: a wire from a to b in parallel with a wire from b to c is equivalent to a unique wire from a to c (under the assumption that pid b is not known from the environment).

Corollary 2. *We have*

$$(\emptyset, a \triangleright b) \mid (\emptyset, b \triangleright c) \approx_{\{b\}}^{\{b\}} (\emptyset, a \triangleright c)$$

Proof. Follows from Theorem 1. □

As a corollary of Theorem 2, on the other hand, we can prove that in the presence of a wire from a to b, a floating message targeting a is equivalent to a floating message, with the same content, directly targeting b.

Corollary 3. *We have*

$$(\emptyset, a \triangleright b) \mid (a, v) \approx^{\{a\}} (\emptyset, a \triangleright b) \mid (b, v)$$

Proof. Follows from Theorem 2. □

The last equivalence that we prove still deals with wires, but used in a different way. If a process sends a pid c to the outside environment, this is equivalent to sending a pid d (unknown by the environment) under the assumption that there is a wire from d to c.

Theorem 3. *Suppose $a, d \subseteq U$ and d is fresh for $\langle a, (\theta, b\,!\,c), q\rangle$. We have:*

$$\langle a, (\theta, b\,!\,c), q\rangle \approx^U_{\{d\}} \langle a, (\theta, b\,!\,d), q\rangle \mid (\emptyset, d \triangleright c)$$

Proof. We have to show that for any C, with $a \notin \mathtt{ppid}(C)$ and without occurrences of pid d, we have

$$\langle a, (\theta, b\,!\,c), q\rangle \mid C \overset{\cdot}{\sim} \langle a, (\theta, b\,!\,d), q\rangle \mid (\emptyset, d \triangleright c) \mid C$$

Starting from the r.h.s., by using Lemma 11, we have $\langle a, (\theta, b\,!\,d), q\rangle \mid (\emptyset, d \triangleright c) \mid C = (\langle a, (\theta, b\,!\,d), q\rangle \mid C) \mid (\emptyset, d \triangleright c) \overset{\cdot}{\sim} (\langle a, (\theta, b\,!\,d), q\rangle \mid C)\{c\!/d\} \overset{\text{def}}{=} B$. By applying the substitution to B, we obtain $B = \langle a, (\theta\{c\!/d\}, b\,!\,c), q\{c\!/d\}\rangle \mid C\{c\!/d\} = \langle a, (\theta, b\,!\,c), q\rangle \mid C$ since pid d does not occur in θ, q and C. □

6 Alternative Approaches

In this section we discuss some possible alternatives to the choices made in the main development described in previous sections. As stated in Sect. 2 we pose various restrictions on the use of pids. Essentially, pids can only be generated by functions spawn and self, passed around, and used to send messages.

Erlang also allows, e.g., equality test on pids. This is forbidden in our context since equality would be a built-in function taking pids as arguments, which we disallow. It is not possible to have such test via pattern matching, since variables in patterns are always fresh, we forbid pid literals, and patterns cannot contain functions. Equality test would break some of ours results. For instance, in Theorem 1, we have:

$$A \mid (\emptyset, a \triangleright b) \approx^U_{\{a\}} A\{b/a\}$$

If we take $A = \langle c, (\theta, a\,!a), q\rangle$, then on the l.h.s. after a few steps b would get a message with value a, while on the r.h.s. it would get a message with value b. Comparing the two values with b would distinguish the two processes. In contrast, if b could only use the received name to send messages, no distinction would be possible, since in both cases messages would reach b, either directly or through the wire.

Even worst, built-in functions taking pids in input, such as the function pid_to_list(Pid), which converts a pid to a string, would break most of our results. In the case above, just converting pids to strings and comparing the strings would break the bisimilarity. However these functions are mainly intended for debugging.

Another assumption we made is that order of messages is not preserved. Erlang specification states that if two messages are sent from a same process a to a same process b, and both are received, then the order is preserved. However, current implementations only guarantee this inside the same node, thus our approach would correspond to running each process on its own node. Adding this constraint would require changing the semantics at the system level, replacing floating messages with explicit queues. This would impact on the theory we present. For instance, in Theorem 1, on the l.h.s. A could send a message directly to b, and another one via the wire. They could reach b in any order. On the r.h.s., both messages would go directly to b, hence the order would be preserved. We could recover the result by requiring A not to contain b.

7   Conclusion

We have investigated the definition of observational semantics for Erlang. This work has been initially conceived with the aim to honor the career of Rocco De Nicola. According to the citations received by his papers, the two main contributions of Rocco are about testing equivalences [13] and KLAIM [12]. Testing equivalences are an example of observational semantics, while KLAIM is a concurrent and distributed language that, similarly to Erlang, is based on message exchange through local repositories accessed via pattern-matching. In order to do some original work, i.e. avoid to simply replicate work already done by Rocco and his co-authors, we have followed a slightly different approach for defining observational semantics (i.e. barbed bisimulation) on a language having some differences w.r.t. KLAIM. There are two main differences between the concurrent model of Erlang and that of KLAIM: locality (when a message is created, only its expected receiver has the capability to read it) and mailbox ordering (pattern matching is applied to messages according to their order of reception).

Despite the initial celebrating objective, we think the paper contains interesting original contribution towards the development of observational theories for Erlang. As a future work, we would like to continue the study of the introduced equivalence by investigating a labelled characterisation of barbed congruence and algebraic characterisations, or transferring type-based techniques from the π-calculus (e.g. to control termination, lock-freedom and deadlock [14,18,19,32]). Moreover, we would like to investigate other approaches to observational semantics such as may and must testing. Concerning this last point, we could apply our approach to define observational equivalences following [6], where different congruences are studied simply by considering a unique definition parametric in the notion of observable. The main novelties in our proposal concern the management of Erlang pids, whereas the notion of observable (i.e. output messages) is standard. Being pid management and the observability criteria two orthogonal concepts, we are confident that our techniques could be applied also to alternative notions of observables like those studied by Boreale et al. [6].

References

1. Amadio, R.M., Castellani, I., Sangiorgi, D.: On bisimulations for the asynchronous π-calculus. Theor. Comput. Sci. **195**(2), 291–324 (1998)
2. Armstrong, J.: A history of Erlang. In: Third ACM SIGPLAN Conference on History of Programming Languages, pp. 6-1–6-26. ACM (2007)

3. Armstrong, J., Virding, R., Wikström, C., Williams, M.: Concurrent Programming in Erlang, 2nd edn. Prentice Hall, Upper Saddle River (1996)
4. Bergstra, J.A., Klop, J.W.: Process algebra for synchronous communication. Inf. Control **60**(1–3), 109–137 (1984)
5. de Boer, F.S., Klop, J.W., Palamidessi, C.: Asynchronous communication in process algebra. In: LICS, pp. 137–147. IEEE Computer Society (1992)
6. Boreale, M., De Nicola, R., Pugliese, R.: Basic observables for processes. Inf. Comput. **149**(1), 77–98 (1999)
7. Boreale, M., De Nicola, R., Pugliese, R.: A theory of "may" testing for asynchronous languages. In: Thomas, W. (ed.) FoSSaCS 1999. LNCS, vol. 1578, pp. 165–179. Springer, Heidelberg (1999). https://doi.org/10.1007/3-540-49019-1_12
8. Boreale, M., De Nicola, R., Pugliese, R.: Trace and testing equivalence on asynchronous processes. Inf. Comput. **172**(2), 139–164 (2002)
9. Caballero, R., Martin-Martin, E., Riesco, A., Tamarit, S.: Declarative debugging of concurrent Erlang programs. J. Log. Algebr. Meth. Program. **101**, 22–41 (2018)
10. Carlsson, R., et al.: Core Erlang 1.0.3. language specification (2004). https://www.it.uu.se/research/group/hipe/cerl/doc/core_erlang-1.0.3.pdf
11. Castellani, I., Hennessy, M.: Testing theories for asynchronous languages. In: Arvind, V., Ramanujam, S. (eds.) FSTTCS 1998. LNCS, vol. 1530, pp. 90–101. Springer, Heidelberg (1998). https://doi.org/10.1007/978-3-540-49382-2_9
12. De Nicola, R., Ferrari, G.L., Pugliese, R.: KLAIM: a kernel language for agents interaction and mobility. IEEE Trans. Softw. Eng. **24**(5), 315–330 (1998)
13. De Nicola, R., Hennessy, M.: Testing equivalences for processes. Theor. Comput. Sci. **34**, 83–133 (1984)
14. Demangeon, R., Hirschkoff, D., Sangiorgi, D.: Termination in impure concurrent languages. In: Gastin, P., Laroussinie, F. (eds.) CONCUR 2010. LNCS, vol. 6269, pp. 328–342. Springer, Heidelberg (2010). https://doi.org/10.1007/978-3-642-15375-4_23
15. Fredlund, L.A.: A framework for reasoning about Erlang code. Ph.D. thesis, Royal Institute of Technology, Stockholm, Sweden (2001)
16. Fredlund, L., Earle, C.B.: Model checking Erlang programs: the functional approach. In: ACM SIGPLAN Workshop on Erlang, pp. 11–19. ACM (2006)
17. Fredlund, L., Gurov, D., Noll, T., Dam, M., Arts, T., Chugunov, G.: A verification tool for Erlang. STTT **4**(4), 405–420 (2003)
18. Kobayashi, N.: A partially deadlock-free typed process calculus. Trans. Program. Lang. Syst. **20**(2), 436–482 (1998)
19. Kobayashi, N., Sangiorgi, D.: A hybrid type system for lock-freedom of mobile processes. ACM Trans. Program. Lang. Syst. **32**(5), 16 (2010)
20. Lanese, I., Nishida, N., Palacios, A., Vidal, G.: CauDEr: a causal-consistent reversible debugger for Erlang. In: Gallagher, J.P., Sulzmann, M. (eds.) FLOPS 2018. LNCS, vol. 10818, pp. 247–263. Springer, Cham (2018). https://doi.org/10.1007/978-3-319-90686-7_16
21. Lanese, I., Nishida, N., Palacios, A., Vidal, G.: A theory of reversibility for Erlang. J. Log. Algebr. Meth. Program. **100**, 71–97 (2018)
22. Letuchy, E.: Erlang at Facebook (2009). http://www.erlang-factory.com/conference/SFBayAreaErlangFactory2009/speakers/EugeneLetuchy
23. Merro, M., Sangiorgi, D.: On asynchrony in name-passing calculi. Math. Struct. Comput. Sci. **14**(5), 715–767 (2004)
24. Milner, R., Sangiorgi, D.: Barbed bisimulation. In: Kuich, W. (ed.) ICALP 1992. LNCS, vol. 623, pp. 685–695. Springer, Heidelberg (1992). https://doi.org/10.1007/3-540-55719-9_114

25. Milner, R.: Communication and Concurrency. PHI Series in Computer Science. Prentice Hall, Upper Saddle River (1989)
26. Milner, R., Parrow, J., Walker, D.: A calculus of mobile processes. I. Inf. Comput. **100**(1), 1–40 (1992)
27. Nishida, N., Palacios, A., Vidal, G.: A reversible semantics for Erlang. In: Hermenegildo, M.V., Lopez-Garcia, P. (eds.) LOPSTR 2016. LNCS, vol. 10184, pp. 259–274. Springer, Cham (2017). https://doi.org/10.1007/978-3-319-63139-4_15
28. Sangiorgi, D., Milner, R.: The problem of "weak bisimulation up to". In: Cleaveland, W.R. (ed.) CONCUR 1992. LNCS, vol. 630, pp. 32–46. Springer, Heidelberg (1992). https://doi.org/10.1007/BFb0084781
29. Svensson, H., Fredlund, L.A.: A more accurate semantics for distributed Erlang. In: SIGPLAN Workshop on Erlang, pp. 43–54. ACM (2007)
30. Svensson, H., Fredlund, L.A., Benac Earle, C.: A unified semantics for future Erlang. In: ACM SIGPLAN Workshop on Erlang, pp. 23–32. ACM (2010)
31. Tóth, M., Bozó, I.: Static analysis of complex software systems implemented in Erlang. In: Zsók, V., Horváth, Z., Plasmeijer, R. (eds.) CEFP 2011. LNCS, vol. 7241, pp. 440–498. Springer, Heidelberg (2012). https://doi.org/10.1007/978-3-642-32096-5_9
32. Yoshida, N., Berger, M., Honda, K.: Strong normalisation in the π-calculus. Inf. Comput. **191**(2), 145–202 (2004)

Genesis and Evolution of ULTRAS: Metamodel, Metaequivalences, Metaresults

Marco Bernardo[✉]

Dipartimento di Scienze Pure e Applicate, Università di Urbino, Urbino, Italy

Abstract. We discuss the genesis of the ULTRAS metamodel and summarize its evolution arising from the introduction of coherent resolutions of nondeterminism and reachability-consistent semirings.

1 The ULTRAS Metamodel

In 2009, within the Italian project PaCo – *Performability-Aware Computing: Logics, Models, and Languages*, I started working with Rocco De Nicola and Michele Loreti on the definition of a general, state-transition behavioral model, hopefully paving the way to the development of a *unifying theory* as well as *reuse facilities* in the field of concurrency, without resorting to abstract representations such as the categorical ones based on coalgebras and bialgebras.

Together with Diego Latella and Mieke Massink, Rocco and Michele had already done much work in that framework, aiming at providing a uniform definition of the structural operational semantics for various stochastic process calculi. To this purpose, they developed *rate-based transition systems* [14], which then evolved into the semiring-based metamodel known as FuTS – *state-to-function labeled transition system* [15, 35].

Rocco, Michele, and I wanted to explore a different direction, not related to languages and their semantics. Our first objective was to define a metamodel general enough to encompass specific behavioral models widely used in the concurrency literature, featuring nondeterminism, probabilities, deterministic/stochastic time, or a combination of them. We thus came up in [4] with a metamodel that we called ULTRAS – *uniform labeled transition system* (then exemplified in [5] as an extension of rate-based transition systems to formalize process semantics), which was fully elaborated in [6] and further fine-tuned in [3].

ULTRAS is a *discrete-state metamodel* parameterized with respect to a set D, where D-values are interpreted as different degrees of *one-step reachability*. These values are assumed to be ordered according to a reflexive and transitive relation $\sqsubseteq_D$, which is equipped with minimum $\bot_D$ expressing *unreachability*. Let us denote by $(S \rightarrow D)$ the set of functions from a set S to D. When S is a set of states, every element Δ of $(S \rightarrow D)$ can be interpreted as a function that *distributes reachability* over all possible next states. The set of states $supp(\Delta) = \{s \in S \mid \Delta(s) \neq \bot_D\}$ that are reachable according to Δ is called the *support* of Δ.

The set $(S \rightarrow D)_{\text{nefs}}$ of D-distributions Δ over S is considered, which satisfies the constraint $0 < |supp(\Delta)| < \omega$. The first part of the constraint establishes that

M. Boreale et al. (Eds.): De Nicola-Festschrift, LNCS 11665, pp. 92–111, 2019.
https://doi.org/10.1007/978-3-030-21485-2_7

the target distribution of each transition has a *nonempty support*, so to avoid distributions always returning $\perp_D$ and hence transitions leading to nowhere. The second part of the constraint ensures that the same distribution has a *finite support*, a fact that will enable a correct definition of behavioral metaequivalences.

Definition 1. *Let* $(D, \sqsubseteq_D, \perp_D)$ *be a preordered set equipped with minimum. A uniform labeled transition system on it, or D-ULTRAS for short, is a triple* $\mathcal{U} = (S, A, \longrightarrow)$ *where:*

- $S \neq \emptyset$ *is an at most countable set of states.*
- $A \neq \emptyset$ *is a countable set of transition-labeling actions.*
- $\longrightarrow \subseteq S \times A \times (S \to D)_{\text{nefs}}$ *is a transition relation.*   ∎

Every transition (s, a, Δ) of $\mathcal{U}$ is written $s \xrightarrow{a} \Delta$, where $\Delta(s')$ is a D-value quantifying the degree of reachability of s' from s via that a-transition, with $\Delta(s') = \perp_D$ meaning that s' is not reachable with that transition. In the directed graph description of $\mathcal{U}$ (see the forthcoming Figs. 1, 2, 3, 4, 5 and 6), vertices represent states and action-labeled edges represent action-labeled transitions. Given a transition $s \xrightarrow{a} \Delta$, the corresponding a-labeled edge goes from the vertex representing state s to a set of vertices linked by a dashed line, each of which represents a state $s' \in supp(\Delta)$ and is labeled with $\Delta(s')$.

In [6,9] we showed what follows about the choice of D:

- $\mathbb{B} = \{\perp, \top\}$, with $\perp \sqsubseteq_{\mathbb{B}} \top$, captures nondeterministic models such as:
  - labeled transition systems (LTS) [30], i.e., fully nondeterministic processes;
  - timed automata (TA) [1] – provided that S and A are allowed to be uncountable – where time is deterministic.
- $\mathbb{R}_{[0,1]}$, with the usual $\leq$, captures probabilistic models such as:
  - action-labeled discrete-time Markov chains (ADTMC) [48], i.e., fully probabilistic processes;
  - Markov decision processes (MDP) [17]/Rabin probabilistic automata [41], i.e., reactive probabilistic processes according to the terminology of [21];
  - Segala probabilistic automata (PA) [42], i.e., nondeterministic and probabilistic processes;
  - probabilistic timed automata (PTA) [33] – provided that S and A are allowed to be uncountable – where time is deterministic.
  - Markov automata (MA) [18], where time is stochastic.
- $\mathbb{R}_{\geq 0}$, with the usual $\leq$, captures stochastic models such as:
  - action-labeled continuous-time Markov chains (ACTMC) [48], i.e., fully stochastic processes;
  - continuous-time Markov decision processes (CTMDP) [40]/Knast probabilistic automata [31], i.e., reactive stochastic processes;
  - nondeterministic and stochastic processes intended as extensions of PA.

The definition of the ULTRAS metamodel is extremely parsimonious, in the sense that it does not require any algebraic structure, really necessary only for behavioral relations and language semantics. It simply relies on a *preordered set equipped with minimum*, because this is sufficient to express reachability degrees for the various states when performing a transition, as well as unreachability.

2   Behavioral Metaequivalences on ULTRAS

The second objective of Rocco, Michele, and myself was to define, on ULTRAS, *behavioral metaequivalences* general enough to encompass equivalences for specific classes of processes appeared in the literature. In [6] we focused on three approaches – bisimulation [36,38], testing [13], and trace [26] – so to cover to some extent the linear-time/branching-time spectrum [20]. We showed that:

- Bisimulation metaequivalence can be instantiated to bisimilarities for:
  - fully nondeterministic processes [23];
  - fully probabilistic processes [19];
  - reactive probabilistic processes [34];
  - fully stochastic processes [24,25];
  - reactive stochastic processes [37].
- Trace metaequivalence can be instantiated to trace equivalences for:
  - fully nondeterministic processes [10];
  - fully probabilistic processes [29];
  - reactive probabilistic processes [46];
  - fully stochastic processes [2,50].
- Testing metaequivalence can be instantiated to testing equivalences for:
  - fully nondeterministic processes [13];
  - fully probabilistic processes [11,12];
  - reactive probabilistic processes [32];
  - fully stochastic processes [2].

Surprisingly enough, it turned out that our behavioral metaequivalences, as defined in [6], were *not* able to capture the following well known equivalences for nondeterministic and probabilistic processes:

- The bisimulation equivalences of [22,45] are finer than the one derivable from our bisimulation metaequivalence. The latter, studied in [8] and akin to the ones in [47,49], contains the former as coarsest congruence with respect to parallel composition, and has the nice property of being characterized by (a minor variant of) the probabilistic modal logic PML [34] like in the case of fully/reactive probabilistic processes [34] and alternating PA [39].
- The trace equivalence of [43] is finer than the one derivable from our trace metaequivalence. The latter, studied in [7], has the nice property of being a congruence with respect to parallel composition.
- The testing equivalences of [16,28,44,51] are finer than the one derivable from our testing metaequivalence. The latter, studied in [7], has the nice property of being backward compatible with testing equivalences for fully nondeterministic, fully probabilistic, and reactive probabilistic processes without imposing any restriction on the set of tests.

In order to retrieve also the aforementioned equivalences, in [3] I introduced the notion of *resolution of nondeterminism* in the ULTRAS framework – with a formalization inspired by testing theories for nondeterministic and probabilistic processes – and, similar to what we did with Rocco and Michele in [7,8], I played with the order of certain universal quantifiers in the definition of the metaequivalences thereby obtaining *pre-* and *post-metaequivalences*.

2.1   Resolutions of Nondeterminism

When several transitions depart from the same state, they describe a choice among different behaviors, but the presence of these choices may hamper the calculations that will be required by behavioral metaequivalences. A *resolution* of a state s of a D-ULTRAS $\mathcal{U}$ is the result of a possible way of resolving choices starting from s, as if a *scheduler* were applied that, at the current state, selects one of its outgoing transitions or no transitions at all.

Following [27], in [3] I formalized a resolution as a D-ULTRAS $\mathcal{Z}$ with a tree-like structure – whose branching points correspond to target distributions of transitions – obtained by unfolding from s the graph structure of $\mathcal{U}$ and by selecting at each reached state at most one of its outgoing transitions. Since $\mathcal{U}$ can be cyclic, I made use of a *correspondence function* from the acyclic state space of $\mathcal{Z}$ to the original state space of $\mathcal{U}$. This function must be bijective[1] between the support of the target distribution of each transition in $\mathcal{Z}$ and the support of the target distribution of the corresponding transition in $\mathcal{U}$.

Definition 2. *Let* $\mathcal{U} = (S, A, \longrightarrow)$ *be a D-ULTRAS and* $s \in S$. *A D-ULTRAS* $\mathcal{Z} = (Z, A, \longrightarrow_{\mathcal{Z}})$, *with no cycles and Z disjoint from S, is a resolution of s, written* $\mathcal{Z} \in Res(s)$, *iff there exists a correspondence function* $corr_{\mathcal{Z}} : Z \to S$ *such that* $s = corr_{\mathcal{Z}}(z_s)$, *for some* $z_s \in Z$, *and for all* $z \in Z$ *it holds that:*

- *If* $z \overset{a}{\longrightarrow}_{\mathcal{Z}} \Delta$ *then* $corr_{\mathcal{Z}}(z) \overset{a}{\longrightarrow} \Delta'$, *with* $corr_{\mathcal{Z}}$ *being bijective between* $supp(\Delta)$ *and* $supp(\Delta')$ *and* $\Delta(z') = \Delta'(corr_{\mathcal{Z}}(z'))$ *for all* $z' \in supp(\Delta)$.
- *At most one transition departs from* z.   ∎

For bisimulation semantics, choices need to be resolved only at the first step or, more generally, only at each of the first k steps in case of a multistep definition of bisimilarity. A notion of *partial resolution* is thus introduced. It has the same characteristics as a resolution in its initial part – i.e., states not in S for ensuring the absence of cycles and choices – but, after the first k steps, its states and transitions are identical to the original ones.

Definition 3. *Let* $\mathcal{U} = (S, A, \longrightarrow)$ *be a D-ULTRAS,* $s \in S$, *and* $k \in \mathbb{N}_{\geq 1}$. *A D-ULTRAS* $\mathcal{Z} = (Z, A, \longrightarrow_{\mathcal{Z}})$ *is a k-resolution of s, written* $\mathcal{Z} \in k\text{-}Res(s)$, *iff there exists a correspondence function* $corr_{\mathcal{Z}} : Z \to S$ *such that* $s = corr_{\mathcal{Z}}(z_s)$, *for some* $z_s \in Z$, *and for all* $z \in Z$ *it holds that:*

- *If* $z \overset{a}{\longrightarrow}_{\mathcal{Z}} \Delta$ *then* $corr_{\mathcal{Z}}(z) \overset{a}{\longrightarrow} \Delta'$, *with* $corr_{\mathcal{Z}}$ *being bijective between* $supp(\Delta)$ *and* $supp(\Delta')$ *and* $\Delta(z') = \Delta'(corr_{\mathcal{Z}}(z'))$ *for all* $z' \in supp(\Delta)$.
- *If z is reachable from z_s with a sequence of less than k transitions, then:*
    • $z \notin S$;
    • *z cannot be part of a cycle;*
    • *z has at most one outgoing transition;*
  otherwise z is equal to $corr_{\mathcal{Z}}(z) \in S$ and has the same outgoing transitions that it has in $\mathcal{U}$.   ∎

---

[1] Requiring only injectivity as in [3] is not enough because it does not ensure that the former distribution preserves the overall reachability mass of the latter distribution (unlike the probabilistic case, in general there is no predefined reachability mass).

2.2 Reachability-Consistent Semirings

To express the calculations needed by behavioral metaequivalences, in [3] I further assumed that D has a *commutative semiring* structure – thereby reconciling ULTRAS with FuTS to a large extent – i.e., that D is equipped with two binary operations denoted by $\oplus$ and $\otimes$, with the latter distributing over the former, which satisfy the following properties:

- $\otimes$ is associative and commutative and admits neutral element 1_D and absorbing element 0_D. This multiplicative operation enables the calculation of multistep reachability from values of consecutive single-step reachability along the same trajectory.
- $\oplus$ is associative and commutative and admits neutral element 0_D. This additive operation is useful for aggregating values of multistep reachability along different trajectories starting from the same state, as well as for shorthands of the form $\Delta(S') = \bigoplus_{s' \in S'} \Delta(s')$ given a transition $s \xrightarrow{a} \Delta$.

In [3] I also assumed that these two binary operations are *reachability consistent*, in the sense that they satisfy the following additional properties in accordance with the intuition behind the concept of reachability:

- $0_D = \bot_D$ (i.e., the zero of the semiring denotes unreachability).
- $d_1 \otimes d_2 \neq 0_D$ whenever $d_1 \neq 0_D \neq d_2$ (hence two consecutive steps cannot result in unreachability).
- The sum via $\oplus$ of finitely many values 1_D is always different from 0_D (known as *characteristic zero*; it ensures that two nonzero values sum up to zero only if they are one the inverse of the other w.r.t. $\oplus$, thus avoiding inappropriate zero results when aggregating values of trajectories from the same state).

For example, the following reachability-consistent semirings can be used:

- $(\mathbb{B}, \vee, \wedge, \bot, \top)$ for nondeterministic models;
- $(\mathbb{R}_{\geq 0}, +, \times, 0, 1)$ for probabilistic and stochastic models;

while characteristic zero rules out all semirings $(\mathbb{Z}_n, +_n, \times_n, 0, 1)$ of the classes of integer numbers that are congruent modulo $n \in \mathbb{N}_{\geq 2}$.

2.3 Measure Schemata for Multistep Reachability

The definition of behavioral metaequivalences requires the capability of measuring the degree of reachability of a given set of states from a given state when executing a sequence of transitions labeled with a certain sequence of actions. On the basis of [6], in [3] I provided a notion of *measure schema* for a D-ULTRAS $\mathcal{U}$ as a set of homogeneously defined *measure functions*, one for each resolution $\mathcal{Z}$ of $\mathcal{U}$. In the following, A^* denotes the set of traces over an action set A, ε the empty trace, and $|\alpha|$ the length of a trace $\alpha \in A^*$.

Definition 4. *Let* $(D, \oplus, \otimes, 0_D, 1_D)$ *be a reachability-consistent semiring and* $\mathcal{U} = (S, A, \longrightarrow)$ *be a* D-ULTRAS. *A* D-measure schema $\mathcal{M}$ for $\mathcal{U}$ is a set of measure functions of the form $\mathcal{M}_{\mathcal{Z}} : Z \times A^* \times 2^Z \to D$, one for each $\mathcal{Z} =$

$(Z, A, \longrightarrow_Z) \in Res(s)$ and $s \in S$, which are inductively defined on the length of their second argument by letting $\mathcal{M}_Z(z, \alpha, Z')$ be equal to:

$$
\begin{cases}
f_Z(\ \bigoplus_{z' \in supp(\Delta)} (\Delta(z') \otimes \mathcal{M}_Z(z', \alpha', Z')), z, a, \Delta) & \text{if } \alpha = a\,\alpha' \text{ and } z \xrightarrow{a}_Z \Delta \\
1_D & \text{if } \alpha = \varepsilon \text{ and } z \in Z' \\
0_D & \text{otherwise}
\end{cases}
$$

where $f_Z : D \times Z \times A \times (Z \to D)_{\text{nefs}} \to D$.   ■

In the first clause, the value of $\mathcal{M}_Z(z, \alpha, Z')$ is built around a sum of products of D-values, with the summation being well defined because $supp(\Delta)$ is finite as established in Definition 1. The definition above applies to $Z \in k\text{-}Res(s)$ by restricting to traces $\alpha \in A^*$ such that $|\alpha| \leq k$ (note that $Z' \subseteq S$ when $|\alpha| = k$). For simplicity, $\mathcal{M}$ will often indicate both the measure schema and any of its measure functions $\mathcal{M}_Z$, with $\mathcal{M}_{\text{nd}}$ being used when the semiring is $(\mathbb{B}, \vee, \wedge, \bot, \top)$ and $\mathcal{M}_{\text{pb}}$ when it is $(\mathbb{R}_{\geq 0}, +, \times, 0, 1)$.

To provide some degree of flexibility, further parameters, internal or external to $\mathcal{U}$, may be taken into account. On the one hand, the auxiliary function f_Z returns its first argument unless otherwise stated, but can also exploit information related to the source state z, the action label a, or the target distribution Δ of the transition elicited in the first clause. On the other hand, when necessary $\mathcal{M}_Z$ is allowed to depend on arguments external to $\mathcal{U}$, such as time [3], which are consistently inherited by f_Z (the codomain of both functions remains D).

2.4   Bisimulation and Trace Pre-/Post-metaequivalences: Coherency

In [3] I focused on the two endpoints of the linear-time/branching-time spectrum and redefined bisimulation and trace semantics for ULTRAS with respect to [6] on the basis of the newly introduced concepts: resolutions of nondeterminism, reachability-consistent semirings, measure schemata. This allowed me to capture *also* the equivalences for nondeterministic and probabilistic processes.

For bisimulation semantics there are two different metaequivalences, $\sim_{\text{B}}^{\text{pre}}$ and $\sim_{\text{B}}^{\text{post}}$. Both are defined in the style of [34], which requires bisimulations to be equivalence relations, but deal with *sets of equivalence classes*, rather than only with individual equivalence classes, to avoid an undesirable decrease of the discriminating power in certain circumstances. The difference between the two metaequivalences lies in the position – underlined in the definition below – of the universal quantification over sets of equivalence classes.

In the first case, inspired by [8, 47, 49] and referred to as *pre*-bisimulation, the quantification occurs *before* the transition of the challenger and the transition of the defender. In the second case, which is the widely accepted approach of [45] referred to as *post*-bisimulation, the quantification occurs *after* those two transitions. Given an equivalence relation $\mathcal{B}$ over a state space S together with a set of equivalence classes $\mathcal{G} \in 2^{S/\mathcal{B}}$, $\bigcup \mathcal{G} \subseteq S$ denotes the union of all the equivalence classes in $\mathcal{G}$. The two considered transitions are represented via 1-resolutions.

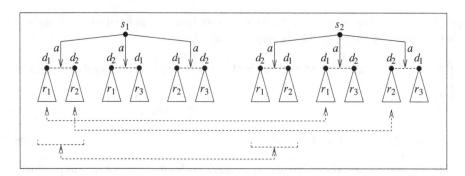

Fig. 1. Difference between bisimulation metaequivalences: $s_1 \not\sim_{\mathrm{B},\mathcal{M}}^{\mathrm{post}} s_2$, $s_1 \sim_{\mathrm{B},\mathcal{M}}^{\mathrm{pre}} s_2$

Definition 5. *Let $(D, \oplus, \otimes, 0_D, 1_D)$ be a reachability-consistent semiring, $\mathcal{U} = (S, A, \longrightarrow)$ be a D-ULTRAS, $\mathcal{M}$ be a D-measure schema for $\mathcal{U}$, and $s_1, s_2 \in S$:*

- *$s_1 \sim_{\mathrm{B},\mathcal{M}}^{\mathrm{pre}} s_2$ iff there exists an $\mathcal{M}$-pre-bisimulation $\mathcal{B}$ over S such that $(s_1, s_2) \in \mathcal{B}$. An equivalence relation $\mathcal{B}$ over S is an $\mathcal{M}$-pre-bisimulation iff, whenever $(s_1, s_2) \in \mathcal{B}$, then for all $a \in A$ and for all $\mathcal{G} \in 2^{S/\mathcal{B}}$ it holds that for each $\mathcal{Z}_1 \in 1\text{-}Res(s_1)$ there exists $\mathcal{Z}_2 \in 1\text{-}Res(s_2)$ such that:*

$$\mathcal{M}(z_{s_1}, a, \bigcup \mathcal{G}) = \mathcal{M}(z_{s_2}, a, \bigcup \mathcal{G})$$

- *$s_1 \sim_{\mathrm{B},\mathcal{M}}^{\mathrm{post}} s_2$ iff there exists an $\mathcal{M}$-post-bisimulation $\mathcal{B}$ over S such that $(s_1, s_2) \in \mathcal{B}$. An equivalence relation $\mathcal{B}$ over S is an $\mathcal{M}$-post-bisimulation iff, whenever $(s_1, s_2) \in \mathcal{B}$, then for all $a \in A$ it holds that for each $\mathcal{Z}_1 \in 1\text{-}Res(s_1)$ there exists $\mathcal{Z}_2 \in 1\text{-}Res(s_2)$ such that for all $\mathcal{G} \in 2^{S/\mathcal{B}}$:*

$$\mathcal{M}(z_{s_1}, a, \bigcup \mathcal{G}) = \mathcal{M}(z_{s_2}, a, \bigcup \mathcal{G}) \qquad \blacksquare$$

To understand the difference between the two bisimulation metaequivalences, consider the two D-ULTRAS models in Fig. 1. Both models feature *internal nondeterminism* (due to the three a-transitions departing from s_1 and s_2), the same distinct D-values d_1 and d_2, and the same inequivalent continuations given by the D-ULTRAS submodels with initial states r_1, r_2, r_3. Notice that both the D-values and the continuations are *shuffled within* each model, while only the D-values are *shuffled across* the two models too. It holds that $s_1 \not\sim_{\mathrm{B},\mathcal{M}}^{\mathrm{post}} s_2$ because, e.g., the leftmost a-transition of s_1 is not matched by any of the three a-transitions of s_2. In contrast, $s_1 \sim_{\mathrm{B},\mathcal{M}}^{\mathrm{pre}} s_2$. For instance, the leftmost a-transition of s_1 is matched by the central (resp. rightmost) a-transition of s_2 with respect to the equivalence class of r_1 (resp. r_2) and by the leftmost a-transition of s_2 with respect to the union of the equivalence classes of r_1 and r_2 (see the dashed arrow-headed lines in Fig. 1).

Also for trace semantics there are two different metaequivalences, $\sim_{\mathrm{T}}^{\mathrm{pre}}$ and $\sim_{\mathrm{T}}^{\mathrm{post}}$, which differ for the position of the universal quantification over traces. In the first case, inspired by [7], the quantification occurs *before* the computation of the challenger and the computation of the defender, so that superscript *pre* is used. In the second case, which is the widely accepted approach of [43], the quantification occurs *after* those two computations, hence superscript *post*.

In the definition of trace semantics, the considered computations are represented through resolutions. The ULTRAS submodels rooted in the support of the target distribution of a transition are not necessarily distinct and can have several outgoing transitions. Therefore, on the resolution side, the scheduler has the freedom of making *different* decisions in different occurrences of the *same* submodel within a target distribution. Unfortunately, this results in overdiscriminating trace metaequivalences.

Unlike [3], in this paper I limit the excessive power of schedulers by restricting myself to *coherent resolutions*, i.e., resolutions in which the decisions made in different occurrences of the same submodel are coherent with each other. This can be expressed by reasoning on suitable sets of traces, each extended with its *degree of executability* in a given resolution.

Given $a \in A$, $d \in D \setminus \{0_D\}$, and $T, T_1, T_2 \subseteq A^* \times (D \setminus \{0_D\})$, let:

$$
\begin{aligned}
a \,.\, T &= \{(a\,\alpha, d') \mid (\alpha, d') \in T\} \\
d \otimes T &= \{(\alpha, d \otimes d') \mid (\alpha, d') \in T\} \\
tr(T) &= \{\alpha \in A^* \mid (\alpha, d') \in T \text{ for some } d' \in D \setminus \{0_D\}\} \\
T_1 \oplus T_2 &= \{(\alpha, d_1 \oplus d_2) \mid (\alpha, d_1) \in T_1 \wedge (\alpha, d_2) \in T_2\} \\
&\cup \{(\alpha, d_1) \in T_1 \mid \text{there exists no } (\alpha, d_2) \in T_2 \text{ or there exists} \\
&\qquad\qquad\qquad \alpha' \neq \alpha \text{ in either } tr(T_1) \text{ or } tr(T_2) \text{ such that } |\alpha'| \leq |\alpha|\} \\
&\cup \{(\alpha, d_2) \in T_2 \mid \text{there exists no } (\alpha, d_1) \in T_1 \text{ or there exists} \\
&\qquad\qquad\qquad \alpha' \neq \alpha \text{ in either } tr(T_1) \text{ or } tr(T_2) \text{ such that } |\alpha'| \leq |\alpha|\}
\end{aligned}
$$

The set of *coherent D-traces* of a state s of a D-ULTRAS is defined as follows:

$$
T_D^{\mathrm{c}}(s) = \bigcup_{n \in \mathbb{N}} T_{D,n}^{\mathrm{c}}(s)
$$

where $T_{D,n}^{\mathrm{c}}(s)$ is the set of coherent D-traces of s having length at most n:

$$
\begin{aligned}
T_{D,0}^{\mathrm{c}}(s) &= \{(\varepsilon, 1_D)\} \\
T_{D,n+1}^{\mathrm{c}}(s) &= \{(\varepsilon, 1_D)\} \cup \bigcup_{s \xrightarrow{a} \Delta} a \,.\, \left(\bigoplus_{\Theta \subseteq A^*} \overset{tr(T_{D,n}^{\mathrm{c}}(s'))=\Theta}{\bigoplus_{s' \in supp(\Delta)}} (\Delta(s') \otimes T_{D,n}^{\mathrm{c}}(s')) \right)
\end{aligned}
$$

Definition 6. *Let* $\mathcal{U} = (S, A, \longrightarrow)$ *be a D-ULTRAS, $s \in S$, $\mathcal{Z} = (Z, A, \longrightarrow_{\mathcal{Z}}) \in Res(s)$ with correspondence function $corr_{\mathcal{Z}} : Z \to S$. $\mathcal{Z}$ is said to be a coherent resolution of s, written $\mathcal{Z} \in Res^{\mathrm{c}}(s)$, iff for all $z \in Z$, whenever $z \xrightarrow{a}_{\mathcal{Z}} \Delta$, then for all $z', z'' \in supp(\Delta)$ and $n \in \mathbb{N}$:*

$$
tr(T_{D,n}^{\mathrm{c}}(corr_{\mathcal{Z}}(z'))) = tr(T_{D,n}^{\mathrm{c}}(corr_{\mathcal{Z}}(z''))) \implies tr(T_{D,n}^{\mathrm{c}}(z')) = tr(T_{D,n}^{\mathrm{c}}(z''))
$$

∎

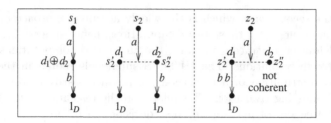

Fig. 2. Validity of Prop. 1(3) thanks to resolution coherency: $s_1 \sim_{B,\mathcal{M}}^{\text{post}} s_2$, $s_1 \sim_{T,\mathcal{M}}^{\text{post}} s_2$

Definition 7. *Let* $(D, \oplus, \otimes, 0_D, 1_D)$ *be a reachability-consistent semiring,* $\mathcal{U} = (S, A, \longrightarrow)$ *be a D-ULTRaS,* $\mathcal{M}$ *be a D-measure schema for* $\mathcal{U}$, *and* $s_1, s_2 \in S$:

- $s_1 \sim_{T,\mathcal{M}}^{\text{pre}} s_2$ *iff* <u>*for all*</u> $\alpha \in A^*$ *it holds that for each* $\mathcal{Z}_1 = (Z_1, A, \longrightarrow_{\mathcal{Z}_1}) \in Res^c(s_1)$ *there exists* $\mathcal{Z}_2 = (Z_2, A, \longrightarrow_{\mathcal{Z}_2}) \in Res^c(s_2)$ *such that:*
$$\mathcal{M}(z_{s_1}, \alpha, Z_1) = \mathcal{M}(z_{s_2}, \alpha, Z_2)$$
and also the condition obtained by exchanging $\mathcal{Z}_1$ *with* $\mathcal{Z}_2$ *is satisfied.*
- $s_1 \sim_{T,\mathcal{M}}^{\text{post}} s_2$ *iff it holds that for each* $\mathcal{Z}_1 = (Z_1, A, \longrightarrow_{\mathcal{Z}_1}) \in Res^c(s_1)$ *there exists* $\mathcal{Z}_2 = (Z_2, A, \longrightarrow_{\mathcal{Z}_2}) \in Res^c(s_2)$ *such that* <u>*for all*</u> $\alpha \in A^*$:
$$\mathcal{M}(z_{s_1}, \alpha, Z_1) = \mathcal{M}(z_{s_2}, \alpha, Z_2)$$
and also the condition obtained by exchanging $\mathcal{Z}_1$ *with* $\mathcal{Z}_2$ *is satisfied.* ∎

2.5 Comparing Bisimulation and Trace Metaequivalences

The outcome of the comparison of the discriminating power of the four behavioral metaequivalences is recalled below from [3].

Proposition 1. *Let* $(D, \oplus, \otimes, 0_D, 1_D)$ *be a reachability-consistent semiring,* $\mathcal{U} = (S, A, \longrightarrow)$ *be a D-ULTRaS, and* $\mathcal{M}$ *be a D-measure schema for* $\mathcal{U}$. *Then:*

1. $\sim_{B,\mathcal{M}}^{\text{post}} \subseteq \sim_{B,\mathcal{M}}^{\text{pre}}$, *with* $\sim_{B,\mathcal{M}}^{\text{post}} = \sim_{B,\mathcal{M}}^{\text{pre}}$ *if* $\mathcal{U}$ *has no internal nondeterminism.*
2. $\sim_{T,\mathcal{M}}^{\text{post}} \subseteq \sim_{T,\mathcal{M}}^{\text{pre}}$.
3. $\sim_{B,\mathcal{M}}^{\text{post}} \subseteq \sim_{T,\mathcal{M}}^{\text{post}}$. ∎

The validity of the third property[2] above is ensured by the coherency of the resolutions used in the definition of the trace metaequivalences. Consider for instance the two *D*-ULTRaS models in the leftmost part of Fig. 2, where $s_1 \sim_{B,\mathcal{M}}^{\text{post}} s_2$ and $s_1 \sim_{T,\mathcal{M}}^{\text{post}} s_2$. The latter identification is made possible by resolution coherency in $\sim_{T,\mathcal{M}}^{\text{post}}$. Indeed, $T_D^c(s_2') = \{(\varepsilon, 1_D), (b, 1_D)\} = T_D^c(s_2'')$. Therefore, the resolution of s_2 coinciding with the entire second model is coherent, while the one in the rightmost part of Fig. 2 is not, because $T_D^c(z_2') = \{(\varepsilon, 1_D), (b, 1_D)\} \neq \{(\varepsilon, 1_D)\} = T_D^c(z_2'')$, and would lead to $s_1 \not\sim_{T,\mathcal{M}}^{\text{post}} s_2$ if it were admitted.

---

[2] The proof is the same as the third property of Proposition 3.5 of [3], which is now correct in its inductive part ($|\alpha| = n + 1$, $a' = a$, "either α' ...") due to resolution coherency.

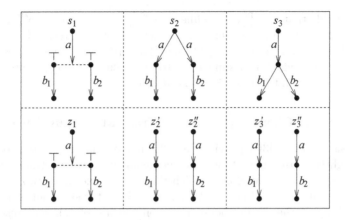

Fig. 3. Strictness of inclusions in Proposition 1 and incomparability of metaequivalences

As far as the strictness of the inclusions in Proposition 1 and the incomparability of certain metaequivalences are concerned, consider the three $\mathbb{B}$-ULTraS models in the upper part of Fig. 3 – where only the second one features internal nondeterminism and $b_1 \neq b_2$ – together with their maximal resolutions in the lower part of Fig. 3 ($\top$ is omitted in the case of target distributions with singleton support). It turns out what follows:

- $s_1 \sim_{\mathrm{B},\mathcal{M}_{\mathrm{nd}}}^{\mathrm{pre}} s_2$ but $s_1 \not\sim_{\mathrm{B},\mathcal{M}_{\mathrm{nd}}}^{\mathrm{post}} s_2$ because the only a-transition of s_1 cannot be matched, in the $\mathcal{M}_{\mathrm{nd}}$-post-bisimulation game, by any of the two a-transitions of s_2, as the transition of s_1 can reach two different equivalence classes, while each transition of s_2 can reach only one class.
- $s_1 \not\sim_{\mathrm{B},\mathcal{M}_{\mathrm{nd}}}^{\mathrm{pre}} s_3$, and hence $s_1 \not\sim_{\mathrm{B},\mathcal{M}_{\mathrm{nd}}}^{\mathrm{post}} s_3$, because the state reached by the a-transition of s_3 enables two actions and, as a consequence, cannot be equivalent to any of the two states reached by the a-transition of s_1. Indeed, although s_2 and s_3 have the same resolutions, their maximal 1-resolutions are different; for s_2 they coincide with the two maximal resolutions, while for s_3 the only maximal 1-resolution coincides with the original model.
- $s_1 \sim_{\mathrm{T},\mathcal{M}_{\mathrm{nd}}}^{\mathrm{pre}} s_2$ but $s_1 \not\sim_{\mathrm{T},\mathcal{M}_{\mathrm{nd}}}^{\mathrm{post}} s_2$ because the only maximal resolution of s_1 cannot be matched, in the case of $\sim_{\mathrm{T},\mathcal{M}_{\mathrm{nd}}}^{\mathrm{post}}$, by any of the two maximal resolutions of s_2, as the maximal resolution of s_1 has two different maximal traces, while each maximal resolution of s_2 has only one maximal trace.
- $s_1 \sim_{\mathrm{T},\mathcal{M}_{\mathrm{nd}}}^{\mathrm{pre}} s_3$ but $s_1 \not\sim_{\mathrm{T},\mathcal{M}_{\mathrm{nd}}}^{\mathrm{post}} s_3$ because s_3 has the same resolutions as s_2. This shows that, unlike bisimulation semantics, $\sim_{\mathrm{T},\mathcal{M}}^{\mathrm{pre}}$ and $\sim_{\mathrm{T},\mathcal{M}}^{\mathrm{post}}$ do not coincide even in the absence of internal nondeterminism, unless excluding $\mathbb{B}$-ULTraS models such as the first one that cannot be considered the canonical representation of any labeled transition system and, more generally, all semirings with a set $D \neq \mathbb{B}$ containing a value $d \neq 0_D$ such that $d \oplus d = d$ (so that trace a would distinguish s_1 from s_3 – and also s_2 – w.r.t. $\sim_{\mathrm{T},\mathcal{M}}^{\mathrm{pre}}$).
- $s_2 \sim_{\mathrm{T},\mathcal{M}_{\mathrm{nd}}}^{\mathrm{post}} s_3$ as they have the same resolutions, but $s_2 \not\sim_{\mathrm{B},\mathcal{M}_{\mathrm{nd}}}^{\mathrm{post}} s_3$.
- $\sim_{\mathrm{B},\mathcal{M}}^{\mathrm{pre}}$ is generally incomparable with $\sim_{\mathrm{T},\mathcal{M}}^{\mathrm{post}}$ and $\sim_{\mathrm{T},\mathcal{M}}^{\mathrm{pre}}$. On the one hand, $s_2 \not\sim_{\mathrm{B},\mathcal{M}_{\mathrm{nd}}}^{\mathrm{pre}} s_3$ while $s_2 \sim_{\mathrm{T},\mathcal{M}_{\mathrm{nd}}}^{\mathrm{post}} s_3$ and $s_2 \sim_{\mathrm{T},\mathcal{M}_{\mathrm{nd}}}^{\mathrm{pre}} s_3$. On the other hand, in

Fig. 1 it holds that $s_1 \sim^{\text{pre}}_{\text{B},\mathcal{M}} s_2$ while $s_1 \not\sim^{\text{post}}_{\text{T},\mathcal{M}} s_2$; moreover $s_1 \not\sim^{\text{pre}}_{\text{T},\mathcal{M}} s_2$ if r_1 (resp. r_2) has a b-transition that reaches with degree d'_b (resp. d''_b) a terminal state, whenever degrees $(d_1 \otimes d'_b) \oplus (d_2 \otimes d''_b)$ and $(d_2 \otimes d'_b) \oplus (d_1 \otimes d''_b)$ associated with trace $a\,b$ – which is assumed not to be executable via r_3 – are different from each other and from $d_1 \otimes d'_b$ and $d_2 \otimes d''_b$.

2.6   Alternative Characterizations of Trace Metaequivalences

On the basis of [7], in [3] I provided an alternative characterization of $\sim^{\text{pre}}_{\text{T},\mathcal{M}}$, which is slightly revised here. Since this metaequivalence treats traces individually regardless of the resolutions in which they can be executed, two states turn out to be equivalent according to $\sim^{\text{pre}}_{\text{T},\mathcal{M}}$ iff they have the same set of D-traces.

The validity of the lemma below relies on the use of coherent resolutions, together with the fact that the definition of $T_1 \oplus T_2$ before Definition 6 also includes (α, d_1) taken from T_1 and (α, d_2) taken from T_2 without summing up their degrees, provided that there exists another trace α' not longer than α in only one of T_1 and T_2 – meaning that T_1 and T_2 stem from two inequivalent states.[3]

Lemma 1. *Let* $(D, \oplus, \otimes, 0_D, 1_D)$ *be a reachability-consistent semiring,* $\mathcal{U} = (S, A, \longrightarrow)$ *be a D-ULTRAS,* $\mathcal{M}$ *be a D-measure schema for $\mathcal{U}$. Let* $(\alpha, d) \in A^* \times (D \setminus \{0_D\})$ *and* $s \in S$. *Then* $(\alpha, d) \in T^c_D(s)$ *iff there exists* $(Z, A, \longrightarrow_Z) \in Res^c(s)$ *such that* $\mathcal{M}(z_s, \alpha, Z) = d$. ∎

Theorem 1. *Let* $s_1, s_2 \in S$. *Then* $s_1 \sim^{\text{pre}}_{\text{T},\mathcal{M}} s_2$ *iff* $T^c_D(s_1) = T^c_D(s_2)$. ∎

An analogous characterization can be provided for $\sim^{\text{post}}_{\text{T},\mathcal{M}}$ by reasoning in terms of *coherent D-trace distributions*, so to bind extended D-traces to the resolutions in which they can be executed. For a state s, what is obtained is a family of sets of extended D-traces instead of a flat set:

$$TD^c(s) = \{T^c(z_s) \mid \text{there exists } \mathcal{Z} \in Res^c(s) \text{ whose initial state is } z_s\}$$

from which the result below immediately follows.

Theorem 2. *Let* $s_1, s_2 \in S$. *Then* $s_1 \sim^{\text{post}}_{\text{T},\mathcal{M}} s_2$ *iff* $TD^c_D(s_1) = TD^c_D(s_2)$. ∎

3   Metaresults for Behavioral Metaequivalences

After the identification of models and equivalences captured or generated by the ULTRAS framework, the ongoing research is aimed at investigating the properties of behavioral metaequivalences. The objective of this activity is to produce *metaresults*, in the sense that the obtained results should be valid *regardless of specific classes of processes*, thereby leading to a *unifying process theory*.

---

[3] The definition of $T_1 \oplus T_2$ before Lemma 4.11 of [3] should be rectified by removing the two instances of "α occurring only in ..." as resolutions are not coherent there (otherwise the if part of Lemma 4.11(2) would not hold).

Table 1. Structural operational semantic rules for UPROC

$$\frac{\mathcal{D} \longmapsto \Delta}{a \, . \, \mathcal{D} \xrightarrow{a} \Delta}$$

$$\frac{P_1 \xrightarrow{a} \Delta}{P_1 + P_2 \xrightarrow{a} \Delta} \qquad\qquad \frac{P_2 \xrightarrow{a} \Delta}{P_1 + P_2 \xrightarrow{a} \Delta}$$

$$\frac{P_1 \xrightarrow{a} \Delta_1 \quad a \notin L}{P_1 \,\|_L\, P_2 \xrightarrow{a} \Delta_1 \otimes \delta_{P_2}} \qquad\qquad \frac{P_2 \xrightarrow{a} \Delta_2 \quad a \notin L}{P_1 \,\|_L\, P_2 \xrightarrow{a} \delta_{P_1} \otimes \Delta_2}$$

$$\frac{P_1 \xrightarrow{a} \Delta_1 \quad P_2 \xrightarrow{a} \Delta_2 \quad a \in L}{P_1 \,\|_L\, P_2 \xrightarrow{a} \Delta_1 \otimes \Delta_2}$$

$$d \triangleright P \longmapsto \{(P, d)\} \qquad\qquad \frac{\mathcal{D}_1 \longmapsto \Delta_1 \quad \mathcal{D}_2 \longmapsto \Delta_2}{\mathcal{D}_1 \mathbin{\mathaccent\cdot\oplus} \mathcal{D}_2 \longmapsto \Delta_1 \oplus \Delta_2}$$

The compositionality metaresults established in [3] for bisimulation and trace pre-/post-metaequivalences are now discussed, by rephrasing them in the setting of a general process calculus relying on the same underpinnings as ULTRAS. The definition of the semantics for this language makes use of the two binary operations provided by the underlying reachability-consistent semiring.

3.1 A Process Algebraic View of ULTRAS

Given a preordered set D equipped with minimum that yields a reachability-consistent semiring $(D, \oplus, \otimes, 0_D, 1_D)$, together with a countable set A of actions, the syntax for UPROC – *uniform process calculus* features two levels, one for the set $\mathbb{P}$ of processes and one for the set $\mathbb{D}$ of reachability distributions:

$$\begin{aligned} P &::= \underline{0} \mid a \, . \, \mathcal{D} \mid P + P \mid P \,\|_L\, P \\ \mathcal{D} &::= d \triangleright P \mid \mathcal{D} \mathbin{\mathaccent\cdot\oplus} \mathcal{D} \end{aligned}$$

where $a \in A$, $L \subseteq A$, $d \in D \setminus \{0_D\}$.

The structural operational semantic rules in Table 1 generate a D-ULTRAS $(\mathbb{P}, A, \longrightarrow)$ by exploiting the semiring operations. The primary transition relation $\longrightarrow$ is defined as the smallest subset of $\mathbb{P} \times A \times (\mathbb{P} \to D)_{\mathrm{nefs}}$ satisfying the rules in the upper part, where $\otimes$ is lifted to reachability distributions over the parallel composition of processes by letting $(\Delta_1 \otimes \Delta_2)(P_1 \,\|_L\, P_2) = \Delta_1(P_1) \otimes \Delta_2(P_2)$, while δ_P is the reachability distribution identically equal to 0_D except in P where its value is 1_D. The secondary transition relation $\longmapsto$ is the smallest subset of $\mathbb{D} \times (\mathbb{P} \to D)_{\mathrm{nefs}}$ satisfying the rules in the lower part, with $\{(P, d)\}$ being a shorthand for the reachability distribution identically equal to 0_D except in P where its value is d; furthermore, $\oplus$ is lifted to reachability distributions by letting $(\Delta_1 \oplus \Delta_2)(P) = \Delta_1(P) \oplus \Delta_2(P)$. Let $supp(\mathcal{D}) = supp(\Delta)$ if $\mathcal{D} \longmapsto \Delta$.

As far as the process operator $+$ is concerned, it expresses a generic choice to be interpreted on the basis of D. For example, if $D = \mathbb{B}$ then the choice is nondeterministic. If instead $D = \mathbb{R}_{\geq 0}$, in the presence of alternative identical actions – corresponding to identically labeled transitions departing from the same state – the choice is nondeterministic and a (variant of) probabilistic automata can be derived; otherwise, the choice may be regarded as probabilistic, in the sense that a Markov chain or a Markov decision process may be obtained. Moreover, note that a probabilistic process term like $P_1 \, _p{+} \, P_2$, where $p \in \mathbb{R}_{]0,1[}$, can be rendered as $\tau . (p \triangleright P_1 \mathbin{\diamond} (1 - p) \triangleright P_2)$ in UProC, where τ is the invisible action.

3.2   Congruence with Respect to Distribution/Dynamic Operators

Let us investigate the compositionality properties of the four behavioral metaequivalences with respect to the operators of UProC. Due to the two-level format of the syntax, as a preliminary step the metaequivalences are lifted from processes to reachability distributions over processes. Extending [34], this can be done by considering $\mathcal{D}_1, \mathcal{D}_2 \in \mathbb{D}$ related by an equivalence relation $\sim$ over $\mathbb{P}$ when $\mathcal{D}_1$ and $\mathcal{D}_2$ assign the same reachability degree to the same equivalence class, i.e., $\Delta_1(C) = \Delta_2(C)$ for all $C \in \mathbb{P}/\sim$ with $\mathcal{D}_1 \longmapsto \Delta_1$ and $\mathcal{D}_2 \longmapsto \Delta_2$. Note that, given $\mathcal{D} \longmapsto \Delta$, it holds that $\Delta \in (\mathbb{P} \to D)_{\mathrm{nefs}}$ and hence $\Delta(C)$, i.e., $\bigoplus_{P \in C} \Delta(P)$, can only have finitely many summands different from 0_D.

Compositionality with respect to the distribution operators $\triangleright$ and $\mathbin{\diamond}$ can be established in a way that abstracts from the specific behavioral metaequivalence.

Theorem 3. *Let* $\sim_{\mathcal{M}} \in \{\sim_{\mathrm{B},\mathcal{M}}^{\mathrm{pre}}, \sim_{\mathrm{B},\mathcal{M}}^{\mathrm{post}}, \sim_{\mathrm{T},\mathcal{M}}^{\mathrm{pre}}, \sim_{\mathrm{T},\mathcal{M}}^{\mathrm{post}}\}$ *for a measure schema* $\mathcal{M}$ *over the* D-ULTRAS *semantics of* UProC. *Let* $P_1, P_2 \in \mathbb{P}$ *and* $\mathcal{D}_1, \mathcal{D}_2 \in \mathbb{D}$. *If* $P_1 \sim_{\mathcal{M}} P_2$ *and* $\mathcal{D}_1 \sim_{\mathcal{M}} \mathcal{D}_2$, *then:*

1. $d \triangleright P_1 \sim_{\mathcal{M}} d \triangleright P_2$ *for all* $d \in D \setminus \{0_D\}$.
2. $\mathcal{D}_1 \mathbin{\diamond} \mathcal{D} \sim_{\mathcal{M}} \mathcal{D}_2 \mathbin{\diamond} \mathcal{D}$ *and* $\mathcal{D} \mathbin{\diamond} \mathcal{D}_1 \sim_{\mathcal{M}} \mathcal{D} \mathbin{\diamond} \mathcal{D}_2$ *for all* $\mathcal{D} \in \mathbb{D}$.   ∎

As far as the two dynamic process operators are concerned, there are different proofs for bisimulation and trace semantics, which are reworkings of those in [3].

Theorem 4. *Let* $\sim_{\mathcal{M}} \in \{\sim_{\mathrm{B},\mathcal{M}}^{\mathrm{pre}}, \sim_{\mathrm{B},\mathcal{M}}^{\mathrm{post}}, \sim_{\mathrm{T},\mathcal{M}}^{\mathrm{pre}}, \sim_{\mathrm{T},\mathcal{M}}^{\mathrm{post}}\}$ *for a measure schema* $\mathcal{M}$ *over the* D-ULTRAS *semantics of* UProC. *Let* $P_1, P_2 \in \mathbb{P}$ *and* $\mathcal{D}_1, \mathcal{D}_2 \in \mathbb{D}$. *If* $P_1 \sim_{\mathcal{M}} P_2$ *and* $\mathcal{D}_1 \sim_{\mathcal{M}} \mathcal{D}_2$, *then:*

1. $a . \mathcal{D}_1 \sim_{\mathcal{M}} a . \mathcal{D}_2$ *for all* $a \in A$.
2. $P_1 + P \sim_{\mathcal{M}} P_2 + P$ *and* $P + P_1 \sim_{\mathcal{M}} P + P_2$ *for all* $P \in \mathbb{P}$.   ∎

Unlike Theorem 4.2 of [3], trace metaequivalences are *full congruences* with respect to *action prefix*. If ordinary resolutions were considered instead of coherent ones, a lack of compositionality would arise in the general setting of ULTRAS because the continuation after an action is *not a single process*, but a reachability distribution over processes.

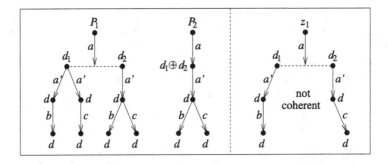

Fig. 4. Full compositionality w.r.t. action prefix thanks to resolution coherency

This can be illustrated through the following UPROC terms P_1 and P_2:

$$P_1 = a \cdot (d_1 \rhd Q_1 \oplus d_2 \rhd Q_2)$$
$$P_2 = a \cdot (d_1 \rhd Q_2 \oplus d_2 \rhd Q_2)$$
$$Q_1 = a' \cdot b \cdot \underline{0} + a' \cdot c \cdot \underline{0}$$
$$Q_2 = a' \cdot (b \cdot \underline{0} + c \cdot \underline{0})$$

where a sequence of action prefixes like $a' \cdot b \cdot \underline{0}$ is a shorthand for $a' \cdot (d \rhd b \cdot (d \rhd \underline{0}))$ for some $d \in D \setminus \{0_D\}$. Their underlying D-ULTRaS models are shown in the leftmost part of Fig. 4. It is easy to see Q_1 and Q_2 are trace equivalent, hence the two distributions describing the a-continuations of P_1 and P_2 are trace equivalent too. However, if one considers the trace $\alpha = a\, a'b$ and the resolution of P_1 shown in the rightmost part of Fig. 4 – in which α is executable with degree $d_1 \otimes d \otimes d$ – then no resolution of P_2 is capable of matching it – as the executability degree would be $(d_1 \oplus d_2) \otimes d \otimes d$ or 0_D – unless $D = \mathbb{B}$ in which case $d_1 = d_2 = \top$ and $d_1 \oplus d_2 = \top \vee \top = \top$. As can be noted, that resolution of P_1 is not coherent, as the scheduler makes different decisions in the two trace equivalent submodels respectively rooted at Q_1 and Q_2, thereby producing two resolutions of those two submodels that are no longer trace equivalent.

3.3 Congruence with Respect to Parallel Composition

Addressing parallel composition is much more involved. Following [3], the first metaresult states that $\sim_{\mathrm{B},\mathcal{M}}^{\mathrm{post}}$ is a congruence with respect to parallel composition always, i.e., for every possible ULTRaS. As a consequence of Proposition 1, this is the case also for $\sim_{\mathrm{B},\mathcal{M}}^{\mathrm{pre}}$ in the absence of internal nondeterminism.

Theorem 5. *Let $\mathcal{M}$ be a measure schema for the D-ULTRaS semantics of UPROC. Let $P_1, P_2 \in \mathbb{P}$. If $P_1 \sim_{\mathrm{B},\mathcal{M}}^{\mathrm{post}} P_2$, then $P_1 \|_L P \sim_{\mathrm{B},\mathcal{M}}^{\mathrm{post}} P_2 \|_L P$ and $P \|_L P_1 \sim_{\mathrm{B},\mathcal{M}}^{\mathrm{post}} P \|_L P_2$ for all $L \subseteq A$ and $P \in \mathbb{P}$.* ∎

Corollary 1. *Let $\mathcal{M}$ be a measure schema for the D-ULTRaS semantics of UPROC. Let $P_1, P_2 \in \mathbb{P}$ have no internal nondeterminism. If $P_1 \sim_{\mathrm{B},\mathcal{M}}^{\mathrm{pre}} P_2$, then $P_1 \|_L P \sim_{\mathrm{B},\mathcal{M}}^{\mathrm{pre}} P_2 \|_L P$ and $P \|_L P_1 \sim_{\mathrm{B},\mathcal{M}}^{\mathrm{pre}} P \|_L P_2$ for all $L \subseteq A$ and $P \in \mathbb{P}$.* ∎

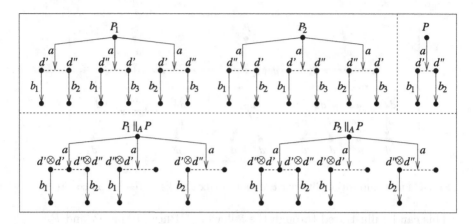

Fig. 5. $\sim_{\text{B},\mathcal{M}}^{\text{pre}}$ is not compositional when $|D| \geq 3$ and there is internal nondeterminism

As for the compositionality of $\sim_{\text{B},\mathcal{M}}^{\text{pre}}$ in the presence of internal nondeterminism, let us consider the case $|D| = 2$, i.e., the simplest reachability-consistent semiring $(\mathbb{B}, \vee, \wedge, \perp, \top)$ together with the corresponding measure schema $\mathcal{M}_{\text{nd}}$. In this specific case, $\sim_{\text{B},\mathcal{M}}^{\text{pre}}$ turns out to be a congruence with respect to parallel composition. Intuitively, in addition to the coinductive nature of bisimulation, the reason is that, starting from transitions whose target distributions can only contain $\top$ and $\perp$ as values, their parallel composition cannot generate, for the target distributions of the resulting transitions, values different from $\top$ and $\perp$.

Theorem 6. *Let $\mathcal{M}_{\text{nd}}$ be the measure schema for the $\mathbb{B}$-ULTRAS semantics of UPROC. Let $P_1, P_2 \in \mathbb{P}$. If $P_1 \sim_{\text{B},\mathcal{M}_{\text{nd}}}^{\text{pre}} P_2$, then $P_1 \|_L P \sim_{\text{B},\mathcal{M}_{\text{nd}}}^{\text{pre}} P_2 \|_L P$ and $P \|_L P_1 \sim_{\text{B},\mathcal{M}_{\text{nd}}}^{\text{pre}} P \|_L P_2$ for all $L \subseteq A$ and $P \in \mathbb{P}$.* ∎

In all the other cases, i.e., when $|D| \geq 3$ and internal nondeterminism is present, the relation $\sim_{\text{B},\mathcal{M}}^{\text{pre}}$ is no longer guaranteed to be a congruence with respect to parallel composition.

Consider for instance the first two D-ULTRAS models in the upper part of Fig. 5 (D-values of terminal states are omitted), where $d', d'' \in D$ satisfy $d' \neq d''$ and $d' \neq 0_D \neq d''$ (these values exist because $|D| \geq 3$). Given a D-measure schema $\mathcal{M}$, it holds that $P_1 \sim_{\text{B},\mathcal{M}}^{\text{pre}} P_2$. However, if the last D-ULTRAS in the upper part is taken into account, the two D-ULTRAS models in the lower part of Fig. 5 are obtained, which satisfy $P_1 \|_A P \not\sim_{\text{B},\mathcal{M}}^{\text{pre}} P_2 \|_A P$. The reason is that, when examining the set of equivalence classes whose states can perform b_1 or b_2, the leftmost a-transition of $P_1 \|_A P$ is not matched by any a-transition of $P_2 \|_A P$ whenever $(d' \otimes d') \oplus (d'' \otimes d'') \notin \{(d'' \otimes d') \oplus (d' \otimes d''), d' \otimes d', d'' \otimes d''\}$.

A *coarsest congruence metaresult* relating $\sim_{\text{B},\mathcal{M}}^{\text{post}}$ and $\sim_{\text{B},\mathcal{M}}^{\text{pre}}$ for $|D| \geq 3$ can be established whenever the reachability-consistent semiring $(D, \oplus, \otimes, 0_D, 1_D)$ is a *field* – like, e.g., $(\mathbb{Q}, +, \times, 0, 1)$, $(\mathbb{R}, +, \times, 0, 1)$, and $(\mathbb{C}, +, \times, 0, 1)$ – which means that the inverse operations with respect to $\oplus$ and $\otimes$ exist:

- $d \ominus d = d \oplus inv_{\oplus}(d) = inv_{\oplus}(d) \oplus d = 0_D$ for all $d \in D$.
- $d \oslash d = d \otimes inv_{\otimes}(d) = inv_{\otimes}(d) \otimes d = 1_D$ for all $d \in D \setminus \{0_D\}$.

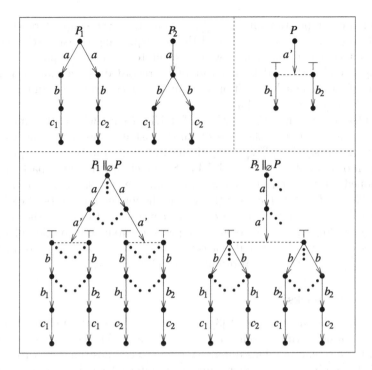

Fig. 6. $\sim_{T,\mathcal{M}}^{post}$ is not compositional

Such a metaresult holds under *image finiteness* – i.e., when the number of identically labeled transitions departing from any state is finite – and relies on the fact that transitions have target distributions with *finite support*. The proof exploits the algebraic and topological properties of the *vector spaces* that can be built on top of the field, as well as *characteristic zero*, which guarantees that the field and hence the vector spaces on it are infinite.

Theorem 7. *Let $(D, \oplus, \ominus, \otimes, \oslash, 0_D, 1_D)$ be a reachability-consistent field and $\mathcal{M}$ be a measure schema for the D-ULTRAS semantics of UProC. Let $P_1, P_2 \in \mathbb{P}$ be image finite. Then $P_1 \sim_{B,\mathcal{M}}^{post} P_2$ iff $P_1 \|_L P \sim_{B,\mathcal{M}}^{pre} P_2 \|_L P$ for all $L \subseteq A$ and $P \in \mathbb{P}$.* ∎

In the case of trace semantics, it is $\sim_{T,\mathcal{M}}^{pre}$ that, for every possible ULTRAS, is a congruence with respect to parallel composition, hence no compositionality connection can be established with $\sim_{T,\mathcal{M}}^{post}$ as the latter is finer than the former. The proof of this congruence metaresult for $\sim_{T,\mathcal{M}}^{pre}$ exploits the alternative characterization of Theorem 1.

Theorem 8. *Let $\mathcal{M}$ be a measure schema for the D-ULTRAS semantics of UProC. Let $P_1, P_2 \in \mathbb{P}$. If $P_1 \sim_{T,\mathcal{M}}^{pre} P_2$, then $P_1 \|_L P \sim_{T,\mathcal{M}}^{pre} P_2 \|_L P$ and $P \|_L P_1 \sim_{T,\mathcal{M}}^{pre} P \|_L P_2$ for all $L \subseteq A$ and $P \in \mathbb{P}$.* ∎

As for the compositionality of $\sim_{T,\mathcal{M}}^{post}$, even under the simplest reachability-consistent semiring $(\mathbb{B}, \vee, \wedge, \perp, \top)$ and the corresponding measure schema $\mathcal{M}_{nd}$ the relation is not a congruence with respect to parallel composition, unless excluding $\mathbb{B}$-ULTRAS models that cannot be regarded as the canonical representation of any labeled transition system (for a congruence counterexample based on $\mathcal{M}_{pb}$, see Fig. 3 of [43]).

Consider for instance the first two $\mathbb{B}$-ULTRAS models in the upper part of Fig. 6 ($\top$ is omitted in the case of target distributions with singleton support), which satisfy $P_1 \sim_{T,\mathcal{M}_{nd}}^{post} P_2$. If the last $\mathbb{B}$-ULTRAS in the upper part is taken into account, the two $\mathbb{B}$-ULTRAS models in the lower part of Fig. 6 are obtained (dots stands for transitions that are not shown), which satisfy $P_1 \parallel_{\emptyset} P \not\sim_{T,\mathcal{M}_{nd}}^{post} P_2 \parallel_{\emptyset} P$. This is witnessed by the maximal resolutions of $P_1 \parallel_{\emptyset} P$ and $P_2 \parallel_{\emptyset} P$ that start with trace $a\,a'$ and continue with one of the traces in $\{b\,b_1\,c_1, b\,b_1\,c_2, b\,b_2\,c_1, b\,b_2\,c_2\}$. As an example, the maximal resolution of $P_2 \parallel_{\emptyset} P$ whose associated set of maximal traces is $\{a\,a'\,b\,b_1\,c_1, a\,a'\,b\,b_2\,c_2\}$ is not matched under $\sim_{T,\mathcal{M}_{nd}}^{post}$ by any maximal resolution of $P_1 \parallel_{\emptyset} P$.

3.4 Final Remarks

In conclusion, the metaresults of [3] – which have been reformulated here in a process algebraic setting – confirm a foundational difference between bisimulation and trace semantics. This difference refers to compositionality with respect to parallel combinators and shows up under internal nondeterminism, as had emerged in the specific case of nondeterministic and probabilistic processes [7,8].

A question naturally arises: *is there a semantics for which both pre- and post-metaequivalences are always congruences with respect to parallel composition?*

4   Future Directions

I plan to keep putting ULTRAS at work on behavioral metaequivalences to further extend the resulting unifying process theory. In particular, I would like to investigate:

- Equational characterization metaresults.
- Logical characterization metaresults.
- Metaresults for other bisimulation-/trace-based metaequivalences.
- Metaresults for testing metaequivalences.
- The spectrum of metaequivalences on ULTRAS.

As far as behavioral metarelations are concerned, it is also worth studying:

- Behavioral metapreorders.
- Weak variants of behavioral metarelations.
- Approximate variants of behavioral metarelations.

Finally, on the metamodel side, it would be interesting to capture also:

- Interleaving models with continuous state spaces.
- Truly concurrent models such as Petri nets and event structures.

References

1. Alur, R., Dill, D.L.: A theory of timed automata. Theor. Comput. Sci. **126**, 183–235 (1994)
2. Bernardo, M.: Non-bisimulation-based Markovian behavioral equivalences. J. Logic Algebraic Program. **72**, 3–49 (2007)
3. Bernardo, M.: ULTraS at work: compositionality metaresults for bisimulation and-trace semantics. J. Logical Algebraic Methods Program. **94**, 150–182 (2018)
4. Bernardo, M., De Nicola, R., Loreti, M.: Uniform labeled transition systems for nondeterministic, probabilistic, and stochastic processes. In: Wirsing, M., Hofmann, M., Rauschmayer, A. (eds.) TGC 2010. LNCS, vol. 6084, pp. 35–56. Springer, Heidelberg (2010). https://doi.org/10.1007/978-3-642-15640-3_3
5. Bernardo, M., De Nicola, R., Loreti, M.: Uniform labeled transition systems for nondeterministic, probabilistic, and stochastic process calculi. In: Proceedings of the 1st International Workshop on Process Algebra and Coordination, PACO 2011, EPTCS, vol. 60, pp. 66–75 (2011)
6. Bernardo, M., De Nicola, R., Loreti, M.: A uniform framework for modeling nondeterministic, probabilistic, stochastic, or mixed processes and their behavioral equivalences. Inf. Comput. **225**, 29–82 (2013)
7. Bernardo, M., De Nicola, R., Loreti, M.: Revisiting trace and testing equivalences for nondeterministic and probabilistic processes. Logical Methods Comput. Sci. **10**(1:16), 1–42 (2014)
8. Bernardo, M., De Nicola, R., Loreti, M.: Revisiting bisimilarity and its modal logic for nondeterministic and probabilistic processes. Acta Informatica **52**, 61–106 (2015)
9. Bernardo, M., Tesei, L.: Encoding timed models as uniform labeled transition systems. In: Balsamo, M.S., Knottenbelt, W.J., Marin, A. (eds.) EPEW 2013. LNCS, vol. 8168, pp. 104–118. Springer, Heidelberg (2013). https://doi.org/10.1007/978-3-642-40725-3_9
10. Brookes, S.D., Hoare, C.A.R., Roscoe, A.W.: A theory of communicating sequential processes. J. ACM **31**, 560–599 (1984)
11. Christoff, I.: Testing equivalences and fully abstract models for probabilistic processes. In: Baeten, J.C.M., Klop, J.W. (eds.) CONCUR 1990. LNCS, vol. 458, pp. 126–138. Springer, Heidelberg (1990). https://doi.org/10.1007/BFb0039056
12. Cleaveland, R., Dayar, Z., Smolka, S.A., Yuen, S.: Testing preorders for probabilistic processes. Inf. Comput. **154**, 93–148 (1999)
13. De Nicola, R., Hennessy, M.: Testing equivalences for processes. Theor. Comput. Sci. **34**, 83–133 (1984)
14. De Nicola, R., Latella, D., Loreti, M., Massink, M.: Rate-based transition systems for stochastic process calculi. In: Albers, S., Marchetti-Spaccamela, A., Matias, Y., Nikoletseas, S., Thomas, W. (eds.) ICALP 2009. LNCS, vol. 5556, pp. 435–446. Springer, Heidelberg (2009). https://doi.org/10.1007/978-3-642-02930-1_36
15. De Nicola, R., Latella, D., Loreti, M., Massink, M.: A uniform definition of stochastic process calculi. ACM Comput. Surv. **46**(1:5), 1–35 (2013)
16. Deng, Y., van Glabbeek, R.J., Hennessy, M., Morgan, C.: Characterising testing preorders for finite probabilistic processes. Logical Methods Comput. Sci. **4**(4:4), 1–33 (2008)
17. Derman, C.: Finite State Markovian Decision Processes. Academic Press, Cambridge (1970)

18. Eisentraut, C., Hermanns, H., Zhang, L.: On probabilistic automata in continuous time. In: Proceedings of the 25th IEEE Symposium on Logic in Computer Science (LICS 2010), pp. 342–351. IEEE-CS Press (2010)
19. Giacalone, A., Jou, C.-C., Smolka, S.A.: Algebraic reasoning for probabilistic concurrent systems. In: Proceedings of the 1st IFIP Working Conference on Programming Concepts and Methods (PROCOMET 1990), North-Holland, pp. 443–458 (1990)
20. van Glabbeek, R.J.: The linear time - branching time spectrum I. In: Handbook of Process Algebra, pp. 3–99. Elsevier (2001)
21. van Glabbeek, R.J., Smolka, S.A., Steffen, B.: Reactive, generative and stratified models of probabilistic processes. Inf. Comput. **121**, 59–80 (1995)
22. Hansson, H., Jonsson, B.: A calculus for communicating systems with time and probabilities. In: Proceedings of the 11th IEEE Real-Time Systems Symposium (RTSS 1990), pp. 278–287. IEEE-CS Press (1990)
23. Hennessy, M., Milner, R.: Algebraic laws for nondeterminism and concurrency. J. ACM **32**, 137–162 (1985)
24. Hermanns, H., Rettelbach, M.: Syntax, semantics, equivalences, and axioms for MTIPP. In: Proceedings of the 2nd International Workshop on Process Algebra and Performance Modelling (PAPM 1994), pp. 71–87. University of Erlangen, Technical Report 27-4 (1994)
25. Hillston, J.: A Compositional Approach to Performance Modelling. Cambridge University Press, Cambridge (1996)
26. Hoare, C.A.R.: Communicating Sequential Processes. Prentice Hall, Upper Saddle River (1985)
27. Jonsson, B., Ho-Stuart, C., Yi, W.: Testing and refinement for nondeterministic and probabilistic processes. In: Langmaack, H., de Roever, W.-P., Vytopil, J. (eds.) FTRTFT 1994. LNCS, vol. 863, pp. 418–430. Springer, Heidelberg (1994). https://doi.org/10.1007/3-540-58468-4_176
28. Jonsson, B., Yi, W.: Compositional testing preorders for probabilistic processes. In: Proceedings of the 10th IEEE Symposium on Logic in Computer Science (LICS 1995), pp. 431–441. IEEE-CS Press (1995)
29. Jou, C.-C., Smolka, S.A.: Equivalences, congruences, and complete axiomatizations for probabilistic processes. In: Baeten, J.C.M., Klop, J.W. (eds.) CONCUR 1990. LNCS, vol. 458, pp. 367–383. Springer, Heidelberg (1990). https://doi.org/10.1007/BFb0039071
30. Keller, R.M.: Formal verification of parallel programs. Commun. ACM **19**, 371–384 (1976)
31. Knast, R.: Continuous-time probabilistic automata. Inf. Control **15**, 335–352 (1969)
32. Kwiatkowska, M., Norman, G.: A testing equivalence for reactive probabilistic processes. In: Proceedings of the 5th International Workshop on Expressiveness in Concurrency (EXPRESS 1998), ENTCS, vol. 16, no. 2, pp. 114–132. Elsevier (1998)
33. Kwiatkowska, M., Norman, G., Segala, R., Sproston, J.: Automatic verification of real-time systems with discrete probability distributions. Theor. Comput. Sci. **282**, 101–150 (2002)
34. Larsen, K.G., Skou, A.: Bisimulation through probabilistic testing. Inf. Comput. **94**, 1–28 (1991)
35. Latella, D., Massink, M., de Vink, E.P.: Bisimulation of labelled state-to-function transition systems coalgebraically. Logical Methods Comput. Sci. **11**(4:16), 1–40 (2015)

36. Milner, R.: Communication and Concurrency. Prentice Hall, Upper Saddle River (1989)
37. Neuhäußer, M.R., Katoen, J.-P.: Bisimulation and logical preservation for continuous-time markov decision processes. In: Caires, L., Vasconcelos, V.T. (eds.) CONCUR 2007. LNCS, vol. 4703, pp. 412–427. Springer, Heidelberg (2007). https://doi.org/10.1007/978-3-540-74407-8_28
38. Park, D.: Concurrency and automata on infinite sequences. In: Deussen, P. (ed.) GI-TCS 1981. LNCS, vol. 104, pp. 167–183. Springer, Heidelberg (1981). https://doi.org/10.1007/BFb0017309
39. Parma, A., Segala, R.: Logical characterizations of bisimulations for discrete probabilistic systems. In: Seidl, H. (ed.) FoSSaCS 2007. LNCS, vol. 4423, pp. 287–301. Springer, Heidelberg (2007). https://doi.org/10.1007/978-3-540-71389-0_21
40. Puterman, M.L.: Markov Decision Processes: Discrete Stochastic Dynamic Programming. Wiley, Hoboken (1994)
41. Rabin, M.O.: Probabilistic automata. Inf. Control **6**, 230–245 (1963)
42. Segala, R.: Modeling and verification of randomized distributed real-time systems. PhD thesis (1995)
43. Segala, R.: A compositional trace-based semantics for probabilistic automata. In: Lee, I., Smolka, S.A. (eds.) CONCUR 1995. LNCS, vol. 962, pp. 234–248. Springer, Heidelberg (1995). https://doi.org/10.1007/3-540-60218-6_17
44. Segala, R.: Testing probabilistic automata. In: Montanari, U., Sassone, V. (eds.) CONCUR 1996. LNCS, vol. 1119, pp. 299–314. Springer, Heidelberg (1996). https://doi.org/10.1007/3-540-61604-7_62
45. Segala, R., Lynch, N.: Probabilistic simulations for probabilistic processes. In: Jonsson, B., Parrow, J. (eds.) CONCUR 1994. LNCS, vol. 836, pp. 481–496. Springer, Heidelberg (1994). https://doi.org/10.1007/978-3-540-48654-1_35
46. Seidel, K.: Probabilistic communicating processes. Theor. Comput. Sci. **152**, 219–249 (1995)
47. Song, L., Zhang, L., Godskesen, J.C., Nielson, F.: Bisimulations meet PCTL equivalences for probabilistic automata. Logical Methods Comput. Sci. **9**(2:7), 1–34 (2013)
48. Stewart, W.J.: Introduction to the Numerical Solution of Markov Chains. Princeton University Press, Princeton (1994)
49. Tracol, M., Desharnais, J., Zhioua, A.: Computing distances between probabilistic automata. In: Proceedings of the 9th International Workshop on Quantitative Aspects of Programming Languages (QAPL 2011), EPTCS, vol. 57, pp. 148–162 (2011)
50. Wolf, V., Baier, C., Majster-Cederbaum, M.: Trace machines for observing continuous-time Markov chains. In: Proceedings of the 3rd International Workshop on Quantitative Aspects of Programming Languages (QAPL 2005), ENTCS, vol. 153, no. 2, pp. 259–277. Elsevier (2005)
51. Yi, W., Larsen, K.G.: Testing probabilistic and nondeterministic processes. In: Proceedings of the 12th International Symposium on Protocol Specification, Testing and Verification (PSTV 1992), North-Holland, pp. 47–61 (1992)

Coordination Models and Languages

X-Klaim Is Back

Lorenzo Bettini[1]([✉])[iD], Emanuela Merelli[2][iD], and Francesco Tiezzi[2][iD]

[1] Dipartimento di Statistica, Informatica, Applicazioni,
Università di Firenze, Firenze, Italy
`lorenzo.bettini@unifi.it`
[2] School of Science and Technology, Computer Science Division,
Università di Camerino, Camerino, Italy
`{emanuela.merelli,francesco.tiezzi}@unicam.it`

Abstract. KLAIM is a coordination language specifically designed to model and program distributed systems consisting of mobile components interacting through multiple distributed tuple spaces. The KLAIM's theoretical foundations provided a solid ground for the implementation of the KLAIM's programming model. To practically program KLAIM-based applications, the X-KLAIM programming language has been proposed. It extends KLAIM with enriched primitives and standard control flow constructs, and is compiled in Java to be executed. However, due to the limits of X-KLAIM in terms of usability and the aging of the technology at the basis of its compiler, X-KLAIM has been progressively neglected. Motivated by the success that KLAIM has gained, the popularity that still has in teaching distributed computing, and its possible future exploitations in the development of modern ICT systems, in this paper we propose a renewed and enhanced version of X-KLAIM. The new implementation, coming together with an Eclipse-based IDE tooling, relies on recent powerful frameworks for the development of programming languages.

Keywords: Network-aware programming · Coordination language · KLAIM · X-KLAIM · Eclipse IDE

1 Introduction

In the mid-90s Rocco De Nicola, to whom this LNCS volume is dedicated, came up with the idea of combining the work on process algebras, to which he had turned his research interest so far, with Linda's notion of asynchronous generative communication. Linda is a coordination paradigm providing a set of primitives for decoupling communicating processes both in space and time [41]. Communication is achieved via a shared data repository, called *tuple space*, where processes *insert*, *read* and *withdraw* tuples (i.e., sequences of data items). The data retrieving mechanism uses *pattern-matching* to find the required data in the tuple space.

The first attempt is PAL (Process Algebra based on Linda, [35]), a process algebra obtained by embedding the Linda primitives for interprocess communication in a CSP-like process description language. Then, this language was

© Springer Nature Switzerland AG 2019
M. Boreale et al. (Eds.): De Nicola-Festschrift, LNCS 11665, pp. 115–135, 2019.
https://doi.org/10.1007/978-3-030-21485-2_8

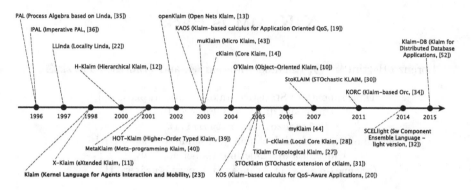

Fig. 1. The KLAIM family.

extended with *localities* (i.e., network addresses) as first-class citizens, which can be dynamically created and communicated. This capability is essential for achieving the so-called *network-aware programming*, where processes of a distributed application can explicitly refer and control the spatial structure of the network where they are currently deployed. The resulting formalism, LLINDA (Locality Linda, [22]), considers multiple tuple spaces that are distributed over a collection of network nodes, and uses localities to distribute/retrieve data over/from these nodes. As the code of processes is itself data, higher-order communication is enabled in order to support the definition of applications with *mobile* components. Syntax and semantics of LLINDA were later revised and cleaned up, thus obtaining the coordination language KLAIM (Kernel Language for Agents Interaction and Mobility, [23]). It allows one to design distributed systems consisting of stationary and mobile components interacting through multiple distributed tuple spaces.

Since then, a lot of effort has been made on KLAIM. On the one hand, several variants of KLAIM have been proposed to face the new challenges posed by the continuously evolving scenario of network-based technology. We show in Fig. 1 a timeline reporting the significant results on this research line. On the other hand, the theoretical foundations of KLAIM enabled the definition of several verification techniques (e.g., type systems [21,24–26,29,42,43], behavioral equivalences [27], flow logic [37], model checking [30,33,38]), as well as they provided a solid ground for the implementation of the KLAIM's programming model. As a further evidence of the success and influence that KLAIM has gained, we report here the number of citations that the seminal paper [23] has received at the time of writing: in Scopus it is cited by 362 documents, in Web of Science by 225, and in Google Scholar by 666.

In this paper, we focus on KLAIM's implementation. In order to program applications according to the KLAIM's paradigm, the toolchain depicted in Fig. 2 was initially developed. Since KLAIM was originally conceived as a formalism rather than as a full-fledged programming language, it had been extended with high-level process constructs to make the programming task more friendly.

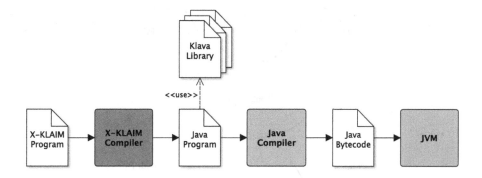

Fig. 2. X-Klaim toolchain.

The resulting programming language, called X-Klaim (eXtended Klaim, [11]), provides variable declarations, enriched communication primitives, assignments, conditionals, sequential and iterative process composition. The X-Klaim compiler translates X-Klaim programs into Java programs that exploit the Java package Klava (Klaim in Java, [8]), which provides the runtime environment for X-Klaim operations. The produced Java code can be then compiled and executed in the standard way.

Klava has evolved over the years and is still a maintained framework used for directly programming in Java according to the Klaim paradigm. Instead, the X-Klaim compiler has been progressively neglected, due to the aging of its underlying technologies, the lack of an IDE supporting the programming and debugging activity, and the limitations of X-Klaim on exchangeable data and supported expressions. These deficiencies undermined the usability of the language and, hence, its usage by the coordination community. To fill this gap, in this paper we propose a renewed and enhanced version of X-Klaim, by relying on powerful modern frameworks for the development of domain-specific programming languages. This is not only motivated by the success of Klaim, as shown above, but also by the fact that Klaim is still a popular language for teaching distributed computing in academia[1]. Moreover, we also envisage possible exploitations of the renewed X-Klaim as coordination language for developing modern ICT systems, in such domains as IoT, Smart Cities, e-Health, etc.

The new version of X-Klaim is available as an open source project. Sources and links to Eclipse update site and to complete Eclipse distributions are available from: https://github.com/LorenzoBettini/xklaim.

The rest of the paper is organized as follows. Section 2 provides an informal overview of Klaim, and introduces a simple running example concerning a leader election algorithm. Section 3 describes the renewed version of X-Klaim we propose, together with details on the implementation and the related Eclipse-based

---

[1] Klaim has been and is still taught on courses about coordination and distributed computing at, e.g., Università di Firenze, Università di Camerino, Università di Pisa, IMT Scuola Alti Studi Lucca, and Danmarks Tekniske Universitet.

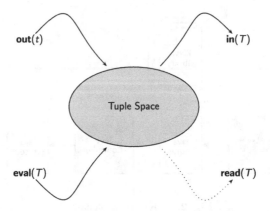

Fig. 3. Tuple space and Linda primitives.

IDE tooling. Finally, Sect. 4 concludes the paper by touching upon directions for future works.

2 KLAIM

In this section, we summarize the key features of KLAIM. It is a formal language specially devised to design distributed applications consisting of several (possibly mobile) components deployed over the nodes of network infrastructure. Although KLAIM is based on process algebras, it makes use of Linda-like asynchronous communication and supports distributed data management via multiple shared tuple spaces. A *tuple space* is a multiset of tuples, the latter consisting of sequences of data items. Processes interact by inserting, reading and withdrawing tuples to/from tuple spaces. The tuple retrieving mechanism relies on *pattern-matching* to find the required data in the tuple space. KLAIM enriches Linda primitives (see Fig. 3) with information about the network *localities* where processes and tuples are allocated. Localities can be explicitly referred and exchanged, thus supporting *network-aware programming*.

KLAIM syntax is shown in Table 1. We use the following disjoint sets: the set of *physical localities* (ranged over by l), the set of *logical localities* (ranged over by u), the set of *locality variables* (ranged over by r), the set of *value variables* (ranged over by x), the set of *process variables* (ranged over by X), and the set of *process identifiers* (ranged over by A). We also use a set of *expressions* (ranged over by e), whose exact syntax is omitted; we assume that expressions contain, at least, values (ranged over by V) and value variables. We shall use ℓ to denote a locality, either physical or logical, or a locality variable.

Nets N are finite collections of nodes where processes and data can be located (see Fig. 4). Nets are formed by composing nodes by means of the parallel operator $N_1 \parallel N_2$.

A computational node $l ::_\rho P$ is characterized by its physical locality l, a running process P and an *allocation environment* ρ. The latter acts as a name solver

Table 1. KLAIM syntax.

(Nets)

$N ::= l ::_\rho P \quad | \quad l :: \langle et \rangle \quad | \quad N_1 \parallel N_2$

(Processes)

$P ::= \textbf{nil} \quad | \quad a.P \quad | \quad P_1 \,|\, P_2 \quad | \quad X \quad | \quad A(\bar{p})$

(Actions)

$a ::= \textbf{out}(t)@\ell \quad | \quad \textbf{in}(T)@\ell \quad | \quad \textbf{read}(T)@\ell \quad | \quad \textbf{eval}(P)@\ell \quad | \quad \textbf{newloc}(r)$

(Tuples)

$t ::= e \quad | \quad \ell \quad | \quad P \quad | \quad t_1, t_2$

(Evaluated tuples)

$et ::= V \quad | \quad l \quad | \quad P \quad | \quad et_1, et_2$

(Templates)

$T ::= e \quad | \quad \ell \quad | \quad P \quad | \quad !x \quad | \quad !r \quad | \quad !X \quad | \quad T_1, T_2$

binding logical localities, occurring in the processes hosted in the corresponding node, into specific physical localities. The distinguished logical locality **self** is used by processes to refer to the physical locality of their current hosting node. The term $l::\langle et \rangle$ indicates that the evaluated tuple et is located to the physical locality l. The *tuple space* for a given locality consists of all the evaluated tuples located there.

Processes P are the active computational units of KLAIM. They can be executed concurrently, either at the same physical locality or at different localities. Processes are built up from the empty process **nil** (which does nothing), basic actions a, process variables X, and process calls $A(\bar{p})$, by means of the action prefixing operator $a.P$ and the parallel composition $P_1 \,|\, P_2$. Recursive behaviors are modeled via process definitions; it is assumed that each process identifier A has a single defining equation $A(\bar{f}) \triangleq P$, where $\bar{f}$ and $\bar{p}$ denote lists of formal and actual parameters, respectively. Hereafter, we do not explicitly represent process definitions (and their migration to make migrating processes complete), and assume that they are available at any node of a net. Process variables support *higher-order* communication, namely the capability to exchange (the code of) a process and possibly execute it. It is realized by first adding a tuple containing the process to a tuple space and then retrieving/withdrawing this tuple while binding the process to a process variable.

During their execution, processes perform some basic *actions* (see Fig. 5). Action **out**$(t)@\ell$ adds the tuple resulting from the evaluation of t to the tuple

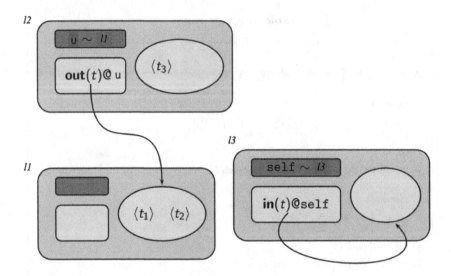

Fig. 4. The KLAIM net.

space of the target node identified by ℓ. A tuple is a sequence of the actual field, i.e., expressions, localities, locality variables, or processes. The evaluation of a tuple amounts to computing the values of its expressions. Action $\mathbf{in}(T)@\ell$ (resp. $\mathbf{read}(T)@\ell$) permits to withdraw (resp. read) tuples from the tuple space hosted at the (possibly remote) locality ℓ. If matching tuples are found, one is non-deterministically chosen, otherwise, the process is blocked. These retrieval actions exploit templates as patterns to select tuples in a tuple space. *Templates* are sequences of actual and formal fields, where the latter are written $!x$, $!r$ or $!X$ and are used to bind variables to values, physical localities, or processes, respectively. Templates must be evaluated before they can be used for retrieving tuples; their evaluation is like that of tuples, where formal fields are left unchanged by the evaluation. Intuitively, an evaluated template matches against an evaluated tuple if both have the same number of fields and corresponding fields do match; two values/localities match only if they are identical, while formal fields match any value of the same type. A successful matching returns a substitution associating the variables contained in the formal fields of the template with the values contained in the corresponding actual fields of the accessed tuple; such substitution is applied to the continuation process of the executed action. Action $\mathbf{eval}(P)@\ell$ sends the process P for execution to the (possibly remote) node identified by ℓ. Finally, action $\mathbf{newloc}(r)$ creates a new network node with physical locality bound to the locality variable r. Differently, from all the other actions, this latter action is not indexed with a target locality because it always acts locally.

We conclude the section with a simple example (inspired by those in [16]) aiming at showing KLAIM at work on the specification of a leader election algorithm.

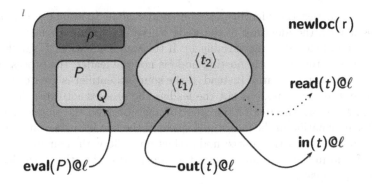

Fig. 5. The KLAIM node.

Example 1 (Running example in KLAIM*).* We consider a system where n participants distributed on the nodes of a network have to elect a leader. The system
is rendered in KLAIM as the following net:

$$l_0::_{[\mathbf{self}\mapsto l_0, u_{next}\mapsto l_1]}P \parallel l_1::_{[\mathbf{self}\mapsto l_1, u_{next}\mapsto l_2]}P \parallel \cdots \parallel l_{n-1}::_{[\mathbf{self}\mapsto l_{n-1}, u_{next}\mapsto l_0]}P$$
$$\parallel$$
$$l_{rg}::_{[\mathbf{self}\mapsto l_{rg}]}\langle "ID", 0\rangle \parallel l_{rg}::_{[\mathbf{self}\mapsto l_{rg}]}\langle "ID", 1\rangle \parallel \cdots \parallel l_{rg}::_{[\mathbf{self}\mapsto l_{rg}]}\langle "ID", n-1\rangle$$

The topology of the network is a ring, which is a common assumption for leader
election algorithms. Thus, the allocation environment of node l_i, in addition to
the standard mapping $\mathbf{self} \mapsto l_i$, maps the logical locality u_{next} to the physical
locality $l_{i+1 \bmod n}$ of the next node in the ring. The node identified by l_{rg} acts as a
random generator: it provides different identifiers, retrieved by the participants
at the outset. In this way, each participant will be uniquely identified by an
identifier selected randomly. The leader will be the participant with the smallest
identifier.

The process P deployed in each participant node is defined as follows:

$$\mathbf{in}("ID", !\, x_{id})@l_{rg}.$$
$$\mathbf{out}("ID", x_{id})@\mathbf{self}.$$
$$\mathbf{eval}(A_{checker}(x_{id}))@u_{next}.\mathbf{nil}$$

Once a participant has retrieved an identifier, it spawns a mobile *checker* process
to the next node. This process will travel along the ring to determine if the source
node has to be the leader.

The checker process is defined as follows:

$$A_{checker}(myId) \triangleq \mathbf{read}("ID", !\, x)@\mathbf{self}.$$
$$\mathbf{if}\ myId < x\ \mathbf{then}$$
$$\mathbf{eval}(A_{checker}(myId))@u_{next}.\mathbf{nil}$$
$$\mathbf{else\ if}\ myId > x\ \mathbf{then}$$
$$\mathbf{eval}(A_{notifier}(myId))@u_{next}.\mathbf{nil}$$
$$\mathbf{else}$$
$$\mathbf{out}("LEADER")@\mathbf{self}.\mathbf{nil}$$

The process carries the identifier of the source node (parameter $myId$) and compares it with the identifier of the node where it is running (retrieved via a **read** action and stored in the variable x). If the source identifier is smaller than the current one, the currently hosting node is not the leader: the process moves to the next node and restarts. Instead, if the source identifier is greater than the current one, the source node is not the leader: the process activates the *notifier* process that crosses the rest of the ring to come back to the source node and insert this information in the local tuple space. If the two identifiers are identical, the process is back on the source node (thus no node with a smaller identifier has been found in the ring) and inserts the information that this is the leader in the local tuple space.

The notifier process is defined as follows:

$$A_{notifier}(myId) \triangleq \textbf{read}(\text{``}ID\text{''}, !\, x)@\textbf{self}.$$
$$\textbf{if } x = myId \textbf{ then}$$
$$\textbf{out}(\text{``}FOLLOWER\text{''})@\textbf{self}.\textbf{nil}$$
$$\textbf{else}$$
$$\textbf{eval}(A_{notifier}(myId))@u_{next}.\textbf{nil}$$

It simply looks for the node with identifier $myId$; when it finds this node, it inserts in the local tuple space the information that this node is a follower.

Notably, for the sake of simplicity, we resort in this example of the conditional construct **if** e_{bcond} **then** P **else** Q. This is a macro that can be expressed here by exploiting pattern-matching and parallel composition as follows:

$$\textbf{out}(\text{``}ITE\text{''}, e_{bcond})@\textbf{self}.$$
$$(\textbf{in}(\text{``}ITE\text{''}, true)@\textbf{self}.P$$
$$\mid \textbf{in}(\text{``}ITE\text{''}, false)@\textbf{self}.Q)$$

3   X-Klaim 2.0

In this section we present the new version of X-Klaim. In particular, we first briefly recap the limitations of the old implementation of X-Klaim. Then, we illustrate the main features of the new version of X-Klaim by showing the implementation of the leader election example, which has been presented in Klaim in Example 1, Sect. 2. Finally, we present a few interesting additional features of the new version of X-Klaim, including its debugging mechanism integrated in the Eclipse IDE.

3.1   The Old Implementation

As mentioned in the Introduction, X-Klaim programs are compiled into Java programs that make use of the Java library Klava, which provides the runtime environment for X-Klaim operations. Klava is a Java library with some classes and methods to develop Java programs according to the Klaim programming model.

KLAVA is also meant to be used directly for programming in Java according to the KLAIM primitives and mechanisms. It allows the programmer to fully exploit Java mechanisms and the libraries of its huge ecosystem, while using the KLAIM programming model. While using KLAVA in Java, the programmer can benefit from IDE tooling, such as content assist, code navigation and debugging. However, this also implies that the programmer will have to deal with the verbosity of Java, which also makes it hard to directly use KLAIM primitives. For example, using KLAIM tuple space operations with KLAVA requires some additional Java instructions to set up the tuple (in particular, its formal fields if any) and to update possible variables representing formal fields with the values retrieved from pattern-matching. KLAVA strives for making Java programmers life easy but it can only do that by obeying the rules of Java. Originally, X-KLAIM was designed to give the programmers a language as close as possible to the KLAIM programming model, while still providing typical programming features such as variable declarations, control structures, etc. Thus, with X-KLAIM, the programmer could easily write KLAIM tuple space operations without additional boilerplate code. However, X-KLAIM programs could not rely on the Java ecosystem and making X-KLAIM program and Java program communicate with each other required too much programming effort. Moreover, no IDE mechanisms for the X-KLAIM compiler were implemented, forcing the X-KLAIM programmer to write an X-KLAIM program with a text editor, without any assistance from any IDE, explicitly call the X-KLAIM command line compiler waiting for possible compilation errors, and finally manually compile the generated Java code. Finally, debugging X-KLAIM programs was not possible: the programmer had to debug the generated Java code, and debugging automatically generated code is known to be quite hard. Summarizing, the benefits of the X-KLAIM programming language were evident only for very small prototype programs.

On the other hand, KLAVA kept on evolving during the years. For example, starting from our experience in implementing KLAVA network and code mobility mechanisms, we proposed a general framework for implementing Java network applications with code mobility, called IMC (Implementing Mobile Code) [7]. Then, we refactored KLAVA completely, implementing it in terms of IMC. Due to the limitations of X-KLAIM, though, we decided it was not worthwhile to port its compiler to the new version of KLAVA. This decision was also due to the limitations of the compilation technologies at that time and to the programming effort required to implement IDE mechanisms for the compiler, e.g., on top of Eclipse.

3.2 The New Implementation

Compiler and IDE technologies have evolved since then. In particular, the framework XTEXT quickly gained popularity. XTEXT [9] is an Eclipse framework for the development of programming languages and domain-specific languages (DSLs). Starting from a grammar definition, XTEXT generates a parser, an abstract syntax tree, and a complete IDE support based on Eclipse (e.g., editor with syntax highlighting, code completion, error reporting and incremental

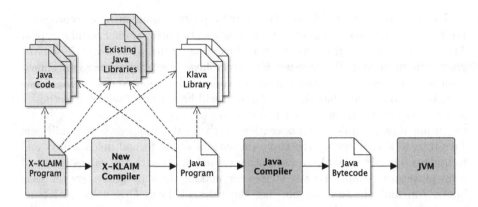

Fig. 6. X-KLAIM 2.0 toolchain (green color highlights the new elements, dashed arrows represent 'use' relationships and solid arrows represent 'input-output' relationships). (Color figure online)

building). XTEXT comes with good defaults for all the above mechanisms and the language developer can easily customize all such mechanisms.

Thus, we decided to re-implement X-KLAIM, targeting the new version of KLAVA. Since we implemented this new version of X-KLAIM from scratch, we also took the chance to make its syntax similar to mainstream languages, in particular, we gave it a Java-like shape. This means that programs written in the previous version of X-KLAIM are not compliant with this new version (however, we do not think that it is a considerable problem). Concerning the integration into Eclipse, we used XTEXT with all its powerful and useful mechanisms, mentioned above, which help the programmer. Furthermore, we also rely on another mechanism provided by XTEXT, that is, XBASE. XBASE is an extensible and reusable expression language, which provides a Java-like syntax and which is meant to be embedded in your own XTEXT DSL. By using XBASE in X-KLAIM, besides inheriting XBASE rich Java-like syntax, we also inherit its interoperability with Java and its type system. This means that an X-KLAIM program can seamlessly access any Java type available in the classpath of the project. This allows us to get rid of one of the worst drawbacks mentioned above of the previous implementation: Java and X-KLAIM programs can now interoperate automatically, and X-KLAIM programs can reuse the whole Java ecosystem. This also implies that one can write a Java application where some parts are written directly in Java using KLAVA, and other parts are written in X-KLAIM (using the parts written in Java).

The syntax of XBASE is similar to Java, but it removes much "syntactic noise" from Java (for example, terminating semicolons are optional, as well as other syntax elements like parenthesis when invoking a method without arguments). XBASE should be easily understood by Java programmers. Moreover, XBASE comes with a powerful type inference mechanism, compliant with the Java type

```
proc InitialProc(String nodeName) {
    val rg = getPhysical(logloc("rg"))
    val next = logloc("next")
    in("ID", var Integer xid)@rg
    out("ID", xid)@self
    eval(new CheckerProc(xid))@next
    in(var String result)@self
    println(nodeName + ": result is " + result)
}
```

Fig. 7. The process P of Example 1 deployed in each participant node implemented in X-KLAIM.

```
proc CheckerProc(Integer myId) {
    val next = logloc("next")
    read("ID", var Integer x)@self
    if (myId < x) {
        eval(new CheckerProc(myId))@next
    } else if (myId > x) {
        eval(new NotifierProc(myId))@next
    } else {
        out("LEADER")@self
    }
}

proc NotifierProc(Integer myId) {
    val next = logloc("next")
    read("ID", var Integer x)@self
    if (x == myId) {
        out("FOLLOWER")@self
    } else {
        eval(new NotifierProc(myId))@next
    }
}
```

Fig. 8. The processes $A_{checker}$ and $A_{notifier}$ of Example 1 implemented in X-KLAIM.

system, that allows the programmer to avoid specifying types in declarations when they can be inferred from the context.

The X-KLAIM compiler implemented with XTEXT/XBASE is now completely integrated into Eclipse. Thus, IDE mechanisms like content assist and code navigation are available in the X-KLAIM editor. Moreover, the compiler is now integrated in the automatic building mechanism of Eclipse: saving an X-KLAIM file automatically triggers the Java code generation, which in turns triggers the generation of Java byte-code. This avoids the manual compilation tasks of the previous implementation. Finally, it is now possible to debug an X-KLAIM program while the generated Java code is executed (as shown in Sect. 3.5). We show the renewed X-KLAIM toolchain in Fig. 6.

3.3   The Leader Election Example in X-KLAIM

We will now describe the main features of the new version of X-KLAIM by showing the implementation of the leader election example, which has been presented in KLAIM in Example 1, Sect. 2.

First of all, the process P deployed in each participant node is defined in X-KLAIM as shown in Fig. 7. Note that the types such as String and Integer are actually Java types, since, as mentioned above, X-KLAIM programs can refer

```
net LeaderElectionNet {
  node L1 [next -> L2] {
    eval(new InitialProc("L1"))@self
  }
  node L2 [next -> L3] {
    eval(new InitialProc("L2"))@self
  }
  node L3 [next -> L1] {
    eval(new InitialProc("L3"))@self
  }
  node RG logical "rg" {
    out("ID", 0)@self
    out("ID", 1)@self
    out("ID", 2)@self
  }
}
```

Fig. 9. The net of Example 1 implemented in X-KLAIM.

directly to Java types. Expressions and statements in X-KLAIM are based on the XBASE syntax. Variable declarations in XBASE start with **val** or **var**, for final and non-final variables, respectively. The type of the variable can be omitted if it can be inferred from the initialization expression. XBASE syntax has been extended with KLAIM operations. Formal fields in a tuple are specified as variable declarations, since, just like in KLAIM, formal fields implicitly declare variables that are available in the code after **in** and **read** operations. Boolean non-blocking versions of **in** and **read** are also available: **in_nb** and **read_nb**, respectively. **logloc** (and **phyloc**, not shown in the example) are syntactic sugar for creating instances of localities. Finally, **getPhysical** and **println** are Java methods available in the runtime library of X-KLAIM, which, of course, includes KLAVA. Notably, since X-KLAIM aims at being a programming language, localities, which in KLAIM can be used without explicit declarations, must be explicitly declared and initialized in X-KLAIM. The only exception is **self**, which is a predefined locality also in X-KLAIM. Since we are in a Java-like context, process invocation corresponds to the creation of an instance of the process (using the **new** operator); we did not use the same "invocation" syntax of KLAIM since that would conflict with the standard Java-like syntax for method invocation.

The processes $A_{checker}$ and $A_{notifier}$ of Example 1 are defined in X-KLAIM as shown in Fig. 8.

Finally, the net of Example 1 is defined in X-KLAIM as shown in Fig. 9 (here we fix the number of the nodes to 3). Note that the mapping for **self** is implicit in every node, so it does not have to be defined. Explicit locality mappings (corresponding to KLAIM allocation environments, Sect. 2) are specified for each node with the syntax [11 -> 12]. For example, the node L1 maps **next** to L2. A node can specify the logical locality with which it will be known in the containing net, with the **logical** clause, as in the node RG. If this clause is not specified, a node is automatically known to the net with a logical locality corresponding to its name (like L1, L2 and L3).

3.4 Additional Features

The syntax of net and nodes shown above allows the programmer to quickly specify a "flat" net, where all nodes are at the same level. However, X-KLAIM implements the hierarchical version of the KLAIM model as presented in [12, 13]. This implies that, if a node is not able to resolve a logical locality into a physical locality then it delegates it to the "parent" node, that is, to the containing **net**. However, the programmer can also define a **node** outside a **net** element and explicitly use the operations of **login** and **accept** (or the versions dealing explicitly with logical localities, **subscribe** and **register**). This will allow X-KLAIM programs to define a custom hierarchical net. For example, this is an X-KLAIM program defining a node accepting remote connections from other nodes, which will then be part of its network (note how physical localities are expressed in terms of the standard TCP syntax `host:port`):

```
node Receiver physical "localhost:9999" {
  while (true) {
    val remote = new PhysicalLocality
    accept(remote)
  }
}
```

and this is a possible client node connecting to this network and evaluating a process remotely:

```
node Sender [server -> phyloc("localhost:9999")] {
  login(server)
  val myLoc = getPhysical(self)
  eval({
    println(String.format("Hello %s...", server))
    println("...from a process coming from " + myLoc)
    out("DONE")@myLoc
  })@server
  in("DONE")@self
  logout(server)
  System.exit(0)
}
```

The above example also shows how X-KLAIM code can access Java code, like the static methods `String.format` and `System.exit`. Moreover, it also shows how X-KLAIM allows the programmer to specify anonymous processes, e.g., for remote evaluation with **eval** (just like KLAIM):

```
in(var String s)@self
eval( in(s)@self )@l
```

In the code snippet above, the process in(s)@self will be evaluated at the remote locality 1. Note that when a process migrates, it is closed with respect to the variables of the original enclosing scope, like the s in the example. Anonymous processes with several statements must be enclosed in a code block { . . . }, like in the previous Sender example. In order to insert an anonymous process, with code p_code, into a tuple space, the syntax proc { p_code } must be used. This is required to disambiguate with a code block that would be evaluated to produce a value to be part of the tuple:

> in(var String s)@self
> out(proc { in(s)@self })@1

A process can be retrieved from a tuple space with a formal field of type KlavaProcess (defined in the KLAVA library), e.g.,

> in(var KlavaProcess X)@self
> eval(X)@self

The above X-KLAIM code corresponds to the KLAIM process

$$\text{in}(!X)@\text{self}. \text{eval}(X)@\text{self}.\text{nil}$$

Code mobility is completely delegated to KLAVA and IMC, which automatically collect the Java classes of the migrating process so that they can be loaded at the remote destination (as described in details in [5]). However, in this new version of X-KLAIM, *strong mobility* is not supported yet. We will implement this feature in the compiler according to the transformation described in [6].

As a further improvement, the new version of X-KLAIM allows the programmer to fully exploit the recursive nature of processes in a way that was not possible in the previous version nor in KLAIM itself. In fact, a process can refer to itself with the Java keyword this, which has the same semantics as in Java. It allows a process to spawn itself to a remote site. This can also be used in anonymous processes. This mechanism allows one to write complex (possibly anonymous) recursive processes. For example, the process in Fig. 10 implements the leader election example without additional process definitions, showing how this correctly refers to the current anonymous process, even in the presence of nesting. This also shows how X-KLAIM automatically deals with the closure of the enclosing scope (e.g., the myId and next used by the anonymous migrating processes).

3.5   Debugging X-KLAIM Programs

As already anticipated, thanks to XTEXT/XBASE, the new version of X-KLAIM, and in particular its integration in Eclipse, allows the programmer to debug an X-KLAIM program, as shown in Fig. 11. In this example, based on the X-KLAIM code of Fig. 10, we set a breakpoint in the X-KLAIM program, and during the execution, we can see the current values of variables, either in the "Variables" Eclipse view or by hovering over a variable in the program (like myId).

```
proc InitialProc(String nodeName) {
  val rg = getPhysical(logloc("rg"))
  val next = logloc("next")
  in("ID", var Integer myId)@rg
  out("ID", myId)@self
  eval({ // anonymous process (1)
    read("ID", var Integer x)@self
    if (myId < x) {
      eval(this)@next // this refers to (1)
    } else if (myId > x) {
      eval({ // anonymous nested process (2)
        read("ID", var Integer x1)@self
        if (x1 == myId) {
          out("FOLLOWER")@self
        } else {
          eval(this)@next // this refers to (2)
        }
      })@next
    } else {
      out("LEADER")@self
    }
  })@next
  in(var String result)@self
  println(nodeName + ": result is " + result)
}
```

Fig. 10. The recursive process in X-Klaim with migrating operations, implementing altogether the processes of Figs. 7 and 8.

We believe that being able to debug an X-Klaim program directly is a crucial feature when programming distributed applications accessing remote tuple spaces and dealing with code mobility. The debugging mechanisms of X-Klaim are as powerful as the standard Java debugging mechanism of Eclipse. For example, during an X-Klaim debugging session, we can evaluate expressions on the fly. For example, as shown in Fig. 12, we can retrieve the current physical locality where the debugged process is executing, by calling the Klava method `getPhysical`.

Of course, the current debugging mechanism allows the developer to debug only a local running process. Currently, it is not possible to debug a process that runs on a remote node. In order to achieve also this mechanism, a dedicated debugging protocol should be implemented in the Klava runtime library. It will be interesting to investigate this feature as a future work.

Note that the X-Klaim Eclipse support also includes the ability to directly run or debug an X-Klaim file, with dedicated context menus: there's no need to run the generated Java code manually.

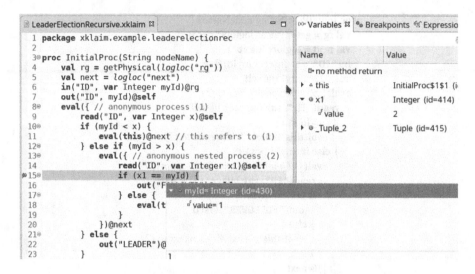

Fig. 11. Debugging an X-Klaim program.

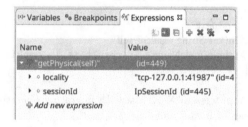

Fig. 12. Evaluating expressions while debugging an X-Klaim program.

4   Concluding Remarks

Motivated by the success that the Klaim language gained over the last years, and believing that still nowadays it can provide further contributions to the coordination research field and application area, we have brought X-Klaim back to life. In doing that, by resorting to modern compiler and IDE technologies, we have enhanced X-Klaim making it a usable and effective coordination language.

The fundamental novelties of this renewed version of X-Klaim are:

- Java-like syntax, which should be easily understood by programmers;
- full interoperability with Java, so that X-Klaim code can access the whole Java ecosystem;
- type inference mechanism, allowing programmers to avoid specifying types that can be inferred from the context;
- IDE support and debugging facilities;
- recursive definition of processes.

The support of these features clarifies how the contribution of this work represents a significant advancement with respect to the previous version of X-KLAIM introduced in [11]. Comparisons with other implementations of Linda-like languages and code mobility frameworks are provided in [8,11], such as Jada [17], MARS [15], Jini [3], JavaSpaces [48], IBM T Spaces [53], IBM Aglets [46], μCODE [49], Lime [50], Sumatra [2]. More recently, other implementations of the Linda paradigm have been proposed. GigaSpaces [1] is a commercial implementation of tuple spaces mainly used for big data analytics. Differently, from X-KLAIM, GigaSpaces supports database-like features, such as complex queries, transactions, and replication. This could be obtained in X-KLAIM by using its interoperability mechanisms to access Java code. Tupleware [4] is a framework providing a scalable (both distributed and centralized) tuple space. It is based on distributed hash tables, similar to other distributed implementations of tuple space like Blossom [51] and DTuples [45]. The focus of these frameworks is on the performance of the search in the distributed tuple space, rather than on the programming facilities to support the development of tuple-space-based applications. Differently from X-KLAIM, they do not consider code mobility features. Instead, LuaTS [47] provides a reactive event-driven tuple space system that also supports code mobility. While X-KLAIM is based on the mainstream Java technology, LuaTS relies on Lua. Finally, we refer to [18] for a recent survey of coordination tools, including both those based on Linda and the ones relying on different coordination models.

As future work, we plan to assess the effectiveness of X-KLAIM in programming distributed, possibly mobile, applications in different domains, such as IoT and Bioinformatics. To this aim, we will use X-KLAIM to implement different case studies from academia and industry. We also intend to appropriately validate the usability of the language, by involving students of BSc and MSc in Computer Science, as well as developers from different industrial settings.

Acknowledgements. The authors would like to take the opportunity to thank Rocco in this Festschrift contribution.

Lorenzo Bettini: Rocco was one of my professors at the University and the supervisor of my Master Thesis and of my PhD. He's the main person who introduced me to the charming world of research. He drove me, helped me and supported me for most of my academic career. He taught me so many things that I could hardly list them here. X-KLAIM was the main subject of my Master and PhD thesis and the starting point of my research cooperation with Rocco, thus I'm very happy to take this opportunity to "remove the dust" from X-KLAIM and to revive it in a modern shape. For all these reasons, it is an extreme pleasure (and honor) to take part to this Festschrift contribution.

Emanuela Merelli: While I was doing my Master's thesis at CNR in Pisa, in Via Santa Maria, Rocco De Nicola worked in a nearby building. From there I heard about his fame as a brilliant researcher. At that time, I never imagined that I could be adopted by one of his doctoral students. When Flavio arrived in Camerino he changed my scientific life and the evolution of the local Computer Science group. He generously introduced me to Rocco and to the whole scientific family of Italian researchers working on formal methods. I am very grateful to Rocco for having understood what it meant for me to be alone in Camerino coping with the difficulties that arose at that time. I am very grateful to him also for having supported my scientific growth, my career and having listened to my odd scientific thoughts, even if they were often not so rigorous as the community usually expects. He always encouraged me to go ahead without limits to creativity. Many important events happened since our first meeting, some beautiful and some painful. I thank Rocco for having contributed to the growth of part of the scientific family also in this side of Italy that sometimes quakes. I'm very proud to be part of Rocco's scientific family!

Francesco Tiezzi: I first met Rocco when I was a student at the University of Florence, where he introduced me to the realm of formal methods. He then gave me the opportunity of working with his research group, at Florence during my PhD and at IMT Lucca later. During these years, his guidance was fundamental for my professional and personal growth. Apart from what he taught me of a technical nature, for which I will always be grateful, the most important lesson that I have learnt from Rocco his the attitude he always had in his job. Everyday he shows the curiosity and the interest of a young researcher for the continuously evolving scenarios of computer science. What I appreciate most about Rocco is that he does with levity a 'serious' job like that of an academician. All this allows Rocco to be able to have a direct dialogue with everybody, from a student to a Turing-awarded researcher or a minister. For all of this, and for having supported me in all occasions, I would sincerely say "Grazie Rocco!".

References

1. GigaSpaces XAP v14.0 Documentation. https://docs.gigaspaces.com/xap/14.0/
2. Acharya, A., Ranganathan, M., Saltz, J.H.: Sumatra: a language for resource-aware mobile programs. In: Vitek, J., Tschudin, C. (eds.) MOS 1996. LNCS, vol. 1222, pp. 111–130. Springer, Heidelberg (1997). https://doi.org/10.1007/3-540-62852-5_10
3. Arnold, K., Scheifler, R., Waldo, J., O'Sullivan, B., Wollrath, A.: Jini Specification. Addison-Wesley, Boston (1999)
4. Atkinson, A.: Tupleware: A Distributed Tuple Space for the Development and Execution of Array-Based Applications in a Cluster Computing Environment. University of Tasmania, School of Computing and Information Systems thesis (2010)
5. Bettini, L.: A Java package for transparent code mobility. In: Guelfi, N., Reggio, G., Romanovsky, A. (eds.) FIDJI 2004. LNCS, vol. 3409, pp. 112–122. Springer, Heidelberg (2005). https://doi.org/10.1007/978-3-540-31869-9_11
6. Bettini, L., De Nicola, R.: Translating strong mobility into weak mobility. In: Picco, G.P. (ed.) MA 2001. LNCS, vol. 2240, pp. 182–197. Springer, Heidelberg (2001). https://doi.org/10.1007/3-540-45647-3_13
7. Bettini, L., De Nicola, R., Falassi, D., Lacoste, M., Loreti, M.: A flexible and modular framework for implementing infrastructures for global computing. In: Kutvonen, L., Alonistioti, N. (eds.) DAIS 2005. LNCS, vol. 3543, pp. 181–193. Springer, Heidelberg (2005). https://doi.org/10.1007/11498094_17
8. Bettini, L., De Nicola, R., Pugliese, R.: KLAVA: a Java package for distributed and mobile applications. Softw. Pract. Exp. **32**(14), 1365–1394 (2002)
9. Bettini, L.: Implementing Domain-Specific Languages with Xtext and Xtend, 2nd edn. Packt Publishing, Birmingham (2016)
10. Bettini, L., Bono, V., Venneri, B.: O'KLAIM: a coordination language with mobile mixins. In: De Nicola, R., Ferrari, G.-L., Meredith, G. (eds.) COORDINATION 2004. LNCS, vol. 2949, pp. 20–37. Springer, Heidelberg (2004). https://doi.org/10.1007/978-3-540-24634-3_5

11. Bettini, L., De Nicola, R., Pugliese, R., Ferrari, G.L.: Interactive mobile agents in X-Klaim. In: WETICE, pp. 110–117. IEEE Computer Society (1998)

12. Bettini, L., Loreti, M., Pugliese, R.: Structured nets in KLAIM. In: SAC, pp. 174–180. ACM (2000)

13. Bettini, L., Loreti, M., Pugliese, R.: An infrastructure language for open nets. In: SAC, pp. 373–377. ACM (2002)

14. Bettini, L., et al.: The klaim project: theory and practice. In: Priami, C. (ed.) GC 2003. LNCS, vol. 2874, pp. 88–150. Springer, Heidelberg (2003). https://doi.org/10.1007/978-3-540-40042-4_4

15. Cabri, G., Leonardi, L., Zambonelli, F.: Reactive tuple spaces for mobile agent coordination. In: Rothermel, K., Hohl, F. (eds.) MA 1998. LNCS, vol. 1477, pp. 237–248. Springer, Heidelberg (1998). https://doi.org/10.1007/BFb0057663

16. Calzolai, F., Loreti, M.: Simulation and analysis of distributed systems in KLAIM. In: Clarke, D., Agha, G. (eds.) COORDINATION 2010. LNCS, vol. 6116, pp. 122–136. Springer, Heidelberg (2010). https://doi.org/10.1007/978-3-642-13414-2_9

17. Ciancarini, P., Rossi, D.: Jada: coordination and communication for Java agents. In: Vitek, J., Tschudin, C. (eds.) MOS 1996. LNCS, vol. 1222, pp. 213–226. Springer, Heidelberg (1997). https://doi.org/10.1007/3-540-62852-5_16

18. Ciatto, G., Mariani, S., Louvel, M., Omicini, A., Zambonelli, F.: Twenty years of coordination technologies: state-of-the-art and perspectives. In: Di Marzo Serugendo, G., Loreti, M. (eds.) COORDINATION 2018. LNCS, vol. 10852, pp. 51–80. Springer, Cham (2018). https://doi.org/10.1007/978-3-319-92408-3_3

19. De Nicola, R., Ferrari, G., Montanari, U., Pugliese, R., Tuosto, E.: A formal basis for reasoning on programmable QoS. In: Dershowitz, N. (ed.) Verification: Theory and Practice. LNCS, vol. 2772, pp. 436–479. Springer, Heidelberg (2003). https://doi.org/10.1007/978-3-540-39910-0_21

20. De Nicola, R., Ferrari, G., Montanari, U., Pugliese, R., Tuosto, E.: A process calculus for QoS-aware applications. In: Jacquet, J.-M., Picco, G.P. (eds.) COORDINATION 2005. LNCS, vol. 3454, pp. 33–48. Springer, Heidelberg (2005). https://doi.org/10.1007/11417019_3

21. De Nicola, R., Ferrari, G.L., Pugliese, R.: Coordinating mobile agents via blackboards and access rights. In: Garlan, D., Le Métayer, D. (eds.) COORDINATION 1997. LNCS, vol. 1282, pp. 220–237. Springer, Heidelberg (1997). https://doi.org/10.1007/3-540-63383-9_83

22. De Nicola, R., Ferrari, G.L., Pugliese, R.: Locality based Linda: programming with explicit localities. In: Bidoit, M., Dauchet, M. (eds.) CAAP 1997. LNCS, vol. 1214, pp. 712–726. Springer, Heidelberg (1997). https://doi.org/10.1007/BFb0030636

23. De Nicola, R., Ferrari, G.L., Pugliese, R.: KLAIM: a kernel language for agents interaction and mobility. IEEE Trans. Softw. Eng. 24(5), 315–330 (1998)

24. De Nicola, R., Ferrari, G.L., Pugliese, R.: Types as specifications of access policies. In: Vitek, J., Jensen, C.D. (eds.) Secure Internet Programming. LNCS, vol. 1603, pp. 117–146. Springer, Heidelberg (1999). https://doi.org/10.1007/3-540-48749-2_6

25. De Nicola, R., Ferrari, G.L., Pugliese, R.: Programming access control: the KLAIM experience. In: Palamidessi, C. (ed.) CONCUR 2000. LNCS, vol. 1877, pp. 48–65. Springer, Heidelberg (2000). https://doi.org/10.1007/3-540-44618-4_5

26. De Nicola, R., Ferrari, G.L., Pugliese, R., Venneri, B.: Types for access control. Theor. Comput. Sci. 240(1), 215–254 (2000)

27. De Nicola, R., Gorla, D., Pugliese, R.: Basic observables for a calculus for global computing. In: Caires, L., Italiano, G.F., Monteiro, L., Palamidessi, C., Yung, M. (eds.) ICALP 2005. LNCS, vol. 3580, pp. 1226–1238. Springer, Heidelberg (2005). https://doi.org/10.1007/11523468_99

28. De Nicola, R., Gorla, D., Pugliese, R.: On the expressive power of klaim-based calculi. Electr. Notes Theor. Comput. Sci. **128**(2), 117–130 (2005)

29. De Nicola, R., Gorla, D., Pugliese, R.: Confining data and processes in global computing applications. Sci. Comput. Program. **63**(1), 57–87 (2006)

30. De Nicola, R., Katoen, J., Latella, D., Loreti, M., Massink, M.: Model checking mobile stochastic logic. Theor. Comput. Sci. **382**(1), 42–70 (2007)

31. De Nicola, R., Latella, D., Massink, M.: Formal modeling and quantitative analysis of KLAIM-based mobile systems. In: SAC, pp. 428–435. ACM (2005)

32. De Nicola, R., et al.: Programming and verifying component ensembles. In: Bensalem, S., Lakhneck, Y., Legay, A. (eds.) ETAPS 2014. LNCS, vol. 8415, pp. 69–83. Springer, Heidelberg (2014). https://doi.org/10.1007/978-3-642-54848-2_5

33. De Nicola, R., Loreti, M.: A modal logic for mobile agents. ACM Trans. Comput. Log. **5**(1), 79–128 (2004)

34. De Nicola, R., Margheri, A., Tiezzi, F.: Orchestrating tuple-based languages. In: Bruni, R., Sassone, V. (eds.) TGC 2011. LNCS, vol. 7173, pp. 160–178. Springer, Heidelberg (2012). https://doi.org/10.1007/978-3-642-30065-3_10

35. De Nicola, R., Pugliese, R.: A process algebra based on Linda. In: Ciancarini, P., Hankin, C. (eds.) COORDINATION 1996. LNCS, vol. 1061, pp. 160–178. Springer, Heidelberg (1996). https://doi.org/10.1007/3-540-61052-9_45

36. De Nicola, R., Pugliese, R.: Testing semantics of asynchronous distributed programs. In: Dam, M. (ed.) LOMAPS 1996. LNCS, vol. 1192, pp. 320–344. Springer, Heidelberg (1997). https://doi.org/10.1007/3-540-62503-8_15

37. De Nicola, R., et al.: From flow logic to static type systems for coordination languages. Sci. Comput. Program. **75**(6), 376–397 (2010)

38. Eckhardt, J., Mühlbauer, T., Meseguer, J., Wirsing, M.: Semantics, distributed implementation, and formal analysis of KLAIM models in maude. Sci. Comput. Program. **99**, 24–74 (2015)

39. Ferrari, G.L., Moggi, E., Pugliese, R.: Global types and network services. Electr. Notes Theor. Comput. Sci. **54**, 35–48 (2001)

40. Ferrari, G., Moggi, E., Pugliese, R.: MetaKlaim: meta-programming for global computing. In: Taha, W. (ed.) SAIG 2001. LNCS, vol. 2196, pp. 183–198. Springer, Heidelberg (2001). https://doi.org/10.1007/3-540-44806-3_11

41. Gelernter, D.: Generative communication in Linda. ACM Trans. Program. Lang. Syst. **7**(1), 80–112 (1985)

42. Gorla, D., Pugliese, R.: Enforcing security policies via types. In: Hutter, D., Müller, G., Stephan, W., Ullmann, M. (eds.) Security in Pervasive Computing. LNCS, vol. 2802, pp. 86–100. Springer, Heidelberg (2004). https://doi.org/10.1007/978-3-540-39881-3_10

43. Gorla, D., Pugliese, R.: Resource access and mobility control with dynamic privileges acquisition. In: Baeten, J.C.M., Lenstra, J.K., Parrow, J., Woeginger, G.J. (eds.) ICALP 2003. LNCS, vol. 2719, pp. 119–132. Springer, Heidelberg (2003). https://doi.org/10.1007/3-540-45061-0_11

44. Hansen, R.R., Probst, C.W., Nielson, F.: Sandboxing in myKlaim. In: ARES, pp. 174–181. IEEE (2006)

45. Jiang, Y., Xue, G., Jia, Z., You, J.: DTuples: a distributed hash table based Tuple space service for distributed coordination. In: GCC, pp. 101–106. IEEE (2006)

46. Lange, D.B., Mitsuru, O.: Programming and Deploying Java Mobile Agents Aglets. Addison-Wesley, Boston (1998)
47. Leal, M.A., de La Rocque Rodriguez, N., Ierusalimschy, R.: LuaTS - a reactive event-driven tuple space. J. UCS **9**(8), 730–744 (2003)
48. Mamoud, Q.H.: Getting Started With JavaSpaces Technology: Beyond Conventional Distributed Programming Paradigms (2005). https://www.oracle.com/technetwork/articles/java/javaspaces-140665.html
49. Picco, G.P.: μCODE: a lightweight and flexible mobile code toolkit. In: Rothermel, K., Hohl, F. (eds.) MA 1998. LNCS, vol. 1477, pp. 160–171. Springer, Heidelberg (1998). https://doi.org/10.1007/BFb0057656
50. Picco, G.P., Murphy, A.L., Roman, G.: LIME: Linda meets mobility. In: ICSE, pp. 368–377. ACM (1999)
51. van der Goot, R.: High performance Linda using a class library. Ph.D. thesis, Erasmus University Rotterdam (2001)
52. Wu, X., Li, X., Lafuente, A.L., Nielson, F., Nielson, H.R.: Klaim-DB: a modeling language for distributed database applications. In: Holvoet, T., Viroli, M. (eds.) COORDINATION 2015. LNCS, vol. 9037, pp. 197–212. Springer, Cham (2015). https://doi.org/10.1007/978-3-319-19282-6_13
53. Wyckoff, P., McLaughry, S.W., Lehman, T.J., Ford, D.A.: T spaces. IBM Syst. J. **37**(3), 454–474 (1998)

A Distributed Ledger Technology Based on Shared Write-Once Objects

Eva Maria Kuehn(⊠)

Faculty of Informatics, Compilers and Languages Group,
Institute of Information Systems Engineering, TU Wien,
Argentinierstr. 8, 1040 Wien, Austria
eva.kuehn@tuwien.ac.at

Abstract. Research on blockchain technologies and applications has exploded since Satoshi Nakamoto's seminal paper on Bitcoin. Everybody agrees that blockchain is a foundational technology, but neither has a unified definition of blockchain been established yet, nor does a commonly agreed upon standard exist. The basic principle of a blockchain is to maintain transactions on digital assets, without utilizing a central coordinator. Despite the assumed trustless environment, high security is promised.

The core technologies behind blockchain are well known in distributed computing. They comprise peer-to-peer replication and peer-to-peer consensus. In addition, cryptography is used to sign transactions and to achieve a timely order between them.

In this paper we show how a coordination middleware that relies on the virtual shared memory (VSM) paradigm can contribute to realizing a flexible and generally distributed ledger technology (DLT) that can serve as the basis for many different kinds of blockchain applications. As a proof-of-concept, the realization of different blockchain types, such as public and permissioned, and different consensus protocols are sketched on top of this VSM-based DLT.

Keywords: Virtual shared memory · Shared objects ·
Coordination system · Distributed ledger technology · Blockchain

1 Introduction

"Blockchain" is one of the most innovative and much-discussed future topics in computer science. In 2008, a decentralized method for transmitting electronic means of payment was published under the pseudonym Nakamoto [32]. It made it possible for the first time to securely exchange the electronic transfer of Bitcoins between two unknown parties without the need for a third trustworthy entity, such as a financial institution. This was possible by solving the double-spending problem.

© Springer Nature Switzerland AG 2019
M. Boreale et al. (Eds.): De Nicola-Festschrift, LNCS 11665, pp. 136–151, 2019.
https://doi.org/10.1007/978-3-030-21485-2_9

The underlying technology is called "distributed ledger technology" (DLT) and describes a sequence of data blocks, which is stored decentral in a peer-to-peer network.

Blockchain pursues a radically new philosophy over current IT approaches: There is no single central coordinator, but self-organizing, distributed "peers". The rules for their cooperation are agreed upon consensually. Data and transactions are replicated to all peers that independently verify their accuracy. Business processes become automated and thus faster, tamper-proof and transparent. The peers do not have to trust each other, but can still enter into secure business relationships.

Several transactions are collected in a so-called "block". It is not predetermined how many transactions a block shall comprise. Rather, this grouping is an optimization, as a consensus must be found on transaction execution, which requires a certain amount of effort. Therefore, the rationale for arranging transactions into groups (i.e., the block) is efficiency.

The participants in the network ("peers") agree on the content of the data blocks in a consensus process (for example, proof of work [1], proof of stake [2]). Cryptographic methods (public/private-key encryption) are used to ensure the immutability and verification of the data. Distributed data management allows a peer in the network to check the correctness of the data at any time.

The number of participating peers can be unlimited (public) or restricted (permissioned) [35]. Public blockchains are mainly found in the area of cryptocurrencies. Known representatives of these are Bitcoin [1], Litecoin [7], Ripple [9], and Ethereum[1] [3]. However, public blockchains are not suitable for use in companies. Business systems typically have a small number of authorized users sharing confidential information with each other. Therefore, permissioned blockchains such as Hydrachain [4], Quorum [6] or Hyperledger Fabric [5] are used.

Blockchains are characterized by the following advantages, which can be derived from the basic technologies used (peer-to-peer networks, cryptographic methods, etc.):

- **Immutability of the data:** Data blocks are verified and permanently stored in the blockchain after the consensus procedure. They cannot be subsequently changed by any of the participating peers. To ensure this property, a hash is created over the contents of the previous block and included in the current block. This creates the chaining of blocks, hence the name blockchain.
- **Distributed data management:** The blockchain is replicated to all peers in the network. Each peer keeps a copy of the entire "ledger", i.e., the entire blockchain.
- **Transparency:** Each peer sees all data at any time and can verify it. Data access can be limited by encryption for permissioned blockchains.

---

[1] Although the Ethereum protocol is not intended for permissioned blockchains, there exist permissioned Ethereum based variants like Quorum or Hydrachain.

There are numerous blockchain implementations (Ethereum [3], Hyperledger Fabric [5], Corda R3 [2], NEM [8], Stellar [10], etc.) that support the development of applications for different application areas. While Corda R3 is more specialized in the financial sector, Hyperledger Fabric offers a modular architecture that also enables blockchain applications in healthcare and supply chain management (SCM). Ethereum relies on a generic platform that is equally suitable for a variety of different applications.

With the popularization of blockchains, more and more businesses are looking for applications that take advantage of replicated, distributed peer-to-peer systems. High expectations have been raised on this fundamental technology, which rearranges the complex network of today's information and its impacts into an easy-to-understand structure—a "chain" of processes.

Everybody agrees that blockchain is a foundational technology, but neither has a unified definition of blockchain been established, nor does a commonly agreed upon standard exist, as Rocco De Nicola also points out in [34] for cloud-based approaches.

This paper therefore aims to present a unifying DLT approach that is based on a general virtual shared memory layer [27]. This middleware layer is flexible enough to realize the different interpretations of a blockchain.

The paper is structured as follows: Sect. 2 analyses requirements on a flexible distributed ledger technology (DLT). Section 3 summarizes virtual shared memory (VSM) approaches and their suitability to implement a DLT. In Sect. 4 the Coordination Kernel-based VSM is used to demonstrate that VSM offers a good abstraction level to realize DLTs with different requirements. A simplified public blockchain is additionally modeled. Section 5 summarizes the work and presents planned future work.

2   Distributed Ledger Technology (DLT)

This section discusses requirements on a flexible DLT:

Digital asset management. The DLT maintains assets that must exist in digitized form. It stores the value of the asset and its owner peer.

Trust in a trustless environment. Peers have different and diverging interests. They need not trust each other nor do they need to know each other. We have to expect that there are unauthorized individuals that might change the records.

Trustworthy transactions. A transaction is a transfer of rights on assets among peers. The transaction must be trustworthy so that one can determine at any time who is the owner of the asset.

Security. Transactions must be secured with help of cryptographic mechanisms. All peers possess a private and a public key. Each transaction contains the public key of the new owner and is signed with the private key of the current owner.

Chronological order. The time when a transaction was executed is relevant. The DLT must track the chronological order of (related) transactions. Therefore, the chronologically sorted chain data structure is valuable. It provides the irreversibility of records.

No central coordinator. A DLT shall avoid one single central coordinator who might influence or censor transactions on the assets. The assumption is that there is no trustworthy third party. All intermediaries and brokers shall be excluded. Instead, a direct interaction—based on P2P transmissions between all peers—takes place.

P2P replication. As there is no single server, the peers must administrate and store all data. Therefore, it is necessary that the data are copied to all distributed peer sites. We assume here that all peers are "full peers" that keep all the records. In reality, not every peer will store all data on its hard disk, but rather connect to another full peer.

Shared access. The data in a blockchain are shared among the peers that (eventually) must have a commonly agreed upon view of them (see consensus below). The type of allowed access to the data depends on the type of the blockchain, which is, e.g., global for public blockchains.

Concurrent access. All distributed peers concurrently and asynchronously access the data with regard to both reading and writing. Nevertheless, a defined level of eventual consistency must be guaranteed.

P2P consensus. All peers must eventually gain a consensual view of the assets and their ownerships. There is no strict consensus possible among distributed peers if we have to cope with system or network failures and do not trust the peers [24,31]. The ingenious solution of the Bitcoin blockchain layer is a statistical consensus based on proof-of-work. Every peer has to solve a complex mathematical task in order to be allowed to close a block. It is rewarded with Bitcoins for doing this work. Unfortunately, this solution is not environmentally friendly and, therefore, cannot be a sustainable solution to build on in the future. Consensus finding can be split into two layers: (1) on the infrastructure layer for which the DLT is responsible (all peers agree on the right blocks and their order), and (2) on the application layer.

Immutability. The chain data structure must not be altered. In other words, it is "write-once", which makes it tamper-free.

Persistence. After a crash, a peer must be able to restore the entire blockchain. It must be permanent and recoverable.

Provenance. The history of each asset must be transparent, meaning that from its first occurrence in the blockchain, all transactions on it and their respective order must be visible. This is important and enables every peer to autonomously verify the correctness of a transaction, i.e., whether all its preconditions are fulfilled. Proving the provenance of anything helps to build an "Internet of trust".

Privacy and anonymity. Depending on the kind of blockchain (public or permissioned), the contents of transactions are visible to all peers or only a group. In a public blockchain, for instance, all data are visible to everyone. Another aspect is the identity of the peers, which also depends on the type of the blockchain. E.g., in a public one, the peers are anonymous. However, in Bitcoin's blockchain, for example, we can only speak about pseudonymity: The chain of transactions can be retraced, meaning that one sees which transactions were issued by the same peer (albeit this peer's identity is not known).

Transparency. All transactions are visible and can be verified by everyone.

Peer verification. Each peer can verify the correctness of a block, i.e., all transactions it contains and whether its chronological order is correct. In fact, it is obliged to do so, because otherwise it must not accept a block.

User-defined rules. An advanced feature of a blockchain, which makes it useful for applications beyond cryptocurrencies, is the definition of rules. These rules are small application programs (also termed "smart contracts") that define and trigger transactions between nodes if certain conditions are fulfilled on the blockchain. The rules are automatically executed by the blockchain. Basically, rules cannot be changed (cf. write-once property on the blockchain), but if the peers find a consensus, the overall effect of the rules can be altered due to the addition of other ones. Rules can be complex: They represent business rules that require a lot of events. Moreover, multi-party interactions are possible, i.e., processes that involve two or more parties.

Availability. The availability of the blockchain is given through the P2P replication. As long as there is a peer that is interested in the blockchain and keeps a copy of it, the blockchain exists.

In detail, these requirements will clearly depend on the overall requirements of the respective blockchain application. A general DLT must be able to map concrete needs in an easy way.

3   Virtual Shared Memory Approaches

Virtual shared memory (VSM) provides a different communication paradigm than messaging. Instead of sending messages, a shared "space" is provided. The participants communicate by accessing data in this space, which serves as communication medium.

3.1   Shared Tuples Without Identity

The pioneering work on VSM is the well-known classic Linda Tuple Space [25]. It is a seminal work in the area of coordination languages and models, and has triggered a plethora of research work in the coordination community, where Rocco De Nicola is one of the leading and inspiring researchers (see, e.g., [20]). In a nutshell, the shared data are so-called "tuples" which are semi-structured data with an arity and determined field positions and types. Tuples have no identity, but are retrieved by means of template matching. The operations of a Tuple Space foresee the writing of a tuple into the space and the (destructive) reading of a tuple with the template matching query mechanism. Initially, the Tuple Space was designed to program with parallelism. Later on, when networks became faster, it became a new communication and coordination model for distributed programming. Its advantages are the high-level abstraction it provides and the simple API. With Java Spaces [11], the model has experienced a breakthrough in the developer community. A notification operation, which informs in real-time about the arrival of new tuples that fulfill a template, has been introduced by Java Spaces as well as a transaction mechanism.

Rocco De Nicola has contributed valuable research on Tuple Spaces and coordination models and languages with regard to formal foundations (e.g., [23]), mobility and programming with localities (e.g., KLAIM [12–14, 18, 19, 22]), software engineering (e.g., [21]) and recently on benchmarking [16, 17] of the Tuple Space implementations GigaSpaces, KLAIM, MozartSpaces (XVSM) and Tupleware.

3.2   Shared Objects with Identity

Another VSM approach is the "Coordination Kernel", a middleware for write-once, coordinated, shared "communication objects". It was first introduced in [27] and later extended towards updateable objects in [28]. In the following, the original specification of the Coordination Kernel [27] with write-once objects is illustrated.

Like in Tuple Spaces, asynchronous access to shared data in a space is provided. The shared data in the Coordination Kernel are denoted as "objects", because they have a network-wide unique identity termed OID (object identity). It is important to clarify that a communication object is not an object in the classic object-oriented sense, as it does not support the inheritance of methods and functionality—this could be a matter of further research. A communication object only provides encapsulation of data—it is in this sense a shared data with a unique URL. Such an object can be structured and contains OIDs of other objects as sub-data fields.

Objects are write-once. This means that after creation, only one peer is allowed to write data to the object. The life-cycle of a communication object is as follows:

1. **Creation.** First, the object is created at one peer site and the Coordination Kernel generates a unique OID for it. The object is undefined after creation: it still has no data value. Trying to read it will cause an exception or blocking (depending on whether a synchronous or asynchronous API is used).
   On object creation, the persistence (volatile or permanent) and a replication strategy (see "asynchronous replication" below) are also configured for the object. If the object is permanent, it can be recovered after system failures. For the blockchain use case, we will use permanent objects.
   Network failures are masked in any case. Each communication object may have its own replication strategy.
2. **Sharing.** An OID can be published on one or more name servers with respective access rights from where it can be retrieved by name. A further sharing possibility is to call a process (termed "entry" in [27]) at another peer's site,

passing the OID in the parameter list of the process. A last possibility is to write an OID into the data of an object that a peer already knows. These are the three ways a peer can gain the access rights of an object.

The concurrent access is controlled by means of transactions: Read and write operations can be grouped into atomic actions.

3. **Asynchronous replication.** A peer that possesses an OID maintains a local copy of the object. The replication strategy implements a certain P2P topology for the distributed sharing of this object. It is responsible for ensuring that all peers in the network eventually have the same view of the object. As the object has only two states (namely undefined and defined), in case of network failures or partitions it might only happen that some peers do not have the information about the data of the object yet, thinking it is still undefined. However, it is impossible for peers to have different views of a defined object's data.

The time when the P2P transmission of the data takes place depends on the chosen strategy. One supported and implemented strategy is, e.g., "passive replication with a deep object tree" (PRD). PRD builds up a tree topology, whereby the peer that possesses the root of the object tree is the primary copy owner. This means it is allowed to write to the object by using a transaction. If a peer that is not the primary copy owner wants to write to the object, it must trigger a distributed protocol in order to get the primary copy.

The flags for PRD supported so far are eager and lazy replication. With eager replication, a written value is immediately propagated to all other sharing sites downstream in the PRD tree, whereas with lazy replication the changes are only propagated on-demand in a lazy way, i.e., when the respective site wants to read this object. There is no difference between the eager and lazy options for the application; they only cause different messaging behavior in the network.

Many peers might want to concurrently write data into an object using a transaction. Upon commitment of the transaction, the primary copy of all objects that shall be written in this transaction must be obtained by means of the PRD protocol. Having a primary copy of an object means having an implicit lock on it. Note that explicit locks are avoided, as this could lead to complex deadlock situations in a distributed system. If one of these objects is already defined, the transaction commit will fail.[2] The strategy resolves conflicts by considering the ID of the transaction in which the object is written as a network wide time-stamp [29]. This allows a priority among transactions (older ones have higher priority) to be determined. Therefore, if two or more peers compete to acquire the primary copy of an undefined object, the oldest transaction will win. The others continue to (re)gain the needed primary copies within their specified transaction timeout. A younger transaction must

---

[2] As an advanced feature, the transaction mechanism also supports weaker forms of commit. In this case, the transaction will not fail and rollback, but report an error and allow certain operations to be withdrawn and new ones to be possibly added in order to "repair" the transaction.

give away a primary copy that it has already acquired in its commit phase if an older transaction requires it. Once a transaction has all primary copies it needs, it will no longer give away primary copies and will successfully commit. One of the peer transactions will therefore "win", i.e., be the first to successfully write and commit data into the object. These data cannot be overwritten later on, as the object is write-once. Depending on eager or lazy replication, the written data are propagated respectively to the descendant peer sites in the PRD tree.

Note that message sending must also be persisted if the object is recoverable. Critical messages are retried until an acknowledgment is received. This way, the Coordination Kernel follows the principles of the "end-to-end argument in system design" [33].

4. **Resolving of administrative information.** After a peer site has received data for an object from an ancestor and if it has issued the propagation to its descendants, it clears the administrative information about the PRD tree structure.

5. **Garbage collection.** As objects have an OID, it is possible to implement an automatic garbage collection mechanism based on a reference counting of which peer still holds a copy of the object. If a peer process terminates properly, it gives up its reference to the object. Everlasting processes are recovered with their image, see [27]; they thus regain access to all objects they had before. Each name server clearly is an everlasting process. Deleting objects must be done explicitly in this case. Note that the removal of the object will be deferred by the Coordination Kernel until no descendants exist any more in the object's P2P topology.

The supported operations on a communication object are: create, read, write and delete. In addition, a notification that informs about the writing of data into an object is supported.

Each distributed site has the same program of the Coordination Kernel running on it and maintaining the shared objects. The Coordination Kernel itself is a language-independent framework used by applications possibly written in different programming languages.

An extension of the Flex transaction model [15] is employed as distributed transaction mechanism. This model provides nested transactions and relaxes the isolation ("I") property of ACID transactions [26]. A sub-transaction may commit early; should the enclosing top-transaction fail, an optional compensation action is executed for the successfully committed sub-transaction. In addition to compensation actions, on-commit and on-abort actions are also supported. These trigger the start of a process either if the transaction commit succeeds or fails. Moreover, the transaction model controls the execution of remote processes and sub-transactions.

Communication objects may be structured and contain the OIDs of other communication objects as members. Thus, arbitrary and infinite data structures can be created; for the blockchain use case, e.g., linked lists ("streams") will be used. Even more efficient data structures that are nevertheless able to keep record of the ordering of a blockchain's blocks, e.g., trees, can be built up with OIDs.

There is no optimal replication strategy that fits every application. For example, applications in which the participating peers and their number are known have different requirements than those in which all peers are anonymous and everyone can dynamically join at any time.

The Coordination Kernel architecture foresees the addition of new strategies to the framework. In Sect. 4 we will use the implemented PRD protocol, but in future work other P2P protocols, e.g., based on Paxos [30], will be used—in fact, any consensus known from current blockchain implementations is thinkable. These protocols are responsible for the consensus finding at the DLT layer about the chain of blocks. Due to its tree structure topology, the PRD protocol has the following peculiarities: A peer that wants to write data into an object is dependent on the availability of its ancestors in the tree. This can e.g., be improved by providing alternative primary copies and adding a voting protocol.

3.3 Suitability for DLT

The major difference between Tuple Space-based VSMs and the Coordination Kernel-based VSM is that the latter provides unique OIDs, defines a P2P architecture, provides built-in exchangeable P2P replication strategies, provides a flexible transaction model, has strong network links (i.e., the OID references), a security concept based access control lists for these OIDs (only authorized processes may access an object), and enforces write-once behavior.

These properties map to the fundamental concepts of blockchains in a natural way:

Peer-to-peer (serverless): P2P Coordination Kernel architecture conception.
Distribution: distributed peer sites.
Consensus and replication: flexible, distributed, nested transaction on objects and built-in and selectable replication strategies.
Block: object with persistence, a well-defined data structure, and a certain strategy.
Timely order of blocks: block linking (time/order preserving) with help of OIDs.
Security: objects are protected against illegal access: Only processes that have legally gained an OID are allowed to read, write or delete the object.
Tamper proof: write-once property of communication objects.
Smart contract: transactional process that is automatically fired (using notifications) if the necessary conditions are fulfilled.

4   Proof-of-Concept: Blockchain Realizations

As a proof-of-concept for the flexibility of a VSM-based DLT, a fictive blockchain is informally modeled with help of the Coordination Kernel and variants are discussed. The blockchain use case is related to the multi-database (MDBS) use case shown in [27]. The MDBS use case realizes a global consensus about a set of application transactions (txs) to be executed by autonomous local systems (LSYSs), which are the distributed peer sites. The set of txs is termed global tx (GTX). The GTX shall be executed atomically ("all or nothing"). Eventual consistency due to the assumed asynchronicity of the system is allowed.

In the blockchain use case, the LSYSs issue txs on assets, so the trigger comes from the peers instead of from one site where the LSYS txs are formulated. These txs form the GTX which must be accepted by all peers. Both use cases have in common that a kind of consensus protocol is needed at application level. In the MDBS use case an asynchronous two-phase-commit protocol (2PC) is implemented, which automatically semantically undoes early committed sub-txs at the LSYSs if the GTX fails. Eventually all LSYSs will reach a consistent state.

We show a model of a simplified public cryptocurrency blockchain. The verification is carried out by a definable group of peers which is determined for each block. The consensus rule says that a majority of these peers must have positively verified the block.

We assume that the PRD protocol fulfills the availability requirement sufficiently. This assumption is valid, as the protocol can easily be exchanged by another one, that e.g., supports a replication group for the primary copy.

4.1 Data Structures

Figures 1, 2, 3, 4 and 5 show the data structures for peer, linked block, tx, coin and verification. In the graphical notation, rectangles mark data structures and basic data types, whereas circles denote OIDs.

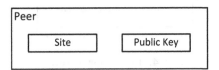

Fig. 1. Peer data structure.

A peer (see Fig. 1) has a site and a public key. Its OID is published on a name server under a unique nickname so that it can be retrieved by other peers without knowing its identity.

A block (see Fig. 2) of the blockchain has a set of tx OIDs, and two OIDs that link it with the other blocks in the chain, termed "Next" and "Alt". Next is the OID of the next block for the normal case. Alt also refers to a block; its semantics will be explained below. In addition, a block has a "Verification" OID that refers to an object that controls the verification process of this block. As optimization, also a Prev OID could be added that is the OID of the previous block, to ease the navigation in the chain.

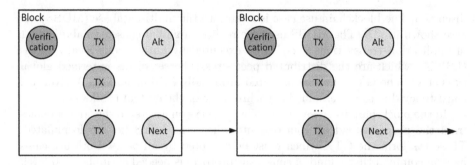

Fig. 2. Chain of blocks data structure.

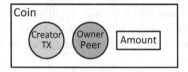

Fig. 3. Coin data structure.

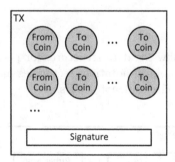

Fig. 4. TX data structure.

A coin (see Fig. 3) has a creator tx OID (this is the application tx in which this coin was created), the OID of its current owner peer, and the amount that is transferred to the current owner by the creator tx.

A tx (see Fig. 4) consists of records where each record has a "FromCoin OID" and several "ToCoin" OIDs. In addition it includes the signature of the peer that issues the tx. The semantics of the tx are that the coins denoted by FromCoin OID are transferred to the respective ToCoin OIDs.

A verification structure (see Fig. 5) has a field termed "N" stating how many peers must successfully verify the block so that it is considered valid, and a number of pairs, each consisting of a verifier peer OID and a verify result OID. The verifier peer OID refers to a peer site at which a verification process is triggered. The verify result OID serves to hold the result of the verification.

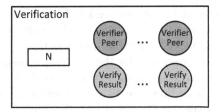

Fig. 5. Verification data structure.

4.2   Program Logic

If a peer wants to transfer one or more coins to other peers[3], it creates a new tx object. For each coin that shall be transferred, a ToCoin OID is created for each recipient peer and the information about the creator transaction, owner peer and amount are written into it in a Coordination Kernel transaction. Note that the owner peer object contains the public key of the peer. The tx object is committed and signed with the private key of the peer. This mechanism is similar to that in Bitcoin: Since the public key of the peer is known to everyone, the tx can be verified as stemming from this peer. Finally, the peer publishes the OID of the tx object on one or more "dashboards" (not explicitly modeled; they are streams of tx OIDs) to which the peers subscribe.

Each peer is continuously notified about new txs and tries to add a next block to the chain. The peer will receive rewards for issuing a correct block. It includes this rewarding tx into the new block as well. For a new coin of this kind, the creator tx is a fixed system tx OID. The more txs the block contains the higher its reward is (in an exponential way) in order to motivate the peer to wait until several txs are available and not to build blocks that are too small. First the peer builds up a data structure for the new block. The peer verifies the tx OIDs that it puts into the block data structure: (1) that the txs must have valid FromCoins, (2) the txs must not yet be included in a previous block, and (3) that the signature is correct. Then it creates new objects for Verification, Alt and Next. Their OIDs are set in the data structure for the new block. Then it creates and initializes a verification data structure. Finally the peer creates a Coordination Kernel transaction which it uses to write:

- the verification data structure into the verification OID, and
- the new block data structure into the Next OID of the currently last block in the chain.

Note that the Coordination Kernel will only accept valid data structures. If the commit succeeds, a new block has been linked to the blockchain.

The verification process works as follows: All peers listen to information being written into verification objects. If they occur in the verifier peers list, they start

---

[3] If a peer wants to transfer only a sub-amount of a coin, then it will transfer the rest to itself by creating a ToCoin at its own site.

to verify the correctness of the respective block and write in a Coordination Kernel transaction their signed verification result in the respective OID. Each peer that receives a next block[4] can either perform the verification of the block by itself and proceed[5], or it may wait for the verification result of the verifier peer group. This group quorum mechanism serves to "seal" a block. If the defined majority has been reached, then the block is correct. If no majority can be reached any more, then the Alt OID of the block comes into use. The Alt OID refers to the alternative chain that replaces the current block that could not be verified. On the alternative chain again the same alternative mechanism is applied.

This verification mechanism implements the consensus protocol at the application level. Each peer is responsible to actively check the verification result and to autonomously decide which chain to follow.

4.3 Variants

Modeling blockchains with different requirements will only cause slight changes to the model. This is a proof-of-concept that the underlying VSM-based DLT provides a good and flexible abstraction.

A permissioned blockchain prescribes that only a pre-defined and identified number of peers may access the blockchain. This would require the objects to be published on name servers with access control, and the dashboard to be protected with passwords.

A different consensus mechanism at the application level—that replaces the shown group quorum mechanism—would require another verification data structure with different semantics. For the proof-of-work consensus, e.g., the miner peer must solve a mathematical puzzle and write the result into the verification object (relating to the "nonce" used in the Bitcoin protocol). Peers only accept a block if the nonce is correct. Note that in the case of OID links the inefficient mechanism of switching to the longest blockchain is not necessary. Due to the OID mechanism and the replication strategy of the Coordination Kernel, all peers always have a consistent view of what the next block is. However, they need to actively switch to the alternative chain if the verification has failed.

5   Conclusion

In this paper we have shown how a virtual shared memory (VSM)-based coordination middleware eases the implementation of distributed ledgers which form the backbone of blockchains. The reference to Rocco De Nicola's work is found in coordination models and languages, shared data, Linda Tuple Space, distributed systems, peer-to-peer networks, replication and his recent contributions to cloud-based blockchain solutions and standards. As no commonly agreed upon

---

[4] Eager replication is used for all objects.

[5] The peer shall reexamine the verification result of the peer group, which must be the same as its own, if the verifier peers did not lie.

blockchain standard exists yet, we believe that it is therefore important to have distributed ledger technologies (DLTs) that can be tailored to the needs of the respective blockchain application.

The classic Tuple Space model supports tuples that are retrieved by means of template matching. The Coordination Kernel foresees also shared data in a space with asynchronous access and notification facilities. As a VSM middleware concept it manages distributed communication objects in a peer-to-peer (P2P) fashion. It has been designed as a general coordination layer to support complex distributed coordination scenarios.

However, it differs from the classical Tuple Space-based approaches in that the shared objects have a unique identifier called the object id (OID). The advantages of the here presented approach over Tuple Spaces is that these OIDs form strong links in the network and are used to chain the blocks of the blockchain. The blocks usually form a chain, but sometimes even more flexible structures, which can easily be accomplished with OID links, have a greater benefit.

The realization of a simplified public blockchain with the Coordination Kernel-based DLT was presented. Variants of it are easy to establish, as is demonstrated by the flexibility of the VSM-based DLT. The reason is that the Coordination Kernel already provides the core technologies needed, like P2P replication and consensus, security, network-wide links, a flexible transaction model and the write-once paradigm for data. These properties map to the fundamental concepts of blockchains in a natural way.

Future work will deal with formal foundations of the Coordination Kernel, the specification and verification of other replication strategies, and the usage of coordination language primitives to model smart contracts.

In memoriam Peter Kühn (1982–2018).

References

1. Bitcoin is an innovative payment network and a new kind of money. https://bitcoin.org/en/
2. Corda R3. https://www.r3.com/corda-platform/. Accessed 01 Apr 2019
3. Ethereum. https://www.ethereum.org/. Accessed 01 Apr 2019
4. Hydrachain. https://github.com/HydraChain/. Accessed 01 Apr 2019
5. Hyperledger Fabric. https://www.hyperledger.org/projects/fabric/. Accessed 01 Apr 2019
6. J.P. Morgan Quorum Whitepaper. https://github.com/jpmorganchase/quorum-docs/blob/master/Quorum%20Whitepaper%20v0.1.pdf. Accessed 01 Apr 2019
7. Litecoin. https://litecoin.org/. Accessed 01 Apr 2019
8. NEM. https://nem.io/. Accessed 01 Apr 2019
9. Ripple. https://ripple.com/. Accessed 01 Apr 2019
10. Stellar. https://www.stellar.org/. Accessed 01 Apr 2019
11. Arnold, K., Hupfer, S., Freeman, E.: JavaSpaces Principles, Patterns, and Practice. Addison-Wesley Professional, Boston (1999)
12. Bettini, L., et al.: The KLAIM project: theory and practice. In: Priami, C. (ed.) GC 2003. LNCS, vol. 2874, pp. 88–150. Springer, Heidelberg (2003). https://doi.org/10.1007/978-3-540-40042-4_4

13. Bettini, L., De Nicola, R.: Mobile distributed programming in X-KLAIM. In: Bernardo, M., Bogliolo, A. (eds.) SFM-Moby 2005. LNCS, vol. 3465, pp. 29–68. Springer, Heidelberg (2005). https://doi.org/10.1007/11419822_2

14. Bettini, L., De Nicola, R., Ferrari, G.L., Pugliese, R.: Mobile applications in X-KLAIM. In: WOA 2000: Dagli Oggetti agli Agenti. 1st AI*IA/TABOO Joint Workshop "From Objects to Agents": Evolutive Trends of Software Systems, Parma, Italy, pp. 1–6 (2000)

15. Bukhres, O., Elmagarmid, A.K., Kühn, E.: Implementation of the Flex Transaction Model. IEEE Data Eng. Bull. **16**(2), 28–32 (1993)

16. Buravlev, V., De Nicola, R., Mezzina, C.A.: Tuple spaces implementations and their efficiency. In: Lluch Lafuente, A., Proença, J. (eds.) COORDINATION 2016. LNCS, vol. 9686, pp. 51–66. Springer, Cham (2016). https://doi.org/10.1007/978-3-319-39519-7_4

17. Buravlev, V., De Nicola, R., Mezzina, C.A.: Evaluating the efficiency of Linda implementations. Concurr. Comput. Pract. Exp. **30**(8), e4381 (2018)

18. De Nicola, R.: From process calculi to KLAIM and back. Electr. Notes Theor. Comput. Sci. **162**, 159–162 (2006). US patent US6848109B1. https://patents.google.com/patent/US6848109

19. De Nicola, R., Ferrari, G.L., Pugliese, R.: KLAIM: a kernel language for agents interaction and mobility. IEEE Trans. Softw. Eng. **24**(5), 315–330 (1998)

20. De Nicola, R., Julien, C. (eds.): COORDINATION 2013. LNCS, vol. 7890. Springer, Heidelberg (2013). https://doi.org/10.1007/978-3-642-38493-6

21. De Nicola, R., Kühn, E. (eds.): SEFM 2016. LNCS, vol. 9763. Springer, Cham (2016). https://doi.org/10.1007/978-3-319-41591-8

22. De Nicola, R., Loreti, M.: A modal logic for KLAIM. In: Rus, T. (ed.) AMAST 2000. LNCS, vol. 1816, pp. 339–354. Springer, Heidelberg (2000). https://doi.org/10.1007/3-540-45499-3_25

23. De Nicola, R., Pugliese, R.: Linda-based applicative and imperative process algebras. Theor. Comput. Sci. **238**(1–2), 389–437 (2000)

24. Fischer, M.J., Lynch, N.A., Paterson, M.S.: Impossibility of distributed consensus with one faulty process. J. ACM **32**(2), 374–382 (1985)

25. Gelernter, D.: Generative communication in Linda. ACM Trans. Program. Lang. Syst. **7**(1), 80–112 (1985)

26. Gray, J., Reuter, A.: Transaction Processing: Concepts and Techniques. The Morgan Kaufmann Series in Data Management Systems (1992)

27. Kühn, E.: Fault-tolerance for communicating multidatabase transactions. In: Proceedings of the Twenty-Seventh Annual Hawaii International Conference on System Sciences (HICSS), Wailea, Maui, Hawaii, vol. 2, pp. 323–332. IEEE (1994)

28. Kühn, E.: Coordination System. European Patent, Number EP0929864 B1 (March 21th 2001), PCT Number PCT/AT1997/000209

29. Lamport, L.: Time, clocks, and the ordering of events in a distributed system. Commun. ACM **21**(7), 558–565 (1978)

30. Lamport, L.: Byzantizing Paxos by refinement. In: Peleg, D. (ed.) DISC 2011. LNCS, vol. 6950, pp. 211–224. Springer, Heidelberg (2011). https://doi.org/10.1007/978-3-642-24100-0_22

31. Lamport, L., Shostak, R., Pease, M.: The Byzantine generals problem. ACM Trans. Program. Lang. Syst. **4**(3), 382–401 (1982)

32. Nakamoto, S.: Bitcoin: A Peer-to-Peer Electronic Cash System (2008). https://bitcoin.org/bitcoin.pdf

33. Saltzer, J.H., Reed, D.P., Clark, D.D.: End-to-end arguments in system design. ACM Trans. Comput. Syst. **2**(4), 277–288 (1984)

34. Uriarte, R.B., De Nicola, R.: Blockchain-based decentralized cloud/fog solutions: challenges, opportunities, and standards. IEEE Commun. Stan. Mag. **2**(3), 22–28 (2018)
35. Xu, X., et al.: A taxonomy of blockchain-based systems for architecture design. In: 2017 IEEE International Conference on Software Architecture (ICSA), pp. 243–252 (2017)

Testing for Coordination Fidelity

Yehia Abd Alrahman[1]($^{\boxtimes}$)(iD), Claudio Antares Mezzina[2](iD),
and Hugo Torres Vieira[3](iD)

[1] Chalmers University of Technology, University of Gothenburg, Gothenburg, Sweden
yehia.abd.alrahman@gu.se
[2] Dipartimento di Scienze Pure e Applicate, Università di Urbino, Urbino, Italy
[3] IMT School for Advanced Studies Lucca, Lucca, Italy

Abstract. Operation control in modern distributed systems must rely on decentralised coordination among system participants. In particular when the operation control involves critical infrastructures such as power grids, it is vital to ensure correctness properties of such coordination mechanisms. In this paper, we present a verification technique that addresses coordination protocols for power grid operation control. Given a global protocol specification, we show how we can rely on testing semantics for the purpose of ensuring protocol fidelity, i.e., to certify that the interaction among the grid nodes follows the protocol specification.

1 Introduction

Power generation and distribution have been undergoing a revolution in the past years, on the one hand due to the introduction of different solutions for generation, on the other hand because of the impact that such solutions have on distribution grids. More concretely, having a unique power supplier in a grid is an outdated configuration, instead now the scenario of interest involves multiple power supplies and distribution to potentially all nodes of the grid, in particular when renewable energy sources come into play. The real time requirements of such systems demand automatic mechanisms for operation control, that must be certifiably reliable given their critical nature.

Clearly, the outdated centralised control models of power grids cannot scale with the complexity and heterogeneity of emerging configurations. Instead, decentralised operation control must rely on the *coordination* of distributed remote collaborating parties, for example for the purpose of balancing supply-and-demand. It is however vital that such coordination mechanisms are encompassed with techniques that allow to ensure reliability in a rigorous way.

Several proposals of formal models for distributed coordination can be found in the existing literature, for instance based on tuple spaces (e.g., [10]). We may also find recent proposals for new paradigms for interaction models, such

Yehia Abd Alrahman is funded by the ERC consolidator grant D-SynMA under the European Union's Horizon 2020 research and innovation programme (grant agreement No 772459).

M. Boreale et al. (Eds.): De Nicola-Festschrift, LNCS 11665, pp. 152–169, 2019.
https://doi.org/10.1007/978-3-030-21485-2_10

as attribute-based communication [1,2]. The common goal is to support system modelling in a precise way and exclude unexpected behaviours. Building on such characterisation of system behaviour, one may then ensure reliability properties by means of verification techniques. We distinguish here the approaches based on behavioural type specifications (cf. [16]) that allow to certify protocol fidelity, i.e., that ensure that interacting parties follow a prescribed protocol of interaction.

In this paper, we build on previous work that introduces a model of coordination protocols for power grid operation control [3]. The key principles underlying the proposal are a global programming model, that allows to reason on grid behaviour as a whole, and a notion of operation control transference via interaction. Intuitively, idle nodes react to synchronisations so as to carry out their part in the operation control, hence interactions authorise nodes much like interactions in a token ring protocol authorise nodes to access the shared resource. Together with a notion of network configuration, in particular network topology and state, the principles above are embedded in a protocol language that is role-agnostic, i.e., that does not specify a priori the parties involved in the communications. This means that the development of coordination protocols may consider generic networks, as expectable, and the concrete association with the network nodes involved in the communications is carried out on-the-fly at runtime based on the transference of the operation control.

Likewise to the (global) protocol specification, also the controllers running in network nodes should be developed targeting a generic setting. The key issue, for the purpose of ensuring that the node controllers interact among them according to the protocol specification, is to certify that the implementation of a node controller exhibits the (local) actions expected at network level. Hence, a notion of observational reasoning over implementations is required in order to certify that an implementation complies with a prescribed protocol of interaction. Ideally, such observational power should be as flexible as possible so to allow for the greatest number of implementations to be deemed compliant with the specification. We therefore rely on *testing* [11] since we may streamline the verification by deriving the testers from the specification and abstract away from implementation details that are not pertinent for the protocol validation.

The global protocol language, presented in the next section, is equipped with an operational semantics that provides the reference model of interaction. We refer the interested reader to previous work [3] for a more detailed presentation of the model, but nevertheless the presentation in this paper is self-contained. To that end we illustrate here the flavour of the language in Sect. 3 by modelling a protocol that addresses the reconfiguration of a power grid which is new to this paper. In Sect. 4 we present our novel technical development, starting by the definition of the language model for testers and a technique that may be used to synthesise testers from global protocol specifications. We then show how we can rely on a testing semantics to ensure that an implementation complies with a protocol (Definition 1). Based on this notion of compliance, we may then ensure protocol fidelity (Theorem 1), which attests that implementations follow the prescribed protocol of interaction. Finally, Sect. 5 includes some concluding remarks.

2   A Model for Operation Control Protocols

In this section, we present a global language to model operation control protocols governing power networks. Interaction in our language is driven by the structure of the power network, in particular considering radial power networks, i.e., tree-structures where the root provides power to respective subtree. The interaction model also accounts for a notion of proximity so as to capture backup links. Thus, we consider that nodes can interact if they are in a provide/receive power relation or in a neighbouring relation. In order to identify the target of a synchronisation, specifications include a direction that determines the type of the relation.

Table 1. Global language syntax

(Protocol)	P ::=	**0**
	|	P | Q
	|	**rec** X.P
	|	X
	|	S
	|	(id)P
(Summation)	S ::=	$[f^d]_i^o$P
	|	S + S
(Direction)	$d \in$	$\{\star, \blacktriangle, \blacktriangleright, \bullet\}$

As anticipated in the Introduction, the language model embeds the principle that control is transferred by means of synchronisations. For example, a node enabling synchronisation on an action and another one reacting to it may synchronise and the enabling node yields the control to the reacting one. Consequently, the reacting node may enable the next step of the protocol. We may therefore consider that *active* nodes enable synchronisations and, as a consequence of a synchronisation, transfer the *active* role to the reacting node. This allows to specify protocols as a (structured) set of interactions without prescribing the actual identities of the nodes involved, as these are determined operationally due to the transference of the active role in synchronisations.

The syntax of the language is given in Table 1. We use id to range over node identifiers, f to range over synchronisation action labels, and $c, i, o, \ldots$ to range over logical conditions. The protocols, ranged over by P and Q, consist of static specifications and the *active* node construct (id)P, which says that the node with identifier id is active to carry out the protocol P. Static specifications represent the behaviour of the protocol which is defined by termination **0**, fork P \| Q to specify that both P and Q are to be carried out, and infinite behaviour defined in terms of the recursion **rec** X.P and recursion variable X, with the usual meaning. Static specifications also include synchronisation summations (S, ...), where $S_1 + S_2$ states that either S_1 or S_2 is to be carried out (exclusively), and where $[f^d]_i^o$ represents a synchronisation action: a node active on $[f^d]_i^o P$ that satisfies condition o may synchronise on f with the node(s) identified by the direction d for which condition i holds, leading to the activation of the latter node(s) on protocol P. Intuitively, the node active on $[f^d]_i^o P$ enables the synchronisation, which results in the reaction of the targeted nodes that are activated to carry out the continuation protocol P.

A direction d specifies the target(s) of a synchronisation; $\star$ targets all (children) of the enabling node; $\blacktriangle$ targets the parent; $\blacktriangleright$ targets a neighbour; and $\bullet$ targets the enabler itself and is used to capture local computation steps. We remark that since one node can supply power to several others, synchronisations with $\star$ direction may actually involve several reacting nodes. Any $\star$ synchronisations are therefore interpreted as broadcasts, i.e., $\star$ targets all (direct) children that satisfy the reacting condition, which can be the empty set (e.g., the node has no children or none of them satisfy the reacting condition). Binary interaction, on the other hand, is interpreted as synchronisation and can only occur if the identified target node satisfies the reacting condition.

Example 1. Consider the protocol: $(id)([f_1{}^\star]_{i_1}^{o_1} P_1 + [f_2{}^\bullet]_{i_2}^{o_2}(P_2 \mid P_3))$ which specifies that node id is active to synchronise on f_1 or f_2, exclusively.

There are two language mechanisms, illustrated in Example 1, that may introduce concurrency in the model. One is the broadcast which may lead to the activation of several nodes: in the example, each one of the nodes reacting to f_1 will carry out P_1. Another is the fork construct which allows a node to concurrently carry out two subprotocols: in the example, a node active on $(P_2 \mid P_3)$ will carry out both P_2 and P_3, and potentially synchronise with different nodes in each one.

The semantics of the language relies on a structural congruence relation $\equiv$. Structural congruence is the least congruence relation on protocols that satisfies the rules given in Table 2. The first set of rules states that fork and summation are associative and commutative, and that fork has identity element $\mathbf{0}$ (notice that $\mathbf{0}$ is syntactically excluded from summations). Rule $(id)(P \mid Q) \equiv (id)P \mid (id)Q$ states that a node id is active on both branches of the fork construct. Rule $(id_1)(id_2)P \equiv (id_2)(id_1)P$ states that the order of active nodes is immaterial and rule $(id)\mathbf{0} \equiv \mathbf{0}$ states that a node active on $\mathbf{0}$ is equivalent to $\mathbf{0}$. Intuitively, structural congruence rewriting allows active nodes to "float" in the term towards the synchronisation actions. The rule for recursion unfolding is standard.

Example 2. Considering the active node distribution in a fork, we have that $[f_1{}^\star]_{i_1}^{o_1} P_1 + [f_2{}^\bullet]_{i_2}^{o_2}(id)(P_2 \mid P_3) \equiv [f_1{}^\star]_{i_1}^{o_1} P_1 + [f_2{}^\bullet]_{i_2}^{o_2}((id)P_2 \mid (id)P_3)$

The definition of the semantics depends on the state of the network and on the fact that nodes satisfy certain logical conditions. We consider state information for each node so as to capture both "local" information about the topology (such as the identities of the power provider and of the set of neighbours) and other information relevant for condition assessment (such as the status of the power supply). The network state, denoted by Δ, is a mapping from node identifiers

Table 2. Structural congruence

$P \mid \mathbf{0} \equiv P$	$P_1 \mid (P_2 \mid P_3) \equiv (P_1 \mid P_2) \mid P_3$	$P_1 \mid P_2 \equiv P_2 \mid P_1$
$\mathbf{rec}\ X.P \equiv P[\mathbf{rec}\ X.P/X]$	$S_1 + (S_2 + S_3) \equiv (S_1 + S_2) + S_3$	$S_1 + S_2 \equiv S_2 + S_1$
$(id)(P \mid Q) \equiv (id)P \mid (id)Q$	$(id_1)(id_2)P \equiv (id_2)(id_1)P$	$(id)\mathbf{0} \equiv \mathbf{0}$

to states, where a state, denoted by s, is a register $id[id', t, n, k, a, e, g]$ containing the following information: id is the node identifier; id' identifies the power provider; t captures the status of the input power connection; n is the set of identifiers of neighbouring nodes; k is the power supply capacity of the node; a is the number of power supply links (i.e., the number of nodes that receive power from this one); g is the identity of a nearby power generator; and e is the number of power supply links that are in a faulty state. We consider that the elements in the register are natural numbers (and a set of natural numbers for the neighbours) albeit in the examples we use some special symbols (e.g., ∞).

We check conditions against states for the purpose of allowing synchronisations. Given a state s we denote by $s \models c$ that state s satisfies condition c, where we leave the underlying logic unspecified. For example, we may say that $s \models (k > 0)$ to check that s has capacity greater than 0. We also consider a notion of side-effects, in the sense that synchronisation actions may result in state changes so as to model system evolution. By $\mathsf{upd}(id, id', f^d, \Delta)$ we denote the operation that yields the network state obtained by updating Δ considering node id synchronises on f with id', hence the update regards the side-effects of f in the involved nodes. Namely, given $\Delta = (\Delta', id \mapsto s, id' \mapsto s')$ we have that $\mathsf{upd}(id, id', f^d, \Delta)$ is defined as $(\Delta', id \mapsto f^d!(s, id'), id' \mapsto f^d?(s', id))$, where $f^d!(s, id')$ modifies state s according to the side-effects of enabling f^d and considering id' is the reactive node (likewise for the reacting update, distinguished by ?). We consider side-effects only for binary synchronisations (▶ and ▲ directions), where both interacting parties are known, but state changes could also be considered for other directions following similar lines.

The definition of the semantics relies on an auxiliary operation, denoted $d(\Delta, id)$, that yields the recipient(s) of a synchronisation action, given the direction d, the network state Δ and the enabler of the action id. The operation yields the power provider of a node in case the direction is ▲, (any) one of the neighbours in case the direction is ▶, all the nodes that have as parent the enabler in case the direction is ⋆, and is undefined for direction •.

The operational semantics is given in terms of configurations consisting of a protocol P and a network state Δ. We use $\Delta; P \to \Delta'; P'$ to represent that configuration $\Delta; P$ evolves in one step to configuration $\Delta'; P'$, potentially involving state changes (Δ and Δ' may differ) and (necessarily) involving a step in the protocol from P to P'.

The semantics of our language is reported in Table 3. Rule BIN captures binary interaction where the direction (d) of the synchronisation action targets either the parent (▲) or a neighbour (▶). Protocol $(id)([f^d]_i^\circ P + S)$ states that node id can enable a synchronisation on f provided that the state of id satisfies

Table 3. Reduction rules

$$\frac{d \in \{\blacktriangle, \blacktriangleright\} \quad \Delta(id) \models o \quad d(\Delta, id) = id' \quad \Delta(id') \models i \quad \Delta' = \mathsf{upd}(id, id', f^d, \Delta)}{\Delta; (id)([f^d]_i^o P + S) \to \Delta'; [f^d]_i^o((id')P) + S} \text{ (BIN)}$$

$$\frac{\Delta(id) \models o \quad \star(\Delta, id) = I' \quad I = \{id' \mid id' \in I' \land \Delta(id') \models i\}}{\Delta; (id)([f^\star]_i^o P + S) \to \Delta'; [f^\star]_i^o((I)P) + S} \text{ (BRD)}$$

$$\frac{\Delta(id) \models o \quad \Delta(id) \models i}{\Delta; (id)([f^\bullet]_i^o P + S) \to \Delta; [f^\bullet]_i^o((id)P) + S} \text{ (LOC)}$$

$$\frac{\Delta; P \to \Delta'; P'}{\Delta; [f^d]_i^o P \to \Delta'; [f^d]_i^o P'} \text{ (SYNCH)} \qquad \frac{\Delta; P \to \Delta'; P'}{\Delta; (id)P \to \Delta'; (id)P'} \text{ (ID)}$$

$$\frac{\Delta; P_1 \to \Delta'; P_1'}{\Delta; P_1 + P_2 \to \Delta'; P_1' + P_2} \text{ (SUM)} \qquad \frac{\Delta; P_1 \to \Delta'; P_1'}{\Delta; P_1 \mid P_2 \to \Delta'; P_1' \mid P_2} \text{ (PAR)}$$

$$\frac{P \equiv P' \quad \Delta; P' \to \Delta'; Q' \quad Q' \equiv Q}{\Delta; P \to \Delta'; Q} \text{ (STRUCT)}$$

condition o, as specified in premise $\Delta(id) \models o$. Furthermore, the reacting node id', specified in the premise $d(\Delta, id) = id'$, is required to satisfy condition i. As a result of the synchronisation, the configuration evolves to $[f^d]_i^o((id')P) + S$, specifying that id' is active on the continuation protocol P. The resulting network state is obtained by considering the side-effects of the synchronisation. Note that the synchronisation action construct is preserved after the respective synchronisation (see Example 3). We omit the rule that captures the case for the singleton summation (likewise for BRD and LOC).

Rule BRD captures broadcast interaction ($\star$) and is similar to rule BIN. Except for the absence of side-effects, the main difference is that now a set of potential reacting nodes is identified (I' denotes a set of node identifiers), out of which all those satisfying condition i are singled out (I). The latter are activated to carry the continuation protocol. We use (I) to abbreviate (id_1)...(id_m) considering $I = id_1, \ldots, id_m$. We remark that the set of reacting nodes may be empty (e.g., if none of the potential ones satisfies condition i), in which case ($\emptyset$)P is defined as P. Note that the reduction step nevertheless takes place, even without reacting nodes, modelling a non-blocking broadcast. This differs from the binary interaction which is blocked until all conditions are met, including the reacting one.

Rule LOC captures local computation steps ($\bullet$). For the sake of uniformity we keep (both) output and input conditions. Note that the node that carries out the f step retains control, i.e., the same id active in f is activated in the continuation P. Like for broadcast, we consider local steps do not involve any state update.

Rules for language closure state that nodes can be active at any stage of the protocol, hence reduction may take place at any level, including after a synchronisation action (rule SYNCH) and within a summation (rule SUM). By preserving the structure of the protocol, including synchronisation actions that have been carried out, we allow for participants to be active on (exactly) the same stage of the protocol simultaneously and at different moments in time, as the next example shows. Rules ID and PAR follow the same principle and finally, rule STRUCT closes reduction under structural congruence.

Example 3. Assuming that node id_2 satisfies conditions i_2 and o_2 in Δ we may derive, using axiom LOC, rule SUM, rule STRUCT, and rule ID the reduction:

$$\Delta; (id_1)(id_2)([f_1{}^\star]_{i_1}^{o_1}P_1 + [f_2{}^\bullet]_{i_2}^{o_2}P_2) \rightarrow \Delta; (id_1)([f_1{}^\star]_{i_1}^{o_1}P_1 + [f_2{}^\bullet]_{i_2}^{o_2}(id_2)P_2)$$

where node id_2 carries out the f_2 local action. Notice that node id_1 is still active on the summation protocol, and both synchronisations are possible regardless of the summation branch involved in the reduction step involving id_2 shown above.

Since we are interested in developing protocols that may be used in different networks, we will focus on static protocols for the purpose of the development, where static protocols are given by the (id)-free fragment of the language. Then, to represent a concrete operating system, active nodes may be added at "top-level" to the static specification (e.g., $(id)P_s$ where P_s denotes a static specification, hence does not specify any active nodes), together with a concrete network state (e.g., $\Delta; (id)P_s$).

Also, to simplify protocol design, we consider that action labels are unique (up to recursion unfolding) and that, as usual, recursion is guarded by (at least) one synchronisation action (excluding, e.g., **rec** $X.X$). In the remainder, we only consider well-formed protocols that follow the above guidelines, namely: originate from specifications where recursion is guarded, all action labels are distinct, and where the active node construct only appears top-level (e.g., $(id_1)\ldots(id_k)P_s$).

3　Management of Distributed Generation in Power Grids

In this section, we model a protocol for managing distributed generation when major faults in power sources happen. The goal is to find a replacement for failed power sources and transfer the control to it.

We consider a cross section of a radial network of a power grid in Fig. 1. The network consists of a primary power substation **PS**, two generators Hydro and Wind Farms, and six secondary power substations, numbered from **1** to **6**. The type of this network is called radial because every substation has only one incoming power input and possibly multiple power outputs. Each secondary substation has fault indicators (fault • and no fault ○), line switches (closed | and open ‖), and an embedded controller that implements the substation's behaviour and manages interactions with others. Fig. 1 illustrates a configuration where the secondary substations **1–5** are energised by the primary substation **PS**, while substation **6** is energised by Wind Farms. Secondary substations cannot operate the switches or exchange information without authorisation from the primary substation which supplies the power.

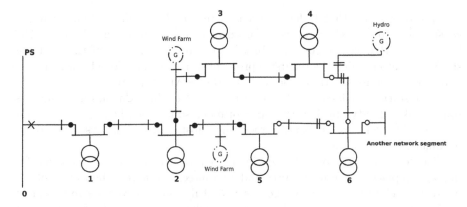

Fig. 1. Power distribution grid

Let us consider that the power source of the primary substation **PS** failed which caused a blackout in its domain. The substation **PS** initiates a reconfiguration protocol by synchronising with its directly connected secondary substations and delegates them to locate the substation managing the hydroelectric generator so to transfer the control to it and restore power. To simplify the presentation, our reconfiguration protocol is designed specifically to handle the configuration in Fig. 1. However, it can be easily extended to handle any configuration.

Every substation delegates the substations connected to its output power lines to collaborate to locate the generator. Once the signal is received by the substation managing the generator (in our case, substation **4**), it reconfigures itself, triggers the generator, and the relocation protocol starts. A swap signal is propagated in the direction of **PS** to reconfigure the connections of secondary substations to the direction of the new source. Once this signal is received by **PS**, it sends a permit signal to the substation where the signal came from so that the control is transferred to the new source. At this point the transference protocol starts and a release signal is propagated to the new source. Once received, the new source claims the manager role and retains the control.

We fix the following terminology before we model the protocol in our global language: the state of a source link t can be 0 (to indicate a faulty link, i.e., no power) or 1 otherwise. We use z as the source *id* when a substation is not connected to a power supply. We also use ∞ in place of the source for all primary stations. Initially, substations, with direct links to backup generators, e.g., substation **4**, record the generators identities in their states regardless of their current sources; otherwise the generation field is reset to $\perp$, e.g., substation **3**. The initial state of each substation follows from Fig. 1. For instance, substations **3**, **4**, and **PS** have the following initial states $3[2, 0, \{2, 4\}, 1, 1, 0, \perp]$, $4[3, 0, \{3, 6\}, 1, 0, 0, H]$, and $\mathbf{PS}[\infty, 0, \{1\}, 2, 1, 0, \perp]$, respectively.

The reconfiguration protocol is reported below:

$$\textsc{Reconfiguration} \triangleq [\mathsf{Unlink}^\star]_{i_1}^{o_1} \mathbf{rec}\ X.([\mathsf{Locate}^\star]_{i_1}^{o_2} X + [\mathsf{Found}^\blacktriangle]_{i_1}^{o_3} \textsc{Relocation})$$

The protocol states that Unlink is broadcasted to the children of the enabling substation, after which a recursive protocol is activated on the children. The latter states that either Locate is broadcasted to the children of the enabling substation, after which the recursive protocol starts over, or Found is sent to the parent which consequently carries out the RELOCATION protocol.

A substation enabled on RECONFIGURATION enables Unlink only when its source link is faulty and it serves as a primary substation, i.e., $o_1 = (t = 0) \wedge (i = \infty)$. Furthermore, a reactive/receiving substation can always synchronise on Unlink, i.e., $i_1 = \mathsf{true}$.

The children carry out the continuation protocol which is responsible for finding a replacement power source and guaranteeing safe reconfiguration of the network. A child can broadcast Locate only if it cannot serve as a replacement power source, i.e., $o_2 = (g \neq H)$; otherwise, when $o_3 = (g = H)$, Found is sent to the parent. Note that Locate has no side-effects on both sides while Found requires that the enabling station sets its source to ∞ and the receiver sets its generation field (g) to the id of the enabling substation. Note that once Found is executed, the substation triggers the hydroelectric generator to supply power and marks itself as a new replacement. The power will be restored once the last substation in the network segment is configured correctly. Furthermore, both actions can always be received. The RELOCATION protocol is reported below:

$$\text{RELOCATION} \triangleq \mathbf{rec}\ Y.([\mathsf{Swap}^{\blacktriangle}]_{i_1}^{o_4} Y + [\mathsf{Permit}^{\blacktriangleright}]_{i_2}^{o_5} \text{TRANSFERENCE})$$

Except for the primary substation, any substation enabled on RELOCATION can send Swap, i.e., $o_4 = (i \neq \infty)$; otherwise, when $o_5 = (i = \infty)$, Permit is sent to its neighbour which would carry out the TRANSFERENCE protocol. The receiver can always synchronise on Swap while for Permit the generation field (g) and the source (i) of the substation should be equal, i.e., $i_2 = (i = g)$. Swap requires that senders sets the value of their source to the one of their generation field. The side-effects of Swap on the receiver are the same as of Found. For Permit, the enabling station disconnects itself and sets its source to z. Furthermore, Permit requires that the receiver resets its generation field. The TRANSFERENCE protocol is reported below:

$$\text{TRANSFERENCE} \triangleq \mathbf{rec}\ Z.([\mathsf{Release}^{\blacktriangle}]_{i_1}^{o_6} Z + [\mathsf{Claim}^{\bullet}]_{i_1}^{o_7} \text{RECONFIGURATION})$$

Similarly, the TRANSFERENCE protocol propagates a Release signal to release the manager role of the network segment to the new source. Once the signal is received, the new substation declares the end of the protocol by enabling Claim which is a local signal. This way, the substation retains the control and becomes ready to carry out the whole RECONFIGURATION protocol. Except for the replacement substation, any substation can enable Release, i.e., $o_6 = (g \neq H)$; otherwise, when $o_7 = (g = H)$, Claim is enabled. Note that Release only requires that the receiver resets its generation field while Claim has not side-effects at all.

The static protocol RECONFIGURATION abstracts from the concrete network configuration. To represent a concrete network, active substations identifiers must be added at "top-level" together with a network state Δ, i.e.,

Δ; (**PS**)Reconfiguration. Note that the primary station, **PS**, is initially active because in our scenario it is the only station that can initiate the protocol.

4   Testing for Protocol Fidelity

In this section, we present a technique ensuring that individual node controllers follow a global protocol specification. We start by introducing a testing language that provides a means of interaction with an implementation. Implementations are left abstract as our focus is on the verification technique that only relies that such implementations exhibit determined actions. Then, we show how we can synthesise testers out of a global protocol specification, building on which we introduce a notion of protocol compliance that characterises implementations that pass the synthesised tests. We then present our protocol fidelity result (Theorem 1) that attests implementations compliant with a protocol exhibit the local actions prescribed by the global specification.

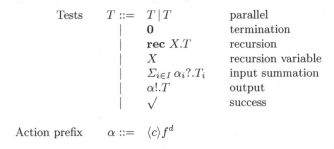

Tests	$T ::=$	$T \mid T$	parallel
	|	$\mathbf{0}$	termination
	|	**rec** $X.T$	recursion
	|	X	recursion variable
	|	$\Sigma_{i \in I}\, \alpha_i?.T_i$	input summation
	|	$\alpha!.T$	output
	|	$\sqrt{}$	success

Action prefix	$\alpha ::=$	$\langle c \rangle f^d$

Fig. 2. Target language syntax

The syntax of tests is given in Fig. 2. A test can be a parallel composition $T \mid T$, the terminated process $\mathbf{0}$, the recursive definition **rec** $X.T$, a recursion variable X, an input summation $\Sigma_{i \in I}\, \alpha_i?.T_i$, an output $\alpha!.T$ and the success $\sqrt{}$. We remark that since we are interested in interacting with an implementation, we do not expect interaction among different tests. Hence, a parallel composition of tests captures two simultaneously active tests, but where no interaction can occur, as will be made clear by the semantics of the language. Furthermore, we remark on the $\sqrt{}$ introduced for the sake of signalling the success of a test. Finally, notice that action prefixes ($\langle c \rangle f^d$) are defined so as to match the observables expected in the global interaction, identifying the synchronisation label f, the direction d and the condition c that either refers to input or output conditions.

The semantics of testers is defined in terms of the following observable actions: $\lambda ::= \alpha! \mid \alpha? \mid \sqrt{}$. An observation λ can then be an input or an output or a success label. We then define the semantics of tests by the rules given in Fig. 3, which we now briefly discuss. Rule Parl allows the left part of a parallel composition to evolve by itself by showing a label different from the success ($\sqrt{}$) one. The

$$\frac{T_1 \xrightarrow{\lambda} T_1' \quad \lambda \neq \sqrt{}}{T_1 \mid T_2 \xrightarrow{\lambda} T_1' \mid T_2} \ \text{PARL} \qquad\qquad \frac{T_1 \xrightarrow{\sqrt{}} T_1' \quad T_2 \xrightarrow{\sqrt{}} T_2'}{T_1 \mid T_2 \xrightarrow{\sqrt{}} T_1' \mid T_2'} \ \text{PARS}$$

$$\frac{T[\textbf{rec } X.T/X] \xrightarrow{\lambda} T'}{\textbf{rec } X.T \xrightarrow{\lambda} T'} \ \text{REC} \qquad\qquad \frac{}{\sqrt{} \xrightarrow{\sqrt{}} \textbf{0}} \ \text{SUCCESS}$$

$$\frac{j \in I}{\Sigma_{i \in I} \, \alpha_i?.T_i \xrightarrow{\alpha_j?} T_j} \ \text{INPUT} \qquad\qquad \frac{}{\alpha!.T \xrightarrow{\alpha!} T} \ \text{OUTPUT}$$

Fig. 3. Tester language LTS

symmetric rule for the right part of the parallel composition is omitted. The only way a success label can be propagated through a parallel composition is when both parts are able to produce such label as reported in PARS. Rule REC deals with recursive processes in a standard way. Rule SUCCESS allows a success prefix to reduce to the idle process, while rules INPUT and OUTPUT show how the prefixes exhibit the corresponding labels and activate the continuation. We say test T succeeds, written $T \downarrow_{\sqrt{}}$, if $T \xrightarrow{\sqrt{}} T'$ for some T'.

As one can notice, in the given LTS there is no rule for synchronisation. As previously announced, this is due to our goal of testing implementations, so the goal is to allow testers to interact with an implementation and not among themselves. We abstract away from how implementations are defined, and consider implementations, ranged over by I, as *black-boxes* that exhibit labels of the form $\alpha!$, $\alpha?$ and τ. For the purpose of testing an implementation, we define a new level of semantics given by the rules in Fig. 4, describing the interactions between a test T and an implementation I, where we use $\|$ to specify the parallel composition operator for the testing level. We consider that the actions of implementations and tester are identical (up to the represented duality), which in particular means that the conditions are exactly the same. Considering logical equivalence instead would be more appropriate to support more flexibility, but for the sake of simplifying the presentation we adopt here syntactic equality. We leave for future work the refinement of this notion, together with a more in depth exploration of the possible logical support for the correspondence, and consider here that implementations refer to conditions as specified in the protocol.

$$\frac{I \xrightarrow{\alpha!} I' \quad T \xrightarrow{\alpha?} T'}{I \parallel T \xrightarrow{\tau} I' \parallel T'} \ \text{COMML} \qquad\qquad \frac{I \xrightarrow{\tau} I'}{I \parallel T \xrightarrow{\tau} I' \parallel T} \ \text{INTERNAL}$$

Fig. 4. Testing semantics

The rules of Fig. 4 on the one hand capture the interaction between test and implementation (rule COMML and the omitted symmetric version), and on the other hand abstract away from the implementation internal behaviours (rule INTERNAL). The latter, conceivably, can be further generalised by disregarding actions that are not relevant for the particular tester considered, e.g., by identifying the set of labels of relevant actions and, like for τ, allowing evolutions of the implementation that carry a non-relevant action label to be interleaved.

For the purpose of defining protocol compliance, we rely on the traces observed for the composition of an implementation and a test. In order to abstract from the internal moves of implementations, we rely on the weak variant of the transitions, defined next following standard lines. As usual, we add τ to the set of relevant observations (because protocols also involve local steps) and use λ^τ to represent either a λ or τ. We then denote by $I \parallel T \overset{\lambda^\tau}{\Rightarrow} I' \parallel T'$ the evolution from $I \parallel T$ to $I' \parallel T'$ comprising a (possibly empty) sequence of τ steps and a λ^τ, hence $I \parallel T \overset{\tau}{\rightarrow} \cdots \overset{\tau}{\rightarrow} \overset{\lambda^\tau}{\rightarrow} \overset{\tau}{\rightarrow} \cdots \overset{\tau}{\rightarrow} I' \parallel T'$. Also, we denote by $I \parallel T \overset{\tilde{\lambda}^\tau}{\Rightarrow} I_n \parallel T_n$ the sequence $I \parallel T \overset{\lambda_1^\tau}{\Rightarrow} I_1 \parallel T_1 \overset{\lambda_2^\tau}{\Rightarrow} \cdots \overset{\lambda_n^\tau}{\Rightarrow} I_n \parallel T_n$ when $\tilde{\lambda}^\tau = \lambda_1^\tau, \cdots, \lambda_n^\tau$.

Table 4. Tester synthesis

$[\![f^d]\!]_i^o P]\!]_\sigma^?$	$\triangleq \langle i \rangle f^d! . [\![P]\!]_\sigma^! \mid [\![P]\!]_\sigma^?$		ISYNCH
$[\![f^d]\!]_i^o P]\!]_\sigma^!$	$\triangleq \langle o \rangle f^d? . \sqrt{}$		OSYNCH
$[\![0]\!]_\sigma^r$	$\triangleq 0$		PNIL
$[\![X]\!]_\sigma^?$	$\triangleq 0$		PVAR
$[\![X]\!]_\sigma^!$	$\triangleq [\![P]\!]_\sigma^!$	$(\sigma(X) = P)$	OVAR
$[\![\text{rec } X.P]\!]_\sigma^r$	$\triangleq [\![P]\!]_{\sigma[X \mapsto P]}^r$		PREC
$[\![P \mid Q]\!]_\sigma^r$	$\triangleq [\![P]\!]_\sigma^r \mid [\![Q]\!]_\sigma^r$		PPAR
$[\![S_1 + S_2]\!]_\sigma^!$	$\triangleq [\![S_1]\!]_\sigma^! + [\![S_2]\!]_\sigma^!$		OSUM
$[\![S_1 + S_2]\!]_\sigma^?$	$\triangleq [\![S_1]\!]_\sigma^? \mid [\![S_2]\!]_\sigma^?$		PSUM

We now show how we can automatically generate testers out of a protocol specification. Tests T are synthesised directly from a protocol P through the function $[\![P]\!]_\sigma^r$ defined in Table 4, where σ is a mapping from recursion variables to protocols and r identifies the type of projection. When r is ? the result of the projection tests if the implementation has an (expected) input. On the other hand when r is ! the result of the projection tests if the implementation has an (expected) output. The result of the (combination of these two types of) projection allows one to verify *static* protocols (cf. Sect. 2).

We briefly discuss the definition of projection. In case ISYNCH, the projection yields the output $(\langle i \rangle f^d! . [\![P]\!]_\sigma^!)$ that is intended to interact with the expected corresponding input. For this purpose, notice that the condition specified in the tester output is precisely the one expected for the input i. Also, the continuation of the tester output $([\![P]\!]_\sigma^!)$ checks if the implementation can afterwards (i.e., after the input) exhibit the active behaviour of the continuation. Therefore the type of the projection for the continuation is !, and hence will test the implementation exhibits the expected outputs. Finally, the remainder of the protocol is (inductively) projected for generating testers for other inputs ($[\![P]\!]_\sigma^?$), which are collected in parallel so inputs are tested without a causality relation, while the causality is present between the input and the output reactions.

In case OSYNCH the yielded tester input specifies the condition of the output expected from the implementation. If the implementation matches the expectancy then the synchronisation may occur, in which case (this part of) the test succeeds and hence the continuation of the tester input is $\checkmark$. The remaining cases show how the two types of projections inductively proceed in the structure of the protocol so as to generate the tester inputs and outputs for the whole of the protocol. We remark that σ is used to generate the ! projection when a recursion variable occurs in the continuation of a synchronisation action (cf., PREC and OVAR).

We may now define the notion of protocol compliance in a way similar to the notion of passing a test [11]. Protocol compliance relies on the ?-projection to check if all expected inputs may be exhibited by the implementation, while ?-projection relies on !-projection to check for the expected outputs.

Definition 1 (Protocol Compliance). *We say implementation I is compliant with protocol P, written $(I \parallel P) \Downarrow_\checkmark$, if*

$$I \parallel [\![P]\!]_\emptyset^? \overset{\tau}{\Rightarrow} I' \parallel T' \qquad and \qquad T' \downarrow_\checkmark$$

The key idea of protocol compliance is to rely on an extensional observational characterisation which allows to abstract away from implementation details.

The compositionality principle stated next is of particular use in our setting, considering different protocols are developed using different action label alphabets (cf. well-formed protocols). We remark that the projection is conservative in this respect, i.e., protocols with disjoint action label alphabets yield testers that also have disjoint action label alphabets. We then say that two tests T_1 and T_2 are non-interfering if the sets of their action prefixes are disjoint, denoted by $T_1 \# T_2$.

Proposition 1 (Compositionality). *If I passes tests T_1 and T_2 with $T_1 \# T_2$, then I passes test $T_1 \mid T_2$.*

Proposition 1 thus allows to focus the verification of implementations considering each protocol separately, given an implementation that is compliant with two protocols individually will also be compliant with the (parallel) combination of the protocols.

As mentioned previously, protocol compliance addresses static protocols, hence ensures that implementations exhibit all expected reactions. For the purpose of our protocol fidelity result, we need to have a means of specifying the initial enabling behaviour that is introduced by adding to a static protocol active nodes at top-level. To this end, we define a third kind of projection, shown in

Table 5, that yields the outputs corresponding to the top-level actions of a protocol.

Table 5. Enabler synthesis

$[\![[f^d]_i^o P]\!]_\sigma^e$	$\triangleq \langle o \rangle f^d!.\mathbf{0}$		ISYNCH
$[\![\mathbf{0}]\!]_\sigma^e$	$\triangleq \mathbf{0}$		INIL
$[\![X]\!]_\sigma^e$	$\triangleq [\![P]\!]_\sigma^e$	$(\sigma(X) = P)$	IVAR
$[\![\mathbf{rec}\ X.P]\!]_\sigma^e$	$\triangleq [\![P]\!]_{\sigma[X \mapsto P]}^e$		IREC
$[\![P \mid Q]\!]_\sigma^e$	$\triangleq [\![P]\!]_\sigma^e \mid [\![Q]\!]_\sigma^e$		PPAR
$[\![S_1 + S_2]\!]_\sigma^e$	$\triangleq [\![S_1]\!]_\sigma^e + [\![S_2]\!]_\sigma^e$		ISUM

Example 4. To illustrate the synthesis of a test from a protocol specification, we consider a simplified version of the RECONFIGURATION protocol in Sect. 3 as follows:

$$\text{RECONFIGURATION} \triangleq [\mathsf{Unlink}^\star]_{i_1}^{o_1} \mathbf{rec}\ X.([\mathsf{Locate}^\star]_{i_1}^{o_2} X + [\mathsf{Found}^\blacktriangle]_{i_1}^{o_3} \mathbf{0})$$

The e-synthesized test according to Table 5 is:

$$\langle o_1 \rangle \mathsf{Unlink}^\star!.\mathbf{0}$$

The ?-synthesized test according to Table 4 is:

$$\langle i_1 \rangle \mathsf{Unlink}^\star!.(\langle o_2 \rangle \mathsf{Locate}^\star?.\sqrt{}\ +\ \langle o_3 \rangle \mathsf{Found}^\blacktriangle?.\sqrt{})\ \mid$$
$$\langle i_1 \rangle \mathsf{Locate}^\star!.(\langle o_2 \rangle \mathsf{Locate}^\star?.\sqrt{}\ +\ \langle o_3 \rangle \mathsf{Found}^\blacktriangle?.\sqrt{})\ \mid\ \langle i_1 \rangle \mathsf{Found}^\blacktriangle?.\mathbf{0}$$

At this point we have all the technical ingredients on the implementation side that allow to characterise protocol fidelity. However, we need to revisit the semantics of the global language, instrumenting it in a way so that evolutions (reductions) carry the respective information (in labels). Namely, we introduce labels that reveal the interacting parties and the synchronisation action that triggered the reduction step. Such labels thus refer to both parties involved in an interaction, while our purpose is to ensure that the implementation of each one of such parties exhibits the prescribed behaviours. So, we need a means to focus a global label on an individual party. Furthermore, we introduce traces of global (labeled) reductions and define a way to trim such traces so as to focus on the contributions of a specific party. All of the above are defined next.

Definition 2 (Labeled Reduction). *Given a reduction* $\Delta; P \to \Delta'; P'$ *derived using the rules of Table 3 we write*

1. $\Delta; P \xrightarrow{(id)[f^d]_i^o(id')} \Delta'; P'$ *if the derivation has axiom* BIN;
2. $\Delta; P \xrightarrow{(id)[f^d]_i^o(\tilde{I})} \Delta'; P'$ *if the derivation has axiom* BRD;

3. $\Delta; P \xrightarrow{\tau} \Delta'; P'$ *if the derivation has axiom* LOC.

We use ξ to range over such labels.

We now define the operation that allow us to focus global protocol labels on an individual participant. Given a protocol label ξ we define $(\xi) \wr_{id}$ as follows:

$$((id)[f^d]_i^o(id')) \wr_{id} \ = !\langle o \rangle f^d \quad ((id')[f^d]_i^o(id)) \wr_{id} \ = ?\langle i \rangle f^d$$
$$((id)[f^d]_i^o(\tilde{I})) \wr_{id} \ = !\langle o \rangle f^d \quad ((id')[f^d]_i^o(\tilde{I})) \wr_{id} \ = ?\langle i \rangle f^d \quad \text{if} \quad id \in \tilde{I}$$
$$(\tau) \wr_{id} \ = \tau \qquad\quad (\xi) \wr_{id} \ = \epsilon \qquad \text{otherwise}$$

We also extend the definition of $(\cdot) \wr_{id}$ for a trace $\tilde{\xi}$ as $(\tilde{\xi}) \wr_{id} = (\xi) \wr_{id} \cdot (\tilde{\xi}') \wr_{id}$ when $\tilde{\xi}$ is $\xi, \tilde{\xi}'$, using '$\cdot$' to represent trace concatenation and taking ϵ as the idempotent element (empty trace). We may now state our main result.

Theorem 1 (Protocol Fidelity). *Let Δ be a network state, id a node identifier, P a protocol and I an implementation such that $(I \parallel P) \Downarrow_{\surd}$. We have that:*

$$if \quad \Delta; (id)P \xrightarrow{\xi_1} \Delta_1; P_1 \xrightarrow{\xi_2} \cdots \xrightarrow{\xi_n} \Delta_n; P_n$$
$$then \quad I \mid \llbracket P \rrbracket_\emptyset^e \xRightarrow{\tilde{\lambda}} I' \mid T' \quad with \quad (\tilde{\xi}) \wr_{id} = \tilde{\lambda}$$

Notice that in Theorem 1 we use the e type of projection to inject the initial behaviours correspondent to the ones obtained by the top-level active node. This is because the implementation I is ensured to exhibit the actions of the static part of the protocol P but not the enabling actions corresponding to $(id)P$. So we consider the implementation is composed (in parallel) with the implementation, where synchronisation between them is not supported (hence, parallel supports interleaving here). The result ensures that any sequence of actions prescribed for any node at the level of the global trace is matched by the corresponding actions of the implementation composed with the initial enabling behaviour.

Example 5. We return to the protocol shown in Example 4, namely:

$$\text{RECONFIGURATION} \triangleq [\text{Unlink}^\star]_{i_1}^{o_1} \mathbf{rec} \ X.([\text{Locate}^\star]_{i_1}^{o_2} X + [\text{Found}^\blacktriangle]_{i_1}^{o_3} \mathbf{0})$$

Let I be an implementation such that $(I \parallel \text{RECONFIGURATION}) \Downarrow_{\surd}$. Considerin the e-synthesized test shown in Example 4 we have that Theorem 1 ensures that $I \mid \langle o_1 \rangle \text{Unlink}^\star!.\mathbf{0}$ can exhibit the actions corresponding to the reductions of $\Delta; (id)\text{RECONFIGURATION}$. Notice that the initial action of id is given by the e-projection, while remaining actions will be exhibited by the implementation since it complies to the test given by the ?-projection (see Example 4).

We remark that the inverse direction of the implication stated in Theorem 1 does not hold in general considering the protocol compliance given in Definition 1. Intuitively, consider that implementations can exhibit more actions than the ones prescribed by the tests, e.g., an implementation can exhibit simultaneously (in parallel) two actions while the corresponding test prescribes that they must happen in sequence. The strict correspondence is naturally a desirable property that we leave for future work. We also remark that we focus here on observable actions and do not introduce the state information explicitly (which may be separated from the operational implementation). Refining the statement so as to consider explicitly the state information may allow us to abstract away from the logical conditions currently under consideration in the testing that supports the protocol compliance, and explore different notions of logical support for assessing when implementations meet the specifications.

5   Concluding Remarks

Ensuring that implementations meet specifications is of crucial importance in software development. Techniques used to guarantee such correspondence should be flexible enough to allow for a great number of implementations to (safely) match a specification, so as to promote their usability. For the purpose of analysing interacting systems, reasoning in terms of observational equivalences has been used ever since the seminal work of Milner (cf. [18]). The key idea is that systems are deemed equivalent if an external observer cannot distinguish between them. Testing [11] embeds this principle and seems particularly fit for the purpose of ensuring that implementations meet specifications, given that the testers may be crafted so as to faithfully represent the specifications. The idea is that two implementations are equivalent if no specification can distinguish between them.

The above principle is at the basis of the development presented in this paper. The goal is to allow for several implementations to conform to a protocol specification, abstracting away from details that do not compromise the safe operation of the system. We have merely scratched the surface of the advantages of using testing in this setting, in particular when taking into account the broadness of the related literature (e.g., [4–6,9,12–15,17,19,20]). However, we can already state a protocol fidelity result that ensures compliant implementations exhibit the actions prescribed by the protocol specifications. Introducing a notion of testing preorder, relating implementations that pass all the tests of other implementations, we may also characterise a substitution principle for the safe replacement of controller implementations.

Our global protocol language can be anchored to the proposal of choreographic programming [7], in the sense that programming is carried out directly at the protocol language level, and operationally correspondent distributed implementations can be automatically generated from the global specification (cf. [3]). We take a different perspective here, admitting that node controllers are developed as usual in a separate way with respect to the specification. In fact, we view implementations in an opaque way so as to allow for greater generality, e.g., allowing for implementations that interleave their participation in different protocols.

Nevertheless, following lines similar to previous work [3], given a protocol specification we may consider a distributed network where each node is equipped with a (compliant) controller implementation. Then, we may also show that the yielded distributed model operationally corresponds to the global (centralised) model of Sect. 2.

A Tribute to Rocco De Nicola. This paper is a contribution to the Festschrift that celebrates Rocco De Nicola's 65th birthday. We tried to gather topics in which Rocco has been a pioneer and a prolific author: *coordination models* and *testing equivalences*. Coordination is the goal of the model presented in Sect. 2 while Sect. 4 is undoubtedly inspired by Rocco's seminal work on testing preorders [8,11]. Besides being a very prolific and influential scientist, Rocco has also been a mentor and a source of inspiration for many researchers. His dedication to research and his quest for scientific rigour will inspire generations.

References

1. Abd Alrahman, Y., De Nicola, R., Loreti, M.: On the power of attribute-based communication. In: 36th IFIP WG 6.1 International Conference on Formal Techniques for Distributed Objects, Components, and Systems, FORTE 2016, pp. 1–18 (2016)
2. Alrahman, Y.A., De Nicola, R., Loreti, M., Tiezzi, F., Vigo, R.: A calculus for attribute-based communication. In: Proceedings of the 30th Annual ACM Symposium on Applied Computing, pp. 1840–1845. ACM (2015)
3. Alrahman, Y.A., Vieira, H.T.: Operation control protocols in power distribution grids. CoRR abs/1811.01942 (2018)
4. Bernardi, G., Hennessy, M.: Mutually testing processes. Log. Methods Comput. Sci. **11**(2), 1–23 (2015)
5. Boreale, M., De Nicola, R.: Testing equivalence for mobile processes. Inf. Comput. **120**(2), 279–303 (1995)
6. Boreale, M., De Nicola, R., Pugliese, R.: Trace and testing equivalence on asynchronous processes. Inf. Comput. **172**(2), 139–164 (2002)
7. Carbone, M., Montesi, F.: Deadlock-freedom-by-design: multiparty asynchronous global programming. In: The 40th Annual ACM SIGPLAN-SIGACT Symposium on Principles of Programming Languages, POPL 2013, pp. 263–274. ACM (2013)
8. De Nicola, R.: Testing equivalences and fully abstract models for communicating systems. Ph.D. thesis, University of Edinburgh, UK (1986). http://ethos.bl.uk/OrderDetails.do?uin=uk.bl.ethos.649251
9. De Nicola, R.: Extensional equivalences for transition systems. Acta Inf. **24**(2), 211–237 (1987)
10. De Nicola, R., Ferrari, G.L., Pugliese, R.: KLAIM: a kernel language for agents interaction and mobility. IEEE Trans. Softw. Eng. **24**(5), 315–330 (1998)
11. De Nicola, R., Hennessy, M.: Testing equivalences for processes. Theor. Comput. Sci. **34**, 83–133 (1984)
12. De Nicola, R., Hennessy, M.: CCS without tau's. In: Ehrig, H., Kowalski, R., Levi, G., Montanari, U. (eds.) CAAP 1987. LNCS, vol. 249, pp. 138–152. Springer, Heidelberg (1987). https://doi.org/10.1007/3-540-17660-8_53
13. De Nicola, R., Melgratti, H.: Multiparty testing preorders. In: Ganty, P., Loreti, M. (eds.) TGC 2015. LNCS, vol. 9533, pp. 16–31. Springer, Cham (2016). https://doi.org/10.1007/978-3-319-28766-9_2

14. De Nicola, R., Segala, R.: A process algebraic view of input/output automata. Theor. Comput. Sci. **138**(2), 391–423 (1995)

15. Hennessy, M.: Algebraic Theory of Processes. MIT Press Series in the Foundations of Computing. MIT Press, Cambridge (1988)

16. Hüttel, H., et al.: Foundations of session types and behavioural contracts. ACM Comput. Surv. **49**(1), 3:1–3:36 (2016)

17. Laneve, C., Padovani, L.: The *Must* preorder revisited. In: Caires, L., Vasconcelos, V.T. (eds.) CONCUR 2007. LNCS, vol. 4703, pp. 212–225. Springer, Heidelberg (2007). https://doi.org/10.1007/978-3-540-74407-8_15

18. Milner, R.: Communication and Concurrency. PHI Series in Computer Science. Prentice Hall, Upper Saddle River (1989)

19. Natarajan, V., Cleaveland, R.: Divergence and fair testing. In: Fülöp, Z., Gécseg, F. (eds.) ICALP 1995. LNCS, vol. 944, pp. 648–659. Springer, Heidelberg (1995). https://doi.org/10.1007/3-540-60084-1_112

20. Rensink, A., Vogler, W.: Fair testing. Inf. Comput. **205**(2), 125–198 (2007)

Data-Driven Choreographies à la Klaim

Roberto Bruni[1], Andrea Corradini[1], Fabio Gadducci[1(✉)], Hernán Melgratti[2],
Ugo Montanari[1], and Emilio Tuosto[3,4]

[1] University of Pisa, Pisa, Italy
fabio.gadducci@unipi.it
[2] University of Buenos Aires & Conicet, Buenos Aires, Argentina
[3] Gran Sasso Science Institute, L'Aquila, Italy
[4] University of Leicester, Leicester, UK

Abstract. We propose Klaim as a suitable base for a novel choreographic framework. More precisely we advocate Klaim as a suitable language onto which to project *data-driven* global specifications based on distributed tuple spaces. These specifications, akin to behavioural types, describe the coordination from a global point of view. Differently from behavioural types though, our specifications express the data flow across distributed tuple spaces rather than detailing the communication pattern of processes. We devise a typing system to validate Klaim programs against projections of our global specifications. An interesting feature of our typing approach is that well-typed systems have an arbitrary number of participants. In standard approaches based on behavioural types, this is often achieved at the cost of considerable technical complications.

1 Introduction

Communication-centered programming is playing a prominent role in the production of nowadays software. Programming peers that need to exchange information is an error-prone activity and the behaviour of even small systems is subject to a combinatorial blow-up as the number of peers increases. Therefore well-structured principles and rigorous foundations are needed to develop well-engineered, trustworthy software. One possibility is to exploit some sort of behavioural types [8,15] to manage abstract descriptions of peers and formally study their properties such as communication safety, absence of deadlocks, progress or session fidelity: given the types of the peers, the emerging behaviour of their composition is analysed. In the seminal paper [14], recently nominated the *most influential POPL paper (Award 2018)*, the authors push forward an

---

Research partly supported by the EU H2020 RISE programme under the Marie Skłodowska-Curie grant agreement No. 778233, by UBACyT projects 200201701-00544BA and 20020170100086BA, and CONICET project PIP 11220130100148CO, by the EU COST Action IC1405, by the MIUR PRINs 201784YSZ5 *ASPRA: Analysis of program analyses* and 2017FTXR7S *IT-MaTTerS: Methods and tools for trustworthy smart systems*, and by University of Pisa PRA_2018_66 *DECLWARE: Metodologie dichiarative per la progettazione e il deployment di applicazioni*.

M. Boreale et al. (Eds.): De Nicola-Festschrift, LNCS 11665, pp. 170–190, 2019.
https://doi.org/10.1007/978-3-030-21485-2_11

abstract notion of global type of interaction that represents a sort of contract between the communicating peers. This is paired with the notion of local type that gives an abstract description of the behaviour of each peer, as taken in isolation. Interestingly, local types can be obtained "for free" by projection from global types, while the properties of interest can be studied and guaranteed just at the level of global types, without the need of studying the composition of local types. The conformance of peers implementation w.r.t. the global type can be studied instead at the level of local types, allowing a more efficient form of type checking. Roughly this means that properties are stated globally but checked locally. Global types have been inspired by session types [13] and by choreography languages in service oriented computing (WS-CDL[1]), where complex interactions are modelled from the point of view of the global sequence of events that must take place in order to successfully complete the computation.

In the literature, global/local types have been studied mostly in the context of point-to-point channel-based interactions. This means that the main action in a choreography is the sending of a message from one peer to another on a specific channel (of a given type). In this paper we explore a different setting, where interaction over tuple-spaces replaces message passing, in the style of Linda-like languages [10]. Instead of primitives for sending and receiving messages, here there are primitives for inserting a tuple on a tuple space, for reading (without consuming) a tuple from a tuple space or for retrieving a tuple from a tuple space. We call these interactions data-driven, as decisions will be taken on the basis of the type of the tuples that are manipulated. We coined the term *klaimographies* in honour of the process language Klaim [1,6], a main contribution of Rocco De Nicola in the fields of process algebras and distributed programming. Inspired by Klaim, klaimographies exploit the notion of distributed tuple spaces to separate the access to data on the basis of the interactions that are carried out.

A Marketplace Scenario. We illustrate this with a motivating example that we will formalise later on (cf. Example 5 on page 8). We consider a scenario where sellers and buyers use a marketplace provided by a broker. Sellers can put on sale (several) items and buyers can inspect them. When an item of interest is found, the client can start a negotiation with the seller. The intended behaviour of this choreography is informally represented by the BPMN diagram[2] in Fig. 1. The diagram does not specify the protocol in a precise way. In our scenario there is a single broker but an arbitrary number of sellers or buyers. This is not reflected in the diagram because the BMPN pools 'Seller' and 'Buyer' represent participants, not roles that maybe enacted by many participants. Taking into account a multiplicity of participants triggers interesting issues. For instance, the bargaining subprocess should happen between two specific instances of participants: the buyer interested in a particular item and the seller that advertised such item. Moreover, the interactions among these specific instances must happen without interference from other participants.

---

[1] http://www.w3.org/2002/ws/chor.

[2] The diagram has been drawn with the BeePMN tool https://www.beepmn.com.

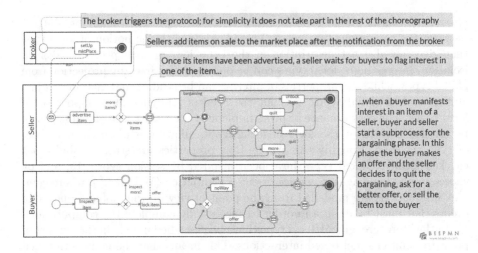

Fig. 1. A marketplace scenario

There are several distinguishing features of klaimographies w.r.t. the literature on global types that tackle the issues described above. First, klaimographies naturally support an arbitrary number of participants. This is uncommon in standard behavioural types approaches where the number of participants in interactions is usually fixed a priori, even when the number of participants is a parameter of the type, as done in [16] (see also Sect. 5). Second, interactions of klaimographies are multiway because each tuple can be read many times. Typically, session types specify point-to-point interactions where messages have exactly one producer and one consumer: see for instance [4] and the discussions on multiway interactions therein. Third, all interactions involve a tuple space locality instead of a channel name. Fourth, klaimographies are data-driven in the sense that they aim to check properties of data-flow. An example of use of klaimographies is to control the access to pieces of data in a tuple space.

The main contribution of this paper is to set up the formal setting of klaimographies and to prepare the ground for several interesting research directions: we fix the syntax of global and local types and define the projection from global to local types, as typical of choreographic frameworks. Global types are equipped with a partial order semantics of events and local types with an ordinary operational semantics. Then, the conditions under which the behaviour of projected local types is faithful to the semantics of global types are spelled out.

Shifting the focus from control to data in the choreographic framework has several implications. Firstly, the emphasis is no longer on properties related to computational actors. For instance, klaimographies admit computations where some processes may not terminate and are left waiting for some data. In standard choreographic frameworks those would be undesired behaviours to rule out with suitable typing disciplines. Nonetheless, we claim that in some application domains computations with deadlocked processes have to be considered non-erroneous. For instance, in reactive systems based on event-notification frameworks some "listener" components must be kept waiting for events to occur. Our work paves the way to the formal study of properties of data, like consumption, persistence and availability, in a choreographic setting.

Another main innovation of klaimographies is that they allow one to easily represent protocols where a role can be enacted by an arbitrary number of components. We give an example of such protocol in Sect. 2.3. Remarkably, those protocols can be specified in some existing choreographic frameworks [5,16], but in a less abstract way that requires the explicit quantification on components.

Structure of the Paper. After some preliminaries in Sect. 2.1, we define klaimographies as global types in Sect. 2.2 and give some examples in Sect. 2.3. In Sect. 3.1 we define the semantics of global types and give the adequacy conditions for projecting global types to local types. In Sect. 3.2 we define the syntax and operational semantics of local types and show how to project global types over local types in Sect. 3.3. The semantic correspondence between global types and local types is accounted for in Sect. 4. Some concluding remarks together with the discussion of related and future work are in Sect. 5.

2 Klaimographies

Our type system hinges on the basic notions of Klaim that are based on tuples, localities, and operations to generate and access tuple spaces. We recall that Klaim features two kinds of access to tuples located on a tuple space dubbed *input* and *read* access and often denoted as in $t @ 1$ and read $t @ 1$ in Klaim's literature. An input access in $t @ 1$ instantiates the variables in t corresponding to the fields in the matching tuple at locality 1 and then removes such tuple from 1, while a read access read $t @ 1$ does not remove the tuple from 1 after instantiating the variables in t. Section 2.1 introduces *tuple types* that basically abstract away from values in Klaim's tuples. Section 2.2 introduces *global types* meant to specify Klaim systems from a global point of view that, using *roles*, abstracts away from the actual instances of processes executing a protocol. Clearly, the form of interactions featured in the global types are inspired by Klaim operations.[3] Sect. 2.3 gives a taste of the expressiveness of our global types.

2.1 Tuple Types

We consider a set of variables $\mathcal{V}$ ranged over by x and a set of localities $\mathcal{Loc}$ ranged over by 1 (and use ℓ to range over $\mathcal{Loc} \cup \mathcal{V}$) and we let s range over basic sorts which include int, bool, str and the sort loc of *localities*. The set $\mathcal{T}$ of *tuple (types)* consists of the terms derived from the following grammar:

$$\mathsf{t} ::= \mathsf{s} \mid \star \mid x : \mathsf{s} \mid \nu x : \mathsf{s} \mid \mathsf{t} \cdot \mathsf{t}$$

---

[3] Klaim allows code mobility, which for the sake of simplicity is disregarded here. See however the discussion in Sect. 5.

Tuple types are trees $t \cdot t$ where leaves are either a sort s, any type $\star$, a sorted variable $x : s$, or a fresh sorted variables $\nu x : s$ (the difference between $x : s$ and $\nu x : s$ is clarified in Sect. 2.3). Note that $\nu x : s$ are binders that *define* $x \in \mathcal{V}$. Hence, we talk about *free* and *defined* (sorted) names occurring in tuples. The functions $fn(\_)$ and $dn(\_)$ return sets of pairs $x \mapsto s$ assigning sort s to $x \in \mathcal{V}$ and are given according to the definition below

$$
\begin{aligned}
dn(s) &= \emptyset & fn(s) &= \emptyset \\
dn(x : s) &= \emptyset & fn(x : s) &= \{x \mapsto s\} \\
dn(\nu x : s) &= \{x \mapsto s\} & fn(\nu x : s) &= \emptyset \\
dn(t_1 \cdot t_2) &= dn(t_1) \cup dn(t_2) & fn(t_1 \cdot t_2) &= fn(t_1) \cup fn(t_2) \\
dn(\star) &= \emptyset & fn(\star) &= \emptyset
\end{aligned}
$$

We write $\llcorner \lrcorner$ to denote the projection of a set of pairs over its first component. We say a tuple t is *well-sorted* if the following two conditions hold:

- $\llcorner fn(t) \lrcorner \cap \llcorner dn(t) \lrcorner = \emptyset$, i.e., free and defined names are disjoint; and
- $t = t_1 \cdot t_2$ implies t_1 and t_2 are well-sorted and their names are disjoint, namely, $\llcorner dn(t_1) \lrcorner \cap \llcorner dn(t_2) \lrcorner = \emptyset$ and $\llcorner fn(t_1) \lrcorner \cap \llcorner fn(t_2) \lrcorner = \emptyset$.

Hereafter, we assume all tuples to be well-sorted. Note that $fn(t)$ and $dn(t)$ are partial functions (from names to sorts) for well-sorted tuples.

A substitution of the free occurrences of a variable x in a (well-sorted) tuple t by a variable $y \notin dn(t)$, written $t\{^y/_x\}$, is defined by

$$
(x : s)\{^y/_x\} = y : s \quad \text{and} \quad (t_1 \cdot t_2)\{^y/_x\} = (t_1\{^y/_x\}) \cdot (t_2\{^y/_x\})
$$

while it is the identity on the remaining cases. Let $\sigma = \{y_1/x_1, \ldots, y_n/x_n\}$ such that $x_i \neq x_j$ for all $i \neq j$ (i.e., σ is a partial endo-function on $\mathcal{V}$). We now write $t\sigma$ for the simultaneous substitution of each x_i by y_i. We use Σ for the set of all substitutions. We write $\sigma_1\sigma_2$ for the composition of partial functions with disjoint domain, and $\sigma_1[\sigma_2]$ for the update of σ_1 with σ_2.

Tuple types t and t' such that $dn(t) \cap dn(t') = \emptyset$ can *match* by producing a substitution; this is realised by the partial function $\bowtie : \mathcal{T} \times \mathcal{T} \to \Sigma$ below

$$
t \bowtie t' = \begin{cases}
\emptyset & \text{if } t = \star \vee t' = \star \vee t, t' \in \{s, x : s\} \\
\sigma & \text{if } t = t_1 \cdot t_2 \wedge t' = t_1' \cdot t_2' \wedge t_1 \bowtie t_1' = \sigma_1 \wedge t_2\sigma_1 \bowtie t_2'\sigma_1 = \sigma \\
\{^y/_x\} & \text{if } (t = \nu y : s \wedge t' = x : s) \vee (t' = \nu y : s \wedge t = x : s) \\
undef & \text{otherwise}
\end{cases}
$$

We write $t \bowtie t'$ when $t \bowtie t' = \sigma$ for a substitution $\sigma \in \Sigma$.

We say that t *generates* when in one of its fields there is a $\nu x : \text{loc}$ type.

2.2   Global Types

We fix two disjoint sets $\mathcal{U} = \{p, q, \ldots\}$ and $\mathcal{M} = \{P, Q, \ldots\}$, respectively of *unit* roles and *multiple* roles, and define the set of *roles* $\mathcal{R} = \mathcal{U} \cup \mathcal{M}$, ranged over by

ρ. We conventionally write multiple roles with initial uppercase letters and unit roles with initial lowercase letters.

Roles have to be thought of as types inhabited by instances of processes enacting the behaviour specified in a choreography. Unit roles are unit types while multiple roles account for multiple instances of processes all performing actions according to their role.

Let us first define the grammar for *prefixes* used in global types:

$$
\begin{array}{llll}
\pi & ::= & \rho\,!\,(\mathbf{t})\,@\,\ell & \text{(autonomous) output} \\
 & | & \rho\,!\,\mathbf{t}\,@\,\ell & \text{(autonomous) read-only output} \\
 & | & \rho\,?\,(\mathbf{t})\,@\,\ell & \text{(autonomous) input} \\
 & | & \rho\,?\,\mathbf{t}\,@\,\ell & \text{(autonomous) read} \\
 & | & \rho \rightarrow \rho' : (\mathbf{t})\,@\,\ell & \text{consuming interaction} \\
 & | & \rho \rightarrow \rho' : \mathbf{t}\,@\,\ell & \text{read-only interaction}
\end{array}
$$

We syntactically distinguish two kinds of prefixes. The prefixes generated by the first four productions in the grammar of π above are the *autonomous* prefixes, that is those prefixes that processes can execute directly on a tuple space without coordinating with other processes. They are analogous to Klaim primitives for Linda-like interactions. The prefixes generated by the remaining two productions are the *interaction* prefixes, namely those involving a role generating a tuple and one accessing it. They are analogous to the usual prefixes of global types. The set $\mathsf{roles}(\pi) \subseteq \mathcal{R}$ of roles in π is defined in the obvious way; note that $\mathsf{roles}(\pi)$ is a singleton if, and only if, π is an autonomous prefix. Inspired by Klaim, processes can access tuple types according to two modalities syntactically distinguished by the round brackets around the tuple in prefixes. More precisely, when a prefix surrounds a tuple $\mathbf{t}$ with round brackets then $\mathbf{t}$ is meant to be consumed, otherwise it is meant to be read-only.

We assume that tuple types used in read-only modalities do not generate.

Global types K have the following syntax

$$
\mathsf{K} ::= \sum_{i \in I} \pi_i.\mathsf{K}_i \;\mid\; \mathsf{K} \prec \mathsf{K} \;\mid\; X \;\mid\; \mu_\rho\, X.\mathsf{K}
$$

for I a finite set of indexes, and we write either 0 or $\pi_j.\mathsf{K}_j$ for $\sum_{i \in I} \pi_i.\mathsf{K}_i$ whenever $I = \emptyset$ (we also omit trailing occurrences of 0) or $I = \{j\}$, respectively. The set $\mathsf{roles}(\mathsf{K}) \subseteq \mathcal{R}$ of roles of K is the set of roles that are mentioned in K and it is defined in the obvious way.

The syntax of global types features prefix guarded choices, sequential composition, and recursion. The semantics in Sect. 3.1 will make clear that the sequential composition $\prec$ allows for some degree of concurrency between actions in the absence of role and communication dependencies. To handle recursive behaviour, the construct $\mu_\rho\, X.\mathsf{K}$ singles out a role $\rho \in \mathsf{roles}(\mathsf{K})$ deciding whether to repeat the execution of the body K or (if ever) to end it. To achieve this, ρ notifies the decision to stop or to do a next iteration by generating tuple types for the other roles (this is formally defined in Sect. 3.1). We omit the decoration ρ when roles(K) = $\{\rho\}$.

We extend the notions of defined and free names to global types as follows:

$$fn(\rho\,!\,(\mathtt{t})\,@\,\ell) = fn(\mathtt{t}) \cup \{\ell \mapsto \mathtt{loc}\} \qquad dn(\rho\,!\,(\mathtt{t})\,@\,\ell) = dn(\mathtt{t})$$

(omitted prefixes are defined analogously)

$$
\begin{aligned}
fn(\sum_{i \in I} \pi_i.\mathsf{K}_i) &= \bigcup_{i \in I} fn(\pi_i) \cup (fn(\mathsf{K}_i) \setminus dn(\pi_i)) & dn(\sum_{i \in I} \pi_i.\mathsf{K}_i) &= \bigcup_{i \in I} dn(\pi_i) \cup dn(\mathsf{K}_i) \\
fn(\mathsf{K}_1 \prec \mathsf{K}_2) &= fn(\mathsf{K}_1) \cup fn(\mathsf{K}_2) & dn(\mathsf{K}_1 \prec \mathsf{K}_2) &= dn(\mathsf{K}_1) \cup dn(\mathsf{K}_2) \\
fn(X) &= \emptyset & dn(X) &= \emptyset \\
fn(\mu_\rho\, X.\mathsf{K}) &= fn(\mathsf{K}) & dn(\mu_\rho\, X.\mathsf{K}) &= dn(\mathsf{K})
\end{aligned}
$$

We remark that in $\mathsf{K}_1 \prec \mathsf{K}_2$ the scope of names defined in K_1 does not include K_2. We write $n(\_)$ for the set of (sorted) defined and free names of a term. A set S of sorted names is *consistent* if $x \mapsto \mathsf{s} \in S$ and $x \mapsto \mathsf{s}' \in S$ implies $\mathsf{s} = \mathsf{s}'$.

The sets of well-sorted prefixes and terms are defined inductively as follows:

- π is well-sorted if $fn(\pi) \cap dn(\pi) = \emptyset$ and $n(\pi)$ is consistent, i.e., there are no clashes/inconsistencies in the sorts of the names in the component $\mathtt{t}$ of π and the locality ℓ mentioned in π;
- $\mathsf{K} = \sum_{i \in I} \pi_i.\mathsf{K}_i$ is well-sorted if for all $i \in I$ both π_i and K_i are well-sorted and $n(\mathsf{K})$ is consistent;
- $\mathsf{K}_1 \prec \mathsf{K}_2$ is well-sorted if K_1 and K_2 are well-sorted and $n(\mathsf{K}_1 \prec \mathsf{K}_2)$ is consistent;
- X is well-sorted and $\mu_\rho\, X.\mathsf{K}$ is well-sorted if K is well-sorted.

We consider terms up-to α-renaming of defined names and recursion variables. Correspondingly, substitutions are capture avoiding, in the sense that defined names can be renamed to fresh names before any substitution is applied to a term. As usual we say that a global type K is *closed* when it does not contain free occurrences of recursion variables X or free occurrences of names.

2.3   Some Examples

We give a few simple global types (Examples 1 to 4) to highlight some basic features of klaimographies as well as a more complex example (Example 5) to illustrate the kind of protocols our global types can capture.

Example 1. Consider the following global type that describes the interaction of a client c with a simple service s that converts integers into strings.

$$\mathsf{K}_{(1)} = \mathsf{c} \to \mathsf{s} : (\mathtt{int})\,@\,\mathsf{l}\,.\,\mathsf{s} \to \mathsf{c} : (\mathtt{str})\,@\,\mathsf{l}$$

The client c produces an integer value on the locality l meant to be consumed by the server s, which in turn produces back the converted string for the client. ◇

Elaborating on the previous example we discuss a few features of our setting.

Example 2. Assume that we consider client and server in Example 1 as multiple instead of unit roles, and write

$$K_{(2)} = C \to S : (\texttt{int}) @ 1 . S \to C : (\texttt{str}) @ 1$$

In this case, $K_{(2)}$ states that each integer produced by a client will be consumed by a server, which will in turn produce a string for one of the clients.   ◇

The type in Example 2 does not ensure that clients consume the string conversion of the integer they produced, because all tuples are put at the same location 1. Name binders can be used to correlate tuples.

Example 3. Consider

$$K_{(3)} = C \to S : (\nu x : \texttt{int}) @ 1 . S \to C : (x : \texttt{int} \cdot \texttt{str}) @ 1$$

The first interaction binds the occurrence of x in the second interaction. The use of x in the second interaction constraints the instances of S and C to share a tuple whose integer expression matches the integer shared in the first interaction. Despite the identifier is known only to the communicating instances, this does not forbid two clients to generate the same integer value.   ◇

The klaimography in Example 3 does not establishes a one-to-one association between instances of C and S. In fact, an instance of C does not necessarily interact with the same instance of S in the two communications when two instances of C generate the same integer in the first interaction.

Example 4. A one-to-one correspondence can be achieved by using defined names for localities. Consider

$$K_{(4)} = C \to S : (\texttt{int} \cdot \nu x : \texttt{loc}) @ 1 . S \to C : (\texttt{str}) @ x$$

As in Example 3, client and server instances establish a common fresh identity x in the first interaction; this time the identity is a locality meant to share tuples in subsequent communications: the second interaction can only take place between the two instances sharing x, because such locality is known only to them.   ◇

The following example focuses on a more realistic scenario, allowing us to combine together most of the features of our framework. For readability, we use the notation $\mu_\rho^1 X.K$ for a recursive protocol where the body K is repeated at least once. Formally,[4]

$$\mu_\rho^1 X.K = K\{^{\mu_\rho\ X.K}/_X\}.$$

---

[4] The reader should not be confused by the meaning of $\mu_\rho X.K$ being different from that of $K\{^{\mu_\rho\ X.K}/_X\}$: this is because iteration and termination require some implicit interactions driven by ρ towards the other roles in K, as discussed in Sect. 3.1.

Example 5. The marketplace scenario described in Sect. 1 can be formalised by the following global type.

$$
\begin{aligned}
&\mathsf{broker} \rightarrow \mathsf{Seller} : \mathtt{start} \, @\, \mathtt{m}. \\
&\mu^1 \, X.\mathsf{Seller}\,! \,(\mathtt{str} \cdot \mathtt{int} \cdot \nu l : \mathtt{loc}) \, @\, \mathtt{m}. \, X \prec \\
&\mu^1_{\mathsf{Buyer}} \, Y. \left(
\begin{array}{l}
\mu \, Z.\mathsf{Buyer}\,? \, \mathtt{str} \cdot \mathtt{int} \cdot \mathtt{loc} \, @\, \mathtt{m}. \, Z \prec \\
\mathsf{Buyer}\,? \, (i : \mathtt{str} \cdot p : \mathtt{int} \cdot \nu l : \mathtt{loc}) \, @\, \mathtt{m}. \\
\quad \mu^1_{\mathsf{Seller}} \, W. \left(
\begin{array}{l}
\left(
\begin{array}{l}
\mathsf{Buyer} \rightarrow \mathsf{Seller} : (i : \mathtt{str} \cdot o : \mathtt{int}) \, @\, l. \\
\mathsf{Seller} \rightarrow \mathsf{Buyer} : (\mathtt{quit}) \, @\, l. \\
\mathsf{Seller}\,! \, (i : \mathtt{str} \cdot p : \mathtt{int} \cdot \nu l : \mathtt{loc}) \, @\, \mathtt{m}. \\
Y \\
+ \\
\mathsf{Seller} \rightarrow \mathsf{Buyer} : (\mathtt{sold}) \, @\, l. \, Y \\
+ \\
\mathsf{Seller} \rightarrow \mathsf{Buyer} : (\mathtt{more}) \, @\, l. \, W
\end{array}
\right) \\
+ \\
\mathsf{Buyer} \rightarrow \mathsf{Seller} : (\mathtt{noway}) \, @\, l. \\
\mathsf{Seller}\,! \, (i : \mathtt{str} \cdot p : \mathtt{int} \cdot \nu l : \mathtt{loc}) \, @\, \mathtt{m}. \\
Y
\end{array}
\right)
\end{array}
\right)
\end{aligned}
$$

The broker is a unit role that triggers sellers to start advertising their items on the marketplace location $\mathtt{m}$. Sellers and buyers are modelled as multiple roles. Each seller advertises one or more items at $\mathtt{m}$ (see recursion at line 2). Each buyer can inspect the advertised items (line 3) and eventually start bargaining on a selected item of interest. Note that the consumption at line 4 instantiates a private location l between the instance of Seller advertising the item and the instance of Buyer interested in buying it. Location l is used to perform the bargaining phase. See Sects. 3.1 and 3.2 for the exact semantics.

The seller instance controls the recursion $\mu^1_{\mathsf{Seller}} \, W. \cdots$; the body of the recursive type lets the buyer sharing location l decide whether to stop the bargaining (by exchanging a $\mathtt{noway}$ tuple, in which case the seller re-advertises the unsold item at $\mathtt{m}$) or to make an offer to the seller (which can then decide either to stop the bargaining, or to struck a deal, or to ask for an higher offer).   ◇

3   Semantics

We equip global types with a semantics based on pomsets, define projections from global to local types (that is abstractions of Klaim processes enacting the roles of global types), and define the operational semantics of local types.

3.1   Pomsets for Klaimographies

We give semantics to global types using *partially-ordered multi-sets* (*pomsets* for short). Following [9], a pomset is an isomorphism class of labelled partially-ordered sets (lposet) where, fixed a set of labels $\mathcal{L}$, an lposet is a triple $(\mathcal{E}, \leq, \lambda)$, with $\mathcal{E}$ a set of events, $\leq$ is a partial order on $\mathcal{E}$, and $\lambda : \mathcal{E} \rightarrow \mathcal{L}$ a labelling function mapping events in $\mathcal{E}$ to labels in $\mathcal{L}$. Two lposets $(\mathcal{E}, \leq, \lambda)$ and $(\mathcal{E}', \leq', \lambda')$ are *isomorphic* if there is a bijection $\phi : \mathcal{E} \to \mathcal{E}'$ such that $e \leq e' \iff \phi(e) \leq' \phi(e')$ and $\lambda = \lambda' \circ \phi$. Intuitively, the partial order $\leq$ yields a causality relation among events; for $e \neq e'$, if $e \leq e'$ then e' is caused by e or, in other words, the occurrence of e' must be preceded by the one of e in any execution respecting the order $\leq$. Note that λ is not required to be injective: for $e \neq e' \in \mathcal{E}$, $\lambda(e) = \lambda(e')$ means that e and e' model different occurrences of the same action. In the following, $[\mathcal{E}, \leq, \lambda]$ denotes the isomorphism class of $(\mathcal{E}, \leq, \lambda)$, symbols $r, r', \dots$ ($R, R', \dots$) range over (sets of, respectively) pomsets, and we assume that pomset r contains at least one lposet, which will possibly be referred to as $(\mathcal{E}_r, \leq_r, \lambda_r)$. The empty pomset is denoted as ϵ.

An event e is an *immediate predecessor* of an event e' (or equivalently, e' is an *immediate successor* of e) in a pomset r if $e \neq e'$, $e \leq_r e'$, and for all $e'' \in \mathcal{E}_r$ such that $e \leq_r e'' \leq_r e'$ either $e = e''$ or $e' = e''$. We draw pomsets as (a variant[5] of) Hasse diagrams of the immediate predecessor relation; for instance, the pomset

$$[\{e_1, e_2, e_3, e_4, e_5\}, \{(e_1, e_2), (e_1, e_3), (e_1, e_4), (e_1, e_5), (e_4, e_5)\}, \lambda]$$

is more conveniently written as

In the definition of our semantics we follow a principle that distinguishes the nature of autonomous and interaction prefixes.

- A tuple type t generated by an autonomous output can be accessed by any instance of *any* other role. However, there is no obligation to access the tuple t, hence our semantics has to contemplate the cases where either no read or no input of t happens.
- Interactions are slightly more subtle. Firstly, a tuple type t in a read-only interaction is meant to be eventually accessed by (an instance of) the receiving role. Secondly, the tuple type t of a consuming interaction must be eventually consumed by an instance of the receiving role. Thirdly, if t is in a consuming interaction, any instance of the receiving role is allowed to read t prior to its consumption.

To capture this semantics we label events with autonomous prefixes π, possibly decorated as $^{[i]}\pi$. Intuitively, e.g., a label $^{[i]}\rho \, ? \, t \, @ \, \ell$ ($^{[i]}\rho \, ! \, t \, @ \, \ell$) represents the fact that the ith instance of ρ reads (produces, respectively) a tuple of type t. Labels π that are not prefixed with $[\_]$ specify that the event can be performed by any instance of the role in π. Hereafter, we only deal with pomsets labelled

---

[5] Edges of Hasse diagrams are usually not oriented; here we use arrows so to draw order relations between events also horizontally.

as above. Also, we assign *basic pomsets* $\mathsf{bp}(i, \pi)$ to prefixes π. A basic pomset yields the causal relations of π imposed by the above design principle. For an autonomous prefix π we define $\mathsf{bp}(i, \pi) = \left\{ \left[\begin{array}{c} {}^{[i]}\pi \end{array} \right] \right\}$, and for interaction prefixes

$$\mathsf{bp}(i, \rho \to \rho' : \mathsf{t} @ \ell) = \bigcup_{h \geq 1} \left\{ \left[\begin{array}{c} {}^{[i]}\rho! \rho' \cdot \mathsf{t} @ \ell \\ \diagup \qquad \diagdown \\ e_1 \cdots\cdots\cdots e_h \end{array} \right]_\lambda \right\}$$

$$\mathsf{bp}(i, \rho \to \rho' : (\mathsf{t}) @ \ell) = \bigcup_{h \geq 1} \left\{ \left[\begin{array}{c} {}^{[i]}\rho! (\rho' \cdot \mathsf{t}) @ \ell \\ \diagup \qquad \diagdown \\ e_1 \cdots\cdots\cdots e_h \\ \diagdown \qquad \diagup \\ {}^{[i]}\rho'? (\rho' \cdot \downarrow\mathsf{t}) @ \ell \end{array} \right]_\lambda \right\} \cup \left\{ \left[\begin{array}{c} {}^{[i]}\rho! (\rho' \cdot \mathsf{t'}) @ \ell \\ \downarrow \\ {}^{[i]}\rho'? (\rho' \cdot \downarrow\mathsf{t}) @ \ell \end{array} \right] \right\}$$

where each read-only event e_j (with $1 \leq j \leq h$) is labelled as $\lambda(e_j) = \rho' ? \rho' \cdot \downarrow\mathsf{t} @ \ell$ with $\downarrow\mathsf{t}$ the binder-free version of t. Formally, $\downarrow\_$ is defined such that $\downarrow (\nu x : \mathsf{s}) = x : \mathsf{s}$, it is the identity on s, $\star$ and $x : \mathsf{s}$ and it behaves homomorphically over $\_ \cdot \_$. Note that the tuples in the labels of the events are "prefixed" by the role ρ' meant to access them; this requires to extend s so to include $\mathcal{R}$.

We can now give the semantics of prefixes as follows

$$[\![\pi]\!] = \begin{cases} \mathsf{bp}(1, \pi) & \text{if } \pi \text{ autonomous } \wedge \mathsf{roles}(\pi) \subseteq \mathcal{U} \\ \bigcup_{i \geq 1} \mathsf{bp}(i, \pi) & \text{if } \pi \text{ autonomous } \wedge \mathsf{roles}(\pi) \not\subseteq \mathcal{U} \end{cases}$$

$$[\![\rho \to \rho' : \mathsf{t} @ \ell]\!] = \begin{cases} \mathsf{bp}(1, \rho \to \rho' : \mathsf{t} @ \ell) & \text{if } \rho \in \mathcal{U} \\ \bigcup_{i \geq 1} \mathsf{bp}(i, \rho \to \rho' : \mathsf{t} @ \ell) & \text{otherwise} \end{cases}$$

$$[\![\rho \to \rho' : (\mathsf{t}) @ \ell]\!] = \begin{cases} \mathsf{bp}(1, \rho \to \rho' : (\mathsf{t}) @ \ell) & \text{if } \rho \in \mathcal{U} \\ \bigcup_{i \geq 1} \mathsf{bp}(i, \rho \to \rho' : (\mathsf{t}) @ \ell) & \text{otherwise} \end{cases}$$

As customary in other choreographic approaches (see [8, 12, 15] and references therein), the semantics of (closed) global types considers only *well-formed* global types, namely those enjoying *well-sequencedness* and *well-branchedness*. With respect to standard notions, however, these concepts have some peculiarities that we are now going to discuss.

The key points of well-sequencedness are highlighted in the following type

$$\rho_1 \to \rho_2 : (\mathsf{str} \cdot \star) @ 1 \prec \rho_2 \to \rho_3 : (\mathsf{str} \cdot \mathsf{int}) @ 1 \tag{1}$$

where an instance of ρ_2 transforms a pair generated by ρ_1 into a pair for ρ_3. The choreography (1) may be violated when ρ_1 generates a tuple of type $\mathsf{str} \cdot \mathsf{int}$.

In fact, such a tuple could match the type consumed by ρ_3 and therefore ρ_3 could "steal" the tuple from ρ_2. The problem is due to the fact that the tuples are generated on the same location and they match each other. More generally, the problem arises when different interactions introduce races on tuple types. Formally, write $(\mathbf{t}, \mathbf{1}) \in \mathsf{K}$ when there is a prefix in K whose tuple type is $\mathbf{t}$ and whose location is $\mathbf{1}$; we say that $(\mathbf{t}, \mathbf{1})$ is *local* to K if either of the following holds:

- $\mathsf{K} = \sum_{i \in I} \pi_i.\mathsf{K}_i$ and there is $i \in I$ such that either $(\mathbf{t}, \mathbf{1})$ is local to K_i or π_i
  outputs $\mathbf{t}$ at $\mathbf{1}$ for consumption and there is $\mathbf{t}'$ in an input from $\mathbf{1}$ in K_i such
  that $\mathbf{t} \bowtie \mathbf{t}'$
- $\mathsf{K} = \mathsf{K}_1 \prec \mathsf{K}_2$ and either $(\mathbf{t}, \mathbf{1})$ is local to K_1 or $(\mathbf{t}, \mathbf{1})$ is local to K_2
- $\mathsf{K} = \mu_\rho X.\mathsf{K}'$ and $(\mathbf{t}, \mathbf{1})$ is local to K'.

Our notion of well-sequencedness requires absence of races on tuple types: we say that K_1 and K_2 are *well-sequenced* ($ws(\mathsf{K}_1, \mathsf{K}_2)$ in symbols) if for $i \neq j \in \{1, 2\}$

- for all $(\mathbf{t}, \mathbf{1})$ local to K_i and for all $(\mathbf{t}', \mathbf{1}) \in \mathsf{K}_j$, $\mathbf{t} \bowtie \mathbf{t}'$ implies $(\mathbf{t}', \mathbf{1})$ is in a
  read-only prefix in K_j
- for all $(\mathbf{t}, \mathbf{1})$ in an autonomous input prefix of K_i and for all $(\mathbf{t}', \mathbf{1})$ generated
  in K_j, $\mathbf{t} \bowtie \mathbf{t}'$ implies $(\mathbf{t}', \mathbf{1})$ is in an autonomous output prefix in K_j for
  consumption.

Finally, the semantics of the sequential composition $\mathsf{K}_1 \prec \mathsf{K}_2$ is as follows:

$$\llbracket \mathsf{K}_1 \prec \mathsf{K}_2 \rrbracket = \begin{cases} \{\mathsf{seq}(\llbracket \mathsf{K}_1 \rrbracket, \llbracket \mathsf{K}_2 \rrbracket) & \text{if } ws(\mathsf{K}_1, \mathsf{K}_2)\} \\ undef & \text{otherwise} \end{cases}$$

where the auxiliary operation $\mathsf{seq}(\_, \_)$ sequentially composes pomsets r and r' so to make the actions of a role in r to precede its actions in r':

$$\mathsf{seq}(r, r') = [\mathcal{E}_r \cup \mathcal{E}_{r'}, \leq, \lambda_r \cup \lambda_{r'}]$$

where we assume that $\mathcal{E}_r \cap \mathcal{E}_{r'} = \emptyset$ and $\leq$ is the reflexive and transitive closure of $\leq_r \cup \leq_{r'} \cup \{(e, e') \in \mathcal{E}_r \times \mathcal{E}_{r'} \mid \mathsf{roles}(e) = \mathsf{roles}(e')\}$ (recall that the labels of events are autonomous prefixes for which roles is a singleton).

We now consider well-branchedness, the other condition of well-formedness. As usual [12], well-branchedness requires two conditions: single selector and knowledge of choices. This can be formalised by requiring that one process in the choice is *active*, namely it selects the branch to take, while the others are *passive*, namely they are informed of the chosen branch by inputting some information that unambiguously identifies each branch of the choice. We syntactically[6] enforce uniqueness of selectors: a choice with several branches takes the form

$$\sum_{i \in I} \rho \to \rho_i : (\mathbf{t}_i) @ \ell_i.\mathsf{K}_i \tag{2}$$

---

[6] This is just for simplicity as we could adopt definitions similar to the ones in [11,12] at the cost of higher technical complexity.

namely the instance of ρ acts as *unique* selectors. Intuitively, a passive instance (for example one enacting role ρ_i) in (2) has to be able to ascertain which branch the selector decided when the choice was taken. A simple way to ensure this is to require that the first input actions of each passive role are pairwise "disjoint" (i.e. non matching tuples or different locations) among branches.

The conditions on active and passive processes alone are not enough: in our framework, the notion of well-branchedness is slightly complicated by the presence of multiple roles. For instance, even assuming unique selectors, many instances of a selector role could exercise choices concurrently. This may create confusion if different branches generate matching tuples on a locality as illustrated by the next example.

Example 6. Let $K_{bad} = A \to B : (\text{int}) @ 1.K_1 + A \to B : (\text{str}) @ 1.K_2$ where

$$K_1 = B \to C : (\text{str}) @ 1.C \to B : (\text{bool}) @ 1 \quad \text{and} \quad K_2 = B \to C : (\text{bool}) @ 1$$

In K_{bad} confusion may arise that could alter the intended data flow. In fact, if two groups of participants execute the choice taking different branches, the instance of C executing K_2 in the second branch may receive the boolean that the instance of C in K_1 executing the first branch generates for B.   ◇

Therefore we require that tuple types in different branches of a choice do not match when they are at the same locality and that if a branch of a choice involves a unit role then none of the branches of the choice involves multiple roles. This condition, dubbed *confusion-free branching*, ensures that different "groups" of instances involved in concurrent resolutions of a choice do not "interfere" with each other. If a unit role is involved, only one group can resolve the choice. We remark that the above condition is not a limitation; in fact, we can pre-process branches of choices by adding an extra field in all tuples of the branch so to unequivocally identify on which branch the tuple type is used.

Summing up, a choice as in (2) is *well-branched*, written $wb(\{\bigcup_{i \in I} \pi_i.K_i\})$, when it is confusion-free, there is a unique active role, and all the other roles are passive. So we define

$$\left[\!\!\left[\sum_{i \in I} \pi_i.K_i\right]\!\!\right] = \begin{cases} \{\epsilon\} & \text{if } I = \emptyset \\ \bigcup_{r \in [\![\pi_i]\!], r' \in [\![K_i]\!]} \text{seq}(r, r') & \text{if } wb(\{\bigcup_{i \in I} \pi_i.K_i\}) \\ undef & \text{otherwise} \end{cases}$$

Finally, the semantic equation for $\mu_\rho X.K$ requires some auxiliary functions:

$$STOP(\rho, K, \widetilde{y}) = \rho \to \rho_1 : (\text{stop}) @ y_1 \prec \ldots \prec \rho \to \rho_n : (\text{stop}) @ y_n$$

$$LOOP(\rho, K, \widetilde{y}, \widetilde{y}') = \rho \to \rho_1 : (\nu y_1' : \text{loc}) @ y_1) \prec \ldots \prec \rho \to \rho_n : (\nu y_n' : \text{loc}) @ y_n$$

where $\text{roles}(K) = \{\rho, \rho_1, \ldots, \rho_n\}$ with $\rho \notin \{\rho_1, \ldots, \rho_n\}$ and $\widetilde{y} = y_1 \cdots y_n$ and $\widetilde{y}' = y_1' \cdots y_n'$. Then, we define

$$[\![\mu_\rho X.K]\!] = \begin{cases} \bigcup_{h \geq 0} [\![\text{unfold}_h(\mu_\rho X.K, fn(K), \widetilde{y}, \widetilde{y}')]\!] & \text{if } ws(K\{^0/x\}, K\{^0/x\}) \\ & \text{and } \widetilde{y} \cap fn(K) = \emptyset \\ undef & \text{otherwise} \end{cases}$$

where

$$\text{unfold}_h(\mu_\rho \ X.\text{K}, L, \widetilde{y}, \widetilde{y}') = \begin{cases} STOP(\rho, \widetilde{y}) & \text{if } h = 0 \\ LOOP(\rho, \text{K}, \widetilde{y}, \widetilde{y}') \prec \text{K}\{{}^{\text{K}'}/X\} & \text{otherwise} \end{cases}$$

where $\text{K}' = \text{unfold}_{h-1}(\mu_\rho \ X.\text{K}, L \cup \widetilde{y} \cup \widetilde{y}', \widetilde{y}', \widetilde{y}'')$ with $\widetilde{y}''$ fresh.

3.2   Local Types

A *local type* L, which describes the interaction from the perspective of a single role, is a term generated by the following grammar:

$$\kappa \ ::= \ \mathbf{t}\,!\,\ell \ \mid \ (\mathbf{t})\,?\,\ell \ \mid \ \mathbf{t}\,?\,\ell$$
$$\text{L} \ ::= \ \sum_{i \in I} \kappa_i.\text{L}_i \ \mid \ \text{L}\,\text{\textfractionsolidus}\,\text{L} \ \mid \ \big(\mu X(\widetilde{x}).\text{L}\big)\langle\widetilde{\ell}\rangle \ \mid \ X\langle\widetilde{\ell}\rangle$$

Prefixes $\mathbf{t}\,!\,\ell$, $(\mathbf{t})\,?\,\ell$ and $\mathbf{t}\,?\,\ell$ respectively stand for the production, consumption and read of a tuple $\mathbf{t}$ at the locality ℓ. Differently from global types, local types do not distinguish the generation of read-only tuples from the ones that can be consumed. Also, we use the symbol $\,\text{\textfractionsolidus}\,$ instead of $\prec$ to remark the fact that, on local types, the sequential operator $\,\text{\textfractionsolidus}\,$ serialises all activities.

Formation rules for branching and sequential local types L are exactly the same as for global types; analogously we write 0 for an empty sum. The syntax of recursive local types deviates from global types to make explicit the localities used for coordinating the execution; consequently, process variables are parametric (the syntax for recursive types is borrowed from [2]). The term $\big(\mu X(\widetilde{x}).\text{L}\big)\langle\widetilde{\ell}\rangle$ defines a process variable X with parameters $\widetilde{x}$ to be used in L; the initial values of $\widetilde{x}$ are given by $\widetilde{\ell}$. Accordingly, the usage of a process variable is parameterised, i.e., $X\langle\widetilde{\ell}\rangle$. For any $\big(\mu X(\widetilde{x}).\text{L}\big)\langle\widetilde{\ell}\rangle$, we assume that $|\widetilde{x}| = |\widetilde{\ell}|$ and $|\widetilde{x}| = |\widetilde{\ell}'|$ for any bound occurrence of $X\langle\widetilde{\ell}'\rangle$ in L.

The notions of free and defined names, well-sorted and closed terms are straightforwardly extended to local types; in $\big(\mu X(\widetilde{x}).\text{L}\big)\langle\widetilde{\ell}\rangle$, X and $\widetilde{x}$ act as binders for the occurrence in L. Substitution on local types is defined as follows:

$$\begin{aligned} (\mathbf{t}\,!\,\ell)\{{}^y/_x\} &= \mathbf{t}\{{}^y/_x\}\,!\,(\ell\{{}^y/_x\}) & &\text{if } x \notin dn(\mathbf{t}) \\ ((\mathbf{t})\,?\,\ell)\{{}^y/_x\} &= (\mathbf{t}\{{}^y/_x\})\,?\,(\ell\{{}^y/_x\}) & &\text{if } x \notin dn(\mathbf{t}) \\ (\mathbf{t}\,?\,\ell)\{{}^y/_x\} &= \mathbf{t}\{{}^y/_x\}\,?\,(\ell\{{}^y/_x\}) & &\text{if } x \notin dn(\mathbf{t}) \\ \big(\sum_{i \in I}\kappa_i.\text{L}_i\big)\{{}^y/_x\} &= \sum_{i \in I}(\kappa_i\{{}^y/_x\}).(\text{L}_i\{{}^y/_x\}) & &\text{if } \forall i.x \notin dn(\kappa_i) \\ (\text{L}_1\,\text{\textfractionsolidus}\,\text{L}_2)\{{}^y/_x\} &= \text{L}_1\{{}^y/_x\}\,\text{\textfractionsolidus}\,\text{L}_2\{{}^y/_x\} & & \\ X\langle\widetilde{\ell}\rangle\{{}^y/_x\} &= X\langle\widetilde{\ell}\{{}^y/_x\}\rangle & & \\ \big((\mu X(\widetilde{z}).\text{L})\langle\widetilde{\ell}\rangle\big)\{{}^y/_x\} &= \big(\mu X(\widetilde{z}).\text{L}\{{}^y/_x\}\big)\langle\widetilde{\ell}\{{}^y/_x\}\rangle & &\text{if } \{x,y\} \cap \widetilde{z} = \emptyset \end{aligned}$$

As for global types, we consider terms up-to α-renaming.

We consider the following syntax for the run-time semantics of a set of local types running on a tuple space, dubbed *specification*.

$$\Delta ::= \emptyset \mid \Delta, \rho : \mathtt{L} \mid \Delta, \mathtt{t} @ \mathtt{1}$$

A specification is a multiset containing two kinds of pairs: $\rho : \mathtt{L}$ associates a role with a local type, while $\mathtt{t} @ \mathtt{1}$ indicates that a tuple of type $\mathtt{t}$ is available at locality $\mathtt{1}$. We assume that when $\rho \in \mathcal{U}$ then there is at most one pair $\rho : \mathtt{L}$ in Δ. We write Γ to denote a specification containing only terms of the form $\mathtt{t} @ \mathtt{1}$.

The definition of $fn(\_)$ is straightforwardly extended to specifications.

We give an operational semantics to local types defined inductively by the rules in Fig. 2, where labels α are of the form $\rho : \kappa$. Rule [LOut] accounts for the behaviour of a role ρ that generates a tuple type $\mathtt{t}$ at locality $\mathtt{1}$. The operational semantics for the generation of a tuple $\mathtt{t}$ that contains binders ensures that each defined name is substituted by a fresh free variable (i.e., a variable that does not occur free in $\Delta, \rho : \mathtt{t} \,!\, \mathtt{1}.\mathtt{L}$). This is achieved by requiring (i) all bound names in $\mathtt{t}$ to be fresh, by α-renaming them if necessary (i.e., $dn(\mathtt{t})$ fresh), and (ii) the generated tuple $\downarrow \mathtt{t}$ is the binder-free version of $\mathtt{t}$. Rule [LIn] handles the case in which a role ρ consumes a tuple specified as $\mathtt{t}$ from locality $\mathtt{1}$. In order for the consumption to take place, the requested tuple $\mathtt{t}$ should match a tuple $\mathtt{t}'$ available at the locality $\mathtt{1}$. Note that the substitution σ generated from the match is applied to the continuation $\mathtt{L}$ associated with the role ρ; the consumed tuple is eliminated from the locality $\mathtt{1}$. Rule [LRd] is analogous to [LIn], but the read tuple is not removed from the tuple space. Rule [LSum] accounts for a role that follows by choosing one of its enabled branches. The semantics of a recursive term $(\mu X(\widetilde{x}) . \mathtt{L})\langle \widetilde{\mathtt{1}} \rangle$ is given by the rule [LRec], which unfolds the definition (i.e., $\mathtt{L}\{ (^{\mu X(\widetilde{x}) . \mathtt{L}})/_X \}$) and substitutes the formal parameters $\widetilde{x}$ of the recursive definition by the actual parameters $\widetilde{\mathtt{1}}$ via the substitution $\{ ^{\widetilde{\mathtt{1}}}/_{\widetilde{x}} \}$.

3.3   Obtaining Local Types Out of Global Types

The projection of a global type K over a role ρ, written $\mathsf{K} \downarrow_\rho$, denotes the local type that specifies the behaviour of ρ in K. Our projection operation is fairly standard but for the case of recursive types, which coordinate their execution by communicating over dedicated locations. Note that the semantics of recursive global types $\mu_\rho X.\mathsf{K}$ introduces auxiliary interactions to coordinate their execution (see $STOP(\rho, \mathsf{K}, \widetilde{y})$ and $LOOP(\rho, \mathsf{K}, \widetilde{y}, \widetilde{y}')$ in Sect. 3.1). However, there is not such an implicit mechanism in the execution of local types, where recursion is standard. Consequently, those auxiliary interactions need to be defined explicitly in local types; and consequently, they are introduced by projection (similarly to the approach in [3]). Another subtle aspect of the semantics of a recursive global type is that each iteration is parametric with respect to the set of localities used for coordination. In fact, $LOOP(\rho, \mathsf{K}, \widetilde{y}, \widetilde{y}')$ generates a set of fresh localities that are used by the next iteration. Such behaviour is mimicked by local types by relying on parameterised process variables. As a consequence, projection depends on the locations that are chosen as parameters of process variables. Hence, $\mathsf{K} \downarrow_\rho$ is

[LOut]

$$\frac{dn(\mathtt{t})\ \mathit{fresh}}{\varDelta, \rho : \mathtt{t}\,!\,1.L \xrightarrow{\rho:\downarrow\mathtt{t}\,!\,1} \varDelta, \rho : L, \downarrow\mathtt{t}\,@\,1}$$

[LRd]

$$\frac{\mathtt{t} \bowtie \mathtt{t}' = \sigma}{\varDelta, \rho : \mathtt{t}\,?\,1.L, \mathtt{t}'\,@\,1 \xrightarrow{\rho:\mathtt{t}'\,?\,1} \varDelta, \rho : L\sigma, \mathtt{t}'\,@\,1}$$

[LSeq₁]

$$\frac{\varDelta, \rho : L_1 \xrightarrow{\alpha} \varDelta', \rho : L_1'}{\varDelta, \rho : L_1\,\mathring{,}\,L_2 \xrightarrow{\alpha} \varDelta', \rho : L_1'\,\mathring{,}\,L_2}$$

[LIn]

$$\frac{\mathtt{t} \bowtie \mathtt{t}' = \sigma}{\varDelta, \rho : (\mathtt{t})\,?\,1.L, \mathtt{t}'\,@\,1 \xrightarrow{\rho:(\mathtt{t}')\,?\,1} \varDelta, \rho : L\sigma}$$

[LSum]

$$\frac{\Gamma, \rho : \kappa_j.L_j \xrightarrow{\alpha} \varDelta'}{\varDelta, \Gamma, \rho : \sum_{i\in I}\kappa_i.L_i \xrightarrow{\alpha} \varDelta, \varDelta'} \quad j \in I$$

[LSeq₂]

$$\frac{\varDelta, \rho : L_1 \xrightarrow{\alpha} \varDelta', \rho : 0}{\varDelta, \rho : L_1\,\mathring{,}\,L_2 \xrightarrow{\alpha} \varDelta', \rho : L_2}$$

[LRec]

$$\frac{\varDelta, \rho : L\{(\mu X(\tilde{x}).L)/X\}\{\tilde{1}/\tilde{x}\} \xrightarrow{\alpha} \varDelta'}{\varDelta, \rho : (\mu X(\tilde{x}).L)\langle\tilde{1}\rangle \xrightarrow{\alpha} \varDelta'}$$

Fig. 2. Semantics of local types

defined in terms of $K \downarrow_\rho^\eta$, where η is a partial function that maps process variables into sequences of locations, i.e., $\eta X = \tilde{\ell}$; and $K \downarrow_\rho = K \downarrow_\rho^\emptyset$. We now comment on the definition of $K \downarrow_\rho^\eta$ in Fig. 3. As usual, the local type corresponding to a role ρ that is not part of K is 0. The projection of a prefix π depends on the role played by ρ in π: it is omitted when ρ does not participate on π; it is the production of a tuple when π is an interaction or an autonomous output and ρ is the producer; it is the consumption of a tuple when π is an autonomous input or a consuming interaction and ρ is the consumer; or else it is the read of a tuple. Projection is homomorphic with respect to choices and sequential composition.

A global type $\mu_\rho X.K$ is projected as a recursive local type $(\mu X(\tilde{x}).L)\langle\tilde{\ell}\rangle$ where the formal parameters $\tilde{x}$ stand for the locations used for coordination and $\tilde{\ell}$ are the initial values. Note that $\mu_\rho X.K$ does not make explicit the set of initial locations but they are so in local types. For this reason, we define projection for a decorated version of global types, where each recursive sub-term $\mu_\rho X.K$ is annotated by a function $\phi : \mathcal{R} \mapsto \mathcal{L}oc$ defined such that $dom(\phi) = \mathsf{roles}(K) \setminus \{\rho\}$ and for all $\rho \in dom(\phi)$, $\phi(\rho)$ is globally fresh. Such annotations can be automatically added by pre-processing global types so to associate a fresh set of locations to each recursive process. Then, the projection of $\mu_{\rho'}^\phi X.K'$ onto ρ depends on whether ρ coordinates the recursion (i.e., $\rho = \rho'$) or not. When ρ is not the coordinator, the recursive process needs just one location x to await for either $\mathtt{stop}$ or a new location y for the next iteration. Note that the body of the recursion K' is then projected by considering an extended version of η where process variable X is parameterised with the received location y. The initial value of x is fixed according to ϕ (i.e., $\phi\rho$). Differently, when ρ coordinates the recursion, the projection generates a process variable that has several parameters, i.e., one location x_i for each passive role. In this case the body of the recursion consists

$$
K \downarrow_\rho^\eta =
\begin{cases}
0 & \text{if } \rho \notin \text{roles}(K) \\
K' \downarrow_\rho^\eta & \text{if } K = \pi.K' \text{ and } \rho \notin \text{roles}(\pi) \\
t\,!\,\ell.(K' \downarrow_\rho^\eta) & \text{if } K = \rho\,!\,t\,@\,\ell.K' \quad \text{ or } \quad K = \rho \to \rho'\,:\,t\,@\,\ell.K' \\
& \text{or } K = \rho\,!\,(t)\,@\,\ell.K' \quad \text{ or } \quad K = \rho \to \rho'\,:\,(t)\,@\,\ell.K' \\
(t)\,?\,\ell.(K' \downarrow_\rho^\eta) & \text{if } K = \rho\,?\,(t)\,@\,\ell.K' \quad \text{ or } \quad K = \rho' \to \rho\,:\,(t)\,@\,\ell.K' \\
t\,?\,\ell.(K' \downarrow_\rho^\eta) & \text{if } K = \rho\,?\,t\,@\,\ell.K' \quad \text{ or } \quad K = \rho' \to \rho\,:\,t\,@\,\ell.K' \\
\sum_{i \in I}(\pi_i.K_i) \downarrow_\rho^\eta & \text{if } K = \sum_{i \in I}\pi_i.K_i \\
K_1 \downarrow_\rho^\eta \,\,{}_9^o\, K_2 \downarrow_\rho^\eta & \text{if } K = K_1 \prec K_2 \\
(\mu X(x).(\text{stop})\,?\,x.0 + ((\nu y : \text{loc})\,?\,x.K' \downarrow_\rho^{\eta,X \mapsto y}))\langle \phi\rho \rangle & \\
\quad \text{if } K = \mu_{\rho'}^\phi X.K',\ \rho \neq \rho',\ \text{and } \{x,y\} \cap (\mathit{fn}(K') \cup \mathit{cod}(\eta)) = \emptyset & \\
(\mu X(\widetilde{x}).\text{stop}\,!\,x_1 \ldots \text{stop}\,!\,x_n.0 + \nu y_1 : \text{loc}\,!\,x.K' \downarrow_\rho^{\eta,X \mapsto \widetilde{y}})\langle \phi\rho_1 \ldots \phi\rho_n \rangle & \\
\quad \text{if } K = \mu_\rho^\phi X.K',\ \mathit{dom}(\phi) = \{\rho_1,\ldots,\rho_n\},\ \widetilde{x} = x_1 \ldots x_n, & \\
\quad \widetilde{y} = y_1 \ldots y_n,\ \text{and } (\widetilde{x} \cup \widetilde{y}) \cap (\mathit{fn}(K') \cup \mathit{cod}(\eta)) = \emptyset & \\
X\langle \eta X \rangle & \text{if } K = X
\end{cases}
$$

Fig. 3. Projection

of two branches: one that communicates the termination of the recursion to each participant, while another executes the body of the recursion after distributing fresh localities to each participants. Recursion parameters are initialised analogously. Finally, a process variable X is projected as its parameterised version $X\langle \eta X \rangle$, where the value of parameters are established according to η.

4   Semantic Correspondence

This section establishes the correspondence between the denotational semantics of global types and the operational semantics of local types. The partial order on the events of a pomset yields an interpretation of linear executions in terms of *linearisations* similar to interleaved semantics of concurrent systems. Intuitively a linearisation of a pomset r is a sequence of the events $\mathcal{E}_r$ that preserves the pomset's order $\leq_r$. We show that the traces of projections of a global type correspond to linearisations of its pomset semantics and that for each linearisation in the pomset semantics there is a system executing a corresponding trace.

We first introduce the notion of linearisation. Given a set of events $E \subseteq \mathcal{E}_r$ of a pomset r, a permutation $e_1 \cdots e_n$ of the events in E is a *linearisation of r* if

- $E \subseteq \mathcal{E}_r$ preserves $\leq_r$ namely $\forall 1 \leq i < j \leq n : \neg(e_j \leq_r e_i)$
- each event in $\mathcal{E}_r$ corresponding to an access of an interaction is in E, namely if $e \in \mathcal{E}_r$ and the tuple type in $\lambda_r(e)$ is of the form $\rho \cdot t$ then $e \in E$
- each output event in $\mathcal{E}_r$ is in E and, letting $I(e)$ be the set of events in $\mathcal{E}_r$ that are labelled by inputs of a tuple type matching the one in $\lambda_r(e)$, $I(e) \cap E = \emptyset \iff I(e) = \emptyset$
- accesses in $e_1 \cdots e_n$ are preceded by a matching output, namely, (i) for each $1 \leq i \leq n$ if e_i accesses t at 1 then there is some j with $1 \leq j < i$ such that

e_j outputs $\mathbf{t}'$ at 1 with $\mathbf{t}' \bowtie \mathbf{t}$, and (ii) for all h such that $j < h < i$ if e_h inputs $\mathbf{t}''$ at 1 then $\neg(\mathbf{t}' \bowtie \mathbf{t}'')$.

Fix a sequence

$$[\text{-}]\pi_1 \ldots [\text{-}]\,\pi_n \tag{3}$$

of labels of events (decorations are immaterial hence omitted in the following). We say that (3) is in *normal form* if the defined names of any two generating labels are disjoint; formally, for all $1 \le i \ne j \le n$

$$\pi_i \text{ generates } \mathbf{t}_i \text{ at } 1 \ \wedge \pi_j \text{ generates } \mathbf{t}_j \text{ at } 1 \implies dn(\mathbf{t}_i) \cap dn(\mathbf{t}_j) = \emptyset$$

Also, for $1 \le i < j \le n$, we say that π_j *is in the scope of* π_i if π_i generates $\mathbf{t}_i$ at 1 and π_j generates $\mathbf{t}_j$ at 1 with $\mathbf{t}_i \bowtie \mathbf{t}_j$ and $\forall i < h < j : \pi_h$ generates $\mathbf{t}_h$ at $1 \implies \neg(\mathbf{t}_h \bowtie \mathbf{t}_j)$. Without loss of generality we can assume that each sequence like (3) is in normal form (since we can rename all defined names generated by some π_i and the names of the labels π_j in their scope).

Let $\pi \vdash \alpha$ hold if

$$\begin{cases} (\pi = \rho\,!\,(\mathbf{t})\,@\,1 \vee \pi = \rho\,!\,\mathbf{t}\,@\,1) & \wedge\ \alpha = \rho : \mathbf{t}'\,!\,1 \\ \pi = \rho\,?\,(\mathbf{t})\,@\,1 & \wedge\ \alpha = \rho : (\mathbf{t}')\,?\,1 \\ \pi = \rho\,?\,\mathbf{t}\,@\,1 & \wedge\ \alpha = \rho : \mathbf{t}'\,?\,1 \\ \text{and } \exists\sigma : dn(\mathbf{t}) \to fn(\mathbf{t}') : \ \downarrow \mathbf{t}\sigma = \mathbf{t}' \end{cases}$$

This definition extends to sequences (3) with $n \ge 1$ as follows: $[\text{-}]\pi_1 \ldots [\text{-}]\,\pi_n \vdash \alpha_1 \cdots \alpha_n$ if $n = 1$ and $\pi_1 \vdash \alpha_1$ or $n > 1$ and

$$\pi_1 \vdash \alpha_1 \wedge \forall\sigma : dn(\mathbf{t}) \to fn(\mathbf{t}') : \ \downarrow \mathbf{t}\sigma = \mathbf{t}' \implies ([\text{-}]\pi_2 \ldots [\text{-}]\,\pi_n)\sigma \vdash \alpha_2 \cdots \alpha_n$$

where $\mathbf{t}$ is the tuple in π and $\mathbf{t}'$ is the one in α_1.

The K-*specification* of a given global type K is a specification Δ made of the projections of K only: formally

(i) $\rho : L \in \Delta$ iff $\rho \in \mathsf{roles}(K)$ and $L = K \downarrow_\rho$, and
(ii) Δ has no tuple.

Our main results give a correspondence between the pomset semantics of a global type K and its K-specification.

Theorem 1. *Given a well-formed global type K, for all $r \in [\![K]\!]$ there is a K-specification Δ such that for all linearisations $e_1 \cdots e_n$ of r there is $\Delta \xrightarrow{\alpha_1} \cdots \xrightarrow{\alpha_n}$ such that $\lambda_r(e_1) \cdots \lambda_r(e_n) \vdash \alpha_1 \cdots \alpha_n$.*

Proof (Sketch). The proof shows that the specification $\Delta = \big(\rho : K \downarrow_\rho\big)_{\rho \in \mathsf{roles}(K)}$ satisfies the property in the conclusion of the statement above. By induction on the structure of K, one shows that

- each output event is matched by an application on Δ of the [LOut] rule in Fig. 2, which adds a tuple type to the specification
- each input or read event has a correspondent transition in Δ from the receiving role according to rules [LIn] and [LRd] respectively; note that (cf. Fig. 2) in the former case the tuple type is removed from the specification.

For input and read events, the existence of the substitution required by the $\vdash$ relation is guaranteed by the hypothesis of rules [LIn] and [LRd]. The above follows immediately in the cases of prefixes. In the case of sum, the thesis follows by induction because the semantics of a choice is the union of the semantics of each branch.   □

Theorem 2. *Let Δ be a K-specification with K a well-formed global type. For all $\Delta \xrightarrow{\alpha_1} \cdots \xrightarrow{\alpha_n}$ there is a linearisation $e_1 \cdots e_n$ of a pomset $r \in [\![K]\!]$ such that $\lambda_r(e_1) \cdots \lambda_r(e_n) \vdash \alpha_1 \cdots \alpha_n$.*

Proof (Sketch). As for Theorem 1, the proof goes by induction on the structure of K. Guided by the structure of K, we can relate the application of the rules of Fig. 2 with the pomset semantics of the projections.   □

5   Conclusions

This paper, a modest attempt to thank Rocco for his work and friendship, addresses the following question:

> What notion of behavioural types corresponds to Linda-based coordination mechanisms?

To answer such question we advocate Klaim-based global and local types, dubbed klaimographies. Klaim has been designed to program distributed systems consisting of processes interacting via multiple distributed tuple spaces.

For simplicity, we have neglected code mobility, a distinctive feature of Klaim. Accommodating the mobility mechanism of Klaim would require to control the multiplicity of running instances and to generalise the well-formedness conditions to dynamically spawned processes. A further challenge would be to include mobility of processes-as-values featured by Klaim, which shares many similarities with session delegation. However, this can be associated to control-driven problems. These challenges are the scope for future work.

Furthermore, we also neglected to consider parallel types. A simple way to compose klaimographies in parallel would be to follow standard approaches by restricting roles on single threads and disjoint tuple spaces. We consider this option not very interesting, and we plan instead to explore more expressive settings for parallel types such as the one in [11, 12]. In particular, we conjecture that to add parallel composition $K \mid K'$ of klaimographies is enough to require that $\neg(t \bowtie t')$ for all $(t, 1) \in K, (t', 1) \in K'$. This condition is the counterpart of the *well-forkedness* condition of [11, 12] that requires different threads of a choreography to have disjoint input actions.

Klaim has been extended with several features designed on theoretical foundations and implemented in a suite of prototypes [1]. On the one hand, klaimographies share similarities with standard behavioural types centred on point-to-point channel based communications; on the other hand, they also have some peculiarities, some of which we highlighted here.

The closest work to ours is [5], which develops the initial proposal on parameterised choreographies in [7,16]. Notably, [5] is the first paper to support indexed roles and to statically infer the participants inhabiting them. The main difference with the approach in [5] is that klaimographies do not focus on processes, but rather on data. We envisage behavioural types as specifications of how to guarantee general properties of tuple spaces. For instance, take the marketplace example (cf. Example 5), one would like to check properties such as

for each tuple type $t = i : str \cdot p : int \cdot \nu l : loc$ consumed from locality m either a tuple type sold is eventually generated at locality l or t is eventually generated at m.

This property does not concern typical properties controlled by behavioural types (e.g., progress of processes, message orphanage, or unspecified reception).

As for future works, we aim to characterise the (classes of) properties of interest that klaimographies enforce. We conjecture that the well-formedness conditions defined here are strong enough to guarantee the property above. Another interesting line of research is to identify typing principles for Klaim processes. We believe that klaimographies can enable the possibility that the same process may enact different roles. For instance, considering again the marketplace example, a process can act both as seller and as buyer.

We have adopted a few simplifying assumptions. Other variants seem rather interesting. For instance, guards of sums could be autonomous inputs and not just consuming interactions, or even read-only access prefixes. Relaxing the constraint that read-only tuples cannot generate would lead to a sort of multi-cast mechanism of fresh localities. We plan to study those variants in future work.

References

1. Bettini, L., et al.: The Klaim project: theory and practice. In: Priami, C. (ed.) GC 2003. LNCS, vol. 2874, pp. 88–150. Springer, Heidelberg (2003). https://doi.org/10.1007/978-3-540-40042-4_4
2. Bocchi, L., Honda, K., Tuosto, E., Yoshida, N.: A theory of design-by-contract for distributed multiparty interactions. In: Gastin, P., Laroussinie, F. (eds.) CONCUR 2010. LNCS, vol. 6269, pp. 162–176. Springer, Heidelberg (2010). https://doi.org/10.1007/978-3-642-15375-4_12
3. Bocchi, L., Melgratti, H., Tuosto, E.: Resolving non-determinism in choreographies. In: Shao, Z. (ed.) ESOP 2014. LNCS, vol. 8410, pp. 493–512. Springer, Heidelberg (2014). https://doi.org/10.1007/978-3-642-54833-8_26
4. Castagna, G., Dezani-Ciancaglini, M., Padovani, L.: On global types and multiparty session. Log. Methods Comput. Sci. 8(1), 1–45 (2012)

5. Castro, D., Hu, R., Jongmans, S., Ng, N., Yoshida, N.: Distributed programming using role-parametric session types in go: statically-typed endpoint APIs for dynamically-instantiated communication structures. In: POPL 2019, PACMPL, vol. 3, pp. 29:1–29:30. ACM (2019)
6. De Nicola, R., Ferrari, G.L., Pugliese, R.: KLAIM: a kernel language for agents interaction and mobility. IEEE Trans. Softw. Eng. **24**(5), 315–330 (1998)
7. Denielou, P.-M., Yoshida, N., Bejleri, A., Hu, R.: Parameterised multiparty session types. Log. Methods Comput. Sci. **8**(4), 1–46 (2012)
8. Dezani-Ciancaglini, M., de'Liguoro, U.: Sessions and session types: an overview. In: Laneve, C., Su, J. (eds.) WS-FM 2009. LNCS, vol. 6194, pp. 1–28. Springer, Heidelberg (2010). https://doi.org/10.1007/978-3-642-14458-5_1
9. Gaifman, H., Pratt, V.R.: Partial order models of concurrency and the computation of functions. In: LICS 1987, pp. 72–85. IEEE Computer Society (1987)
10. Gelernter, D.: Generative communication in Linda. ACM Trans. Program. Lang. Syst. **7**(1), 80–112 (1985)
11. Guanciale, R., Tuosto, E.: An abstract semantics of the global view of choreographies. In: Bartoletti, M., Henrio, L., Knight, S., Vieira, H.T. (eds.) ICE 2016, EPTCS, vol. 223, pp. 67–82 (2016)
12. Guanciale, R., Tuosto, E.: Semantics of global views of choreographies. Log. Algebraic Methods Program. **95**, 17–40 (2018)
13. Honda, K., Vasconcelos, V.T., Kubo, M.: Language primitives and type discipline for structured communication-based programming. In: Hankin, C. (ed.) ESOP 1998. LNCS, vol. 1381, pp. 122–138. Springer, Heidelberg (1998). https://doi.org/10.1007/BFb0053567
14. Honda, K., Yoshida, N., Carbone, M.: Multiparty asynchronous session types. In: Necula, G.C., Wadler, P. (eds.) POPL 2008, pp. 273–284 (2008)
15. Hüttel, H., et al.: Foundations of session types and behavioural contracts. ACM Comput. Surv. **49**(1), 3:1–3:36 (2016)
16. Yoshida, N., Deniélou, P.-M., Bejleri, A., Hu, R.: Parameterised multiparty session types. In: Ong, L. (ed.) FoSSaCS 2010. LNCS, vol. 6014, pp. 128–145. Springer, Heidelberg (2010). https://doi.org/10.1007/978-3-642-12032-9_10

Different Glasses to Look into the Three Cs: Component, Connector, Coordination

Farhad Arbab[1], Marco Autili[2], Paola Inverardi[2], and Massimo Tivoli[2(✉)]

[1] Centrum Wiskunde & Informatica,
Science Park 123, 1098 XG Amsterdam, The Netherlands
Farhad.Arbab@cwi.nl

[2] Department of Information Engineering, Computer Science and Mathematics,
University of L'Aquila, L'Aquila, Italy
{marco.autili,paola.inverardi,massimo.tivoli}@univaq.it

Abstract. Component, connector, and coordination have been key concepts exploited in different communities to manage the complexity of concurrent and distributed system development. In this paper, we discuss three approaches within three different classes: composition in software architectures, coordination models, and programming abstractions for concurrency. These classes encompass different perspectives and solutions to face crucial challenges in developing concurrent and distributed systems. The approaches are discussed with respect to some characteristics of interest for the above classes: compositionality, incrementality, scalability, compositional reasoning, reusability, and evolution.

Keywords: Software components · Connectors ·
Software architectures · Coordination models ·
Programming abstractions

1 Introduction

Since late 70's, the development of concurrent and distributed systems has been receiving much attention from the research community [72,77]. Later, since 90's, component, connector, and coordination have been key concepts exploited in different communities to manage the complexity of concurrent and distributed systems development [2,4,9,17,18,24,32,37,43,47,49,52,75,78,79,83,84,87]. Process calculi and algebras laid the theoretical foundation for concurrency. The concept of *coordination* was introduced to offer software developers programming language constructs and models at a level of abstraction higher than the primitives offered by the parsimony of process algebras [3,39]. The concept of *connectors* emerged in software architectures as a useful construct to facilitate communication among independently developed *components*.

In this paper, we discuss three different approaches within three different classes: composition in software architectures, coordination models, and programming abstractions for concurrency. These classes encompass different perspectives and solutions to face crucial challenges in developing concurrent and

© Springer Nature Switzerland AG 2019
M. Boreale et al. (Eds.): De Nicola-Festschrift, LNCS 11665, pp. 191–216, 2019.
https://doi.org/10.1007/978-3-030-21485-2_12

distributed systems. Strictly concerning the purpose of this festschrift paper, we limit our discussion to previous work by De Nicola et al. and previous work by the authors. Specifically, we focus on programming abstractions for concurrent and autonomic systems [84]; exogenous coordination [5]; and the architectural synthesis of software coordinators for the distributed composition of heterogeneous components [18].

Since these approaches are radically different in nature, it is not possible, neither would it make sense, to make a point-to-point comparison or to force a description of them by adopting a uniform writing strategy at the same level of detail. However, this paper makes an effort to discuss the three approaches with respect to the same set of characteristics of interest for the above classes: compositionality, incrementality, scalability, compositional reasoning, reusability, and evolution.

This paper is organized as follows. Section 2 preludes our discussion by collocating the three works above within the state of the art. Section 3 provides a concise, yet complete, description of the three works, which are then characterized in Sect. 5 with respect to the six dimensions defined in Sect. 4. Section 6 concludes the paper.

2   Praeludium

In this section, we give a brief account of the three approaches that we consider followed by a brief discussion on related approaches.

The first approach by De Nicola et al. [84] is based on the definition of programming abstractions for concurrent and autonomic systems. The starting point of the work is represented by the notions of autonomic components (ACs) and autonomic-component ensembles (ACEs). The defined programming abstractions permit to model their evolution and their interactions. The authors define SCEL (Software Component Ensemble Language), a kernel language for programming the behavior of ACs and the formation of ACEs, and for controlling the interaction among different ACs. These abstractions permit describing autonomic systems in terms of behaviors, knowledge, and aggregations by complying with specific policies.

The second approach essentially concerns the work conducted by Arbab as described in [5], among other references. The author emphasizes the separation between computation and coordination defining a data-flow paradigm. Arbab defines the notion of *Abstract Behavior Types* (ABTs) as a higher-level alternative to ADT (*Abstract Data Type*) and proposes it as a proper foundation model for both components and their composition. An ABT defines an abstract behavior as a relation among a set of *timed-data-streams*, without specifying any detail about the operations that may be used to implement such behavior or the data types it may manipulate for its realization. ABTs allows for loosely coupling and exogenous coordination that are considered as two essential properties for components and their composition. ABTs serve as the primary formal semantic model for the coordination language Reo.

The third approach that we consider is described in the work conducted by Inverardi et al. [18]. The authors provide a complete formalization of an automated synthesis method for the distributed composition and coordination of software services. The method takes as input a specification of the global collaboration that the involved services must realize. This specification is given in the form of a state machine. The methods automatically generates a set of *Coordination Delegates* (CDs). CDs are additional software entities with respect to the participant services, and are synthesized in order to proxify and control their interaction. When interposed among the services, the synthesized entities enforce the collaboration prescribed by the specification. The synthesized CDs are proved to be correct by construction, meaning that the resulting distributed system realizes the specification. The synthesis method is able to deal with heterogeneous services that communicate synchronously and/or asynchronously. CDs are able to handle asynchrony through 1-bounded FIFO queues.

As already introduced, beyond the above mentioned approaches, there are many other approaches in the literature that should be considered (see [85] for an early comprehensive survey). For instance, in [2], the authors define a control-flow event-based paradigm for both computation and coordination. The WRIGHT architecture description language [1] is used as a specialized notation for architectural specification. As underlining formalism, the authors embed in WRIGHT an approach based on process algebra. In fact, in [2], CSP [86] (*Communicating Sequential Processes*) is used by the authors in order to provide an operational formalization of the separation between computation and coordination.

A family of process calculi called "*Kell calculus*" is presented in [33,34,87, 90]. It has been intended as a basis for studying distributed (and ubiquitous) component-based programming. Essentially, the Kell calculus is an *high-order* extension of π-Calculus. Its aim is to support the modeling of different forms of process *mobility* (e.g., logical and physical mobility). This is done by considering the possibility to directly transmit *processes* as messages and not only channels (used by processes in order to communicate) as it is in π-Calculus.

A further approach concerns the work described in [36]. The authors propose an algebraic formalization of the structure of the interactions enabled by connectors in component-based system implemented in the BIP framework [26,89]. It is a control-flow paradigm based on active/inactive communication ports of components.

The work described in [79] presents a modeling approach based upon the Bigraphical Reactive Systems framework developed by Milner, which consists of a bigraph together with a collection of bigraphical rewrite rules. Analogously to Kell calculus, this approach introduces mobility, locality and dynamism.

Further approaches are described in [37,47,75] and, as pure algebraic modeling approaches, they are theoretically very powerful although, they result to be hard to be used by practitioners.

Beyond the notational/algebraic/mathematical class of works on connector/component modeling, another interesting class of works that should be considered concerns *quantitative* approaches, e.g., [9,24]. These approaches are quantitative in the sense that they are able to express, and reason about, characteristics such as the probability of an event occurring, the elapse of time, performance, QoS, etc. In particular, in [9], the work described in [5] is extended in order to take into account QoS attributes of both computation and coordination, e.g., *shortest time for data transmission, allocated memory cost for data transmission*, and *reliability* represented by the probability of successful transmission. Furthermore, this work defines a semantic model for connectors different from ABTs, i.e., it is an operational model based on a QoS extension of *constraint automata* [24] called *Quantitative Constraint Automata*. In spirit, this model is a variant of a *labelled transition-system* model. Other extensions of Reo are also based on the constraint-automata semantics, and allow two forms of probability distributions, continuous-time (with no nondeterminism) and discrete-time (with nondeterminism) [25].

3   Looking into the Three Cs

Within the *"three Cs sphere"*, the three approaches considered in this paper represent three possible ways of dealing with component-based system development, component connection and coordination. For different purposes and at different levels, these approaches target the complexity of concurrent and distributed system development, and address crucial challenges to be faced when developing component-based systems, possibly reusing existing third-party components, connecting them and coordinating their interaction.

This section provides a concise, yet complete, description of the three approaches. For each of them, we first provide an overview by summarizing notions and aspects borrowed from the corresponding original work; then, we discuss the approach with respect to the best-fitting "**C**".

3.1   Software Component Ensemble Language

The aims of the work in [84] is to provide language designers with appropriate programming abstractions and constructs to deal with the development of concurrent and autonomic systems, adaptation with respect to possibly unforeseen changes of the working environment, evolving requirements, emergent behaviors resulting from complex interactions. The work in [84] is based on the two fundamentals notions of *Autonomic Components* (ACs) and *Autonomic-Component Ensembles* (ACEs), and defines programming abstractions to model their evolutions and their interactions. The authors define the *Software Component Ensemble Language* (SCEL) that is a programming language for programming the behavior of ACs and the formation of ACEs, and for controlling the interaction among different ACs. These abstractions permit describing autonomic systems in terms of *Behaviors, Knowledge*, and *Aggregations* by complying with specific *Policies*.

Overview of the SCEL's Design Principles – ACs and ACEs serve to structure systems into independent and distributed building blocks that interact and adapt.

ACs are entities with dedicated knowledge units and resources; awareness is guaranteed by providing them with information about their state and behavior via their knowledge repositories. These repositories also can be used to store and retrieve information about ACs' working environments, and thus can be exploited to adapt their behavior to the perceived changes. Each AC is equipped with an *interface*, consisting of a collection of *attributes*, describing the component's features such as identity, functionalities, spatial coordinates, group memberships, trust level, response time, and so on.

Attributes are used by the ACs to dynamically organize themselves into ACEs. Indeed, one of the main novelties of SCEL is the way groups of partners are selected for interaction and thus how ensembles are formed. Individual ACs can single out communication partners by using their identities, but partners can also be selected by taking advantage of the attributes exposed in the interfaces. Predicates over such attributes are used to specify the targets of communication actions, thus permitting a sort of *attribute-based* communication. In this way, the formation rule of ACEs is endogenous to ACs: members of an ensemble are connected by the interdependency relations defined through predicates. An ACE is therefore not a rigid fixed network but rather a highly flexible structure where ACs' linkages are dynamically established.

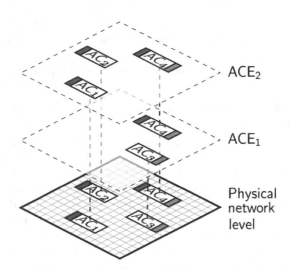

Fig. 1. Autonomic component ensembles

A typical scenario that gives rise to ACEs is reported in Fig. 1. It suggests that ACEs can be thought of as logical layers (built on top of the physical ACs' network) that identify dynamic ubnetworks of ACs by exploiting specific attributes; in the picture, these are the different colours associated to individual ACs.

The main linguistic abstractions that SCEL provides developer with for programming the evolution and the interactions of ACs and the architecture of ACEs are listed as follows.

- *Behaviors* describe how computations may progress and are modeled as processes executing actions, in the style of process calculi.
- *Knowledge* repositories provide the high-level primitives to manage pieces of information coming from different sources. Each knowledge repository is equipped with operations for adding, retrieving, and withdrawing knowledge items.
- *Aggregations* describe how different entities are brought together to form ACs and to construct the software architecture of ACEs. Composition and interaction are implemented by exploiting the attributes exposed in ACs' interfaces.
- *Policies* control and adapt the actions of the different ACs for guaranteeing accomplishment of specific tasks or satisfaction of specific properties.

By accessing and manipulating their own knowledge repository or the repositories of other ACs, components acquire information about their status (self-awareness) and their environment (context awareness) and can perform self-adaptation, initiate self- healing actions to deal with system malfunctions, or install self-optimizing behaviors. All these self-* properties, as well as self-configuration, can be naturally expressed by exploiting SCEL's higher-order features, namely, the capability to store/retrieve (the code of) processes in/from the knowledge repositories and to dynamically trigger execution of new processes. Moreover, by implementing appropriate security policies (e.g., limiting information flow or external actions), components can set up self-protection mechanisms against different threats, such as unauthorised access or denial-of-service attacks.

Discussion – More on the Component side, the work by De Nicola et al. addresses the challenges to develop large systems composed of a massive numbers of components, featuring complex interactions among components, as well as with humans and other systems. These complex systems are often referred to as ensembles. The complexity of the ensembles is due to their large dimension and their need to adapt to the changes of the working environment and to the evolving requirements. Self-* abilities are thus desirable to make this kind of systems *autonomic*, hence capable to self-manage by continuously monitoring their behavior and context, and by selecting corrective actions if needed.

Due to such an inherent complexity, today's engineering methods and tools do not scale well, and new engineering techniques are needed to address the challenges of developing, integrating, and deploying them. As the blending of different concepts that have emerged in different fields of computer science and engineering, the work by De Nicola et al. proposes programming abstractions specific to autonomic system development, and reconcile them under a single and uniform formal semantics. Main advances brought by De Nicola et al. are (i) ability to deal with heterogenous systems and different application domains;

(ii) flexibility and suitability to support adaptive context-aware activities in pervasive and mobile computing scenarios together with transparent monitoring; (iii) strict relation with component-based design, which has been indicated as a key approach for adaptive software design; (iv) flexible and expressive forms of communication and adaptation that are adequate to deal with highly dynamic ensembles; (v) strict relation with context-oriented programming, which has been advocated to program autonomic systems.

3.2   Reo Connectors

Reo [4,6,7] is a dataflow-inspired language for incremental construction of complex connectors by composing simpler ones, with a graphical as well as a textual syntax [45]. Every Reo connector encapsulates a concrete interaction protocol. In contrast to traditional models of concurrency, where actions or processes constitute the basic building blocks, Reo espouses and advocates an *interaction-centric* model of concurrency, where the only first class primitive is *interaction*.

Reo views components in a concurrent system as black boxes, each of which has an interface consisting of a set of ports. A *port* is a uni-directional means of communication through which a component exchanges with its environment by performing blocking I/O operations *get* and *put*. Because a component has access to only its own ports and Reo offers no other means of inter-process communication, components cannot communicate with each other directly. Instead, a separate construct, a *connector*, connects to the ports of various components and mediates the flow of data amongst them. Every connector imposes the interaction protocols that it encapsulates upon the communication of the components, exogenously (from the outside of the components, which remain oblivious to the interaction protocol that engages them).

Fig. 2. A typical set of Reo channels

Overview of Reo – A complex connector in Reo is constructed as a graph whose edges comprise of primitive binary connectors, called *channels*, and whose vertices consist of particular synchronous dataflow components, called *nodes*.

A channel is a medium of communication that consists of two ends and a constraint on the dataflows observed at those ends. There are two types of channel ends: *source* and *sink*. A source channel end accepts data into its channel, and a sink channel end dispenses data out of its channel. Every channel (type) specifies its own particular behavior as constraints on the flow of data through its ends.

Although all channels used in Reo are user-defined and users can indeed define channels with any complex behavior (expressible in the semantic model) that they wish, a very small set of channels, each with very simple behavior, suffices to construct useful Reo connectors with significantly complex behavior. Figure 2 shows a common set of primitive channels often used to build Reo connectors.

A `Sync` channel has a source and a sink end and no buffer. It accepts a data item through its source end iff it can simultaneously (i.e., atomically) dispense it through its sink.

A `LossySync` channel is similar to a synchronous channel except that it always accepts all data items through its source end. This channel transfers a data item if it is possible for the channel to dispense the data item through its sink end; otherwise the channel loses the data item. Thus, the context of (un)availability of a ready consumer at its sink end determines the (context-sensitive) behavior a `LossySync` channel.

A `FIFO1` channel represents an asynchronous channel with a buffer of capacity 1: it can contain at most one data item. When its buffer is empty, a `FIFO1` channel blocks I/O operations on its sink, because it has no data to dispense. It dispenses a data item and allows an I/O operation at its sink to succeed, only when its buffer is full, after which its buffer becomes empty. When its buffer is full, a `FIFO1` channel blocks I/O operations on its source, because it has no more capacity to accept the incoming data. It accepts a data item and allows an I/O operation at its source to succeed, only when its buffer is empty, after which its buffer becomes full.

More exotic channels are also permitted in Reo, for instance, synchronous and asynchronous *drains*. Each of these channels has two source ends and no sink end. No data value can be obtained from a drain channel because it has no sink end. Consequently, all data accepted by a drain channel are lost. `SyncDrain` is a synchronous drain that can accept a data item through one of its ends iff a data item is also available for it to simultaneously accept through its other end as well. `AsyncDrain` is an asynchronous drain that accepts data items through its source ends and loses them exclusively one at a time, but never simultaneously.

For a *filter channel*, or `Filter(P)`, its pattern P ⊆ *Data* specifies the type of data items that can be transmitted through the channel. This channel accepts a value $d \in$ P through its source end iff it can simultaneously dispense d through its sink end, exactly as if it were a `Sync` channel; it always accepts all data items $d \notin$ P through its source end and loses them immediately.

A Reo node is a logical place where channel ends coincide and coordinate their dataflows as prescribed by its *node type*. Figure 3 shows the three possible node types in Reo. A node is either *source*, *sink*, or *mixed*, depending

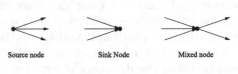

Source node   Sink Node   Mixed node

Fig. 3. Reo nodes

on whether all channel ends that coincide on that node are source ends, sink ends, or a combination of the two. Reo fixes the semantics of (i.e., the constraints on the dataflow through) Reo nodes, as described below.

The source and sink nodes of a connector are collectively called its *boundary nodes*. Boundary nodes define the interface of a connector. Components attach their ports to the boundary nodes of a connector and interact anonymously with each other through the interface of the connector. Attaching a component to a (source or sink) node of a connector consists of the identification of one of the (respectively, output or input) ports of the component with that node. The blocking I/O operations performed by components on their own local ports, triggers dataflow through their attached connector nodes.

A component can write data items to a source node that it is attached to. The write operation succeeds only if all (source) channel ends coincident on the node accept the data item, in which case the data item is transparently written to every source end coincident on the node. A source node, thus, acts as a synchronous replicator. A component can obtain data items, by an input operation, from a sink node that it is attached to. A take operation succeeds only if at least one of the (sink) channel ends coincident on the node offers a suitable data item; if more than one coincident channel end offers suitable data items, one is selected nondeterministically. A sink node, thus, acts as a nondeterministic merger. A mixed node nondeterministically selects and takes a suitable data item offered by one of its coincident sink channel ends and replicates it into all of its coincident source channel ends. Note that a component cannot attach to, take from, or write to mixed nodes.

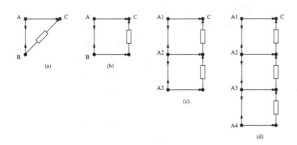

The connector shown in Fig. 4(a) is an *alternator* that imposes an ordering on the flow of the data from its input nodes A and B to its output node C. The SyncDrain enforces that data flow through A and B only synchronously (i.e., atomically). The empty buffer of the the FIFO1 channel together with the

Fig. 4. Reo circuits for alternators

SyncDrain guarantee that the data item obtained from A is delivered to C while the data item obtained from B is stored in the FIFO1 buffer. After this, the buffer of the FIFO1 is full and data cannot flow in through either A or B, but C can dispense the data stored in the FIFO1 buffer, which makes it empty again. Thus, subsequent take operations at C obtain the data items written to $A, B, A, B, ...$, etc.

The connector in Fig. 4(b) has an extra Sync channel between node B and the FIFO1 channel, compared to the one in Fig. 4(a). It is trivial to see that these two connectors have the exact same behavior. However, the structure of the connector in Fig. 4(b) allows us to generalize its alternating behavior to any number of producers, simply by replicating it and "juxtaposing" the top and the bottom Sync channels of the resulting copies, as seen in Fig. 4(c) and Fig. 4(d).

The connector in Fig. 4(d) is obtained by replicating the one in Fig. 4(b) 3 times. Following the reasoning for the connector in Fig. 4(c), it is easy to see that the connector in Fig. 4(d) delivers the data items obtained from $A1$, $A2$, $A3$, and $A4$ through C, in that order.

Semantics. Reo allows arbitrary user-defined channels as primitives; arbitrary mix of synchrony and asynchrony; and relational constraints between input and output. This makes Reo more expressive than, e.g., dataflow models, Kahn networks, synchronous languages, stream processing languages, workflow models, and Petri nets. On the other hand, it makes the semantics of Reo quite nontrivial. Various models have been developed to capture (various aspects of) the semantics of Reo, each to serve some specific purposes [55]. In this paper, we briefly describe only the ABTs [5], which constitute the primary formal semantics of Reo.

Formally, an ABT is a relation on a set of *time-data-streams*. ABTs yield an expressive compositional semantics for Reo where coinduction is the main definition and proof principle to reason about properties involving both data and time streams [14].

Discussion – Building upon earlier work on classical dataflow [15, 44, 56, 57], synchronous languages [30, 31, 40, 48], and Ptolemy [38, 74], interaction-centric concurrency allows treatment of protocols as concrete objects of discourse. Besides Reo, more recent work, such as BIP [16, 27], multiparty session types [51], Scribble [50, 91], and Pabble [81, 82] represent other examples of interaction-centric models that to various degrees of expressiveness and generality. Allowing arbitrary user-defined primitive building blocks and arbitrary mix of synchronous and asynchronous communication in its compositions, Reo relaxes restrictions and limitations implicit in most other above-mentioned models. See, for instance, [46] for an in-depth comparison of BIP and Reo.

The examples in Fig. 4 demonstrate how more complex connectors can be constructed by incremental composition of simpler ones. They also show how (1) arbitrary mix of synchrony and asynchrony, (2) preservation of synchrony through composition, which results in (3) propagation synchrony and exclusion though composition make Reo an expressive language. Several model checking tools are available for verification of Reo connectors [20–23, 35, 58–61, 67–69].

A high-level language like Reo that supports this form of protocol specification offers clear software engineering advantages (e.g., programmability, maintainability, verbatim-reusability, verifiability, scalability, etc.). The results of on-going work on compiling Reo connectors suggest that smart optimizing compilers for high-level protocol languages can generate executable code with better performance than hand-crafted code produced by programmers written in contemporary general-purpose languages with constructs of traditional models of concurrency [54]. For some protocols, existing Reo compilers already generate code that can compete with code written by a competent programmer [53].

Reo has been used for composition of Web services [12, 64, 73], modeling and analysis of long-running transactions in service-oriented systems [66], coordination of multi-agent systems [8], performance analysis of coordinated compositions [9,10,13,80], modeling of business processes and verification of their compliance [11,65,88], and modeling of coordination in biological systems [42].

3.3 Coordination Delegates

The work in [18] is based on the notion of *Coordination Delegate* and aims to formalize an automated synthesis method for the distributed composition and coordination of software services or, more in general, of software components. Following a modular and reuse-based approach, the business functionality of the system is assumed to be implemented by a set of software services, possibly black-box since provided by third parties. The system to be realized – out of the set of considered services – is specified as a global collaboration that the involved services have to realize by interacting via either synchronous or asynchronous message passing. This specification is given in the form of a state machine. Starting from this specification, and accounting for the specification of the interaction protocol performed by the involved services, the synthesis method is able to automatically generates a set of Coordination Delegates (CDs). CDs are additional software entities with respect to the participant services, and are synthesized in order to proxify and control their interaction. When interposed among the services by following the rules of a well-defined architectural style, the synthesized entities enforce the collaboration prescribed by the system specification. The synthesized CDs are correct by construction, meaning that the resulting distributed system realizes the specification. CDs are able to handle asynchrony through 1-bounded FIFO queues.

Overview of the Synthesis Method – Figure 5 shows an overview of the method for the automatic synthesis of CDs that, when interposed among the participant services, control those interactions that need coordination in order to enforce the realizability [28,29] of the specified global collaboration.

The method is organized into four steps that are performed in the following order: Projection, Selection, Synthesis, and Concretization.

1: Projection – It takes as input the system specification given in terms of a state machine where transitions model possibly simultaneous message exchanges among participants. As such, the system specification describes the way participants perform their interactions from a global perspective defining the (partial) order in which the message exchanges occur. Each single message exchange involves two participants: the sender and the receiver of the message. The specification abstracts from the way participants communicate to exchange messages, e.g., synchronous communication versus asynchronous one.

Out of the specification, Projection generates a behavioral model for each participant. This model is a state machine where transitions model (sets of possibly simultaneous) actions sending or receiving message, or actions internal to the participant that are not observable from outside. Message send and receive are, instead, observable actions. Simultaneous actions serve to deal with parallel

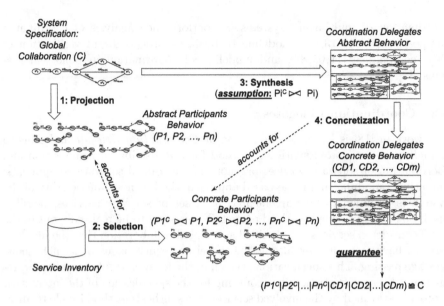

Fig. 5. Synthesis method overview

flows specified in the global collaboration and, hence, simultaneous executions. A projection represents the participant expected behavior according to the flows of message exchanges specified by the collaboration. Being derived from the system specification, also this model abstracts from the type of the send and receive actions (synchronous or asynchronous). We call this model Abstract Participant Behavior.

2: Selection – We recall that our approach is reuse-oriented, meaning that it allows to enforce system realizability in contexts in which the system is not implemented from scratch but it is realized by reusing, as much as possible, third-party services published in a Service Inventory. Services are selected from the inventory to play the roles of the abstract participants in the system specification. This calls for exogenous coordination of the selected concrete participants since, in general, we cannot access the participant code or change it.

A concrete service in the inventory comes with a behavioral specification of its interaction protocol. We call this model Concrete Participant Behavior. It is a state machine where transitions model (sets of possibly simultaneous) actions sending or receiving message, or internal actions. Similarly to the choreography specification, it can also specifies parallel flows that are joined afterwards. Differently from the Abstract Participant Behavior, for each transition, its type is specified: synchronous, asynchronous, or internal. That is, our approach does not impose constraints on the way concrete participants communicate, hence dealing with hybrid participants that can support both synchrony and asynchrony. For instance, a concrete participant could be a SOAP Web Service whose

WSDL[1] interface defines both Request/Response (synchronous interaction) and One-way operations (asynchronous interaction). In order to exchange messages asynchronously, concrete participants make use of bounded message queues. Our approach does not impose constraints on the size of the participants queues.

In order to select concrete participants that can suitably play the roles of abstract participants, our approach exploits a notion of behavioral refinement in order to automatically check whether the behavior of a concrete participant Pi^C is a refinement ($\bowtie$ in the figure) of the behavior of an abstract participant Pi. In the best case, for each abstract participant, a suitable concrete participant is found in the inventory. Otherwise, it might be the case that the set of selected participants covers a subset of the abstract participants in the specification. In this case, the abstract behavior of the remaining participants can support code generation activities to implement the missing concrete participants from scratch. Furthermore, the newly implemented concrete participant can be published in the inventory for possible future reuse.

An important consideration here is that, even in the case of limited reuse of third-party participants, our approach realizes separation of concern between the pure business logic implemented locally to each participant and the coordination logic needed for the realization of the global collaboration specified for the system. This logic is automatically generated as a set of CDs (Synthesis step). Keeping the needed coordination logic separated from the business one saves developers from writing code that goes beyond the development of the pure business logic internal to single participants. This allows developers to realize the specified system, without requiring any specific attention to what concerns coordination aspects. This aspect permits practitioners to develop the specified distributed system according to their daily development practices.

3 and 4: Synthesis and Concretization – The Synthesis step takes as input the system specification and automatically generates a set of CD Abstract Behavior models. Similarly to the Abstract Participant Behavior, each of them is a state machine where transitions model (sets of possibly simultaneous) actions sending or receiving message, or internal actions. These actions are related to the *standard* communication performed to achieve the choreography business logic. Differently from the Abstract Participant Behavior, there are also transitions modeling the synchronous exchange of coordination/synchronization messages. These actions model additional communication required to realize the coordination logic that is needed to enforce the realizability of the specified global collaboration. Standard communication takes place between a CD and the participant it controls and supervises, or directly among participants in case coordination is not required. When needed, additional communication messages are exchanged among the involved CD.

The Synthesis step is performed after a set of suitable concrete participants is obtained. Since the CD Abstract Behavior is generated out of the system specification, it abstracts from the way the supervised participants communicate (synchronously or asynchronously). This information will be added by the

---

[1] www.w3.org/TR/wsdl.

Concretization step that enriches the CD Abstract Behavior to achieve the so called CD Concrete Behavior.

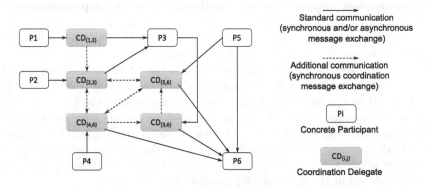

Fig. 6. Collaboration-based architectural style (a sample instance of)

For the set of synthesized CDs, correctness by construction means that when they are composed with the selected participants, the behavior of the resulting system realizes the specified global collaboration. That is, the generated CDs enforce by construction the realizability of the specified collaboration. Leveraging results on choreography realizability and its decidability from the work in [28,29], to correctly deal with asynchrony, the concrete CDs (Concretization step) in the controlled system make use of 1-bounded message queues. According to a predefined architectural style, CDs are interposed only among the participants needing coordination. Figure 6 shows an instance of the architectural style underlying our synthesis method.

CDs perform coordination (i.e., additional communication in the figure) of the participants interaction (i.e., standard communication in the figure) in a way that the resulting collaboration realizes the specified system. According to the type of actions performed by the concrete participants, standard communication can be synchronous or asynchronous. Additional communication is always synchronous. It is worth to note that CDs coordinate the interaction among the participants only when it is strictly needed for realizability enforcement purposes. That is, some participants are left free to communicate directly on those interactions that do not prevent the realizability of the specified global collaboration. Furthermore, depending on the specified collaboration, CDs do not necessarily require to be connected one to each other.

Discussion – Last but not least, on the Coordination side, the work by Inverardi et al. targets the development of reuse-based concurrent and distributed systems, from specification to composition and coordination code synthesis. The approach finds its most effective application in the distributed computing environment offered by the current Internet, which is increasingly populated by a virtually infinite number of software services that can be opportunistically composed to realize more complex and powerful distributed applications.

According to John Musser, founder of the ProgrammableWeb[2], the production of application programming interfaces (APIs) growths exponentially and some companies are accounting for billions of dollars in revenue per year via API links to their services. The evolution of today Internet is expected to lead to an ultra large number of available services, hence increasing their number from 104 services on 2007 to billions of services in the near future. This situation radically changes the way software will be produced. Modern service-oriented systems will be more and more often built by reusing and assembling existing pieces of software, exposed through their APIs. Thus, the ability to automatically *compose* and *coordinate* these pieces of software enables the productive construction of innovative and revolutionary everyday-life scenarios within smart cities and related software ecosystems [76].

Most of the existing approaches to software composition are heavily based on central coordination. A centralized approach composes multiple components into a larger application, in which one component centrally coordinates the whole system interaction. The approach by Inverardi et al. permits to describe the interactions among the different system parties from a global perspective. It permits to model a peer-to-peer communication by defining a multiparty protocol that, when put in place by the cooperating parties, allows reaching the overall goal in a fully distributed way. In this sense, it differs significantly from a centralized approach, where all participants (but one) play the passive role of serving requests. Future software systems will be increasingly composed of active entities that, communicating peer-to-peer, proactively make decisions and autonomously perform tasks according to their own imminent needs and the emergent global collaboration. Each involved party knows exactly when to execute its operations and with whom to interact. The system execution becomes a collaborative effort focusing on the exchange of messages among several business participants to reach a common global goal. Thus, (i) the ability to reuse, compose and coordinate existing pieces of software are all basic ingredients to achieve this vision; (ii) automated supported is needed to realize correct-by-construction coordination logic.

4   Characteristics of Interest

The approaches presented in previous sections will be characterized in next section by using the six characteristics of interest defined in the following.

- **Compositionality:** this characteristic concerns the ability to compose a system in a hierarchical way out of simpler components/sub-systems and, roughly speaking, it does not matter the way we conduct this hierarchical construction, the result is always equivalent. This means that the system

---

[2] https://www.programmableweb.com.

construction process is based on a composition operator '$*$' that is *associative*, i.e., for all x, y, z then $x*(y*z) \equiv (x*y)*z$. Compositionality is crucial for system analysis purposes since it may improve the efficiency of the analysis.

- **Incrementality:** incrementality is implied by compositionality but the former does not imply the latter. This characteristic concerns hierarchical system construction. However, differently from compositionality, the associativity property is not required. Icrementality is another crucial aspect for system design purposes since it promotes reuse. It is implied by the existence of a composition operator that hides the internal details of the composition and exposes its observational (external) behavior.
- **Scalability:** also scalability is implied by compositionality and it refers to the ability for a composition to scale to systems with an increasing number of components (i.e., systems of systems).
- **Compositional reasoning:** this characteristic is related to compositionality but not necessarily. It refers to the ability to infer properties held by the *whole* by locally checking properties held by its *constituents*. This characteristic promotes efficient system analysis by performing local checks instead of a global one, hence facing complexity issues in some cases.
- **Reusability:** this characteristic concerns the reuse degree of components/ sub-systems. A sub-system can be: (i) reusable in any context (i.e., it is context-free), (ii) parameterized with respect to an abstract characterization of a set of contexts and, hence, reusable only in some contexts (i.e., it is partially context-free), or (iii) not reusable at all (i.e., it is not context-free) since it is tailored to a specific context.
- **Evolution:** this characteristic refers to the ability to express and deal with dynamicity and reconfiguration, two aspects that promote system evolution. It is related to programming constructs useful to model specific forms of system evolution.

Note that the characteristics of interest above must be considered to be general in nature and, as such, in the following are inflected in different ways and interpreted according to the purposes of the three approaches.

5   Matching the Characteristics of Interest

In this section, we characterize the approaches described in Sect. 3 with respect to the characteristics of interest introduced in Sect. 4. The results of the characterization are summarized in the tables below, and discussed just after in the following subsections.

We make use of "Yes", "No", and "Limited" to rank at a glance how the considered approaches match the characteristics of interest. Obviously, "Yes" and "No" are used to indicate that an approach enjoys or does not enjoy at all, respectively, the ability/property associated to the indicated characteristic. "Limited" is used to indicate either limited or constrained (i.e., if some assumptions hold) support for the indicated characteristic (Tables 1 and 2).

Table 1. Matching the characteristics of interest (Part 1)

Approach	Compositionality	Incrementality	Scalability
SCEL	Yes	Yes	Yes
Reo connectors	Yes	Yes	Yes
Coordination delegates	Yes	Yes	Yes

Table 2. Matching the characteristics of interest (Part 2)

Approach	Compositional reasoning	Reusability	Evolution
SCEL	Either Yes or Limited (to reachability properties)	Yes	Yes
Reo connectors	Yes	Yes	Yes
Coordination delegates	Yes	Limited (under refinement)	Limited (under variation points specification)

5.1   Software Component Ensemble Language Characterization

The main benefits of SCEL can be summarized as follows with respect to the characteristics of interest introduced in Sect. 4.

- *Compositionality:* as formalized in [84], SCEL builds systems by composing in parallel subsystems/components in a process algebra style. The parallel composition operator is both commutative and associative, hence directly achieving incrementality and compositionality.
- *Incrementality:* it is directly implied by compositionality.
- *Scalability:* systems programmed in SCEL are able to self-manage by continuously monitoring their behavior and their working environment and by selecting the actions to perform for best dealing with the current status of affairs. The self-* properties supported by SCEL allows developer to overcome typical scalability issues of ensembles, by improving their development, integration and deployment.
- *Compositional reasoning:* compositional reasoning is not explicitly discussed in [84]. However, it is shown that SCEL supports the verification of reachability properties such as checking the probability of reaching a configuration where a given predicate on collected data is satisfied within a given deadline. The fact that a SCEL system is built by means of an associative composition operator and its constituents are well-understood, independent and distributed suggests that compositional reasoning might be supported at least for such reachability properties.

– **Reusability:** SCEL supports different forms of reusability. It defines abstractions to program behaviors (ACs) and aggregations (ACEs) and its syntax is parametric with respect to knowledge and policies. Thus, reusability of ACs and ACEs with respect to different approaches to knowledge handling and policies specification is supported. Similarly to what is done by the object-oriented paradigm, SCEL components are exposed through their interface that allows developers to control the access to their internal knowledge, policies and processes. Thus, another form of reusability that is directly supported concerns the one achievable through subtyping. Furthermore, SCEL provides high-order features to store/retrieve the code of processes in/from the knowledge repositories and to dynamically trigger the execution of new processes.

– **Evolution:** as briefly discussed above, SCEL components are self-aware and context-aware and enjoy a number of self-* properties, e.g., they are capable to perform self-adaptation and self-reconfiguration. Thus, dynamic evolution is completely supported by the programming abstractions provided by the language.

5.2   Reo Connectors Characterization

For what concerns Reo, main benefits are as follows:

– **Compositionality:** Reo connectors are fully compositional. Starting with a set of (user-defined) primitive binary connectors—i.e., channels—Reo's composition rules, manifested as nodes, hierarchically construct more complex connectors. Examples in Figs. 3 and 4 demonstrate this property. Composition in Reo is associative.

– **Incrementality:** This property is impled by Reo's compositionality.

– **Scalability:** This property is impled by Reo's compositionality. Figure 4 serves as an example that demonstrates scalability.

– **Compositional reasoning:** Hiding the internal nodes of a connector, e.g., the exclusive router in Fig. 4(a), simplifies its semantics to the behavior of the connectors that is externally observable through its boundary nodes which comprise its interface, e.g., $XRout(\langle \alpha, a \rangle; \langle \beta, b \rangle, \langle \gamma, c \rangle)$, above. Once this behavior is verified, using this simplified semantcs avoids the need to repeat in-situ re-verification of its internal details whenever the connector is used as a sub-connector in a construction.

– **Reusability:** Figures 3 to 4 demonstrate verbatim reusability of Reo connectors.

– **Evolution:** Reo offers operations to dynamically reconfigure the topology of its connectors, thereby changing the interaction protocol of a running application. A semantic model for Reo cognizant of its reconfiguration capability, a logic for reasoning about reconfigurations, together with its model checking algorithm, are presented in [41]. Graph transformation techniques have been used in combination with the connector coloring model to formalize the dynamic reconfiguration semantics of Reo circuits triggered by dataflow [62,63,70,71].

5.3   Coordination Delegates Characterization

The main benefits of the synthesis method, and of using the notion of Coordination Delegate for distributed coordination, can be summarized as follows.

- *Compositionality:* the composition operator that is used to model the coordination logic of the controlled system, i.e., the parallel composition of the synthesized CDs, is based on a enhanced version of the synchronous product of LTSs that is able to deal with aptly defined synchronization messages (additional communication in Fig. 6) that are exchanged synchronously among the CDs in different ways (one-to-one, one-to-many, many-to-one, or many-to-many interactions). Compositionality can be straightforwardly achieved by making the non-synchronized communication observable from outside. This means that the coordination logic can be modeled by composing in parallel the CDs in an incremental way and it does not matter the order in which the composition is performed.
- *Incrementality:* it is directly implied by compositionality.
- *Scalability:* concerning the CDs synthesis method, the experimental example discussed in [18] show that: (i) the "performance" of the CDs scale, meaning that they are not affected when the number of system consumers increases; (ii) the time required for executing the needed distributed coordination logic is neglectable with respect to the overall collaboration execution time, hence confirming that the CDs enforces the specified global collaboration effectively and efficiently.
- *Compositional reasoning:* the coordination logic synthesized by the method supports compositional reasoning for verifying a global property of the controlled system by just performing local checks. Each check considers: (i) a projection (similarly to what is done in step 1) of the property with respect to a set of participants; and (ii) a projection of the coordination logic with respect to the same set of participants. Both (i) and (ii) provide local (to each participant) models of the property and local models of the coordination logic, respectively. Standard model-checking techniques can be then used to singularly check each projection of the property against the related projection of the coordination logic.
- *Reusability:* the abstract CDs as synthesized after step 3 (Synthesis) of the method are concrete services independent since they are generated by only looking at the global collaboration specification. This means that, as long as the interaction protocol of the selected concrete participants refines the one of the corresponding abstract participants in the specification, the generated abstract CDs can be reused and only their Concretization (step 4) need to be performed again. Thus, we can conclude that reusability is achieved, although in a limited form.
- *Evolution:* in another recent work [19] from the authors of [18], which is based on a slightly revised version of the summarized synthesis method, a novel global collaboration specification is presented where the designer can specify the so called *variation points*. They are points in the specification that

can be realized by alternative collaborations. Each alternative can be dynamically enabled/disabled during system execution depending on the "sensed" context. The CDs that are automatically synthesized out of this new specification are thus able to deal with this (limited) form of dynamic evolution by performing not only exogenous distributed coordination, as already discussed above, but by also handling the enabling/disabling of the different specified alternatives.

6   Conclusions

Component, connector, and coordination have been key concepts exploited in different communities to manage the complexity of concurrent and distributed system development.

In this paper we discussed three approaches within three different classes: composition in distributed software architectures, exogenous coordination models, and programming abstractions for concurrent and autonomic systems. These classes encompass different perspectives and solutions to face crucial challenges in developing concurrent and distributed systems.

Our discussion considered previous work by De Nicola et al. about the SCEL language [84] for developing autonomic systems, and previous work by the authors about Reo connectors [5] for achieving exogenous coordination and distributed Coordination Delegates [18] for the distributed composition of heterogeneous components.

The approaches have been discussed with respect to some characteristics of interest for the above classes: compositionality, incrementality, scalability, compositional reasoning, reusability, and evolution.

All the three discussed approaches have been found to be representative for the three classes above since they support to some extent all the six dimension of interests for the engineering and development of concurrent and distributed systems.

References

1. Allen, R.: A formal approach to software architecture. Ph.D. thesis, Carnegie Mellon, School of Computer Science, January 1997. Issued as CMU Technical Report CMU-CS-97-144
2. Allen, R., Garlan, D.: A formal basis for architectural connection. ACM Trans. Softw. Eng. Methodol. 6(3), 213–249 (1997)
3. Arbab, F.: What do you mean, coordination? Bulletin of the Dutch Association for Theoretical Computer Science (NVTI), 19 March 1998
4. Arbab, F.: Reo: a channel-based coordination model for component composition. Math. Struct. Comput. Sci. 14(3), 329–366 (2004)
5. Arbab, F.: Abstract behavior types: a foundation model for components and their composition. Sci. Comput. Program. 55(1–3), 3–52 (2005)

6. Arbab, F.: Puff, the magic protocol. In: Agha, G., Danvy, O., Meseguer, J. (eds.) Formal Modeling: Actors, Open Systems, Biological Systems. LNCS, vol. 7000, pp. 169–206. Springer, Heidelberg (2011). https://doi.org/10.1007/978-3-642-24933-4_9

7. Arbab, F.: Proper protocol. In: Ábrahám, E., Bonsangue, M., Johnsen, E.B. (eds.) Theory and Practice of Formal Methods. LNCS, vol. 9660, pp. 65–87. Springer, Cham (2016). https://doi.org/10.1007/978-3-319-30734-3_7

8. Arbab, F., Aştefănoaei, L., de Boer, F.S., Dastani, M., Meyer, J.-J., Tinnermeier, N.: Reo connectors as coordination artifacts in 2APL systems. In: Bui, T.D., Ho, T.V., Ha, Q.-T. (eds.) PRIMA 2008. LNCS (LNAI), vol. 5357, pp. 42–53. Springer, Heidelberg (2008). https://doi.org/10.1007/978-3-540-89674-6_8

9. Arbab, F., Chothia, T., Meng, S., Moon, Y.-J.: Component connectors with QoS guarantees. In: Murphy and Vitek [84], pp. 286–304

10. Arbab, F., Chothia, T., van der Mei, R., Meng, S., Moon, Y.-J., Verhoef, C.: From coordination to stochastic models of QoS. In: Field and Vasconcelos [49], pp. 268–287

11. Arbab, F., Kokash, N., Meng, S.: Towards using Reo for compliance-aware business process modeling. In: Margaria, T., Steffen, B. (eds.) ISoLA 2008. CCIS, vol. 17, pp. 108–123. Springer, Heidelberg (2008). https://doi.org/10.1007/978-3-540-88479-8_9

12. Arbab, F., Meng, S.: Synthesis of connectors from scenario-based interaction specifications. In: Chaudron, M.R.V., Szyperski, C., Reussner, R. (eds.) CBSE 2008. LNCS, vol. 5282, pp. 114–129. Springer, Heidelberg (2008). https://doi.org/10.1007/978-3-540-87891-9_8

13. Arbab, F., Meng, S., Moon, Y.-J., Kwiatkowska, M.Z., Qu, H.: Reo2MC: a tool chain for performance analysis of coordination models. In: van Vliet, H., Issarny, V. (eds.) ESEC/SIGSOFT FSE, pp. 287–288. ACM (2009)

14. Arbab, F., Rutten, J.J.M.M.: A coinductive calculus of component connectors. In: Wirsing, M., Pattinson, D., Hennicker, R. (eds.) WADT 2002. LNCS, vol. 2755, pp. 34–55. Springer, Heidelberg (2003). https://doi.org/10.1007/978-3-540-40020-2_2

15. Arvind, A., Gostelow, K.P., Plouffe, W.: Indeterminacy, monitors, and dataflow. In: Rosen, S., Denning, P.J. (eds.) Proceedings of the Sixth Symposium on Operating System Principles, SOSP 1977, Purdue University, West Lafayette, Indiana, USA, 16–18 November 1977, pp. 159–169. ACM (1977)

16. Attie, P., Baranov, E., Bliudze, S., Jaber, M., Sifakis, J.: A general framework for architecture composability. In: Giannakopoulou, D., Salaün, G. (eds.) SEFM 2014. LNCS, vol. 8702, pp. 128–143. Springer, Cham (2014). https://doi.org/10.1007/978-3-319-10431-7_10

17. Autili, M., Chilton, C., Inverardi, P., Kwiatkowska, M., Tivoli, M.: Towards a connector algebra. In: Margaria, T., Steffen, B. (eds.) ISoLA 2010. LNCS, vol. 6416, pp. 278–292. Springer, Heidelberg (2010). https://doi.org/10.1007/978-3-642-16561-0_28

18. Autili, M., Inverardi, P., Tivoli, M.: Choreography realizability enforcement through the automatic synthesis of distributed coordination delegates. Sci. Comput. Program. 160, 3–29 (2018)

19. Autili, M., Salle, A.D., Gallo, F., Pompilio, C., Tivoli, M.: On the model-driven synthesis of evolvable service choreographies. In: Proceedings of the 12th European Conference on Software Architecture: Companion Proceedings, ECSA 2018, Madrid, Spain, 24–28 September 2018, pp. 20:1–20:6 (2018)

20. Baier, C., Blechmann, T., Klein, J., Klüppelholz, S.: Formal verification for components and connectors. In: de Boer, F.S., Bonsangue, M.M., Madelaine, E. (eds.) FMCO 2008. LNCS, vol. 5751, pp. 82–101. Springer, Heidelberg (2009). https://doi.org/10.1007/978-3-642-04167-9_5

21. Baier, C., Blechmann, T., Klein, J., Klüppelholz, S.: A uniform framework for modeling and verifying components and connectors. In: Field and Vasconcelos [49], pp. 247–267

22. Baier, C., Blechmann, T., Klein, J., Klüppelholz, S., Leister, W.: Design and verification of systems with exogenous coordination using Vereofy. In: Margaria, T., Steffen, B. (eds.) ISoLA 2010. LNCS, vol. 6416, pp. 97–111. Springer, Heidelberg (2010). https://doi.org/10.1007/978-3-642-16561-0_15

23. Baier, C., Klein, J., Klüppelholz, S.: Modeling and verification of components and connectors. In: Bernardo, M., Issarny, V. (eds.) SFM 2011. LNCS, vol. 6659, pp. 114–147. Springer, Heidelberg (2011). https://doi.org/10.1007/978-3-642-21455-4_4

24. Baier, C., Sirjani, M., Arbab, F., Rutten, J.J.M.M.: Modeling component connectors in Reo by constraint automata. Sci. Comput. Program. **61**(2), 75–113 (2006)

25. Baier, C., Wolf, V.: Stochastic reasoning about channel-based component connectors. In: Ciancarini, P., Wiklicky, H. (eds.) COORDINATION 2006. LNCS, vol. 4038, pp. 1–15. Springer, Heidelberg (2006). https://doi.org/10.1007/11767954_1

26. Basu, A., Bozga, M., Sifakis, J.: Modeling heterogeneous real-time components in BIP. In: SEFM 2006: Proceedings of the Fourth IEEE International Conference on Software Engineering and Formal Methods, Washington, DC, USA, pp. 3–12. IEEE Computer Society (2006)

27. Basu, A., Bozga, M., Sifakis, J.: Modeling heterogeneous real-time components in BIP. In: Proceedings of SEFM 2006, pp. 3–12. IEEE (2006)

28. Basu, S., Bultan, T.: Automated choreography repair. In: Stevens, P., Wąsowski, A. (eds.) FASE 2016. LNCS, vol. 9633, pp. 13–30. Springer, Heidelberg (2016). https://doi.org/10.1007/978-3-662-49665-7_2

29. Basu, S., Bultan, T., Ouederni, M.: Deciding choreography realizability. In: POPL. ACM (2012)

30. Benveniste, A., Caspi, P., Le Guernic, P., Halbwachs, N.: Data-flow synchronous languages. In: de Bakker, J.W., de Roever, W.-P., Rozenberg, G. (eds.) REX 1993. LNCS, vol. 803, pp. 1–45. Springer, Heidelberg (1994). https://doi.org/10.1007/3-540-58043-3_16

31. Berry, G.: Esterel and Jazz: two synchronous languages for circuit design (abstract). In: Pierre, L., Kropf, T. (eds.) CHARME 1999. LNCS, vol. 1703, p. 1. Springer, Heidelberg (1999). https://doi.org/10.1007/3-540-48153-2_1

32. Bhaduri, P., Ramesh, S.: Interface synthesis and protocol conversion. Form. Asp. Comput. **20**(2), 205–224 (2008)

33. Bidinger, P., Schmitt, A., Stefani, J.-B.: An abstract machine for the Kell calculus. In: Steffen, M., Zavattaro, G. (eds.) FMOODS 2005. LNCS, vol. 3535, pp. 31–46. Springer, Heidelberg (2005). https://doi.org/10.1007/11494881_3

34. Bidinger, P., Stefani, J.-B.: The Kell calculus: operational semantics and type system. In: Najm, E., Nestmann, U., Stevens, P. (eds.) FMOODS 2003. LNCS, vol. 2884, pp. 109–123. Springer, Heidelberg (2003). https://doi.org/10.1007/978-3-540-39958-2_8

35. Blechmann, T., Baier, C.: Checking equivalence for Reo networks. Electr. Notes Theor. Comput. Sci **215**, 209–226 (2008)

36. Bliudze, S., Sifakis, J.: The algebra of connectors - structuring interaction in BIP. IEEE Trans. Comput. **57**(10), 1315–1330 (2008)

37. Bruni, R., Lanese, I., Montanari, U.: A basic algebra of stateless connectors. Theor. Comput. Sci. **366**(1), 98–120 (2006)
38. Buck, J.T., Ha, S., Lee, E.A., Messerschmitt, D.G.: Ptolemy: a framework for simulating and prototyping heterogenous systems. Int. J. Comput. Simul. **4**(2), 155–182 (1994)
39. Carriero, N., Gelernter, D.: A computational model of everything. Commun. ACM **44**(11), 77–81 (2001)
40. Caspi, P., Pilaud, D., Halbwachs, N., Plaice, J.: LUSTRE: a declarative language for programming synchronous systems. In: Conference Record of the Fourteenth Annual ACM Symposium on Principles of Programming Languages, Munich, Germany, 21–23 January 1987, pp. 178–188. ACM Press (1987)
41. Clarke, D.: A basic logic for reasoning about connector reconfiguration. Fundam. Inform. **82**(4), 361–390 (2008)
42. Clarke, D., Costa, D., Arbab, F.: Modelling coordination in biological systems. In: Margaria, T., Steffen, B. (eds.) ISoLA 2004. LNCS, vol. 4313, pp. 9–25. Springer, Heidelberg (2006). https://doi.org/10.1007/11925040_2
43. de Alfaro, L., Henzinger, T.A.: Interface automata. SIGSOFT Softw. Eng. Notes **26**(5), 109–120 (2001)
44. Dennis, J.B., Gao, G.R.: An efficient pipelined dataflow processor architecture. In: Michael, G.A. (ed.) Proceedings Supercomputing 1988, Orlando, FL, USA, 12–17 November 1988, pp. 368–373. IEEE Computer Society (1988)
45. Dokter, K., Arbab. F.: Treo: textual syntax for Reo connectors. In: Bliudze, S., Bensalem, S. (eds.) Proceedings of the 1st International Workshop on Methods and Tools for Rigorous System Design, MeTRiD@ETAPS 2018. EPTCS, Thessaloniki, Greece, 15th April 2018, vol. 272, pp. 121–135 (2018)
46. Dokter, K., Jongmans, S., Arbab, F., Bliudze, S.: Combine and conquer: relating BIP and Reo. J. Log. Algebr. Meth. Program. **86**(1), 134–156 (2017)
47. Fiadeiro, J.L., Lopes, A., Wermelinger, M.: A mathematical semantics for architectural connectors. In: Generic Programming, pp. 178–221 (2003)
48. Gautier, T., Le Guernic, P., Besnard, L.: SIGNAL: a declarative language for synchronous programming of real-time systems. In: Kahn, G. (ed.) FPCA 1987. LNCS, vol. 274, pp. 257–277. Springer, Heidelberg (1987). https://doi.org/10.1007/3-540-18317-5_15
49. Hirsch, D., Uchitel, S., Yankelevich, D.: Towards a periodic table of connectors. In: Ciancarini, P., Wolf, A.L. (eds.) COORDINATION 1999. LNCS, vol. 1594, p. 418. Springer, Heidelberg (1999). https://doi.org/10.1007/3-540-48919-3_32
50. Honda, K., Mukhamedov, A., Brown, G., Chen, T.-C., Yoshida, N.: Scribbling interactions with a formal foundation. In: Natarajan, R., Ojo, A. (eds.) ICDCIT 2011. LNCS, vol. 6536, pp. 55–75. Springer, Heidelberg (2011). https://doi.org/10.1007/978-3-642-19056-8_4
51. Honda, K., Yoshida, N., Carbone, M.: Multiparty asynchronous session types. In: Necula, G.C., Wadler, P. (eds.) Proceedings of the 35th ACM SIGPLAN-SIGACT Symposium on Principles of Programming Languages, POPL 2008, San Francisco, California, USA, 7–12 January 2008, pp. 273–284. ACM (2008)
52. Inverardi, P., Tivoli, M.: Automatic synthesis of modular connectors via composition of protocol mediation patterns. In: 35th International Conference on Software Engineering, ICSE 2013, San Francisco, CA, USA, 18–26 May 2013, pp. 3–12 (2013)
53. Jongmans, S.-S., Halle, S., Arbab, F.: Reo: a dataflow inspired language for multicore. In: Proceedings of DFM 2013, pp. 42–50. IEEE (2014)

54. Jongmans, S.-S.T.: Automata-theoretic protocol programming: parallel computation, threads and their interaction, optimized compilation, [at a] high level of abstraction. Ph.D. thesis, Leiden University (2015, submitted)
55. Jongmans, S.-S.T., Arbab, F.: Overview of thirty semantic formalisms for Reo. Sci. Ann. Comput. Sci. **22**(1), 201–251 (2013)
56. Kahn, G.: The semantics of a simple language for parallel programming. In: Rosenfeld, J.L. (ed.) Information Processing, Stockholm, Sweden, pp. 471–475. North Holland, Amsterdam, August 1974
57. Kahn, G., MacQueen, D.B.: Coroutines and networks of parallel processes. In: IFIP Congress, pp. 993–998 (1977)
58. Kemper, S.: SAT-based verification for timed component connectors. Electr. Notes Theor. Comput. Sci. **255**, 103–118 (2009)
59. Kemper, S.: Compositional construction of real-time dataflow networks. In: Clarke, D., Agha, G. (eds.) COORDINATION 2010. LNCS, vol. 6116, pp. 92–106. Springer, Heidelberg (2010). https://doi.org/10.1007/978-3-642-13414-2_7
60. Klein, J., Klüppelholz, S., Stam, A., Baier, C.: Hierarchical modeling and formal verification. An industrial case study using Reo and Vereofy. In: Salaün, G., Schätz, B. (eds.) FMICS 2011. LNCS, vol. 6959, pp. 228–243. Springer, Heidelberg (2011). https://doi.org/10.1007/978-3-642-24431-5_17
61. Klüppelholz, S., Baier, C.: Symbolic model checking for channel-based component connectors. Electr. Notes Theor. Comput. Sci **175**(2), 19–37 (2007)
62. Koehler, C., Arbab, F., de Vink, E.: Reconfiguring distributed Reo connectors. In: Corradini, A., Montanari, U. (eds.) WADT 2008. LNCS, vol. 5486, pp. 221–235. Springer, Heidelberg (2009). https://doi.org/10.1007/978-3-642-03429-9_15
63. Koehler, C., Costa, D., Proença, J., Arbab, F.: Reconfiguration of Reo connectors triggered by dataflow. In: Ermel, C., Heckel, R., de Lara, J. (eds.) Proceedings of the 7th International Workshop on Graph Transformation and Visual Modeling Techniques (GT-VMT 2008), vol. 10, pp. 1–13 (2008). ECEASST. ISSN 1863-2122. http://www.easst.org/eceasst/
64. Koehler, C., Lazovik, A., Arbab, F.: ReoService: coordination modeling tool. In: Krämer et al. [72], pp. 625–626
65. Kokash, N., Arbab, F.: Formal behavioral modeling and compliance analysis for service-oriented systems. In: de Boer, F.S., Bonsangue, M.M., Madelaine, E. (eds.) FMCO 2008. LNCS, vol. 5751, pp. 21–41. Springer, Heidelberg (2009). https://doi.org/10.1007/978-3-642-04167-9_2
66. Kokash, N., Arbab, F.: Formal design and verification of long-running transactions with extensible coordination tools. IEEE Trans. Serv. Comput. **6**(2), 186–200 (2013)
67. Kokash, N., Krause, C., de Vink, E.: Data-aware design and verification of service compositions with Reo and mCRL2. In: SAC 2010: Proceedings of the 2010 ACM Symposium on Applied Computing, pp. 2406–2413. ACM, New York (2010)
68. Kokash, N., Krause, C., de Vink, E.P.: Verification of context-dependent channel-based service models. In: de Boer, F.S., Bonsangue, M.M., Hallerstede, S., Leuschel, M. (eds.) FMCO 2009. LNCS, vol. 6286, pp. 21–40. Springer, Heidelberg (2010). https://doi.org/10.1007/978-3-642-17071-3_2
69. Kokash, N., Krause, C., de Vink, E.P.: Time and data-aware analysis of graphical service models in Reo. In: Fiadeiro, J.L., Gnesi, S., Maggiolo-Schettini, A. (eds.) SEFM, pp. 125–134. IEEE Computer Society (2010)
70. Krause, C.: Reconfigurable component connectors. Ph.D. thesis, Leiden University (2011). https://openaccess.leidenuniv.nl/handle/1887/17718

71. Krause, C., Maraikar, Z., Lazovik, A., Arbab, F.: Modeling dynamic reconfigurations in Reo using high-level replacement systems. Sci. Comput. Program. **76**(1), 23–36 (2011)
72. Lamport, L.: Time, clocks, and the ordering of events in a distributed system. Commun. ACM **21**(7), 558–565 (1978)
73. Lazovik, A., Arbab, F.: Using Reo for service coordination. In: Krämer et al. [72], pp. 398–403
74. Liu, X., Xiong, Y., Lee, E.A.: The Ptolemy II framework for visual languages. In: 2002 IEEE CS International Symposium on Human-Centric Computing Languages and Environments (HCC 2001), Stresa, Italy, 5–7 September 2001, p. 50. IEEE Computer Society (2001)
75. Lopes, A., Wermelinger, M., Fiadeiro, J.L.: Higher-order architectural connectors. ACM Trans. Softw. Eng. Methodol. **12**(1), 64–104 (2003)
76. Manikas, K., Hansen, K.M.: Software ecosystems - a systematic literature review. J. Syst. Softw. **86**(5), 1294–1306 (2013)
77. Milner, R.: A Calculus of Communicating Systems. Springer, New York (1982)
78. Milner, R.: Communicating and Mobile Systems: The Pi-Calculus. Cambridge University Press, Cambridge (1999)
79. Milner, R.: The Space and Motion of Communicating Agents. Cambridge University Press, New York (2009)
80. Moon, Y.-J., Silva, A., Krause, C., Arbab, F.: A compositional semantics for stochastic Reo connectors. In: Mousavi, M.R., Salaün, G. (eds.) FOCLASA. EPTCS, vol. 30, pp. 93–107 (2010)
81. Ng, N., de Figueiredo Coutinho, J.G., Yoshida, N.: Protocols by default - safe MPI code generation based on session types. In: Franke, B. (ed.) CC 2015. LNCS, vol. 9031, pp. 212–232. Springer, Heidelberg (2015). https://doi.org/10.1007/978-3-662-46663-6_11
82. Ng, N., Yoshida, N.: Pabble: parameterised scribble for parallel programming. In: 22nd Euromicro International Conference on Parallel, Distributed, and Network-Based Processing, PDP 2014, Torino, Italy, 2–14 February 2014, pp. 707–714. IEEE Computer Society (2014)
83. Nicola, R.D., Duong, T., Inverso, O., Trubiani, C.: AErlang: empowering Erlang with attribute-based communication. Sci. Comput. Program. **168**, 71–93 (2018)
84. De Nicola, R., Loreti, M., Pugliese, R., Tiezzi, F.: A formal approach to autonomic systems programming: the SCEL language. ACM Trans. Auton. Adapt. Syst. **9**(2), 7:1–7:29 (2014)
85. Papadopoulos, G.A., Arbab, F.: Coordination models and languages. Adv. Comput. **46**, 329–400 (1998)
86. Roscoe, A.W.: The Theory and Practice of Concurrency. Prentice-Hall Inc., New York (1998)
87. Schmitt, A., Stefani, J.-B.: The Kell calculus: a family of higher-order distributed process calculi. In: Priami, C., Quaglia, P. (eds.) GC 2004. LNCS, vol. 3267, pp. 146–178. Springer, Heidelberg (2005). https://doi.org/10.1007/978-3-540-31794-4_9
88. Schumm, D., Turetken, O., Kokash, N., Elgammal, A., Leymann, F., van den Heuvel, W.-J.: Business process compliance through reusable units of compliant processes. In: Daniel, F., Facca, F.M. (eds.) ICWE 2010. LNCS, vol. 6385, pp. 325–337. Springer, Heidelberg (2010). https://doi.org/10.1007/978-3-642-16985-4_29

89. Sifakis, J.: A framework for component-based construction extended abstract. In: SEFM 2005: Proceedings of the Third IEEE International Conference on Software Engineering and Formal Methods, Washington, DC, USA, pp. 293–300. IEEE Computer Society (2005)

90. Stefani, J.-B.: A calculus of Kells. Electr. Notes Theor. Comput. Sci. **85**(1), 40–60 (2003)

91. Yoshida, N., Hu, R., Neykova, R., Ng, N.: The scribble protocol language. In: Abadi, M., Lluch Lafuente, A. (eds.) TGC 2013. LNCS, vol. 8358, pp. 22–41. Springer, Cham (2014). https://doi.org/10.1007/978-3-319-05119-2_3

Logics and Types

From the Archives of the Formal Methods and Tools Lab
Axiomatising and Contextualising ACTL

Stefania Gnesi$^{(\boxtimes)}$ (iD) and Maurice H. ter Beek (iD)

Formal Methods and Tools Lab, ISTI–CNR, Pisa, Italy
{stefania.gnesi,maurice.terbeek}@isti.cnr.it

Abstract. We present a sound and complete axiomatisation of ACTL, an action-based version of the well-known branching-time temporal logic CTL, and place it into a historical context. ACTL was originally introduced by Rocco De Nicola together with Frits Vaandrager 30 years ago, and it has played a major role in shaping the activity of our Formal Methods and Tools Lab from the nineties to this very day.

Keywords: Temporal logic · ACTL · Axiomatisation

1 Introduction

To appreciate the contribution of this paper, we first provide some necessary context through a brief recollection of memories from the last 40 years.

1.1 Rocco and Stefania

Rocco and Stefania were fellow students in Computer Science at the University of Pisa. They followed the same classes and had the same thesis supervisor. In fact, both were advised by Ugo Montanari and both graduated in 1978. After that, they followed a different road for some time. Their paths crossed again in 1984 when Stefania started working at the CNR, in the *Istituto di Elaborazione dell'Informazione* (later incorporated in what is nowadays called the *Istituto di Scienza e Tecnologie dell'Informazione* (ISTI)), where Rocco had been employed a couple of years earlier. Those were the years of the birth of formal verification techniques and tools. Temporal logics [11,12,15,16,26–28,47,53] were very much *à la mode* at that time and the first automatic tools for the verification of concurrent systems, mostly model checkers [15,17,18,33,48], were being realised.

The late eighties was the time during which Rocco and Frits Vaandrager worked on the definition of the so-called *action-based* branching-time temporal logics, namely ACTL and its extended version ACTL* [23–25]. Such temporal logics are highly suitable to express properties of concurrent systems specified by means of process algebras.

© Springer Nature Switzerland AG 2019
M. Boreale et al. (Eds.): De Nicola-Festschrift, LNCS 11665, pp. 219–235, 2019.
https://doi.org/10.1007/978-3-030-21485-2_13

1.2   Action-Based Temporal Logics

Process algebras [1, 2, 43, 44, 51] are generally recognised as being a convenient means for describing concurrent systems at different levels of abstraction. Their basic operational semantics is usually defined in terms of Labelled Transition Systems (LTSs), which are then quotiented by means of observational equivalences and allow the behaviour of a system to be analysed in relation to the *actions* the specified system may perform.

Specific logics for process algebras were proposed (cf., e.g., [42, 53]), typically interpreted on LTSs, and ACTL and ACTL* were defined in this framework as the action-based counterparts of CTL and CTL* [15, 16, 27, 28]. In another Festschrift contribution [6], we provided a more detailed historical account of temporal logics for reasoning on state-based as well as action-based properties and their interpretation structures, typically variants of the Doubly-Labelled Transition Systems (L^{2}TS) introduced by Rocco and Frits Vaandrager in [24, 25].

1.3   Model Checking Action-Based Temporal Logics

Model-checking techniques [17, 18] were defined to verify system properties, expressed as temporal logic formulae, on finite-state models of the behaviour of systems. Once a model of a system has been generated, the properties are automatically verified by model-checking tools.

An efficient model checker, called AMC, was defined for ACTL to verify the satisfaction of ACTL formulae over states in an LTSs as a collaboration between Stefania, Rocco and other colleagues from Pisa and was first presented at CAV'91 [20, 21]. The model checker AMC was later integrated in the JACK verification environment [14], whose extended version also contains a symbolic model checker for ACTL, called SAM [36], and they were successfully used to verify properties expressed as ACTL formulae on several concurrent systems, among which some interesting industrial case studies [13, 19, 36, 38].

Following this initial experience and to better deal with the so-called *state-space explosion problem* which is typical of explicit-state model checkers, the on-the-fly model checker FMC [41] was developed by Franco Mazzanti, another Formal Methods and Tools Lab member. This tool formed the basis on which a family of model checkers, named KandISTI, has been developed at ISTI–CNR for over two decades now; that family now includes besides FMC, the UML model checker UMC [4], the model checker CMC for verifying specifications in the Calculus for Orchestration of Web Services (COWS) [35] and—the most recent member of the family—the variability model checker VMC [9, 10]. Each tool allows for the efficient verification, by means of explicit-state on-the-fly model checking of a family of logics based on ACTL. The KandISTI model checkers, available online at http://fmt.isti.cnr.it/kandisti/, allow for model checking with a complexity that is linear with respect to the size of the model and the size of the formula, when ignoring the fixed point operators and the parametric aspects of the logics (in which cases the complexity depends on the number of nested fixed point operators and the number of instantiations of parametric subformulae). In yet another Festschrift contribution [7], we described the development of the KandISTI family of model checkers from its origins.

1.4   The ERCIM Workshop on Theory and Practice in Verification

The eighties and nineties of the last century saw the birth of numerous events concerning the formal verification of systems and protocols. The IFIP WG6.1 established the series of symposia on Protocol Specification, Testing and Verification (PSTV) and conferences on Formal Description Techniques for Distributed Systems and Communication Protocols (FORTE). In 1989, exactly 30 years ago, the conference series on Computer Aided Verification (CAV) began as a workshop on Automatic Verification Methods for Finite State Systems, including a contribution by Rocco and some of his colleagues from Pisa [22]. Subsequently, a steering committee composed of Edmund Clarke, Robert Kurshan, Amir Pnueli and Joseph Sifakis decided that CAV was to be organised annually. Started as a workshop, nowadays it is the premier international conference on formal verification. Together with colleagues from Pisa, Rocco and Stefania contributed to CAV'91 with a paper that shows how to model check ACTL formulae [20].

A year later, in 1992, Stefania and colleagues from Pisa organised a workshop on the Theory and Practice in Verification at the CNR, in the context of the European Research Consortium for Informatics and Mathematics (ERCIM), founded in 1989 to foster collaborative work within the European ICT research community and to increase co-operation with European industry, which CNR joined in 1992. This workshop was the first 'European' meeting in the context of formal verification and Rocco was among the participants, together with many of the main actors in verification in the context of process algebras (cf. Figs. 1 and 2).

1.5   The Formal Methods and Tools Lab of ISTI–CNR

From that moment, formal verification became one of the main research fields for us and we may say that this particular event, as well as the collaborations with Rocco on ACTL, have played a major role in shaping the activity of the Formal Methods and Tools Lab of ISTI–CNR from the nineties to this very day.

Since Maurice joined the lab in the beginning of this century, he has worked together with Rocco and Stefania in a number of European and national projects, most notably the FP6-IP-IST-016004 project SENSORIA (Software Engineering for Service-Oriented Overlay Computers) and the FP7-FET-ICT-600708 project QUANTICOL (A Quantitative Approach to Management and Design of Collective and Adaptive Behaviours), as well as the MIUR–PRIN 2010LHT4KM project CINA (Compositionality, Interaction, Negotiation, Autonomicity for the future ICT society) and the most recently approved MIUR–PRIN 2017FTXR7S project IT MaTTerS (Methods and Tools for Trustworthy Smart Systems), both coordinated by Rocco. During this period, he has become acquainted with ACTL and he has helped to promote the model checkers from the KandISTI family [5,7–10], which are characterised by their logics based on ACTL that allow for the verification of action-based as well as state-based properties [3,4,6].

1.6   Contribution: An Axiomatisation of ACTL

An alternative to the model-theoretic approach to verification is the proof-theoretic one, according to which a system is modelled in terms of set-theoretic structures on which deduction rules are defined and theorems can be proved [49]. A proof assistant or theorem prover is an (interactive) tool which assists the user in the development of formal proofs of properties of finite- as well as infinite-state specifications, a known advantage over model checking. Furthermore, deductive proofs can *certify* or *justify* the validity of a model-checking result [45,46]. However, there is no automatic procedure that can always determine whether there exists a derivation of a given formula in a given logic setting, which is the reason for which theorem proving typically involves interaction with a trained user.

The technical contribution of this paper is to present a set of axioms and inference rules for ACTL, which provide a sound and complete axiom system for ACTL, and which may thus form the basis for realising a proof-theoretic approach to the verification of ACTL formulae. It complements the sound and complete axiomatisations of CTL and CTL* first presented in [29,50], respectively.[1]

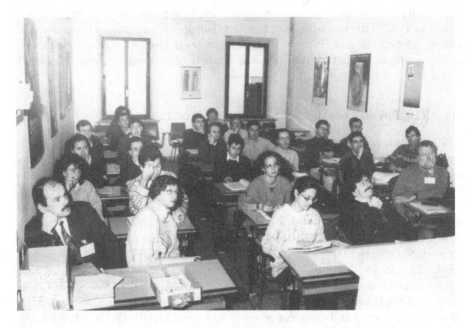

Fig. 1. Rocco, Stefania and several other contributors, as well as 3/4 of the editors of this Festschrift, at the 1992 ERCIM Workshop on Theory and Practice in Verification.

---

[1] A preliminary version of the axiom system was presented in [40]; here we provide a more succinct set of axioms, based on the fact that the *eventually* and *always* operators F and G can be expressed in terms of the Until operator U, cf. Sect. 3.

Fig. 2. Contents of the 1992 ERCIM Workshop on Theory and Practice in Verification and the abstract of Rocco's contribution (including his likely first-ever email address).

Outline

This paper is organised as follows. Section 2 provides some relevant preliminary definitions. Section 3 contains the definition of the sound and complete axiomatisation of ACTL. Section 4 concludes the paper.

2   Basic Definitions

The semantic models for the action-based branching-time temporal logic ACTL are Labelled Transition Systems (LTSs).

Definition 1. *A* Labelled Transition System *(LTS) is a triple*

$$L = (Q, \longrightarrow, A \cup \{\tau\}),$$

where

- *Q is a set of* states, *and $u, v, w, s, t, \ldots$ range over Q.*
- *A is a* finite and non-empty *set of* visible actions, *and $a, b, c, \ldots$ range over A; τ is the* silent action, *which is not in A. We let $A_\tau = A \cup \{\tau\} = \{\ell_1, \ell_2, \ldots\}$.*
- *$\longrightarrow \subseteq Q \times A_\tau \times Q$ is the* state transition relation. *Instead of $(s, \ell, t) \in \longrightarrow$, we also write $s \xrightarrow{\ell} t$ and we call such transition an ℓ-transition.*

Remark 1. Hereafter, when we write that a state t is a successor *of s, we intend that $\exists \ell \in A_\tau$ such that $s \xrightarrow{\ell} t$; if $s = t$, such transition is called a* loop *(on ℓ).*

Definition 2. *Let $L = (Q, \longrightarrow, A \cup \{\tau\})$ be an LTS and let*

$$\longrightarrow^n = \underbrace{\longrightarrow \times \longrightarrow \times \cdots \times \longrightarrow}_{n \text{ times}} \quad and \quad \longrightarrow^\infty = \underbrace{\longrightarrow \times \longrightarrow \times \cdots}_{\infty \text{ times}}$$

be Cartesian products of the state transition relation $\longrightarrow$. Then:

- *an infinite sequence σ of ordered triples of the form*

$$\sigma = (s_0, \ell_0, s_1)(s_1, \ell_1, s_2)(s_2, \ell_2, s_3) \cdots \in \longrightarrow^\infty$$

is called a path *beginning in s_0, and σ, π, δ range over paths.*
- *a finite sequence σ of ordered triples of the form*

$$\sigma = (s_0, \ell_0, s_1)(s_1, \ell_1, s_2) \cdots (s_{k-1}, \ell_{k-1}, s_k) \in \longrightarrow^k$$

is called a (finite) path *from s_0 to s_k (of length k).*
- *a path σ that cannot be extended, i.e. σ is infinite or ends in a state without outgoing transitions, is called a* full path.
- *$\sigma(0)$ is the starting state of the path σ, also denoted by $first(\sigma)$.*
- *$\sigma(n)$, for some $n \geq 0$, is the nth state of the path σ.*
- *if σ is a finite path, $last(\sigma)$ denotes its last state.*
- *the nth* suffix *of σ, denoted by σ^n, with $n \leq k$ for finite paths of length k, is the sequence that contains all the states of σ starting from $\sigma(n)$, which is thus included. Thus $\sigma^0 = \sigma$.*
- *if σ is a finite path and δ is a path such that $last(\sigma) = first(\delta)$, the path $\pi = \sigma\delta$ is called a* concatenation *of σ and δ (and δ is a* suffix *of π).*

3   The Temporal Logic ACTL

The *branching-time* temporal logic ACTL [23] is the *action-based* version of CTL [15,16] and its semantic models are LTSs. ACTL is suitable for describing the behaviour of systems that perform actions during their execution. In fact, ACTL embeds the idea of "evolution over time by actions" and is suitable for describing the various possible temporal sequences of actions that characterise a system. The original definition of ACTL includes an action calculus to improve the expressiveness of its operators.

In this section, we consider an LTS $L = (Q, \longrightarrow, A \cup \{\tau\})$ as defined above.

Definition 3. *Let $a \in A$. Then* action formulae f, g *are defined by the grammar:*

$$f, g ::= a \mid \neg f \mid f \vee g$$

Let A_{for} be the set of action formulae over A.

Intuitively, the action formulae are Boolean expressions over (visible) actions.

Next we define the satisfaction of an action formula f by a single action a, and we denote this satisfaction by $a \models f$.

Definition 4. *Let $a \in A$ and let $f, g \in A_{for}$. Then:*

$$
\begin{array}{ll}
a \models a & \textit{always holds} \\
a \models \neg b & \textit{holds for each } b \in A \textit{ such that } a \neq b \\
a \models \neg f & \textit{iff } a \not\models f \\
a \models f \vee g & \textit{iff } a \models f \textit{ or } a \models g
\end{array}
$$

It is common to let $t\!\!t$ denote a formula that is always satisfied in a calculus and to let $f\!\!f$ correspond to $\neg t\!\!t$. In our action calculus A_{for}, we define the formula $t\!\!t$ by choosing an $a \in A$ and letting $t\!\!t = a \vee \neg a$ (i.e. all actions of A are permitted).

Given $f \in A_{for}$, the set of actions satisfying f is defined as $[\![f]\!] = \{\, a \mid a \models f \,\}$.

Well-formed ACTL formulae are defined by the state formulae generated by the following grammar.

Definition 5. *Well-formed formulae ϕ, ψ of ACTL are defined by the grammar:*

$$
\begin{aligned}
\phi, \psi &::= t\!\!t \mid \phi \wedge \phi \mid \neg \phi \mid \forall \pi \mid \exists \pi \\
\pi &::= X_\tau \phi \mid X_f \phi \mid X \phi \mid \phi_f U \psi \mid \phi_f U_g \psi
\end{aligned}
$$

where $f, g \in A_{for}$ are action formulae.

Here, $\forall$ and $\exists$ are universal and existential *path quantifiers*, while X and U are (action-based) *neXt(time)* and *Until* operators (first introduced in [23]).

3.1 Models for ACTL

Let L be a *total* LTS (i.e. each state has a successor) and let R_L be a non-empty and suffix-closed set of paths on L (i.e. $\sigma \in R_L$ implies $\sigma^i \in R_L$ for all $i \geq 0$). The tuple (L, R_L) is called an *extended LTS* and it is a model for ACTL formulae. We consider only total LTSs to simplify the ACTL axiom system presented next. Note that this is not a limitation, since there is a simple way to transform any finite path of an LTS into an infinite one: it suffices to add a loop on τ in its final state. First, we define the satisfaction relation for ACTL formulae.

Definition 6. *Let M be an extended LTS, let $s \in Q$ be a state of M, and let σ be a path of M. Then the* satisfaction relation $\models$ *for well-formed ACTL formulae ϕ, ψ is inductively defined as follows:*

$$M, s \models t\!\!t \qquad \textit{always holds}$$

$$M, s \models \neg\phi \qquad \textit{iff } M, s \not\models \phi$$

$$M, s \models \phi \wedge \psi \quad \textit{iff } M, s \models \phi \textit{ and } M, s \models \psi$$

$$M, s \models \forall\pi \qquad \textit{iff } \forall\sigma \textit{ such that } \sigma(0) = s : M, \sigma \models \pi$$

$$M, s \models \exists\pi \qquad \textit{iff } \exists\sigma \textit{ such that } \sigma(0) = s \textit{ and } M, \sigma \models \pi$$

$$M, \sigma \models X\phi \qquad \textit{iff } M, \sigma(1) \models \phi$$

$$M, \sigma \models X_\tau \phi \quad \textit{iff } M, \sigma(1) \models \phi \textit{ and } \sigma(0) \xrightarrow{\tau} \sigma(1)$$

$$M, \sigma \models X_f \phi \quad \textit{iff } M, \sigma(1) \models \phi \textit{ and } \sigma(0) \xrightarrow{\ell} \sigma(1) \textit{ such that } \ell \neq \tau \textit{ and } \ell \models f$$

$$M, \sigma \models \phi_f U \psi \quad \textit{iff } \exists k \geq 0 \textit{ such that } M, \sigma(k) \models \psi \textit{ and } \forall 0 \leq j < k :$$
$$M, \sigma(j) \models \phi \textit{ and } (\sigma(j) \xrightarrow{\ell} \sigma(j+1)) \rightarrow (\ell = \tau \textit{ or } \ell \models f)$$

$$M, \sigma \models \phi_f U_g \psi \textit{ iff } \exists k \geq 0 \textit{ such that } M, \sigma(k+1) \models \psi, \ M, \sigma(k) \models \phi,$$
$$(\sigma(k) \xrightarrow{\ell} \sigma(k+1)) \rightarrow (\ell \models g) \textit{ and } \forall 0 \leq j < k :$$
$$(M, \sigma(j) \models \phi \textit{ and } (\sigma(j) \xrightarrow{\ell} \sigma(j+1)) \rightarrow (\ell = \tau \textit{ or } \ell \models f))$$

The meaning of the propositional operators and the CTL path quantifiers is standard. Intuitively, the neXt operator says that in the next state of the path (reached by the silent action τ or by an action satisfying f) the formula ϕ holds; the Until operator says that ψ holds at some future state of the path (reached by an action satisfying g), while ϕ holds from the current state until that state is reached and all actions executed meanwhile along the path satisfy f.

As usual, numerous modalities can be derived starting from these basic ones. In particular, we may write $f\!\!f$ for $\neg t\!\!t$ and $\phi \vee \psi$ for $\neg(\neg\phi \wedge \neg\psi)$. Furthermore, we define the following derived operators:

- $\exists F \phi$ stands for $\exists[t\!\!t_{t\!\!t} U \phi]$
- $\forall G \phi$ stands for $\neg \exists F \neg\phi$
- $\langle\tau\rangle \phi$ stands for $\exists[t\!\!t_{f\!\!f} U \phi]$
- $\langle a\rangle \phi$ stands for $\exists[t\!\!t_{f\!\!f} U_a \phi]$

The meaning of $\exists F \phi$ is that ϕ must *eventually* be true in a possible Future, while $\forall G \phi$ means that ϕ must *always* be true in all possible futures (Globally).

The meaning of $\langle \tau \rangle \phi$ is that ϕ must be true in some future state reached by zero or more τ-transitions. The meaning of $\langle a \rangle \phi$ is that ϕ must be true in some future state reached by zero or more τ-transitions followed by an a-transition; this resembles the *diamond* modality (*possibly*) of Hennessy–Milner logic [42], which however does not require ϕ to be true immediately in the state reached by the a-transition, but allows another zero or more τ-transitions also after the a-transition before reaching the state in which ϕ is true (i.e. $\langle a \rangle \langle \tau \rangle \phi$ in ACTL). More details on the variants of Hennessy–Milner logic introduced in [24,42,52] and their relation to ACTL can be found in [37]. Finally, the dual *box* modalities (*necessarily*) of Hennessy–Milner logic, denoted by $[\cdot] \phi$, are defined by $\neg \langle \cdot \rangle \neg \phi$.

ACTL can thus be used to define the well-known properties of *liveness* ("something good eventually happens") and *safety* ("nothing bad can happen").

Definition 7. *Let M be an extended LTS and let s be a state of M. If $M, s \models \phi$, then we say that M is a model for ϕ in state s and that state formula ϕ is satisfiable. Analogously for path formulae. We say that ϕ is* valid, *denoted by $\models \phi$, if ϕ is satisfiable for all models and all its states (for a state formula) and similarly for a path formula.*

Note that a formula is satisfiable iff its negation is not valid.

Notation 1. Neither $\forall X_{f \vee \tau} \phi$ nor $\exists X_{f \vee \tau} \phi$ is a well-formed ACTL formula. Therefore, we define the following shorthands to be used in the rest of the paper:

$$\exists X_{f \vee \tau} \phi \stackrel{\text{def}}{=} \exists X_f \phi \vee \exists X_\tau \phi$$
$$\forall X_{f \vee \tau} \phi \stackrel{\text{def}}{=} \neg \exists X_{tt} \neg \phi \wedge \neg \exists X_\tau \neg \phi \wedge \neg \exists X_{\neg f} \, tt$$

We are now ready to present the main (technical) contribution of this paper.

3.2 An Axiom System for ACTL

We define an axiom system for ACTL, after which we present the main result of this paper: the set of axioms and inference rules provides a sound and complete axiomatisation of ACTL.

The axiom system for ACTL is shown in Fig. 3. We now provide some explanations of this axiomatisation, discussing first the axioms and then the rules.

A0 represents any set of axioms that characterises the propositional tautologies. A possible choice could be the following:

$$\begin{aligned}
&\text{(A0/1)} \quad (\phi \vee \phi) \to \phi \\
&\text{(A0/2)} \quad \phi \to (\phi \vee \psi) \\
&\text{(A0/3)} \quad (\phi \vee \psi) \to (\psi \vee \phi) \\
&\text{(A0/4)} \quad (\phi \to \psi) \to ((\phi \vee \gamma) \to (\psi \vee \gamma))
\end{aligned}$$

Together with the MP rule, this is a consistent and complete axiomatisation of the calculus of the sentences.

ACTL axiom system

Axioms:

(A0) All tautology instances

(A1) $\exists X_f\, \phi \leftrightarrow \bigvee_{a\in[\![f]\!]} \exists X_a\, \phi$

(A2) $\exists X_f\, (\phi \vee \psi) \leftrightarrow (\exists X_f\, \phi \vee \exists X_f\, \psi)$

(A3) $\exists X_\tau\, (\phi \vee \psi) \leftrightarrow (\exists X_\tau\, \phi \vee \exists X_\tau\, \psi)$

(A4) $\neg \forall X_f\, t\!\!t \leftrightarrow \exists X_\tau\, t\!\!t \vee \exists X_{\neg f}\, t\!\!t$

(A5) $\neg \forall X_\tau t\!\!t \leftrightarrow \exists X_{t\!\!t}\, t\!\!t$

(A6) $\forall X_f\, \phi \leftrightarrow \forall X\, \phi \wedge \forall X_f\, t\!\!t$

(A7) $\forall X_\tau\, \phi \leftrightarrow \forall X\, \phi \wedge \forall X_\tau\, t\!\!t$

(A8) $\exists X\, \phi \leftrightarrow \exists X_{t\!\!t}\, \phi \vee \exists X_\tau\, \phi$

(A9) $\forall X\, \phi \leftrightarrow \neg \exists X\, \neg\phi$

(A10) $\forall X\, (\phi \rightarrow \psi) \rightarrow (\exists X_f\, \phi \rightarrow \exists X_f\, \psi)$

(A11) $\forall X\, (\phi \rightarrow \psi) \rightarrow (\exists X_\tau\, \phi \rightarrow \exists X_\tau\, \psi)$

(A12) $\exists X\, t\!\!t \wedge \forall X\, t\!\!t$

(A13) $\exists(\phi\, _f U\, \psi) \leftrightarrow \psi \vee (\phi \wedge \exists X_{f\vee\tau}\, \exists(\phi\, _f U\, \psi))$

(A14) $\forall(\phi\, _f U\, \psi) \leftrightarrow \psi \vee (\phi \wedge \forall X_{f\vee\tau}\, \forall(\phi\, _f U\, \psi))$

(A15) $\exists(\phi\, _f U_g\, \psi) \leftrightarrow \phi \wedge (\exists X_g\, \psi \vee \exists X_{f\vee\tau}\, \exists(\phi\, _f U_g\, \psi))$

(A16) $\forall(\phi\, _f U_g\, \psi) \leftrightarrow (\phi \wedge \forall X_{f\vee g\vee\tau}\, t\!\!t \wedge \neg \exists X_{\neg f\wedge g}\, \neg\psi \wedge$
$\qquad \neg \exists X_{f\wedge g}\, (\neg\forall(\phi\, _f U_g\, \psi) \wedge \neg\psi) \wedge \neg \exists X_{(f\wedge\neg g)\vee\tau}\, (\neg\forall(\phi\, _f U_g\, \psi)))$

(A17) $\forall G\, (\gamma \rightarrow (\neg\psi \wedge \neg\exists X_{f\vee\tau}\, (\exists(\phi\, _f U\, \psi) \wedge \neg\gamma))) \rightarrow (\gamma \rightarrow \neg\exists(\phi\, _f U\, \psi))$

(A18) $\forall G\, (\gamma \rightarrow (\neg(\phi \wedge \exists X_g\, \psi) \wedge \neg\exists X_{f\vee\tau}\, (\exists(\phi\, _f U_g\, \psi) \wedge \neg\gamma))) \rightarrow$
$\qquad (\gamma \rightarrow \neg\exists(\phi\, _f U_g\, \psi))$

(A19) $\forall G\, (\gamma \rightarrow (\neg\psi \wedge \exists X\, \gamma)) \rightarrow (\gamma \rightarrow \neg\forall(\phi\, _f U\, \psi))$

(A20) $\forall G\, (\gamma \rightarrow (\exists X_{(f\wedge\neg g)\vee\tau}\, \gamma \vee \exists X_{f\wedge g}\, (\neg\psi \wedge \gamma))) \rightarrow (\gamma \rightarrow \neg\forall(\phi\, _f U_g\, \psi))$

(A21) $\forall G\, (\gamma \rightarrow (\neg\psi \wedge \exists X\, \gamma)) \rightarrow (\gamma \rightarrow \neg\forall F\, \psi)$

(A22) $\forall G\, (\gamma \rightarrow (\neg\psi \wedge \forall X\, \gamma)) \rightarrow (\gamma \rightarrow \neg\exists F\, \psi)$

Rules:

$(R\forall X)\ \dfrac{\vdash \phi}{\vdash \forall X\, \phi} \qquad (MP)\ \dfrac{\vdash \phi \rightarrow \psi \quad \vdash \phi}{\vdash \psi} \qquad (R\forall G)\ \dfrac{\vdash \phi}{\vdash \forall G\, \phi}$

Fig. 3. The axiom system of ACTL.

A1 defines the $\exists X_f$ operator in terms of single action $\exists X_a$ operators.

A2–A12 concern the quantified neXt operators. More precisely:

A2 distribution law related to visible actions satisfying f.

A3 distribution law related to the silent action τ.

A4 defines the relation between the universal and existential next operators. It says that if not all the states that are successors of a state s are reachable from s by satisfying f, then at least one of them is reachable either by the silent action τ or by an action that does not satisfy f; the reverse holds too.

A5 defines the separation between the visible actions and the silent action. It says that if not all the states that are successors of a state s are reachable from s by the silent action τ, then there is one such successor state that is reachable by a visible action satisfying f, and vice versa.

A6 defines the $\forall X_f$ operator. It says that if a state s satisfies $\forall X_f\, \phi$, then all the successors of s satisfy ϕ ($\forall X \phi$) and, moreover, they are all reachable by actions that satisfy f ($\forall X_f\, t\!t$).

A7 defines the $\forall X_\tau$ operator in a way that is analogous to A6.

A8 defines the $\exists X$ operator.

A9 defines the $\forall X$ operator as the dual of the $\exists X$ operator.

A10 distribution law.

A11 distribution law.

A12 guarantees that each model for ACTL formulae must be *total*.

A13–A16 show the inductive way by which $\exists(\phi\,_f U\,\psi)$, $\forall(\phi\,_f U\,\psi)$, $\exists(\phi\,_f U_g\,\psi)$ and $\forall(\phi\,_f U_g\,\psi)$ (in a slightly different way, cf. [40] for details) propagate themselves along the paths of models. Note that A13–A16 do not forbid the infinite unfolding of the Until operators, which is handled by A17–A20.

A17–A20 avoid the infinite unfolding of the Until operators. The trick is to use a *placeholder* γ to characterise the case of infinite unfolding of an operator O that should actually have a *finite* unfolding; we then say that if γ holds in a state (i.e. such a state is the initial one for an infinite unfolding of O), then in such a state O cannot hold.

A21–A22 avoid the infinite unfolding of the eventually operators F in a way similar to the way this is done for the Until operators in A17–A20.

MP the usual Modus Ponens.

R∀X ensures that the theorems of the inference systems are closed under the most general universal neXt operator.

R∀G ensures that the theorems of the inference systems are closed under the always operator G.

We say that a formula ϕ can be inferred from an axiom system, denoted by $\vdash \phi$, if there exists a finite sequence of formulae, ending with ϕ, such that each formula is an instance of one of the axioms or follows from previous formulae by applying one of the rules.

Finally, the next theorem ensures the soundness and completeness of the axiom system for ACTL.

Theorem 1 (Soundness and Completeness). *Each well-formed ACTL formula ϕ is valid if and only if it can be inferred from the ACTL axiom system, i.e.*

$$\vdash \phi \quad \leftrightarrow \quad \models \phi$$

Proof Sketch. ($\vdash \phi \rightarrow \models \phi$) The soundness proof is a rather standard proof by induction on the structure of the derivation of ϕ.

($\models \phi \rightarrow \vdash \phi$) The completeness proof is quite long and tedious; therefore, we only provide an outline. It uses a technique from [26,30] based on a decision algorithm for the satisfiability of CTL formulae. This technique is a variant of the tableau approach, which was applied to the branching-time logics considered in [12,34].

A formula ψ is *consistent* if $\neg\psi$ cannot be inferred from the axiom system. To show that any valid ACTL formula can be inferred from the axiom system, it thus suffices to show that any consistent ACTL formula is satisfiable.

Let ϕ be a consistent ACTL formula. Then we need to define a procedure to characterise a model for ϕ in a structural way, i.e. in a way that allows us to automatically build and manipulate an LTS to achieve a model for ϕ. To do so, we define a Fischer–Ladner *finite* closure set for ϕ (cf. [39]) and a particular class of LTSs, so-called Hintikka Structures (HS), as in [12,30]. HS have the property that each of their states is labelled by a subset of the Fischer–Ladner closure of ϕ and we say that an HS is an HS *for* ϕ if one of its states contains the formula ϕ. The following property holds: each model for ϕ is an HS for ϕ, and each HS for ϕ is extendible to a model for ϕ without changing the number of its states. Hence, if we have an algorithm that returns an HS for ϕ, then we know that ϕ is satisfiable.

In order to write a procedure that takes ϕ, calculates its Fischer–Ladner closure and tries to build an HS for ϕ, we must ensure that such a procedure will terminate, i.e. that it is possible to build a *finite* HS for ϕ if ϕ is satisfiable. To achieve this, we prove that ϕ is satisfiable if and only if it is possible to build a *finite* HS that satisfies ϕ.

We conclude this proof sketch with an outline of the above mentioned decision procedure:

1. Calculate the Fischer–Ladner closure of ϕ.
2. Let M be the set of all maximal subsets of this closure. Build an LTS L that satisfies a minimal subset of conditions among those defining an HS and whose states are elements of M. This ensures that whenever a finite HS for ϕ exists, it is contained in L.
3. Purge all states of L that do not match the definition of HS. We prove that (i) if ϕ is consistent, then there exists a consistent element S of M that contains ϕ, and (ii) if a state is purged, then it was not consistent. Hence, S cannot be purged by the procedure, and S will be a state of the resulting HS that is calculated by the procedure. But S contains ϕ, so we obtain an HS for ϕ and hence ϕ is satisfiable.   □

4   Conclusion

In this paper, we have revisited De Nicola & Vaandrager's action-based logic ACTL. We have sketched the context in which it was introduced 30 years ago and the impact it has had on our research and that of many of our colleagues of the Formal Methods and Tools Lab. Furthermore, we have revamped an axiom system for ACTL that has originally been published in the proceedings of a national conference [40], by providing a more concise sound and complete axiom system for ACTL.

Axiomatisation of a logic is often said to offer a better understanding of the logic. Moreover, the ACTL axiom system may form the basis for developing a theorem prover for the verification of ACTL formulae. In [40], a preliminary proof assistant for ACTL implemented in HOL (http://hol-theorem-prover.org) was described. Other directions for future work include the consideration of infinite-state systems, to overcome limitations of model checking, and to investigate the use of ACTL theorem proving to certify or justify the validity of an ACTL model-checking result.

Finally, it would be interesting to develop an axiom system also for ACTL*. This logic, as is the case for CTL*, includes both linear- and branching-time operators, and it is well known that the model-checking algorithms for this class of logics are PSPACE-complete. A proof-theoretic approach for ACTL* formulae might ease verification for at least some classes of properties. However, it is known from [26] and [31,32] that the complexity of checking satisfiability of CTL and CTL* is EXPTIME-complete and 2-EXPTIME-complete, respectively, in the length of the formula.

Acknowledgements. Stefania wishes to thank Salvatore Larosa, who worked on the ACTL axiomatisation; Alessandro Fantechi, Franco Mazzanti, and Monica Nesi, for interesting discussions on the preliminary version of the ACTL axiomatisation; and Maurizio La Bella, who developed the ACTL proof assistant. And, *last but not least*, Stefania would like to thank Rocco, for having initiated this line of research that has led to so many interesting papers, projects, and collaborations with many different people, and which in hindsight has made it worthwhile to remain at the CNR.

Maurice also would like to thank Alessandro and Franco, for numerous pleasant collaborations on, among others, ACTL-like logics and the KandISTI family. And, *of course*, also Rocco, for quality time spent together during a number of projects, not limited to research.

References

1. Baeten, J.C.M., Weijland, W.P.: Process Algebra. Cambridge Tracts in Theoretical Computer Science, vol. 18. Cambridge University Press, Cambridge (1990). https://doi.org/10.1017/CBO9780511624193
2. Baeten, J.C.M., Basten, T., Reniers, M.A.: Process Algebra: Equational Theories of Communicating Processes. Cambridge Tracts in Theoretical Computer Science, vol. 50. Cambridge University Press, Cambridge (2010). https://doi.org/10.1017/CBO9781139195003

3. ter Beek, M.H., Fantechi, A., Gnesi, S., Mazzanti, F.: An action/state-based model-checking approach for the analysis of communication protocols for service-oriented applications. In: Leue, S., Merino, P. (eds.) FMICS 2007. LNCS, vol. 4916, pp. 133–148. Springer, Heidelberg (2008). https://doi.org/10.1007/978-3-540-79707-4_11

4. ter Beek, M.H., Fantechi, A., Gnesi, S., Mazzanti, F.: A state/event-based model-checking approach for the analysis of abstract system properties. Sci. Comput. Program. **76**(2), 119–135 (2011). https://doi.org/10.1016/j.scico.2010.07.002

5. ter Beek, M.H., Fantechi, A., Gnesi, S., Mazzanti, F.: Using FMC for family-based analysis of software product lines. In: Proceedings of the 19th International Software Product Line Conference (SPLC 2015), pp. 432–439. ACM (2015). https://doi.org/10.1145/2791060.2791118

6. ter Beek, M.H., Fantechi, A., Gnesi, S., Mazzanti, F.: States and events in KandISTI: a retrospective. In: Margaria, T., Graf, S., Larsen, K.G. (eds.) Models, Mindsets, Meta: The What, the How, and the Why Not? LNCS, vol. 11200. Springer, Cham (2019). https://doi.org/10.1007/978-3-030-22348-9_9

7. ter Beek, M.H., Gnesi, S., Mazzanti, F.: From EU projects to a family of model checkers. In: De Nicola, R., Hennicker, R. (eds.) Software, Services, and Systems. LNCS, vol. 8950, pp. 312–328. Springer, Cham (2015). https://doi.org/10.1007/978-3-319-15545-6_20

8. ter Beek, M.H., Mazzanti, F., Gnesi, S.: CMC-UMC: a framework for the verification of abstract service-oriented properties. In: Proceedings of the 24th Annual ACM Symposium on Applied Computing (SAC 2009), pp. 2111–2117. ACM (2009). https://doi.org/10.1145/1529282.1529751

9. ter Beek, M.H., Mazzanti, F., Sulova, A.: VMC: a tool for product variability analysis. In: Giannakopoulou, D., Méry, D. (eds.) FM 2012. LNCS, vol. 7436, pp. 450–454. Springer, Heidelberg (2012). https://doi.org/10.1007/978-3-642-32759-9_36

10. ter Beek, M.H., Mazzanti, F.: VMC: recent advances and challenges ahead. In: Proceedings of the 18th International Software Product Line Conference (SPLC 2014), pp. 70–77. ACM (2014). https://doi.org/10.1145/2647908.2655969

11. Ben-Ari, M., Pnueli, A., Manna, Z.: The temporal logic of branching time. In: Proceedings of the 8th Annual ACM SIGACT/SIGPLAN Symposium on Principles of Programming Languages (POPL 1981), pp. 164–176. ACM (1981). https://doi.org/10.1145/567532.567551

12. Ben-Ari, M., Pnueli, A., Manna, Z.: The temporal logic of branching time. Acta Inform. **20**(3), 207–226 (1983). https://doi.org/10.1007/BF01257083

13. Bernardeschi, C., Fantechi, A., Gnesi, S., Larosa, S., Mongardi, G., Romano, D.: A formal verification environment for railway signaling system design. Formal Methods Syst. Des. **12**(2), 139–161 (1998). https://doi.org/10.1023/A:1008645826258

14. Bouali, A., Gnesi, S., Larosa, S.: JACK: Just Another Concurrency Kit - the integration project. Bull. EATCS **54**, 207–223 (1994)

15. Clarke, E.M., Emerson, E.A.: Design and synthesis of synchronization skeletons using branching time temporal logic. In: Kozen, D. (ed.) Logic of Programs 1981. LNCS, vol. 131, pp. 52–71. Springer, Heidelberg (1982). https://doi.org/10.1007/BFb0025774

16. Clarke, E.M., Emerson, E.A.: Using branching time temporal logic to synthesize synchronization skeletons. Sci. Comput. Program. **2**(3), 241–266 (1982). https://doi.org/10.1016/0167-6423(83)90017-5

17. Clarke, E.M., Emerson, E.A., Sistla, A.P.: Automatic verification of finite state concurrent systems using temporal logic specifications: a practical approach. In: Proceedings of the 10th Annual ACM SIGACT/SIGPLAN Symposium on Principles of Programming Languages (POPL 1983), pp. 117–126. ACM (1983). https://doi.org/10.1145/567067.567080

18. Clarke, E.M., Emerson, E.A., Sistla, A.P.: Automatic verification of finite state concurrent systems using temporal logic specifications. ACM Trans. Program. Lang. Syst. **8**(2), 244–263 (1986). https://doi.org/10.1145/5397.5399

19. De Nicola, R., Fantechi, A., Gnesi, S., Larosa, S., Ristori, G.: Verifying hardware components with JACK. In: Camurati, P.E., Eveking, H. (eds.) CHARME 1995. LNCS, vol. 987, pp. 246–260. Springer, Heidelberg (1995). https://doi.org/10.1007/3-540-60385-9_15

20. De Nicola, R., Fantechi, A., Gnesi, S., Ristori, G.: An action based framework for verifying logical and behavioural properties of concurrent systems. In: Larsen, K.G., Skou, A. (eds.) CAV 1991. LNCS, vol. 575, pp. 37–47. Springer, Heidelberg (1992). https://doi.org/10.1007/3-540-55179-4_5

21. De Nicola, R., Fantechi, A., Gnesi, S., Ristori, G.: An action-based framework for verifying logical and behavioural properties of concurrent systems. Comput. Netw. ISDN Syst. **25**(7), 761–778 (1993). https://doi.org/10.1016/0169-7552(93)90047-8

22. De Nicola, R., Inverardi, P., Nesi, M.: Using the axiomatic presentation of behavioural equivalences for manipulating CCS specifications. In: Sifakis, J. (ed.) CAV 1989. LNCS, vol. 407, pp. 54–67. Springer, Heidelberg (1990). https://doi.org/10.1007/3-540-52148-8_5

23. De Nicola, R., Vaandrager, F.: Action versus state based logics for transition systems. In: Guessarian, I. (ed.) LITP 1990. LNCS, vol. 469, pp. 407–419. Springer, Heidelberg (1990). https://doi.org/10.1007/3-540-53479-2_17

24. De Nicola, R., Vaandrager, F.W.: Three logics for branching bisimulation (extended abstract). In: Proceedings of the 5th Annual Symposium on Logic in Computer Science (LICS 1990), pp. 118–129. IEEE (1990). https://doi.org/10.1109/LICS.1990.113739

25. De Nicola, R., Vaandrager, F.W.: Three logics for branching bisimulation. J. ACM **42**(2), 458–487 (1995). https://doi.org/10.1145/201019.201032

26. Emerson, E.A.: Temporal and modal logic. In: Handbook of Theoretical Computer Science. Formal Models and Semantics, vol. B, pp. 995–1072. Elsevier (1990). https://doi.org/10.1016/B978-0-444-88074-1.50021-4

27. Emerson E.A., Halpern, J.Y.: "Sometimes" and "not never" revisited: on branching versus linear time (preliminary report). In: Proceedings of the 10th Annual ACM SIGACT/SIGPLAN Symposium on Principles of Programming Languages (POPL 1983), pp. 127–140. ACM (1983). https://doi.org/10.1145/567067.567081

28. Emerson, E.A., Halpern, J.Y.: "Sometimes" and "not never" revisited: on branching versus linear time temporal logic. J. ACM **33**(1), 151–178 (1986). https://doi.org/10.1145/4904.4999

29. Emerson, E.A., Halpern, J.Y.: Decision procedures and expressiveness in the temporal logic of branching time. In: Proceedings of the 14th Annual ACM Symposium on Theory of Computing (STOC 1982), pp. 169–180. ACM (1982). https://doi.org/10.1145/800070.802190

30. Emerson, E.A., Halpern, J.Y.: Decision procedures and expressiveness in the temporal logic of branching time. J. Comput. Syst. Sci. **30**(1), 1–24 (1985). https://doi.org/10.1016/0022-0000(85)90001-7

31. Emerson, E.A., Jutla, C.S.: The complexity of tree automata and logics of programs (extended abstract). In: Proceedings of the 29th Annual Symposium on Foundations of Computer Science (FOCS 1988), pp. 328–337. IEEE (1988). https://doi.org/10.1109/SFCS.1988.21949

32. Emerson, E.A., Jutla, C.S.: The complexity of tree automata and logics of programs. SIAM J. Comput. **29**(1), 132–158 (1999). https://doi.org/10.1137/S0097539793304741

33. Emerson, E.A., Lei, C.-L.: Efficient model checking in fragments of the propositional mu-calculus (extended abstract). In: Proceedings of the First Annual IEEE Symposium on Logic in Computer Science (LICS 1986), pp. 267–278. IEEE (1986)

34. Emerson, E.A., Sistla, A.P.: Deciding full branching time logic. Inf. Control **61**(3), 175–201 (1984). https://doi.org/10.1016/S0019-9958(84)80047-9

35. Fantechi, A., Gnesi, S., Lapadula, A., Mazzanti, F., Pugliese, R., Tiezzi, F.: A logical verification methodology for service-oriented computing. ACM Trans. Softw. Eng. Methodol. **21**(3), 161–1646 (2012). https://doi.org/10.1145/2211616.2211619

36. Fantechi, A., Gnesi, S., Mazzanti, F., Pugliese, R., Tronci, E.: A symbolic model checker for ACTL. In: Hutter, D., Stephan, W., Traverso, P., Ullmann, M. (eds.) FM-Trends 1998. LNCS, vol. 1641, pp. 228–242. Springer, Heidelberg (1999). https://doi.org/10.1007/3-540-48257-1_14

37. Fantechi, A., Gnesi, S., Ristori, G.: Model checking for action-based logics. Formal Methods Syst. Des. **4**(2), 187–203 (1994). https://doi.org/10.1007/BF01384084

38. Fantechi, A., Gnesi, S., Semini, L.: Formal description and validation for an integrity policy supporting multiple levels of criticality. In: Dependable Computing and Fault-Tolerant Systems: Proceedings of the 7th IFIP International Conference on Dependable Computing for Critical Applications (DCCA-7), vol. 12, pp. 129–146. IEEE (1999). https://doi.org/10.1109/DCFTS.1999.814293

39. Fischer, M.J., Ladner, R.E.: Propositional dynamic logic of regular programs. J. Comput. Syst. Sci. **18**(2), 194–211 (1979). https://doi.org/10.1016/0022-0000(79)90046-1

40. Gnesi, S., Larosa, S.: A sound and complete axiom system for the logic ACTL. In: Proceedings of the 5th Italian Conference on Theoretical Computer Science (ICTCS 1995), pp. 343–358. World Scientific (1996). https://doi.org/10.1142/9789814531184

41. Gnesi, S., Mazzanti, F.: On the fly verification of networks of automata. In: Proceedings of the International Conference on Parallel and Distributed Processing Techniques and Applications (PDPTA 1999), pp. 1040–1046. CSREA Press (1999)

42. Hennessy, M., Milner, R.: Algebraic laws for nondeterminism and concurrency. J. ACM **32**(1), 137–161 (1985). https://doi.org/10.1145/2455.2460

43. Hoare, C.A.R.: Communicating Sequential Processes. Prentice Hall, Englewood Cliffs (1985)

44. Milner, R.: Communication and Concurrency. Prentice Hall, Englewood Cliffs (1989)

45. Namjoshi, K.S.: Certifying model checkers. In: Berry, G., Comon, H., Finkel, A. (eds.) CAV 2001. LNCS, vol. 2102, pp. 2–13. Springer, Heidelberg (2001). https://doi.org/10.1007/3-540-44585-4_2

46. Peled, D., Pnueli, A., Zuck, L.: From falsification to verification. In: Hariharan, R., Vinay, V., Mukund, M. (eds.) FSTTCS 2001. LNCS, vol. 2245, pp. 292–304. Springer, Heidelberg (2001). https://doi.org/10.1007/3-540-45294-X_25

47. Pnueli, A.: Linear and branching structures in the semantics and logics of reactive systems. In: Brauer, W. (ed.) ICALP 1985. LNCS, vol. 194, pp. 15–32. Springer, Heidelberg (1985). https://doi.org/10.1007/BFb0015727

48. Queille, J.P., Sifakis, J.: Specification and verification of concurrent systems in CESAR. In: Dezani-Ciancaglini, M., Montanari, U. (eds.) Programming 1982. LNCS, vol. 137, pp. 337–351. Springer, Heidelberg (1982). https://doi.org/10.1007/3-540-11494-7_22

49. Ray, S.: Scalable Techniques for Formal Verification. Springer, Heidelberg (2010). https://doi.org/10.1007/978-1-4419-5998-0

50. Reynolds, M.: An axiomatization of full computation tree logic. J. Symb. Log. **66**(3), 1011–1057 (2001). https://doi.org/10.2307/2695091

51. Roscoe, A.W.: The Theory and Practice of Concurrency. Prentice Hall, Englewood Cliffs (1997)

52. Stirling, C.: An introduction to modal and temporal logics for CCS. In: Yonezawa, A., Ito, T. (eds.) CONCURRENCY 1989. LNCS, vol. 491, pp. 1–20. Springer, Heidelberg (1991). https://doi.org/10.1007/3-540-53932-8_41

53. Stirling, C.: Modal and temporal logics. In: Handbook of Logic in Computer Science. Background: Computational Structures, vol. 2, pp. 477–563. Oxford University Press (1993)

Featherweight Scribble

Rumyana Neykova[1] and Nobuko Yoshida[2](✉)

[1] Brunel University London, London, UK
[2] Imperial College London, London, UK
n.yoshida@imperial.ac.uk

Abstract. This paper gives a formal definition of the protocol specification language Scribble. In collaboration with industry, Scribble has
been developed as an engineering incarnation of the formal *multiparty
session types*. In its ten years of development, Scribble has been applied
and extended in manyfold ways as to verify and ensure correctness of
concurrent and distributed systems, e.g. type checking, runtime monitoring, code generation, and synthesis. This paper introduces a core version
of Scribble, *Featherweight Scribble*. We define the semantics of Scribble by translation to communicating automata and show a behavioural-
preserving encoding of Scribble protocols to multiparty session type.

1 Introduction

The computational model, Klaim, introduced by De Nicola and others [8] advocates a hybrid (dynamic and static) approach for access control against *capabilities* (policies) to support static checking integrated within a dynamic access-
control procedure. Their capabilities can specify crucial operations for mobile
computation such as *read*, *write* and *execute* of processes in relation to the various
localities, as *types*. Around the same period, (binary) *session types* [14,27] were
proposed to describe a sequence of read (output), write (input) and choice operations for channel passing protocols. Later binary session types were extended
to *multiparty session types* [7,15], as a model of *abstract choreographies* of Web
Services Choreography Description Language [6]. See [16, §1] for more historical
backgrounds.

Scribble [13,26] is a protocol description language, formally based on the
multiparty session type theory. A protocol in Scribble represents an agreement
on how participating systems interact with each other. It specifies a format and
a predefined order for messages to be exchanged. The name of the language
embodies the motivation for its creation, as explained by the following quote
from the inventor of the Scribble language Kohei Honda:

*The name (Scribble) comes from our desire to create an effective tool for
architects, designers and developers alike to quickly and accurately write
down protocols.*

M. Boreale et al. (Eds.): De Nicola-Festschrift, LNCS 11665, pp. 236–259, 2019.
https://doi.org/10.1007/978-3-030-21485-2_14

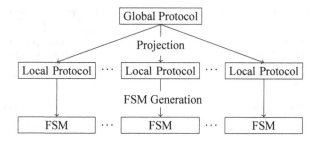

Fig. 1. Scribble development methodology

The development of Scribble is a result of a persistent dialogue between researchers and industry partners. Currently Scribble tools are applied to verification of main stream languages such as Java [18,19], Python [9,17], MPI [24], Go [5], F# [22], Erlang [23].

All great ideas of architectural construction come from that unconscious moment, when you do not realise what it is, when there is no concrete shape, only a whisper which is not a whisper, an image which is not an image, somehow it starts to urge you in your mind, in so small a voice but how persistent it is, at that point you start scribbling

Although Scribble is often referred as "the practical incarnation of multiparty session types (MPST)" [13,26], a formal correspondence between the two is not proven in the literature. In this paper we present the semantics of Scribble protocols, given by translation to communicating automata, and show a behavioural-preserving encoding of Scribble protocols to multiparty session type.

Section 2 gives an overview of Scribble and explains the Scribble framework. Section 3 presents the formal semantics of the Scribble language. Section 4 proves the encoding of Scribble local and global protocols to global and local session types to be behaviour-preserving. Section 5 gives the translation between local Scribble protocols and Communicating Finite State machines (CFSMs) [10]. Section 6 concludes. Appendix contains omitted proofs.

2 Scribble Overview

Scribble protocols describe an abstract structure of message exchanges between *roles*: roles abstract from the actual identity of the endpoints that may participate in a run-time conversation instantiating the protocol. Scribble enables the description of abstract interaction structures including asynchronous message passing, choice, and recursion.

Here we demonstrate the basic Scribble constructs via an example of an online payment service. Figure 2 (left) shows the global Scribble protocol `OnlineWallet`. The first line declares, under the name `OnlineWallet`, the Scribble global protocol and the two participating roles. The protocol has a recursion at thetop-level. In

```
global protocol OnlineWallet(              local protocol OnlineWallet(
  role S, role C){                           self S, role C) {
  rec LOOP {                                 rec LOOP {
    Balance(int) from S to C;                  Balance(int) to C;
    Overdraft(int) from S to C;                Overdraft(ints) to C;
    choice at C {                              choice {
    Payment(int) from C to S;                  Payment(int) from C;
    continue LOOP;                             continue LOOP;
  } or {                                     } or {
    CloseAccount() from C to S;                CloseAccount() from C;
  } or {                                     } or {
    Quit() from C  to S;                       Quit() from C;
}}}                                         }}}
```

Fig. 2. A global (left) and local (right) Scribble protocol

each iteration, the `Server` (`S`) sends the`Client` (`C`) the current balance and the overdraft limit for client's account. The `Balance` message has an `int` payload; similarly for the `Overdraft`. `Client` then can choose to either make a payment, close the account or quit this session.

Figure 1 gives an abstract overview of the Scribble verification process. From a global Scribble protocol, the toolchain produces (1) a set of local protocols or (2) a set of finite state machines (FSMs). We outline the tasks performed by the Scribble toolchain.

Well-Formedness Check: A global Scribble protocol is verified for correctness to ensure that the protocol is *well-formed*, which *intuitively* represents that a protocol describes a meaningful interaction, beyond the basic syntax defined by the language grammar. This well-formed checking is necessary because some of the protocols are unsafe or inconsistent even if they follow the grammar. For example, two choice branches from the same sender to the same receiver with the same message signature lead to ambiguity at the receiver side. A protocol is well-formed if local protocols can be generated for all of its roles, i.e., the projection function is defined for all roles. The formal definition of projection is given in Definition 4.10. Here we give intuition as to what the main syntactic restrictions are. First, in each branch of a choice the first interaction (possibly after a number of unfoldings) is from the same sender (e.g., A) and to the same set of receivers. Second, in each branch of a choice the labels are pair-wise distincs (i.e., protocols are deterministic).

Projection: A global Scribble protocol is projected to a set of local protocols. More precisely, a local Scribble protocol is generated per each role declared in the definition of the global protocol. Local protocols correspond to local (MPST) types, they describe interactions from the viewpoint of a single entity. They can be used directly by a type checker to verify that an endpoint code implementation complies to the interactions prescribed by a specification. Figure 2 (right) lists the Scribble local protocol `OnlineWallet` projected for role `Server`.

FSM Generation: An alternative representation of a local protocol can be given in the form of a communicating finite state machine (FSM). This representation is useful for runtime verification. Specifically, at runtime the traces emitted by a program are checked against the language accepted by the FSM.

An implementation of Java and Python based Scribble tools for projection and validation [26], as well as static verification for various languages can be found in [1].

3   Syntax and Semantics of Scribble

3.1   Scribble Global Protocols

We now define the syntax of Scribble global protocols. The grammar is given below.

Definition 3.1 (Scribble Global Protocols)

$$
\begin{array}{lll}
\text{P} :: = & \text{global protocol pro (role } A_1, ..., \text{role } A_n)\{G\} & \textit{specification} \\
\text{G} :: = & \text{a(S) from A to B; } G & \textit{interaction} \\
& | \quad \text{choice at A } \{G\} \text{ or } ... \text{ or } \{G\} & \textit{choice} \\
& | \quad \text{rec t } \{G\} & \textit{recursion} \\
& | \quad \text{continue t} & \textit{call}
\end{array}
$$

Protocol names are ranged over by **pro**. A (global) specification P declares a protocol with name **pro**, involving a list $(A_1, ..A_n)$ of roles, and prescribing the behaviour in G. The other constructs are explained below:

- An interaction a(S) **from A to B**; G specifies that a message a(S) should be sent from role A to role B and that the protocol should then continue as prescribed by the continuation G. Messages are of the form a(S) with a being a label and S being the constant type of exchanged messages (such as **real**, **bool** and **int**).
- A choice **choice at A** {G} **or** ... **or** {G} specifies a branching where role A chooses to engage in the interactions prescribed by one of the options G. The decision itself is an internal process to role A, i.e. how A decides which scenario to follow is not specified by the protocol.
- A recursion **rec t** {G} defines a scope with a name t and a body G. Any call **continue t** occurring inside G executes another recursion instance (if **continue t** is not in an appropriate scope than it remains idle).

Formal Semantics of Global Protocols. The formal semantics of global protocols characterises the desired/correct behaviour of the roles in a multiparty protocol. We give the semantics for Scribble protocols as a Labelled Transition System (LTS). The LTS is defined over the following set of transition labels:

$$\ell:: = \text{AB!a(S)} \mid \text{AB?a(S)}$$

Label AB!a(S) is for a send action where role A sends to role B a message a(S). Label AB?a(S) is for a receive action where B receives (i.e., collects from the queue associated to the appropriate channel) message a(S) that was previously sent by A. We define the subject of an action, modelling the role that has the responsibility of performing that action, as follows:

$$subj(\mathtt{AB!a(S)}) = \mathtt{A} \qquad subj(\mathtt{AB?a(S)}) = \mathtt{B}$$

As, due to asynchrony, send and receive are two distinct actions, the LTS shall also model the intermediate state where a message has been sent but it has not been yet received. To model these intermediate states we introduce the following additional global Scribble interaction:

$$\mathtt{transit : a(S) \ from \ A \ to \ B}; \ \mathtt{G}$$

to describe the state in which a message a(S) has been sent by A but not yet received by B. We call *runtime* global protocol a protocol obtained by extending the syntax of Scribble with these intermediate states.

The transition rules are given in Fig. 3. Rule ⌊SEND⌋ models a sending action; it produces a label AB!a(S). The sending action yields a state in which the global protocol is in an intermediate state.

Rule ⌊RECV⌋ models the dual receive action, from an intermediate state to a continuation G. Rule ⌊CHOICE⌋ continues the execution of the protocol as a continuation of one of the branches. Rule ⌊REC⌋ is standard and unfolds recursive protocols.

We explain the remaining rules with more detailed illustration.

Due to asynchrony and distribution, in a particular state of a Scribble global protocol it may be possible to trigger more than one action. For instance, the protocol in (1) allows two possible actions: AB!a(S) or CD!a(S).

$$\begin{aligned}
&\mathtt{a(S) \ from \ A \ to \ B};\\
&\mathtt{a(S) \ from \ C \ to \ D};
\end{aligned} \tag{1}$$

This is due to the fact that the two send actions are not *causally related* as they have different subjects (which are independent roles). We want the semantics of Scribble to allow, in the state with protocol (1), not only the first action that occurs syntactically (e.g., AB!a(S)) but also any action that occurs later, syntactically, but it is not causally related with previous actions in the protocol (e.g., CD!a(S)). Rule ⌊ASYNC1⌋ captures this asynchronous feature. CD!a(S), which occurs syntactically later than AB!a(S) to possibly occur before. In fact, the LTS allows (1) to take one of these two actions: either AB!a(S) by rule ⌊SEND⌋ or CD!a(S) is allowed by ⌊ASYNC1⌋. Rule ⌊ASYNC2⌋ is similar to ⌊ASYNC1⌋ but caters for intermediate states, and is illustrated by the protocol in (2).

$$\begin{aligned}
&\mathtt{transit :a(S) \ from \ A \ to \ B};\\
&\mathtt{a(S) \ from \ C \ to \ D};
\end{aligned} \tag{2}$$

The protocol in (2) is obtained from (1) via transition AB!a(S) by rule ⌊SEND⌋. The above protocol can execute either AB?a(S) by rule ⌊RECV⌋, or CD!a(S) by rule ⌊ASYNC2⌋.

$$a(S) \text{ from A to B}; G \xrightarrow{\text{AB}!a(S)} transit : a(S) \text{ from A to B}; G \qquad \lfloor\text{SEND}\rfloor$$

$$\frac{i \in \{1,..,n\} \quad G_i \xrightarrow{\ell} G_i'}{transit : a(S) \text{ from A to B}; G \xrightarrow{\text{AB}?a(S)} G \text{ choice at A } \{G_1\} \text{ or } ... \text{ or } \{G_n\} \xrightarrow{\ell} G_i'} \quad \lfloor\text{RECV}\rfloor/\lfloor\text{CHOICE}\rfloor$$

$$\frac{G[\text{rec } t \ \{G\}/\text{continuet}] \xrightarrow{\ell} G'}{\text{rec } t \ \{G\} \xrightarrow{\ell} G'} \qquad \frac{G \xrightarrow{\ell} G' \quad A,B \notin subj(\ell)}{a(S) \text{ from A to B}; G \xrightarrow{\ell} a(S) \text{ from A to B}; G'} \qquad \lfloor\text{REC}\rfloor/\lfloor\text{ASYNC1}\rfloor$$

$$\frac{G \xrightarrow{\ell} G' \quad B \notin subj(\ell)}{transit : a(S) \text{ from A to B}; G \xrightarrow{\ell} transit : a(S) \text{ from A to B}; G'} \qquad \lfloor\text{ASYNC2}\rfloor$$

Fig. 3. Labelled transitions for global protocols.

$$a(S) \text{ to B}; T \xrightarrow{\text{AB}!a(S)} T \quad \lfloor\text{SEND}\rfloor \quad a(S) \text{ from B}; T \xrightarrow{\text{BA}?a(S)} T \ \lfloor\text{RECV}\rfloor$$

$$\frac{i\in\{1,..,n\} \quad T_i \xrightarrow{\ell} T_i'}{\text{choice at A } \{T_1\} \text{ or}...\{T_n\} \xrightarrow{\ell} T_i'} \ \lfloor\text{CHOICE}\rfloor \quad \frac{T[\text{rec } t \ \{T\}/\text{continuet}] \xrightarrow{l} T'}{\text{rec } t \ \{T\} \xrightarrow{l} T'} \ \lfloor\text{REC}\rfloor$$

Fig. 4. Labelled transitions for local protocols (from A's point of view)

$$G \ ::= \ A \to B : \{a_i\langle S_i\rangle.G_i\}_{i\in I} \ | \ \mu t.G \ | \ t \ | \ \text{end} \qquad \text{global types}$$
$$T \ ::= \ B!\{a_i : \langle S_i\rangle.T_i'\}_{i\in I} \ | \ B?\{a_i : \langle S_i\rangle.T_i'\}_{i\in I} \ | \ \mu t.T \ | \ t \ | \ \text{end} \qquad \text{local types}$$

Fig. 5. Syntax for global and local types

$$\frac{j \in I}{(A \to B : \{a_i\langle S_i\rangle.G_i\}_{i\in I}) \xrightarrow{\text{AB}!a_j\langle S_j\rangle} (A \rightsquigarrow B : a_j\langle S_j\rangle.G_j)} \qquad \lfloor\text{SELECT}\rfloor$$

$$\frac{(G[\mu t.G/t]) \xrightarrow{\ell} (G')}{(\mu t.G) \xrightarrow{\ell} (G')} \qquad \frac{\forall k \in I \quad G_k \xrightarrow{\ell} G_k' \quad A,B \notin subj(\ell) \quad \ell \neq t}{(A \to B : \{a_i\langle S_i\rangle.G_i\}_{i\in I}) \xrightarrow{\ell} (A \to B : \{a_i\langle S_i\rangle.G_i'\}_{i\in I})} \qquad \lfloor\text{REC}\rfloor/\lfloor\text{ASYNC1}\rfloor$$

$$\frac{}{(A \rightsquigarrow B : a\langle S\rangle.G) \xrightarrow{\text{AB}?a(S)} (G)} \qquad \frac{G \xrightarrow{\ell} G' \quad B \notin subj(\ell)}{(A \rightsquigarrow B : a\langle S\rangle.G) \xrightarrow{\ell} (A \rightsquigarrow B : a\langle S\rangle.G')} \qquad \lfloor\text{BRANCH}\rfloor/\lfloor\text{ASYNC2}\rfloor$$

Fig. 6. Labelled transitions for global types (adapted from [11])

$$B!\{a_i : \langle S_i\rangle.T_i\}_{i\in I} \xrightarrow{\text{AB}!a\langle S\rangle} T_j \ \ (j \in I) \ \lfloor\text{LSEL}\rfloor \quad B?\{a_i : \langle S_i\rangle.T_i\}_{i\in I} \xrightarrow{\text{AB}?a\langle S\rangle} T_j \ \ (j \in I) \ \lfloor\text{LBRA}\rfloor$$

$$T[\mu t.T/t] \xrightarrow{\ell} T' \ imply \ \mu t.T \xrightarrow{\ell} T' \ \lfloor\text{LREC}\rfloor$$

Fig. 7. LTS for local session types (adapted from [11])

3.2 Scribble Local Protocols

Scribble local protocols describe a session from the perspective of a single participant. The syntax of Scribble local protocols is given below.

Definition 3.2 (Scribble Local Protocols)

$$L ::= \text{local protocol pro at } A_i(\text{role } A_1, ..., \text{role} A_1)\{T\}$$
$$T ::= a(S) \text{ to } B; T \mid a(S) \text{ from } B; T \mid \text{choice at } A \{T_1\} \text{ or} ... \text{or } \{T_n\}$$
$$\mid \text{ rec pro } \{T\} \mid \text{continue pro} \mid \text{end}$$

The construct $a(S)$ to $B; T$ models a send action from A to B; the dual local protocol is $a(S)$ from $B; T$ that models a receive action of A from B. The other protocol constructs are similar to the corresponding global protocol constructs. Recursive variables are guarded in the standard way, i.e. they only occur under a prefix. For convenience we will, sometimes, use the notation choice at $\{a_i(S_i)$ from $A; T_i\}_{i\in\{1,..,n\}}$ to denote protocols of the form choice at $\{a_1(S_1)$ from $A; T_1\}$ or ... or $\{a_n(S_n)$ from $A; T_n\}$ with $n > 1$, or of the form $a(S)$ from $A; T$ when $n = 1$.

Decomposing global protocols into a set of local protocols is called *projection*. Projection is a key mechanism to enable distributed enforcement of global properties. Projection preserves the interaction structures and message exchanges required for the target role to fulfil his/her part in the conversation. The formal definition of projection, for a normal (canonical) form of global protocols, is given by Definition 4.10.

Formal Semantics of Local Protocols. The LTS for local protocols is defined by the rules in Fig. 4, and uses the same labels as the global semantics in Fig. 3. The rules ⌊SEND⌋, ⌊RECV⌋, ⌊CHOICE⌋, ⌊REC⌋ are similar to the respective rules for global protocols. No rules for asynchrony are required as each participant is assumed to be single threaded.

Formal Semantics of Configurations. The LTS in Fig. 4 describes the behaviour of each single role in isolation. In the rest of this section we give the semantics of systems resulting from the composition of Scribble local protocols and communication channels. Given a set of roles $\{1, ..., n\}$ we define configurations $(T_1, ..., T_n, \vec{w})$ where $\vec{w} ::= \{w_{ij}\}_{i\neq j\in\{1,...,n\}}$ are unidirectional, possibly empty (denoted by ϵ), unbounded FIFO queues with elements of the form $a(S)$.

Definition 3.3 (Semantics of configurations). *The LTS of* $(T_1, ..., T_n, \vec{w})$ *is defined as follows:* $(T_1, ..., T_n, \vec{w}) \xrightarrow{\ell} (T'_1, ..., T'_n, \vec{w}')$ *iff:* :

(1) $T_B \xrightarrow{AB!a(S)} T'_B \wedge w'_{AB} = w_{AB} \cdot a(S) \wedge (ij \neq AB \Rightarrow w_{ij} = w'_{ij} \wedge T_i = T'_i)$

(2) $T_B \xrightarrow{AB?la(S)} T'_B \wedge a(S) \cdot w'_{AB} = w_{AB} \wedge (ij \neq AB \Rightarrow w_{ij} = w'_{ij} \wedge T_j = T'_j)$
with $A, B, i, j \in \{1, ..., n\}$.

In (1) the configuration makes a send action given that one of the participants can perform that send action. Case (1) has the effect of adding a message, that

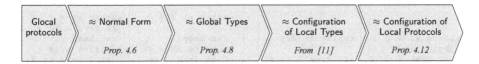

Fig. 8. Workflow of proving soundness of the projection

is sent, to the corresponding queue. In (2) the configuration makes a receive action given that one of its participant can perform such an action and that the message being received is currently stored in the corresponding queue. Thus, (2) has the effect of removing the message received from the queue.

4   Correspondence Between Scribble and MPST

In this section we show that a trace of a global protocol corresponds exactly to a trace of its projected local protocols. Correspondence is important as it ensures that the composition of processes, each implementing some local protocol, will behave as prescribed by the original global specification. In the context of MPST, this property is known as *soundness of the projection* (Theorem 3.1, [11]) and has already been proven for global types as defined in [11]. As explained in Sect. 4.1 a translation of this result to Scribble, however, is not obvious.

Figure 8 gives a high level overview of the results presented in this section. First, we discuss the (syntactic) differences between global types and global protocols. We present a normal form for global protocols such that a Scribble global protocol in a normal form can be encoded into (MPST) global types and it preserves semantics. We then prove a similar correspondence between Scribble local protocols and (MPST) local types. The soundness of the projection of global protocols then follows from soundness of the projection of MPST global types (Theorem 3.1 from [11]).

4.1   Scribble Normal Form

We recall the syntax of global types from [11] in Fig. 5. It is very similar to the syntax of Scribble global protocols in Sect. 3 except: (1) Scribble does not cater for delegation and higher order protocols whereas global types do; and (2) the choice and interaction protocols are two separated constructs in Scribble while they are modelled as a unique construct in global types and (3) differently than MPST, Scribble allows unguarded choice. The case of (2) is a consequence of the specific focus of Scribble as a protocol design language directed at practitioners that are familiar with e.g., Java notation, who proved to find this notation friendlier [12,13,26,28]. Regarding (3) the choice construct in Scribble directly supports recursion and choice while in MPST the choice is always directly followed by an interaction. In the following section we explain that these differences are indeed syntactic and do not affect the soundness of the language.

```
choice at A {          choice at A {
  choice at A {          m1 from A to B;
    m1 from A to B;      } or {
  } or {                 m2 from A to B;
    m2 from A to B;      } or {
  }                      m3 from A to B;
} or {                   }
  m3 from A to B;
}
```

```
choice at A {
  rec Loop{
    choice at A {
      m1 from A to B;
      continue Loop;
    } or {
      m2 from A to B;
    }
  } or {
    m3 from A to B;}
```

```
choice at A {
  m1 from A to B;
  rec Loop {
    choice at A {
      m1 from A to B;
      continue Loop;
    } or {
      m2 from A to B;
    }
  } or {
    m2 from A to B;
  } or {
    m3 from A to B;}
```

Fig. 9. Scribble protocol (left), and its flatten form (right)

Fig. 10. Scribble protocol (left), and its normal form (right)

Definition 4.1 (Scribble Normal Form (SNF))

$$G ::= \texttt{choice at A } \{N_i\}_{i \in \{1,..,n\}} \mid N \mid \texttt{rec t } \{N\}$$
$$N ::= \texttt{a(S) from A to B}; G \mid \texttt{continue t} \mid end$$

First, we observe that a Scribble syntax with a guarded and a singleton choice directly corresponds to MPST. We refer to a Scribble protocol, where all choices are guarded, as a Scribble Normal Form (SNF). Later we show that there is a behaviour preserving translation between a well-formed Scribble protocol and its normal form. The Scribble Normal Form (SNF) for global protocols is given below.

The encoding of Scribble global protocols to SNF requires two auxiliary functions: flatten(G) and unfold(G). The latter collects top level global types from a choice type, and is utilised in the encoding as to remove nested choice. The former performs one unfolding of a recursion. We demonstrate flatten(G) in the example in Fig. 9.

Definition 4.2 (Flatten). *Given a Scribble protocol* G *then* flatten(G) *is defined as* flatten(G_0)∪...∪flatten(G_n) *if* G=choice at A $\{G_i\}_{i \in \{1,..,n\}}$. *In all other cases,* flatten(G) *is homomorphic,* flatten(G) = G

Definition 4.3 (Unfold). *Given a global Scribble protocols* G *then* unfold(G) *is defined as* unfold(G'[rec t $\{G'\}$/continue t])) *if* G = rec t $\{G'\}$ *and homomrhic otherwise*

Thus for any recursive type, unfold is the result of repeatedly unfolding the top level recursion until a non-recursive type constructor is reached. Unfold terminates given the assumption that recursive types are contractive, as in our case. Intuitively, a protocol is translated to a normal form after first unfolding all recursions once and then flattening nested choice. Figure 10 shows a Scribble protocol and its translation to its normal form, and the encoding is given in Definition 4.4.

Definition 4.4 (Encoding ⟨⟩ of Global Protocols to SNF)

$$\langle\texttt{a(S) from A to B}; G\rangle \qquad\quad = \texttt{a(S) from A to B}; \langle G\rangle$$

$$\langle\texttt{choice at A } \{G_i\}_{i\in\{1,..,n\}}\rangle = \texttt{choice at A } \{\texttt{flatten}(\langle G_i\rangle)\}_{i\in\{1,..,n\}}$$

$$\langle\texttt{end}\rangle = \texttt{end} \quad \langle\texttt{rec t } \{G\}\rangle = \texttt{unfold}(\texttt{rec t } \{\langle G\rangle\}) \quad \langle\texttt{continue t}\rangle = \texttt{continue t}$$

Trace Equivalence. The definition of trace equivalence, denoted by ≈ is standard. We write $G \approx G'$ if $TR(G) = TR(G')$ where $TR(G)$ is the set of traces obtained by reducing G

$$TR(G) = \{\vec{\ell} \mid \exists G', G \xrightarrow{\vec{\ell}} G'\}$$

We assume G is closed, i.e does not contain free type variables, where a type variable t is bound in $\texttt{rec t } \{G'\}$, and free otherwise. We extend the definition of traces for local protocols, global and local types, and we also extend ≈ and $\lesssim$ to local protocols, as well as global and local types, and configuration of local protocols.

Lemma 4.5. *Given a global protocol G then: (1) $G \approx \texttt{flatten}(G)$ (2) $G \approx \texttt{unfold}(G)$; and (3) $\langle G'\rangle[\texttt{rec t } \{\langle G'\rangle\}/\texttt{continue t}] \approx \langle G'[\texttt{rec t } \{G'\}/\texttt{continue t}]\rangle$*

Proposition 4.6 (SNF Translation). *Let G be a Scribble local protocol, then $G \approx \langle G\rangle$.*

4.2 From Global Protocols to Global Types

Definition 4.7 (Encoding of Global Protocols to Global Types). *The encoding $[\![\,]\!]$ from SNF to global types is given below:*

$$[\![\texttt{ a(S) from A to B}; G]\!] = A \rightarrow B : \{\texttt{a}\langle S\rangle.[\![G]\!]\}$$

$$[\![\texttt{choice at A } \{\texttt{a}_j(S_j) \texttt{ from A to B}; G_j\}_{j\in\{1\cdots n\}}]\!] = A \rightarrow B : \{\texttt{a}_j\langle S_j\rangle.[\![G_j]\!]\}_{j\in\{1\cdots n\}}$$

$$[\![\texttt{rec t } \{G\}]\!] = \mu t.[\![G]\!] \quad [\![\texttt{continue t}]\!] = t \quad [\![\texttt{end}]\!] = \texttt{end}$$

For convenience, we recall the semantics of global types in Fig. 6. The semantics of global protocols and global types are similar except that the one for MPSTs from [11] have no rule ⌊CHOICE⌋ as choice is handled directly in the rule for send/selection and branch/receive. To match Scribble global protocols and MPST step by step we extend the definition of encoding to account for intermediate steps:

$$[\![\texttt{transit :a(S) from A to B}; G'']\!] = A \rightsquigarrow B : \texttt{a}\langle S\rangle.[\![G'']\!]$$

Proposition 4.8 (Correspondence of Global Protocols and Global Types). *Let G be a Scribble global protocol, then $G \approx [\![G]\!]$.*

4.3   From Local Protocols to Local Types

The syntactic differences between Scribble local protocols and local types (given in Fig. 5) reflect the difference between Scribble global protocols and MPST global types. We define an encoding of local protocols (Definition 3.2) to local types on the normal form of a Scribble local protocol (Definition 4.9).

Definition 4.9 (Local Scribble Normal Form (LSNF))

$$T :: = \texttt{choice at } A\{N_i\}_{i \in I} \mid N \mid \texttt{rec t } \{N\}$$
$$N :: = a(S) \texttt{ from } B; T \mid a(S) \texttt{ to } B; T \mid \texttt{continue t} \mid \texttt{end}$$

Local types are generated from global types following a syntactic procedure, called *projection*. In a similar way we define projection on global protocols. The definition of projection is given in Definition 4.10. We denote by $\mathscr{P}(G)$ the set of roles in a protocol G.

Definition 4.10 (Projection). *The projection of G onto* $A \in \mathscr{P}(G)$, *written* $G \downarrow_A$, *is defined by induction on* G *as follows:*

$(a(S) \texttt{ from } B \texttt{ to } C; G') \downarrow_A =$
$$\begin{cases} a(S) \texttt{ from } B; (G' \downarrow_A) & \textit{if } A = C \\ a(S) \texttt{ to } C; (G' \downarrow_A) & \textit{if } A = B \\ G' \downarrow_A & \textit{if } A \neq B, C \end{cases}$$

$(\texttt{rec t } \{G'\}) \downarrow_A =$
$$\begin{cases} \texttt{rec t } \{(G' \downarrow_A)\} & G' \neq \texttt{continue t} \\ \texttt{end} & \textit{otherwise} \end{cases}$$

$(\texttt{choice at } B \ \{a_i(S_i) \texttt{ from } B \texttt{ to } C; G_i\}_{i \in I}) \downarrow_A =$
$$\begin{cases} \texttt{choice at } B \ \{a_i(S_i) \texttt{ from } B; (G_i \downarrow_A)\}_{i \in I} & \textit{if } A = C \\ \texttt{choice at } B \ \{a_i(S_i) \texttt{ to } C; (G_i \downarrow_A)\}_{i \in I} & \textit{if } A = B \\ \texttt{choice at } D \ (\sqcup\{(G_i \downarrow_A)\}_{i \in I}) \textit{ if } A \neq B, C; \ G_i \downarrow_A = a_i(S_i) \texttt{ from } D; G_i' \downarrow_A, \forall i \in I \end{cases}$$

$(\texttt{continue t}) \downarrow_A = \texttt{continue t}$ $(\texttt{end}) \downarrow_A = \texttt{end}$

If no side condition applies then G is *not projectable* on A and the global protocol G is not well-formed. The case for **choice** uses the merge operator $\sqcup$ to ensure that (1) the locally projected behaviour is independent of the chosen branch (i.e $G_i = G_j$, for all $i, j \in I$), or (2) the chosen branch is identifiable by A via a unique label. The merge operator $\sqcup$ [11] is defined as a partial commutative operator over two types s.t.

$$\{a_i(S_i) \texttt{ from } B; T_i\}_{i \in I} \sqcup \{a_j'(S_j') \texttt{ from } B; T_j'\}_{j \in J} = \{a_k(S_k) \texttt{ from } B; T_k\}_{k \in I \setminus J}$$
$$\cup \ \{a_j'(S_j') \texttt{ from } B; T_j'\}_{j \in J \setminus I} \cup \ \{a_k(S_k) \texttt{ from } B; T_k \sqcup T_k'\}_{k \in I \cap J}$$

where for each $k \in I \cap J, a_k = a_k', S_k = S_k'$. Merge is homomorphic for all other types (i.e $\mathscr{E}[T_k] \sqcup \mathscr{E}[T_k'] = \mathscr{E}[T_k \sqcup T_k']$, where $\mathscr{E}$ is a context for local protocols.). We say that G is *well-formed* if for all $A \in \mathscr{P}(G)$, $G \downarrow_A$ is defined. Note that a normal form is preserved during projection, i.e a Sribble global protocol in a normal form is projected to a Scribble local protocol in a normal form. Next we give the encoding between Scribble local protocols and MPST local types. Hereafter we write Scribble local protocol when referring to LSNF protocols.

Definition 4.11 (Encoding of Local Protocols to Local Types). *The encoding* $(\!|\cdot|\!)$ *from (Scribble) local protocols to MPST local types is given below:*

$(\!|\text{a}(S) \text{ to } B; T|\!) = B!\{a : \langle S \rangle.(\!|T|\!)\}$ $(\!|\text{a}(S) \text{ from } B; T|\!) = B?\{a : \langle S \rangle.(\!|T|\!)\}$

$(\!|\text{choice at A } \{T'_i\}_{i \in I}|\!) = \begin{cases} B!\{a_i : \langle S_i \rangle.(\!|T'_i|\!)\}_{i \in I} & \textit{if } T'_i = a_i(S_i) \text{ to } B; T_i \\ A?\{a_i : \langle S_i \rangle.(\!|T'_i|\!)\}_{i \in I} & \textit{if } T'_i = a_i(S_i) \text{ from } A; T_i \end{cases}$

$(\!|\text{rec t } \{T\}|\!) = \mu t.(\!|T|\!)$ $(\!|\text{continue t}|\!) = t$ $(\!|\text{end}|\!) = \text{end}$

Proposition 4.12 (Correspondence of Local Protocols and Local Types). *Let* T *be a Scribble local protocol, then* $T \approx (\!|T|\!)$.

Proposition 4.13 (Correspondence of Configurations). *Let* $(T_1, \ldots, T_n, \vec{w})$ *be a configuration of Scribble local protocols, then* $(T'_1, \ldots, T'_n, \vec{w}) \approx ((\!|T_1'|\!), \ldots, (\!|T_n'|\!), \vec{w'})$.

4.4 Correspondence of Global and Local Protocols

Theorem 4.14 gives the correspondence between the traces produced by a global protocol G and those produced by the configuration that consists of the composition of the projections of G onto $\mathscr{P}(G)$.

Theorem 4.14 (Soundness of projection). *Let* G *be a Scribble global protocol and* $\{T_1, \ldots, T_n\} = \{G \downarrow_A\}_{A \in \mathscr{P}(G)}$ *be the set of its projections, then*

$$G \approx (T_1, \ldots, T_n, \vec{\varepsilon})$$

Theorem 4.14 directly follows by: (i) the correspondence between (Scribble) global protocols and MPSTs global types given in Sect. 4; (ii) trace equivalence between global types and configuration of projected global types (Theorem 3.1 in [11]); (iii) the correspondence between configurations of MPSTs local types and configurations of Scribble local protocols given in Sect. 4.

5 From Scribble to CFSMs

This section gives the translation of local protocols to CFSMs [4]. First, we start from some preliminary notations. ϵ is the empty word. A is a finite alphabet and A^* is the set of all finite words over A. $|x|$ is the length of a word x and $x.y$ or xy the concatenation of two words x and y. Let $\mathscr{P}$ be a set of participants fixed throughout the section: $\mathscr{P} = \{A, B, C, \ldots p, q, \ldots\}$.

Definition 5.1 (CFSM). *A communicating finite state machine is a finite transition system given by a 5-tuple* $M = (Q, C, q_0, A, \delta)$ *where (1)* Q *is a finite set of states; (2)* $C = \{AB \in \mathscr{P}^2 | A \neq B\}$ *is a set of channels; (3)* $q_0 \in Q$ *is an initial state; (4)* A *is a finite alphabet of message labels, and (5)* $\delta = Q \times (C \times \{!, ?\} \times A) \times Q$ *is a finite set of transitions.*

Final State is a state $q \in Q$, which does not have any outgoing transitions. If all states in Q are final, δ is the empty relation. *A (communicating) system* S is a tuple $S = (M_p)_{p \in \mathscr{P}}$ of CFSMs such that $M_p = (Q_p, C, q_{0_p}, A, \delta_p)$. We define *a configuration* for M_p to be a tuple $s = (\vec{q}, \vec{w})$ where $\vec{q} = (q_p)_{p \in \mathscr{P}}$ and where $w = (w_{pq})_{p \neq q \in \mathscr{P}}$ with $w_{pq} \in A^*$. *A path* in M is a finite sequence of $q_0, \ldots, q_n (n \geq 0)$ such that $(q_i, \ell, q_{i+1}) \in \delta (0 \leq i \leq n - 1)$ and we write $q \xrightarrow{\ell} q'$ if $(q, \ell, q') \in \delta$.

Definition 5.2 gives the translation of local Scribble protocols to CFSMs. For convenience, we do not separate a label from a payload and we write msg instead of a(S). Without loss of generality we assume all nested recursive types are given as $\operatorname{rec} \vec{t} \{T\}$, where $\operatorname{rec} \vec{t} \{T\} = T$ if $|\vec{t}| = 0$. If $\vec{t} = (t_0, \ldots, t_n), T' \neq \operatorname{rec} t \{T''\}$, then $\operatorname{rec} \vec{t} \{T\} = \operatorname{rec} t_0 \{\ldots \operatorname{rec} t_n \{T'\} \ldots\}$.

We use the auxiliary function $\mathrm{body}(T)$ to denote the body of a recursive term. Hence $\mathrm{body}(T) = T'$ if $T = \operatorname{rec} \vec{t} \{T'\}$; in all other cases $\mathrm{body}(T) = T$. We remind that recursive variables are guarded in the standard way, i.e. they only occur under a prefix and therefore $\mathrm{body}(T)$ cannot be $\mathtt{continue}\ t$.

Definition 5.2 (Translation from local types to CFSMs). *We write* $T' \in T$ *if* T' *occurs in* T. *Let* T_0 *be the normal form of the local type of participant* A *projected from* G. *The automaton corresponding to* T_0 *is* $\mathcal{A}(T_0) = (Q, C, q_0, A, \delta)$ *where: (1)* $Q = \{T' | T' \in T_0, T' \neq \mathtt{continue}\ t\} \setminus (\{T' | \operatorname{rec} \vec{t} \{T'\} \in T_0\} \cup \{T_i | \mathtt{choice\ at\ A}\ \{T_i\}_{i \in I} \in T_0\})$; *(2)* $q_0 = T_0$ *(3)* $C = \{AB\ |\ A, B \in G\}$; *(4)* $A = \{msg\ |\ msg\ occurs\ in\ G\}$ *is the set of labels* msg *in* G; *and (5)* δ *is defined below:*

1. *if* $\mathrm{body}(T) = msg$ to $B; T' \in Q$, *then*

$$\begin{cases} 1)(T, (AB!msg), \operatorname{rec}_{t \in \vec{t}} \vec{t} \{T''\}) \in \delta & \textit{if } T' = \mathtt{continue}\ t, \operatorname{rec}_{t \in \vec{t}} \vec{t} \{T''\} \in T_0 \\ 2)(T, (AB!msg), T') \in \delta & \textit{otherwise} \end{cases}$$

2. *if* $\mathrm{body}(T) = msg$ from $B; T' \in Q$, *then*

$$\begin{cases} 1)(T, (BA?msg), \operatorname{rec}_{t \in \vec{t}} \vec{t} \{T''\}) \in \delta & \textit{if } T' = \mathtt{continue}\ t, \operatorname{rec}_{t \in \vec{t}} \vec{t} \{T''\} \in T_0 \\ 2)(T, (BA?msg), T') \in \delta & \textit{otherwise} \end{cases}$$

3. *if* $T = \mathtt{choice\ at\ A}\ \{T_i\}_{i \in I}$, *then:*
   (a) *if* $T_i = msg_i$ to $B; T'$

$$\begin{cases} 1)T, (AB!msg_i), \operatorname{rec}_{t \in \vec{t}} \vec{t} \{T''\}) \in \delta & \textit{if } T' = \mathtt{continue}\ t, \operatorname{rec}_{t \in \vec{t}} \vec{t} \{T''\} \in Q, \\ 2)T, (AB!msg_i), T') \in \delta & \textit{otherwise} \end{cases}$$

   (b) *if* $T_i = msg_i$ from $A; T'$

$$\begin{cases} 1)(T, (BA?msg_i), \operatorname{rec}_{t \in \vec{t}} \vec{t} \{T''\}) \in \delta & \textit{if } T' = \mathtt{continue}\ t, \operatorname{rec}_{t \in \vec{t}} \vec{t} \{T''\} \in Q \\ 2)(T, (BA?msg_i), T') \in \delta & \textit{otherwise} \end{cases}$$

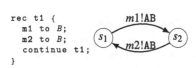

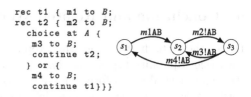

```
rec t1 {
  m1 to B;
  m2 to B;
  continue t1;
}
```

Fig. 11. Scribble protocol (left) and corresponding CFSM (right)

```
rec t1 { m1 to B;
rec t2 { m2 to B;
  choice at A {
    m3 to B;
    continue t2;
  } or {
    m4 to B;
    continue t1}}}
```

Fig. 12. Scribble protocol (left) and corresponding CFSM (right)

Examples. We illustrate the translation with two examples, in Figs. 11 and 12. The CFSM $\mathscr{A}(\mathtt{T})$ for the local protocol $\mathtt{T}$ from Fig. 11 (left) is $\mathscr{A}(\mathtt{T}) = (Q, C, q_0, A, \delta)$. We first generate the states Q of $\mathscr{A}(\mathtt{T})$ from the suboccurrences of the initial local protocol $\mathtt{T}$. The states are denotes as s_1 and s_2 where $s_1 = \mathtt{T}$ and $s_2 = (\mathtt{m2\ to\ B;\ continue\ t1;})$. $\mathscr{A}(\mathtt{T})$ is defined as the 5-tuple: 1) $Q = \{s_1, s_2\}$; 2) $C = \{\mathtt{AB}, \mathtt{BA}\}$; 3) $q_0 = s_1$; 4) $A = \{\mathtt{m1}, \mathtt{m2}\}$; 5) $\delta = \{(s_1, \mathtt{m1!AB}, s_2), (s_2, \mathtt{m2!AB}, s_1)\}$.

Next we consider the local type $\mathtt{T}$, given on Fig. 12 (left). From the suboccurrences of the local protocol $\mathtt{T}$ we generate three states s_1, s_2, and s_3, where $s_1 = \mathtt{T}$; $s_2 = \mathtt{rec\ t2\ m2\ to\ B;\ choice\ at\ A\ m3\ to\ B;\ continue\ t2\ or\ m4\ to\ B;\ continue\ t1}$; and $s_3 = \mathtt{choice\ at\ A\ m3\ to\ B;\ continue\ t2\ or\ m4\ to\ B;\ continue\ t1}$. Then the corresponding automaton $\mathscr{A}(\mathtt{T})$ is the 5-tuple (Q, C, A, q_0, δ) where 1) $Q = \{s_1, s_2, s_3\}$; 2) $C = \{\mathtt{AB}, \mathtt{BA}\}$; 3) $q_0 = s_1$ 4) $A = \{\mathtt{m1}, \mathtt{m2}, \mathtt{m3}, \mathtt{m4}\}$; 5) $\delta = \{(s_1, \mathtt{m1!AB}, s_2), (s_2, \mathtt{m2!AB}, s_3), (s_3, \mathtt{m3!AB}, s_2), (s_3, \mathtt{m4!AB}, s_1)\}$.

We proceed by proving operational correspondence between a local type $\mathtt{T}$ and its corresponding $\mathscr{A}(\mathtt{T})$. We use an auxiliary function to map recursive variables to types.

Definition 5.3 (Unfold mapping). *We define a function* $\mathtt{unfMap} : \mathtt{T} \times \sigma \rightarrow \sigma$, *where* $\mathtt{T}$ *is a type and* σ *is a mapping from recursive variables to types* $\mathtt{unfMap}(\mathtt{T}, \sigma) =$

$$\begin{cases} \bigcup_{i \in I} \mathtt{unfMap}(\mathtt{T_i}, \sigma) \text{ if } \mathtt{T} = \mathtt{choice\ at\ A}\ \{\mathtt{T_i}\}_{i \in I} \\ \mathtt{unfMap}(\mathtt{T'}, \sigma) \text{ if either } \mathtt{T} = \mathit{msg}\ \mathtt{to\ B}; \mathtt{T'}, \text{ or } \mathtt{T} = \mathit{msg}\ \mathtt{from\ B}; \mathtt{T'} \\ \mathtt{unfMap}(\mathtt{T'}[\mathtt{rec}\ \vec{\mathtt{t}}\ \{\mathtt{T'}\}/\mathtt{continue\ t}]_{\forall \mathtt{t} \in \vec{\mathtt{t}}}, \sigma \bigcup_{\mathtt{t_i} \in \vec{\mathtt{t}}} \{\mathtt{t_i} \mapsto \mathtt{T}\}) \\ \qquad \text{if } \mathtt{T} = \mathtt{rec}\ \vec{\mathtt{t}}\ \{\mathtt{T'}\}; \mathtt{t_i} \notin \sigma \\ \sigma \text{ if either } \mathtt{T} = \mathtt{rec}\ \vec{\mathtt{t}}\ \{\mathtt{T'}\} \text{ and } \exists \mathtt{t'} \in \vec{\mathtt{t}} : \mathtt{t'} \in \sigma, \text{ or } \mathtt{T} = \mathtt{end} \end{cases}$$

We assume all recursive variables are distinct and also $\mathtt{rec}\ \vec{\mathtt{t}}\ \{\mathtt{T'}\}\sigma = \mathtt{T'}\sigma$. Hence, σ can contain $\mathtt{t} \in \vec{\mathtt{t}}$ and we apply the substitution σ without α-renaming.

Lemma 5.4 (Suboccurrences). *Given a local protocol* $\mathtt{T}$, *with a suboccurrence* $\mathtt{rec}\ \vec{\mathtt{t}}\ \{\mathtt{T'}\}_{(\mathtt{t} \in \vec{\mathtt{t}})} \in T$ *and a substitution* σ *s.t* $\sigma = \mathtt{unfMap}((\mathtt{T}, \varnothing))$, *then*

$$\mathtt{rec}\ \vec{\mathtt{t}}\ \{\mathtt{T'}\}_{(\mathtt{t} \in \vec{\mathtt{t}})}\sigma = \mathtt{T''} \text{ with } \{\mathtt{t} \mapsto \mathtt{T''}\} \in \sigma$$

Theorem 5.5 (Soundness of translation). *Given a local protocol* $\mathtt{T}$, *then* $\mathtt{T} \approx \mathscr{A}(\mathtt{T})$.

6   Conclusion and Related Work

De Nicola is the first person who proposed a location-based distributed model with rich capability types, and *implemented* that model in Java as to demonstrate a practical use of formal foundations for mobile computing. Following his spirits, this paper gave a formal definition of a practical protocol description language, Scribble. We proved a correspondence between Scribble and MPST and showed that a global protocol corresponds to a system of CFSMs.

The work [10] is the first to explore the connection of MPST and CFSMs. [10] gives a sound and complete characterisation of a class of communicating automata that can be expressed by the language of multiparty session types. The presented work is closely based on the translation of session types to CFSMs presented in [10], and hence we adhere to the same conditions as theirs, namely the CFSM is deterministic and directed without mixed states (each state is either sending or receiving to the same participant with distinct labels). Lange et al. [20] presents an algotithm for synthesising *global graphs* from local multiparty specifications, given as CFSMs, that allows more general constructs, such as fork and join. Scribble currently does not support such constructs. The correspondence of MPST and CFSMs with time constraints is further explored in [2,3]. The work [21] uses the result in [3] to implement a runtime monitor based on an extension of Scribble with time annotations, but the work does not prove formal correspondence between timed Scribble and timed automata.

The encoding of Scribble protocols to CFSMs presented in this article is an important basis when building and verifying distributed systems. It guarantees that global safety properties can be ensured through local, i.e, decentralised verification. The setting defined by CFSMs does not require synchronisation at runtime. Therefore our approach is more efficient to implement than a centralised approach. In [9,17], we rely on this result to design and build a sound Scribble-based framework for runtime and hybrid verification.

Several implementation works use the Scribble toolchian and the local CFSM representation to generate APIs for programming distributed protocols [18,22]. In recent years, Scribble-based code generation has been extended with various contructs, e.g. parameterised role [5] for distributed Go programming, delegation in Scala [25], time constarints in Python [3], explicit connections [19] for dynamic joining of roles in Java, and payload constraints in F# [22]. The above mentioned works are either practical (hence no formal semantics nor operational correspondence results are given) and/or informally rely on the correspondence between MPST and Scribble as to justify the soundness of their respective implementations and extensions.

Future work includes formalisations of extended Scribble in the literature explained above. In particular, there exists no operational semantics of multiple multiparty session types with *delegations* and *higher-order code mobility* since a single system of CFSMs corresponds to a single multiparty session type with fixed participants. We plan to tackle this problem first extending CFSM models from a fixed set to a family of participants.

Acknowledgments. We thank the reviewers for their comments. This work is partially supported by EPSRC projects EP/K034413/1, EP/K011715/1, EP/L00058X/1, EP/N027833/1 and EP/N028201/1. The first author was supported by an EPSRC Doctoral Prize Fellowship.

A   Scribble Normal Form

Proposition 4.6 **(SNF Translation):** Let G be a Scribble local protocol, then $G \approx \langle G \rangle$.

Proof. First we consider $G \lesssim \langle G \rangle$. The proof is mechanical and is done by induction on the transition rules applied for closed terms of G.

1. (base case) If $G = $ **end** then both $trmG$ and $\langle G \rangle$ produce an empty set of traces and no rules can be applied.
2. (inductive case) if $G \xrightarrow{\ell} G'$ then $\langle G \rangle \xrightarrow{\ell} G''$ such that $G' \approx G''$.
   (a) if $G = $ **a(S) from A to B**$; G'$
       G can do **AB!msg** or ℓ by $\lfloor$SEND$\rfloor$ or $\lfloor$ASYNC1$\rfloor$ respectively.
       Then $G \lesssim \langle G \rangle$ follows by the induction hypothesis (IH) and by the definition of encoding
   (b) $G = $ **rec t** $\{G'\}$
       $G \xrightarrow{\ell} G''$
       By $\lfloor$REC$\rfloor$ $G'[$**rec t** $\{G'\}/$**continue t**$] \xrightarrow{\ell} G''$
       By IH $\langle G'[$**rec t** $\{G'\}/$**continue t**$]\rangle \xrightarrow{\ell} G'''$ s.t $G'' \approx G'''$
       By Lemma 4.5
       $\langle G' \rangle[$**rec t** $\{\langle G' \rangle\}/$**continue t**$] \approx \langle G'[$**rec t** $\{G'\}/$**continue t**$]\rangle$
       Thus, $\langle G' \rangle[$**rec t** $\{\langle G' \rangle\}/$**continue t**$] \xrightarrow{\ell} G''''$ s.t $G''' \approx G''''$
       By $\lfloor$REC$\rfloor$**rec t** $\{\langle G' \rangle\} \xrightarrow{\ell} G''''$
       By Lemma 4.5 **rec t** $\{\langle G' \rangle\} \approx$ **unfold**(**rec t** $\{\langle G' \rangle\}) = \langle G \rangle$
   (c) $G = $ **choice at A** $\{G_i\}_{i \in \{1,..,n\}}$
       From $\lfloor$CHOICE$\rfloor G \xrightarrow{\ell} G'$ with $G_i \xrightarrow{\ell} G'$
       From IH $\langle G_i \rangle \xrightarrow{\ell} G''$ s.t $G'' \approx G'$ From **flatten**$(G) \approx G$ it follows that
       flatten$(G_i) \xrightarrow{\ell} G'''$ s.t $G''' \approx G''$
       From $\lfloor$CHOICE$\rfloor$ it follows $\langle G \rangle \xrightarrow{\ell} G'''$

Now we consider $\langle G \rangle \lesssim G$. The proof is by induction on the definition of encoding of closed terms of G.

1. (base case) If $\langle G \rangle = $ **end** then both G and $\langle G \rangle$ produce an empty set of traces and no rules can be applied.
2. (inductive case) if $\langle G \rangle \xrightarrow{\ell} G'$ then $G \xrightarrow{\ell} G''$ such that $G' \approx G''$.
   (a) $\langle$**a(S) from A to B**$; G \rangle = $ **a(S) from A to B**$; \langle G \rangle$
       $\langle G \rangle$ can do **AB!msg** or ℓ by $\lfloor$SEND$\rfloor$ or $\lfloor$ASYNC1$\rfloor$ respectively.
       Then $G \lesssim \langle G \rangle$ follows by the IH and by the definition of encoding

(b) $\langle \texttt{rec t } \{G\}\rangle = \texttt{unfold}(\texttt{rec t } \{\langle G\rangle\}) = \langle G\rangle[\texttt{rec t } \{\langle G\rangle\}/\texttt{continue t}]$

From IH: $G[\texttt{rec t } \{G\}/\texttt{continue t}] \approx \langle G\rangle[\texttt{rec t } \{\langle G\rangle\}/\texttt{continue t}]$

Thus, if $\langle G\rangle[\texttt{rec t } \{\langle G\rangle\}/\texttt{continue t}] \xrightarrow{\ell} G'$

then $G[\texttt{rec t } \{G\}/\texttt{continue t}] \xrightarrow{\ell} G''$ s.t $G' \approx G''$

From $\lfloor\text{REC}\rfloor$ rule: $\texttt{rec t } \{G\} \xrightarrow{\ell} G''$

(c) $\langle G\rangle = \langle \texttt{choice at A } \{G_i\}_{i\in\{1,..,n\}}\rangle = \texttt{choice at A } \{\texttt{flatten}(\langle G_i\rangle)\}_{i\in\{1,..,n\}}$

From $\lfloor\text{CHOICE}\rfloor\langle G\rangle \xrightarrow{\ell} G'$ with $\texttt{flatten}(\langle G_i\rangle) \xrightarrow{\ell} G'$

By Lemma 4.5 $\texttt{flatten}(\langle G\rangle) \approx \langle G\rangle$ it follows that

$\langle G_i\rangle \xrightarrow{\ell} G''$ s.t $G'' \approx G'$

From IH it follows that $G \xrightarrow{\ell} G'''$ s.t $G''' \approx G'' \approx G'$.

B   From Global Protocols to Global Types

Proposition 4.8 (Correspondence of Global Protocols and Global Types): Let G be a Scribble global protocol, then $G \approx \llbracket G\rrbracket$.

Proof. First, we consider $G \lesssim \llbracket G\rrbracket$. The proof is done by induction (on the depth of the tree) on the transition rule applied.

1. (Base case) If $G = \texttt{end}$ then both G and $\llbracket G\rrbracket$ produce an empty set of traces.
2. (Inductive case) if $G \xrightarrow{\ell} G'$ and we have to prove that $\llbracket G\rrbracket \xrightarrow{\ell} \llbracket G'\rrbracket$.

– if $G = \texttt{a(S) from A to B}; G''$ then we either have a send action by $\lfloor\text{SEND}\rfloor$ or ℓ transition by $\lfloor\text{ASYNC1}\rfloor$

  • $\lfloor\text{SEND}\rfloor G \xrightarrow{AB!a\langle S\rangle} \texttt{transit :a(S) from A to B}; G''$
    By (1) $\llbracket G\rrbracket = A \rightarrow B : \{a\langle S\rangle.\llbracket G''\rrbracket\}$ and
    (2) $\llbracket \texttt{transit :a(S) from A to B}; G''\rrbracket = A \rightsquigarrow B : a\langle S\rangle.\llbracket G''\rrbracket$ and
    (3) $\lfloor\text{SELECT}\rfloor_{MPST}: A \rightarrow B : \{a\langle S\rangle.\llbracket G''\rrbracket\} \xrightarrow{AB!a\langle S\rangle} A \rightsquigarrow B : a\langle S\rangle.\llbracket G''\rrbracket$
    we have $\llbracket G\rrbracket \xrightarrow{AB!a\langle S\rangle} \llbracket G'\rrbracket$
  • $\lfloor\text{ASYNC1}\rfloor a(S) \texttt{ from A to B}; G'' \xrightarrow{\ell} a(S) \texttt{ from A to B}; G''$ By (1) $\llbracket G\rrbracket = A \rightarrow B : \{a\langle S\rangle.\llbracket G''\rrbracket\}$ and $\llbracket G'\rrbracket = A \rightarrow B : a\langle S\rangle.\llbracket G'''\rrbracket$ By (2) $\llbracket G''\rrbracket \xrightarrow{\ell} \llbracket G'''\rrbracket$, which follows from the premise $G'' \xrightarrow{\ell} G'''$ of the $\lfloor\text{ASYNC1}\rfloor$ and by IH and (3) $B \notin subj(\ell)$, which follows from the premise of $\lfloor\text{ASYNC1}\rfloor$:
    we can apply the $\lfloor\text{ASYNC1}\rfloor_{MPST}$ rule: $\llbracket G\rrbracket \xrightarrow{\ell} \llbracket G'\rrbracket$

– if $G = \texttt{transit :a(S) from A to B}; G''$
  We proceed as in the above case. We either have a receive action by the rule $\lfloor\text{RECV}\rfloor$ or ℓ transition by the rule $\lfloor\text{ASYNC2}\rfloor$.

  • $\lfloor\text{RECV}\rfloor G \xrightarrow{AB?a\langle S\rangle} G'$ where $G' = G''$
    By (1) $\llbracket G\rrbracket = A \rightsquigarrow B : a\langle S\rangle.\llbracket G''\rrbracket$ and $\llbracket G'\rrbracket = \llbracket G''\rrbracket$ and
    (3) $\lfloor\text{BRANCH}\rfloor_{MPST}: A \rightsquigarrow B : a\langle S\rangle.\llbracket G''\rrbracket \xrightarrow{AB?a\langle S\rangle} \llbracket G''\rrbracket$
    therefore $\llbracket G\rrbracket \xrightarrow{AB?a\langle S\rangle} \llbracket G'\rrbracket$

- $\lfloor\text{ASYNC2}\rfloor G \xrightarrow{\ell} G'$ where $G' = \texttt{transit :a(S) from A to B}; G''$

  By (1) $\llbracket G \rrbracket = A \rightsquigarrow B : a\langle S\rangle.\llbracket G''\rrbracket$ and $\llbracket G'\rrbracket = A \rightarrow B : \{a\langle S\rangle.\llbracket G'''\rrbracket\}$ By (2)
  $\llbracket G''\rrbracket \xrightarrow{\ell} \llbracket G'''\rrbracket$, which follows from the premises $G'' \xrightarrow{\ell} G'''$ of the $\lfloor\text{ASYNC1}\rfloor$
  and by the induction hypothesis and
  (3) $A, B \notin subj(\ell)$, which follows from the premise of $\lfloor\text{ASYNC2}\rfloor$:

  we can apply the $\lfloor\text{ASYNC2}\rfloor_{MPST}$ rule: $\llbracket G\rrbracket \xrightarrow{\ell} \llbracket G'\rrbracket$

- if $G = \texttt{choice at A } \{G^b_j\}_{j\in\{1,..,n\}})$

  By $\lfloor\text{CHOICE}\rfloor$ we have $G \xrightarrow{\ell} G'$ where by the rule premise we have for G' that
  $a_i(S_i) \texttt{ from A to B}; G'' \xrightarrow{\ell} G'$ for $(i \in I)$ which brings us back to the first case.
- if $G = \texttt{rec t } \{G''\}$ the thesis directly follows by induction since
  (1) by $\lfloor\text{REC}\rfloor G \xrightarrow{\ell} G'$ where $G[\texttt{rec t } \{G\}/\texttt{continue t}] \xrightarrow{\ell} G'$
  (2) $\llbracket G\rrbracket = \mu t\llbracket G''\rrbracket$
  By $\lfloor\text{REC}\rfloor \llbracket G''\rrbracket[\mu t.\llbracket G''\rrbracket/t]) \xrightarrow{\ell} \llbracket G'\rrbracket$
  (3) From IH, $G' \lesssim \llbracket G'\rrbracket$ and therefore $G \lesssim \llbracket G\rrbracket$

Now we consider $\llbracket G\rrbracket \lesssim G$.
The proof is done by induction on transition rules applied to the encoding
of G.

1. $\llbracket G\rrbracket = \texttt{end}$ then both $\llbracket G\rrbracket$ and G then no rules can be applied.
2. if $\llbracket G\rrbracket = A \rightarrow B : \{a\langle S\rangle.\llbracket G\rrbracket\}$, then we either have a send action by $\lfloor\text{SELECT}\rfloor_{MPST}$
   or ℓ transition by $\lfloor\text{ASYNC1}\rfloor$.

   - $\lfloor\text{SELECT}\rfloor_{MPST}\llbracket G\rrbracket \xrightarrow{AB!a\langle S\rangle} \llbracket G'\rrbracket$
     By $G = \texttt{a(S) from A to B}; G''$ and $G' = \texttt{transit :a(S) from A to B}; G''$ and
     $\lfloor\text{SEND}\rfloor$ it follows that $G \xrightarrow{AB!a\langle S\rangle} G'$
   - $\lfloor\text{ASYNC1}\rfloor_{MPST}\llbracket G\rrbracket \xrightarrow{\ell} \llbracket G'\rrbracket$ where
     $\llbracket G\rrbracket = A \rightarrow B : \{a\langle S\rangle.\llbracket G''\rrbracket\}$ and $\llbracket G'\rrbracket = A \rightsquigarrow B : a\langle S\rangle.\llbracket G''\rrbracket$
     By (1) the rule premise $\llbracket G''\rrbracket \xrightarrow{\ell} \llbracket G'''\rrbracket$ and by (2) IH it follows that $G'' \xrightarrow{\ell} G'''$.
     Given also that $A, B \notin subj(\ell)$, we can apply $\lfloor\text{ASYNC1}\rfloor$. Thus, $G \xrightarrow{\ell} G'$

3. if $\llbracket G\rrbracket = \llbracket\texttt{choice at A } a_j(S_j) \texttt{ from A to B}; G_j\rrbracket = A \rightarrow B : \{a_j\langle S_j\rangle.\llbracket G_j\rrbracket\}_{j\in\{1,..,n\}}$
   Then by $\lfloor\text{CHOICE}\rfloor$ we have that $\llbracket G\rrbracket \xrightarrow{\ell} \llbracket G'\rrbracket$ when $\llbracket a_i(S_i) \texttt{ from A to B}; G_i\rrbracket \xrightarrow{\ell} \llbracket G'\rrbracket$
   for $i \in I$.
   Thus, we have to prove that
   if $\llbracket a_i(S_i) \texttt{ from A to B}; G_i\rrbracket \xrightarrow{\ell} \llbracket G'\rrbracket$ then $a_i(S_i) \texttt{ from A to B}; G_i \xrightarrow{\ell} \llbracket G'\rrbracket$, which
   follows from a).

4. if $\llbracket G\rrbracket = A \rightsquigarrow B : a\langle S\rangle.\llbracket G''\rrbracket$ $\llbracket G\rrbracket$ can do a receive action by $\lfloor\text{BRANCH}\rfloor_{MPST}$ or ℓ
   transition by $\lfloor\text{ASYNC2}\rfloor$.

   - $\lfloor\text{BRANCH}\rfloor_{MPST}\llbracket G\rrbracket \xrightarrow{AB!a\langle S\rangle} \llbracket G'\rrbracket$
     By $G = \texttt{transit :a(S) from A to B}; G''$ and
     $G' = \texttt{transit :a(S) from A to B}; G''$ and $\lfloor\text{RECV}\rfloor$ it follows that $G \xrightarrow{AB?a\langle S\rangle} G'$

- $\lfloor \text{ASYNC2} \rfloor_{MPST} \llbracket G \rrbracket \xrightarrow{\ell} \llbracket G' \rrbracket$ where
  $\llbracket G \rrbracket = A \rightsquigarrow B : a\langle S \rangle.\llbracket G'' \rrbracket$ and $\llbracket G' \rrbracket = A \rightarrow B : a\langle S \rangle.\llbracket G'' \rrbracket$
  By (1) the rule premise $\llbracket G'' \rrbracket \xrightarrow{\ell} \llbracket G''' \rrbracket$ and by (2) IH it follows that $G'' \xrightarrow{\ell} G'''$.
  Given also that $A, B \notin subj(\ell)$, we can apply $\lfloor \text{ASYNC2} \rfloor$. Thus, $G \xrightarrow{\ell} G'$

5. if $\llbracket G \rrbracket = \mu t.\llbracket G'' \rrbracket$ the thesis directly follows by induction.

C   From Local Protocols to Local Types

Proposition 4.12 (Correspondence of Local Protocols and Local Types): Let T be a Scribble local protocol, then $T \approx (\!|T|\!)$.

Proof. First, we consider $T \lesssim \llbracket T \rrbracket$.

The proof is done by induction (on the depth of the tree) on the transition rule applied.

1. (Base case) If $T = \textbf{end}$ then both T and $(\!|T|\!)$ produce an empty set of traces.
2. (Inductive case) $T \xrightarrow{\ell} T'$ and we have to prove that $(\!|T|\!) \xrightarrow{\ell} (\!|T'|\!)$. We proceed by case analysis on the structure of T

   (a) if $T = a(S)$ to $B; T'' \xrightarrow{AB!a\langle S \rangle} T''$ by $\lfloor \text{SEND} \rfloor$
      $(\!|T|\!) = B!\{a : \langle S \rangle.(\!|T''|\!)\} \xrightarrow{AB!a\langle S \rangle} (\!|T''|\!)$ by $\lfloor \text{LSEL} \rfloor$

   (b) if $T = a(S)$ from $B; T'' \xrightarrow{AB?a\langle S \rangle} T''$ by $\lfloor \text{RECV} \rfloor$
      $(\!|T|\!) = B?\{a : \langle S \rangle.(\!|T''|\!)\} \xrightarrow{AB?a\langle S \rangle} (\!|T''|\!)$ by $\lfloor \text{LBRA} \rfloor$

   (c) if $T = \textbf{choice at } A \{T_i\}_{i \in I}) \xrightarrow{\ell} T'$
      Depending on the structure of T_i, this case folds back to previous cases a) and b).
      if $T_i = a_i(S_i)$ from $B; T'' \xrightarrow{AB!a\langle S \rangle} T'' = T'$ then $(\!|T_i|\!) \xrightarrow{AB!a\langle S \rangle} (\!|T'|\!)$ by $\lfloor \text{LSEL} \rfloor$
      if $T_i = B?\{a_i : \langle S_i \rangle.(\!|T''|\!)\} \xrightarrow{AB?a\langle S \rangle} = T'' = T'$ then $(\!|T_i|\!) \xrightarrow{AB?a\langle S \rangle} (\!|T'|\!)$ by $\lfloor \text{LBRA} \rfloor$

   (d) if $T = \mu t.T''$ the thesis directly follows by induction.

   Now we consider $(\!|T|\!) \lesssim T$.
   The proof is done by induction on transition rules applied to the encoding.

1. (Base case) If $(\!|T|\!) = \textbf{end}$ then both $(\!|T|\!)$ and T produce an empty set of traces.
2. (Inductive case) $(\!|T|\!) \xrightarrow{\ell} (\!|T'|\!)$ and we have to prove that $T \xrightarrow{\ell} T'$. We proceed by case analysis on the structure of $(\!|T|\!)$

   - if $(\!|T|\!) = B!\{a : \langle S \rangle.(\!|T''|\!)\}$
      $B!\{a : \langle S \rangle.(\!|T''|\!)\} \xrightarrow{AB!a\langle S \rangle} (\!|T''|\!)$ by $\lfloor \text{LSEL} \rfloor$
      $T = a(S)$ to $B; T'' \xrightarrow{AB!a\langle S \rangle} (\!|T''|\!)$ by $\lfloor \text{SEND} \rfloor$

- if $(\!|T|\!) = B?\{a : \langle S\rangle.(\!|T''|\!)\}$

  $B?\{a : \langle S\rangle.(\!|T''|\!)\} \xrightarrow{\text{AB?a}\langle S\rangle} (\!|T''|\!)$ by $\lfloor \text{LBRA} \rfloor$

  $T = a(S) \text{ from } B; T'' \xrightarrow{\text{AB?a}\langle S\rangle} T''$ by $\lfloor \text{RECV} \rfloor$

- if $(\!|T|\!) = B?\{a_i : \langle S_i\rangle.(\!|T_i|\!)\}_{i \in I}$

  $B?\{a_i : \langle S_i\rangle.(\!|T_i|\!)\}_{i \in I} \xrightarrow{\text{AB?a}\langle S\rangle} (\!|T_j|\!)(j \in I)$

  By $\lfloor \text{RECV} \rfloor$ and the structure of T_i we have that $a_i(T_i)$ to $B; T_i \xrightarrow{\text{AB!a}\langle S\rangle} T_i$ and therefore we can apply $\lfloor \text{CHOICE} \rfloor$

  Thus, $T \xrightarrow{\text{AB!a}\langle S\rangle} T_j$

- if $(\!|T|\!) = A!\{a_i : \langle S_i\rangle.(\!|T|\!)\}_{i \in I}$ the case is analogical to the previous one.
- if $(\!|T|\!) = \mu t.T''$ the thesis directly follows by induction.

Proposition 4.13 **(Correspondence of Configurations):** Let $(T_1, \ldots, T_n, w)$ be a configuration of Scribble local protocols, then $(T_1', \ldots, T_n', w) \approx ((\!|T_1'|\!), \ldots, (\!|T_n'|\!), w')$.

Proof. The proof is by induction on the number of transition steps. Inductive hypothesis: $(T_1, \ldots, T_n, w) \approx ((\!|T_1|\!), \ldots, (\!|T_n|\!), w)$

Now we want to prove that if $(T_1, \ldots, T_n, w) \xrightarrow{\ell} (T_1', \ldots, T_n', w')$ then

$((\!|T_1|\!), \ldots, (\!|T_n|\!), w) \xrightarrow{\ell} ((\!|T_1'|\!), \ldots, (\!|T_n'|\!), w')$

We do a case analysis on the transition label ℓ:

(1) if $\ell = \text{AB!a}\langle S\rangle$

  By $T_B \xrightarrow{\text{AB!a}\langle S\rangle} T_B$ and Proposition 4.12 it follows: $(\!|T_B|\!) \xrightarrow{\text{AB!a}\langle S\rangle} (\!|T_B|\!)$

  By definition of configuration of local protocols:

$w_{AB}' = w_{AB} \cdot a(T) \wedge (w_{ij} = w_{ij}')_{\text{for } ij \neq AB}$.

(2) if $\ell = \text{AB?a}\langle S\rangle$

  By $T_B \xrightarrow{\text{AB?a}\langle S\rangle} T_B'$ and Proposition 4.12 it follows: $(\!|T_B|\!) \xrightarrow{\text{AB?a}\langle S\rangle} (\!|T_B'|\!)$

  By definition of configuration of local protocols:

$w_{AB}' = w_{AB} \cdot a(S) \wedge (\Rightarrow w_{ij} = w_{ij}')_{ij \neq AB}$

In (1) and (2) we have by definition that $T_i = T_i'(\text{ for } \neq AB)$, which by the inductive hypothesis implies that $(\!|T_i|\!) = (\!|T_i'|\!)$

Then by the definition of configuration of local protocols (from (1) and (2)) it follows that $((\!|T_1|\!), \ldots, , \ldots, (\!|T_n|\!), w) \xrightarrow{\ell} ((\!|T_1'|\!), \ldots, (\!|T_n'|\!), w')$.

D From Sribble to CFSM

Lemma 5.5 **(Soundness of the translation).** Given a local protocol T , then $T \approx \mathscr{A}(T)$.

Proof. In the proof we assume $\sigma = \text{unfMap}(T, \varnothing)$. Also we assume $T \neq \text{end}$. When $T = \text{end}$ the lemma is trivially true since T produces an empty set of traces, δ is an empty relation and q_0, the initial state, is also a final state.

First, we consider $T \lesssim \mathscr{A}(T)$. Next we prove that if $T \xrightarrow{\ell} T'$ then $\exists T_A, T_A' \in Q$ such that $T_A \sigma = T$ and $T_A' \sigma = T'$, and $(T_A, \ell, T_A') \in \delta$.

The proof is by induction on the transition relation for local types. In all cases we assume that $T = T_A \sigma$.

- $\lfloor \text{SEND} \rfloor$ if the reduction is by $\lfloor \text{SEND} \rfloor$ we have
  $$T_A \sigma = (\text{msg to B}; T_A')\sigma = \text{msg to B}; (T_A' \sigma).$$
  Thus, $T_A \sigma \xrightarrow{\ell} T_A' \sigma$ where $\ell = \text{msg!AB}$.
  Since $\text{body}(T_A) = \text{msg to B}; T_A'$ we proceed by case analysis on T_A'.
  Case 1: $T_A' \neq \text{continue t}$;
  By Definition 5.2(1-2) and $\text{body}(T_A) = \text{msg to B}; T_A' \Rightarrow (T_A, \ell, T_A') \in \delta$.
  Case 2: $T_A' = \text{continue t}$;
  We have that $T_A' \sigma = \text{continue t } \sigma = T''$, where $\{t \mapsto T''\} \in \sigma$.

  By $\lfloor \text{SEND} \rfloor$ we have $T_A \sigma \xrightarrow{\ell} T''$.
  By Definition 5.2(1-1) and $body T_A = \text{msg to B}; T_A'$ it follows that
  $(T_A, \ell, \text{rec } \overrightarrow{t} \{T_A''\}) \in \delta$ with $\text{rec } \overrightarrow{t} \{T_A''\} \in T_0$.
  By Lemma 5.4 we have $\text{rec } \overrightarrow{t} \{T_A''\}\sigma = T''$ and we conclude the case.
- $\lfloor \text{RECV} \rfloor$ is similar to Case $\lfloor \text{SEND} \rfloor$ and thus we omit.
- $\lfloor \text{CHOICE} \rfloor$ if the reduction is by $\lfloor \text{CHOICE} \rfloor$ we have
  $$T_A \sigma = (\text{choice at A}\{T_{Ai}\}_{i \in I})\sigma = \text{choice at A}\{(T_{Ai}\sigma)\}_{i \in I}.$$
  Case 1: if $T_{Ai}\sigma$ has the shape $(\text{msg}_i \text{ to B}; T_{Ai}')\sigma = \text{msg}_i \text{ to B}; (T_{Ai}'\sigma), \forall i \in I$

  then we have $T_A \sigma \xrightarrow{\ell} T_{Aj}'\sigma$ for some $j \in I$ with $\ell = \text{msg}_j!\text{AB}$.
  Since $\text{body}(T_A) = T_A$, we proceed by case analysis on T_{Aj}'.
  Case 1.1: $T_{Aj}' \neq \text{continue t}$;
  By Definition 5.2(3-a-2) and $\text{body}(T_A) = T_A$ we have $(T_A, \ell, T_{Aj}') \in \delta$.
  Case 1.2: $T_A j' = \text{continue t}$;
  (1*) We have that $T_{Aj}'\sigma = \text{continue t } \sigma = T''$, where $\{t \mapsto T''\} \in \sigma$.

  (2*) By $\lfloor \text{CHOICE} \rfloor$ we have $T_A \sigma \xrightarrow{\ell} T''$.
  By Definition 5.2(3-a-2) and $\text{body}(T_A) = T_A \Rightarrow (T_A, \ell, \text{rec } \overrightarrow{t} \{T_A''\}) \in \delta$
  with $\text{rec } \overrightarrow{t} \{T_A''\} \in T_0$.
  By Lemma 5.4 we have $\text{rec } \overrightarrow{t} \{T_A''\}\sigma = T''$.
  Applying the IH to (1*) and (2*) we conclude the case.
  Case 2: if $T_{Ai}\sigma$ has the shape $(\text{msg}_i \text{ to B}; T_{Ai}')\sigma = \text{msg}_i \text{ to B}; (T_{Ai}'\sigma)$
  this case is similar to Case 1 and thus we omit.
  Note that since the normal form of local types does not allow for unguarded choice, hence, all possible transitions of $T_A \sigma$ are the transitions from Case 1 and Case 2.
- $\lfloor \text{REC} \rfloor$ if the reduction is by $\lfloor \text{REC} \rfloor$ we have then $T_A \sigma = (\text{rec t } \{T_A'\})\sigma = T_A' \sigma$. We note that $T_A' \sigma$ does not contain the term continue t since unguarded recursive variables are not allowed. Hence, $T_A' \sigma$ is either send, receive or choice and by IH and $\lfloor \text{SEND} \rfloor$, $\lfloor \text{RECV} \rfloor$, $\lfloor \text{CHOICE} \rfloor$ we conclude this case.

We next consider $\mathscr{A}(T) \lesssim T$. We prove that given a local protocol T_0 if $(T_A, \ell, T_A') \in \delta$ then $\exists T$ s.t. $T = T_A \sigma$ and $T \xrightarrow{\ell} T'$ and $T' = T_A' \sigma$ with $\sigma = \text{unfMap}(T_0, \varnothing)$. We proceed by case analysis on the transitions in δ.

Case 1: $T_A = \mathtt{msg}$ to $B; T_A''$ and $\ell = \mathtt{msg?AB}$.

Then $T' = T_A\sigma$ and we have by $\lfloor\text{SEND}\rfloor T_A\sigma \xrightarrow{\ell} T_A''\sigma$.

Case 1.1: if $T_A'' = T_A' \neq \mathtt{continue}\ t$

The hypothesis follows from $T_A\sigma \xrightarrow{\ell} T_A'\sigma$.

Case 1.2: if $T_A'' = \mathtt{continue}\ t$

By Definition 5.2 $T_A' = \mathtt{rec}\ \vec{t}\ \{T_A'''\} \in T_0, t \in \mathbf{t}$.

By Definition 5.3 and Lemma 5.4 we have $t \mapsto T''$ s.t. $\mathtt{rec}\ \vec{t}\ \{T_A'''\}\sigma = T''$.

From IH and $T_A\sigma \xrightarrow{\ell} T_A''\sigma = T'' = \mathtt{rec}\ \vec{t}\ \{T_A'''\}\sigma = T_A'\sigma$ we conclude the case.

Case 2: $T_A = \mathtt{msg}$ from $B; T_A''$ and $\ell = \mathtt{msg!AB}$.

Proceeds in a similar way as Case 2 and thus we omit.

Case 3: $T_A = \mathtt{choice\ at}\{\mathtt{msg}_i$ to $B; T_{Ai}\}_{i \in I}$

Then we have by $\lfloor\text{CHOICE}\rfloor$

$T_A\sigma = \mathtt{choice\ at}\{\mathtt{msg}_i$ to $B; T_{Ai}\sigma\}_{i \in I} \xrightarrow{\mathtt{msg!AB}} T_{Aj}\sigma$ for some $j \in I$.

Case 3.1: if $T_{Aj} = T_A' \neq \mathtt{continue}\ t$

From IH and $T_A\sigma \xrightarrow{\ell} T_A'\sigma$ we conclude the case.

Case 3.2: if $T_{Aj} = \mathtt{continue}\ t$

By Definition 5.2 $T_{Aj} = \mathtt{rec}\ \vec{t}\ \{T_A'''\} \in T_0, t \in \mathbf{t}$

By Definition 5.3 and Lemma 5.4 we have $t \mapsto T''$ s.t. $\mathtt{rec}\ \vec{t}\ \{T_A'''\}\sigma = T''$.

We have that $T_A\sigma \xrightarrow{\ell} T_{Aj}\sigma = T'' = \mathtt{rec}\ \vec{t}\ \{T_A'''\}\sigma = T_A'\sigma$, hence we conclude the case.

Case 4: $T_A = \mathtt{choice\ at}\{\mathtt{msg}_i$ from $B; T_{Ai}\}_{i \in I}$

Proceeds in a similar way as Case 3 and thus we omit.

Case 5: $T_A = \mathtt{rec}\ \vec{t}\ \{T_A''\}$

Note that the T_A'' is either message send or message receive. Hence, By applying the IH and Case 1, 2 we conclude the case.

References

1. Behavioural Types: From Theory to Tools. River Publishers, Delft (2017)
2. Bocchi, L., Lange, J., Yoshida, N.: Meeting deadlines together. In: 26th International Conference on Concurrency Theory. LIPIcs, vol. 42, pp. 283–296. Schloss Dagstuhl (2015)
3. Bocchi, L., Yang, W., Yoshida, N.: Timed multiparty session types. In: Baldan, P., Gorla, D. (eds.) CONCUR 2014. LNCS, vol. 8704, pp. 419–434. Springer, Heidelberg (2014). https://doi.org/10.1007/978-3-662-44584-6_29
4. Brand, D., Zafiropulo, P.: On communicating finite-state machines. J. ACM **30**(2), 323–342 (1983)
5. Castro, D., Hu, R., Jongmans, S.-S., Ng, N., Yoshida, N.: Distributed programming using role parametric session types in go. In: 46th ACM SIGPLAN Symposium on Principles of Programming Languages, pp. 1–30. ACM (2019)
6. W3C WS-CDL. http://www.w3.org/2002/ws/chor/
7. Coppo, M., Dezani-Ciancaglini, M., Padovani, L., Yoshida, N.: A gentle introduction to multiparty asynchronous session types. In: Bernardo, M., Johnsen, E.B. (eds.) SFM 2015. LNCS, vol. 9104, pp. 146–178. Springer, Cham (2015). https://doi.org/10.1007/978-3-319-18941-3_4

8. De Nicola, R., Ferrari, G., Pugliese, R.: Klaim: a kernel language for agents interaction and mobility. IEEE Trans. Softw. Eng. **24**, 315–330 (1998)
9. Demangeon, R., Honda, K., Raymond, H., Neykova, R., Yoshida, N.: Practical interruptible conversations: distributed dynamic verification with multiparty session types and Python. FMSD **46**(3), 197–225 (2015)
10. Deniélou, P.-M., Yoshida, N.: Multiparty session types meet communicating automata. In: Seidl, H. (ed.) ESOP 2012. LNCS, vol. 7211, pp. 194–213. Springer, Heidelberg (2012). https://doi.org/10.1007/978-3-642-28869-2_10
11. Deniélou, P.-M., Yoshida, N.: Multiparty compatibility in communicating automata: characterisation and synthesis of global session types. In: Fomin, F.V., Freivalds, R., Kwiatkowska, M., Peleg, D. (eds.) ICALP 2013. LNCS, vol. 7966, pp. 174–186. Springer, Heidelberg (2013). https://doi.org/10.1007/978-3-642-39212-2_18
12. Honda, K., et al.: Structuring communication with session types. In: Agha, G., et al. (eds.) Concurrent Objects and Beyond. LNCS, vol. 8665, pp. 105–127. Springer, Heidelberg (2014). https://doi.org/10.1007/978-3-662-44471-9_5
13. Honda, K., Mukhamedov, A., Brown, G., Chen, T.-C., Yoshida, N.: Scribbling Interactions with a Formal Foundation. In: Natarajan, R., Ojo, A. (eds.) ICDCIT 2011. LNCS, vol. 6536, pp. 55–75. Springer, Heidelberg (2011). https://doi.org/10.1007/978-3-642-19056-8_4
14. Honda, K., Vasconcelos, V.T., Kubo, M.: Language primitives and type discipline for structured communication-based programming. In: Hankin, C. (ed.) ESOP 1998. LNCS, vol. 1381, pp. 122–138. Springer, Heidelberg (1998). https://doi.org/10.1007/BFb0053567
15. Honda, K., Yoshida, N., Carbone, M.: Multiparty asynchronous session types. In: POPL 2008, pp. 273–284. ACM (2008)
16. Honda, K., Yoshida, N., Carbone, M.: Multiparty asynchronous session types. JACM **63**, 1–67 (2016)
17. Hu, R., Neykova, R., Yoshida, N., Demangeon, R., Honda, K.: Practical interruptible conversations. In: Legay, A., Bensalem, S. (eds.) RV 2013. LNCS, vol. 8174, pp. 130–148. Springer, Heidelberg (2013). https://doi.org/10.1007/978-3-642-40787-1_8
18. Hu, R., Yoshida, N.: Hybrid session verification through endpoint API generation. In: Stevens, P., Wąsowski, A. (eds.) FASE 2016. LNCS, vol. 9633, pp. 401–418. Springer, Heidelberg (2016). https://doi.org/10.1007/978-3-662-49665-7_24
19. Hu, R., Yoshida, N.: Explicit connection actions in multiparty session types. In: Huisman, M., Rubin, J. (eds.) FASE 2017. LNCS, vol. 10202, pp. 116–133. Springer, Heidelberg (2017). https://doi.org/10.1007/978-3-662-54494-5_7
20. Lange, J., Tuosto, E., Yoshida, N.: From communicating machines to graphical choreographies. In: POPL, pp. 221–232. ACM (2015)
21. Neykova, R., Bocchi, L., Yoshida, N.: Timed runtime monitoring for multiparty conversations. FAOC **29**, 877–910 (2017)
22. Neykova, R., Hu, R., Yoshida, N., Abdeljallal, F.: A session type provider: compile-time API generation for distributed protocols with interaction refinements in F#. In: 27th International Conference on Compiler Construction, pp. 128–138. ACM (2018)
23. Neykova, R., Yoshida, N.: Let it recover: multiparty protocol-induced recovery. In: CC. ACM (2017, to appear)
24. Ng, N., de Figueiredo Coutinho, J.G., Yoshida, N.: Protocols by default. In: Franke, B. (ed.) CC 2015. LNCS, vol. 9031, pp. 212–232. Springer, Heidelberg (2015). https://doi.org/10.1007/978-3-662-46663-6_11

25. Scalas, A., Dardha, O., Hu, R., Yoshida, N.: A linear decomposition of multiparty sessions for safe distributed programming. In: 31st European Conference on Object-Oriented Programming. LIPIcs, vol. 74, pp. 24:1–24:31. Schloss Dagstuhl (2017)
26. Scribble Project.. http://www.scribble.org
27. Takeuchi, K., Honda, K., Kubo, M.: An interaction-based language and its typing system. In: Halatsis, C., Maritsas, D., Philokyprou, G., Theodoridis, S. (eds.) PARLE 1994. LNCS, vol. 817, pp. 398–413. Springer, Heidelberg (1994). https://doi.org/10.1007/3-540-58184-7_118
28. Yoshida, N., Hu, R., Neykova, R., Ng, N.: The scribble protocol language. In: Abadi, M., Lluch Lafuente, A. (eds.) TGC 2013. LNCS, vol. 8358, pp. 22–41. Springer, Cham (2014). https://doi.org/10.1007/978-3-319-05119-2_3

Embedding RCC8D in the Collective Spatial Logic CSLCS

Vincenzo Ciancia$^{(\boxtimes)}$, Diego Latella, and Mieke Massink

Consiglio Nazionale delle Ricerche - Istituto di Scienza e Tecnologie dell'Informazione
'A. Faedo', CNR, Pisa, Italy
vincenzo.ciancia@isti.cnr.it

Abstract. Discrete mereotopology is a logical theory for the specification of qualitative spatial functions and relations defined over a discrete space, intended as a set of basic elements, the *pixels*, with an adjacency relation defined over it. The notions of interest are that of *region*, intended as an arbitrary aggregate of pixels, and of specific *relations* between regions. The mereotopological theory RCC8D extends the mereological theory RCC5D—a theory of region parthood for discrete spaces—with the topological notion of *connection* and the remaining relations (disconnection, external connection, tangential and nontangential proper parthood and their inverses). In this paper, we propose an encoding of RCC8D into CSLCS, the *collective* extension of the *Spatial Logic of Closure Spaces* SLCS. We show how topochecker, a model-checker for CSLCS, can be used for effectively checking the existence of a RCC8D relation between two given regions of a discrete space.

Keywords: RCC8D · Adjacency Spaces · Closure Spaces ·
Spatial logics · SLCS · CSLCS

1 Introduction

The study of logical approaches to modelling *space* and spatial aspects of computation is a well established area of research in computer science and artificial intelligence. A standard reference is the *Handbook of Spatial Logics* [1]. Therein, several spatial logics are described, with applications far beyond topological spaces; such logics treat not only aspects of morphology, geometry and distance, but also advanced topics such as dynamic systems, and discrete structures, that are particularly difficult to deal with, especially from a topological perspective (see, for example [15,19]). For this reason, most of the work present in the literature deals with continuous notions of space, such as Euclidean spaces. In this context, a prominent area of research is represented by the logical theories of "parthood"—*Mereology*—and of "connection" between "regions", i.e. sets of points in a continuous space—*Mereotopology*—representative of which are the Region Connection Calculi RCC5 and RCC8, respectively. In particular, RCC8 [17] is widely referred to in the AI literature on Qualitative Spatial Reasoning [5].

M. Boreale et al. (Eds.): De Nicola-Festschrift, LNCS 11665, pp. 260–277, 2019.
https://doi.org/10.1007/978-3-030-21485-2_15

More recently, attention has been devoted also to logical approaches to *discrete* spaces, including e.g. graphs or digital images, given the importance of such structures in computer science. In particular, in [18] the notions of *Discrete Mereology* and *Discrete Meretopology* have been presented and discrete versions of RCC5 and RCC8, namely RCC5D and RCC8D, have been defined.

On the other hand, in recent work [9,10], Ciancia et al. proposed the *Spatial Logic for Closure Spaces* (SLCS), defined along the same lines as the classical work of Tarski on the spatial interpretation of the modal *possibility* operator as the topological *closure* operator, but with two major differences. The first one is that the underlying model for the logic is not that of topological spaces, as in the classical approach, but rather *Closure Spaces* [15,16], a generalisation of topological spaces including also discrete structures such as graphs, and, consequently, digital images. The second one is the inclusion of the *surrounded* operator—denoted by S, to be read "surrounded"—an operator similar to the *spatial until* discussed in [20] in the context of continuous spaces; a point satisfies $\Phi_1 \; S \; \Phi_2$ if it satisfies Φ_1 and there is no way for moving away to a point not satisfying Φ_1 without first passing by a point satisfying Φ_2. In other words, the points satisfying Φ_1 are *surrounded by* points satisfying Φ_2. In addition, in [10] the logic has been extended with the *collective* fragment, leading to the definition of the *Collective Spatial Logic for Closure Spaces* (CSLCS), where properties of (connected) *sets* of points can be specified. Efficient model checking algorithms have been defined for both SLCS and CSLCS and have been implemented in the prototype tool `topochecker`[1].

In this paper we present an encoding of RCC8D into CSLCS. This shows that CSLCS is a suitable logic not only for reasoning about points in (closure) spaces and connected sets of such points, but also for regions in the sense of the Region Calculus and, in particular, of RCC8D.

The paper is organised as follows: in Sect. 2, SLCS and its extension CSLCS are briefly described; furthermore, we state a proposition relating the temporal *weak until* connective with the interpretation of spatial *surrounded* on discrete spatial models—the proof is provided in the appendix. Section 3 recalls Adjacency Spaces and RCC8D of [5]. The encoding procedure is described in Sect. 4 where some examples of use of `topochecker` are also shown as well as the (graphical) result of RCC8D relations over sample regions. Finally, in Sect. 6 some conclusions are drawn.

2   Spatial Logics for Closure Spaces

Spatial logics have been mainly studied from the point of view of *modal* logics. In his seminal work of 1938, Tarski presented a spatial, and in particular topological, interpretation of modal logic; in 1944 Tarski and McKinsey proved that the simple (and decidable) modal system $S4$ is complete when interpreting

---

[1] Topochecker: *a topological model checker*, see http://topochecker.isti.cnr.it, https://github.com/vincenzoml/topochecker.

the *possibility* modality $\Diamond$ of $\mathcal{S}4$ as *closure* on the reals or any similar metric space. More specifically, a topological model $\mathcal{M} = ((X, O), \mathcal{V})$ of modal logic is any topological space (X, O) where each *point* $x \in X$ is associated with the set of *atomic propositions* p it satisfies, namely the set $\{p | x \in \mathcal{V}(p)\}$, negation and conjunction are interpreted in the usual way, and the *possibility* operator $\Diamond$ is interpreted as *topological closure*, as follows (see [1], Chap. 5):

$$\mathcal{M}, x \models \Diamond\Phi \Leftrightarrow \text{ for all open sets } o \in O \text{ such that } x \in o$$
$$\text{there exists } x' \in o \text{ such that } \mathcal{M}, x' \models \Phi.$$

Of course, by duality, the *necessity* operator $\Box$ turns out to be interpreted as the *topological interior* operator, namely $\mathcal{M}, x \models \Box\Phi \Leftrightarrow$ there exists a open set $o \in O$ such that $x \in o$ and $\mathcal{M}, x' \models \Phi$ for all $x' \in o$. We refer the reader to [20] for further details. A legitimate question is whether the restriction to topological spaces is too strong. For answering this question, it is appropriate to focus on *discrete* spaces, e.g. graphs; any logical approach to reasoning about spatial properties of distributed systems should obviously be capable to deal with discrete structures. There exist of course relational models of $\mathcal{S}4$, namely reflexive and transitive Kripke structures and it is possible to derive a topological space from any such a structure in a sound and complete way. The topological spaces that are used are the so-called *Alexandroff spaces*. These are topological spaces in which each point has a least open neighbourhood. Unfortunately, the correspondence between topological spaces and reflexive and transitive Kripke structures is not easily extended to arbitrary Kripke structures, as transitivity and reflexivity always hold in topo-logics where the basic modality is the closure. On the other hand, requiring transitivity in all models may be too limiting a constraint. This is the main reason to further investigate non-transitive concepts of spatial models and for resorting to models which are more general than topological spaces. In our approach we use *closure spaces* as a generalisation of topological spaces.

Definition 1. *A* closure space *is a pair* $(X, \mathcal{C})$ *where* X *is a non-empty set (of points) and* $\mathcal{C} : 2^X \to 2^X$ *is a function satisfying the following axioms:*

1. $\mathcal{C}(\emptyset) = \emptyset$;

2. $Y \subseteq \mathcal{C}(Y)$ *for all* $Y \subseteq X$;

3. $\mathcal{C}(Y_1 \cup Y_2) = \mathcal{C}(Y_1) \cup \mathcal{C}(Y_2)$ *for all* $Y_1, Y_2 \subseteq X$. ●

It is worth pointing out that topological spaces coincide with the sub-class of closure spaces for which also the *idempotence* axiom $\mathcal{C}(\mathcal{C}(Y)) = \mathcal{C}(Y)$ holds.

Given any relation $R \subseteq X \times X$, function $\mathcal{C}_R : 2^X \to 2^X$ with $\mathcal{C}_R(Y) \triangleq Y \cup \{x | \exists y \in Y. y \, R \, x\}$ satisfies the axioms of Definition 1 thus making $(X, \mathcal{C}_R)$ a closure space. It can be shown that the sub-class of closure spaces that can be generated by a relation as above coincides with the class of *quasi-discrete* closure spaces, i.e. closure spaces where every $x \in X$ has a minimal neighbourhood or, equivalently, for each $Y \subseteq X, \mathcal{C}(Y) = \bigcup_{y \in Y} \mathcal{C}(\{y\})$. Thus (finite) discrete structures, like graphs or Kripke structures can be (re-)interpreted as *quasi-discrete* closure spaces. For example, consider the graph of Fig. 1 where a set Y of nodes is shown in red (1a); the closure $\mathcal{C}(Y)$ of Y is shown in green (1b).

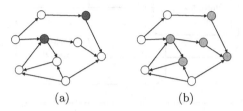

(a)   (b)

Fig. 1. A set of nodes Y in a graph (1a) and its closure $\mathcal{C}(Y)$ (1b). (Color figure online)

Being a special case of graphs, also digital images can be modelled by (finite) quasi-discrete closure spaces. In particular, the pixels of the image are the nodes of the space, whereas the relevant relation is typically both reflexive and symmetric. It may relate any pixel with all the pixels with which it shares an edge, i.e. 5 pixels in 2D images, or with all the pixels with which it shares an edge or a corner, i.e. 9 pixels in 2D images. In the first case, the relation is called *othogonal*, whereas in the second case it is called *orthodiagonal*; in Sect. 3 we will use the orthodiagonal relation, also called the *adjacency relation* in [18]. For instance, the closure of the set of red pixels Y in Fig. 2a is shown in green in Fig. 2b, where the orthogonal relation is used, and in Fig. 2c, where the orthodiagonal relation is used instead.

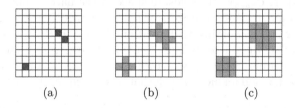

(a)   (b)   (c)

Fig. 2. A set of red pixels Y in a digital image (2a) and its closure $\mathcal{C}(Y)$ according to the orthogonal relation (2b) and the orthodiagonal relation (2c). (Color figure online)

The hierarchy of closure spaces is shown in Fig. 3.

2.1   The Spatial Logic for Closure Spaces - SLCS

In [9,10] the Spatial Logic for Closure Spaces (SLCS) was proposed. In the remainder of this section we briefly recall the fragment of the logic we use in the present paper, which consists essentially of $\mathcal{S}4$—where the $\Diamond$ operator is

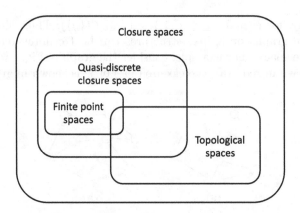

Fig. 3. The hierarchy of closure spaces.

renamed $\mathcal{N}$ (to be read as *near*) for clarity reasons—enriched with an additional operator, the *surrounded* operator $\mathcal{S}$, where $\Phi_1 \, \mathcal{S} \, \Phi_2$ characterises the set of points belonging to an area satisfying Φ_1 and such that one cannot "escape" from such an area without hitting a point satisfying Φ_2, i.e. they are *surrounded* by Φ_2. The syntax of SLCS is given below, for P a set of *atomic predicates* p:

$$\Phi ::= p \mid \neg\Phi \mid \Phi_1 \vee \Phi_2 \mid \mathcal{N}\Phi \mid \Phi_1 \, \mathcal{S} \, \Phi_2 \tag{1}$$

In the sequel we provide a formal definition of the satisfaction relation for SLCS. To that purpose, we need to first introduce the notion of path. A (quasi-discrete) *path* π in $(X, \mathcal{C}_R)$ is a function $\pi : \mathbb{N} \to X$, such that for all $Y \subseteq \mathbb{N}$, $\pi(\mathcal{C}_{Succ}(Y)) \subseteq \mathcal{C}_R(\pi(Y))$, where $\pi(Y)$ is the pointwise extension of π on a set of points Y and $(\mathbb{N}, \mathcal{C}_{Succ})$ is the closure space of the natural numbers with the *successor* relation: $(n, m) \in Succ \Leftrightarrow m = n + 1$. Informally: the ordering in the path imposed by $\mathbb{N}$ is compatible with relation R, i.e. $\pi(i) \, R \, \pi(i{+}1)$. Technically, a (quasi-discrete) path is a *continuous* function from $(\mathbb{N}, \mathcal{C}_{Succ})$ to $(X, \mathcal{C}_R)$. We refer to [10] for details. Set $Y \subseteq X$ is *path-connected* if for all points $y_1, y_2 \in Y$ there exists a path π and an index i such that: $\pi(0) = y_1$, $\pi(i) = y_2$ and $\pi(j) \in Y$, for all $0 \leq j \leq i$.

Definition 2. *A* closure model *$\mathcal{M}$ is a tuple $\mathcal{M} = ((X, \mathcal{C}), \mathcal{V})$, where $(X, \mathcal{C})$ is a closure space and $\mathcal{V} : P \to 2^X$ is a valuation assigning to each atomic predicate the set of points where it holds.* •

Definition 3. Satisfaction $\mathcal{M}, x \models \Phi$ *of a formula Φ at point $x \in X$ in model $\mathcal{M} = ((X, \mathcal{C}), \mathcal{V})$ is defined by induction on the structure of formulas:*

$$\mathcal{M}, x \models p \in P \quad \Leftrightarrow x \in \mathcal{V}(p)$$
$$\mathcal{M}, x \models \neg \Phi \qquad \Leftrightarrow \mathcal{M}, x \models \Phi \text{ does not hold}$$
$$\mathcal{M}, x \models \Phi_1 \vee \Phi_2 \Leftrightarrow \mathcal{M}, x \models \Phi_1 \text{ or } \mathcal{M}, x \models \Phi_2$$
$$\mathcal{M}, x \models \mathcal{N} \Phi \qquad \Leftrightarrow x \in \mathcal{C}(\{y | \mathcal{M}, y \models \Phi\})$$
$$\mathcal{M}, x \models \Phi_1 \mathcal{S} \Phi_2 \Leftrightarrow \mathcal{M}, x \models \Phi_1 \text{ and}$$

> *for all paths π and indexes ℓ the following holds:*
> $$\pi(0) = x \text{ and } \mathcal{M}, \pi(\ell) \models \neg \Phi_1$$
> *implies*
> *there exists index j such that:*
> $$0 < j \leq \ell \text{ and } \mathcal{M}, \pi(j) \models \Phi_2 \qquad \bullet$$

Standard derived operators can be defined in the usual way e.g.: $\Phi_1 \wedge \Phi_2 \equiv \neg(\neg \Phi_1 \vee \neg \Phi_2)$, $\top \equiv p \vee \neg p$, $\bot \equiv \neg \top$, and so on.

In Fig. 4a an example is shown of a model, based on a 2D space of 100 points arranged as a 10×10 grid, with reflexive, symmetric and orthogonal relation. We assume the set of atomic predicates P is the set $\{black, white, red\}$ and, in Fig. 4a, we color in black the points satisfying *black* and similarly for *white* and *red*. In Fig. 4b the points satisfying formula *black* $\vee$ *red* are shown in green[2]; similarly, Fig. 4c shows the points satisfying $\neg(black \vee red)$, and Fig. 4a shows those satisfying $\mathcal{N} black$. Finally, the points in Fig. 4d satisfying *black* satisfy also *black* $\mathcal{S}(\mathcal{N} red)$. Several examples of use of SLCS, extensions thereof, and related model-checking tools can be found in [3,9–14]

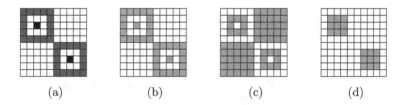

(a)   (b)   (c)   (d)

Fig. 4. An example model (4a); the points shown in green are those satisfying *black* $\vee$ *red* (4b), $\neg(black \vee red)$ (4c), and $\mathcal{N} black$ (4d). (Color figure online)

Finally, we show the formal relationship between the SLCS *surrounded* operator interpreted on quasi-discrete closure spaces and the temporal logic *weak until* operator. Let us consider a set X and a relation $R \subseteq X \times X$; the pair $(X, \mathcal{C}_R)$ is a quasi-discrete closure space, but also a *Kripke frame*; any valuation $\mathcal{V}$ of atomic propositions makes such a space (frame) a closure model (Kripke model). The until operator $\Phi_1 \mathcal{U} \Phi_2$ is well-known. Let us recall the *weak until* operator $\Phi_1 \mathcal{W} \Phi_2$, whose satisfaction for path π is defined as $\mathcal{M}, \pi \models \Phi_1 \mathcal{W} \Phi_2$ iff $\mathcal{M}, \pi(i) \models \Phi_1$ for all i, or $\mathcal{M}, \pi \models \Phi_1 \mathcal{U} \Phi_2$ (note that $\mathcal{W}$ and $\mathcal{U}$ are path-formulas). The following holds:

---

[2] Note that this colour does *not* correspond to any atomic predicate and so it is not part of the model; we use it only for illustration purposes.

Proposition 1.
$$\Phi_2 \vee (\Phi_1\, \mathcal{S}\, \Phi_2) \equiv A(\Phi_1\, \mathcal{W}\, \Phi_2)$$
where A is the *path universal quantifier*. The proof is provided in the Appendix.

2.2 The Collective Extension - CSLCS

In this section we show how the logic defined above is extended in order to reason about *sets* of (connected) points, instead of individual points (see [10] for details). We introduce an additional class of formulas, namely the *collective formulas* by extending the grammar given in (1) as follows:

$$\Psi ::= \neg\,\Psi \mid \Psi_1 \wedge \Psi_2 \mid \Phi \prec \Psi \mid \mathcal{G}\Phi \tag{2}$$

Let Φ be an SLCS formula ("individual" formula, in the sequel), and Ψ a collective formula. Informally, $\Phi \prec \Psi$ (read: Φ *share* Ψ) is satisfied by set Y when the subset of points of Y satisfying the individual property Φ also satisfies the collective property Ψ. Formula $\mathcal{G}\Phi$ (read: *group* Φ) holds on set Y when the elements of the latter belong to a *group*, that is, a possibly larger, path-connected set of points, all satisfying the individual formula Φ. The satisfaction relation $\models_C$ for CSLCS is defined below:

Definition 4. *Satisfaction* $\mathcal{M}, Y \models_C \Psi$ *of a collective formula* Ψ *at set* $Y \subseteq X$ *in model* $\mathcal{M} = ((X, \mathcal{C}), \mathcal{V})$ *is defined by induction on the structure of formulas:*

$$
\begin{aligned}
&\mathcal{M}, Y \models_C \neg\,\Psi &&\Leftrightarrow \mathcal{M}, Y \models_C \Psi \text{ does not hold}\\
&\mathcal{M}, Y \models_C \Psi_1 \wedge \Psi_2 &&\Leftrightarrow \mathcal{M}, Y \models_C \Psi_1 \text{ and } \mathcal{M}, Y \models_C \Psi_2\\
&\mathcal{M}, Y \models_C \Phi \prec \Psi &&\Leftrightarrow \mathcal{M}, \{x \in Y \mid \mathcal{M}, x \models \Phi\} \models_C \Psi\\
&\mathcal{M}, Y \models_C \mathcal{G}\,\Phi &&\Leftrightarrow \text{there exists } Z \subseteq X \text{ such that}\\
&&&\quad Y \subseteq Z \text{ and } Z \text{ is path-connected and}\\
&&&\quad \text{for all } z \in Z \text{ we have: } \mathcal{M}, z \models \Phi \quad\bullet
\end{aligned}
$$

Back to Fig. 4a, we note that, although *each* point satisfying *black* satisfies also $(black \vee white)\mathcal{S}red$, *the set* consisting exactly of the two points satisfying *black* does *not* satisfy the collective formula $\mathcal{G}((black \vee white)\mathcal{S}red)$, i.e. the members of the set are not surrounded *collectively* by red points. The set of black points in Fig. 5 instead satisfies $\mathcal{G}((black \vee white)\mathcal{S}red)$.

Fig. 5. A model where the set of the black points satisfies $\mathcal{G}((black \vee white)\mathcal{S}red)$. (Color figure online)

Finally, it is useful to note that $\mathcal{M}, Y \models_C \Phi \prec \mathcal{G}\bot$ for every $\mathcal{M}$ and every Y if and only if $\Phi \equiv \bot$. Thus the formula $\Phi \prec \mathcal{G}\bot$ can be used for checking whether Φ denotes the empty set.

3   Discrete Spaces with Adjacency and RCC8D

In this section we briefly introduce a subclass of quasi-discrete closure spaces, namely those spaces $(X, \mathcal{C}_R)$ where the underlying relation R, called the *adjacency relation*, is *reflexive* and *symmetric*. The points of any such space can be thought of as *pixels* and the space itself can be used as (a model for) a digital picture [18].

Discrete Mereotopology (DM) is concerned with the study of the relations among *regions*, where a region is interpreted as an arbitrary aggregate $Y \subseteq X$ of pixels. In particular, Mereology is the theory of *parthood* and those relations which can be defined in terms of it. Parthood is defined as set inclusion restricted to non-null regions:

$$\mathsf{P}(Y_1, Y_2) \equiv_{\mathrm{def}} Y_1 \subseteq Y_2 \text{ and } Y_1 \neq \emptyset.$$

The intuition behind the definition of $\mathsf{P}(Y_1, Y_2)$ is fairly simple and comes from set theory: Y_1 is part of Y_2 and should not be empty. The derived relations are defined below. They are readily explained in terms of set theory; the interested reader is referred to [18] for a discussion on the region relations and on their relationships:

$$
\begin{array}{lll}
\mathsf{PP}(Y_1, Y_2) & \equiv_{\mathrm{def}} \mathsf{P}(Y_1, Y_2) \wedge Y_1 \neq Y_2 & [\text{PROPER PARTHOOD}] \\
\mathsf{Pi}(Y_1, Y_2) & \equiv_{\mathrm{def}} \mathsf{P}(Y_2, Y_1) & [\text{INVERSE PARTHOOD}] \\
\mathsf{PPi}(Y_1, Y_2) & \equiv_{\mathrm{def}} \mathsf{PP}(Y_2, Y_1) & [\text{INVERSE PROPER} \\
& & \text{PARTHOOD}] \\
\\
\mathsf{O}(Y_1, Y_2) & \equiv_{\mathrm{def}} Y_2 \cap Y_1 \neq \emptyset & [\text{OVERLAP}] \\
\mathsf{PO}(Y_1, Y_2) & \equiv_{\mathrm{def}} \mathsf{O}(Y_1, Y_2) \wedge \neg\mathsf{P}(Y_1, Y_2) \wedge \neg\mathsf{P}(Y_2, Y_1) & [\text{PARTIALLY OVERLAP}] \\
\mathsf{DR}(Y_1, Y_2) & \equiv_{\mathrm{def}} \neg\mathsf{O}(Y_1, Y_2) & [\text{DISCRETE}] \\
\mathsf{EQ}(Y_1, Y_2) & \equiv_{\mathrm{def}} \mathsf{P}(Y_1, Y_2) \wedge \mathsf{P}(Y_2, Y_1) & [\text{EQUAL}]
\end{array}
$$

The relation set $\{\mathsf{DR}, \mathsf{PO}, \mathsf{PP}, \mathsf{PPi}, \mathsf{EQ}\}$ is referred to as RCC5D, i.e. the Discrete Region Connection Calculus based on 5 relations, which is a purely mereological language. It is extended to the mereotopological language RCC8D through the addition of the topological notion of *connection* and operators derived thereof, as follows:

$$
\begin{aligned}
&\mathtt{C}(Y_1, Y_2) &&\equiv_{\text{def}} \exists y_1 y_2 (y_1 \in Y_1 \wedge y_2 \in Y_2 \wedge y_1 R y_2) &&[\text{CONNECTION}] \\
&\mathtt{DC}(Y_1, Y_2) &&\equiv_{\text{def}} \neg\mathtt{C}(Y_1, Y_2) &&[\text{DISCONNECTION}] \\
&\mathtt{EC}(Y_1, Y_2) &&\equiv_{\text{def}} \mathtt{C}(Y_1, Y_2) \wedge \neg\mathtt{O}(Y_1, Y_2) &&[\text{EXTERNAL} \\
& && && \quad\text{CONNECTION}] \\
&\mathtt{TPP}(Y_1, Y_2) &&\equiv_{\text{def}} \mathtt{PP}(Y_1, Y_2) \wedge \exists Z (\mathtt{EC}(Z, Y_1) \wedge \mathtt{EC}(Z, Y_2)) &&[\text{TANGENTIAL} \\
& && && \quad\text{PARTHOOD}] \\
&\mathtt{NTPP}(Y_1, Y_2) &&\equiv_{\text{def}} \mathtt{PP}(Y_1, Y_2) \wedge \neg\exists Z (\mathtt{EC}(Z, Y_1) \wedge \mathtt{EC}(Z, Y_2)) &&[\text{NON TANGENTIAL} \\
& && && \quad\text{PARTHOOD}] \\
&\mathtt{TPPi}(Y_1, Y_2) &&\equiv_{\text{def}} \mathtt{TPP}(Y_2, Y_1) &&[\text{INV. TANGENTIAL} \\
& && && \quad\text{PARTHOOD}] \\
&\mathtt{NTPPi}(Y_1, Y_2) &&\equiv_{\text{def}} \mathtt{NTPP}(Y_2, Y_1) &&[\text{INV. NON TANG.} \\
& && && \quad\text{PARTHOOD}]
\end{aligned}
$$

The relation set $\{\mathtt{DC}, \mathtt{EC}, \mathtt{PO}, \mathtt{TPP}, \mathtt{NTPP}, \mathtt{TPPi}, \mathtt{NTPPi}, \mathtt{EQ}\}$ forms what is known as RCC8D. In Fig. 6 we give an illustration of these relations using models based on a 2D space of 100 points arranged as a 10×10 grid, with reflexive, symmetric and orthodiagonal relation, as in [18], which we refer to for a more detailed description.

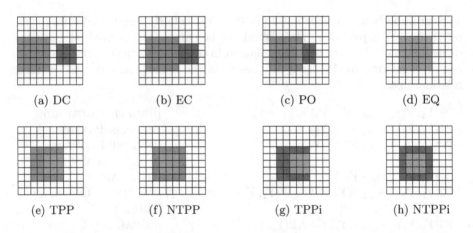

(a) DC   (b) EC   (c) PO   (d) EQ

(e) TPP   (f) NTPP   (g) TPPi   (h) NTPPi

Fig. 6. The eight RCC8D relations.

4   Encoding RCC8D into CSLCS

Let us now focus on the encoding of RCC8D in CSLCS. Let $(X, \mathcal{C})$ be a finite closure space. We associate the atomic predicate p_Y to each set $Y \subseteq X$, such that in all closure models $\mathcal{M} = ((X, \mathcal{C}), \mathcal{V})$ we have $\mathcal{V}(p_Y) = Y$. The encoding $[\![\cdot]\!]$ of RCC8D in CSLCS is defined in the sequel.

We first encode standard set theoretic and closure operations into CSLCS in the obvious way; in the sequel $\gamma, \gamma_1, \gamma_2$ range over expressions on sets built out of constants, complement, intersection and closure:

$$
\begin{aligned}
[\![Y]\!] &= p_Y, \text{for all } Y \subseteq X \ [\text{CONSTANT}] \\
[\![\overline{\gamma}]\!] &= \neg[\![\gamma]\!] & [\text{COMPLEMENT}] \\
[\![\gamma_1 \cap \gamma_2]\!] &= [\![\gamma_1]\!] \wedge [\![\gamma_2]\!] & [\text{INTERSECTION}] \\
[\![\mathcal{C}(\gamma)]\!] &= \mathcal{N}([\![\gamma]\!]) & [\text{CLOSURE}]
\end{aligned}
$$

Now we add the tests on the empty set, on set-inclusion and set-equality; note the use of the format $\varPhi \prec \mathcal{G}\bot$ to check for the empty set, discussed at the end of Sect. 2:

$$
\begin{aligned}
[\![\gamma = \emptyset]\!] &= [\![\gamma]\!] \prec \mathcal{G}\bot & [\text{EMPTY}] \\
[\![\gamma_1 \subseteq \gamma_2]\!] &= [\![(\gamma_1 \cap \overline{\gamma_2}) = \emptyset]\!] & [\text{INCLUSION}] \\
[\![\gamma_1 = \gamma_2]\!] &= [\![\gamma_1 \subseteq \gamma_2]\!] \wedge [\![\gamma_2 \subseteq \gamma_1]\!] & [\text{EQUALITY}]
\end{aligned}
$$

Finally, the actual encoding of (RCC5D and) RCC8D is given below and is self-explanatory; the right-hand side of the equation for the encoding of a relation is just the logical encoding of the set-theoretical expression used in the definition of the relation presented in [18] and recalled in Sect. 3 of the present paper:

$$
\begin{aligned}
[\![\text{P}(Y_1, Y_2)]\!] &= [\![Y_1 \subseteq Y_2]\!] \wedge \neg[\![Y_1 = \emptyset]\!] & [\text{PARTHOOD}] \\
[\![\text{PP}(Y_1, Y_2)]\!] &= [\![\text{P}(Y_1, Y_2)]\!] \wedge \neg[\![Y_1 = Y_2]\!] & [\text{PROPER PARTHOOD}] \\
[\![\text{Pi}(Y_1, Y_2)]\!] &= [\![\text{P}(Y_2, Y_1)]\!] & [\text{INVERSE PARTHOOD}] \\
[\![\text{PPi}(Y_1, Y_2)]\!] &= [\![\text{PP}(Y_2, Y_1)]\!] & [\text{INVERSE PROPER} \\
& & \text{PARTHOOD}] \\[4pt]
[\![\text{O}(Y_1, Y_2)]\!] &= \neg[\![Y_1 \cap Y_2 = \emptyset]\!] & [\text{OVERLAP}] \\
[\![\text{PO}(Y_1, Y_2)]\!] &= [\![\text{O}(Y_1, Y_2)]\!] \wedge \neg[\![\text{P}(Y_1, Y_2)]\!] \wedge \neg[\![\text{P}(Y_2, Y_1)]\!] & [\text{PARTIAL OVERLAP}] \\
[\![\text{DR}(Y_1, Y_2)]\!] &= \neg[\![\text{O}(Y_1, Y_2)]\!] & [\text{DISCRETE}] \\
[\![\text{EQ}(Y_1, Y_2)]\!] &= [\![\text{P}(Y_1, Y_2)]\!] \wedge [\![\text{P}(Y_2, Y_1)]\!] & [\text{EQUALITY ON} \\
& & \text{NON-NULL REGIONS}] \\[4pt]
[\![\text{C}(Y_1, Y_2)]\!] &= \neg([\![\mathcal{C}(Y_1) \cap Y_2 = \emptyset]\!] \vee [\![\mathcal{C}(Y_2) \cap Y_1 = \emptyset]\!]) & [\text{CONNECTION}] \\
[\![\text{DC}(Y_1, Y_2)]\!] &= \neg[\![\text{C}(Y_1, Y_2)]\!] & [\text{DISCONNECTION}] \\
[\![\text{EC}(Y_1, Y_2)]\!] &= [\![\text{C}(Y_1, Y_2)]\!] \wedge \neg[\![\text{O}(Y_1, Y_2)]\!] & [\text{EXTERNAL} \\
& & \text{connection}] \\[4pt]
[\![\text{TPP}(Y_1, Y_2)]\!] &= [\![\text{PP}(Y_1, Y_2)]\!] \wedge \neg[\![\mathcal{C}(Y_1) \cap \overline{Y_2} = \emptyset]\!] & [\text{TANGENTIAL PP}] \\
[\![\text{NTPP}(Y_1, Y_2)]\!] &= [\![\text{PP}(Y_1, Y_2)]\!] \wedge [\![\mathcal{C}(Y_1) \cap \overline{Y_2} = \emptyset]\!] & [\text{NONTANGENTIAL PP}] \\
[\![\text{TPPi}(Y_1, Y_2)]\!] &= [\![\text{TPP}(Y_2, Y_1)]\!] & [\text{INVERSE} \\
& & \text{TANGENTIAL PP}] \\[4pt]
[\![\text{NTPPi}(Y_1, Y_2)]\!] &= [\![\text{NTPP}(Y_2, Y_1)]\!] & [\text{INVERSE} \\
& & \text{NONTANGENTIAL PP}]
\end{aligned}
$$

Correctness of the above encoding is stated below:

Proposition 2. *For all RCC8D formulas F the following holds: F holds in an adjacency model $\mathcal{M}$ if and only if $\mathcal{M}, \emptyset \models_C [\![F]\!]$.*

Proof. Note that if $\mathcal{M}, Y \models_C [\![F]\!]$ holds for a set Y, then it holds for any other set Y', thence we conventionally take $Y = \emptyset$. The proposition is straightforward to prove. The only case which requires a bit of explanation concerns the TPP predicate (and NTPP). The definition of TPP given in [18] is the following:

$$\text{TPP}(Y_1, Y_2) = \text{PP}(Y_1, Y_2) \wedge \exists Z. (\text{EC}(Z, Y_1) \wedge \text{EC}(Z, Y_2)).$$

We show that the two definitions characterise the same property. Note that, according to our embedding, $\text{TPP}(Y_1, Y_2)$ implies that $\mathcal{C}(Y_1) \cap \overline{Y_2} \neq \emptyset$ and $Y_1 \subseteq Y_2$; the latter also implies, by monotonicity of closure, $\mathcal{C}(Y_1) \subseteq \mathcal{C}(Y_2)$. Take $Z = \mathcal{C}(Y_1) \cap \overline{Y_2}$. We show that $\text{EC}(Z, Y_1)$ holds, i.e. $\text{C}(Z, Y_1)$ and $\neg \text{O}(Z, Y_1)$: $Z \subseteq \mathcal{C}(Y_1)$ implies[3] $\mathcal{C}(Z) \cap Y_1 \neq \emptyset$; moreover $\mathcal{C}(Y_1) \cap Z = Z$ and $Z \neq \emptyset$ by hypothesis; so $\text{C}(Z, Y_1)$ holds. $Y_1 \subseteq Y_2$ implies $Y_1 \cap \overline{Y_2} = \emptyset$, which in turn implies $Z \cap Y_1 = \emptyset$, i.e. $\neg \text{O}(Z, Y_1)$.

Now we show that $\text{EC}(Z, Y_2)$ holds, i.e. $\text{C}(Z, Y_2)$ and $\neg \text{O}(Z, Y_2)$: We have already proved $\mathcal{C}(Z) \cap Y_1 \neq \emptyset$; so we get $\emptyset \neq \mathcal{C}(Z) \cap Y_1 \subseteq \mathcal{C}(Z) \cap Y_2$ because $Y_1 \subseteq Y_2$, i.e. $\mathcal{C}(Z) \cap Y_2 \neq \emptyset$; moreover $\emptyset \neq \mathcal{C}(Y_1) \cap \overline{Y_2} = \mathcal{C}(Y_1) \cap (\mathcal{C}(Y_1) \cap \overline{Y_2}) \subseteq \mathcal{C}(Y_2) \cap (\mathcal{C}(Y_1) \cap \overline{Y_2})$ because $\mathcal{C}(Y_1) \subseteq \mathcal{C}(Y_2)$ and $\mathcal{C}(Y_2) \cap (\mathcal{C}(Y_1) \cap \overline{Y_2}) = \mathcal{C}(Y_2) \cap Z$; so $\text{C}(Z, Y_2)$ holds. $Z \subseteq \overline{Y_2}$ implies $Z \cap Y_2 = \emptyset$, i.e. $\neg \text{O}(Z, Y_2)$. In conclusion, we proved that there exists Z such that $\text{EC}(Z, Y_1)$ and $\text{EC}(Z, Y_2)$ which, together with $P(Y_1, Y_2)$, completes the first half of the proof.

Now, suppose that $\text{PP}(Y_1, Y_2)$ and there exists Z such that $\text{EC}(Z, Y_1)$ and $\text{EC}(Z, Y_2)$; then $Z \subseteq \overline{Y_2}$, because $\text{EC}(Z, Y_2)$ implies $\neg \text{O}(Z, Y_2)$; moreover, EC is commutative, so we have also $\text{EC}(Y_1, Z)$, which implies $\mathcal{C}(Y_1) \cap Z \neq \emptyset$, and then $\mathcal{C}(Y_1) \cap \overline{Y_2} \neq \emptyset$, since $Z \subseteq \overline{Y_2}$. The above, together with $P(Y_1, Y_2)$, completes the proof.

Correctness of our definition of NTPP can be proved in a similar way and is left to the reader.

Note that our definition of $[\![\text{C}(Y_1, Y_2)]\!]$ could be simplified to $\neg [\![\mathcal{C}(Y_1) \cap Y_2 = \emptyset]\!]$ due to symmetry of the adjacency relation. We prefer the more general definition covering also the case in which the underlying relation is not symmetric. Finally, our definition of $[\![\text{TPP}(Y_1, Y_2)]\!]$ resembles the alternative definition by equation (32) in [18].

5   Model Checking RCC8D Using topochecker

The tool **topochecker** is a global spatio-temporal model checker, capable of analysing either directed graphs, or digital images. The tool is implemented in the functional programming language OCaml[4], catering for a good balance between declarative features and computational efficiency. The algorithms implemented by **topochecker** are linear in the size of the input space. The spatial model checking algorithm is run in central memory, and it uses memoization and on-disk caching to store intermediate results, achieving high efficiency.

---

[3] It is trivial to prove that, for quasi-discrete closure space $(X, \mathcal{C}_R)$, whenever R is symmetric, if $B \subseteq \mathcal{C}_R(A)$ then $\mathcal{C}_R(B) \cap A \neq \emptyset$, for all non-empty $A, B \subseteq X$.

[4] See http://www.ocaml.org.

For SLCS formulas, the output of the tool consists of a copy of its input, where the points on which each user-defined formula holds are indicated, e.g. by colouring pixels (for images), or labelling nodes (for graphs). Although such mechanism is quite useful (for instance, because it permits one to colour so called "regions of interest" in medical images), it is not apt to report the result of checking CSLCS formulas of the form $\mathcal{M}, \emptyset \models_C \phi$. This is so because the application of Proposition 2 results in a truth value, not a set of points that satisfy the property. In order not to change the way topochecker produces its results, and to permit the use of both "truth-valued" CSLCS formulas and "point-valued" SLCS formulas at the same time, the tool has been augmented with a *conditional* formula constructor. Using this constructor, one can define a new point-valued formula Φ by

$$\text{Let } \Phi = \text{IF } \Psi \text{ THEN } \Phi_1 \text{ ELSE } \Phi_2 \text{ FI}$$

where Ψ is a CSLCS truth-valued formula, whereas Φ_1 and Φ_2 are SLCS point-valued formulas. The result of such a definition is that Φ is true on the points where Φ_1 holds, if $\mathcal{M}, \emptyset \models_C \Psi$, and on the points where Φ_2 holds, otherwise. Formulas Φ_1 and Φ_2 can for instance be atomic propositions that denote "indicator" areas that make truth of the CSLCS formula Ψ observable as graphical output. Application of the conditional constructor is not limited to image models; for instance, given a quasi-discrete closure-space $(X, \mathcal{C}_R)$, one can augment the space with new *isolated* points (these are by definition not connected to X via R), and new special *indicator* atomic propositions, which characterize each new point. These indicator atomic propositions can then be used to produce output in topochecker via the conditional constructor. The formal details are left as an exercise.

We use this conditional constructor in the example in Fig. 7 to illustrate the TPP operator using topochecker. On the left, an RGB image is displayed, where each pixel has three colour components, red, green and blue, respectively, each ranging over 8 bits (i.e. taking values from 0 to 255). This is the input of the model checking session. Such input image consists of six rows, each one containing a green-ish rectangle g_i on the left, a red-ish rectangle r_i on the right of it (for i in $\{1, \ldots, 6\}$) and two more squares further to the right yes_i (the leftmost square) and no_i (the rightmost square).

All the information is encoded in the red, green and blue components of each pixel. Each of the six rows is identified by a different shade of the blue component of the pixels in that row (for example, in the topmost row the value of the blue component of each pixel is equal to 0, whereas in row 3 the blue component of each pixel is equal to 80); the pixels in each green-ish rectangle have their green component equal to 255, whereas the pixels in each red-ish rectangle have their red component equal to 255 (therefore, when g_i and r_i overlap, the overlapping area has both red and green components equal to 255, that is, it shows up as a yellow-ish area in Fig. 7). Each pixel in a yes_i square has both red and green components that are equal to 100, whereas each pixel in a no_i square has both red and green components that are equal to 200.

Atomic properties for RGB images in `topochecker` are equalities and comparisons on colour components. For instance one can define the points of $g_3 \cup r_3 \cup yes_3 \cup no_3$ by[5]

```
Let row3 = [blue == 80]
```

because all pixels in the third row have their blue component set to 80. The points of $\bigcup_i r_i$, i.e. all red pixels in all rows, can be identified by

```
Let right = [red == 255]
```

therefore, the red rectangle in row 3, namely r_3, is characterised by the formula `row3 & right`.

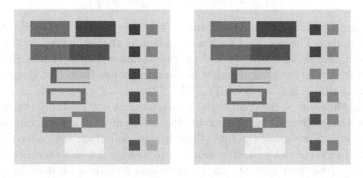

Fig. 7. Checking the `TPP` operator using `topochecker`. (Color figure online)

On the right of Fig. 7, the image produced by `topochecker` as a result of spatial model checking is shown. For each row i, one of the two (right-most) squares has been coloured in orange. More precisely, yes_i is coloured if $\text{TPP}(g_i, r_i)$ holds, and no_i is coloured otherwise (indeed, only $\text{TPP}(g_3, r_3)$ actually holds). Such image is produced by the following statement:

```
Check "orange" checktpp(row1) | checktpp(row2) | checktpp(row3)

     | checktpp(row4) | checktpp(row5) | checktpp(row6)
```

where `checktpp` is a conditional definition that, for each row i, identifies either yes_i or no_i according to the satisfaction value of $\text{TPP}(g_i, r_i)$. Since the current version[6] of `topochecker` permits only the definition of point-valued macros (not of truth-valued ones), the encoding of RCC8D in the definition of `checktpp` has been expanded manually, as follows:

---

[5] In the remainder of this section, we employ the syntax of `topochecker`, using & for conjunction, | for disjunction, ! for negation, -< for the "share" connective, and `Gr` for the "group" connective.

[6] This may change in a future release of the model checker.

```
Let green(row) = row & left;

Let red(row) = row & right;

Let checktpp(row) =
    IF  ((green(row) & (!red(row))) -< Gr FF) &
        (!((red(row) & (!green(row))) -< Gr FF)) &
        (!(((N green(row)) & (!red(row))) -< Gr FF))
    THEN yes & row
    ELSE no & row
    FI;
```

The condition of the IF-statement is a direct encoding of the TPP operator into basic CSLCS operators following the encoding defined in Sect. 4. If the condition holds then $TPP(g_i, r_i)$ holds in the given row, i.e. the green area is indeed a tangential proper part of the red area, and therefore the small square in the third column is coloured orange, otherwise the square in the fourth, rightmost column is coloured orange. This produces the results in Fig. 7 (right). Of course, this is only one way to visualise the model checking results that exploits the current features of topochecker and used here for the purpose of illustration. Other ways can be defined or added as preferred or required by the application at hand.

6   Conclusions

We defined an encoding of the mereotopological theory RCC8D as a fragment of the *Collective Spatial Logic of Closure Spaces* (CSLCS). CSLCS comes equipped with a model checking algorithm and tool, which also contains an experimental spatio-temporal extension of the logic. The newly defined encoding adds a region-based point of view to the point-based methodology of the existing framework. Such developments can be used right away in current applications of spatial and spatio-temporal model checking, including spatio-temporal properties of smart transportation systems [11,14], and medical imaging case studies [2]. Especially for the latter, it is worth mentioning that a new tool is being developed, which is specialised for digital images (including 3D—e.g., magneto-resonance—scans for medical purposes). The tool, called VoxLogicA and described in [4], achieves a two-orders-of-magnitude speedup in the specialised setting. VoxLogicA does not yet implement the collective operators of CSLCS, but this is a planned development, enabling, by the encoding of RCC8D we propose, efficient image analysis with both the point of views of points and regions. Another interesting domain of application could be that of the characterisation of spatial properties and relations in the context of simulation of biological systems [6–8].

One open question regards RCC8D interpreted in arbitrary closure spaces, not just the symmetric ones. We consider worth investigating in future work what operators may be obtained when the underlying relation is directed. Indeed, many relations can be defined (for instance, region A may be "half-connected" to region B when there is an edge from A to B even if there is no edge from B to A). Application domains and case studies will help to clarify which ones make more sense in practice.

Acknowledgements. This paper was written for the Festschrift in honour of Prof. Rocco De Nicola. We would like to thank Rocco for the many years of fruitful collaboration in the context of numerous European and Italian research projects and we are looking forward to future collaboration in the context of the new Italian MIUR PRIN project "IT MATTERS". But most of all, we are grateful for his great sense of humanity with which he dedicated part of his professional live to keep computer science research alive in areas struck by devastating earthquakes and to give a second professional chance to people from conflict areas.

A   Proof of Proposition 1

Proof. We prove that, for all models $\mathcal{M} = ((X, \mathcal{C}), \mathcal{V})$ and points $x \in X$, the following holds:

$$\mathcal{M}, x \not\models \Phi_2 \vee (\Phi_1 \, \mathcal{S} \, \Phi_2) \text{ iff } \mathcal{M}, x \not\models A(\Phi_1 \, \mathcal{W} \, \Phi_2).$$

For the direct implication, we proceed as follows:

$\mathcal{M}, x \not\models \Phi_2 \vee (\Phi_1 \, \mathcal{S} \, \Phi_2)$

$\Rightarrow$ {Logic}

$\mathcal{M}, x \not\models \Phi_2$ and $\mathcal{M}, x \not\models \Phi_1 \, \mathcal{S} \, \Phi_2$

$\Rightarrow$ {def. of $\mathcal{S}$}

$\mathcal{M}, x \not\models \Phi_2$ and

there exists π, ℓ s.t.

$\pi(0) = x, \mathcal{M}, \pi(\ell) \not\models \Phi_1$, and $\mathcal{M}, \pi(j) \not\models \Phi_2$, for all j s.t. $0 < j \leq \ell$

$\Rightarrow$ {Logic}

there exists π, ℓ s.t.

$\pi(0) = x, \mathcal{M}, \pi(\ell) \not\models \Phi_1$, and $\mathcal{M}, \pi(j) \not\models \Phi_2$, for all j s.t. $0 \leq j \leq \ell$

$\Rightarrow$ {def. of $\mathcal{W}$}

$\mathcal{M}, \pi \not\models \Phi_1 \, \mathcal{W} \, \Phi_2$

$\Rightarrow$ {def. of A}

$\mathcal{M}, x \not\models A(\Phi_1 \, \mathcal{W} \, \Phi_2)$

For the one but last step of the above derivation, note that: (i) $\mathcal{M}, \pi(\ell) \not\models \Phi_1$ implies that $\mathcal{M}, \pi(i) \models \Phi_1$ for all i does *not* hold; and (ii) $\mathcal{M}, \pi(j) \not\models$

Φ_2, for all j s.t. $0 \le j \le \ell$ implies that, if there exists k s.t. $\mathcal{M}, \pi(k) \models \Phi_2$, then, it necessarily must be $k > \ell$; but then $\mathcal{M}, \pi \models \Phi_1 \mathcal{U} \Phi_2$ cannot hold because this would *not* allow $\mathcal{M}, \pi(\ell) \not\models \Phi_1$, with $\ell < k$.

The derivation for the reverse implication is given below:

$\mathcal{M}, x \not\models A(\Phi_1 \mathcal{W} \Phi_2)$

$\Rightarrow$ {def. of A}

there exists π s.t.

$\pi(0) = x$ and $\mathcal{M}, \pi \not\models \Phi_1 \mathcal{W} \Phi_2$

$\Rightarrow$ {def. of $\mathcal{W}$}

there exist π, ℓ s.t.

$\pi(0) = x$ and $\mathcal{M}, \pi(\ell) \not\models \Phi_1$ and $\mathcal{M}, \pi \not\models \Phi_1 \mathcal{U} \Phi_2$

$\Rightarrow$ {$\mathcal{M}, \pi \not\models \Phi_1 \mathcal{U} \Phi_2$ implies $\mathcal{M}, \pi(0) \not\models \Phi_2$}

there exists π, ℓ s.t.

$\pi(0) = x$ and $\mathcal{M}, \pi(\ell) \not\models \Phi_1$ and $\mathcal{M}, \pi(0) \not\models \Phi_2$ and $\mathcal{M}, \pi \not\models \Phi_1 \mathcal{U} \Phi_2$

Take the minimal ℓ as above. If $\ell = 0$, then clearly $\mathcal{M}, x \not\models \Phi_1 \mathcal{S} \Phi_2$, by definition of $\mathcal{S}$, and since we also have $\mathcal{M}, x \not\models \Phi_2$, we get $\mathcal{M}, x \not\models \Phi_2 \vee (\Phi_1 \mathcal{S} \Phi_2)$, i.e. the assert. If instead $\ell > 0$, then clearly $\mathcal{M}, \pi(j) \models \Phi_1$ for $0 \le j < \ell$, by minimality of ℓ, and since we also have $\mathcal{M}, \pi \not\models \Phi_1 \mathcal{U} \Phi_2$, we get $\mathcal{M}, \pi(j) \not\models \Phi_2$ for $0 \le j \le \ell$. So, there exist π, ℓ s.t. $\pi(0) = x$, $\mathcal{M}, \pi(\ell) \models \neg\Phi_1$ and for all j, $0 < j \le \ell$, $\mathcal{M}, \pi(j) \not\models \Phi_2$, which, by definition of $\mathcal{S}$, is equivalent to $\mathcal{M}, x \not\models \Phi_1 \mathcal{S} \Phi_2$. Moreover, since we also know that $\mathcal{M}, \pi(0) \not\models \Phi_2$, we get $\mathcal{M}, x \not\models \Phi_2 \vee (\Phi_1 \mathcal{S} \Phi_2)$, i.e. the assert.

References

1. Aiello, M., Pratt-Hartmann, I., van Benthem, J. (eds.): Handbook of Spatial Logics. Springer, Dordrecht (2007). https://doi.org/10.1007/978-1-4020-5587-4
2. Banci Buonamici, F., Belmonte, G., Ciancia, V., Latella, D., Massink, M.: Spatial logics and model checking for medical imaging. Int. J. Softw. Tools Technol. Transf. (2019). https://doi.org/10.1007/s10009-019-00511-9
3. Belmonte, G., Ciancia, V., Latella, D., Massink, M.: From collective adaptive systems to human centric computation and back: spatial model checking for medical imaging. In: ter Beek, M.H., Loreti, M. (eds.) Proceedings of the Workshop on FORmal Methods for the Quantitative Evaluation of Collective Adaptive Systems, FORECAST@STAF 2016, Vienna, Austria, 8 July 2016. EPTCS, vol. 217, pp. 81–92 (2016). https://doi.org/10.4204/EPTCS.217.10
4. Belmonte, G., Ciancia, V., Latella, D., Massink, M.: VoxLogicA: A Spatial Model Checker for Declarative Image Analysis. In: Vojnar, T., Zhang, L. (eds.) TACAS 2019. LNCS, vol. 11427, pp. 281–298. Springer, Cham (2019). https://doi.org/10.1007/978-3-030-17462-0_16. http://arxiv.org/abs/1811.05677

5. Bennett, B., Düntsch, I.: Axioms, algebras and topology. In: Springer [1], pp. 99–159

6. Binchi, J., Merelli, E., Rucco, M., Petri, G., Vaccarino, F.: jHoles: a tool for understanding biological complex networks via clique weight rank persistent homology. Electr. Notes Theor. Comput. Sci. **306**, 5–18 (2014). https://doi.org/10.1016/j.entcs.2014.06.011

7. Buti, F., Cacciagrano, D., Corradini, F., Merelli, E., Tesei, L., Pani, M.: Bone remodelling in BioShape. Electr. Notes Theor. Comput. Sci. **268**, 17–29 (2010). https://doi.org/10.1016/j.entcs.2010.12.003

8. Buti, F., Cacciagrano, D., Callisto De Donato, M., Corradini, F., Merelli, E., Tesei, L.: *BioShape*: end-user development for simulating biological systems. In: Costabile, M.F., Dittrich, Y., Fischer, G., Piccinno, A. (eds.) IS-EUD 2011. LNCS, vol. 6654, pp. 379–382. Springer, Heidelberg (2011). https://doi.org/10.1007/978-3-642-21530-8_45

9. Ciancia, V., Latella, D., Loreti, M., Massink, M.: Specifying and verifying properties of space. In: Diaz, J., Lanese, I., Sangiorgi, D. (eds.) TCS 2014. LNCS, vol. 8705, pp. 222–235. Springer, Heidelberg (2014). https://doi.org/10.1007/978-3-662-44602-7_18

10. Ciancia, V., Latella, D., Loreti, M., Massink, M.: Model checking spatial logics for closure spaces. Logical Methods Comput. Sci. **12**(4) (2016). http://lmcs.episciences.org/2067

11. Ciancia, V., Gilmore, S., Grilletti, G., Latella, D., Loreti, M., Massink, M.: Spatio-temporal model checking of vehicular movement in public transport systems. STTT **20**(3), 289–311 (2018). https://doi.org/10.1007/s10009-018-0483-8

12. Ciancia, V., Latella, D., Loreti, M., Massink, M.: Spatial logic and spatial model checking for closure spaces. In: Bernardo, M., De Nicola, R., Hillston, J. (eds.) SFM 2016. LNCS, vol. 9700, pp. 156–201. Springer, Cham (2016). https://doi.org/10.1007/978-3-319-34096-8_6

13. Ciancia, V., Latella, D., Massink, M., Paskauskas, R.: Exploring spatio-temporal properties of bike-sharing systems. In: 2015 IEEE International Conference on Self-Adaptive and Self-Organizing Systems Workshops, SASO Workshops 2015, Cambridge, MA, USA, 21–25 September 2015, pp. 74–79. IEEE Computer Society (2015). https://doi.org/10.1109/SASOW.2015.17

14. Ciancia, V., Latella, D., Massink, M., Paškauskas, R., Vandin, A.: A tool-chain for statistical spatio-temporal model checking of bike sharing systems. In: Margaria, T., Steffen, B. (eds.) ISoLA 2016. LNCS, vol. 9952, pp. 657–673. Springer, Cham (2016). https://doi.org/10.1007/978-3-319-47166-2_46

15. Galton, A.: The mereotopology of discrete space. In: Freksa, C., Mark, D.M. (eds.) COSIT 1999. LNCS, vol. 1661, pp. 251–266. Springer, Heidelberg (1999). https://doi.org/10.1007/3-540-48384-5_17

16. Galton, A.: A generalized topological view of motion in discrete space. Theor. Comput. Sci. **305**(1–3), 111–134 (2003). https://doi.org/10.1016/S0304-3975(02)00701-6

17. Randell, D.A., Cui, Z., Cohn, A.G.: A spatial logic based on regions and connection. In: Nebel, B., Rich, C., Swartout, W.R. (eds.) Proceedings of the 3rd International Conference on Principles of Knowledge Representation and Reasoning (KR 1992), Cambridge, MA, USA, 25–29 October 1992, pp. 165–176. Morgan Kaufmann (1992)

18. Randell, D.A., Landini, G., Galton, A.: Discrete mereotopology for spatial reasoning in automated histological image analysis. IEEE Trans. Pattern Anal. Mach. Intell. **35**(3), 568–581 (2013). https://doi.org/10.1109/TPAMI.2012.128

19. Smyth, M.B., Webster, J.: Discrete spatial models. In: Springer [1], pp. 713–798
20. van Benthem, J., Bezhanishvili, G.: Modal logics of space. In: Springer [1], pp. 217–298

From Behavioural Contracts
to Session Types

Alessandro Fantechi[1], Elie Najm[2(✉)], and Jean-Bernard Stefani[3]

[1] Università di Firenze, Florence, Italy
`alessandro.fantechi@unifi.it`
[2] Institut Polytechnique de Paris, Telecom Paris, LTCI, Paris, France
`elie.najm@telecom-paristech.fr`
[3] INRIA, Rocquencourt, France
`Jean-Bernard.Stefani@inria.fr`

Abstract. We present a research trajectory of the authors and colleagues dealing with the correctness and meaningful composition of software components, trajectory that incrementally traverses successive paradigms and approaches: open distributed processing, contract based reasoning, behavioural typing and session types. This research is grounded on the foundational work of Robin Milner on processes and observation equivalence, and the followup work by De Nicola and Hennessy on testing relations. Indeed, these initial works have set benchmarks that define the meaning of behaviour, which has fostered a full body of research in concurrency and verification. Behavioural typing is one of the avenues opened by these early contributions. This paper is a brief and staged report of the research accomplished by the authors and colleagues, presented in chronological order, starting with their work on the computational model of open distributed processing and ending at their latest work on sessions for web services.

Keywords: Distributed software components · Services ·
Coordination · Composition · Behavioural contracts · Session types ·
Verification

1 Introduction

In this paper, we present a trajectory of research undertaken by a group of co-authors over the last two decades, which is directly or indirectly connected to Rocco De Nicola's seminal work. Numerous are the domains touched by Rocco De Nicola in his long research career: process algebras, testing equivalence [19], Linda [20], Klaim [21] and coordination languages, attribute-based communication [3], cloud computing [55], autonomic computing [18], service orientation [7,34], sessions and session-types [9], to name a few. The early 1980s witnessed a significant debate related to the meaning and representation of processes. Robin Milner's answer constituted a first major landmark, which comprises of a calculus of Communication Systems for encoding processes, and an Observation

© Springer Nature Switzerland AG 2019
M. Boreale et al. (Eds.): De Nicola-Festschrift, LNCS 11665, pp. 278–297, 2019.
https://doi.org/10.1007/978-3-030-21485-2_16

equivalence to abstract their behaviour [43]. By proposing the testing equivalence [19], a coarser but still meaningful relation that refines the overly strong observation equivalence, De Nicola, together with Hennessy, achieved a second major landmark. Both, observational and testing relations influenced a full body of research, and, most notably, fostered the emergence of a new approach for the static verification of concurrent software, which is based on integrating types and behaviour. The trajectory accounted for in this paper is grounded on this basis.

This paper is a commented history of the contributions by the co-authors, focused on behavioural typing. Its starting point is their contribution to the formal semantics of the computational model of the Open Distributed Processing, presented in Sect. 2. Then comes their work on behavioural typing and contracts, which is given in Sect. 3. Section 4 then presents their results in service oriented computing, session types and web services. This paper does not provide an up-to-date account on the subject matter; connections to related work are deliberately minimal. We think that the exposure of how research have been progressed by the authors as a coherent research agenda carried out over two decades is interesting in itself. In the conclusion, however, we touch upon the latest developments in this field and refer the interested reader to the latest survey [29].

2   Open Distributed Processing

The 1980s witnessed the development of the early foundations of networking: protocols versus services, layered architectures, naming and addressing, packet forwarding, end to end communication, etc. This first development and the advent of the object paradigm, paved the way for a new approach which addresses both software engineering and distributed computing in an integrated vision. This endeavor was conducted by many researchers from academia and industry and was capitalized in the Open Distributed Processing (ODP) international standard published in 1998 [30]. The ODP reference model prescribes that a distributed system needs to be considered and described under five complementary viewpoints, each endowed with its abstract modeling language:

- Enterprise is the requirements viewpoint. The Enterprise model, among others, decomposes a system into its stakeholders, delimits boundaries between them, and establishes assume/guarantee relationships among them.
- Information is a viewpoint that describes the structure of the information defining the system and how this information may change over time.
- Computation is the viewpoint that defines the units of distribution and separation and also the requirements on how these units interact.
- The Engineering viewpoint defines generic solutions of the infrastructure that support the system and which satisfies the requirements defined in the Computation viewpoint.
- Technology is the viewpoint that provides market or developed solutions that conform to the generic solutions of the Engineering viewpoint.

This novel approach to system development comes in contrast with the OSI layered architecture where each layer is a proper part of the system. In ODP, each viewpoint considers the system as a whole, and different models of the system, conforming to different viewpoints, need to be consistent [5,22]. The authors focused their research on the ODP Computational Model (ODP-CM). Informally, the ODP-CM constitutes a language independent distributed programming model turned towards system designers and developers. It exhibits a number of distinctive features: (i) the ODP-CM is populated with objects, (ii) objects encapsulate state and behaviour, (iii) objects come with dynamic creation of multiple, strongly typed interfaces; (iv) objects are the unit of structure, and interfaces the unit of reference, (v) interfaces are either operational or stream based, (vi) operational interfaces are for one way signals or request-response operations; (vii) stream interfaces are for continuous (media) flows; (viii) objects are bound implicitly or explicitly, allowing for the dynamic configuration of communicating objects; (ix) quality of service declarations can be associated with both the operational and stream interfaces.

In [49], the authors provided a formal semantics of a subset of the features of the ODP-CM. It encompasses an interface type language with its type system and algorithm, inspired by [4], and a rewriting logic semantics [38] which captures the behaviour of the dynamically evolving configurations of interacting objects and with changing communication patterns. Features (ii), (iii) and (viii) above suggest a strong connection with the pi-calculus. Indeed, another formalization [46] was given to DPL, a language compliant to the ODP computational model, using a translation into the pi-calculus [24].

The advent of the ODP reference model opened an avenue of contributions from industry and academia. Many dimensions were tackled that refine and develop the abstract concepts provided in the reference model. In the sequel, we present contributions that deal with some of these dimensions. In particular, the following dimensions were addressed: (i) providing a framework for defining and verifying quality of service contracts; (ii) adjoining behaviour dependent types and contracts to interface types; (iii) experimenting with language bindings that conform to the ODP computational model and its interface types.

3   Behavioural Contracts and Behavioural Types

3.1   Contracts for ODP

The quality of service dimension was approached in [24]. An extension to the ODP-CM was first provided that views the behaviour of the computational model as a collection of timed and observable interactions. In this setting, an interaction takes place between two interfaces of two objects and has one of two possible observable results: success or failure. A calculus of object contracts (COC) is introduced. COC is a process algebra over a special set of *Actions*. An action is either an observed interaction or an error notification. A typical observed interaction is !?g.m(x:T) which represents the observation of the sending by an object of a message m from its reference g and its successful reception by the target object. Another typical observed interaction is the dual interaction, $!\overline{?}g.m(x:T)$, which represents a sending of message m which has not been received by the target object. An error notification is of the form: $!w.m(F)$ where w is the error notification interface, m the missed message, and where F designates the incriminated object, which can be either the sender, noted $!g$, or the target object, noted $?g$. A contract is a COC process which is added as an observer (à la *aspect*) to a configuration of objects, thus it observes and monitors the interactions occurring between the objects of the configuration. In case of interaction failure, it identifies and incriminates the faulty object. Thus the elegant formal definition of contract fulfillment inspired by [1]: a configuration S, which is put to run in an environment E, fulfills contract C if and only if, in any trace of $(C||S||E)$, any occurrence of an error notification incriminating S is preceded by an occurrence of an error notification incriminating E. Contracts as processes gave rise to an interesting theory, rich with modeling concepts, which are built using the process algebraic counterparts : contracts can be compared, composed, strengthened, weakened, split into assumptions and obligations. Another interesting link can be made with run-time verification as COC processes can be viewed as an early manifestation of run-time monitors.

3.2 Behavioural Types with Modalities

The influence of state and behaviour on the types of interfaces was not dealt with in the work on formal semantics of the computational model presented in the previous section. In the quest for the most expressive way to define behavioural types acting as contracts between distributed interacting objects, we choose to move the focus from objects to components, as the latter emphasizes both the sending and receiving capacities of objects, and is more suitable for contract based analysis.

In [13,14] we defined a framework in which a component can exhibit several *ports* through which it communicates with other components. To each port is associated a type, which is a localized abstraction of the behaviour of the component. The interface type language introduces modalities on the sequences of actions to be performed by ports using **must** and **may** prefixes and allows the distinction between *required* messages and *possible* ones. The complexity of the interface typing language is kept deliberately low, in order to facilitate compatibility verification among ports. We were not interested to define a specific language for components, but we chose an abstract definition which is general enough to accommodate different languages: components are abstracted as a set of ports, by which they communicate, and whose behaviour is provided by a set of internal threads of execution of which only the effects on ports can be observed.

The approach was in part inspired by the work of De Alfaro and Henzinger [2], who associate interface automata to components and define compatibility rules between interfaces. Our approach, which belongs instead to the streamline of process algebraic type systems, also brings in the picture the compliance between components and interfaces: the interface of a port is thought as a *contract* with the external environment that the component should honor. The work on Modal Transition Systems by Larsen, Steffen and Weise [36] has inspired our definition of modalities and the way interface compatibility is checked.

Ports of components exhibit multiple features and capacities, thus ports:

- are the sources and targets of messages exchanged between components;
- can be in sending or in receiving states;
- can be dynamically created and deleted;
- can be bound to other ports located in other components;
- can send messages to, and receive messages from, only these other bound ports;
- can be moved and become relocated at other components;
- are of two kinds, server and client, where client ports can be bound to server ports but server ports cannot be bound.

A client port bound to a server port allows for a request to be sent to the server, and this has the effect to create a new port that is collocated with this server and where the newly created port and the requesting client port become bound in a peer-to-peer manner.

The dynamic semantics of a single component is defined through labeled transition systems. The state of a component depends on the current state of its behaviour, the set of known ports, and the set of bindings established between the local ports and the known ports. No syntax is defined for the behaviours of components. The state of an assembly of components is the parallel composition of the components and of the communication medium (expressed in a typical process-algebraic style as $C_1||\cdots||C_n||Com$). The labeled transition system defining the behaviour of a component dictates the possible transitions depending on the states of the components and the state of the communication channels.

Fulfillment of a contract by a component, and hence the enforcement of the correct usage of ports and their capacities as listed before, is operationally defined by a set of rules that check the match between the transitions of the component and the transitions allowed or enforced by its declared types. A configuration made up of communicating components satisfies well-typedness if each of its components abides by the contracts exposed by its ports, and if the interface types of any couple of bounded ports are pairwise compatible. Provable properties include *subject reduction* (no error state is ever reached), *message consumption* (every message will be consumed eventually, under proper fairness assumptions), inter-component *deadlock freedom*, *livelock freedom* under specific assumptions on the computations.

In short, [13,14] brought about the following accomplishments: an abstract component model is introduced, its operational semantics is given in terms of labeled transition systems, an interface type language featuring modalities is defined; each port can be explicitly associated with an interface type, a formal definition of well-typedness of components is provided, a notion of sound assembly of components is defined based on compatibility between bounded ports (using subtyping), properties are proven on well typed configurations that guarantee: subject reduction, all messages sent are consumed, and absence of external deadlock.

The work covered by this contribution is incomplete however, in the sense that it misses an instantiation on a language for encoding the behaviour of components. This is the topic handled in the next section.

3.3   Behavioural Types for Object Calculi

In this section, we account for work done on the definition and properties of object calculi with explicit behavioural typing of their interfaces. As presented in the previous sections, the ODP computational model is a language independent reference model for distributed computing. What remains is the work of finding languages (or adapting existing ones) that comply with the reference model. To that end, although we were inspired by the π-calculus, we have set our work rather on object calculi, where interfaces, methods and invocations are primitive concepts. Indeed, many approaches existed that considered behavioural typing and its application. Most of the work was directly conducted on variants of the π-calculus, or else on actors. The survey [29] provides a good discussion comparing these approaches. However, we continued our efforts in substantiating the ODP-CM and hence we proposed three embodiments of object calculi each with its expressive power, its interface behavioural type language, its typing rules and algorithms, and the properties guaranteed by the well-typedness verdict.

The first calculus introduced is COB [45] (Calculus of Object Bindings) which features objects with multiple interfaces that can be dynamically created and that can be migrated between objects. The interface type language is defined in the format of a finite transition systems labeled with message types. The novelty of COB is in the distinction that is made between the private and public interfaces and between the client and server roles of interfaces. Hence, the type discipline dictates that when an object sends the sending role of a private interface, it looses that role and therefore can no longer send messages over that interface. Configurations are made of COB objects that communicate in rendez-vous. The messages they can exchange are tuples made of a message name and an ordered list of arguments. Arguments are just interface roles. When an object creates an interface, it possesses both the sending and receiving roles. Then it can choose to migrate one or both of these roles by sending them over another interface. A configuration is well typed if each object abides with the typing rules and if any pair of dual roles present in any pair of objects of the configuration have compatible interface types. Beyond the *subject reduction* property, any well typed configuration also ensures the safety property at run time: when an object is ready to send a message on an interface, and another object is ready to receive a message on the receiving role of that interface, then there is a match between the message to be sent and the receiving action.

The second calculus introduced is OL1 [48]. In COB, one could not define interfaces having possibly infinite states, i.e., the labeled transition system defining the interface is finite. For instance, the type of a buffer in COB can be given by the equation:

$$\texttt{Buffer} = \texttt{put}(\ldots); \ \texttt{Buffer} + \texttt{get}(\ldots); \ \texttt{Buffer}$$

and thus, the type system cannot discard the case of a get access to an empty buffer. OL1 extends COB by allowing such a feature. Each interface type is a labeled transition system parameterized with a natural number (thus introducing a dependent type). In OL1, the type of an unbounded buffer can be given by:

$$\texttt{Buffer}[n] = \texttt{put}(\ldots); \ \texttt{Buffer}[n+1] + [n > 0] \ \texttt{get}(\ldots); \ \texttt{Buffer}[n-1]$$

which enforces that any get access is only done when the buffer is full. The language OL1 itself is also extended with guards that act on natural numbers. The typing rules defined on OL1 ensure the same properties guaranteed by COB; in a well-typed configuration, there may not be, at run-time, any state where a message is not understood by its receiving object.

The third calculus introduced is OL2 [47] which is also an enhancement to COB in two ways. First, communication between objects is asynchronous and through FIFO channels, which is more realistic than the synchronous communication scheme of COB. Second, a distinction is made, both in the type language and the calculus itself, between mobile and immobile (called *stable*) interfaces. The type discipline enforces that no role of a stable interface can migrate and that no role of a mobile interface can be sent to a mobile interface. Indeed, this type discipline avoids situations where, for instance, a role is sent to an interface which turns out to be already sent in a message by the target object and is pending in a buffer destined to another mobile interface. This is obviously a deadlock situation that is prevented by the type system. Hence, OL2 ensures a liveness property which can be stated as follows: if a message is in a queue targeting an object of the configuration, then the configuration can evolve to a situation where this message has been consumed. It is worth noting that all three calculi enjoy the *configuration extension property*: if a well typed object is added to a well typed configuration and it refers to a compatible public interface of an object of that configuration, then the new configuration is also well typed.

An important contribution of the above works on OL1 and OL2 is the idea that types, as processes, enjoy notions of equivalence and subtyping corresponding to behavioural relations of bisimilarity and similarity. More generally, this is the idea that compatibility relations between behavioural types must correspond to notions of similarity or refinement between processes. Although natural, this idea was not necessarily prominent at the time. It relates to the first proposal for subtyping in binary session types by Gay and Hole [25,26], which was proposed independently, and which defined a subtype relation on binary session types using a coinductive definition clearly inspired by the simulation preorder on transition systems. It also plays a key role in understanding subtyping for behavioural contracts, for example, as proposed by Castagna and Padovani [15], and in eliciting the relationships between session types and behavioural contracts as in the work of Bernardi and Hennessy [6].

The typed object calculi presented in this section are limited in their expressive power in that they do not have internal concurrency. This restriction is relaxed in session-based-service-oriented computing: in fact, service oriented computing features services that result from the orchestration of other services, and orchestration is naturally multi-threaded. Work on sessions and service orchestration is covered in the following section.

4   Sessions, Session Types and Service Orchestration

Once the basics of the theory of contracts as behavioural types were established, we needed to verify their potential application to concrete examples of distributed software architectures. Our efforts therefore led us to service-oriented computing, whose importance at that time was growing. Services are exposed over a network via well-defined interfaces and specific communication protocols, and the design of software is obtained as an orchestration of services, that is, defining a local view of a structured set of interactions with remote services.

In this context, the interest is on guaranteeing that services interact safely. To this aim, we were investigating means to check, at deployment time, whether or not interacting services are compatible and will not yield interaction errors at run time. The elementary construct in a Web service interaction is a message exchange between two partner services. The message specifies the name of the operation to be invoked and bears arguments as its payload. An interaction can be long-lasting because multiple messages of different types can be exchanged in both directions before a service is delivered. Also, an orchestration typically requires support for concurrency in order to invoke multiple services simultaneously rather than sequentially [23]. The set of interactions supported by a service defines its behaviour. We argue that the high concurrency and complex behaviour found in orchestrations make them easily susceptible to programming errors.

In this setting, the concept of *sessions* emerged to capture the exchange of messages among components, starting from the request for a service and ending at its fulfillment. The concept of sessions has also gained recognition also in programming languages such as Java [50] and Erlang [44]. Sessions and session types became a powerful means for developing correct-by-construction components destined at collectively providing software services.

4.1   Session Types and Orchestration Charts

Orcharts. In the service orchestration community, a significant body of work looks at formal models that support sessions for services as a first-class element of the language, such as in the Service-Centered Calculus (SCC) [7], SSCC [33], CaSPiS [8], the latter two being process calculi inspired by the π-calculus [41,42] and Orc [32].

Most of these efforts adhere to the process algebraic paradigm. Hence, they miss capturing one of the main features of orchestration which is how different active sessions can influence each other at run-time. Indeed, one needs to explicitly capture how running sessions intertwine with control flows and data flows within an orchestration program. In [23], we presented *Orcharts*, a service orchestration language, specially designed to meet its modeling need. *Orcharts* is graph-based, as graphs are well suited for conveying complex control and data flows. *Orcharts* is accompanied by the *typecharts*, a session behavioural typing language, based on finite labeled transition systems. A novelty in *typecharts* is the presence of terminal states, which are meant to capture the successful termination of sessions.

Due to lack of space, we do not show here the graphical appearance of Orcharts, but only give the main characteristics: an Orchart is a finite directed acyclic graph where nodes can be of three types: input nodes, output nodes and instantiation nodes, and where edges can be of two types: data carrying edges and control edges. Each node is a unit of action; control is transferred from node to node by (control and data) edges:

- Simple input nodes receive messages (read messages from the FIFO queue associated with the referred session), whose value is assigned to write-once variables, that are carried over to next nodes by data carrying edges.
- An input node can be internally structured in one or more *capsules*, that is, expressions of a single receiving action, each in a different session.
- A structured input node behaves like a guarded command: when an input node receives control, its capsules can consume messages that are waiting in the FIFO queue of the referred session.
- When one message in a capsule is consumed, this capsule is fired and the flow concurrently continues on all edges having their source at this capsule.
- When a capsule is fired, all other capsules of the same input node (and their continuation flows) are discarded.
- An output node may contain one or more message emissions. Messages may carry values that can be either simple data values (as carried by variables in incoming data carrying edges) or service names. Each message emission refers to a session name. When an output node receives control, each of its messages is inserted in the FIFO queues corresponding to the named sessions.
- An instantiation node is analogous to a procedure call, that is, it refers to an orchart defined elsewhere, or it may introduce recursion and therefore iterative behaviour.
- Control can fork from a node in alternative or parallel control flows. Parallel control flows can join in a node that acts as a synchronization point for the two flows.

An orchart declares the session type for each *required* session and for each *provided* session, by a reference to a typechart.

Typecharts. Typecharts are a special kind of deterministic finite labeled transition systems where labels represent messages with parameter types. Parameter types can be data types, or names of typecharts. The transition system of a typechart has an initial state and one or more final states, and states are partitioned in two subsets: sending states and receiving states (initial and final states can only be receiving states). The typechart declared for a required service can be different from the one declared as provided in the service definition of this required service, but compatibility is required.

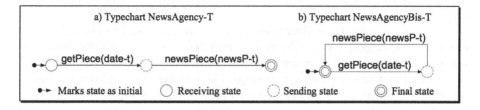

Fig. 1. Two typecharts of News Agency services

In Fig. 1 two example typecharts from [23] are given, derived by a revisited example of the News Agency service presented in [31]. A session typed with the typechart (a) allows for a single exchange of request and reply, while (b) allows for repeatable request/response interactions.

Subtyping. Compatibility is expressed recurring to the notions of *subtyping* and *type duality*:

- Subtyping between typecharts, defined according to [56], in a way resembles the classical simulation relation between transition systems:
  T_1 is a *subtype* of T_2, written $T_1 \preceq T_2$, if in any receiving state, T_1 is able to receive all the messages that T_2 is able to receive, and in any sending state T_2 is able to send all the messages that T_1 is able to send.
- A session has two ends, the end of the client and the end of the service. Session types differ for a session if seen from the two ends, in the fact that what is an input on one side is an output on the other side. $Dual(T)$ is simply defined exchanging sendings and receivings [56].

Substitutability and compatibility of types are defined, as in [56]:

- a session type T can *safely substitute* T' if $T \preceq T'$;
- a session type T is *compatible* with T' if $T \preceq Dual(T')$.

That is, two session types are deemed compatible if any sending of one is matched by the reception of the other; hence, a session having at its two ends compatible types does not internally deadlock. The typecharts NewsAgency-T and NewsAgencyBis-T are defined so that NewsAgencyBis-T *can safely substitute* NewsAgency-T.

Well-Typedness of Orcharts. Substitutability and compatibility allow for automatically checking, in a composition of services represented by two orcharts, the conformance of the required session type of an orchart with the provided session type of the other. The missing step is to ensure that effectively the orcharts defining composed services conform to their own provided and required typecharts.

In [23] a well-typedness algorithm is defined to this aim. The algorithm proceeds by discharging proof obligations: from the initial proof obligation (the initial state of the orchart conforms to the provided typechart), the algorithm proceeds with symbolic co-execution steps, where the orchart and the associated typecharts are executed in a synchronised fashion. Either a step fails, in which case the whole algorithm immediately terminates concluding a typing error, or produces a set of new proof obligations to be discharged. The algorithm can cope with instantiation nodes and with parallel flows so that it is guaranteed to terminate.

The notion of well-typedness is finally extended to configuration of services, by requiring well-typedness of each service and mutual type compatibility. A well-typed configuration of services is claimed to enjoy the *soundness* property: any service invocation potentially reaches a termination state.

4.2   Session Types and Web Service Orchestration

After looking for a specific language for reasoning on session types in service orchestrations, we moved to study how to apply the same concepts to a standard service oriented language.

Widely adopted standards such as the Web Service Description Language WSDL [16] provide support for syntactical compatibility analysis by defining message types in a standard way [35]. However, WSDL defines one-way or request-response exchange patterns and does not support the definition of more complex behaviour. Relevant behavioural information is exchanged between participants in human-readable forms, if at all. Automated verification of behavioural compatibility is impossible in such cases.

As already discussed in the previous section, the session paradigm has the potential to improve the verification of behavioural compatibility of web services (e.g. [33,57]). To that end, we have applied in [39] the session based approach by adapting and *sessionizing* a significant subset of the industry standard orchestration language BPEL [52]. SeB extends BPEL by featuring sessions as first class citizens. Sessions are typed in order to describe not only syntactical information but also behaviour. A SeB service exposes its required and provided session types, and a client wishing to interact with a service begins by opening a session with it. Thus, the interaction that follows the session initiation should behave according to the guidelines declared by the type of the opened session. Achieving the extension of BPEL with sessions and proving the benefits provided by this extension involves many steps:

- Defining the syntax of the untyped SeB,

- providing its static and dynamic semantics, defining the session type language,
- defining the typed SeB,
- providing the algorithm of well typedness of SeB,
- defining the syntax and dynamic semantics of running configurations of SeB services,
- characterisation of the interaction errors,
- defining well typed configurations of SeB services and the algorithm of its verification,
- defining the syntax and dynamic semantics of well typed configurations of SeB services,
- proving that well typed configurations of SeB services are interaction safe.

In the sequel, we give some hints on how these steps have been achieved.

SeB, a Sessionized BPEL. BPEL has its textual syntax defined in XML. Hence, XML would have been the most natural choice of metalanguage for encoding SeB's syntax. However, the verbose nature of the XML is not suitable for the purpose of the formal discussion that is engaged. Indeed, BPEL is essentially a graph-based notation, with nodes representing either simple or structured activities and where edges act as control links between activities. A structured activity is, in turn, a graph of linked activities. Hence, BPEL is not naturally expressible by process algebras and cannot be reduced to traditional structured programming with control constructs. Therefore we have adopted a mixed syntax: records to encode activities, and graph notations for control links. Elementary activities in BPEL are essentially made of service *invocations*. And the main structured activities are:

- *flow*, for running activities in parallel;
- *sequence*, for sequential composition of activities,
- *pick* (also known as external choice), which waits for multiple messages, the continuation behaviour being dependent on the received message.

SeB adopts the same structured activities of BPEL, but also introduces a new activity for session opening, and adapts the two activities of *invocation* and *pick*. Hence the three typical SeB activities are: opening a session, sending an invocation over a session, and awaiting for a response on a session. A typical sequence of SeB activities is (using a loose syntax):

```
r@serv ; r!req ; (r?resp1; Act1 + r?resp2; Act2)
```

which depicts the opening of a new session with service **serv** (and where the session id is bound to variable **r**), then sending an invocation **req** over this session, then awaiting for one of two possible responses **resp1** or **resp2** over this session.

SeB also inherits from BPEL the possibility of having control links between concurrent subactivities contained in a flow, as well as adding a join condition as a guard to any activity. As in BPEL, a join condition requires that all its arguments have a defined value (true or false) and must evaluate to true in order for the activity to be executable. SeB also implements so-called *dead path elimination* (DPE) whereby all links outgoing from a cancelled activity, or from its subactivities, have their values set to false.

Session Types. The untyped SeB language is then equipped with explicit typing by use of session types as a mean to abstract the interactions between a client and a service. Session types used for SeB are very similar to the type-charts introduced in Sect. 4.1. Indeed, the main difference of SeB, w.r.t. BPEL, resides in the addition of the session concept. The mechanism used in BPEL to relate and route distinct messages from one or more clients towards a particular service instance is called correlation. *Correlation sets* are application-level message fields whose values are used as a basis for correlation. Note that the purpose of both sessions and correlation sets is to maintain long-lasting interactions between process instances, but correlation sets are more implicit by nature. For example, with correlation sets, a service's lifecycle is hidden from clients, and the initiation of and reference to a specific instance of an interaction cannot be done explicitly and with any certainty. SeB does not feature correlation sets and instead relies on sessions as an explicit language element. Identifiable sessions are particularly useful as one may then associate types to sessions, which facilitates the fulfillment of our goal of checking that interactions are safe. Indeed, analysis of interactions that stem from correlations seems difficult [11]. Hence, in SeB, session identifiers are the only means to refer to the instances at each end of a conversation.

SeB uses binary sessions, therefore interactions involve strictly two partners. Correlation sets are more expressive than binary sessions in the sense that they can, for example, allow multiple clients that are not aware of each other's existence to communicate with one single service instance if the right correlation data is included in the messages. Multiparty sessions have been studied in the literature [11], as well as multiparty session types [28], and offer a solution as to how this limitation can be lifted from binary sessions Multiparty sessions can in fact be shown to emulate some of the behaviour that can be defined with correlation sets.

Operational Semantics of SeB and of Service Configurations. In [39] we first define a static semantics for SeB that defines well-formed activities. We then define an operational semantics obtained in two steps: the nature of BPEL is such that there is an additional layer of control over concurrent activities within a local process. This layer of control manifests itself in the form of control links and complementary join conditions. Compared to traditional theoretical concurrent languages such as those based on the π-calculus, this adds a layer of complexity when giving BPEL-style languages formal semantics. Undoubtedly, attempting to combine the evaluation of local control flow while simultaneously studying the value and message passing semantics of distributed processes would result in very complicated semantics. Hence, the first step consists in the creation of what we have called a *control graph*: before looking at how distributed services interact, SeB activities are transformed into control graphs. Control graphs are labeled transition systems that reflect the evaluation of the control flow of SeB activities including the evaluation of join conditions, but do not address values and message passing. By isolating this first step, we can study different properties and transformations of control graphs and distinguish between binding, usage, and free occurrences of variables. This graph takes into account the effect of the control flow part of a SeB activity, including the evaluation of join conditions. Control graphs contain symbolic actions and no variables are evaluated in the translation into control graphs. In the second step of the semantics we run service definitions, service instances, and client instances alongside each other (based on the control graphs obtained in the previous step) in what we call a *service configuration* and we enable communication through FIFO message queues. At this stage, the values of variables need to be taken into account as they are exchanged in messages, by adjoining a memory map to each SeB activity, providing the value and message passing semantics of SeB activities. This semantics shows how a dynamic configuration of services can evolve by instantiating sessions and exchanging messages.

Interaction Safety. Based on these semantics we formalise the concepts of interaction error and of *interaction safety*. Informally, interaction safety is verified when the following situation never occurs: a service instance reaches a state where it waits for an input on a session, and the message that is at the head of the queue for that session is not expected, i.e., the service has no matching pick or receive activity and cannot remove the message from the queue.

Similarly to what had been done for orcharts, but with a higher degree of complexity due to the simultaneous presence of parallel flows and control links in SeB, we are able to provide an algorithm that determines whether or not a collection of services is able to interact correctly by verifying the compatibility of the clients'required session types with the providers'provided session types. We say that such a collection of services is well-typed. Finally, we prove that a well-typed collection of interacting services is *interaction safe*, in the sense given above, meaning that no unexpected messages or arguments are exchanged.

5 Conclusion

We have presented the history of a research activity centered on the need of correctly composing distributed software components that has spanned over almost two decades, following the evolution of the software component technologies, from Open Distributed Processing to service-oriented architectures. The focal point of this research activity is the adoption of contracts, in the form of behavioural types, to regulate the interactions between communicating software components. The notion of behavioural contract has been successively refined and subsumed by the concept of session type.

Session types and behavioural contracts have undergone a significantly dense research activity by a vast community, as witnessed by a recent survey [29], in which, out of the extensive bibliography of 180 references, more than one hundred papers have explicitly addressed these concepts in some form or another, only a few are present in the bibliography below.

The aim of our paper was not to give just another exhaustive account of the research in the field, but to closely follow, inside this large research stream, a particular line that has been taken by the authors and pursued with the constant aim to provide methods and techniques to effectively verify the absence of interaction problems in assemblies of distributed software components, following the technological evolution in this field. One characterising factor in our work was the continuous reference to realistic computational models that include both parallelism (e.g. between service invocations) and asynchronous communication, two elements that make the proof of meaningful safety and progress properties much more complex.

The research activity provided in this paper has been in several cases inspired by Rocco De Nicola's work, either as reference to his works on service-oriented calculi [7,8], or indirectly when using process algebra concepts, behavioural equivalences, labeled transition systems, simulation preorders which include a range of mathematically powerful tools that have received prominent attention and contributions by Rocco over the last three decades.

Session types and behavioural contracts later on evolved in several directions, among which we cite *multiparty* sessions [11,28]; indeed, *binary or biparty* sessions introduced in Sect. 4 are restricted to communication between two partners, with dual communication capabilities, while multiparty sessions cover complex communication schemes with three or more partners. A natural way to define multiparty session types is to consider a global view of a conversation between several parties, that is, of all the message exchanges that take place inside the session, projecting then the global view to local views on the side of each partner's interface, similarly to binary sessions [10].

Work on multiparty session types [28] indicates two major difficulties: they lack the duality between each end of a session that makes binary sessions relatively straightforward, and the effects of non-linear use of communication channels is error-prone. As advocated in [28] (albeit for the π-calculus), it is possible to project *global types* (for multiparty sessions) onto local processes, and these local type projections can be used for local type verification. We believe that our work on binary sessions for BPEL could be extended to embrace multiparty sessions.

Another important direction pursued by the research stream on session types and behavioural contracts concerns the properties satisfied by a distributed system made up of communicating components. A classical distinction of program properties is between safety and liveness properties; the former express that a program execution will never exhibit an undesirable event, while the latter establish the eventual occurrence of a desirable situation during the execution of the program. While behavioural type systems provide a suitable way to prove safety of distributed executions, using them to prove liveness properties has been challenging. Indeed, compliance to behavioural types can be used to check (liveness) local progress inside a single session, while this becomes difficult in the case of multiple simultaneously open sessions (binary or, especially, multiparty), since types are associated to single sessions. Dependency between simultaneously open sessions has to be taken into account in order to be able to deduce global progress. In our work, we have first encountered this problem when addressing inter-component deadlock freedom in [14], proposing a solution under asynchronous communication and assumptions on the communication dependency between components, that somehow anticipates in a quite limited setting the much more general and systematic latest results of [17] for asynchronous multiparty sessions.

Finally, while most of the work on session types and behavioural contracts has considered mobile computational models as in the π-calculus and the ODP Computational Model, where process, object of component configurations are essentially flat, with no other dependencies between processes, objects or components than communication dependencies, we believe computational models with non-flat configurations, i.e. featuring containment, failure and encapsulation dependencies between their elements, need to be considered. Example computational models of the sort include variants of the π-calculus with localities such as Dpi [27], Klaim [21], the Kell calculus [53], Mobile Ambients and their variants [12,37], as well as bigraphs [40,54]. Type systems for these models have appeared in the literature but revisiting them in light of the recent advances on session types and behavioural contracts seems worthwhile, as well as dealing with phenomena such as failures and encapsulation, which could require introducing constructs and techniques borrowed from separation logic [51].

Acknowledgments. The work reported in the present paper has been carried out over the years by a group of authors: Arnaud Bailly, Cinzia Bernardeschi, Cyril Carrez, Joubine Dustzadeh, Alessandro Fantechi, Arnaud Février, Jonathan Michaux, Elie Najm, Abdelkrim Nimour, Frank Olsen, Jean-Bernard Stefani.

References

1. Abadi, M., Lamport, L.: Composing specifications. ACM Trans. Program. Lang. Syst. **15**(1), 73–132 (1993). https://doi.org/10.1145/151646.151649
2. de Alfaro, L., Henzinger, T.A.: Interface automata. In: ESEC/FSE-01. Software Engineering Notes, vol. 26, p. 5. ACM Press (2001)
3. Alrahman, Y.A., De Nicola, R., Loreti, M., Tiezzi, F., Vigo, R.: A calculus for attribute-based communication. In: Wainwright, R.L., Corchado, J.M., Bechini, A., Hong, J. (eds.) Proceedings of the 30th Annual ACM Symposium on Applied Computing, Salamanca, Spain, 13–17 April 2015, pp. 1840–1845. ACM (2015). https://doi.org/10.1145/2695664.2695668
4. Amadio, R.M., Cardelli, L.: Subtyping recursive types. ACM Trans. Program. Lang. Syst. **15**(4), 575–631 (1993). https://doi.org/10.1145/155183.155231

5. Bernardeschi, C., Dustzadeh, J., Fantechi, A., Najm, E., Nimour, A., Olsen, F.: Consistent semantics and correct transformations for the ODP information and computational models. In: Proceedings of 2nd IFIP Conference on Formal Methods for Open Object-based Distributed Systems (FMOODS). Chapman & Hall, Canterbury, July 1997

6. Bernardi, G., Hennessy, M.: Using higher-order contracts to model session types. Log. Methods Comput. Sci. **12**(2) (2016)

7. Boreale, M., et al.: SCC: a service centered calculus. In: Bravetti, M., Núñez, M., Zavattaro, G. (eds.) WS-FM 2006. LNCS, vol. 4184, pp. 38–57. Springer, Heidelberg (2006). https://doi.org/10.1007/11841197_3

8. Boreale, M., Bruni, R., De Nicola, R., Loreti, M.: Sessions and pipelines for structured service programming. In: Barthe, G., de Boer, F.S. (eds.) FMOODS 2008. LNCS, vol. 5051, pp. 19–38. Springer, Heidelberg (2008). https://doi.org/10.1007/978-3-540-68863-1_3

9. Boreale, M., Bruni, R., De Nicola, R., Loreti, M.: CaSPiS: a calculus of sessions, pipelines and services. Math. Struct. Comput. Sci. **25**(3), 666–709 (2015). https://doi.org/10.1017/S0960129512000953

10. Bravetti, M., Zavattaro, G.: A foundational theory of contracts for multi-party service composition. Fundam. Inf. **89**, 451–478 (2008)

11. Bruni, R., Lanese, I., Melgratti, H., Tuosto, E.: Multiparty sessions in SOC. In: Lea, D., Zavattaro, G. (eds.) COORDINATION 2008. LNCS, vol. 5052, pp. 67–82. Springer, Heidelberg (2008). https://doi.org/10.1007/978-3-540-68265-3_5

12. Cardelli, L., Gordon, A.: Mobile ambients. Theor. Comput. Sci. **240**(1), 173–213 (2000)

13. Carrez, C., Fantechi, A., Najm, E.: Behavioural contracts for a sound assembly of components. In: König, H., Heiner, M., Wolisz, A. (eds.) FORTE 2003. LNCS, vol. 2767, pp. 111–126. Springer, Heidelberg (2003). https://doi.org/10.1007/978-3-540-39979-7_8

14. Carrez, C., Fantechi, A., Najm, E.: Assembling components with behavioural contracts. Annales des Télécommunications **60**(7–8), 989–1022 (2005). https://doi.org/10.1007/BF03219957

15. Castagna, G., Gesbert, N., Padovani, L.: A theory of contracts for web services. In: Proceedings of the 35th Annual ACM SIGPLAN-SIGACT Symposium on Principles of Programming Languages, POPL 2008, pp. 261–272. ACM, New York (2008). https://doi.org/10.1145/1328438.1328471

16. Chinnici, R., Moreau, J.J., Ryman, A., Weerawarana, S.: Web Service Definition Language (WSDL) Version 2.0, W3C. Technical report, June 2007

17. Coppo, M., Dezani-Ciancaglini, M., Padovani, L., Yoshida, N.: Inference of global progress properties for dynamically interleaved multiparty sessions. In: De Nicola, R., Julien, C. (eds.) COORDINATION 2013. LNCS, vol. 7890, pp. 45–59. Springer, Heidelberg (2013). https://doi.org/10.1007/978-3-642-38493-6_4

18. De Nicola, R., Ferrari, G., Loreti, M., Pugliese, R.: A language-based approach to autonomic computing. In: Beckert, B., Damiani, F., de Boer, F.S., Bonsangue, M.M. (eds.) FMCO 2011. LNCS, vol. 7542, pp. 25–48. Springer, Heidelberg (2013). https://doi.org/10.1007/978-3-642-35887-6_2

19. De Nicola, R., Hennessy, M.: Testing equivalences for processes. Theor. Comput. Sci. **34**, 83–133 (1984). https://doi.org/10.1016/0304-3975(84)90113-0

20. De Nicola, R., Pugliese, R.: A process algebra based on Linda. In: Ciancarini, P., Hankin, C. (eds.) COORDINATION 1996. LNCS, vol. 1061, pp. 160–178. Springer, Heidelberg (1996). https://doi.org/10.1007/3-540-61052-9_45

21. DeNicola, R., Ferrari, G., Pugliese, R.: KLAIM: a Kernel language for agents inter-action and mobility. IEEE Trans. Softw. Eng. **24**(5), 315–330 (1998)
22. Dustzadeh, J., Najm, E.: Consistent semantics for ODP information and computa-tional models. In: Specification, Testing IFIP TC6 WG6.1, Techniques for X) and 18–21 November, 1997, Osaka, Japan. IFIP Conference Proceedings, vol. 107, pp. 107–126. Chapman & Hall (1997)
23. Fantechi, A., Najm, E.: Session types for orchestration charts. In: Lea, D., Zavat-taro, G. (eds.) COORDINATION 2008. LNCS, vol. 5052, pp. 117–134. Springer, Heidelberg (2008). https://doi.org/10.1007/978-3-540-68265-3_8
24. Février, A., Najm, E., Stefani, J.: Contracts for ODP. In: Bertran, M., Rus, T. (eds.) Transformation-Based Reactive Systems Development. Springer, Heidelberg (1997). https://doi.org/10.1007/3-540-63010-4_15
25. Gay, S.J., Hole, M.: Subtyping for session types in the pi calculus. Acta Inf. **42**(2–3), 191–225 (2005)
26. Gay, S., Hole, M.: Types and subtypes for client-server interactions. In: Swierstra, S.D. (ed.) ESOP 1999. LNCS, vol. 1576, pp. 74–90. Springer, Heidelberg (1999). https://doi.org/10.1007/3-540-49099-X_6
27. Hennessy, M., Rathke, J., Yoshida, N.: SafeDpi: a language for controlling mobile code. Acta Inf. **42**(4–5), 227–290 (2005)
28. Honda, K., Yoshida, N., Carbone, M.: Multiparty asynchronous session types. SIG-PLAN Not. **43**, 273–284 (2008). https://doi.org/10.1145/1328897.1328472
29. Hüttel, H., et al.: Foundations of session types and behavioural contracts. ACM Comput. Surv. **49**(1), 3:1–3:36 (2016). https://doi.org/10.1145/2873052
30. ISO, IEC: Information Technology Open Distributed Processing Reference Model. IS 10746 parts 1,2,3 (1998–2010), also published as ITU-T Recommendations X901, X.902, X.903
31. Kitchin, D., Cook, W.R., Misra, J.: A language for task orchestration and its semantic properties. In: Baier, C., Hermanns, H. (eds.) CONCUR 2006. LNCS, vol. 4137, pp. 477–491. Springer, Heidelberg (2006). https://doi.org/10.1007/11817949_32
32. Kitchin, D., Quark, A., Cook, W., Misra, J.: The orc programming language. In: Lee, D., Lopes, A., Poetzsch-Heffter, A. (eds.) FMOODS/FORTE -2009. LNCS, vol. 5522, pp. 1–25. Springer, Heidelberg (2009). https://doi.org/10.1007/978-3-642-02138-1_1
33. Lanese, I., Martins, F., Vasconcelos, V.T., Ravara, A.: Disciplining orchestration and conversation in service-oriented computing. In: Proceedings of the Fifth IEEE International Conference on Software Engineering and Formal Methods, SEFM 2007, pp. 305–314. IEEE Computer Society, Washington, DC (2007), https://doi.org/10.1109/SEFM.2007.13
34. Lapadula, A., Pugliese, R., Tiezzi, F.: A calculus for orchestration of web ser-vices. In: De Nicola, R. (ed.) ESOP 2007. LNCS, vol. 4421, pp. 33–47. Springer, Heidelberg (2007). https://doi.org/10.1007/978-3-540-71316-6_4
35. Lapadula, A., Pugliese, R., Tiezzi, F.: A WSDL-based type system for asyn-chronous WS-BPEL processes. Form. Methods Syst. Des. **38**(2), 119–157 (2011). https://doi.org/10.1007/s10703-010-0110-0
36. Larsen, K.G., Steffen, B., Weise, C.: A constraint oriented proof methodology based on modal transition systems. In: Brinksma, E., Cleaveland, W.R., Larsen, K.G., Margaria, T., Steffen, B. (eds.) TACAS 1995. LNCS, vol. 1019, pp. 17–40. Springer, Heidelberg (1995). https://doi.org/10.1007/3-540-60630-0_2
37. Levi, F., Sangiorgi, D.: Mobile safe ambients. ACM. Trans. Program. Lang. Syst. **25**(1), 1–69 (2003)

38. Meseguer, J.: Conditioned rewriting logic as a united model of concurrency. Theor. Comput. Sci. **96**(1), 73–155 (1992). https://doi.org/10.1016/0304-3975(92)90182-F

39. Michaux, J., Najm, E., Fantechi, A.: Session types for safe web service orchestration. J. Log. Algebr. Program. **82**(8), 282–310 (2013). https://doi.org/10.1016/j.jlap.2013.05.004

40. Milner, R.: The Space and Motion of Communicating Agents. Cambridge University Press, Cambridge (2009)

41. Milner, R., Parrow, J., Walker, J.: A calculus of mobile processes, I. Inf. Comput. **100**(1), 1–40 (1992). Technical report ECS-LFCS-89-85

42. Milner, R., Parrow, J., Walker, J.: A calculus of mobile processes, II. Inf. Comput. **100**(1), 41–77 (1992). Technical report ECS-LFCS-89-86

43. Milner, R.: A Calculus of Communicating Systems. Lecture Notes in Computer Science, vol. 158. Springer, Heidelberg (1983)

44. Mostrous, D., Vasconcelos, V.T.: Session typing for a featherweight erlang. In: De Meuter, W., Roman, G.-C. (eds.) COORDINATION 2011. LNCS, vol. 6721, pp. 95–109. Springer, Heidelberg (2011). https://doi.org/10.1007/978-3-642-21464-6_7

45. Najm, E., Nimour, A.: A calculus of object bindings. In: Proceedings of 2nd IFIP Conference on Formal Methods for Open Object-based Distributed Systems (FMOODS). Chapman & Hall, Canterbury, July 1997

46. Najm, E., Stefani, J.: A formal semantics of DPL. Technical report, Report CNET/RC.V01.ENJBS.004., Esprit Project 2267 (Integrated Systems Architecture) (1992)

47. Najm, E., Nimour, A., Stefani, J.-B.: Guaranteeing liveness in an object calculus through behavioral typing. In: Wu, J., Chanson, S.T., Gao, Q. (eds.) Formal Methods for Protocol Engineering and Distributed Systems. IAICT, vol. 28, pp. 203–221. Springer, Boston (1999). https://doi.org/10.1007/978-0-387-35578-8_12

48. Najm, E., Nimour, A., Stefani, J.-B.: Infinite types for distributed object interfaces. In: Ciancarini, P., Fantechi, A., Gorrieri, R. (eds.) FMOODS 1999. ITIFIP, vol. 10, pp. 353–369. Springer, Boston, MA (1999). https://doi.org/10.1007/978-0-387-35562-7_28

49. Najm, E., Stefani, J.: A formal semantics for the ODP computational model. Comput. Netw. ISDN Syst. **27**(8), 1305–1329 (1995). https://doi.org/10.1016/0169-7552(94)00032-O

50. Ng, N., Yoshida, N., Pernet, O., Hu, R., Kryftis, Y.: Safe parallel programming with session java. In: De Meuter, W., Roman, G.-C. (eds.) COORDINATION 2011. LNCS, vol. 6721, pp. 110–126. Springer, Heidelberg (2011). https://doi.org/10.1007/978-3-642-21464-6_8

51. O'Hearn, P.W.: A primer on separation logic (and automatic program verification and analysis). In: Software Safety and Security - Tools for Analysis and Verification, NATO Science for Peace and Security Series - D: Information and Communication Security, vol. 33. IOS Press (2012)

52. Organization for the Advancement of Structured Information Standards (OASIS): Web Services Business Process Execution Language (WS-BPEL) Version 2.0, April 2007

53. Schmitt, A., Stefani, J.-B.: The kell calculus: a family of higher-order distributed process calculi. In: Priami, C., Quaglia, P. (eds.) GC 2004. LNCS, vol. 3267, pp. 146–178. Springer, Heidelberg (2005). https://doi.org/10.1007/978-3-540-31794-4_9

54. Sevegnani, M., Calder, M.: Bigraphs with sharing. Theor. Comput. Sci. **577**, 43–73 (2015). https://doi.org/10.1016/j.tcs.2015.02.011

55. Uriarte, R.B., Tiezzi, F., De Nicola, R.: SLAC: a formal service-level-agreement language for cloud computing. In: Proceedings of the 7th IEEE/ACM International Conference on Utility and Cloud Computing, UCC 2014, London, United Kingdom, 8–11 December 2014, pp. 419–426. IEEE Computer Society (2014). https://doi.org/10.1109/UCC.2014.53
56. Vallecillo, A., Vasconcelos, V.T., Ravara, A.: Typing the behavior of software components using session types. Fundam. Inf. **73**(4), 583–598 (2006)
57. Yoshida, N., Vasconcelos, V.T.: Language primitives and type discipline for structured communication-based programming revisited: two systems for higher-order session communication. Electron. Notes Theor. Comput. Sci. **171**(4), 73–93 (2007). https://doi.org/10.1016/j.entcs.2007.02.056

Modal Epistemic Logic on Contracts: A Doctrinal Approach

Paolo Bottoni[1] , Daniele Gorla[1(✉)] , Stefano Kasangian[2],
and Anna Labella[1]

[1] Dipartimento di Informatica, "Sapienza" Università di Roma, Rome, Italy
{bottoni,gorla,labella}@di.uniroma1.it
[2] Dipartimento di Matematica, University of Milano, Milan, Italy
stefano.kasangian@unimi.it

Abstract. Problems related to the construction of consensus out of distributed knowledge have become actual again under a new perspective with the diffusion of distributed ledger techniques. In particular, when dealing with contracts, different observers must agree that a contract is in a certain state, even if not all transactions performed under the contract are observable by all of them. In this paper, we revisit previous work on algebraic modelling of labelled non-deterministic concurrent processes, which identified an intuitionistic modal/temporal logic associated with a categorical model. We expand this logic with typical epistemic operators in a categorical framework in order to encompass distributed knowledge to speak about transactions and contracts.

Keywords: Categorical logic · Doctrines · Modal operators ·
Epistemic logic · Distributed knowledge · Contracts

1 Introduction

This paper follows on a series of works [4,5,8,9,15] where a category, naturally equipped with an internal logic, was introduced for reasoning on concurrent computations. Indeed, a concurrent agent can be seen as an automaton, with non-determinism expressing the fact that its states can offer different behaviours at different moments in time. Differently from the classical approach taken in automata theory, non-deterministic computations between a pair of states are not described as a set of strings in a free monoid: rather, we deal with a labelled, structured set of computations, where two computations can part from each other while maintaining the same observable steps [15]. We defined a category

Dedication: With this paper, we all wish to thank Rocco for the stimulating discussions, the original ideas and the collaborations carried out in the last twenty-five years. Furthermore, apart from being a colleague and a guide, he has always primarily been a friend for all of us, and his friendship is the main gift we received from him.

© Springer Nature Switzerland AG 2019
M. Boreale et al. (Eds.): De Nicola-Festschrift, LNCS 11665, pp. 298–314, 2019.
https://doi.org/10.1007/978-3-030-21485-2_17

of (action-labelled) trees that can be used to model unfolding of labelled transition systems and to study behavioural relations over them; in particular, many different equivalences based on bisimulation were investigated in [8,9].

Recently [4,5] we moved to the study of the internal logic arising from our model. In particular, in [5] we proposed a characterisation of visual interaction in terms of games, and showed that the algebraic structure derived from the association of temporal and spatial structures (actually, a variant of the model in [15]) is canonically associated with a logical system that can be naturally extended by the introduction of operators which simultaneously model both temporal and modal qualifications of formulae. This line has been extended in [4] where we proved that, if the labelling set has enough properties, then the model presents a two-fold internal logical structure, induced by two doctrines [16] definable on it: one related to its families of subobjects and one to its families of regular subobjects. The first doctrine is Heyting and makes the model a Heyting category; the second one is Boolean. The difference between these two logical structures, namely the different behaviour of the negation operator, can be interpreted in terms of a distinction between non-deterministic and deterministic behaviours of agents able to perform computations in the context of the same process. Moreover, the sorted first-order logic naturally associated with the model can be extended to a modal/temporal logic, again using the doctrinal setting.

Based on [4], we perform here a step further and consider not only concurrent but also distributed systems, where knowledge about the current state varies from agent to agent. To this end, we combine temporal operators with epistemic ones (e.g., those defined in [12,18,19]), to reflect the evolution of the system in time. Similarly to the original model, we have a system of categories based on a bicategory, but now the logical system need not be built on top of a free monoid (the labelling set); indeed, atomic labels are configurations of a transaction system (which can only be prolonged according to a meet-semilattice structure) and a temporal structure is associated with the order to describe the evolution of the system, so that our model can support the modal/temporal operators from [4]. We then add to them new operators taken from epistemic logics, e.g., those for *public announcement, common knowledge* and *distributed knowledge*.

The derived logic allows us to set up a language of epistemic formulae in which to reason about properties of distributed and common knowledge, typically related to the possibility of maintaining a consistent set of beliefs across different agents, in the presence of public announcements updating information about some state of the world. In particular, we show how such a language can be used to express knowledge maintained by different observers about the execution of some contract following some logics for public announcements [18], as suggested in [17]. In particular, we model a contract as a formal device to restrict the set of allowed transactions leading to the transfer of ownership of some resource across different actors.

In the rest of the paper, Sect. 2 introduces a simple language of transactions, used in Sect. 3 to specify contracts. In Sect. 4 relevant notions about categorical/logical structures and epistemic logic are introduced. In Sect. 5 the algebraic and logical structures of our model are presented, together with examples of the use of the language. Section 6 draws some conclusions.

2   Worlds of Resources

We present a simple model of worlds in which resources are either (1) assigned to actors, or (2) present in the environment for actors to grab them, or (3) irremediably destroyed. Resource exchanges, i.e., changes of assignments (including the possibility of destroying a resource), are modelled as transactions.

With each universe of worlds, three finite disjoint sets are given: a set $\mathbf{A}$ of *proper actors*, a fixed set $\mathbf{A}_{env} = \{\top, \bot\}$ of *environment actors*, and a set $\mathbf{R}$ of *resources*. Here, $\top$ and $\bot$ model the fact that a resource is available but not assigned to any proper actor (yet) and that a resource is no longer assignable to any proper actor (i.e., it has been destroyed), respectively. We talk generically of *actors* when not distinguishing between proper and environment ones. We use $a, a_1, \ldots, a_n$ for actor names (which are unique) and $r, r_1, \ldots, r_n$ for resources. The notation $[r, 1] \ldots, [r, k]$ is used to denote different copies of a resource r.

Configurations are collections of assignments evolving through transactions. To be precise, a configuration $\mathcal{C}$ encodes an *assignment function* $ass_{\mathcal{C}} : \mathbf{R} \to (\mathbf{A} \cup \mathbf{A}_{env})$, so that each resource is uniquely associated with an actor. A transaction is then an operator replacing an assignment function with another. The following treatment, however, is based on a presentation of such functions and operators through sets of individual assignments.

Definition 1 (Assignment). *Given a set of proper actors* $\mathbf{A}$ *and a set of resources* $\mathbf{R}$, *an* assignment *over* $\mathbf{A}, \mathbf{R}$ *is a couple* $(r, a) \in \mathbf{R} \times (\mathbf{A} \cup \mathbf{A}_{env})$. *The set of all assignments over* $\mathbf{A}, \mathbf{R}$ *is denoted by* $ASS_{\mathbf{A}}^{\mathbf{R}}$.

Definition 2 (Configuration). *Given a set of resources,* $\mathbf{R}$, *a set of proper actors,* $\mathbf{A}$, *and a total function,* $ass_{\mathcal{C}} : \mathbf{R} \to (\mathbf{A} \cup \mathbf{A}_{env})$, *the induced set of assignments* $\mathcal{C} = \{(r, a) \in \mathbf{R} \times (\mathbf{A} \cup \mathbf{A}_{env}) \mid a = ass_{\mathcal{C}}(r)\} \subset ASS_{\mathbf{A}}^{\mathbf{R}}$ *is called the* configuration *over* $\mathbf{A}, \mathbf{R}$ *induced by* $ass_{\mathcal{C}}$, *(in short a* configuration*)*.

We denote by $CONF_{\mathbf{A}}^{\mathbf{R}}$ the set of configurations over $\mathbf{A}, \mathbf{R}$ and with † the *dead configuration*, induced by $ass_{\dagger}$, defined as $ass_{\dagger}(r) = \bot$ for all $r \in \mathbf{R}$.

Configurations evolve via transactions modifying individual assignments.

Definition 3 (Atomic transaction). *Given a set of proper actors* $\mathbf{A}$ *and a set of resources* $\mathbf{R}$, *an* atomic transaction *over* $\mathbf{A}, \mathbf{R}$ *is a triple* $(r, a_1, a_2) \in \mathbf{R} \times (\mathbf{A} \cup \{\top\}) \times (\mathbf{A} \cup \mathbf{A}_{env})$ *such that* $a_1 \neq a_2$. *The* effect *of an atomic transaction* $trn = (r, a_1, a_2)$ *on* $\mathcal{C} \in CONF_{\mathbf{A}}^{\mathbf{R}}$ *is the configuration* $\mathcal{C}' = \text{eff}(\mathcal{C}, trn) \in CONF_{\mathbf{A}}^{\mathbf{R}}$:

$$\mathcal{C}' = \begin{cases} (\mathcal{C} \setminus \{(r, a_1)\}) \cup \{(r, a_2)\} & \textit{if } (r, a_1) \in \mathcal{C} \\ \mathcal{C} & \textit{otherwise} \end{cases}$$

We say that trn is an *effective atomic transaction for* $\mathcal{C}$ if $\mathcal{C}' \neq \mathcal{C}$. Note that no atomic transaction can be effective for †. The condition $a_1 \neq a_2$, may appear redundant, as one could well conceive of transactions leaving an assignment unchanged. However, from a semantic point of view, it allows an observer, by looking only at the effect of the application of a transaction, to distinguish between successful (modifying the current configuration) and failed (leaving the configuration unchanged) transactions, which would not be possible otherwise.

A transaction is then a collection of atomic transactions, which collectively define an operator whose application to an assignment function ass_C produces an assignment function $ass_{C'}$.

Definition 4 (Transaction). *Given a set of proper actors* $\mathbf{A}$ *and a set of resources* $\mathbf{R}$, *a transaction over* $\mathbf{A}, \mathbf{R}$, *denoted with* Trn, *is a finite set* $\{(r^i, a_1^i, a_2^i) \mid r^i \in \mathbf{R}, a_1^i \in \mathbf{A} \cup \{\top\}, a_2^i \in \mathbf{A} \cup \mathbf{A}_{env}, a_1^i \neq a_2^i, i \in \{1, \ldots, n\}\}$ *of atomic transactions over* $\mathbf{A}, \mathbf{R}$ *such that* $i \neq j \Leftrightarrow r^i \neq r^j$. *We denote by* $TRN_{\mathbf{A}}^{\mathbf{R}}$ *the set of all transactions on the given sets* $\mathbf{A}, \mathbf{R}$. *The* effect *of a transaction* $Trn = \{trn_1, \ldots, trn_n\} \in TRN_{\mathbf{A}}^{\mathbf{R}}$ *on* $C \in CONF_{\mathbf{A}}^{\mathbf{R}}$ *is* $C' \in CONF_{\mathbf{A}}^{\mathbf{R}}$, *defined as* $\textit{eff}(\ldots (\textit{eff}(\textit{eff}(C, trn_1), trn_2), \ldots), trn_n)$ *if all* trn_i *are effective,* C *otherwise.*

Note that each transaction can contain at most one atomic transaction defining a change of assignment for any given resource r; thus, the order in which we consider the atomic transactions in Trn for its effect is immaterial. Furthermore, the effect of Trn is $C' \neq C$ only if $\textit{eff}(C, trn_i) \neq C$, for all $trn_i \in Trn$; thus, a transaction succeeds or fails as a whole. We say that Trn is an *effective transaction for* C if $C' \neq C$; again, no transaction can be effective for †.

For any given $CONF_{\mathbf{A}}^{\mathbf{R}}$, we introduce a notion of verification by assuming the existence of a set of *verifiers* $\mathbf{V}_{\mathbf{A}}^{\mathbf{R}}$. Each verifier $v \in \mathbf{V}_{\mathbf{A}}^{\mathbf{R}}$ is endowed with some *observational capability*, modeled as an alphabet $alph_v = alph_v^{\mathbf{R}} \cup alph_v^{\mathbf{A}}$, with $alph_v^{\mathbf{R}} \subseteq \mathbf{R}$ and $(\mathbf{A}_{env} \cup \{\bowtie\}) \subseteq alph_v^{\mathbf{A}} \subseteq (\mathbf{A} \cup \mathbf{A}_{env} \cup \{\bowtie\})$. The special name $\bowtie$ is used as a place-holder for proper actors not observable by v. In this way, a verifier is always informed whether a resource $r \in alph_v^{\mathbf{R}}$ is either

- assigned to an actor a observable by v (i.e., $a \in alph_v^{\mathbf{A}} \cap (\mathbf{A} \cup \mathbf{A}_{env})$); or
- assigned to an actor which is not observable by v (in which case the dummy assignment $(r, \bowtie)$ is used by the verifier to record the fact that it does not know the exact assignment for r, but it knows that it has neither been destroyed nor is it free in the environment).

We denote by $ASS_{\mathbf{A}\bowtie}^{\mathbf{R}}$ the extension of $ASS_{\mathbf{A}}^{\mathbf{R}}$ to include assignments of the form $(r, \bowtie)$. An *observation by* $v \in \mathbf{V}_{\mathbf{A}}^{\mathbf{R}}$ over a configuration $C \in CONF_{\mathbf{A}}^{\mathbf{R}}$ is the result of $obs_v : CONF_{\mathbf{A}}^{\mathbf{R}} \to \wp(ASS_{\mathbf{A}\bowtie}^{\mathbf{R}})$, defined as follows: $obs_v(C) = \{(r, a) \mid (r, a) \in C, r \in alph_v^{\mathbf{R}}, a \in alph_v^{\mathbf{A}}\} \cup \{(r, \bowtie) \mid (r, a) \in C, r \in alph_v^{\mathbf{R}}, a \notin alph_v^{\mathbf{A}}\}$.

A set of assignments $\mathcal{K}^v \subset ASS_{\mathbf{A}\bowtie}^{\mathbf{R}}$ (representing the *knowledge* $v \in \mathbf{V}_{\mathbf{A}}^{\mathbf{R}}$ has of a configuration) is *consistent with* $C \in CONF_{\mathbf{A}}^{\mathbf{R}}$ for v if $\mathcal{K}^v = obs_v(C)$. Given $\mathcal{K}^v \subset ASS_{\mathbf{A}\bowtie}^{\mathbf{R}}$, with all the assignments in $\mathcal{K}^v$ formed with elements in $alph_v$, for $v \in \mathbf{V}_{\mathbf{A}}^{\mathbf{R}}$, we denote by $CONS_v(\mathcal{K}^v)$ the set $\{C \in CONF_{\mathbf{A}}^{\mathbf{R}} \mid \mathcal{K}^v = obs_v(C)\}$.

A verifier v becomes informed of the application of a transaction Trn to a configuration C by receiving a *public announcement* of Trn, i.e., the list of the atomic transactions in Trn, incorporating the received information inasmuch it refers to elements of $alph_v$. In particular, the knowledge $\mathcal{K}^v$ that v has of C evolves, for each atomic transaction $(r, a_1, a_2) \in Trn$ applied on C, as follows:

1. if $r, a_2 \in alph_v$ and either $(r, a_1) \in \mathcal{K}^v$ or $(r, \bowtie) \in \mathcal{K}^v$, then $\mathcal{K}'^v \ni (r, a_2)$;
2. if $r \in alph_v$ and $a_1, a_2 \notin alph_v$ and $(r, \bowtie) \in \mathcal{K}^v$, then $\mathcal{K}'^v \ni (r, \bowtie)$;
3. if $r \in alph_v$ and $(r, a) \in \mathcal{K}^v$, then $\mathcal{K}'^v \not\ni (r, a)$, for any $a \in \mathbf{A} \cup \{\top\}$;
4. if $r \in alph_v$ and $(r, a_3) \in \mathcal{K}^v$ and $\bowtie \neq a_3 \neq a_1$, then $\mathcal{K}'^v = \mathcal{K}^v$;
5. if $r \notin alph_v$ then $\mathcal{K}'^v = \mathcal{K}^v$.

The third property guarantees that the condition on uniqueness of the assignment for a resource also holds for the verifier's knowledge, while the fourth one rules out the possibility of continuing observing configurations not compatible with a transaction or of maintaining inconsistent observations. Note that, if we denote with $\dagger_v$ for any v the configuration mapping $alph_v^{\mathbf{R}}$ to $\bot$, it holds that $obs_v(\dagger) = \dagger_v$; by contrast, it is not true in general that $obs_v(\mathcal{C}) = \dagger_v \Rightarrow \mathcal{C} = \dagger$, as $\mathcal{C}$ might contain assignments not observable by v.

Example 1. Let v be a verifier with $alph_v = \{r_1, r_2, a_1, \top, \bot, \bowtie\}$ and let $\mathcal{K}^v = obs_v(\mathcal{C})$. When v receives a public announcement p of the (effective) execution of $Trn = \{(r_1, a_1, a_2), (r_2, a_2, a_1)\}$ on $\mathcal{C}$, then its knowledge $\mathcal{K}^v$ is updated to $\mathcal{K}'^v = (\mathcal{K}^v \setminus \{(r_1, a_1), (r_2, \bowtie)\}) \cup \{(r_2, a_1), (r_1, \bowtie)\}$.

Proposition 1. *Let v be an arbitrary verifier on $CONF_{\mathbf{A}}^{\mathbf{R}}$ and let $\mathcal{C}, \mathcal{C}' \in CONF_{\mathbf{A}}^{\mathbf{R}}$ be such that $\mathcal{C}' = eff(\mathcal{C}, Trn)$ for some $Trn \in TRN_{\mathbf{A}}^{\mathbf{R}}$. Let $\mathcal{K}^v = obs_v(\mathcal{C})$ and let $\mathcal{K}'^v$ be the set of assignments constructed by v after the public announcement of Trn as indicated before. Then $\mathcal{C}' \in CONS_v(\mathcal{K}'^v)$.*

Proof. Suppose $\mathcal{K}'^v \neq obs_v(\mathcal{C}')$. Then there exist $r, a_3, a_2 \in alph_v, a_3 \neq a_2$ such that $(r, a_3) \in \mathcal{K}'^v$ and $(r, a_2) \in \mathcal{C}'$. But this cannot happen if all entities are in $alph_v$, due to the first property of obs_v. Conversely, if $a_2 \notin alph_v$, then $(r, \bowtie) \in \mathcal{K}'^v$, which would leave $\mathcal{C}' \in CONS_o(\mathcal{K}'^v)$, anyway. Since no other case can cause a disagreement between $\mathcal{K}'^v$ and $obs_v(\mathcal{C}')$, the proposition is proved. □

Note that there may emerge a situation in which a sequence of effective transactions is performed starting from a configuration $\mathcal{C}_0 \neq \dagger$ for which $obs_v(\mathcal{C}_0) = \dagger_v$. In this case, in correspondence with the sequence of configurations $\langle \mathcal{C}_0, \ldots, \mathcal{C}_n \rangle$, v would just keep observing the constant configuration $\dagger_v$. We say therefore that a verifier v *is invalidated* by a transaction which would reduce its knowledge to $\dagger_v$. Indeed, while $\dagger_v$ is consistent with all the configurations $\mathcal{C}_i$ (as none of them would change the assignment of a resource to $\bot$), v would not be able to perform any further verification distinguishing effective from non effective transactions. A transaction which does not invalidate a verifier v is said to be *compatible* with v. To summarise, observers maintain consistent knowledge of the evolution of configurations through the reception of public announcements, but they can verify their effect only as far as their knowledge is not reduced to $\dagger_v$.

3   Contracts on Resources

Based on the notions of configuration and transaction, we can now model contracts as a way of specifying admissible sequences of transactions/configurations.

Definition 5 (Contract). *With* **A** *and* **R** *sets of proper actors and resources, a contract over* **A, R** *is a tuple Cnt* = (*TRNS, enbl, Init, Hon, Brc*), *where TRNS* ⊆ *TRN*$_\mathbf{A}^\mathbf{R}$ *is a finite set of transactions, enbl*: *CONF*$_\mathbf{A}^\mathbf{R}$ → $\wp$(*TRNS*), *and Init, Hon, Brc* ⊆ *CONF*$_\mathbf{A}^\mathbf{R}$ *are finite nonempty sets of configurations such that enbl*($\mathcal{C}$) ≠ ∅ *for each* $\mathcal{C}$ ∈*Init, enbl*($\mathcal{C}$) = ∅ *for each* $\mathcal{C}$ ∈ *Hon* ∪ *Brc, and Hon* ∩ *Brc* = ∅. *The set of all contracts over* **A, R** *is denoted by CNT*$_\mathbf{A}^\mathbf{R}$.

Function *enbl* defines the set of transactions *enabled* in each configuration, whereas sets *Init, Hon* specify the admissible *initial* and *honoured* configurations *conforming to* the contract, respectively, and *Brc* specifies the configurations corresponding to a *breach* of the contract.

An admissible *execution* of *Cnt* is a pair ($\sigma, \mathcal{C}_0$), where $\sigma = \langle Trn_1, \ldots, Trn_n \rangle$ is a sequence of effective transactions and $\mathcal{C}_0$ ∈ *Init*, such that there is a corresponding sequence of configurations $\langle \mathcal{C}_0, \mathcal{C}_1, \ldots, \mathcal{C}_n \rangle$ with $\mathcal{C}_n$ ∈ *Hon* ∪ *Brc* and, for each i ∈ {1, ..., n}, Trn_i ∈ *enbl*($\mathcal{C}_{i-1}$) and $\mathcal{C}_i = eff(\mathcal{C}_{i-1}, Trn_i)$. We say that *Cnt* is *honoured* after the execution ($\sigma, \mathcal{C}_0$) if $\mathcal{C}_n$ ∈ *Hon*; it is *broken* if $\mathcal{C}_n$ ∈ *Brc*. We denote the set of all executions which honour *Cnt* by *HNR*(*Cnt*) and say that a contract is *honourable* if and only if *HNR*(*Cnt*) ≠ ∅. Analogously, we use the notation *BRC*(*Cnt*) for the set of executions corresponding to breaches of a contract. The *semantics* of a contract *Cnt* is the couple *Sem*(*Cnt*) = (*HNR*(*Cnt*), *BRC*(*Cnt*)).

A verifier v is a *contract verifier* of *Cnt* = (*TRNS, enbl, Init, Hon, Brc*) if and only if obs_v(*init*) = *init*, obs_v(*hon*) = *hon* and obs_v(*brc*) = *brc*, for each *init* ∈ *Init*, *hon* ∈ *Hon* and *brc* ∈ *Brc*. Note that, for a contract verifier v of *Cnt* ∈ *CNT*$_\mathbf{A}^\mathbf{R}$, *alph*$_v$ only needs to include all the resources and actors involved in the initial and final configurations of *Cnt*.

Contract verifiers of *Cnt* evolve their knowledge through sequences of public announcements corresponding to executions in *HNR*(*Cnt*) ∪ *BRC*(*Cnt*).

Proposition 2. *Given a contract Cnt and a contract verifier v of Cnt, a sequence* $\langle p_1, p_2, \ldots, p_n \rangle$ *of public announcements associated with an execution of Cnt starting with* $\mathcal{C}_0$ ∈*Init and ending in* $\mathcal{C}_n$ ∈ *Hon*∪*Brc, with initial knowledge* $\mathcal{K}_0^v = obs_v(\mathcal{C}_0) = \mathcal{C}_0$, *will leave v with knowledge* $\mathcal{K}_n^v = \mathcal{C}_n$.

Proof. By iteration of the argument in the proof of Proposition 1, considering that, for any $\mathcal{C}$ ∈ *Init* ∪ *Hon* ∪ *Brc*, we have $obs_v(\mathcal{C}) = \mathcal{C}$ and that † cannot appear as an intermediate configuration in the execution of a contract.   □

Now, we can model the knowledge a contract verifier holds for a contract *Cnt* as the set PA_v(*Cnt*) of sequences of *expected* public announcements such that the first element of the sequence is compatible with its current knowledge of the configuration. With each *emitted* public announcement, PA_v(*Cnt*) is evolved to eliminate sequences in which transactions appear that invalidate v.

Example 2. Let us consider a contract *Loan* for a loan from *paul* to *steve* to be remitted, with interests, in five monthly instalments. The debt can also be closed at any month after the first by paying the remaining sum, without interests.

We model this via configurations of obligations (of the lender to provide the agreed sum, and of the borrower to remit the instalments), and publicly announced transactions representing discharges of such obligations (or failures to do so).

Let $\mathbf{R} = \{brk, lndOblg\} \cup \{[loanCnt, i], [hon, i] \mid i \in \{1, 2\}\} \cup \{[insOblg, i] \mid i \in \{1, \ldots, 5\}\} \cup \{[close, i] \mid i \in \{2, \ldots, 4\}\}$ and $\mathbf{A} = \{paul, steve\}$. The set $Init$ of initial configurations contains a single configuration $init = \{([loanCnt, 1], paul), ([loanCnt, 2], steve)\} \cup \{(r, \top) \mid r \in \mathbf{R} \setminus \{[loanCnt, i] \mid i \in \{1, 2\}\}\}$, stating that both actors agree on the terms of $Loan$, without having any obligation been assigned yet (nor, consequently, discharged).

The set of configurations for $Loan$ being honoured is $Hon = \{([hon, 1], paul), ([hon, 2], steve), ([loanCnt, 1], paul), ([loanCnt, 2], steve)\}$ (i.e., the loan has been lended and all obligations have been discharged, by remitting the instalments in the correct order, or closing at some month after the first).

The set of configurations modeling a breach of $Loan$ is $Brc = \{(brk, paul), (lndOblg, paul)\} \cup \{BRK_i \mid i \in \{1, \ldots, 5\}\}$, where $BRK_i = \{(brk, steve), ([insOblg, j], steve) \mid j \in \{i, \ldots, 5\}\} \cup \{([close, i], steve) \mid 2 \leq i \leq 4\}$, i.e., $Loan$ can be broken by $paul$'s not lending the money or by $steve$'s failing to pay an instalment when due or to close before the last instalment (we also add $\{([loanCnt, 1], paul), ([loanCnt, 2], steve)\}$ to each configuration in Brc).

Transactions express the discharge of obligations, abstracting away from actual amounts or the calendar for discharges. Hence, $TRNS = \{START, LEND, FSTNST, \ldots, LSTNST, SNDCLS, \ldots, LSTCLS, LNDBRK, RMTBRK\}$, with individual transactions named as follows:

- $START = \{(lndOblg, \top, paul)\}$
- $LEND = \{(lndOblg, paul, \bot), ([hon, 1], \top, paul)\} \cup$
  $\bigcup_{r \in \{[insOblg, i] \mid i \in \{1, \ldots, 5\}\}} \{(r, \top, steve)\}$
- $FSTNST = \{([insOblg, 1], steve, \bot), ([close, 2], \top, steve)\}$
- $SNDNST = \{([insOblg, 2], steve, \bot), ([close, 2], steve, \bot), ([close, 3], \top, steve)\}$
- $THDDNST = \{([insOblg, 3], steve, \bot), ([close, 3], steve, \bot), ([close, 4], \top, steve)\}$
- $FRTNST = \{([insOblg, 4], steve, \bot), ([close, 4], steve, \bot)\}$
- $LSTNST = \{([insOblg, 5], steve, \bot), ([hon, 2], \top, steve)\}$
- $SNDCLS = \{([close, 2], steve, \bot), ([hon, 2], \top, steve)\} \cup$
  $\{([insOblg, l], steve, \bot) \mid l \in \{2, \ldots, 5\}\}$
- $THDCLS = \{([close, 3], steve, \bot), ([hon, 2], \top, steve)\} \cup$
  $\{([insOblg, l], steve, \bot) \mid l \in \{3, \ldots, 5\}\}$
- $LSTCLS = \{([close, 4], steve, \bot), ([hon, 2], \top, steve)\} \cup$
  $\{([insOblg, l], steve, \bot) \mid l \in \{4, 5\}\}$
- $LNDBRK = \{(brk, \top, paul)\}$
- $RMTBRK = \{(brk, \top, steve)\} \cup \{([close, k], steve, \bot) \mid k \in \{2, \ldots, 4\}\}.$

Note that breaking a contract does not cancel the obligations still standing. Specific clauses can be devised to deal with them. Also, closing represents a possibility, not an obligation. Finally, the $enbl$ function is defined as follows[1]:

- $enbl(init) = START,$

---

[1] Remember that, by definition, $enbl(hon) = enbl(brc) = \emptyset$ for $hon \in Hon, brc \in Brc$.

- if $(lndOblg, paul) \in \mathcal{C}$ then $enbl(\mathcal{C}) = \{LEND, LNDBRK\}$
- if $([insOblg, 1], steve) \in \mathcal{C}$ then $enbl(\mathcal{C}) = \{FSTNST, RMTBRK\}$
- if $([insOblg, 2], steve) \in \mathcal{C}$ and $([insOblg, 1], steve) \notin \mathcal{C}$ then $enbl(\mathcal{C}) = \{SNDNST, SNDCLS, RMTBRK\}$
- if $([insOblg, 3], steve) \in \mathcal{C}$ and $([insOblg, 2], steve) \notin \mathcal{C}$ then $enbl(\mathcal{C}) = \{THDNST, THDCLS, RMTBRK\}$
- if $([insOblg, 4], steve) \in \mathcal{C}$ and $([insOblg, 3], steve) \notin \mathcal{C}$ then $enbl(\mathcal{C}) = \{FRTNST, LSTCLS, RMTBRK\}$
- if $([insOblg, 5], steve) \in \mathcal{C}$ and $([insOblg, 4], steve) \notin \mathcal{C}$ then $enbl(\mathcal{C}) = \{LSTNST, RMTBRK\}$

It can be easily inferred that the sequences of public announcements corresponding to sequences of configurations for $HNR(Loan)$ are:

$$\langle START, LEND, FSTNST, SNDNST, THDNST, FRTNST, LSTNST \rangle,$$
$$\langle START, LEND, FSTNST, SNDNST, THDNST, LSTCLS \rangle,$$
$$\langle START, LEND, FSTNST, SNDNST, THDCLS \rangle,$$
$$\langle START, LEND, FSTNST, SNDCLS \rangle$$

Similarly, the sequences of public announcements corresponding to sequences of configurations in $BRC(Loan)$ are:

$$\langle START, LNDBRK \rangle, \langle START, LEND, RMTBRK \rangle,$$
$$\langle START, LEND, FSTNST, RMTBRK \rangle,$$
$$\langle START, LEND, FSTNST, SNDNST, RMTBRK \rangle,$$
$$\langle START, LEND, FSTNST, SNDNST, THDNST, RMTBRK \rangle,$$
$$\langle START, LEND, FSTNST, SNDNST, THDNST, FRTNST, RMTBRK \rangle$$

For a contract verifier, maintaining knowledge of the current configuration of a contract means to know which worlds correspond to possible evolutions of the configuration. Hence, receiving a public announcement eliminates the possibility that an invalidated verifier can keep following the evolution of certain worlds.

Example 3. For any contract verifier v of *Loan*, $alph_v$ will contain not only brk, $[loanCnt, i]$ and $[hon, i]$ for $i \in \{1, 2\}$, but also $[lndOblig]$ and all the copies of *instOblig*, since they can all appear if an execution results in a breach. As an execution of *Loan* proceeds, a contract verifier of *Loan* will only accept as compatible with reaching a final configuration of *Loan* worlds where, after each public announcement, a transaction in *enbl* is expected.

We are therefore looking for a language able to express such properties in this model. To this aim, we introduce an algebraic model whose internal logic can support a set of modal operators both of temporal and epistemic kind.

4   Logical Background

We recall here some definitions and results from [4] in order to subsequently present our model as an instance and an extension of the theory exposed there.

Let $\mathcal{B} = (B, \leq, \bigwedge)$ be a complete meet-(semi)lattice, i.e. a poset with all possible small non-empty meets $\bigwedge$. Under these hypotheses, we have binary meets (denoted by $\wedge$) and a minimum element $\bullet$, but also bounded joins, since we can define $\bigvee a_i = \bigwedge b_k$, where $a_i \leq b_k$ for every i and k. We also require the following distributivity property to be satisfied: $b \wedge \bigvee_{i \in I} a_i = \bigvee_{i \in I}(b \wedge a_i)$, i.e., binary meets do distribute over joins (when they exist).

Definition 6 (Category on a complete meet-semilattice). *Given a complete meet-semilattice $\mathcal{B} = (B, \leq, \bigwedge)$, a category $\mathbf{C}$ is a category on $\mathcal{B}$ (actually, a generalized metric space) when:*

1. *Each object $\mathcal{X}$ in $\mathbf{C}$ is a set X equipped with a $\mathcal{B}$-valued function $\iota_X : X \to B$ (extent) and a $\mathcal{B}$-valued relation $\alpha_X : X \times X \to B$ (agreement) such that, $\forall x, y, z \in X$:*
   - $\iota_X(x) = \alpha_X(x, x)$ *(reflexivity)*
   - $\alpha_X(x, y) \wedge \alpha_X(y, z) \leq \alpha_X(x, z)$ *(transitivity)*
   - $\alpha_X(x, y) = \alpha_X(y, x)$ *(symmetry).*
2. *A morphism in $\mathbf{C}$ is a function $f : \mathcal{X} \to \mathcal{Y}$ (induced by the function $f : X \to Y$ on the corresponding carrier sets) s.t. $\forall x, y \in X$:*
   - $\iota_X(x) = \iota_Y(f(x))$.
   - $\alpha_X(x, y) \leq \alpha_Y(f(x), f(y))$.
3. *Composition is function composition.*

Intuitively, an object $\mathcal{X}$ is a set of $\mathcal{B}$-labeled elements, allowed to be equal up to α_X. We call L_B the category on $\mathcal{B}$ of categories on a complete meet-semilattice $\mathcal{B}$ with their functors. A subobject $\mathcal{X}'$ of $\mathcal{X}$ is a subset of $\mathcal{B}$-labeled elements in $\mathcal{X}$ such that $\alpha_{X'}$ is contained in α_X as a $\mathcal{B}$-valued relation. We denote with $Sub(\mathcal{X})$ the subcategory of all the subobjects of $\mathcal{X}$ with monos between them.

Fact 1. *If $\mathcal{B}$ is a complete meet-semilattice with the distributive property as above, then, L_B is a Heyting category [4].*

It is well known [14] that an *infinitary Heyting first order logic* can be associated with a Heyting category. Connectives are interpreted via the algebraic operations and quantifiers via functors Π and Σ, right and left adjoints to the pullback functors.

In our case, for every object $\mathcal{X}$ in L_B, $Sub(\mathcal{X})$ is a Heyting algebra in such a way that $Sub : L_B^{op} \to \mathbf{H}$, where $\mathbf{H}$ is the category of Heyting algebras with their homomorphisms, is a functor, and for every $f : J \to I$ in L_B, the functor $f^* = Sub(f) : Sub(I) \to Sub(J)$ has both left and right adjoint, $\exists_f$ and $\forall_f$, satisfying the Beck-Chevalley condition[2]. Hence, Sub is a Heyting doctrine.

With every object $\mathcal{X}$ in L_B we associate the algebras $uSub(\mathcal{X})$ and $dSub(\mathcal{X})$, alongside with $Sub(\mathcal{X})$. These new algebras are obtained by closing the subobjects of $\mathcal{X}$ with respect to the prefix (resp. prolongation) relation (see Definition 7); the prolongation of a label is intuitively associated with time flow.

---

[2] Given a pullback square $gq = fp$ in L_B and $x \in Sub(J)$, the canonical morphisms $g^* \forall_f(x) \to \forall_q p^*(x)$ and $\exists_q p^*(x) \to g^* \exists_f(x)$ are iso.

Definition 7 (Prefix/prolongation/closedness). *Let $\mathcal{X}$ be an object in L_B.*

- *Given two elements x and x' in $\mathcal{X}$, we say that x is a* prefix *of x' (or x' is a* prolongation *of x), in symbols $x \preccurlyeq x'$ (resp. $x' \succcurlyeq x$), iff $\iota(x) = \alpha(x', x)$.*
- *$\mathcal{X}'$ is an up- (or down-)closed subobject of $\mathcal{X}$ iff, for every $x' \in \mathcal{X}, x \in \mathcal{X}$ s.t. $x \preccurlyeq x'$ (resp. $x' \succcurlyeq x$) in $\mathcal{X}$, then $x \in \mathcal{X}'$ and $x \preccurlyeq x'$ (resp. $x' \succcurlyeq x$) in $\mathcal{X}'$.*
- *$uSub(\mathcal{X})$ ($dSub(\mathcal{X})$) is the family of up- (resp. down-)closed subobjects of $\mathcal{X}$.*

In order to prove that from this situation a modal/temporal doctrine, in the sense of [4], arises for $Sub(\mathcal{X})$, one has to define suitable operators that can provide adjoints to injections. This is realised by defining (see [4] for details):

- $\spadesuit_{\mathcal{X}} \mathcal{X}'$ as the minimum up-closed subobject of $\mathcal{X}$ containing $\mathcal{X}'$.
- $\triangle_{\mathcal{X}} \mathcal{X}'$ as the maximum up-closed subobject of $\mathcal{X}$ contained into $\mathcal{X}'$.
- $\heartsuit_{\mathcal{X}} \mathcal{X}'$ as the minimum down-closed subobject of $\mathcal{X}$ containing $\mathcal{X}'$.
- $\triangledown_{\mathcal{X}} \mathcal{X}'$ as the maximum down-closed subobject of $\mathcal{X}$ contained into $\mathcal{X}'$.

Correspondingly, we can extend our first order logic with four modal/temporal operators $\lozenge^u, \square^u, \lozenge^d, \square^d$ to be interpreted in the L_B operators above. In other words: a modal operator like $\lozenge$ (resp. $\square$) is a closure (resp. interior) operator. Prefix and prolongation relations are used as past and future accessibility relations. Let w be an element (world) in $\mathcal{X}$, we define satisfiability as follows:

- $w \models_{\mathcal{X}} \phi$ *iff* $w \in |\phi|$ (i.e. its terminal state enjoys ϕ), where $|\phi|$ is the interpretation of the formula ϕ.
- $w \models_{\mathcal{X}} \lozenge^d \phi$ *iff* $\exists w'(w \preccurlyeq w' \wedge w' \models_{\mathcal{X}} \phi)$. This is equivalent to $w \in \heartsuit_{\mathcal{X}} |\phi|$, i.e, "there is a past of w in which ϕ is true".
- $w \models_{\mathcal{X}} \square^d \phi$ *iff* $\forall w'(w \preccurlyeq w' \Rightarrow w' \models_{\mathcal{X}} \phi)$. This is equivalent to $w \in \triangledown_{\mathcal{X}} |\phi|$ i.e., "in all possible futures of w, ϕ is true".
- $w \models_{\mathcal{X}} \lozenge^u \phi$ *iff* $\exists w'(w' \preccurlyeq w \wedge w' \models_{\mathcal{X}} \phi)$. This is equivalent to $w \in \spadesuit_{\mathcal{X}} |\phi|$, i.e, "there is a future of w in which ϕ is true".
- $w \models_{\mathcal{X}} \square^u \phi$ *iff* $\forall w'(w' \preccurlyeq w \Rightarrow w' \models_{\mathcal{X}} \phi)$. This is equivalent to $w \in \triangle_{\mathcal{X}} |\phi|$, i.e, "for every possible past of w, ϕ is true".

All this can be summarized by the following Fact:

Fact 2. *The diagram $i^u : uSub \to Sub \leftarrow dSub : i^d$ is a modal/temporal doctrine for Sub in L_B (see [4] for details).*

5   A Model for the Language of Transactions

In this section, we first define the algebraic structure of the model $\mathcal{M}$, in which the language of transactions will be interpreted, as a subcategory of an instance of L_B, and then the logics associated with it. Let us remark that the partiality of the alphabet "visible" by a verifier introduces the necessary nondeterminism in our model, so that it makes sense to speak about agreement between two worlds, once they are observed. To this end, we abstract away from the actual mechanism by which a verifier updates its knowledge, and substitute the notion of verifier with that of an *observer* which is aware of the possible worlds whose evolution it can observe. In this view, for a verifier v to reach the $\dagger_v$ configuration is equivalent, for an observer, to ignoring, in evaluating a formula, the possible worlds in which effective transactions continue to occur after $\dagger_v$ has been reached.

Due to the evolution of labels (actually the series of public announcements), in our objects we have both a *temporal* structure and a *distributed* one; hence, we can introduce all the modal/temporal operators we had in Sect. 4 as well as introduce, in the same vein, another set of modal/epistemic operators.

5.1   The Algebraic Structure of $Sub(\mathcal{U}_o)$

Let U denote a *universe*, i.e., a set whose elements are called *worlds*, as above. Given a couple of sets $\mathbf{A}, \mathbf{R}$ as in Sect. 2, let us consider the set of admissible *strings* of configurations in $CONF_{\mathbf{A}}^{\mathbf{R}}$, i.e. the sequences of configurations $\langle \mathcal{C}_0, \mathcal{C}_1 \ldots, \mathcal{C}_n \rangle$ such that, for all $i \in \{1, \ldots, n-1\}$, $\mathcal{C}_{i+1} = \mathit{eff}(\mathcal{C}_i, Trn)$, for some $Trn \in TRN_{\mathbf{A}}^{\mathbf{R}}$. Let o be an observer on U, associated with an alphabet $\mathbf{A}_{env} \cup \{\bowtie\} \subseteq \mathit{alph}_o \subseteq \mathbf{A} \cup \mathbf{A}_{env} \cup \{\bowtie\} \cup \mathbf{R}$ and a function $\mathit{obs}_o : \wp(CONF_{\mathbf{A}}^{\mathbf{R}}) \to \wp(CONF_{\mathbf{A}\bowtie}^{\mathbf{R}})$, defined as obs_v in Sect. 2. Then, parallel to any admissible sequence of configurations $cSeq = \langle \mathcal{C}_0, \mathcal{C}_1, \ldots, \mathcal{C}_n \rangle$, for each o we identify the sequence $oSeq_o = \langle \mathcal{K}_0^o, \mathcal{K}_1^o, \ldots, \mathcal{K}_n^o \rangle$ where $\mathcal{K}_i^o = \mathit{obs}_o(\mathcal{C}_i)$ for all $i \in \{0, 1, \ldots, n\}$. We denote by $B(\mathbf{A}, \mathbf{R}, o)$ the set of all such sequences, given o. We call a sequence in $B(\mathbf{A}, \mathbf{R}, o)$ a *string of observable configurations for o*. Once o is fixed, we simply denote $B(\mathbf{A}, \mathbf{R}, o)$ by $B(\mathbf{A}, \mathbf{R})$. Sequences in $B(\mathbf{A}, \mathbf{R})$ are ordered by the prefix relation, thus forming a locally complete meet-semilattice $\mathbf{B} = (B(\mathbf{A}, \mathbf{R}), \bigwedge)$. The coherence condition and the restriction to a given alphabet are preserved by considering prefixes. As in the general case, prolongation of strings is intuitively related to time flow and defines a temporal accessibility relation. On the other hand, B will be the locally complete meet-semilattice containing all the $B(\mathbf{A}, \mathbf{R}, o)$ for any o. Given an observer o, we also associate with it an *accessibility* preorder relation $R_o \subseteq U \times U$, thus inducing, for each world $w \in U$, the pair of *classes* $w_o^+ = \{w' \in U_o \mid (w, w') \in R_o\}$ and $w_o^- = \{w' \in U_o \mid (w', w) \in R_o\}$. If R_o is symmetric, then $w_o^+ = w_o^-$ for each $w \in U_o$.

Summing up, the universe U, observed by an observer o, results provided with a *labeling function* $\iota_U : U \to B(\mathbf{A}, \mathbf{R})$; hence, $\mathcal{U}_o = (U, \iota_U, \bigwedge)$ can be thought of as an object of L_B and, as such, associated with a Heyting algebra $Sub(\mathcal{U}_o)$ (which is also a subcategory of L_B), whose elements are objects $\mathcal{X} = (X, \iota_X, \alpha_X)$ in L_B such that X is a subset of U and ι_X is the restriction of ι_U to X. Morphisms between them are monomorphisms in L_B, commuting with respect to injections into $\mathcal{U}_o$ so that they preserve R_o: if $f : \mathcal{X} \to \mathcal{Y}$ and wR_ow', then $f(w)R_of(w')$.

5.2   The Logical Structure of $\mathcal{M}$

What has been said about L_B in terms of connectives, quantifiers, logical laws, and modal/temporal operators can now be directly adapted to $Sub(\mathcal{U}_o)$. Moreover, we can also extend the modal logic associated with L_B described in Sect. 4 with a set of modal operators related to the new accessibility notion and the restricted category $Sub(\mathcal{U}_o)$. These operators are substantially taken from the classical epistemic logic treatment [12], rather than from the original presentation in [13], modulo some adaptation to our case.

We use transactions, as defined in Sect. 2, as atomic formulas.

Definition 8 (Language). *Given the sets* $\mathbf{A}, \mathbf{R}$ *and an observer* o, *the language* $L_\Phi(\mathbf{A}, \mathbf{R}, o)$ *of epistemic formulae on the knowledge of* o *with respect to* $\mathbf{A}, \mathbf{R}$ *is the minimum language which contains the following expressions:*

$$\phi ::= (p, i) \mid \neg(p, i) \mid \phi \wedge \phi \mid \phi \vee \phi \mid \Box_o^\star \phi \mid \Diamond_o^\star \phi \mid \Box_{(p,i)}\phi.$$

for every $p \in TRN_\mathbf{R}^\mathbf{A}$, $i \in \mathbb{N}$, $\star \in \{+, -\}$.

The intuitive meaning of the epistemic operators in $L_\Phi(\mathbf{A}, \mathbf{R}, o)$ is:

- $\Box_o\phi$: o "necessarily accepts" ϕ.
- $\Diamond_o\phi$: o "possibly accepts" ϕ.
- $\Box_{(p,i)}\phi$: after p has been publicly announced at time i, ϕ is true.

Let $\sigma = \langle \mathcal{K}_0^o, \mathcal{K}_1^o, \ldots, \mathcal{K}_n^o \rangle$ be a string of observable configurations for an observer o. We say that a transaction p is *in accordance with* $\mathcal{K}_i^o$ in σ, if for every $(r, a_1, a_2) \in p$, $(r, a_1) \in \mathcal{K}_i^o$ and $(r, a_2) \in \mathcal{K}_{i+1}^o$. We say that p is *in contrast with* $\mathcal{K}_i^o$ in σ if there are r, a_1, a_1', a_2, a_2' in $alph_o$, such that $a_1 \neq a_1'$, $a_2 \neq a_2'$, and there is $(r, a_1, a_2) \in p$ and, either $(r, a_1') \in \mathcal{K}_i^o$ or $(r, a_2') \in \mathcal{K}_{i+1}^o$.

For the moment, our model $\mathcal{M}$ will be $Sub(\mathcal{U}_o)$.

Definition 9 (Satisfiability). *The following clauses define the satisfiability of a formula* ϕ *according to a given world* w *with* $\iota(w) = \langle \mathcal{K}_0, \mathcal{K}_1, \ldots, \mathcal{K}_n \rangle$.

- $w \models_\mathcal{M} (p, i)$ iff p is in accordance with $\mathcal{K}_i$.
- $w \models_\mathcal{M} \neg(p, i)$ iff p is in contrast with $\mathcal{K}_i$.
- $w \models_\mathcal{M} \phi \wedge \psi$ iff $w \models_\mathcal{M} \phi$ and $w \models_\mathcal{M} \psi$.
- $w \models_\mathcal{M} \phi \vee \psi$ iff $w \models_\mathcal{M} \phi$ or $w \models_\mathcal{M} \psi$.
- $w \models_\mathcal{M} \Box_o^\star \phi$ iff $w' \models_\mathcal{M} \phi$ for all $w' \in w_o^\star$.
- $w \models_\mathcal{M} \Diamond_o^\star \phi$ iff $w' \models_\mathcal{M} \phi$ for some $w' \in w_o^\star$.
- $w \models_\mathcal{M} \Box_{(p,i)}\phi$ iff $w \models_{\mathcal{M}'} \phi$ where $\mathcal{M}'$ is the restriction of $\mathcal{M}$ to worlds w' where p is in accordance with $\mathcal{K}_i$.

Let us now look for a categorical characterisation of these operators.

Definition 10 (R_o-closedness). *We define the following:*

- $\mathcal{X}'$ is an o^+-closed (resp., o^--closed) subobject of $\mathcal{X}$ iff for every $x' \in \mathcal{X}'$ and $x \in \mathcal{X}$ s.t. $x'R_ox$ (resp., xR_ox'), it holds that $x \in \mathcal{X}'$.
- $o^\star Sub(\mathcal{X})$ is the family of $o^\star$-closed subobjects of $\mathcal{X}$.

Remark 1. In the case of a symmetric relation R_o, o^+Sub and o^-Sub do coincide.

Definition 11 (Modal R_o-accessibility operators in $Sub(\mathcal{U}_o)$). *We define in $Sub(\mathcal{U}_o)$ the following operators:*

- $\spadesuit^o_{\mathcal{X}} \mathcal{X}' = \langle X'', \iota_{\spadesuit^o \mathcal{X}'}, \alpha_{\spadesuit^o \mathcal{X}'} \rangle$ *where:*
  - $X'' = \{x \in X \mid \exists x' \in X'[xR_o x']\}$
  - $\iota_{\spadesuit^o \mathcal{X}'} = \iota_{\mathcal{X}},$
  - $\alpha_{\spadesuit^o \mathcal{X}'}(x', x'') = \begin{cases} \alpha_{\mathcal{X}'}(x', x'') & \text{if } x', x'' \in X' \\ \bullet & \text{otherwise} \end{cases}$
- $\triangle^o_{\mathcal{X}} \mathcal{X}' = \langle \{x' \in X' \mid \forall x \in X[xR_o x' \Rightarrow x \in X']\}, \iota_{\mathcal{X}'}, \alpha_{\mathcal{X}'} \rangle$
- $\heartsuit^o_{\mathcal{X}} \mathcal{X}' = \langle X'', \iota_{\heartsuit^o \mathcal{X}'}, \alpha_{\heartsuit^o \mathcal{X}'} \rangle$ *where*
  - $X'' = \{x \in X \mid \exists x' \in X'[x' R_a x]\}$
  - $\iota_{\heartsuit^o \mathcal{X}'} = \iota_{\mathcal{X}}$
  - $\alpha_{\heartsuit^o \mathcal{X}'}(x', x'') = \begin{cases} \alpha_{\mathcal{X}'}(x', x'') & \text{if } x', x'' \in X' \\ \bullet & \text{otherwise} \end{cases}$
- $\triangledown^o_{\mathcal{X}} \mathcal{X}' = \langle \{x' \in X' \mid \forall x \in X[x' R_o x \Rightarrow x \in X']\}, \iota_{\mathcal{X}'}, \alpha_{\mathcal{X}'} \rangle.$

Lemma 1. *All the operators in Definition 11 are monotonic functions (functors), and so are the injections:*

$$i^{o+}_{\mathcal{X}} : o^+ Sub(\mathcal{X}) \rightarrow Sub(\mathcal{X}) \leftarrow o^- Sub(\mathcal{X}) : i^{o-}_{\mathcal{X}}$$

Moreover, $i^{o-}_{\mathcal{X}}$ and $i^{o+}_{\mathcal{X}}$ have both left and right adjoint, namely (forgetting the index $\mathcal{X}$): $\spadesuit^o \dashv i^{o-} \dashv \triangle^o$ and $\heartsuit^o \dashv i^{o+} \dashv \triangledown^o$ such that

$$\spadesuit^o i^{o-} \simeq id \qquad \triangle^o i^{o-} \simeq id \qquad \heartsuit^a i^{o+} \simeq id \qquad \triangledown^o i^{o+} \simeq id$$

Proof. (Sketch) We have to prove that the definitions of $\spadesuit^o \mathcal{X}'$, $\triangle^o \mathcal{X}'$, $\heartsuit^o \mathcal{X}'$ and $\triangledown^o \mathcal{X}'$ can be extended to functors, and then prove the adjunctions. All the operators are monotonic and adjunctions formalise their representing minimal closure and maximal closed subobjects, respectively. These properties and the required isomorphisms are verified through simple inequations between subobjects. This is essentially due to the fact that, assuming that the accessibility relations are preorders, the operators result into closure (resp. interior) operators.   □

Lemma 2. *$o^+ Sub$ and $o^- Sub$ can be extended to Heyting doctrines in $Sub(\mathcal{U}_o)$.*

Proof. We first prove that $o^+ Sub$ and $o^- Sub$ are Heyting algebras: due to the adjunctions from Lemma 1, $o^+ Sub$ and $o^- Sub$ inherit unions and intersections from Sub. In fact, $\spadesuit^o \mathcal{X}'$, being a left adjoint, preserves unions and, being a left inverse, makes them the same as in $Sub(\mathcal{X})$. Dually, $\triangle^o \mathcal{X}'$, being a right adjoint, preserves intersections and, being a left inverse, it makes them the same as in $Sub(\mathcal{X})$. The same happens with $o^+ Sub$, using $\heartsuit^o \mathcal{X}'$ and $\triangledown^o \mathcal{X}'$. Distributivity holds because it holds in $Sub(\mathcal{X})$. It is now sufficient to show that, given a morphism $f : \mathcal{X} \rightarrow \mathcal{Y}$, the inverse image operator f^* can be restricted to the appropriate family and it has left and right adjoints. Since morphisms preserve accessibility, f^* preserves o^+ (o^-)-closedness, f^* restricted to $o^+ Sub(\mathcal{X})$ ($o^- Sub(\mathcal{X})$) has both adjoints, but they are not the immediate restrictions of those in $Sub(\mathcal{X})$: we need to compose the general ones with the suitable closure operators and restrict the result.

$$\Sigma_f^{o-} = \spadesuit^o \circ \Sigma_f \circ i^{o-}, \Pi_f^{o-} = \triangle^o \circ \Pi_f \circ i^{o-},$$
$$\Sigma_f^{o+} = \heartsuit^o \circ \Sigma_f \circ i^{o+}, \Pi_f^{o+} = \triangledown^o \circ \Pi_f \circ i^{o+}$$

With these definitions, the adjointness result is routine.   □

Theorem 1. *If we interpret a formula with the subobject satisfying it, then the operators above are categorically characterizable as follows:*

1. *The interpretation of $\square_o^-$ and $\triangle^o$ is the right adjoint to the inclusion $o^- Sub(\mathcal{X}) \to Sub(\mathcal{X})$, for every $\mathcal{X}$ in $\mathcal{M}$.*
2. *The interpretation of $\lozenge_o^-$ and $\spadesuit^o$ is the left adjoint.*
3. *The interpretation of $\square_o^+$ and $\triangledown^o$ is the right adjoint to the inclusion $o^+ Sub(\mathcal{X}) \to Sub(\mathcal{X})$, for every $\mathcal{X}$ in $\mathcal{M}$.*
4. *The interpretation of $\lozenge_o^+$ and $\heartsuit^o$ is the left adjoint.*

Hence, the 4-tuple $(\square_o^-, \lozenge_o^-, \square_o^+, \lozenge_o^+)$ is a modal doctrine (see [4]).

For the "public announcement operator", we say that a subobject $\mathcal{X}'$ is "(p,i)-closed" if, for every $w \in X'$, p is in accordance with $\mathcal{K}_i$ in $\iota(w)$; $(p,i)Sub(\mathcal{X})$ is the algebra of the (p,i)-closed subobjects of $\mathcal{X}$.

Proposition 3. $\square_{(p,i)}$ *can be interpreted as the functor associating with $\mathcal{X}'$ its larger (p,i)-closed subobject, i.e., the right adjoint to the inclusion $i_{(p,i)}$: $(p,i)Sub(\mathcal{X}) \to Sub(\mathcal{X})$.*

We are now able to formalize sentences such as the one in Example 3 of Sect. 3. For example, we can express the fact that "necessarily in the future, after the announcement that the third instalment has been remitted, an observer o, which is a contract verifier of *Loan* and for which w is a possible world, will observe, in all the worlds accessible from w, that the expected configurations evolve by first applying one transaction out of the possible executions of *Loan*":

$$\square^d(\square_{(THDNST,5)}((FRTNEST, 6) \vee (LSTCLS, 6) \vee (RMTBRK, 6) \vee (RMTBRK, 7)))$$

This formula is true for all observers corresponding to contract verifiers of *Loan* (some of them might also be able to observe some $[close, i]$ resource).

More generally, a situation in which reaching the final configuration of a contract (on a transaction announced as (p,i)) makes it possible to start a new contract, whose possible sequences of observable configurations are represented by a formula ϕ, can be expressed as $w \models_{\mathcal{M}} \square^d \lozenge_o^+ \square_{(p,i)} \phi$.

If we consider a set O of observers, $\mathcal{M}$ should now accomodate all $Sub(\mathcal{U}_o)$ for $o \in O$. Other epistemic operators can then be introduced into the language.

Definition 12 (Extended Language). *Given* $\mathbf{A}, \mathbf{R}$ *and a set of observers* O, *the language* $L_{\Phi}(\mathbf{A}, \mathbf{R}, O)$ *of* epistemic formulae on the knowledge of O *with respect to* $\mathbf{A}, \mathbf{R}$ *is the minimum language containing the following expressions:*

$$\phi ::= (p,i) \mid \neg(p,i) \mid \phi \wedge \phi \mid \phi \vee \phi \mid \Box_o^{\star} \phi \mid \Diamond_o^{\star} \phi \mid \Box_{O'}^{\star} \phi \mid K_{O'}^{\star} \phi \mid D_{O'}^{\star} \phi \mid \Box_{(p,i)} \phi.$$

for every $p \in TRN_{\mathbf{R}}^{\mathbf{A}}$, $i \in \mathbb{N}$, $\star \in \{+, -\}$, $o \in O$, $O' \subseteq O$.

The intuitive meaning of the new epistemic operators is:

- $\Box_{O'} \phi$: for all $o \in O'$, o "necessarily accepts" ϕ (this is called $E_{O'}$ in [12]).
- $K_{O'} \phi$ is *common* knowledge, the iteration of $\Box_{O'}$ applied to ϕ (see [12]).
- $D_{O'} \phi$ is *distributed* knowledge when ϕ is necessarily accepted with respect to the intersection of the classes of all observers (see [12]).

Theorem 2. *The operators above are categorically characterizable as follows:*

1. $\Box_{O'}^{\star} = \bigwedge_{o' \in O'} \Box_{o'}^{\star} \phi$;
2. $K_{O'}^{\star} \phi = \bigwedge_{n \in \mathbb{N}} \Box_{O'}^{\star n} \phi$;
3. *The interpretation of* $D_{O'}^{\star} \phi$ *is the right adjoint to the inclusion* $O'^{*} Sub(\mathcal{X}) \rightarrow Sub(\mathcal{X})$, *where* $O'^{+} Sub(\mathcal{X})$ *contains all the* $\mathcal{X}'$ *closed w.r.t. all* $R_{o'}$, *i.e. all the* $\mathcal{X}'$ *that contain all the* v *s.t.* $vR_{o'}w$, *for every* $w \in X'$ *and* $o' \in O'$ *(dually for* $O'^{-} Sub(\mathcal{X})$).

Remark 2. Having an infinitary Heyting first order logic, we can use an infinitary conjunction on the parts of the model common to different $Sub(\mathcal{U}_o)$ for $o \in O$.

While we leave to future work a thorough exploration of these new operators, we just observe here that one can derive, for purely mathematical reasons, some relations as in Proposition 4, the proof of which derives from the fact that both operators, being right adjoints, preserve conjunctions.

Proposition 4. $K_{O'}^{\star}(\phi \wedge \psi) \equiv K_{O'}^{\star} \phi \wedge K_{O'}^{\star} \psi$ *and* $D_{O'}^{\star}(\phi \wedge \psi) \equiv D_{O'}^{\star} \phi \wedge D_{O'}^{\star} \psi$.

6 Conclusions and Future Work

A fundamental problem in distributed systems is the presence of inconsistent knowledge across different agents, and how to reconstruct a common knowledge of the global state of the system. We are exploring the potential of a categorical approach in the definition of a logic for reasoning about this kind of problems.

We have shown how a categorical modal/temporal logic, originally developed for reasoning about concurrent processes, can be adapted to an epistemic logic, concerned with notions of distributed and common knowledge, based on a "possible worlds" semantics. We have applied this logic to contracts, considering whether observers of a contract execution agree on its being honoured or broken. This opens the way to verification and validation techniques, for example to check if, given a certain sequence of transactions, these can be prolonged to be executions which honour the contract.

We foresee several developments. Instead of contracts in isolation, one can study problems arising from the interference of different contracts in which one or more actors are simultaneously engaged. In recurring contracts, such as insurance policies, the expiration of a contract enables its renewal, so that one should, in principle, be able to reason on consequences of contracts. Another natural development would be to provide a logic for reasoning about consensus on the composition of a blockchain, using a limited form of common knowledge, where some qualified form of agreement (typically majority) is required of observers on their knowledge of the sequence of transactions the blockchain has gone through. A logical treatment of the updates of blockchains has been recently proposed in [6], but without reference to aspects related to common knowledge.

Deontic logic, i.e., a logic in which intentions and obligations can be discussed, has also been proposed as an important tool in the evaluation of the feasibility of contracts and in the monitoring of their execution [1]. Work is under way, aimed at asserting whether the categorical structure we have devised in this paper can also support this particular form of modal logic. Under this respect, we remark that the ability of observers to distinguish successful and failed transactions can be useful when modeling *attempts*.

As a final remark, we mention that the line of work discussed in this paper resonates with De Nicola's recent work on smart contracts [20] as well as with his research on system modeling [2,7] and with his usage of modal logics to express and verify system properties [3,10,11].

Acknowledgements. Work partially supported by Sapienza, project "Consistency problems in distributed and concurrent systems". We thank the anonymous referees for indication on how to improve this paper.

References

1. Azzopardi, S., Pace, G.J., Schapachnik, F.: On observing contracts: deontic contracts meet smart contracts. In: Palmirani, M. (ed.) Legal Knowledge and Information Systems - JURIX 2018, vol. 313, pp. 21–30. IOS Press (2018)
2. Bernardo, M., De Nicola, R., Loreti, M.: A uniform framework for modeling nondeterministic, probabilistic, stochastic, or mixed processes and their behavioral equivalences. Inf. Comput. **225**, 29–82 (2013)
3. Bernardo, M., De Nicola, R., Loreti, M.: Revisiting bisimilarity and its modal logic for nondeterministic and probabilistic processes. Acta Informatica **52**(1), 61–106 (2015)
4. Bottoni, P., Gorla, D., Kasangian, S., Labella, A.: A doctrinal approach to modal/temporal heyting logic and non-determinism in processes. Math. Struct. Comput. Sci. **28**(4), 508–532 (2018)
5. Bottoni, P., Labella, A., Kasangian, S.: Spatial and temporal aspects in visual interaction. J. Vis. Lang. Comput. **23**(2), 91–102 (2012)
6. Brünnler, K., Flumini, D., Studer, T.: A logic of blockchain updates. In: Artemov, S., Nerode, A. (eds.) LFCS 2018. LNCS, vol. 10703, pp. 107–119. Springer, Cham (2018). https://doi.org/10.1007/978-3-319-72056-2_7

7. De Nicola, R., Di Stefano, L., Inverso, O.: Toward formal models and languages for verifiable multi-robot systems. In: Front. Robotics and AI 2018 (2018)

8. De Nicola, R., Gorla, D., Labella, A.: Tree-functors, determinacy and bisimulations. Math. Struct. Comput. Sci. **20**, 319–358 (2010)

9. De Nicola, R., Labella, A.: Tree morphisms and bisimulations. Electr. Notes Theor. Comput. Sci. **18**, 46–64 (1998)

10. De Nicola, R., Loreti, M.: A modal logic for mobile agents. ACM Trans. Comput. Logic **5**(1), 79–128 (2004)

11. De Nicola, R., Vaandrager, F.W.: Three logics for branching bisimulation. J. ACM **42**(2), 458–487 (1995)

12. Fagin, R., Halpern, J.Y., Moses, Y., Vardi, M.Y.: Reasoning About Knowledge. The MIT Presss, Cambridge (1995)

13. Hendricks, V., Symons, J.: Epistemic logic. In: Zalta, E.N. (ed.) The Stanford Encyclopedia of Philosophy. Metaphysics Research Lab, Stanford University, fall 2015 edn. (2015)

14. Johnstone, P.T.: Sketches of an Elephant: A Topos Theory Compendium. Oxford Logic Guides, vol. 1. Clarendon Press, Oxford (2002). autre tirage: 2008

15. Kasangian, S., Labella, A.: Observational trees as models for concurrency. Math. Struct. Comput. Sci. **9**(6), 687–718 (1999)

16. Lawvere, B.: Equality in hyperdoctrines and the comprehension schema as an adjoint functor. In: Heller, A. (ed.) Applications of Categorical Algebra, Proceedings of Symposium in Pure Mathematics of the American Mathematical Society, No. 17, pp. 1–14 (1970)

17. Magazzeni, D., McBurney, P., Nash, W.: Validation and verification of smart contracts: a research agenda. Computer **50**(9), 50–57 (2017)

18. Plaza, J.: Logics of public communications. Synthese **158**(2), 165–179 (2007)

19. Roelofsen, F.: Distributed knowledge. J. Appl. Non-Class. Logics **17**(2), 255–273 (2007)

20. Uriarte, R.B., De Nicola, R.: Blockchain-based decentralized cloud/fog solutions: challenges, opportunities, and standards. IEEE Commun. Stand. Mag. **2**(3), 22–28 (2018)

Types for Progress in Actor Programs

Minas Charalambides[iD], Karl Palmskog, and Gul Agha[(✉)][iD]

University of Illinois at Urbana-Champaign, Urbana, IL 61801, USA
{charala1,agha}@illinois.edu, palmskog@acm.org

Abstract. Properties in the actor model can be described in terms of the message-passing behavior of actors. In this paper, we address the problem of using a type system to capture liveness properties of actor programs. Specifically, we define a simple actor language in which demands for certain types of messages may be generated during execution, in a manner specified by the programmer. For example, we may want to require that each request to an actor eventually results in a reply. The difficulty lies in that such requests can be generated dynamically, alongside the associated requirements for replies. Such replies might be sent in response to intermediate messages that never arrive, but the property may also not hold for more trivial reasons; for instance, when the code of potential senders of the reply omit the required sending command in some branches of a conditional statement. We show that, for a restricted class of actor programs, a system that tracks typestates can statically guarantee that such dynamically generated requirements will eventually be satisfied.

Keywords: Concurrency · Actors · Liveness · Typestate

1 Introduction

Liveness properties state that a system will eventually produce an event of interest [5,33]. For example, a client may request exclusive use of a resource from a server, with the expectation that there will eventually be a reply indicating whether access has been granted or denied. Liveness properties are an important class of *qualitative* properties of open distributed systems and their models, and are relevant for the languages and logics for agents and coordination proposed and investigated in depth by De Nicola and his collaborators [17–19].

However, liveness properties are generally difficult to express and reason about; this is primarily because they are formulated over, and thus require reasoning on, sequences of runtime configurations. In addition, even elementary liveness properties may hinge on assumptions about *fairness*, which disallow the indefinite postponement of basic operations such as message dispatch [4].

Usually, type systems provide a straightforward way to capture *safety* properties of programs, i.e., properties which rule out executions that reach undesirable states. In contrast to liveness, safety can be established by analyzing single runtime transition steps. However, work in session types [43] has shown the feasibility of using a type system to establish certain notions of progress. These works

© Springer Nature Switzerland AG 2019
M. Boreale et al. (Eds.): De Nicola-Festschrift, LNCS 11665, pp. 315–339, 2019.
https://doi.org/10.1007/978-3-030-21485-2_18

apply type discipline to the use of communication channels in the π-calculus, and view issues of progress under the prism of session fidelity: communication protocols, and hence the types that describe them, are designed so that adhering participants never get stuck. Session types usually constrain cyclic communication dependencies on the level of the protocol itself, so that well-typed processes communicate in a manner that always makes progress [6,26]. However, as Sumii and Kobayashi remark [42], there is more to progress than breaking cyclic dependencies: *programmer intent* should be taken into account.

We are interested in guaranteeing that an implementation adheres to the programmer's intent on the delivery of certain messages. For example, the programmer may demand that whenever a client requests resource access from a server, it must eventually receive a reply. This reply does not necessarily need to come from the server process itself, but it does need to specify whether access to the resource has been granted or not. Certain bugs in the implementation can violate this requirement, for example, due to cyclic dependencies, or an omission of a message sending command by the programmer.

This paper presents a possible solution to the problem in the context of actors [2], which communicate via asynchronous message-passing. Our work is structured around a simple actor calculus that allows the programmer to specify how messaging requirements may be generated at runtime. We regard *progress* to be a persistent property on the (runtime) program state such that a configuration C satisfies progress if every execution trace from C ends in a state where all (dynamically) generated messaging requirements have been satisfied. We propose a type system to guarantee this property for every runtime configuration resulting from the program. We use the notion of a *typestate* [41] both at the language level and in the presented meta-theory, tagging actor names with the multiset of message types that the corresponding actor needs to receive. We therefore regard progress as the question of whether an actor eventually receives all the messages included in their typestate. The type system enforces that, for every requirement that appears at runtime, suitable action is taken: either it is fulfilled in the current scope, or it is delegated to another actor. By recursive reasoning, the type system guarantees that such a postponed requirement will be satisfied by the delegate actor. In essence, we show that in all executions of well-typed programs, all requirements generated at runtime will eventually result in the corresponding messages being received. In that regard, our typing can be seen as an effect system.

A preliminary version of this work appeared at the Workshop on Actors and Active Objects [16], in 2017. The present paper makes the ideas more precise, and discusses possible extensions. The most important shortcoming of the 2017 work is that the typing does not handle cyclic communication patterns. In order to keep the discussion of the key ideas clear, this paper inherits the limitation in the main presentation, and postpones an in-depth discussion with a possible solution until Sect. 6. Moreover, we do not clutter the type system with handling elementary safety properties, such as checking the number of handler arguments—those can be established by a separate type system.

Paper Outline. We first present, in Sect. 2, two example actor programs that demonstrate the usefulness of message requirements with regard to establishing progress. We then define our actor calculus formally in Sect. 3, with its abstract syntax and operational semantics. The type system is defined in Sect. 4, where we give example typings and discuss the system's limitations. The main result is proven in Sect. 5, where we show that executions of well-typed programs eventually satisfy stated requirements. Extensions for overcoming the system's limitations are discussed in Sect. 6. Lastly, we cover related work in Sect. 7, and conclude in Sect. 8.

2   Motivating Examples

We motivate our approach by discussing two simple programs, given in pseudo-code syntax reminiscent of Scala [29] with the Akka toolkit [28] for actors. Later, in Sect. 3, we will define a minimal calculus to make the underlying ideas precise. The first program, shown in Listing 1, embodies a resource sharing scenario among multiple clients via a central server. The second program, shown in Listing 2, implements a classic example from the session types literature, where two buyers coordinate to purchase a book from a seller.

2.1   Resource Sharing Program

In the resource sharing program of Listing 1, there are three kinds of actors: servers, clients, and resources. The clients attempt to acquire exclusive access to resources administered by the server, by repeatedly messaging it until they succeed. The server is responsible for responding to requests, by creating new resource actors and handing out their names, as permitted by system limits. The problem we consider in this example is how to ensure that (a) clients eventually receive some reply after a request, whether positive or negative; (b) resources are properly allocated and de-allocated; and that (c) allocated resources are eventually put to work.

Actors are defined by their *behavior*, i.e., how they respond to messages, and their persistent *state*. For example, server actors have handlers for request and done messages, and a count state variable that represents the number of available resources. The program initially spawns a server actor and two client actors, on lines 40 to 42. The two clients are each sent a start(s) message (lines 43 to 44), informing them of the name of the server s. The clients then send request messages to the server (line 19), to ask for resource access. Upon receiving a request message, the server checks if count is zero or less (line 3), and if so, it sends a later message to the client. If count is positive, the server spawns a new resource actor to which it sends a lock message (line 8) with the client and itself as the payload; then, it decrements count. The resource reacts to the lock message by sending ok to the client (line 33), who replies with a work message (line 22).

Listing 1. Example – *Resource Sharing.*   Listing 2. Example – *Two Buyer Protocol.*

```
1   Server(count : Int) = {
2     request(c : Client) =
3       if count ≤ 0 then
4         c ! later()
5       else
6         let rs = new Resource() in
7         let rs_ = rs.add_req(kill) in
8             rs_ ! lock(c, self);
9         update(count - 1)
10
11    done(r : Resource) =
12      r ! kill();
13      update(count + 1)
14  }
15
16  Client() = {
17    start(s : Server) =
18      let self_ = self.add_req(ok + later)
19      in s ! request( self_ )
20
21    ok(r : Resource, s : Server) =
22      r ! work( self, s )
23
24    later() = ...
25
26    done(r : Resource, s : Server) =
27      s ! done(r)
28  }
29
30  Resource() = {
31    lock(c : Client, s : Server) =
32      let self_ = self.add_req(work) in
33        c ! ok( self_, s )
34
35    work(c : Client, s : Server) =
36      ...
37      c ! done(self, s);
38  }
39
40  let s = new Server(1) in
41  let c1 = new Client() in
42  let c2 = new Client() in
43    c1 ! start(s);
44    c2 ! start(s)
```

```
45  Seller() = {
46    get_quote(title : String,
47              b1 : Buyer1,
48              b2 : Buyer2) =
49      let price = price_of(title) in
50      let self_ = self.add_req(yes + no) in
51        b1 ! quote(price, b2, self_)
52
53    yes() =
54      ...
55
56    no() =
57      ...
58  }
59
60  Buyer1(contr : Int) = {
61    start(s : Seller,
62          b2 : Buyer2) =
63      let self_ = self.add_req(quote) in
64        s ! get_quote("1984", self_, b2)
65
66    quote(price : Int,
67          b2 : Buyer2,
68          s : Seller) =
69      b2 ! ask(price, contr, s)
70  }
71
72  Buyer2(contr : Int) = {
73    ask(price : Int,
74        b1_contr : Int,
75        s : Seller) =
76      if price - b1_contr ≤ contr then
77        s ! yes()
78      else
79        s ! no()
80  }
81
82  let s = new Seller() in
83  let b1 = new Buyer1(11) in
84  let b2 = new Buyer2(5) in
85    b1 ! start(s, b2)
```

The requirements (a), (b), and (c) from above are explicitly embedded in the code via the use of the construct add_req. On line 18, we express that the client actor currently executing this line is required to eventually receive either ok or later. On line 7, add_req expresses the requirement that the actor whose name is stored in rs (a resource actor) must eventually receive a kill message, representing de-allocation. Finally, on line 32, we express that the resource actor executing this line needs to eventually receive a work message.

As it turns out, the stated requirements will be satisfied in all executions of the resource sharing program where message delivery and processing is not indefinitely postponed. With regard to the delivery of either ok or later to the clients, consider what happens when the server actor receives a request message. It is either count ≤ 0, in which case the server sends later to the client actor right away; or count > 0, and the client name is sent to the newly spawned resource actor (line 8), which sends it an ok message on line 33.

Note that if we omit some message sending operation, requirements will be violated; for example, leaving out the statement c!done(self, s) from line 37 would violate the requirement set on line 7, thus resulting in failure to de-allocate the resource. Consequently, satisfaction of requirements captures a form of progress for actor programs, by ruling out that certain actors wait forever for some specific message.

2.2   Two Buyer Protocol

The program in listing 2 builds on the two buyer protocol—a classic example found, e.g., in the work of Honda et al. [27]. The general idea is that two buyers need to coordinate to buy a book from a seller. The first buyer sends a quote request to the seller, who replies with a price. When the first buyer receives this quote, it tells the second buyer how much it is willing to contribute; then, the second buyer decides if the remaining amount is within their budget, and lets the seller know. In this example, the problem we consider is (a) whether the first buyer eventually gets a quote from the seller, and (b) whether the seller eventually receives a response to the quote.

There are three actor behaviors in the program: Seller, Buyer1, and Buyer2 . Execution begins with spawning one actor of each behavior, on lines 82 to 85. The protocol starts when the first buyer actor receives a start message with the names of the two other participants. The first buyer then sends a get_quote message to the seller actor with the title of a book (line 64). Requirement (a) is embedded in the use of add_req on line 63. In response to a get_quote message, the seller actor looks up the price of the title and sends it back in a quote message (lines 49 to 51). Notice the assignment with add_req on line 50, which captures requirement (b) by demanding either one of the messages yes or no.

The first requirement is easily seen to be fulfilled by the seller actor on line 51, assuming the price_of invocation on line 49 terminates. The second requirement is ultimately fulfilled by the buyer-two actor, which will either reply yes, or no, in response to the ask message from the buyer-one actor. Once again, omitting send operations will result in requirement violations; for example, omitting s!yes() from line 77 would have that branch of the conditional (line 76) to proceed without a response to the seller. As in the first example, it makes sense to demand that both branches of a conditional satisfy all stated requirements, perhaps via a different messaging path—in this example, via a yes or no (lines 77 and 79, respectively).

As both presented examples hint at, making messaging requirements explicit allows us to reason about the eventual delivery of certain messages—and to do so *statically*. Our approach is to reduce difficult parts of this reasoning to the checking of program conformance to a type system along the lines of process types [24,39]. If a program passes the check, it is free of the discussed progress issues.

3   Actor Calculus

Our calculus follows standard actor semantics; however, its syntax does not adopt the λ-calculus extension of Agha et al. [2] – instead, to capture the examples above, we allow behaviors to include message handler definitions. The intention here is the following: consider an actor α with behavior b, where the definition of b includes a handler h with parameters $x_1 \ldots x_k$ and body S. Then, the receipt of a message $h(u_1 \ldots u_k)$ by actor α will invoke the code S, replacing the formal parameters $x_1 \ldots x_k$ with the values $u_1 \ldots u_k$, and **self** with α. The reserved name **self** refers to the actor in which it is evaluated.

In what follows, we abbreviate sequences of the form $x_1 \ldots x_k$ with $\overline{x}$, sequences of the form $u_1 \ldots u_k$ with $\overline{u}$, et cetera. The calculus syntax is given in Fig. 1: programs P consist of a list of behavior definitions $\overline{B}$ and an initial statement S. An actor behavior definition includes a name b that identifies the behavior, variables $\overline{x}$ that store the assuming actor's state, and a list of message handler definitions $\overline{H}$. In turn, a message handler definition includes a name h that identifies the handler, a list of message parameters $\overline{x}$, and a statement S to be executed upon invocation of the handler.

Statements generally consist of single operations followed by another statement. For example, $x!h(\overline{e})$.S sends a message for handler h of the actor x, with argument list $\overline{e}$, and then proceeds as S. The statement $\nu x{:}b(\overline{e})$.S creates a new actor (whose name is bound to x in S) with behavior b and initial state variables set to the values of the expressions $\overline{e}$. The statement **update**$(\overline{e})$ updates the values of actor state variables, and the **if** statement has the usual meaning of a conditional. A **ready** statement belongs to the runtime syntax, signifying the end of handler execution.

The call **add**(x, R) adds the requirement R to the list of requirements already associated with the actor x. Informally, to satisfy a disjunctive requirement $(h_1 + h_2)$ of some actor x, we have to send it a message labeled with either h_1 or h_2. Similarly, to satisfy a conjunctive requirement $h_1 \cdot h_2$, one has to send the actor two messages, h_1 and h_2.

3.1 Operational Semantics

To formalize the semantics of our calculus, we first define an algebra on the extended requirement syntax (including the empty, conjunction, and satisfaction rules of Fig. 1). The relation $\equiv$ on requirements is the least congruence relation that includes the rules of Fig. 2. The empty requirement ϵ is the zero element for $+$ (disjunction) and the unit element for $\cdot$ (conjunction). Reductions on requirements are defined in Fig. 3, and hold up to structural congruence. An empty requirement ϵ is always considered satisfied, and we say that the messages $h_1, \ldots, h_k$ satisfy a non-empty requirement R iff $(\ldots (R \div h_1) \div h_2) \div \cdots) \div h_k) \longrightarrow^* \epsilon$.

Furthermore, we assume a reduction relation on expressions, such that the notation $e \rightsquigarrow_\Delta u$ means that the expression e reduces to the value u, given static program information Δ. The latter is assumed to contain information extracted from the program, such as the parameters of message handlers. The transition relation for statements is defined in Fig. 4, where we write $S \xrightarrow{l}_\Delta S'$ to say that a statement S reduces to S' via l. The label l records the action being taken; for

$$P ::= \overline{B}\ S$$
$$B ::= \textbf{bdef}\ b(\overline{x}) = \{\overline{H}\} \qquad\qquad b \in \text{behavior names}$$
$$H ::= \textbf{hdef}\ h(\overline{x}) = S \qquad\qquad h \in \text{handler names}$$

$$
\begin{aligned}
S ::=\ & x!h(\overline{e}).S \\
\mid\ & \textbf{add}(x, R).S \\
\mid\ & \textbf{if}\ e\ \textbf{then}\ S_1\ \textbf{else}\ S_2 \qquad & e \in \text{expressions (values, function calls, etc.)} \\
\mid\ & \nu x{:}b(\overline{e}).S & \text{actor creation} \\
\mid\ & \textbf{update}(\overline{e}) & \text{state update} \\
\mid\ & \textbf{ready} & \text{[runtime syntax]}
\end{aligned}
$$

$$
x ::= \textbf{self}\ \mid\ x, y, z, \ldots\ \mid\ \alpha, \beta, \ldots \qquad
\begin{aligned}
& x, y, z, \ldots \in \text{variables} \\
& \alpha, \beta, \ldots \in \text{runtime actor names}
\end{aligned}
$$

$$
\begin{aligned}
R ::=\ & (R_1 + \cdots + R_k) & \text{requirement disjunction} \\
\mid\ & (R_1 \cdot \ldots \cdot R_k) & \text{requirement conjunction} & \quad\text{[runtime syntax]} \\
\mid\ & (R_1 \div R_2) & \text{requirement satisfaction} & \quad\text{[runtime syntax]} \\
\mid\ & h & \text{simple message requirement} \\
\mid\ & \epsilon & \text{empty requirement} & \quad\text{[runtime syntax]}
\end{aligned}
$$

$$
\begin{aligned}
C ::=\ & (\Delta, R, M, A) & \text{configuration} & \quad\text{[runtime syntax]} \\
\Delta ::=\ & \text{program information} & & \quad\text{[runtime syntax]} \\
R ::=\ & \{\alpha_1 \mapsto R_1 \ldots \alpha_\kappa \mapsto R_\kappa\} & \text{requirement map} & \quad\text{[runtime syntax]} \\
M ::=\ & \{\alpha_1!h_1(\overline{u}_1) \ldots \alpha_\kappa!h_\kappa(\overline{u}_\kappa)\} & \text{multiset of pending messages} & \quad\text{[runtime syntax]} \\
A ::=\ & \{\langle S_1 \rangle_{\alpha_1}^{b_1(\overline{w}_1)} \ldots \langle S_\kappa \rangle_{\alpha_\kappa}^{b_\kappa(\overline{w}_\kappa)}\} & \text{actor map} & \quad\text{[runtime syntax]} \\
& & u, w \in \text{values}
\end{aligned}
$$

Fig. 1. Actor calculus syntax.

$$\epsilon + R \equiv \epsilon \qquad\qquad \epsilon \cdot R \equiv R$$
$$R_1 + R_2 \equiv R_2 + R_1 \qquad\qquad R_1 \cdot R_2 \equiv R_2 \cdot R_1$$
$$R_1 \cdot (R_2 \cdot R_3) \equiv (R_1 \cdot R_2) \cdot R_3 \qquad R_1 + (R_2 + R_3) \equiv (R_1 + R_2) + R_3$$
$$(R_1 \cdot R_2) \div R_3 \equiv (R_1 \div R_3) \cdot R_2$$
$$R \div (R_1 + R_2) \equiv (R \div R_1) + (R \div R_2) \qquad R \div (R_1 \cdot R_2) \equiv (R \div R_1) \div R_2$$
$$(R_1 + R_2) \div R \equiv (R_1 \div R) + (R_2 \div R)$$

Fig. 2. Structural congruence on requirements.

$$(R \cdot h) \div h \longrightarrow R$$

$$\frac{R_1 \longrightarrow R_1'}{R_1 \cdot R_2 \longrightarrow R_1' \cdot R_2} \qquad \frac{R_1 \longrightarrow R_1'}{R_1 + R_2 \longrightarrow R_1' + R_2}$$

$$R_1 \cdot (R_2 + R_3) \longrightarrow R_1 \cdot R_2 + R_1 \cdot R_3$$

Fig. 3. Requirement reductions.

example, $\alpha!h(\bar{e}).S$ reduces to S, and $l = \alpha!h(\bar{u})$ records the sent message. The values $\bar{u}$ are computed from the expressions $\bar{e}$, i.e., $\bar{e} \rightsquigarrow_\Delta \bar{u}$.

$$\frac{\bar{e} \rightsquigarrow_\Delta \bar{u} \quad l = \alpha!h(\bar{u})}{\alpha!h(\bar{e}).S \xrightarrow{l}_\Delta S} \qquad \mathsf{add}(\alpha, \mathrm{R}).S \xrightarrow{\mathsf{add}(\alpha, \mathrm{R})}_\Delta S$$

$$\frac{\alpha \ fresh \quad \bar{e} \rightsquigarrow_\Delta \bar{u} \quad l = \alpha{:}b(\bar{u})}{\nu x{:}b(\bar{e}).S \xrightarrow{l}_\Delta S[\alpha/x]} \qquad \frac{\bar{e} \rightsquigarrow_\Delta \bar{u} \quad l = \mathsf{update}(\bar{u})}{\mathsf{update}(\bar{e}) \xrightarrow{l}_\Delta \mathsf{ready}}$$

$$\frac{e \rightsquigarrow_\Delta \mathsf{true}}{\mathsf{if}\ e\ \mathsf{then}\ S_1\ \mathsf{else}\ S_2 \xrightarrow{\mathsf{if}}_\Delta S_1} \qquad \frac{e \rightsquigarrow_\Delta \mathsf{false}}{\mathsf{if}\ e\ \mathsf{then}\ S_1\ \mathsf{else}\ S_2 \xrightarrow{\mathsf{if}}_\Delta S_2}$$

Fig. 4. Labeled transition semantics for statements. Expressions e follow standard semantics, and Δ is static program information.

The transition relation $S \xrightarrow{l}_\Delta S'$ is referenced in the program-level rules of Fig. 5, which transform runtime configurations. A runtime configuration C is a tuple (Δ, R, M, A), where Δ records static program information; R is a map from actor names to requirements; M is the multiset of pending (sent, but not received) messages; and A maps each actor name to a behavior, state, and executing statement. Elements of M have the form $\alpha!h(\bar{u})$, where α is the destination actor, h is the handler to be invoked upon receipt, and $\bar{u}$ are values constituting the message payload. We denote A as a set of elements of the form

$$\text{SEND}\frac{R(\beta) \div h \rightsquigarrow R' \quad R' = R[\beta \mapsto R'] \quad S \xrightarrow{\beta!h(\bar{u})}_\Delta S'}{\Delta, R, M, A \cup \{\langle S \rangle_\alpha^{b(\bar{w})}\} \longrightarrow \Delta, R', M \cup \{\beta!h(\bar{u})\}, A \cup \{\langle S' \rangle_\alpha^{b(\bar{w})}\}}$$

$$\text{RECEIVE}\frac{S = body(\Delta, h) \quad \bar{y} = params(\Delta, h) \quad \bar{x} = params(\Delta, b)}{\Delta, R, M \cup \{\alpha!h(\bar{u})\}, A \cup \{\langle \mathsf{ready} \rangle_\alpha^{b(\bar{w})}\} \longrightarrow \Delta, R, M, A \cup \{\langle S[\alpha/\mathsf{self}][\bar{u}\bar{w}/\bar{y}\bar{x}] \rangle_\alpha^{b(\bar{w})}\}}$$

$$\text{UPDATE}\frac{S \xrightarrow{\mathsf{update}(\bar{u})}_\Delta S'}{\Delta, R, M, A \cup \{\langle S \rangle_\alpha^{b(\bar{w})}\} \longrightarrow \Delta, R, M, A \cup \{\langle S' \rangle_\alpha^{b(\bar{u})}\}}$$

$$\text{NEW}\frac{S \xrightarrow{\beta{:}b(\bar{u})}_\Delta S'}{\Delta, R, M, A \cup \{\langle S \rangle_\alpha^{b_\alpha(\bar{w})}\} \longrightarrow \Delta, R, M, A \cup \{\langle S' \rangle_\alpha^{b_\alpha(\bar{w})}, \langle \mathsf{ready} \rangle_\beta^{b(\bar{u})}\}}$$

$$\text{ADDREQ}\frac{R(\beta) \cdot R \rightsquigarrow R' \quad S \xrightarrow{\mathsf{add}(\beta, \mathrm{R})}_\Delta S' \quad R' = R[\beta \mapsto R']}{\Delta, R, M, A \cup \{\langle S \rangle_\alpha^{b(\bar{w})}\} \longrightarrow \Delta, R', M, A \cup \{\langle S' \rangle_\alpha^{b(\bar{w})}\}}$$

$$\text{IF}\frac{S \xrightarrow{\mathsf{if}}_\Delta S'}{\Delta, R, M, A \cup \{\langle S \rangle_\alpha^{b(\bar{w})}\} \longrightarrow \Delta, R, M, A \cup \{\langle S' \rangle_\alpha^{b(\bar{w})}\}} \qquad \text{PROG}\frac{\Delta = info(\overline{\mathsf{B}})}{\overline{\mathsf{B}}\ S \longrightarrow \Delta, \emptyset, \emptyset, \{\langle S \rangle_{in}^{in()}\}}$$

Fig. 5. Labeled transition semantics for actor configurations.

$\langle S \rangle_{\alpha}^{b(\overline{w})}$, where α is the actor's name, b corresponds to its behavior, the values $\overline{w}$ constitute its state, and S is the statement the actor is currently executing.

We write $C \longrightarrow C'$ to say that the runtime configuration C reduces to C' via an application of some rule in Fig. 5. By extension, $C_1 \longrightarrow C_2 \longrightarrow \cdots$ denotes a possibly infinite sequence of configurations where each adjacent pair follows the transition rules of Fig. 5. Execution of a program $P = \overline{B} S$ then consists of a sequence of transformations that starts from the program's initial configuration. Such an initial configuration is created via rule PROG in Fig. 5, and it records information Δ from the program, associates no requirements with any actor, has an empty message multiset, and includes a single initial actor executing S. This actor has reserved name and behavior in, and no state variables. When $R = \emptyset$, we define $R(x) = \epsilon$ for all x; i.e., by convention, $\emptyset$ maps no requirements to any actor. We assume a straightforward extension of the requirement algebra to runtime configurations, as shown in Fig. 6. As always, reductions hold up to $\equiv$.

$$(R_1 \cdot R_2)(x) \stackrel{\text{def}}{=} R_1(x) \cdot R_2(x)$$
$$(R_1 + R_2)(x) \stackrel{\text{def}}{=} R_1(x) + R_2(x)$$
$$(R_1 \div R_2)(x) \stackrel{\text{def}}{=} R_1(x) \div R_2(x)$$

$$\frac{R \longrightarrow R'}{R \cup \{x \mapsto R\} \longrightarrow R \cup \{x \mapsto R'\}} \qquad \frac{R \equiv R'}{R \cup \{x \mapsto R\} \equiv R \cup \{x \mapsto R'\}}$$

$$\frac{R \longrightarrow R'}{(\Delta, R, M, A) \longrightarrow (\Delta, R', M, A)} \qquad \frac{R \equiv R'}{(\Delta, R, M, A) \equiv (\Delta, R', M, A)}$$

Fig. 6. Requirement algebra extended to requirement mappings and runtime configurations.

Rule ADDREQ deals with calls of the form **add**(β, R) by appending R to $R(\beta)$, the latter being the requirements already associated with β. Note the use of $\div$ in SEND: the rule adds the sent message to the multiset of pending messages, and reduces the requirements related to β, by re-mapping β to $R(\beta) \div h$. This corresponds to the fact that β will eventually receive h.

Only idle actors can receive messages [3]. Since statements take the form **ready** when completely reduced, RECEIVE describes an idle actor α receiving a message to be processed by handler h. The statement S to execute is extracted from the program information Δ, and on it, the rule performs substitution of current values for handler and state variables. These values are taken from the message contents $\overline{u}$ and actor state $\overline{w}$. Handler and behavior (i.e., state) parameters are looked up via the auxiliary function $params$. Rule UPDATE writes new values $\overline{u}$ to the state variables of α. Rule NEW creates a new actor $\langle \textbf{ready} \rangle_{\beta}^{b(\overline{u})}$ with unique name β, initialized with the given behavior b and values $\overline{u}$ for its state variables. Rule IF has the usual effect of deciding a conditional.

4   Type System

The typing rules are given in Fig. 7. As before, Δ records static program information (such as the abstract syntax tree) which is used to retrieve, for example, the body of message handlers. R maps names to pending requirements, and S is the program statement being typed. Judgments have the form $R \vdash_\Delta S$, read "under program information Δ and requirement map R, the statement S is well typed".

$$\text{T-Prog} \frac{\Delta = info(\overline{B}) \qquad \emptyset \vdash_\Delta S}{\vdash \overline{B}\, S}$$

$$\text{T-New} \frac{R \cup \{x' \mapsto \epsilon\} \vdash_\Delta S[x'/x] \qquad x' \text{ fresh}}{R \vdash_\Delta \nu x{:}b(\overline{e}).S} \qquad \text{T-Add} \frac{R_1 \cdot R \rightsquigarrow R' \qquad R \cup \{x \mapsto R'\} \vdash_\Delta S}{R \cup \{x \mapsto R_1\} \vdash_\Delta \mathbf{add}(x, R).S}$$

$$\text{T-If} \frac{R_1 \vdash_\Delta S_1 \qquad R_2 \vdash_\Delta S_2 \qquad R \equiv R_1 + R_2}{R \vdash_\Delta \mathbf{if}\ e\ \mathbf{then}\ S_1\ \mathbf{else}\ S_2} \qquad \text{T-Update} \frac{\forall x.(x \in dom(R) \implies R(x) \longrightarrow^* \epsilon)}{R \vdash_\Delta \mathbf{update}(\overline{e})}$$

$$\text{T-Send} \frac{\begin{array}{c} \overline{y} = actors(\Delta, \overline{e}) \qquad \overline{z} = actors(\Delta,\, params(\Delta, h)) \\ S_h = body(\Delta, h) \qquad \{x \mapsto R_1,\ \overline{y} \mapsto \overline{R}_2\} \vdash_\Delta S_h[x/\mathbf{self}][\overline{y}/\overline{z}] \\ R \cup \{x \mapsto (R_x \div (h \cdot R_1)),\ \overline{y} \mapsto (\overline{R}_y \div \overline{R}_2)\} \vdash_\Delta S \end{array}}{R \cup \{x \mapsto R_x,\ \overline{y} \mapsto \overline{R}_y\} \vdash_\Delta x!h(\overline{e}).S}$$

Fig. 7. Static typing rules.

Rule T-Prog types programs, writing $\vdash P$ to state that the program P is well-typed. The rule prescribes that $P = \overline{B}\,S$ is well-typed when, using the information Δ extracted from the behavior definitions $\overline{B}$, the statement S is well-typed under the empty requirement map. Rule T-New requires that the statement following the creation command be typed with no requirements associated with the new actor. Rule T-Add demands that the statement following the $\mathbf{add}(x, R)$ command is well-typed under an environment which includes the new requirements R for x. Per rule T-If, typing conditionals requires that each of the two branches satisfies the known requirements. Consistent with the fact that statements end in a construct of the form $\mathbf{update}(\overline{e})$, rule T-Update is the base case of the recursive typing algorithm: it demands that all requirements known in the current scope have been satisfied.

Typing the action of sending a message takes into account that the execution of the related handler may satisfy some requirements known in the current context. Thus, rule T-Send demands that the statement S following the send command must be type-able under a "reduced" requirement map, from which we have removed the sent message h, and the requirements satisfied by the body of h. These include some requirements R_1 associated with x, as well as some requirements R_2 associated with (some of[1]) the arguments $\overline{e}$.

---

[1] The careful reader might observe that the rule does not account for **self** being part of the message payload. Accounting for **self** in messages poses no additional technical difficulty, and is omitted to simplify the presentation.

```
bdef b₁() = {
    hdef h(z) = z!m().update()        [sends m to z and returns]
}
bdef b₂() = {
    hdef m() = update()              [empty update, does nothing]
}
νx:b₁()                              [creates x with behavior b₁]
.νy:b₂()                             [creates y with behavior b₂]
.add(y, m)                           [associates requirement for m with y]
.x!h(y)                              [sends h to x, with y in the payload]
.update()                            [empty update, does nothing]
```

Fig. 8. Example of requirement delegation.

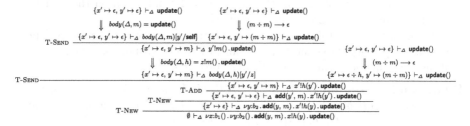

Fig. 9. Typing the example of Fig. 8.

To clarify the use of these rules, consider the example in Fig. 8, and the respective typing in Fig. 9. The program's main statement adds the requirement for a message m to y, but does not subsequently contain a $y!m()$ statement; rather, it sends $h(y)$ to x. When x receives that message, the requirement for m will be satisfied in the body of the handler, i.e., the statement $z!m().\mathbf{update}()$, with z bound to y. For this reason, when the typing reaches $x!h(y)$, it requires both the typing of the body of h, and the remaining commands—as in the application of rule T-SEND from Fig. 9.

5 Calculus Meta-theory

In order to establish our main result, we extend the typing relation to runtime configurations:

Definition 1 (Runtime Typing). *Let C be a runtime configuration. We say that C is well-typed, written $\vdash C$, iff C satisfies the rules shown in Fig. 10.*

$$\text{R-Transition} \frac{C \longrightarrow \quad \forall C'.(C \longrightarrow C' \implies \vdash C')}{\vdash C} \qquad \text{R-Ready} \frac{\forall x.(x \in dom(R) \implies R(x) \longrightarrow^* \epsilon)}{\forall s, b, \overline{w}, \alpha.(\langle s \rangle_\alpha^{b(\overline{w})} \in A \implies s = \mathbf{ready})}{\vdash \Delta, R, \emptyset, A}$$

Fig. 10. Runtime typing rules.

For a runtime configuration C, we write $C \longrightarrow$ to mean that there exists some C' such that $C \longrightarrow C'$, and $C \nrightarrow$ to mean that there exists no C' with $C \longrightarrow C'$. Note rule R-TRANSITION, which is defined with the intention of forcing the runtime typing to unfold program execution—facilitating the proofs of this section. For example, we can show that typing holds up to equivalence and requirement reductions (Fig. 6), captured by the next lemma.

Lemma 1. *The following rules hold true:*

$$\frac{C_1 \equiv C_2 \quad \vdash C_1}{\vdash C_2} \qquad \frac{R \longrightarrow R' \quad \vdash (\Delta, R, M, A)}{\vdash (\Delta, R', M, A)}$$

The rule on the left maintains typing along structurally congruent configurations. The rule on the right maintains typing after performing the operations $(+, \div, \cdot)$ on requirements inside R. The proof is by induction on the structure of runtime typing derivations, and is omitted.

The main result of this section is that during executions of well-typed programs, all requirements generated dynamically are eventually satisfied; that is, runtime configurations satisfy the *progress* property:

Definition 2 (Progress). *Let $C = (\Delta, R, M, A)$ be a runtime configuration. We say that C satisfies the progress property, written $\mathbb{P}(C)$, iff for all executions $C \longrightarrow C_1 \longrightarrow \cdots \longrightarrow C_k$ that start from C, we have $C_k = (\Delta, R_k, M_k, A_k)$ with $R_k(x) \longrightarrow^* \epsilon$ for all $x \in dom(R_k)$.*

We remind the reader that the initial configuration of a program P is denoted with $init(\text{P})$, and that $\longrightarrow^*$ is the transitive reflexive closure of the relation $\longrightarrow$. We can now state the main result:

Theorem 1. *Let P be a program. Assuming statements S terminate, $\vdash$ P and $init(\text{P}) \longrightarrow^* C$ imply $\mathbb{P}(C)$.*

The theorem states that all configurations reachable from the initial configuration of a well-typed program satisfy the progress property, notwithstanding the divergence of expressions (denoted with e in Fig. 1).

Proof Outline. The main idea is to show that

(i) well-typed programs generate well-typed initial configurations, that is, $\vdash$ P implies $\vdash init(\text{P})$;
(ii) the reduction relation of Fig. 5 preserves typing, that is, $\vdash C$ and $C \longrightarrow^* C'$ imply $\vdash C'$; and
(iii) well-typed configurations satisfy the progress property, that is, $\vdash C$ implies $\mathbb{P}(C)$.

In other words, we show that the typing of configurations guarantees progress, and that reduction preserves the progress property. We proceed to prove the above items in sequence.

Recalling that satisfying $R_1 \cdot R_2$ requires the satisfaction of both R_1 and R_2, we state—without proof—an auxiliary lemma, which can be shown by induction on the structure of runtime typing derivations:

Lemma 2. *If* $\vdash (\Delta, R_1, M_1, A_1)$ *and* $\vdash (\Delta, R_2, M_2, A_2)$, *then* $\vdash (\Delta, R_1 \cdot R_2, M_1 \cup M_2, A_1 \cup A_2)$.

The next lemma captures our intuition that the static typing of programs (per Fig. 7) implies that the respective runtime configurations are well-typed (per Fig. 10).

Lemma 3. *Let* S *be a statement where* **self** *has been replaced by a runtime name* α, *and let* A *consist solely of actors executing* **ready**. *Then, for any static program information* Δ, *requirement map* R, *behavior instantiation* $b(\overline{u})$, *and variables* $\overline{x}$ *with* $|\overline{x}| = |\overline{u}|$, *we have that*

$$R[\overline{u}/\overline{x}] \vdash_\Delta S[\overline{u}/\overline{x}] \text{ implies } \vdash (\Delta, R[\overline{u}/\overline{x}], \emptyset, A \cup \{\langle S[\overline{u}/\overline{x}]\rangle_\alpha^{b(\overline{u})}\}).$$

Proof. We proceed by induction on the syntax of statements.

<u>Base case.</u> From Fig. 1, the base case is that of the **update** call. Let Δ, R, A, α, $\overline{x}$ and $b(\overline{u})$ be as per the statement of the lemma. Moreover, fix values $\overline{w}$ with $|\overline{w}| = |\overline{u}|$. We need to show that

$$R[\overline{u}/\overline{x}] \vdash_\Delta \underbrace{\textbf{update}(\overline{w})[\overline{u}/\overline{x}]}_{\textbf{update}(\overline{w})} \quad \text{implies}$$

$$\vdash (\Delta, \quad R[\overline{u}/\overline{x}], \quad \emptyset, \quad A \cup \{\langle\underbrace{\textbf{update}(\overline{w})[\overline{u}/\overline{x}]}_{\textbf{update}(\overline{w})}\rangle_\alpha^{b(\overline{u})}\}).$$

Notice that the variables $\overline{x}$ do not appear in the values $\overline{w}$, and so the substitution $[\overline{u}/\overline{x}]$ leaves **update**$(\overline{w})$ unchanged. Assume $R[\overline{u}/\overline{x}] \vdash_\Delta$ **update**$(\overline{w})$ per rule T-UPDATE in Fig. 7, i.e.,

$$\forall y.(y \in dom(R[\overline{u}/\overline{x}]) \implies R[\overline{u}/\overline{x}](y) \longrightarrow^* \epsilon).$$

From the above and rule R-READY in Fig. 10, we have that

$$\vdash (\Delta, R[\overline{u}/\overline{x}], \emptyset, A \cup \{\langle\textbf{ready}\rangle_\alpha^{b(\overline{w})}\})$$

which, by R-TRANSITION, implies

$$\vdash (\Delta, R[\overline{u}/\overline{x}], \emptyset, A \cup \{\langle\textbf{update}(\overline{w})\rangle_\alpha^{b(\overline{u})}\}).$$

<u>Inductive step – message sending.</u> Let Δ, R, A, α, $\overline{x}$ and $b(\overline{u})$ be as per the statement of the lemma. Moreover, fix a message handler h, values $\overline{w}$, an actor name β, a statement S, a behavior instantiation $b'(\overline{u}')$, and variables $\overline{x}'$ with $|\overline{x}'| = |\overline{u}'|$. Assume that $A = A_1 \cup A_2 \cup \{\langle\textbf{ready}\rangle_\beta^{b'(\overline{u}')}\}$ for some A_1 and A_2 consisting solely of **ready** actors, and that $R = R'[\overline{u}/\overline{x}]$ for some R'. Also, assume that $S = S_0[\overline{u}/\overline{x}]$ for some S_0 where **self** has been replaced with α. Further assumptions on $\overline{x}'$ and $\overline{u}'$ will become clear in the next few steps. We need to prove that

$$R \vdash_\Delta \beta!h(\overline{w}).S \text{ implies } \vdash (\Delta, R, \emptyset, A \cup \{\langle\beta!h(\overline{w}).S\rangle_\alpha^{b(\overline{u})}\}).$$

Assume $R \vdash_\Delta \beta!h(\overline{w}).S$ was derived via an application of rule T-SEND, and thus

$$R = \underbrace{R_0}_{R_{01}[\overline{u}/\overline{x}]} \cup \underbrace{\{\beta \mapsto R_\beta, \overline{\gamma} \mapsto \overline{R}_\gamma\}}_{R_{02}[\overline{u}/\overline{x}]} \tag{1}$$

for some mapping R_0, requirements R_β and $\overline{R}_\gamma$, and $\overline{\gamma} = actors(\Delta, \overline{w})$. From T-SEND, it is

$$\underbrace{R_0}_{R_{01}[\overline{u}/\overline{x}]} \cup \underbrace{\{\beta \mapsto R_\beta \div (h \cdot R_1), \overline{\gamma} \mapsto \overline{R}_\gamma \div \overline{R}_2\}}_{R_{03}[\overline{u}/\overline{x}]} \vdash_\Delta S \tag{2}$$

$$\text{and} \quad \{\beta \mapsto R_1, \overline{\gamma} \mapsto \overline{R}_2\} \vdash_\Delta \underbrace{body(\Delta, h)[\beta/\textbf{self}][\overline{\gamma}/\overline{z}]}_{S'_h = S_h[\overline{u}'/\overline{x}']} \tag{3}$$

where R_1, $\overline{R}_2$, $\overline{\gamma}$ and $\overline{z}$ are as in rule T-SEND. From the inductive hypothesis, Eq. (2) implies

$$\vdash \left(\Delta, R_0 \cup \{\beta \mapsto R_\beta \div (h \cdot R_1), \overline{\gamma} \mapsto \overline{R}_\gamma \div \overline{R}_2\}, \emptyset, A_1 \cup \{\langle S \rangle_\alpha^{b(\overline{u})}\}\right) \tag{4}$$

since A_1 consists solely of **ready** actors. Applying the inductive hypothesis on Eq. (3), we get

$$\vdash \left(\Delta, \{\beta \mapsto R_1, \overline{\gamma} \mapsto \overline{R}_2\}, \emptyset, A_2 \cup \{\langle S'_h \rangle_\beta^{b'(\overline{u}')}\}\right) \tag{5}$$

because A_2 consists solely of **ready** actors, and the mapping $\{\beta \mapsto R_1, \overline{\gamma} \mapsto \overline{R}_2\}$ subsumes the substitution $[\overline{u}'/\overline{x}']$. Combining Eqs. (4) and (5) per Lemma 2, we get

$$\vdash \big(\Delta, R_0 \cup \{\beta \mapsto (R_\beta \div (h \cdot R_1)) \cdot R_1, \overline{\gamma} \mapsto (\overline{R}_\gamma \div \overline{R}_2) \cdot \overline{R}_2\}$$
$$\emptyset, A_1 \cup A_2 \cup \{\langle S \rangle_\alpha^{b(\overline{u})}, \langle S'_h \rangle_\beta^{b'(\overline{u}')}\}\big). \tag{6}$$

We apply Lemma 1 (reducing the requirements) to Eq. (6) to get

$$\vdash \left(\Delta, R_0 \cup \{\beta \mapsto R_\beta \div h, \overline{\gamma} \mapsto \overline{R}_\gamma\}, \emptyset, A_1 \cup A_2 \cup \{\langle S \rangle_\alpha^{b(\overline{u})}, \langle S'_h \rangle_\beta^{b'(\overline{u}')}\}\right). \tag{7}$$

We remind the reader that $\overline{u}'$ contains (among others) names in $\overline{w}$, and that S'_h is the body of handler h with the required substitutions. Thus, by rule R-TRANSITION, Eq. (7) implies

$$\vdash \big(\Delta, R_0 \cup \{\beta \mapsto R_\beta \div h, \overline{\gamma} \mapsto \overline{R}_\gamma\},$$
$$\{\beta!h(\overline{w})\}, A_1 \cup A_2 \cup \{\langle S \rangle_\alpha^{b(\overline{u})}, \langle \textbf{ready} \rangle_\beta^{b'(\overline{u}')}\}\big).$$

Since $A = A_1 \cup A_2 \cup \{\langle \textbf{ready} \rangle_\beta^{b'(\overline{u}')}\}$, the above can be written

$$\vdash \left(\Delta, R_0 \cup \{\beta \mapsto R_\beta \div h, \overline{\gamma} \mapsto \overline{R}_\gamma\}, \{\beta!h(\overline{w})\}, A \cup \{\langle S \rangle_\alpha^{b(\overline{u})}\}\right).$$

Applying R-TRANSITION again, the above implies

$$\vdash (\Delta, \ R_0 \cup \{\beta \mapsto R_\beta, \ \overline{\gamma} \mapsto \overline{R}_\gamma\}, \ \emptyset, \ A \cup \{\langle \beta!h(\overline{w}).S\rangle_\alpha^{b(\overline{u})}\}).$$

From Eq. (1), the above is the same as

$$\vdash (\Delta, \ R, \ \emptyset, \ A \cup \{\langle \beta!h(\overline{w}).S\rangle_\alpha^{b(\overline{u})}\})$$

which completes the proof for message sending. The rest of the cases are simpler, and are thus omitted in the interest of space.

Corollary 1 (Static Typing Implies Runtime Typing). $\vdash P$ *implies* $\vdash init(P)$ *for all programs* P.

Proof. Let $P = \overline{B}\, S$ be a program, and assume **self** does not appear in S (**self** does not make sense in the context of the initial actor). We apply Lemma 3 to $\emptyset \vdash_\Delta S$ and $\vdash (\Delta, \emptyset, \emptyset, \{\langle S\rangle_{in}^{in()}\})$ with $\Delta = info(\overline{B})$.

We now show that the reduction relation of Fig. 5 preserves typing:

Lemma 4 (Type Preservation). *Let* C *be a runtime configuration. Then* $\vdash C$ *and* $C \longrightarrow^* C'$ *imply* $\vdash C'$.

Proof. Assume $\vdash C$, which means that one of the rules in Fig. 10 (page 12) applies. If there exists C' s.t. $C \longrightarrow C'$, then $\vdash C'$ from the definition of typing rule R-TRANSITION. If $C \not\longrightarrow$, i.e., $C \longrightarrow^* C$, the only possibility is that C is a quiescent state, i.e., there are no messages to be delivered, and all actor statements have been reduced to **ready**. Per rule R-READY, C is well-typed.

Let C be a well-typed runtime configuration. Then, a derivation of $\vdash C$ according to the rules of Fig. 10 forms a tree with root $\vdash C$, such that every path on this tree is a sequence of applications of R-TRANSITION that ends in a single application of R-READY. On each such sequence, we focus on the configurations on the rule conclusions, say $C, C_1 \ldots C_k$. We write $Paths(\vdash C)$ for the set of all such sequences of configurations. As it turns out, $Paths(\vdash C)$ includes all possible executions from configuration C:

Lemma 5 (Typing Unfolds Execution). *Let* C_1 *be a well-typed configuration, i.e.,* $\vdash C_1$ *and* $C_1 \longrightarrow \cdots \longrightarrow C_k$ *an execution from* C_1. *Then,* $(C_1, \ldots, C_k) \in Paths(\vdash C)$.

Proof. Directly from Lemma 4.

Finally, item (iii) from the proof outline is captured in the statement below:

Lemma 6 (Runtime Typing Guarantees Progress). *Let* C *be a configuration. Then* $\vdash C$ *implies* $\mathbb{P}(C)$.

Proof. A derivation of $\vdash C$ follows the rules of Fig. 10, and hence, such a derivation ends in an application of rule R-READY. Thus, every sequence in $Paths(\vdash C)$ ends in some configuration C_k for which $\vdash C_k$ is given by rule R-READY. From the definition of the rule, C_k must be a quiescent state with no requirements. By Lemma 5 and the fact that $\vdash C$, every execution from C ends in such a state.

We are now ready to prove the main result:

Proof (Theorem 1). Direct consequence of

$$\vdash \text{P implies } \vdash init(\text{P}) \qquad\qquad (\text{corollary 1})$$
$$\vdash C \text{ and } C \longrightarrow^* C' \text{ implies } \vdash C' \qquad (\text{lemma 4})$$
$$\vdash C \text{ implies } \mathbb{P}(C) \qquad\qquad\qquad (\text{lemma 6}).$$

Error Programs. The progress property $\mathbb{P}(C)$ ensures that a configuration C reduces to a state where all requirements have been satisfied. The property implicitly captures the definition of *error* programs: those that can result in a configuration C for which $\mathbb{P}(C)$ does not hold. More formally,

Definition 3 (Error Program). *Let P be a program in the syntax of page 7. It is error(P) when $P \rightsquigarrow (\Delta, R, M, A)$ and there exists α for which $R(\alpha) \not\longrightarrow^* \epsilon$.*

In other words, an error program is one that can reduce to a configuration with non-empty requirements, and where no reduction rules (page 9) apply. Theorem 1 directly implies that well-typed programs are not error:

Corollary 2. *Let P be a program. Then $\vdash$ P implies that $P \notin error$.*

Proof. Direct consequence of Theorem 1 and Definition 2.

6   Augmented Typing

The typing presented so far is limited in some aspects. For example, it does not consider a requirement fulfilled, if the necessary messaging happens via state variables. To clarify this limitation, consider the program on the left-hand side of Fig. 11. It includes two behavior definitions, b_1 and b_2, with one handler each: h_1 in b_1, and h_2 in b_2. Execution starts with the creation of actor x with behavior b_1, and actor y with behavior b_2. Actor y is created with $b_2(x)$, i.e., storing x in the behavior (state) variable z. The program proceeds to associate the requirement h_1 with x, then sends $h_2()$ to y. When y receives h_2, it will send $h_1()$ to x. However, the presented type system will reject the program, because the typing rules for message sending do not consult with the actor's state. Doing so requires the static tracking of dynamically changing actor state, and is the topic of future research.

A perhaps more important limitation is revealed by considering the example on the right-hand side of Fig. 11. There, two actors exchange messages forever: actor x sends h_2 to y, which replies with h_1, and so on. The complication arises because both actors generate a requirement for themselves before satisfying the requirement they already know for the other actor: on line 3, actor x adds a requirement for h_1 to itself; then, on line 4, it satisfies the requirement h_2 for y, to whom it relies for the satisfaction of its own (just added) requirement for h_1.

Let us see what happens when we attempt to type the body of h_1. First, the system encounters the call **add**(**self**, h_1), which adds a requirement for h_1 to **self**, i.e., x. Because the remaining statement is $z!h_2$(**self**).**update**(), the typing will have to proceed via rule T-SEND. In accordance to the rule premises (page 10), we need to type the body of h_2. In doing so, we will eventually reach the statement **add**(**self**, h_2), adding a requirement for h_2 to **self**, i.e., y. The remaining statement (line 11) is $z!h_1$(**self**).**update**(), and T-SEND demands the typing of the body of h_1. Attempting to type h_1 essentially restarts the process, entering an infinite sequence of rule applications.

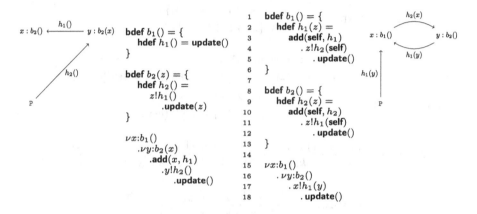

Fig. 11. Untypeable examples.

Note that, although the typing of Sect. 4 fails, this program has the discussed progress property, on an intuitive level: every generated requirement is eventually satisfied, even though a new one takes its place immediately after. The root of the problem with the typing of Sect. 4 is that the rules demand that obligation delegation be linear, in the sense that symbolic tracing of the code should not revisit the same parts in a circular fashion, to avoid infinite loops. As it turns out, this requirement is an artifact of the design of the typing algorithm, which was chosen to make the presentation easier to follow.

6.1 On Cyclic Communication

To detect that requirements are indeed satisfied even though new ones take their place, we can look at each **add** statement separately: by unfolding execution from the **add** statement onward, we can declare success if we find appropriate send commands before looping back to that same **add** statement. If no such command was reached and no more unfolding is possible, then we can safely assume failure. The problem of termination can be tackled by "remembering" the initial **add** call site and breaking the loop if it is encountered again. We make these ideas more precise with the rules in Fig. 12.

The rules assume that each **add** statement is associated with a unique token k, as in $\mathbf{add}(x, R)^k$. Rule AUGM-ADD-START bootstraps the process, with k carried along the relation $\vdash$, which unfolds execution. The algorithm only keeps track of one actor name x and its requirements R, and declares success if it loops back to the same k with an empty R (rule AUGM-ADD-END). Rule AUGM-SEND reduces the tracked requirements by the sent message h, as well as the requirements R_2 satisfied in the handler body S_h. Rule AUGM-DELEGATE reduces the

$$\text{AUGM-SEND}\frac{S_h = body(\Delta, h) \quad k, \{x \mapsto R_2\} \vdash_\Delta S_h[x/\mathbf{self}] \quad k, \{x \mapsto (R_1 \div (h \cdot R_2))\} \vdash_\Delta S}{k, \{x \mapsto R_1\} \vdash_\Delta x!h(\bar{e}).S}$$

$$\text{AUGM-DELEGATE}\frac{\bar{z} = params(\Delta, h) \qquad x \neq y \quad S_h = body(\Delta, h) \quad k, \{x \mapsto R_2\} \vdash_\Delta S_h[y/\mathbf{self}][\bar{e}_1 \times \bar{e}_2 / \bar{z}] \quad k, \{x \mapsto (R_1 \div R_2)\} \vdash_\Delta S}{k, \{x \mapsto R_1\} \vdash_\Delta y!h(\bar{e}_1 \times \bar{e}_2).S}$$

$$\text{AUGM-IF}\frac{k, \{x \mapsto R_1\} \vdash_\Delta S_1 \quad k, \{x \mapsto R_2\} \vdash_\Delta S_2 \quad R_1 \equiv R_1 + R_2}{k, \{x \mapsto R\} \vdash_\Delta \mathbf{if}\ e\ \mathbf{then}\ S_1\ \mathbf{else}\ S_2}$$

$$\text{AUGM-NEW}\frac{k, \{x \mapsto R\} \vdash_\Delta S[y'/y] \quad y'\ \text{fresh}}{k, \{x \mapsto R\} \vdash_\Delta \nu y{:}b(\bar{e}).S}$$

$$\text{AUGM-UPDATE}\frac{R \longrightarrow^* \epsilon}{k, \{x \mapsto R\} \vdash_\Delta \mathbf{update}(\bar{e})}$$

$$\text{AUGM-ADD}\frac{k_1 \neq k_2 \quad k_1, \{x \mapsto R_1 \cdot R_2\} \vdash_\Delta S}{k_1, \{x \mapsto R_1\} \vdash_\Delta \mathbf{add}(x, R_2)^{k_2}.S}$$

$$\text{AUGM-ADD-END}\frac{R \longrightarrow^* \epsilon}{k, \{x \mapsto R\} \vdash_\Delta \mathbf{add}(x, R)^k.S}$$

$$\text{AUGM-ADD-START}\frac{k, \{x \mapsto R\} \vdash_\Delta S}{\vdash_\Delta \mathbf{add}(x, R)^k.S}$$

Fig. 12. Augmented static typing for progress, overcoming issues with cyclic requirement delegation.

requirements of x when it is passed as an argument to the message h. Notice that AUGM-UPDATE demands that no requirements remain unsatisfied.

The difference from the system of Fig. 7 lies in the fact that the rules presented here are intended for application on each **add** call site independently, via application of AUGM-ADD-START. Endless looping is prevented by keeping track of the unique token k, and stopping when it is reached again (rule AUGM-ADD-END).

The Fairness Requirement. The typing strategy of this section only guarantees requirement satisfaction for fair executions [22], i.e., executions where enabled transitions are not infinitely postponed. Without this assumption, the program on the right-hand side of Fig. 11 would not be guaranteed to satisfy all generated requirements; for instance, $h_2(x)$ is not guaranteed to arrive at y, which is the only way h_1 gets sent to x after line 3.

The typing rules in Fig. 12 follow the rationale that after encountering an **add** operation, execution must reach a configuration where a suitable **send** transition is taken, i.e., rule SEND on page 9. One way that AUGM-ADD in Fig. 12 succeeds, is when the typing goes through rule AUGM-SEND, which removes the added requirement. In other words, for a statement **add**(x, R).S, rule AUGM-ADD succeeds if S contains a suitable send command. The silent assumption here is that all necessary intermediate transitions are taken, that the **send** command is reached, and the message is indeed sent. Note that such intermediate transitions can be ones where x is sent over as the payload to another message—captured by the typing rule AUGM-DELEGATE. In those cases, the typing must go through AUGM-SEND eventually, i.e., guarantee that a suitable **send** command is reached, even if in another actor's code.

7 Related Work

In mainstream programming languages, one expects that the arguments passed to a procedure are compatible with the way they are used in the procedure's body. Pierce and Sangiorgi [37] extended this idea to Milner's π-calculus [34], ensuring the proper use of communicable values. Their system guarantees that a value sent from one process to another can be safely used at the receiving end, including when the sent value is a channel name. Through a suitable subtyping relation, Pierce and Sangiorgi guarantee that after communicating the name of a channel, subsequent interactions through that channel recursively satisfy this same (safety) property.

Honda's early work [24] took a different approach, focusing on the typing of concurrent processes instead of channels. His system views types as descriptions of the sequencing of communication actions, and demands that composed processes have *dual* types. Duality corresponds to the sequencing of matching send and receive actions, ensuring safety and deadlock-freedom in two-party interactions. The idea was later applied to communication over π-calculus channels by Takeuchi et al. [43], an approach in turn refined by Honda et al. [25] and later by Yoshida and Vasconcelos [47].

These early works have been captured in practice by WSCDL, i.e., the Web Services Choreography Description Language [45]. In this language, one gives specifications of protocols involving multiple concurrent web services and clients, in XML form [44]. Its original purpose was to ensure standard safety properties: clients only use services that exist, and communicated data is well-formed. Nevertheless, WSCDL has served as the starting point for the treatment of protocol types from a global perspective. For example, Carbone et al. [9] introduced the notion of a *projection*—the restriction of a globally specified protocol onto the individual participants, assigning a type to each concurrent entity in the system. Then, type-checking can be performed on a per process basis, rather than having to look at the protocol as a whole. This idea was extended by Honda et al. [26], who allowed sessions to include more than two participants. In that and other similar systems, a *global type* describes the session protocol, and a projection algorithm mechanically derives end-point types for the individual processes— describing how each process uses the channels known to them. The system by Honda et al. ensures progress on a per session basis, under the condition that communication within a session is not hindered by actions in a different session, an assumption also made by Dezani-Ciancaglini et al. [21].

Subtyping for the system by Honda et al. was considered by Gay and Hole [23], and for the π-calculus in general by Castagna et al. [12], but without further progress guarantees. The assumption on the absence of inter-session hindrance was first lifted by Bettini et al. [6], who analyzed the flow of dependencies on the use of channels, tracking the sending of channel names and preventing cyclic dependencies. These systems have since been improved on to account for parameterized participant numbers, and to capture more complex protocols [14,15,20,46]. A different direction was taken by Carbone and Montesi [11], who allowed the concurrent program itself to be written from a global perspective, while statically ensuring the absence of deadlocks via a suitable type system.

Much like the present paper, some authors observed that deadlock-freedom does not necessarily guarantee progress in the intuitive sense, and have considered more general notions [8]. For instance, Kobayashi [30] identifies three important classes of channel usage, and guarantees a notion of progress for programs that use such channels. In general, Kobayashi's typing associates a time tag with each channel, inferred from the relative order of actions in which the channel is involved. In order to disable cycles, the type system then enforces an ordering relation on these tags. The use of a partial order to break cyclic dependencies is also found in the work of Padovani [36].

Sumii and Kobayashi [42] take these ideas further with the explicit inclusion of programmer intent in the code, so that channels are annotated with capabilities and obligations. The resulting type system ensures that if a process has the capability of performing an I/O action on a channel, that action will eventually succeed; similarly, if a process has the obligation to perform an action on a channel, the action is eventually taken. This strategy for deadlock-freedom is improved on in Kobayashi's later work [31], where even more precise information is used: channels are additionally associated with the minimum number of reduction steps needed until capabilities are met, and also the maximum number of steps required until obligations are fulfilled. The automatic inference of similar type annotations has also been considered [32].

Related to our approach is the work of Puntigam and Peter [39, 40], who allow actors to produce and consume tokens as a reaction to message receipt. Their typing only allows an actor α to be sent a message m when the handler for m does not consume more tokens than α has. The type system keeps track of the tokens known in each scope; the effect is that, after a send command, actors update their knowledge of the tokens associated with the recipient. Puntigam and Peter distinguish between optional and *obligatory* tokens, such that if an actor is aware of the existence of obligatory tokens in another actor, they need to ensure that these tokens are consumed—by sending those actors suitable messages. Puntigam and Peter's system focuses on breaking cycles of requirements, and it does so by imposing a partial order on obligatory tokens. A salient drawback of their strategy is that well-typed programs still allow passing obligations around in circles, never sending the required messages. It is worth mentioning that our system does not suffer from this drawback, while in fact employing a simpler typing strategy.

Similarly to in the work of Puntigam and Peter [40], object capabilities have been considered by De Nicola et al. [18], who investigate the connections between flow logic [35] and typing for a concurrent process calculus with localities. A generic approach that nevertheless does not provide static guarantees is given in the work of Abd Alrahman et al. [1], allowing processes to communicate with each other based on boolean predicates. In that system, processes do not address each other by name; rather, values are communicated among processes that satisfy the given predicates. From the semantics perspective (as opposed to static typing), many of the above calculi can be implemented using the basic primitives of Boreale et al. [7]. For an in-depth discussion on static type systems for concurrent programming, we refer the reader to the works of Charalambides [13] and Carbone et al. [10].

8   Conclusions and Future Work

We presented a type-based approach to ensuring progress in actor systems, allowing the programmer to state requirements on messages that an actor must eventually receive at runtime. To demonstrate the practical usefulness of our approach, we showed that such requirements can be naturally expressed in the classic example scenarios of resource sharing and book selling. We formalized the idea as a type and effect system for a simple language of stateful actors that communicate via asynchronous message passing, and proved that executions of well-typed actor programs will eventually fulfill all requirements that appear at runtime.

We expect that similar type systems and constructs such as add_req can be straightforwardly implemented in practical actor languages. However, as is common of decidable type systems capturing powerful properties in full-featured languages, such implementations will necessarily be incomplete—in the sense that there will be programs that fulfill all requirements, but where type checking cannot attest to this fact. Our system is no different in this respect, and relevant examples were presented in Sect. 6, where cyclic messaging patterns cause problems.

The restriction on cyclic communication patterns can be lifted to a great extent by considering each requirement generation site separately. This way, it is possible to remember each such site and avoid visiting it twice. To ensure our progress property, it is sufficient to match each requirement generation command with message sending commands guaranteed to execute. We presented a preliminary discussion of such extensions in Sect. 6; however, we leave the formal treatment of the augmented type system for future work.

Moreover, the typing accepts programs where requirements are matched by previously sent messages. This allows, for example, an actor to issue a computation, then add a requirement for the result. This is not always the intuitively expected behavior, and we leave a detailed treatment of such cases as future work.

Our type system is able to help programmers find simple but critical errors, such as the omission of a key message sending operation. However, in its present form, the type system does not deal with safety properties, even elementary ones such as ensuring that a message handler receives the correct number of arguments. We opted to not clutter the presentation with additional rules, to focus solely on issues of progress. It is nonetheless clear that such safety checks can be easily incorporated to this work as an additional type system, on top of ours. One can envision superimposing a number of more complex systems; one example is Puntigam's token system [38] which ensures that an actor has sufficient tokens to process the messages sent to it. Combining the two approaches would allow complicated coordination constraints to be statically expressed and enforced.

Acknowledgments. We gratefully acknowledge Rocco De Nicola for inspiration, criticism, and enduring influence on our work. We also thank the anonymous reviewers for their comments. This work was supported in part by the National Science Foundation under grants NSF CCF 14-38982, NSF CCF 16-17401 and NSF-CCF-1647432.

References

1. Abd Alrahman, Y., De Nicola, R., Loreti, M.: A behavioural theory for interactions in collective-adaptive systems. CoRR abs/1711.09762 (2017). http://arxiv.org/abs/1711.09762
2. Agha, G., Mason, I.A., Smith, S.F., Talcott, C.L.: A foundation for actor computation. J. Funct. Program. **7**(1), 1–72 (1997). https://doi.org/10.1017/S095679689700261X
3. Agha, G., Thati, P.: An algebraic theory of actors and its application to a simple object-based language. In: Owe, O., Krogdahl, S., Lyche, T. (eds.) From Object-Orientation to Formal Methods. LNCS, vol. 2635, pp. 26–57. Springer, Heidelberg (2004). https://doi.org/10.1007/978-3-540-39993-3_4

4. Agha, G.A.: ACTORS - A Model of Concurrent Computation in Distributed Systems. MIT Press, Cambridge (1990)
5. Alpern, B., Schneider, F.B.: Defining liveness. Inf. Process. Lett. **21**(4), 181–185 (1985). https://doi.org/10.1016/0020-0190(85)90056-0
6. Bettini, L., Coppo, M., D'Antoni, L., De Luca, M., Dezani-Ciancaglini, M., Yoshida, N.: Global progress in dynamically interleaved multiparty sessions. In: van Breugel, F., Chechik, M. (eds.) CONCUR 2008. LNCS, vol. 5201, pp. 418–433. Springer, Heidelberg (2008). https://doi.org/10.1007/978-3-540-85361-9_33
7. Boreale, M., Bruni, R., De Nicola, R., Loreti, M.: Sessions and pipelines for structured service programming. In: Barthe, G., de Boer, F.S. (eds.) FMOODS 2008. LNCS, vol. 5051, pp. 19–38. Springer, Heidelberg (2008). https://doi.org/10.1007/978-3-540-68863-1_3
8. Carbone, M., Dardha, O., Montesi, F.: Progress as compositional lock-freedom. In: Kühn, E., Pugliese, R. (eds.) COORDINATION 2014. LNCS, vol. 8459, pp. 49–64. Springer, Heidelberg (2014). https://doi.org/10.1007/978-3-662-43376-8_4
9. Carbone, M., Honda, K., Yoshida, N.: Structured communication-centred programming for web services. In: De Nicola, R. (ed.) ESOP 2007. LNCS, vol. 4421, pp. 2–17. Springer, Heidelberg (2007). https://doi.org/10.1007/978-3-540-71316-6_2
10. Carbone, M., Honda, K., Yoshida, N.: Structured communication-centered programming for web services. ACM Trans. Program. Lang. Syst. **34**(2), 8:1–8:78 (2012). https://doi.org/10.1145/2220365.2220367
11. Carbone, M., Montesi, F.: Deadlock-freedom-by-design: multiparty asynchronous global programming. In: Symposium on Principles of Programming Languages, pp. 263–274 (2013). https://doi.org/10.1145/2429069.2429101
12. Castagna, G., De Nicola, R., Varacca, D.: Semantic subtyping for the pi-calculus. Theor. Comput. Sci. **398**(1–3), 217–242 (2008). https://doi.org/10.1016/j.tcs.2008.01.049
13. Charalambides, M.: Actor Programming with Static Guarantees. Ph.D. thesis, Urbana, Illinois (2018). http://hdl.handle.net/2142/101036
14. Charalambides, M., Dinges, P., Agha, G.: Parameterized concurrent multi-party session types. In: International Workshop on Foundations of Coordination Languages and Self Adaptation, pp. 16–30 (2012). https://doi.org/10.4204/EPTCS.91.2
15. Charalambides, M., Dinges, P., Agha, G.A.: Parameterized, concurrent session types for asynchronous multi-actor interactions. Sci. Comput. Program. **115–116**, 100–126 (2016). https://doi.org/10.1016/j.scico.2015.10.006
16. Charalambides, M., Palmskog, K., Agha, G.: Types for progress in actor programs. In: Proceedings of the Workshop on Actors and Active Objects, Torino, Italy (2017)
17. De Nicola, R., Ferrari, G.L., Pugliese, R.: KLAIM: a kernel language for agents interaction and mobility. IEEE Trans. Softw. Eng. **24**(5), 315–330 (1998). https://doi.org/10.1109/32.685256
18. De Nicola, R., et al.: From flow logic to static type systems for coordination languages. Sci. Comput. Program. **75**(6), 376–397 (2010). https://doi.org/10.1016/j.scico.2009.07.009
19. De Nicola, R., Loreti, M.: A modal logic for KLAIM. In: Rus, T. (ed.) AMAST 2000. LNCS, vol. 1816, pp. 339–354. Springer, Heidelberg (2000). https://doi.org/10.1007/3-540-45499-3_25
20. Deniélou, P., Yoshida, N.: Dynamic multirole session types. In: Symposium on Principles of Programming Languages, pp. 435–446 (2011). https://doi.org/10.1145/1926385.1926435

21. Dezani-Ciancaglini, M., Mostrous, D., Yoshida, N., Drossopoulou, S.: Session types for object-oriented languages. In: Thomas, D. (ed.) ECOOP 2006. LNCS, vol. 4067, pp. 328–352. Springer, Heidelberg (2006). https://doi.org/10.1007/11785477_20
22. Francez, N.: Fairness. Texts and Monographs in Computer Science. Springer, Heidelberg (1986). https://doi.org/10.1007/978-1-4612-4886-6
23. Gay, S.J., Hole, M.: Subtyping for session types in the pi calculus. Acta Inf. **42**(2–3), 191–225 (2005). https://doi.org/10.1007/s00236-005-0177-z
24. Honda, K.: Types for dyadic interaction. In: International Conference on Concurrency Theory, pp. 509–523 (1993). https://doi.org/10.1007/3-540-57208-2_35
25. Honda, K., Vasconcelos, V.T., Kubo, M.: Language primitives and type discipline for structured communication-based programming. In: Hankin, C. (ed.) ESOP 1998. LNCS, vol. 1381, pp. 122–138. Springer, Heidelberg (1998). https://doi.org/10.1007/BFb0053567
26. Honda, K., Yoshida, N., Carbone, M.: Multiparty asynchronous session types. In: Symposium on Principles of Programming Languages, pp. 273–284 (2008). https://doi.org/10.1145/1328438.1328472
27. Honda, K., Yoshida, N., Carbone, M.: Multiparty asynchronous session types. J. ACM **63**(1), 9:1–9:67 (2016). https://doi.org/10.1145/2827695
28. Akka, Lightbend Inc. http://akka.io
29. Scala, École Polytechnique Fédérale (EPFL) Lausanne, Switzerland: The scala programming language. https://www.scala-lang.org/
30. Kobayashi, N.: A partially deadlock-free typed process calculus. ACM Trans. Program. Lang. Syst. **20**(2), 436–482 (1998). https://doi.org/10.1145/276393.278524
31. Kobayashi, N.: A type system for lock-free processes. Inf. Comput. **177**(2), 122–159 (2002). https://doi.org/10.1006/inco.2002.3171
32. Kobayashi, N., Saito, S., Sumii, E.: An implicitly-typed deadlock-free process calculus. In: Palamidessi, C. (ed.) CONCUR 2000. LNCS, vol. 1877, pp. 489–504. Springer, Heidelberg (2000). https://doi.org/10.1007/3-540-44618-4_35
33. Lamport, L.: Proving the correctness of multiprocess programs. IEEE Trans. Softw. Eng. **3**(2), 125–143 (1977). https://doi.org/10.1109/TSE.1977.229904
34. Milner, R., Parrow, J., Walker, D.: A calculus of mobile processes. I. Inf. Comput. **100**(1), 1–40 (1992). https://doi.org/10.1016/0890-5401(92)90008-4
35. Nielson, H.R., Nielson, F.: Flow logic: a multi-paradigmatic approach to static analysis. In: Mogensen, T.Æ., Schmidt, D.A., Sudborough, I.H. (eds.) The Essence of Computation. LNCS, vol. 2566, pp. 223–244. Springer, Heidelberg (2002). https://doi.org/10.1007/3-540-36377-7_11
36. Padovani, L.: From lock freedom to progress using session types. In: Workshop on Programming Language Approaches to Concurrency and Communication-cEntric Software, pp. 3–19 (2013). https://doi.org/10.4204/EPTCS.137.2
37. Pierce, B.C., Sangiorgi, D.: Typing and subtyping for mobile processes. Math. Struct. Comput. Sci. **6**(5), 409–453 (1996)
38. Puntigam, F.: Coordination requirements expressed in types for active objects. In: Akşit, M., Matsuoka, S. (eds.) ECOOP 1997. LNCS, vol. 1241, pp. 367–388. Springer, Heidelberg (1997). https://doi.org/10.1007/BFb0053387
39. Puntigam, F.: Concurrent Object-Oriented Programming with Process Types. Habilitationsschrift. Der Andere Verlag, Osnabrück, Germany (2000)
40. Puntigam, F., Peter, C.: Types for active objects with static deadlock prevention. Fundam. Inform. **48**(4), 315–341 (2001)
41. Strom, R.E., Yemini, S.: Typestate: a programming language concept for enhancing software reliability. IEEE Trans. Softw. Eng. **12**(1), 157–171 (1986). https://doi.org/10.1109/TSE.1986.6312929

42. Sumii, E., Kobayashi, N.: A generalized deadlock-free process calculus. Electron. Notes Theor. Comput. Sci. **16**(3), 225–247 (1998). https://doi.org/10.1016/S1571-0661(04)00144-6

43. Takeuchi, K., Honda, K., Kubo, M.: An interaction-based language and its typing system. In: Halatsis, C., Maritsas, D., Philokyprou, G., Theodoridis, S. (eds.) PARLE 1994. LNCS, vol. 817, pp. 398–413. Springer, Heidelberg (1994). https://doi.org/10.1007/3-540-58184-7_118

44. W3C: Extensible Markup Language. https://www.w3.org/XML/

45. W3C: The Web Services Choreography Description Language, November 2005. http://www.w3.org/TR/ws-cdl-10/

46. Yoshida, N., Deniélou, P.-M., Bejleri, A., Hu, R.: Parameterised multiparty session types. In: Ong, L. (ed.) FoSSaCS 2010. LNCS, vol. 6014, pp. 128–145. Springer, Heidelberg (2010). https://doi.org/10.1007/978-3-642-12032-9_10

47. Yoshida, N., Vasconcelos, V.T.: Language primitives and type discipline for structured communication-based programming revisited: two systems for higher-order session communication. Electron. Notes Theor. Comput. Sci. **171**(4), 73–93 (2007). https://doi.org/10.1016/j.entcs.2007.02.056

Event Structure Semantics
for Multiparty Sessions

Ilaria Castellani[1], Mariangiola Dezani-Ciancaglini[2], and Paola Giannini[3(✉)]

[1] Inria, Université Côte d'Azur, Sophia Antipolis, France
[2] Dipartimento di Informatica, Università di Torino, Turin, Italy
[3] DiSIT, Università del Piemonte Orientale, Alessandria, Italy
`ilaria.castellani@inria.fr, dezani@di.unito.it, paola.giannini@uniupo.it`

Abstract. We propose an interpretation of multiparty sessions as *flow event structures*, which allows concurrency between communications within a session to be explicitly represented. We show that this interpretation is equivalent, when the multiparty sessions can be described by global types, to an interpretation of global types as *prime event structures*.

1 Introduction

Session types were proposed in the mid-nineties [32,46], as a tool for specifying and analysing web services and communication protocols. They were first introduced in a variant of the π-calculus to describe binary interactions between processes. Such binary interactions may often be viewed as a client-server protocol. Subsequently, session types were extended to *multiparty sessions* [33,34], where several participants may interact with each other. A multiparty session is an interaction among peers, and there is no need to distinguish one of the participants as representing the server. All one needs is an abstract specification of the protocol that guides the interaction. This is called the *global type* of the session. The global type describes the behaviour of the whole session, as opposed to the local types that describe the behaviours of single participants. In a multiparty session, local types may be retrieved as projections from the global type.

Typical safety properties ensured by session types are *communication safety* (absence of communication errors), *session fidelity* (agreement with the protocol) and, in the absence of session interleaving, *progress* (no participant gets stuck).

Some simple examples of sessions not satisfying the above properties are: (1) a sender emitting a message while the receiver expects a different message (communication error); (2) two participants both waiting to receive a message from the other one (deadlock due to a protocol violation); (3) a three-party session

M. Dezani-Ciancaglini—Partially supported by EU H2020-644235 Rephrase project, EU H2020-644298 HyVar project, IC1402 ARVI and Ateneo/CSP project RunVar.
P. Giannini—This original research has the financial support of the Università del Piemonte Orientale.

M. Boreale et al. (Eds.): De Nicola-Festschrift, LNCS 11665, pp. 340–363, 2019.
https://doi.org/10.1007/978-3-030-21485-2_19

where the first participant waits to receive a message from the second participant, which keeps interacting forever with the third participant (starvation,
although the session is not deadlocked).

What makes session types particularly attractive is that they offer several
advantages at once: (1) static safety guarantees, (2) automatic check of protocol
implementation correctness, based on local types, and (3) a strong connection
with automata [27], graphical models [37] and logics [13,47,49].

In this paper we further investigate the relationship between multiparty session types and other concurrency models, by focussing on Event Structures [52].
We consider a standard multiparty session calculus where sessions are described
as networks of sequential processes [27]. Each process implements a participant
in the session. We propose an interpretation of such networks as *Flow Event
Structures* (FESs) [8,10] (a subclass of Winskel's Stable Event Structures [52]),
which allows concurrency between session communications to be explicitly represented. We then introduce global types for these networks, and define an interpretation of them as *Prime Event Structures* (PESs) [42,50]. Since the syntax
of global types does not allow all the concurrency among communications to be
expressed, the events of the associated PES need to be defined as equivalence
classes of communication sequences up to *permutation equivalence*. We show that
when a network is typable by a global type, the FES semantics of the former is
equivalent, in a precise technical sense, to the PES semantics of the latter.

The paper is organised as follows. Section 2 introduces our multiparty session
calculus. In Sect. 3 we recall the definitions of PESs and FESs, which will be used
in Sect. 4 to interpret processes and networks, respectively. PESs are also used in
Sect. 6 to interpret global types, which are defined in Sect. 5. In Sect. 7 we prove
the equivalence between the FES semantics of a network and the PES semantics
of its global type. Section 8 discusses related work in some detail and sketches
directions for future work. Last but not least, we conclude by expressing our
gratitude to Rocco.

For space reasons, all the proofs except that of the main theorem (Theorem 4)
are omitted. The missing proofs may be found in the research report [15].

2   A Core Calculus for Multiparty Sessions

We now formally introduce our calculus, where multiparty sessions are represented as networks of processes. We assume the following base sets: *session participants*, ranged over by p, q, r and forming the set Part, and *messages*, ranged
over by $\lambda, \lambda', \ldots$ and forming the set Msg.

Let $\pi \in \{p?\lambda, p!\lambda \mid p \in \mathsf{Part}, \lambda \in \mathsf{Msg}\}$ denote an *atomic action*. The action
$p?\lambda$ represents an input of message λ from participant p, while the action $p!\lambda$
represents an output of message λ to participant p.

Definition 1 (Processes). *Processes are defined by:*

$$P ::= \Sigma_{i \in I} p?\lambda_i; P_i \quad | \quad \bigoplus_{i \in I} p!\lambda_i; P_i \quad | \quad \mu X.P \quad | \quad X \quad | \quad 0$$

External choice ($\sum$) and internal choice ($\bigoplus$) are assumed to be associative, commutative, and non-empty. When I is a singleton, $\sum_{i \in I} \mathsf{p}?\lambda_i; P_i$ will be rendered as $\mathsf{p}?\lambda; P$ and $\bigoplus_{i \in I} \mathsf{p}!\lambda_i; P_i$ will be rendered as $\mathsf{p}!\lambda; P$.

A process prefixed by an atomic action is either an *input process* or an *output process*. Note that in an external choice all summands are input processes receiving from the same sender p, and in an internal choice all summands are output processes sending to the same receiver p. Trailing $\mathbf{0}$ processes will be omitted.

Recursion is required to be guarded and processes are treated equirecursively, i.e. they are identified with their generated tree [45] (Chapter 21).

In a full-fledged calculus, messages would carry values, namely they would be of the form $\lambda(v)$. For simplicity, we consider only pure messages here. This will allow us to project global types directly to processes, without having to explicitly introduce local types, see Sect. 5.

$$\mathsf{p}[\![\bigoplus_{i \in I} \mathsf{q}!\lambda_i; P_i]\!] \parallel \mathsf{q}[\![\sum_{j \in J} \mathsf{p}?\lambda_j; Q_j]\!] \parallel \mathsf{N} \xrightarrow{\mathsf{p}\lambda_h\mathsf{q}} \mathsf{p}[\![P_h]\!] \parallel \mathsf{q}[\![Q_h]\!] \parallel \mathsf{N} \quad h \in I \cap J \quad [\textsc{Com}]$$

Fig. 1. LTS for networks.

Networks are comprised of at least two pairs of the form $\mathsf{p}[\![P]\!]$ composed in parallel, each with a different participant p.

Definition 2 (Networks). Networks *are defined by:*

$$\mathsf{N} = \mathsf{p}_1[\![P_1]\!] \parallel \cdots \parallel \mathsf{p}_n[\![P_n]\!] \qquad n \geq 2, \ \mathsf{p}_i \neq \mathsf{p}_j \ \text{for any } i,j$$

We assume the standard structural congruence on networks, stating that parallel composition is associative and commutative and has neutral element $\mathsf{p}[\![\mathbf{0}]\!]$ for any fresh p. To express the operational semantics of networks, we use an LTS whose labels record the message exchanged during a communication together with its sender and receiver. The set of *atomic communications*, ranged over by α, α', is defined to be $\{\mathsf{p}\lambda\mathsf{q} \mid \mathsf{p}, \mathsf{q} \in \mathsf{Part}, \lambda \in \mathsf{Msg}\}$, where $\mathsf{p}\lambda\mathsf{q}$ represents the emission of a message λ from participant p to participant q. We write $\mathsf{part}(\mathsf{p}\lambda\mathsf{q}) = \{\mathsf{p}, \mathsf{q}\}$.

The LTS semantics of networks is specified by the unique rule [COM] given in Fig. 1. Notice that rule [COM] is symmetric with respect to external and internal choices. In a well-typed network (see Sect. 5) it will always be the case that $I \subseteq J$, assuring that participant p can freely choose an output, since participant q offers all corresponding inputs. As usual, we write $\mathsf{N} \xrightarrow{\alpha_1 \cdots \alpha_n} \mathsf{N}'$ as short for $\mathsf{N} \xrightarrow{\alpha_1} \mathsf{N}_1 \cdots \mathsf{N}_{n-1} \xrightarrow{\alpha_n} \mathsf{N}'$.

3   Event Structures

We recall now the definitions of *Prime Event Structure* (PES) from [42] and *Flow Event Structure* (FES) from [8]. The class of FESs is more general than that of PESs: for a precise comparison of various classes of event structures, we refer the reader to [9]. As we shall see in Sect. 4, while PESs are sufficient to interpret processes, the generality of FESs is needed to interpret networks.

Definition 3 (Prime Event Structure). *A prime event structure (PES) is a tuple* $S = (E, \leq, \#)$ *where:*

1. E *is a denumerable set of events;*
2. $\leq \, \subseteq (E \times E)$ *is a partial order relation, called the* causality *relation;*
3. $\# \subseteq (E \times E)$ *is an irreflexive symmetric relation, called the* conflict *relation, satisfying the property:* $\forall e, e', e'' \in E : e \# e' \leq e'' \Rightarrow e \# e''$ *(conflict hereditariness).*

We say that two events are *concurrent* if they are neither causally related nor in conflict.

Definition 4 (Flow Event Structure). *A flow event structure (FES) is a tuple* $S = (E, \prec, \#)$ *where:*

1. E *is a denumerable set of events;*
2. $\prec \, \subseteq (E \times E)$ *is an irreflexive relation, called the* flow *relation;*
3. $\# \subseteq (E \times E)$ *is a symmetric relation, called the* conflict *relation.*

Note that the flow relation is not required to be transitive, nor acyclic (its reflexive and transitive closure is just a preorder, not necessarily a partial order). Intuitively, the flow relation represents a possible *direct causality* between two events. Observe also that in a FES the conflict relation is not required to be irreflexive nor hereditary; indeed, FESs may exhibit self-conflicting events, as well as disjunctive causality (an event may have conflicting causes).

Any PES $S = (E, \leq, \#)$ may be regarded as a FES, with $\prec$ given by $<$ (the strict ordering) or by the covering relation of $\leq$.

We now recall the definition of *configuration* for event structures. Intuitively, a configuration is a set of events having occurred at some stage of the computation. Thus, the semantics of an event structure S is given by its poset of configurations ordered by set inclusion, where $\mathcal{X}_1 \subset \mathcal{X}_2$ means that S may evolve from $\mathcal{X}_1$ to $\mathcal{X}_2$.

Definition 5 (PES Configuration). *Let* $S = (E, \leq, \#)$ *be a prime event structure. A configuration of S is a finite subset* $\mathcal{X}$ *of E such that:*

1. $\mathcal{X}$ *is left-closed:* $e' \leq e \in \mathcal{X} \Rightarrow e' \in \mathcal{X}$;
2. $\mathcal{X}$ *is conflict-free:* $\forall e, e' \in \mathcal{X}, \neg(e \# e')$.

The definition of configuration for FESs is slightly more elaborated. For a subset $\mathcal{X}$ of E, let $\prec_{\mathcal{X}}$ be the restriction of the flow relation to $\mathcal{X}$ and $\prec_{\mathcal{X}}^*$ be its transitive and reflexive closure.

Definition 6 (FES Configuration). *Let* $S = (E, \prec, \#)$ *be a flow event structure. A configuration of S is a finite subset* $\mathcal{X}$ *of E such that:*

1. $\mathcal{X}$ is left-closed up to conflicts: $e' \prec e \in \mathcal{X}, \, e' \notin \mathcal{X} \Rightarrow \exists e'' \in \mathcal{X}. \, e' \# e'' \prec e;$
2. $\mathcal{X}$ is conflict-free: $\forall e, e' \in \mathcal{X}, \neg(e\#e');$
3. $\mathcal{X}$ has no causality cycles: the relation $\prec_{\mathcal{X}}^*$ is a partial order.

Condition (2) is the same as for prime event structures. Condition (1) is adapted to account for the more general – non-hereditary – conflict relation. It states that any event appears in a configuration with a "complete set of causes". Condition (3) ensures that any event in a configuration is actually reachable at some stage of the computation.

If S is a prime or flow event structure, we denote by $\mathcal{C}(S)$ its set of finite configurations. Then, the *domain of configurations* of S is defined as follows:

Definition 7 (ES Configuration Domain). *Let S be a prime or flow event structure with set of configurations $\mathcal{C}(S)$. The domain of configurations of S is the partially ordered set $\mathcal{D}(S) =_{\mathsf{def}} (\mathcal{C}(S), \subseteq)$.*

We recall from [9] a useful characterisation for configurations of FESs, which is based on the notion of proving sequence, defined as follows:

Definition 8 (Proving Sequences).   *Given a flow event structure $S = (E, \prec, \#)$, a proving sequence in S is a sequence $e_1; \cdots ; e_n$ of distinct non-conflicting events (i.e. $i \neq j \Rightarrow e_i \neq e_j$ and $\neg(e_i\#e_j)$ for all i, j) satisfying:*

$$\forall i \leq n \, \forall e \in E : \quad e \prec e_i \quad \Rightarrow \quad \exists j < i. \quad \text{either } e = e_j \text{ or } e \# e_j \prec e_i$$

Note that any prefix of a proving sequence is itself a proving sequence.

We have the following characterisation of configurations of FESs in terms of proving sequences.

Proposition 1 (Representation of configurations as proving sequences [9]). *Given a flow event structure $S = (E, \prec, \#)$, a subset $\mathcal{X}$ of E is a configuration of S if and only if it can be enumerated as a proving sequence $e_1; \cdots ; e_n$.*

Since PESs may be viewed as particular FESs, we may use Definition 8 and Proposition 1 both for the FESs associated with networks (see Sect. 4) and for the PESs associated with global types (see Sect. 6). Note that for a PES the condition of Definition 8 simplifies to

$$\forall i \leq n \, \forall e \in E : \quad e < e_i \quad \Rightarrow \quad \exists j < i. \quad e = e_j$$

4   Event Structure Semantics of Processes and Networks

We interpret both processes and networks as event structures. The event structures associated with processes will be PESs. On the other hand, the event structures associated with networks will be FESs that are not necessarily prime. Process events, ranged over by η, η', are actions $\pi, \pi' \in \{\mathsf{p}?\lambda, \mathsf{p}!\lambda \mid \mathsf{p} \in \mathsf{Part}, \lambda \in \mathsf{Msg}\}$ preceded by their *causal history*, which is a sequence of past actions.

Definition 9 (Process event). Process events η, η' *are defined by:*

$$\eta \quad ::= \pi \quad | \quad \pi \cdot \eta$$

Let ζ denote a (possibly empty) sequence of actions, and $\sqsubseteq$ denote the prefix ordering on such sequences. Each process event η may be written either in the form $\eta = \zeta \cdot \pi$ or in the form $\eta = \pi \cdot \zeta$. We shall feel free to use any of these forms.

We define the action of a process event as follows:

$$\mathsf{act}(\zeta \cdot \pi) = \pi$$

Definition 10 (Event Structure of a Process). *The* event structure of pro-cess P *is the triple*

$$\mathcal{S}^{\mathcal{P}}(P) = (\mathcal{PE}(P), \leq, \#)$$

where:

1. $\mathcal{PE}(P)$ *is defined by induction on the structure of P as follows:*
   (a) $\mathcal{PE}(\Sigma_{i \in I} \mathsf{p}?\lambda_i; P_i) = \bigcup_{i \in I} \{\mathsf{p}?\lambda_i\} \cup \bigcup_{i \in I} \{\mathsf{p}?\lambda_i \cdot \eta_i \mid \eta_i \in \mathcal{PE}(P_i)\};$
   (b) $\mathcal{PE}(\bigoplus_{i \in I} \mathsf{p}!\lambda_i; P_i) = \bigcup_{i \in I} \{\mathsf{p}!\lambda_i\} \cup \bigcup_{i \in I} \{\mathsf{p}!\lambda_i \cdot \eta_i \mid \eta_i \in \mathcal{PE}(P_i)\};$
   (c) $\mathcal{PE}(\mathbf{0}) = \emptyset;$
   (d) $\mathcal{PE}(\mu X.P) = \mathcal{PE}(P\{\mu X.P/X\});$
2. *the $\leq$ relation on the set of events $\mathcal{PE}(P)$ is given by:*
   (a) $\zeta \sqsubseteq \zeta' \Rightarrow \pi \cdot \zeta \leq \pi \cdot \zeta';$
3. *the $\#$ relation on the set of events $\mathcal{PE}(P)$ is given by:*
   (a) $\pi \neq \pi' \Rightarrow \pi \cdot \zeta \# \pi' \cdot \zeta';$
   (b) $\eta \# \eta' \Rightarrow \pi \cdot \eta \# \pi \cdot \eta'.$

Note that, due to Clause 1d of the previous definition, the set $\mathcal{PE}(P)$ is denu-merable.

Example 1. If $P \supset \mu X.\mathsf{q}!\lambda; X \oplus \mathsf{q}!\lambda'$, then $\mathcal{PE}(P) = \{\underbrace{\mathsf{q}!\lambda \cdot \ldots \cdot \mathsf{q}!\lambda}_{n} \cdot \mathsf{q}!\lambda' \mid n \geq 0\}.$

Proposition 2. *Let P be a process. Then $\mathcal{S}^{\mathcal{P}}(P)$ is a prime event structure with an empty concurrency relation.*

The definition of network events requires some preliminary notions. We start by defining the projections of process events on participants, which yield sequences of *undirected actions* of the form $?\lambda$ and $!\lambda$, or the empty sequence ϵ. Let ϑ range over $?\lambda$ and $!\lambda$, and let Θ range over non empty sequences of ϑ's.

Definition 11 (Projection of process events).

$$\mathsf{q}?\lambda \restriction \mathsf{p} = \begin{cases} ?\lambda & \textit{if } \mathsf{p} = \mathsf{q}, \\ \epsilon & \textit{otherwise.} \end{cases} \qquad \mathsf{q}!\lambda \restriction \mathsf{p} = \begin{cases} !\lambda & \textit{if } \mathsf{p} = \mathsf{q}, \\ \epsilon & \textit{otherwise.} \end{cases}$$

$$\pi.\eta \restriction \mathsf{p} = \begin{cases} \eta \restriction \mathsf{p} & \textit{if } \pi \restriction \mathsf{p} = \epsilon, \\ \pi \restriction \mathsf{p} . \eta \restriction \mathsf{p} & \textit{otherwise.} \end{cases}$$

Sequences of undirected actions are related by a standard notion of duality.

Definition 12 (Duality of projections of process events).

$$?\lambda \bowtie !\lambda \qquad \vartheta \bowtie \vartheta' \text{ and } \Theta \bowtie \Theta' \Rightarrow \vartheta.\Theta \bowtie \vartheta'.\Theta'$$

Network events are essentially pairs of matching process events. To formalise the matching condition, we need to specify the locations of process events, namely the participants to which they belong.

Definition 13 (Located event). *We call* located event *a process event* η *pertaining to a participant* p, *written* $p::\eta$.

The duality between projections of process events induces a duality between located events.

Definition 14 (Duality of located events). *Two located events* $p::\eta, q::\eta'$ *are* dual, *written* $p::\eta \bowtie q::\eta'$, *if* $\eta \upharpoonright q \bowtie \eta' \upharpoonright p$ *and either* $\mathsf{act}(\eta) = q?\lambda$ *and* $\mathsf{act}(\eta') = p!\lambda$ *or* $\mathsf{act}(\eta) = q!\lambda$ *and* $\mathsf{act}(\eta') = p?\lambda$.

Dual located events may be sequences of actions of different length. For instance $p::q!\lambda \cdot r!\lambda' \bowtie r::p?\lambda'$ and $p::q!\lambda \bowtie q::r!\lambda' \cdot p?\lambda$.

Definition 15 (Network event). *Network events* ν, ν' *are* unordered pairs of *dual located events, namely:*

$$\nu ::= \{p::\eta, q::\eta'\} \qquad \text{where} \quad p::\eta \bowtie q::\eta'$$

We can now define the event structure associated with a network.

Definition 16 (Event Structure of a Network). *The* event structure of *network* $\mathbb{N} = p_1[\![P_1]\!] \parallel \cdots \parallel p_n[\![P_n]\!]$ *is the triple*

$$\mathcal{S}^{\mathcal{N}}(\mathbb{N}) = (\mathcal{N}\mathcal{E}(\mathbb{N}), \prec, \#)$$

where:

1. $\mathcal{N}\mathcal{E}(\mathbb{N}) = \bigcup_{1 \leq i \neq j \leq n} \{\{p_i::\eta_i, p_j::\eta_j\} \mid \eta_i \in \mathcal{P}\mathcal{E}(P_i), \eta_j \in \mathcal{P}\mathcal{E}(P_j), p_i::\eta_i \bowtie p_j::\eta_j\}$
2. *the* $\prec$ *relation on the set of events* $\mathcal{N}\mathcal{E}(\mathbb{N})$ *is given by:*
   $\eta < \eta'$ & $p::\eta \in \nu$ & $p::\eta' \in \nu' \Rightarrow \nu \prec \nu'$;
3. *the* $\#$ *relation on the set of events* $\mathcal{N}\mathcal{E}(\mathbb{N})$ *is given by:*
   $\eta \# \eta'$ & $p::\eta \in \nu$ & $p::\eta' \in \nu' \Rightarrow \nu \# \nu'$.

We define $\mathsf{comm}(\nu) = p\lambda q$ *if* $\nu = \{p::\zeta \cdot \lambda!q, q::\zeta' \cdot \lambda?p\}$ *and we say that the network event* ν *represents the atomic communication* $p\lambda q$.
Two events ν *and* ν' *are* concurrent *if* $\mathsf{part}(\mathsf{comm}(\nu)) \cap \mathsf{part}(\mathsf{comm}(\nu')) = \emptyset$.

The set of network events can be infinite as in the following example.

Example 2. Let P be as in Example 1, $Q = \mu Y.\mathsf{p}?\lambda; Y \oplus \mathsf{p}?\lambda'$ and $\mathsf{N} = \mathsf{p}[\![P]\!] \parallel \mathsf{q}[\![Q]\!]$. Then

$$\mathcal{NE}(\mathsf{N}) \supset \{\{\mathsf{p} :: \underbrace{\mathsf{q}!\lambda \cdot \ldots \cdot \mathsf{q}!\lambda}_{n} \cdot \mathsf{q}!\lambda', \mathsf{q} :: \underbrace{\mathsf{p}?\lambda \cdot \ldots \cdot \mathsf{p}?\lambda}_{n} \cdot \mathsf{p}?\lambda'\} \mid n \geq 0\}$$

Notably, concurrent events may also be related by the transitive closure of the flow relation, as shown in Example 3.

Proposition 3. *Let* N *be a network. Then* $\mathcal{S}^{\mathcal{N}}(\mathsf{N})$ *is a flow event structure with an irreflexive conflict relation.*

The following example shows how communications inherit the flow relation from the causality relation of their components.

Example 3. Let N be the network

$$\mathsf{p}[\![\mathsf{q}!\lambda_1]\!] \parallel \mathsf{q}[\![\mathsf{p}?\lambda_1; \mathsf{r}!\lambda_2]\!] \parallel \mathsf{r}[\![\mathsf{q}?\lambda_2; \mathsf{s}!\lambda_3]\!] \parallel \mathsf{s}[\![\mathsf{r}?\lambda_3]\!]$$

Then $\mathcal{S}^{\mathcal{N}}(\mathsf{N})$ has three network events

$$\nu_1 = \{\mathsf{p} :: \mathsf{q}!\lambda_1, \mathsf{q} :: \mathsf{p}?\lambda_1\} \qquad \nu_2 = \{\mathsf{q} :: \mathsf{p}?\lambda_1; \mathsf{r}!\lambda_2, \mathsf{r} :: \mathsf{q}?\lambda_2\}$$

$$\nu_3 = \{\mathsf{r} :: \mathsf{q}?\lambda_2; \mathsf{s}!\lambda_3, \mathsf{s} :: \mathsf{r}?\lambda_3\}$$

The flow relation obtained by Definition 16 is: $\nu_1 \prec \nu_2$ and $\nu_2 \prec \nu_3$. Note that each time the flow relation is inherited from the causality within a different participant, q in the first case and r in the second case. By the same definition the events ν_1 and ν_3 are concurrent. However, since $\nu_1 \prec^* \nu_3$, the events ν_1 and ν_3 cannot occur in any order. Indeed, the nonempty configurations are $\{\nu_1\}, \{\nu_1, \nu_2\}$ and $\{\nu_1, \nu_2, \nu_3\}$. Note that $\mathcal{S}^{\mathcal{N}}(\mathsf{N})$ has only one proving sequence per configuration (which is that given by the numbering of events in the configuration).

If N is a binary network, then its flow event structure may be turned into a prime event structure simply by replacing $\prec$ by $\prec^*$:

Theorem 1. *Let* $\mathsf{N} = \mathsf{p}_1[\![P_1]\!] \parallel \mathsf{p}_2[\![P_2]\!]$ *and* $\mathcal{S}^{\mathcal{N}}(\mathsf{N}) = (\mathcal{NE}(\mathsf{N}), \prec, \#)$. *Then the structure* $\mathcal{S}^{\mathcal{N}}_*(\mathsf{N}) =_{\mathsf{def}} (\mathcal{NE}(\mathsf{N}), \prec^*, \#)$ *is a prime event structure.*

If N has more than two participants, then the duality requirement on its events is not sufficient to ensure the absence of circular dependencies[1]. For instance, in the following ternary network (which may be viewed as representing the 3-philosopher deadlock) the relation $\prec^*$ is not a partial order.

Example 4. Let N be the network

$$\mathsf{p}[\![\mathsf{r}?\lambda; \mathsf{q}!\lambda']\!] \parallel \mathsf{q}[\![\mathsf{p}?\lambda'; \mathsf{r}!\lambda'']\!] \parallel \mathsf{r}[\![\mathsf{q}?\lambda''; \mathsf{p}!\lambda]\!].$$

---

[1] This is a well-known issue in multiparty session types, which motivated the introduction of global types in [33], see Sect. 6.

Then $\mathcal{S}^{\mathcal{N}}(\mathbb{N})$ has three network events

$$\nu_1 = \{p :: r?\lambda, r :: q?\lambda''; p!\lambda\} \;\; \nu_2 = \{p :: r?\lambda; q!\lambda', q :: p?\lambda'\} \;\; \nu_3 = \{q :: p?\lambda'; r!\lambda'', r :: q?\lambda''\}$$

By Definition 16(2) we have $\nu_1 \prec \nu_2 \prec \nu_3$ and $\nu_3 \prec \nu_1$. The only configuration is the empty configuration, because the only set of events that satisfies left-closure is $X = \{\nu_1, \nu_2, \nu_3\}$, but this is not a configuration because $\prec_X^*$ is not a partial order (recall that $\prec_X$ is the restriction of $\prec$ to X) and hence the condition (3) of Definition 6 is not satisfied.

The next example illustrates Proposition 3 and shows that a network event may have both conflicting and concurrent causes.

Example 5. Let $\mathbb{N}$ be the network

$$p[\![\, q!\lambda; r!\lambda_1 \oplus q!\lambda'; r!\lambda_1 \,]\!] \;\|\; q[\![\, p?\lambda; s!\lambda_2 + p?\lambda'; s!\lambda_2 \,]\!] \;\|$$
$$r[\![\, p?\lambda_1; s!\lambda_3 \,]\!] \;\|\; s[\![\, q?\lambda_2; r?\lambda_3 \,]\!]$$

Then $\mathcal{S}^{\mathcal{N}}(\mathbb{N})$ has seven network events:

$$\begin{aligned}
\nu_1 &= \{p :: q!\lambda, q :: p?\lambda\} & \nu_1' &= \{p :: q!\lambda', q :: p?\lambda'\} \\
\nu_2 &= \{p :: q!\lambda; r!\lambda_1, r :: p?\lambda_1\} & \nu_2' &= \{p :: q!\lambda'; r!\lambda_1, r :: p?\lambda_1\} \\
\nu_3 &= \{q :: p?\lambda; s!\lambda_2, s :: q?\lambda_2\} & \nu_3' &= \{q :: p?\lambda'; s!\lambda_2, s :: q?\lambda_2\}
\end{aligned}$$

$$\nu_4 = \{r :: p?\lambda_1; s!\lambda_3, s :: q?\lambda_2; r?\lambda_3\}$$

We have $\nu_1 \prec \nu_i$ for $i = 2, 3$ and $\nu_j \prec \nu_4$ for $j = 2, 3$. Similarly, we have $\nu_1' \prec \nu_i'$ for $i = 2, 3$ and $\nu_j' \prec \nu_4$ for $j = 2, 3$. The events ν_2 and ν_2' share $r :: p?\lambda_1$, the events ν_3 and ν_3' share $s :: q?\lambda_2$. Moreover $\nu_i \,\#\, \nu_j'$ for each $i, j = 1, 2, 3$, whereas ν_2 and ν_3 are concurrent, and so are ν_2' and ν_3'. The event ν_4 has two conflicting sets of causes $\{\nu_1, \nu_2, \nu_3\}$ and $\{\nu_1', \nu_2', \nu_3'\}$, and the nonempty configurations are $\{\nu_1\}, \{\nu_1, \nu_2\}, \{\nu_1, \nu_3\}, \{\nu_1, \nu_2, \nu_3\}$ and $\{\nu_1, \nu_2, \nu_3, \nu_4\}$, as well as $\{\nu_1'\}, \{\nu_1', \nu_2'\}, \{\nu_1', \nu_3'\}, \{\nu_1', \nu_2', \nu_3'\}$ and $\{\nu_1', \nu_2', \nu_3', \nu_4\}$. Let $\mathcal{X} = \{\nu_1, \nu_2, \nu_3, \nu_4\}$ and $\mathcal{X}' = \{\nu_1', \nu_2', \nu_3', \nu_4\}$. Note that the event ν_4 has two concurrent causes in both $\mathcal{X}$ and $\mathcal{X}'$. The proving sequences are:

$$\begin{array}{llllllll}
\nu_1, & \nu_1; \nu_2, & \nu_1; \nu_3, & \nu_1; \nu_2; \nu_3, & \nu_1; \nu_3; \nu_2, & \nu_1; \nu_2; \nu_3; \nu_4, & \nu_1; \nu_3; \nu_2; \nu_4 \\
\nu_1', & \nu_1'; \nu_2', & \nu_1'; \nu_3', & \nu_1'; \nu_2'; \nu_3', & \nu_1'; \nu_3'; \nu_2', & \nu_1'; \nu_2'; \nu_3'; \nu_4, & \nu_1'; \nu_3'; \nu_2'; \nu_4
\end{array}$$

Note that there are two proving sequences corresponding to the configuration $\mathcal{X}$ (and similarly for $\mathcal{X}'$ and each of the configurations $\{\nu_1, \nu_2, \nu_3\}$ and $\{\nu_1', \nu_2', \nu_3'\}$).

A graphical representation of $\mathcal{S}^{\mathcal{N}}(\mathbb{N})$ is given in Fig. 2, where the arrows represent the flow relation $\prec$ and the vertical dotted line for $\#$ indicates that all the events on the left of the line are in conflict with all the events on the right.

The next example shows that the relations of flow and conflict on network events are not necessarily disjoint.

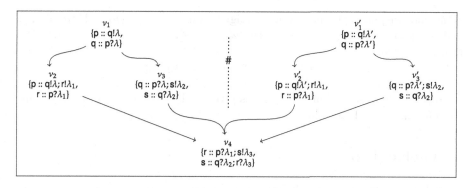

Fig. 2. Flow relation between events of $\mathcal{S}^{\mathcal{N}}(\mathbb{N})$ in Example 5.

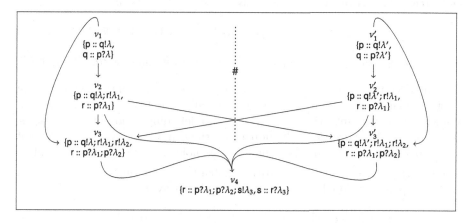

Fig. 3. Flow relation between events of $\mathcal{S}^{\mathcal{N}}(\mathbb{N})$ in Example 6.

Example 6. Let $\mathbb{N}$ be the network

$$\mathsf{p}[\![\, \mathsf{q}!\lambda; \mathsf{r}!\lambda_1; \mathsf{r}!\lambda_2 \oplus \mathsf{q}!\lambda'; \mathsf{r}!\lambda_1; \mathsf{r}!\lambda_2 \,]\!] \parallel \mathsf{q}[\![\, \mathsf{p}?\lambda + \mathsf{p}?\lambda' \,]\!] \parallel \mathsf{r}[\![\, \mathsf{p}?\lambda_1; \mathsf{p}?\lambda_2; \mathsf{s}!\lambda_3 \,]\!] \parallel \mathsf{s}[\![\, \mathsf{r}?\lambda_3 \,]\!].$$

Then $\mathcal{S}^{\mathcal{N}}(\mathbb{N})$ has seven network events:

$$\nu_1 = \{\mathsf{p} :: \mathsf{q}!\lambda, \mathsf{q} :: \mathsf{p}?\lambda\} \qquad\qquad \nu_1' = \{\mathsf{p} :: \mathsf{q}!\lambda', \mathsf{q} :: \mathsf{p}?\lambda'\}$$
$$\nu_2 = \{\mathsf{p} :: \mathsf{q}!\lambda; \mathsf{r}!\lambda_1, \mathsf{r} :: \mathsf{p}?\lambda_1\} \qquad\qquad \nu_2' = \{\mathsf{p} :: \mathsf{q}!\lambda'; \mathsf{r}!\lambda_1, \mathsf{r} :: \mathsf{p}?\lambda_1\}$$
$$\nu_3 = \{\mathsf{p} :: \mathsf{q}!\lambda; \mathsf{r}!\lambda_1; \mathsf{r}!\lambda_2, \mathsf{r} :: \mathsf{p}?\lambda_1; \mathsf{p}?\lambda_2\} \quad \nu_3' = \{\mathsf{p} :: \mathsf{q}!\lambda'; \mathsf{r}!\lambda_1; \mathsf{r}!\lambda_2, \mathsf{r} :: \mathsf{p}?\lambda_1; \mathsf{p}?\lambda_2\}$$

$$\nu_4 = \{\mathsf{r} :: \mathsf{p}?\lambda_1; \mathsf{p}?\lambda_2; \mathsf{s}!\lambda_3, \mathsf{s} :: \mathsf{r}?\lambda_3\}$$

We have $\nu_1 \prec \nu_i$ for $i = 2, 3$ and $\nu_j \prec \nu_4$ for $j = 2, 3$. Similarly, we have $\nu_1' \prec \nu_i'$ for $i = 2, 3$ and $\nu_j' \prec \nu_4$ for $j = 2, 3$. Moreover $\nu_i \,\#\, \nu_j'$ for each $i, j = 1, 2, 3$. Finally, we have $\nu_2 \prec \nu_3$ and $\nu_2' \prec \nu_3'$, and also the cross flows $\nu_2 \prec \nu_3'$ and $\nu_2' \prec \nu_3$. Since we have also $\nu_2 \,\#\, \nu_3'$ and $\nu_2' \,\#\, \nu_3$, this shows that the two relations $\prec$ and

\# are not disjoint. The nonempty configurations are $\{\nu_1\}, \{\nu_1, \nu_2\}, \{\nu_1, \nu_2, \nu_3\}$ and $\{\nu_1, \nu_2, \nu_3, \nu_4\}$, as well as $\{\nu_1'\}, \{\nu_1', \nu_2'\}, \{\nu_1', \nu_2', \nu_3'\}$ and $\{\nu_1', \nu_2', \nu_3', \nu_4'\}$. The proving sequences are:

$$\nu_1, \quad \nu_1; \nu_2, \quad \nu_1; \nu_2; \nu_3, \quad \nu_1; \nu_2; \nu_3; \nu_4$$
$$\nu_1', \quad \nu_1'; \nu_2', \quad \nu_1'; \nu_2'; \nu_3', \quad \nu_1'; \nu_2'; \nu_3'; \nu_4'$$

A graphical representation of $\mathcal{S}^{\mathcal{N}}(\mathbb{N})$ is given in Fig. 3, where we use the same conventions as for Example 5.

5   Global Types

Global types are built from choices among atomic communications.

Definition 17 (Global types). Global types G *are defined by:*

$$G \quad ::= \quad p \to q : \boxplus_{i \in I} \lambda_i; G_i \mid G \parallel G \mid \mu t.G \mid t \mid \mathsf{End}$$

where $\lambda_j \neq \lambda_h$ *for all* $j, h \in I$, $j \neq h$, *i.e. messages in choices are all different.*

Sequential composition (;) has higher precedence than choice ($\boxplus$). Recursion must be guarded by atomic communications and it is treated equi-recursively. While there is no syntactic restriction on parallel composition of global types, our definition of projection will enforce that the component types have disjoint sets of participants. When I is a singleton, a choice $p \to q : \boxplus_{i \in I} \lambda_i; G_i$ will be rendered simply as $p \xrightarrow{\lambda} q; G$. In writing global types, we omit the final End.

Participants of global types are defined inductively as follows:

$$\mathsf{part}(p \to q : \boxplus_{i \in I} \lambda_i; G_i) = \{p, q\} \cup \bigcup_{i \in I} \mathsf{part}(G_i)$$
$$\mathsf{part}(\mu t.G) = \mathsf{part}(G) \qquad \mathsf{part}(t) = \mathsf{part}(\mathsf{End}) = \emptyset$$

The projection of a global type onto participants is given in Fig. 4. As usual, projection is defined only when it is defined on all participants. Because of the simplicity of our calculus, the projection of a global type, when defined, is simply

$$(p \to q : \boxplus_{i \in I} \lambda_i; G_i) \restriction r = \begin{cases} \Sigma_{i \in I} p? \lambda_i; G_i \restriction r & \text{if } r = q, \\ \bigoplus_{i \in I} q! \lambda_i; G_i \restriction r & \text{if } r = p, \\ G_i \restriction r & \text{if } G_i \restriction r = G_j \restriction r \text{ for all } i, j \in I \end{cases}$$

$$(G_1 \parallel G_2) \restriction p = G_i \restriction p \text{ if } p \notin \mathsf{part}(G_j) \text{ for } \{i, j\} = \{1, 2\}$$

$$(\mu t.G) \restriction p = \begin{cases} \mu X_t.G \restriction p & \text{if } p \in \mathsf{part}(G) \\ 0 & \text{otherwise} \end{cases} \qquad t \restriction p = X_t \qquad \mathsf{End} \restriction p = 0$$

Fig. 4. Projection of global types onto participants.

a process. The projection of a choice type on the sender produces an output process sending one of its possible messages to the receiver and then acting according to the projection of the corresponding branch. Similarly for the projection on the receiver, which produces an input process. Projection of a choice type on the other participants is defined only if it produces the same process for all the branches of the choice. This is a standard condition for multiparty session types. The projection of a parallel global type $G_1 \parallel G_2$ on a participant p is undefined if p appears in both G_1 and G_2. Otherwise there are two possibilities: (1) if p appears in G_i but not in G_j, for $i \neq j$, then $(G_1 \parallel G_2) \upharpoonright p$ yields the projection of G_i on p; (2) if p appears in neither G_1 nor G_2, then $(G_1 \parallel G_2) \upharpoonright p$ yields $\mathbf{0}$.

From now on we will only consider projectable global types.

The definition of well-typed network is given in Fig. 5. We first define a preorder on processes, $P \leq P'$, saying when a process P *can be used where we expect process P'*. In particular, $P \leq P'$, if either P is equal to P' or they are both input processes receiving messages from the same participant, P may receive more messages than P' and after receiving the same message the process P continues with a process that can be used when we expect the corresponding one in P'. The double line indicates that the rule is interpreted coinductively [45] (Chap. 21). A network is well typed with global type G, if all its participants have associated processes that behave as specified by the projections of a global type. In Rule [NET], the condition $\mathsf{part}(G) \subseteq \{p_i \mid i \in I\}$ ensures that all participants of the global type appear in the network. Moreover it permits additional participants that do not appear in the global type, allowing the typing of sessions containing $p[\![\mathbf{0}]\!]$ for a fresh p — a property required to guarantee invariance of types under structural congruence of networks.

$$0 \leq 0 \text{ [S-0]} \qquad \frac{P_i \leq Q_i \quad i \in I}{\Sigma_{i \in I \cup J} p?\lambda_i; P_i \leq \Sigma_{i \in I} p?\lambda_i; Q_i} \text{[S-IN]} \qquad \frac{P_i \leq Q_i \quad i \in I}{\bigoplus_{i \in I} p!\lambda_i; P_i \leq \bigoplus_{i \in I} p!\lambda_i; Q_i} \text{[S-OUT]}$$

$$\frac{P_i \leq G \upharpoonright p_i \quad i \in I \qquad \mathsf{part}(G) \subseteq \{p_i \mid i \in I\}}{\vdash \prod_{i \in I} p_i [\![P_i]\!] : G} \text{[NET]}$$

Fig. 5. Preorder on processes and network typing rule.

Example 7. The networks of Examples 2, 3, 5 and 6 can be typed respectively by

$$G = \mu t.p \to q : (\lambda; t \boxplus \lambda')$$
$$G' = p \xrightarrow{\lambda_1} q; q \xrightarrow{\lambda_2} r; r \xrightarrow{\lambda_3} s$$
$$G'' = p \to q : (\lambda; p \xrightarrow{\lambda_1} r; q \xrightarrow{\lambda_2} s; r \xrightarrow{\lambda_3} s \boxplus \lambda'; p \xrightarrow{\lambda_1} r; q \xrightarrow{\lambda_2} s; r \xrightarrow{\lambda_3} s)$$
$$G''' = p \to q : (\lambda; p \xrightarrow{\lambda_1} r; p \xrightarrow{\lambda_2} r; r \xrightarrow{\lambda_3} s \boxplus \lambda'; p \xrightarrow{\lambda_1} r; p \xrightarrow{\lambda_2} r; r \xrightarrow{\lambda_3} s)$$

The network of Example 4 instead cannot be typed.

$$p \to q : \boxplus_{i \in I} \lambda_i; G_i \xrightarrow{\; p\lambda_j q \;} G_j \quad j \in I \; [\text{ECOMM}] \qquad \dfrac{G_1 \xrightarrow{\alpha} G_1'}{G_1 \parallel G_2 \xrightarrow{\alpha} G_1' \parallel G_2} \; [\text{PCOMM}]$$

$$\dfrac{G_i \xrightarrow{\alpha} G_i' \quad i \in I \quad \text{part}(\alpha) \cap \{p, q\} = \emptyset}{p \to q : \boxplus_{i \in I} \lambda_i; G_i \xrightarrow{\alpha} p \to q : \boxplus_{i \in I} \lambda_i; G_i'} \; [\text{ICOMM}]$$

Fig. 6. LTS for global types.

To formalise the classical properties of Subject Reduction and Session Fidelity [33,34], we use the standard LTS for global types given in Fig. 6. Rule [ICOMM] is justified by the fact that in a projectable global type $p \to q : \boxplus_{i \in I} \lambda_i; G_i$, the behaviours of the participants different from p and q are the same in all branches, and hence they are independent from the choice and may be executed before it.

Theorem 2 (Subject Reduction). *If* $\vdash N : G$ *and* $N \xrightarrow{\alpha} N'$, *then* $G \xrightarrow{\alpha} G'$ *and* $\vdash N' : G'$.

Theorem 3 (Session Fidelity). *If* $\vdash N : G$ *and* $G \xrightarrow{\alpha} G'$, *then* $N \xrightarrow{\alpha} N'$ *and* $\vdash N' : G'$.

6   Event Structure Semantics of Global Types

We define now the event structure associated with a global type. The events of this PES will be equivalence classes of particular sequences of communications.

Let σ denote a finite (and possibly empty) sequence of atomic communications, and *Seq* denote the set of these sequences.

Definition 18 (Permutation equivalence). *The permutation equivalence on Seq is the least equivalence* $\sim$ *such that*

$$\sigma \cdot \alpha_1 \cdot \alpha_2 \cdot \sigma' \sim \sigma \cdot \alpha_2 \cdot \alpha_1 \cdot \sigma' \quad \text{if} \quad \text{part}(\alpha_1) \cap \text{part}(\alpha_2) = \emptyset$$

We denote by $[\sigma]_\sim$ *the equivalence class of the sequence* σ, *and by Seq/$\sim$ the set of equivalence classes on Seq. Note that* $[\epsilon]_\sim = \{\epsilon\} \in Seq/\sim$, *and* $[\alpha]_\sim = \{\alpha\} \in Seq/\sim$ *for any* α. *Moreover* $|\sigma'| = |\sigma|$ *for all* $\sigma' \in [\sigma]_\sim$, *where* $|\cdot|$ *yields the length of the sequence.*

The events associated with a global type, called *global events* and denoted by γ, γ', are equivalence classes of particular communication sequences that we call *pointed*. Intuitively, all communications in a pointed sequence are causes of some subsequent communication. Formally:

Definition 19 (Pointed communication sequence). *A communication sequence* $\sigma = \alpha_1 \cdots \alpha_n$, $n > 0$, *is said to be* pointed *if*

$$\text{for all } i,\ 1 \leq i < n,\ \text{part}(\alpha_i) \cap \bigcup_{i+1 \leq j \leq n} \text{part}(\alpha_j) \neq \emptyset$$

Note that the condition of Definition 19 must be satisfied only by the α_i with $i < n$, thus it is vacuously satisfied by any communication sequence of length 1.

Example 8. Let $\alpha_1 = \text{p}\lambda_1\text{q}$, $\alpha_2 = \text{r}\lambda_2\text{s}$ and $\alpha_3 = \text{r}\lambda_3\text{p}$. Then $\sigma_1 = \alpha_1$ and $\sigma_3 = \alpha_1 \cdot \alpha_2 \cdot \alpha_3$ are pointed sequences, while $\sigma_2 = \alpha_1 \cdot \alpha_2$ is *not* a pointed sequence.

Definition 20 (Global event). *Let* $\sigma = \sigma' \cdot \alpha$ *be a pointed communication sequence. Then* $\gamma = [\sigma]_\sim$ *is a* global event *with communication* α, *notation* $\text{comm}(\gamma) = \alpha$.

Notice that $\text{comm}(\cdot)$ is well defined due to the following proposition, where $\text{last}(\sigma)$ denotes the last communication of σ.

Proposition 4. *Let* σ *be pointed communication sequence. If* $\sigma \sim \sigma'$, *then* σ' *is a pointed communication sequence and* $\text{last}(\sigma) = \text{last}(\sigma')$.

In order to interpret global types as ESs, we define a form of prefixing of a global event by a communication, in such a way that the result is again a global event.

Definition 21 (Causal prefixing of a global event by communications).
The causal prefixing of a global event by a nonempty sequence of communications is defined as follows:

1. *The causal prefixing of a global event by a communication is defined by*
$$\text{p}\lambda\text{q} \circ \gamma = \begin{cases} [\text{p}\lambda\text{q} \cdot \sigma]_\sim & \text{if } \gamma = [\sigma]_\sim \text{ and } \text{p}\lambda\text{q} \cdot \sigma \text{ is a pointed sequence} \\ \gamma & \text{otherwise} \end{cases}$$

2. *The mapping* $\circ$ *naturally extends to communication sequences*
$$(\alpha \cdot \sigma) \circ \gamma = \alpha \circ (\sigma \circ \gamma) \qquad \sigma \neq \epsilon$$

Definition 22 (Event Structure of a Global Type). *The* event structure of global type G *is the triple*

$$\mathcal{S}^{\mathcal{G}}(\mathsf{G}) = (\mathcal{GE}(\mathsf{G}), \leq, \#)$$

where:

1. $\mathcal{GE}(\mathsf{G})$ *is defined by induction on the structure of* G *as follows:*
   (a) $\mathcal{GE}(\text{p} \rightarrow \text{q} : \boxplus_{i \in I} \lambda_i; \mathsf{G}_i) = \bigcup_{i \in I}\{\{\text{p}\lambda_i\text{q}\}\} \cup \bigcup_{i \in I}\{\text{p}\lambda_i\text{q} \circ \gamma_i \mid \gamma_i \in \mathcal{GE}(\mathsf{G}_i)\}$;
   (b) $\mathcal{GE}(\mathsf{G}_1 \parallel \mathsf{G}_2) = \mathcal{GE}(\mathsf{G}_1) \cup \mathcal{GE}(\mathsf{G}_2)$;
   (c) $\mathcal{GE}(\text{End}) = \mathcal{GE}(\text{t}) = \emptyset$;
   (d) $\mathcal{GE}(\mu\text{t}.\mathsf{G}) = \mathcal{GE}(\mathsf{G}\{\mu\text{t}.\mathsf{G}/\text{t}\})$;

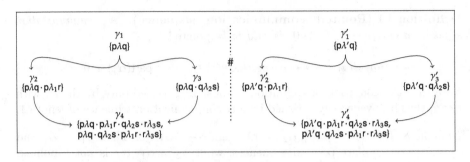

Fig. 7. Relation between events of $\mathcal{S}^{\mathcal{G}}(\mathsf{G}'')$ in Example 9.

2. *the $\leq$ relation on the set of events $\mathcal{GE}(\mathsf{G})$ is given by:*
   $[\sigma]_\sim \leq [\sigma']_\sim$ *if* $\sigma \cdot \sigma'' \sim \sigma'$ *for some* σ'';
3. *the $\#$ relation on the set of events $\mathcal{GE}(\mathsf{G})$ is given by:*
   $[\sigma]_\sim \, \# \, [\sigma']_\sim$ *if* $\sigma \sim \sigma_1 \cdot \mathsf{p}\lambda\mathsf{q} \cdot \sigma_2$ *and* $\sigma' \sim \sigma_1 \cdot \mathsf{p}\lambda'\mathsf{q} \cdot \sigma_2'$ *for some*
   $\sigma_1, \sigma_2, \sigma_2', \mathsf{p}, \mathsf{q}, \lambda, \lambda'$ *such that* $\lambda \neq \lambda'$.

Note that, due to Clause 1d of Definition 22, the set $\mathcal{GE}(\mathsf{G})$ is denumerable.

Example 9. Let $\mathsf{G}_1 = \mathsf{p} \overset{\lambda_1}{\to} \mathsf{q}; \mathsf{r} \overset{\lambda_2}{\to} \mathsf{s}; \mathsf{r} \overset{\lambda_3}{\to} \mathsf{p}$ and $\mathsf{G}_2 = \mathsf{r} \overset{\lambda_2}{\to} \mathsf{s}; \mathsf{p} \overset{\lambda_1}{\to} \mathsf{q}; \mathsf{r} \overset{\lambda_3}{\to} \mathsf{p}$. Then $\mathcal{GE}(\mathsf{G}_1) = \mathcal{GE}(\mathsf{G}_2) = \{\gamma_1, \gamma_2, \gamma_3\}$ where

$$\gamma_1 = \{\mathsf{p}\lambda_1\mathsf{q}\} \qquad \gamma_2 = \{\mathsf{r}\lambda_2\mathsf{s}\} \qquad \gamma_3 = \{\mathsf{p}\lambda_1\mathsf{q} \cdot \mathsf{r}\lambda_2\mathsf{s} \cdot \mathsf{r}\lambda_3\mathsf{p}, \mathsf{r}\lambda_2\mathsf{s} \cdot \mathsf{p}\lambda_1\mathsf{q} \cdot \mathsf{r}\lambda_3\mathsf{p}\}$$

with $\gamma_1 \leq \gamma_3$ and $\gamma_2 \leq \gamma_3$. The configurations are $\{\gamma_1\}$, $\{\gamma_2\}$ and $\{\gamma_1, \gamma_2, \gamma_3\}$ and the proving sequences are

$$\gamma_1 \qquad \gamma_2 \qquad \gamma_1; \gamma_2 \qquad \gamma_2; \gamma_1 \qquad \gamma_1; \gamma_2; \gamma_3 \qquad \gamma_2; \gamma_1; \gamma_3$$

If G' is as in Example 7, then $\mathcal{GE}(\mathsf{G}') = \{\gamma_1, \gamma_2, \gamma_3\}$ where

$$\gamma_1 = \{\mathsf{p}\lambda_1\mathsf{q}\} \qquad \gamma_2 = \{\mathsf{p}\lambda_1\mathsf{q} \cdot \mathsf{q}\lambda_2\mathsf{r}\} \qquad \gamma_3 = \{\mathsf{p}\lambda_1\mathsf{q} \cdot \mathsf{q}\lambda_2\mathsf{r} \cdot \mathsf{r}\lambda_3\mathsf{s}\}$$

with $\gamma_1 \leq \gamma_2 \leq \gamma_3$. The configurations are $\{\gamma_1\}$, $\{\gamma_1, \gamma_2\}$ and $\{\gamma_1, \gamma_2, \gamma_3\}$. There is a proving sequence corresponding to each configuration. Notice that G' types the network of Example 3.
If G'' is as in Example 7, then $\mathcal{GE}(\mathsf{G}'') = \{\gamma_1, \gamma_1', \gamma_2, \gamma_2', \gamma_3, \gamma_3', \gamma_4, \gamma_4'\}$ where

$$\gamma_1 = \{\mathsf{p}\lambda\mathsf{q}\} \qquad \gamma_1' = \{\mathsf{p}\lambda'\mathsf{q}\} \qquad \gamma_2 = \{\mathsf{p}\lambda\mathsf{q} \cdot \mathsf{p}\lambda_1\mathsf{r}\} \qquad \gamma_2' = \{\mathsf{p}\lambda'\mathsf{q} \cdot \mathsf{p}\lambda_1\mathsf{r}\}$$
$$\gamma_3 = \{\mathsf{p}\lambda\mathsf{q} \cdot \mathsf{q}\lambda_2\mathsf{s}\} \qquad \gamma_3' = \{\mathsf{p}\lambda'\mathsf{q} \cdot \mathsf{q}\lambda_2\mathsf{s}\}$$
$$\gamma_4 = \{\mathsf{p}\lambda\mathsf{q} \cdot \mathsf{p}\lambda_1\mathsf{r} \cdot \mathsf{q}\lambda_2\mathsf{s} \cdot \mathsf{r}\lambda_3\mathsf{s}, \mathsf{p}\lambda\mathsf{q} \cdot \mathsf{q}\lambda_2\mathsf{s} \cdot \mathsf{p}\lambda_1\mathsf{r} \cdot \mathsf{r}\lambda_3\mathsf{s}\}$$
$$\gamma_4' = \{\mathsf{p}\lambda'\mathsf{q} \cdot \mathsf{p}\lambda_1\mathsf{r} \cdot \mathsf{q}\lambda_2\mathsf{s} \cdot \mathsf{r}\lambda_3\mathsf{s}, \mathsf{p}\lambda'\mathsf{q} \cdot \mathsf{q}\lambda_2\mathsf{s} \cdot \mathsf{p}\lambda_1\mathsf{r} \cdot \mathsf{r}\lambda_3\mathsf{s}\}$$

with $\gamma_1 \leq \gamma_2 \leq \gamma_4$, $\gamma_1 \leq \gamma_3 \leq \gamma_4$ and $\gamma_1' \leq \gamma_2' \leq \gamma_4'$, $\gamma_1' \leq \gamma_3' \leq \gamma_4'$. The configurations are $\{\gamma_1\}$, $\{\gamma_1'\}$, $\{\gamma_1, \gamma_2\}$, $\{\gamma_1', \gamma_2'\}$, $\{\gamma_1, \gamma_3\}$, $\{\gamma_1', \gamma_3'\}$, $\{\gamma_1, \gamma_2, \gamma_3\}$, $\{\gamma_1', \gamma_2', \gamma_3'\}$, and $\{\gamma_1, \gamma_2, \gamma_3, \gamma_4\}$, $\{\gamma_1', \gamma_2', \gamma_3', \gamma_4'\}$. The configurations with less than three elements correspond to only one proving sequence, while the others correspond to two proving sequences each. Notice that G'' types the network of Example 5. A graphical representation of $\mathcal{S}^{\mathcal{G}}(G'')$ is given in Fig. 7, where the arrows represent the covering relation of $\leq$. Note that the event structure is prime and so conflict is hereditary. Indeed, since the events maintain their complete history the events γ_4 and γ_4' are in conflict.

Proposition 5. *Let* G *be a global type. Then* $\mathcal{S}^{\mathcal{G}}(G)$ *is a prime event structure.*

Observe that while our interpretation of networks as FESs exactly reflects the concurrency expressed by the syntax of networks, our interpretation of global types as PESs exhibits more concurrency than that given by the syntax of global types. This is because the parallel composition of global types is only defined when its arguments have disjoint participants, and thus it cannot be used to specify concurrency between two forking paths that may join again, e.g., two concurrent events that are both causes of a third event, as γ_1 and γ_2 in $\mathcal{GE}(G_1) = \mathcal{GE}(G_2)$ in the above Example 9.

7   Equivalence of the Two Event Structure Semantics

We establish now our main result for typed networks, namely the isomorphism between the domain of configurations of the FES of the network and the domain of configurations of the PES of its global type. We start by stating the correspondence between the communication sequences of networks and the proving sequences of their event structures. To this end, we introduce some auxiliary definitions.

Definition 23 (Truncation of a communication sequence). *Let* $\sigma = \alpha_1 \cdots \alpha_n$ *be a communication sequence with* $n > 0$. *For each* $i = 1, \ldots, n+1$, *we define* $\sigma\rfloor_i =_{\text{def}} \alpha_1 \cdots \alpha_{i-1}$ *to be the ith truncation of* σ, *where by convention* $\alpha_1 \cdots \alpha_{i-1} = \epsilon$ *if* $i = 1$. *Note that* $\sigma\rfloor_{n+1} = \sigma$.

Definition 24 (Projection). *The* projection of the communication sequence σ *on participant* p, *notation* $\sigma \rightsquigarrow p$, *is the process event defined by:*

1. $(p\lambda q \cdot \sigma) \rightsquigarrow p = q!\lambda \cdot \sigma \rightsquigarrow p$;
2. $(q\lambda p \cdot \sigma) \rightsquigarrow p = q?\lambda \cdot \sigma \rightsquigarrow p$;
3. $(r\lambda s \cdot \sigma) \rightsquigarrow p = \sigma \rightsquigarrow p$ *if* $p \neq r, s$;
4. $\epsilon \rightsquigarrow p = \epsilon$.

It is easy to verify that if $\text{part}(\alpha_1) \cap \text{part}(\alpha_2) = \emptyset$, then $(\alpha_1 \cdot \alpha_2) \rightsquigarrow p = (\alpha_2 \cdot \alpha_1) \rightsquigarrow p$ for all p. Therefore $\sigma \sim \sigma'$ implies $\sigma \rightsquigarrow p = \sigma' \rightsquigarrow p$.

Definition 25 (Network events from communications). *If* $\sigma = \alpha_1 \cdots \alpha_n$ *is a communication sequence with* $\text{part}(\alpha_i) = \{p_i, q_i\}$, *we define the* sequence of network events corresponding to σ *by*

$$\text{nec}(\sigma) = \nu_1; \cdots; \nu_n$$

where $\nu_i = \{p_i :: \sigma\rfloor_{i+1} \rightsquigarrow p_i, q_i :: \sigma\rfloor_{i+1} \rightsquigarrow q_i\}$ *for* $1 \leq i \leq n$.

It is immediate to see that, if $\sigma = \mathsf{p}\lambda\mathsf{q}$, then $\mathsf{nec}(\sigma)$ is the event $\{\mathsf{p}::\mathsf{q}!\lambda, \mathsf{q}::\mathsf{p}?\lambda\}$.

Lemma 1. *Let* $\mathsf{N} \xrightarrow{\sigma} \mathsf{N}'$.

1. *If* $\{\mathsf{r}::\eta, \mathsf{s}::\eta'\} \in \mathcal{NE}(\mathsf{N}')$, *then* $\{\mathsf{r}::\sigma \leftrightsquigarrow \mathsf{r} \cdot \eta, \mathsf{s}::\sigma \leftrightsquigarrow \mathsf{s} \cdot \eta'\} \in \mathcal{NE}(\mathsf{N})$;
2. $\mathsf{nec}(\sigma)$ *is a proving sequence in* $\mathcal{S}^{\mathcal{N}}(\mathsf{N})$.

Lemma 2. *If* $\nu_1; \cdots; \nu_n$ *is a proving sequence in* $\mathcal{S}^{\mathcal{N}}(\mathsf{N})$, *then* $\mathsf{N} \xrightarrow{\sigma} \mathsf{N}'$ *where* $\sigma = \mathsf{comm}(\nu_1) \cdots \mathsf{comm}(\nu_n)$.

Similar relations hold between reductions of global types and their events.

Definition 26. (Global events from communications). *If* $\sigma = \alpha_1 \cdots \alpha_n$ *is a communication sequence, we define the sequence of global events corresponding to* σ *by*

$$\mathsf{gec}(\sigma) = \gamma_1; \cdots; \gamma_n$$

where $\gamma_i = \sigma \rfloor_i \circ [\alpha_i]_{\sim}$ *for* $1 \leq i \leq n$.

Lemma 3. *Let* $\mathsf{G} \xrightarrow{\sigma} \mathsf{G}'$.

1. *If* $\gamma \in \mathcal{GE}(\mathsf{G}')$, *then* $\sigma \circ \gamma \in \mathcal{GE}(\mathsf{G})$;
2. $\mathsf{gec}(\sigma)$ *is a proving sequence in* $\mathcal{S}^{\mathcal{G}}(\mathsf{G})$.

Lemma 4. *If* $\gamma_1; \cdots; \gamma_n$ *is a proving sequence in* $\mathcal{S}^{\mathcal{G}}(\mathsf{G})$, *then* $\mathsf{G} \xrightarrow{\sigma} \mathsf{G}'$ *and* $\sigma = \mathsf{comm}(\gamma_1) \cdots \mathsf{comm}(\gamma_n)$.

To prove our main theorem we will also use the following separation result from [9] (Lemma 2.8 p. 12):

Lemma 5 (Separation [9]). *Let* $S = (E, \prec, \#)$ *be a flow event structure and* $X, X' \in \mathcal{C}(S)$ *be such that* $X \subset X'$. *Then there exist* $e \in X' \backslash X$ *such that* $X \cup \{e\} \in \mathcal{C}(S)$.

We may now show the correspondence between the configurations of the FES of a network and the configurations of the PES of its global type.

Let $\simeq$ denote isomorphism on domains of configurations.

Theorem 4. *If* $\vdash \mathsf{N} : \mathsf{G}$, *then* $\mathcal{D}(\mathcal{S}^{\mathcal{N}}(\mathsf{N})) \simeq \mathcal{D}(\mathcal{S}^{\mathcal{G}}(\mathsf{G}))$.

Proof. By Lemma 2 if $\nu_1; \cdots; \nu_n$ is a proving sequence of $\mathcal{S}^{\mathcal{N}}(\mathsf{N})$, then $\mathsf{N} \xrightarrow{\sigma} \mathsf{N}'$ where $\sigma = \mathsf{comm}(\nu_1) \cdots \mathsf{comm}(\nu_n)$. By applying iteratively Subject Reduction (Theorem 2) $\mathsf{G} \xrightarrow{\sigma} \mathsf{G}'$ and $\vdash \mathsf{N}' : \mathsf{G}'$. By Lemma 3(2) $\mathsf{gec}(\sigma)$ is a proving sequence of $\mathcal{S}^{\mathcal{G}}(\mathsf{G})$.

By Lemma 4 if $\gamma_1; \cdots; \gamma_n$ is a proving sequence of $\mathcal{S}^{\mathcal{G}}(\mathsf{G})$, then $\mathsf{G} \xrightarrow{\sigma} \mathsf{G}'$ where $\sigma = \mathsf{comm}(\gamma_1) \cdots \mathsf{comm}(\gamma_n)$. By applying iteratively Session Fidelity (Theorem 3) $\mathsf{N} \xrightarrow{\sigma} \mathsf{N}'$ and $\vdash \mathsf{N}' : \mathsf{G}'$. By Lemma 1(2) $\mathsf{nec}(\sigma)$ is a proving sequence of $\mathcal{S}^{\mathcal{N}}(\mathsf{N})$.

Therefore we have a bijection between $\mathcal{D}(\mathcal{S}^{\mathcal{N}}(\mathsf{N}))$ and $\mathcal{D}(\mathcal{S}^{\mathcal{G}}(\mathsf{G}))$, given by $\mathsf{nec}(\sigma) \leftrightarrow \mathsf{gec}(\sigma)$ for any σ generated by the (bisimilar) LTSs of N and G.

We show now that this bijection preserves inclusion of configurations. By Lemma 5 it is enough to prove that if $\nu_1; \cdots; \nu_n \in \mathcal{C}(\mathcal{S}^{\mathcal{N}}(\mathsf{N}))$ is mapped to $\gamma_1; \cdots; \gamma_n \in \mathcal{C}(\mathcal{S}^{\mathcal{G}}(\mathsf{G}))$, then $\nu_1; \cdots; \nu_n; \nu \in \mathcal{C}(\mathcal{S}^{\mathcal{N}}(\mathsf{N}))$ iff $\gamma_1; \cdots; \gamma_n; \gamma \in \mathcal{C}(\mathcal{S}^{\mathcal{G}}(\mathsf{G}))$, where $\gamma_1; \cdots; \gamma_n; \gamma$ is the image of $\nu_1; \cdots; \nu_n; \nu$ under the bijection.

Suppose $\sigma = \mathsf{comm}(\nu_1) \cdots \mathsf{comm}(\nu_n) = \mathsf{comm}(\gamma_1) \cdots \mathsf{comm}(\gamma_n)$.

Let $\mathsf{comm}(\nu) = \alpha$. By Lemma 2, if $\nu_1; \cdots; \nu_n; \nu$ is a proving sequence of $\mathcal{S}^{\mathcal{N}}(\mathsf{N})$, then $\mathsf{N} \xrightarrow{\sigma} \mathsf{N}_0 \xrightarrow{\alpha} \mathsf{N}'$. Then we get $\nu = \{\, \mathsf{p} :: \sigma \cdot \alpha \looparrowright \mathsf{p}, \mathsf{q} :: \sigma \cdot \alpha \looparrowright \mathsf{q} \,\}$ by Lemma 1(1). By Definition 25 $\mathsf{nec}(\sigma \cdot \alpha) = \nu_1; \cdots; \nu_n; \nu$. By applying iteratively Subject Reduction (Theorem 2) $\mathsf{G} \xrightarrow{\sigma} \mathsf{G}_0 \xrightarrow{\alpha} \mathsf{G}'$ and $\vdash \mathsf{N}' : \mathsf{G}'$. By Definition 26 $\mathsf{gec}(\sigma \cdot \alpha) = \gamma_1; \cdots; \gamma_n; \gamma$. By Lemma 3(2) $\mathsf{gec}(\sigma \cdot \alpha)$ is a proving sequence of $\mathcal{S}^{\mathcal{G}}(\mathsf{G})$.

Let now $\mathsf{comm}(\gamma) = \alpha$. By Lemma 4, if $\gamma_1; \cdots; \gamma_n; \gamma$ is a proving sequence of $\mathcal{S}^{\mathcal{G}}(\mathsf{G})$, then $\mathsf{G} \xrightarrow{\sigma} \mathsf{G}_0 \xrightarrow{\alpha} \mathsf{G}'$. By Lemma 3(1) we have $\gamma = [\sigma \circ \alpha]_\sim$. By Definition 26 $\mathsf{gec}(\sigma \cdot \alpha) = \gamma_1; \cdots; \gamma_n; \gamma$. By applying iteratively Session Fidelity (Theorem 3) $\mathsf{N} \xrightarrow{\sigma} \mathsf{N}_0 \xrightarrow{\alpha} \mathsf{N}'$ and $\vdash \mathsf{N}' : \mathsf{G}'$. By Definition 25 $\mathsf{nec}(\sigma \cdot \alpha) = \nu_1; \cdots; \nu_n; \nu$. By Lemma 1(2) $\mathsf{nec}(\sigma \cdot \alpha)$ is a proving sequence of $\mathcal{S}^{\mathcal{N}}(\mathsf{N})$.

8   Related Work and Conclusions

Event Structures (ESs) were introduced in Winskel's PhD Thesis [50] and in the seminal paper by Nielsen, Plotkin and Winskel [42], roughly in the same frame of time as Milner's calculus CCS [40]. It is therefore not surprising that the relationship between these two approaches for modelling concurrent computations started to be investigated very soon afterwards. The first interpretation of CCS into ESs was proposed by Winskel in [51]. This interpretation made use of Stable ESs, because PESs, the simplest form of ESs, appeared not to be flexible enough to account for CCS parallel composition. Indeed, since CCS parallel composition allows for two concurrent complementary actions to either synchronise or occur independently in any order, each pair of such actions gives rise to two forking computations: this requires duplication of the same continuation process for each computation in PESs, while the continuation process may be shared by the forking computations in Stable ESs, which allow for disjunctive causality. Subsequently, ESs (as well as other nonsequential "denotational models" for concurrency such as Petri Nets) have been used as the touchstone for assessing noninterleaving operational semantics for CCS: for instance, the pomset semantics for CCS by Boudol and Castellani [7,8] and the semantics based on "concurrent histories" proposed by Degano, De Nicola and Montanari [23–25], were both shown to agree with an interpretation of CCS processes into some class of ESs (PESs for [23,24], PESs with non-hereditary conflict for [7] and FESs for [8]). Among the early interpretations of process calculi into ESs, we should also mention the PES semantics for TCSP (Theoretical CSP [11,43]), proposed by Goltz and Loogen [39] and generalised by Baier and Majster-Cederbaum [2], and the Bundle ES semantics for LOTOS, proposed by Langerak [38] and extended by

Katoen [36]. Like FESs, Bundle ESs are a subclass of Stable ESs. We recall the relationships between the above classes of ESs (the reader is referred to [10] for separating examples):

Prime ESs ⊂ Bundle ESs ⊂ Flow ESs ⊂ Stable ESs ⊂ General ESs

More sophisticated ES semantics for CCS, based on FESs and designed to be robust under action refinement [1,22,29], were later proposed by Goltz and van Glabbeek [28]. Importantly, all the above-mentioned classes of ESs, except General ESs, give rise to the same *prime algebraic domains* of configurations, from which one can recover a PES by selecting the complete prime elements.

More recently, ES semantics have been investigated for the π-calculus by Crafa, Varacca and Yoshida [17,18,48] and by Cristescu, Krivine and Varacca [19–21]. Other causal models for the π-calculus had already been put forward by Jategaonkar and Jagadeesan [35], by Montanari and Pistore [41], by Cattani and Sewell [16] and by Bruni, Melgratti and Montanari [12]. The main new issue, when addressing causality-based semantics for the π-calculus, is the implicit causality induced by scope extrusion. Two alternative views of such implicit causality had been proposed in previous work on noninterleaving operational semantics for the π-calculus, respectively by Boreale and Sangiorgi [6] and by Degano and Priami [26]. Essentially, in [6] an *extruder* (that is, an output of a private name) is considered to cause any action that uses the extruded name, whether in subject or object position, while in [26] it is considered to cause only the actions that use the extruded name in subject position. Thus, for instance, in the process $P = \nu a \left(\overline{b}\langle a \rangle \mid \overline{c}\langle a \rangle \mid a \right)$, the two parallel extruders are considered to be causally dependent in the former approach, and independent in the latter. All the causal models for the π-calculus mentioned above, including the ES-based ones, take one or the other of these two stands. Note that opting for the second one leads necessarily to a non-stable ES model, where there may be causal ambiguity within the configurations themselves: for instance, in the above example the maximal configuration contains three events, the extruders $\overline{b}\langle a \rangle$, $\overline{c}\langle a \rangle$ and the input on a, and one does not know which of the two extruders enabled the input. Indeed, the paper [18] uses non-stable ESs. The use of non-stable ESs (General ESs) to express situations where a computational step can merge parts of the state is advocated for instance by Baldan, Corradini and Gadducci in [3]. These ESs give rise to configuration domains that are not prime algebraic, hence the classical representation theorems have to be adjusted.

In our simple setting, where we deal only with single sessions and do not consider session interleaving nor delegation, we can dispense with channels altogether, and therefore the question of parallel extrusion does not arise. In this sense, our notion of causality is closer to that of CCS than to the more complex one of the π-calculus. However, even in a more general setting, where participants would be paired with the channel name of the session they pertain to, the issue of parallel extrusion would not arise: indeed, in the above example b and c should be equal, because participants can only delegate their own channel, but then they could not be in parallel because of linearity, one of the distinguishing features enforced by session types. Hence we believe that in a session-based framework the two above views of implicit causality should collapse into just one.

We now briefly discuss our design choices. Our calculus uses synchronous communication - rather than asynchronous, buffered communication - because this is how communication is modelled in ESs, when they are used to give semantics to process calculi. Concerning the choice operator, we adopted here the basic (and most restrictive) variant for it, as it was originally proposed for multiparty session calculi in [33]. This is essentially a simplifying assumption, and we do not foresee any difficulty in extending our results to a more general choice operator allowing for different receivers, where the projection is more flexible thanks to a merge operator [34]. Finally, concerning subtyping, we envisaged to use the standard preorder on processes, in which a process with fewer outputs is smaller than a process with more outputs. Session Fidelity becomes weaker, since the reduction of global types only assures the reduction of networks, possibly with a different atomic communication. The main drawback is that Theorem 4 would no longer hold, and the domains of network configurations would only be embedded in the domains of their global type configurations.

As regards future work, we plan to define an asynchronous transition system (ATS) [4] for our calculus, along the lines of [10], and show that it provides a noninterleaving operational semantics for networks that is equivalent to their FES semantics. This would enable us also to investigate the issue of reversibility, jointly on our networks and on their FES representations, since the ATS semantics would give us the handle to unwind networks, while the corresponding FESs could be unrolled following one of the methods proposed in existing work on reversible event structures [21,30,31,44].

Acknowledgments. It is a great pleasure for us to contribute to this volume in honour of Rocco, who has been a long-time friend and colleague for all of us. For some of us, this friendship dates back to the early years when Rocco was a Master student at Pisa University. The human qualities that made him become so widely appreciated in the community, namely his friendliness, sense of humour and warmth, as well as his sharpness, dynamism and animating skills, were already quite visible at the time. Since then, Rocco has built up a highly successful career and has acted as an inspiring mentor for several students and young researchers. This is not the place for an exhaustive tribute to Rocco, whose scientific contributions span a wide spectrum of topics and are too numerous to recall. Suffice it to remember, besides his highly influential work on testing in collaboration with Matthew Hennessy, his frontline work on non-interleaving models of computation together with Pierpaolo Degano and Ugo Montanari, and his more recent work on models for service-oriented computing with a number of co-authors from the SENSORIA [5,14] and ASCENS projects. Our paper is a wink to Rocco's achievements in the last two areas of research.

We would like to thank the anonymous referees for their helpful comments.

References

1. Aceto, L., Hennessy, M.: Towards action-refinement in process algebras. In: Meyer, A.R. (ed.) LICS 1989, pp. 138–145. IEEE Computer Society Press, Washington (1989). https://doi.org/10.1109/LICS.1989.39168
2. Baier, C., Majster-Cederbaum, M.E.: The connection between an event structure semantics and an operational semantics for TCSP. Acta Informatica 31(1), 81–104 (1994). https://doi.org/10.1007/BF01178923
3. Baldan, P., Corradini, A., Gadducci, F.: Domains and event structures for fusions. In: Ouaknine, J. (ed.) LICS 2017, pp. 1–12. IEEE Computer Society Press, Washington (2017). https://doi.org/10.1109/LICS.2017.8005135
4. Bednarczyk, M.: Categories of Asynchronous Systems. Ph.D. thesis, University of Sussex (1988)
5. Boreale, M., Bruni, R., De Nicola, R., Loreti, M.: Caspis: a calculus of sessions, pipelines and services. Math. Struct. Comput. Sci. 25(3), 666–709 (2015). https://doi.org/10.1016/0890-5401(92)90008-4
6. Boreale, M., Sangiorgi, D.: A fully abstract semantics for causality in the π-calculus. Acta Informatica 35(5), 353–400 (1998). https://doi.org/10.1007/s002360050124
7. Boudol, G., Castellani, I.: On the semantics of concurrency: Partial orders and transition systems. In: Ehrig, H., Kowalski, R., Levi, G., Montanari, U. (eds.) CAAP 1987. LNCS, vol. 249, pp. 123–137. Springer, Heidelberg (1987). https://doi.org/10.1007/3-540-17660-8_52
8. Boudol, G., Castellani, I.: Permutation of transitions: an event structure semantics for CCS and SCCS. In: de Bakker, J.W., de Roever, W.-P., Rozenberg, G. (eds.) REX 1988. LNCS, vol. 354, pp. 411–427. Springer, Heidelberg (1989). https://doi.org/10.1007/BFb0013028
9. Boudol, G., Castellani, I.: Flow models of distributed computations: event structures and nets. Research Report 1482, INRIA (1991)
10. Boudol, G., Castellani, I.: Flow models of distributed computations: three equivalent semantics for CCS. Inf. Comput. 114(2), 247–314 (1994). https://doi.org/10.1006/inco.1994.1088
11. Brookes, S., Hoare, C., Roscoe, A.: A theory of communicating sequential processes. J. ACM 31(3), 560–599 (1984). https://doi.org/10.1145/828.833
12. Bruni, R., Melgratti, H., Montanari, U.: Event structure semantics for nominal calculi. In: Baier, C., Hermanns, H. (eds.) CONCUR 2006. LNCS, vol. 4137, pp. 295–309. Springer, Heidelberg (2006). https://doi.org/10.1007/11817949_20
13. Caires, L., Pfenning, F.: Session types as intuitionistic linear propositions. In: Gastin, P., Laroussinie, F. (eds.) CONCUR 2010. LNCS, vol. 6269, pp. 222–236. Springer, Heidelberg (2010). https://doi.org/10.1007/978-3-642-15375-4_16
14. Caires, L., De Nicola, R., Pugliese, R., Vasconcelos, V.T., Zavattaro, G.: Core calculi for service-oriented computing. In: Wirsing, M., Hölzl, M. (eds.) Rigorous Software Engineering for Service-Oriented Systems. LNCS, vol. 6582, pp. 153–188. Springer, Heidelberg (2011). https://doi.org/10.1007/978-3-642-20401-2_8
15. Castellani, I., Dezani-Ciancaglini, M., Giannini, P.: Event structure semantics for multiparty sessions (Extended Version). Research Report 9266, INRIA (2019)
16. Cattani, G.L., Sewell, P.: Models for name-passing processes: interleaving and causal. Inf. Comput. 190(2), 136–178 (2004). https://doi.org/10.1016/j.ic.2003.12.003

17. Crafa, S., Varacca, D., Yoshida, N.: Compositional event structure semantics for the internal π-calculus. In: Caires, L., Vasconcelos, V.T. (eds.) CONCUR 2007. LNCS, vol. 4703, pp. 317–332. Springer, Heidelberg (2007). https://doi.org/10.1007/978-3-540-74407-8_22

18. Crafa, S., Varacca, D., Yoshida, N.: Event structure semantics of parallel extrusion in the Pi-calculus. In: Birkedal, L. (ed.) FoSSaCS 2012. LNCS, vol. 7213, pp. 225–239. Springer, Heidelberg (2012). https://doi.org/10.1007/978-3-642-28729-9_15

19. Cristescu, I.: Operational and denotational semantics for the reversible π-calculus. Ph.D. thesis, University Paris Diderot - Paris 7 (2015)

20. Cristescu, I.D., Krivine, J., Varacca, D.: Rigid families for CCS and the π-calculus. In: Leucker, M., Rueda, C., Valencia, F.D. (eds.) ICTAC 2015. LNCS, vol. 9399, pp. 223–240. Springer, Cham (2015). https://doi.org/10.1007/978-3-319-25150-9_14

21. Cristescu, I., Krivine, J., Varacca, D.: Rigid families for the reversible π-calculus. In: Devitt, S., Lanese, I. (eds.) RC 2016. LNCS, vol. 9720, pp. 3–19. Springer, Cham (2016). https://doi.org/10.1007/978-3-319-40578-0_1

22. Darondeau, P., Degano, P.: Refinement of actions in event structures and causal trees. Theor. Comput. Sci. **118**(1), 21–48 (1993). https://doi.org/10.1016/0304-3975(93)90361-V

23. Degano, P., De Nicola, R., Montanari, U.: On the consistency of truly concurrent operational and denotational semantics. In: Chandra, A.K. (ed.) LICS 1988. IEEE Computer Society Press, Washington (1988). https://doi.org/10.1109/LICS.1988.5112

24. Degano, P., De Nicola, R., Montanari, U.: A partial ordering semantics for CCS. Theor. Comput. Sci. **75**(3), 223–262 (1990). https://doi.org/10.1016/0304-3975(90)90095-Y

25. Degano, P., Montanari, U.: Concurrent histories: a basis for observing distributed systems. J. Comput. Syst. Sci. **34**(2/3), 422–461 (1987). https://doi.org/10.1016/0022-0000(87)90032-8

26. Degano, P., Priami, C.: Non-interleaving semantics for mobile processes. Theor. Comput. Sci. **216**(1–2), 237–270 (1999). https://doi.org/10.1016/S0304-3975(99)80003-6

27. Deniélou, P.-M., Yoshida, N.: Multiparty session types meet communicating automata. In: Seidl, H. (ed.) ESOP 2012. LNCS, vol. 7211, pp. 194–213. Springer, Heidelberg (2012). https://doi.org/10.1007/978-3-642-28869-2_10

28. van Glabbeek, R.J., Goltz, U.: Well-behaved flow event structures for parallel composition and action refinement. Theor. Comput. Sci. **311**(1–3), 463–478 (2004). https://doi.org/10.1016/j.tcs.2003.10.031

29. Goltz, U., Gorrieri, R., Rensink, A.: Comparing syntactic and semantic action refinement. Inf. Comput. **125**(2), 118–143 (1996). https://doi.org/10.1006/inco.1996.0026

30. Graversen, E., Phillips, I., Yoshida, N.: Towards a categorical representation of reversible event structures. In: Vasconcelos, V.T., Haller, P. (eds.) PLACES. EPTCS 2017, vol. 246, pp. 49–60. Open Publishing Association, Waterloo (2017). https://doi.org/10.4204/EPTCS.246.9

31. Graversen, E., Phillips, I., Yoshida, N.: Event structure semantics of (controlled) reversible CCS. In: Kari, J., Ulidowski, I. (eds.) RC 2018. LNCS, vol. 11106, pp. 102–122. Springer, Cham (2018). https://doi.org/10.1007/978-3-319-99498-7_7

32. Honda, K., Vasconcelos, V.T., Kubo, M.: Language primitives and type discipline for structured communication-based programming. In: Hankin, C. (ed.) ESOP 1998. LNCS, vol. 1381, pp. 122–138. Springer, Heidelberg (1998). https://doi.org/10.1007/BFb0053567

33. Honda, K., Yoshida, N., Carbone, M.: Multiparty asynchronous session types. In: Necula, G.C., Wadler, P. (eds.) POPL 2008, pp. 273–284. ACM Press, New York (2008). https://doi.org/10.1145/1328438.1328472

34. Honda, K., Yoshida, N., Carbone, M.: Multiparty asynchronous session types. J. ACM **63**(1), 9:1–9:67 (2016). https://doi.org/10.1007/978-3-319-40578-0_1

35. Jategaonkar Jagadeesan, L., Jagadeesan, R.: Causality and true concurrency: a data-flow analysis of the Pi-Calculus. In: Alagar, V.S., Nivat, M. (eds.) AMAST 1995. LNCS, vol. 936, pp. 277–291. Springer, Heidelberg (1995). https://doi.org/10.1007/3-540-60043-4_59

36. Katoen, J.: Quantitative and qualitative extensions of event structures. Ph.D. thesis, University of Twente (1996)

37. Lange, J., Tuosto, E., Yoshida, N.: From communicating machines to graphical choreographies. In: Rajamani, S.K., Walker, D. (eds.) POPL 2015, pp. 221–232. ACM Press, New York (2015). https://doi.org/10.1145/2676726.2676964

38. Langerak, R.: Bundle event structures: a non-interleaving semantics for LOTOS. In: Diaz, M., Groz, R. (eds.) Formal Description Techniques for Distributed Systems and Communication Protocols, pp. 331–346. North-Holland, Amsterdam (1993)

39. Loogen, R., Goltz, U.: Modelling nondeterministic concurrent processes with event structures. Fundamenta Informaticae **14**(1), 39–74 (1991). https://dblp.org/rec/bib/journals/fuin/LoogenG91

40. Milner, R. (ed.): A Calculus of Communicating Systems. LNCS, vol. 92. Springer, Heidelberg (1980). https://doi.org/10.1007/3-540-10235-3

41. Montanari, U., Pistore, M.: Concurrent semantics for the π-calculus. In: Brookes, S., Main, M., Melton, A., Mislove, M. (eds.) MFPS. ENTCS, vol. 1, pp. 411–429. Elsevier, Oxford (1995). https://doi.org/10.1016/S1571-0661(04)00024-6

42. Nielsen, M., Plotkin, G., Winskel, G.: Petri nets, event structures and domains, part I. Theor. Comput. Sci. **13**(1), 85–108 (1981). https://doi.org/10.1016/0304-3975(81)90112-2

43. Olderog, E.-R.: TCSP: theory of communicating sequential processes. In: Brauer, W., Reisig, W., Rozenberg, G. (eds.) ACPN 1986. LNCS, vol. 255, pp. 441–465. Springer, Heidelberg (1987). https://doi.org/10.1007/3-540-17906-2_34

44. Phillips, I., Ulidowski, I.: Reversibility and asymmetric conflict in event structures. J. Log. Algebr. Methods Program. **84**(6), 781–805 (2015). https://doi.org/10.1016/j.jlamp.2015.07.004

45. Pierce, B.C.: Types and Programming Languages. MIT Press, Cambridge (2002). https://dblp.org/rec/bib/books/daglib/0005958

46. Takeuchi, K., Honda, K., Kubo, M.: An interaction-based language and its typing system. In: Halatsis, C., Maritsas, D., Philokyprou, G., Theodoridis, S. (eds.) PARLE 1994. LNCS, vol. 817, pp. 398–413. Springer, Heidelberg (1994). https://doi.org/10.1007/3-540-58184-7_118

47. Toninho, B., Caires, L., Pfenning, F.: Dependent session types via intuitionistic linear type theory. In: Schneider-Kamp, P., Hanus, M. (eds.) PPDP 2011, pp. 161–172. ACM Press, New York (2011). https://doi.org/10.1145/2003476.2003499

48. Varacca, D., Yoshida, N.: Typed event structures and the linear π-calculus. Theor. Comput. Sci. **411**(19), 1949–1973 (2010)

49. Wadler, P.: Propositions as sessions. J. Funct. Program. **24**(2–3), 384–418 (2014). https://doi.org/10.1016/S1571-0661(04)00144-6

50. Winskel, G.: Events in Computation. Ph.D. thesis, University of Edinburgh (1980)

51. Winskel, G.: Event structure semantics for CCS and related languages. In: Nielsen, M., Schmidt, E.M. (eds.) ICALP 1982. LNCS, vol. 140, pp. 561–576. Springer, Heidelberg (1982). https://doi.org/10.1007/BFb0012800
52. Winskel, G.: An introduction to event structures. In: de Bakker, J.W., de Roever, W.-P., Rozenberg, G. (eds.) REX 1988. LNCS, vol. 354, pp. 364–397. Springer, Heidelberg (1989). https://doi.org/10.1007/BFb0013026

Distributed Systems Modelling

Process Calculi for Modelling Mobile, Service-Oriented, and Collective Autonomic Systems

Martin Wirsing$^{(\boxtimes)}$ and Rolf Hennicker$^{(\boxtimes)}$

Ludwig-Maximilians-Universität München, München, Germany
`wirsing@lmu.de`, `hennicker@ifi.lmu.de`

- Dedicated to Rocco De Nicola -

Abstract. Process-algebraic methods have proven to be excellent tools for designing and analysing concurrent systems. In this paper we review several process calculi and languages developed and studied by Rocco De Nicola and his students and colleagues in the three EU projects AGILE, SENSORIA, and ASCENS. These calculi provide a theoretical basis for engineering mobile, service-oriented, and collective autonomic systems. KLAIM is a framework for distributed mobile agents consisting of a kernel language, a stochastic extension, a logic for specifying properties of mobile applications, and an automatic tool for verifying such properties. In the AGILE project of the EU Global Computing Initiative I, KLAIM served as a the process-algebraic basis for an architectural approach to mobile systems development. For modelling and analysing service-oriented systems, a family of process-algebraic core calculi was developed in the SENSORIA project of the EU Global Computing Initiative II. These calculi address complementary aspects of service-oriented programming such as sessions and correlations. They come with reasoning and analysis techniques, specification and verification tools as well as prototypical analyses of case studies. In the ASCENS project, the language SCEL was developed for modelling and programming systems consisting of interactive autonomic components. SCEL is based on process-algebraic principles and supports formal description and analysis of the behaviours of ensembles of autonomic components.

1 Introduction

In the seventies of the last century, Robin Milner and Tony Hoare used process algebraic techniques for defining their concurrent programming languages CCS and (T)CSP. Also main program analysis techniques such as strong and weak bisimulation equivalence have been developed at that time. Since then process algebra is a flourishing field of computer science and the mathematical tool for modelling and analysing concurrent programming systems. Testing equivalence [30] and branching bisimulation [43] are two other important notions of

© Springer Nature Switzerland AG 2019
M. Boreale et al. (Eds.): De Nicola-Festschrift, LNCS 11665, pp. 367–387, 2019.
https://doi.org/10.1007/978-3-030-21485-2_20

program equivalence. They have been introduced by Robin Milner's PhD student Rocco De Nicola, the former notion together with Matthew Hennessy [32] and the latter together with Frits Vandraager.

In the years 2002–2015, three FET EU projects – AGILE [10], SENSORIA [73], and ASCENS [74] – aimed at developing rigorous engineering methods for advanced computing paradigms such as mobile, service-oriented, and interacting autonomic systems. In all three projects, Rocco De Nicola was one of the main contributors and the principal investigator who was responsible for the use of process calculi as a main tool for providing mathematical foundations and analysis techniques. In this paper we review main process calculi and languages of AGILE, SENSORIA, and ASCENS, show their main language primitives and draw some relationships between different calculi. In addition, we shortly describe the projects AGILE, SENSORIA, and ASCENS and the European initiatives which supported these projects.

Personal Note. Martin and Rocco know each other since 1981 when Rocco was a PhD student at the University of Edinburgh and Martin was there as a guest lecturer. Rocco and Martin were working on different research topics - Martin on formal software development and algebraic specifications, Rocco on process calculi and concurrent computations. They became friends and were meeting for common excursions, dinners, and drinks. Almost 20 years later at an EU workshop in Edinburgh for promoting the so-called Global Computing Initiative, they met again and decided to plan a common project. Then at ETAPS 2001, together with José Fiadeiro and Ugo Montanari the idea of AGILE was born and a successful proposal was written. On January 1, 2002, the AGILE project started and also the fruitful collaboration of Rocco and Martin, later joined by Rolf. It continued in the SENSORIA and the ASCENS project where Rocco was responsible for the development of the calculi for service-oriented computing and the SCEL language for autonomic computing. The collaboration continues until today. In 2013 Rocco was a guest professor at LMU Munich; in 2014, Rocco and Martin (together with Matthias Hölzl) organised the track on "Rigorous Engineering of Autonomic Ensembles" [72] at ISoLA 2014 [59]. Then in 2015 Rocco and Rolf edited the Festschrift for Martin [34] and wrote together the paper on Martin's professional career [33]; in 2018 Rocco and Martin (together with Stefan Jähnichen) chaired a track at the ISoLA conference [60], the track on "Rigorous Engineering of Collective Adaptive Systems" [35].

Working and discussing with Rocco is a very pleasant experience. He is not only an outstanding scientist and an excellent coordinator of work; he is also a warm-hearted and kind friend and colleague. We are looking forward to many further inspiring exchanges with him.

Outline. In Sect. 2 we present shortly the Global Computing Initiative, the AGILE project, and the process algebraic framework for network aware programming that was developed in AGILE. In Sect. 3 we discuss service-oriented computing and present basic features of the SENSORIA core calculi for service-oriented computing. In Sect. 4 we introduce ensemble computing, present the main characteristics of the SCEL language for modelling interacting autonomic components, and draw some relationships between SCEL and KLAIM. Some concluding remarks are given in Sect. 5.

2 Mobile Systems: The AGILE Project and Network-Aware Programming

The AGILE project was one of the projects of the first Global Computing Initiative (see Sect. 2.1) the European Commission had launched in 2001. AGILE (see Sect. 2.2) was focussing on software architectures for mobile computing and on process-based calculi and languages for modelling and analysing mobile systems. One of the main results of AGILE is the KLAIM framework for network-aware programming (see Sect. 2.3).

2.1 The Global Computing Initiative I

The Global Computing Initiative [4] was a proactive action within the Information Society Technologies (IST) priority of 5th Framework Programme for Research and Technological Development (FP5) of the European Commission. In 2001–2005, the initiative was carried out as action-line IST-2001-6.2.2 of the Future and Emerging Technologies (FET) unit of the European Commission. The aim was to develop the theoretical foundations needed to enable the design and construction of "rapidly evolving interacting systems" that work over a "massive networked infrastructure composed of highly diverse interconnected objects". Dominant concerns were those of "handling the co-ordination and interaction, security, reliability, robustness, failure modes, and control of risk of the entities in the system and the overall design, description and performance of the system itself".

13 research and development projects[1] were funded by the initiative, among them the projects AGILE and MIKADO. Typically, the projects had four to seven partners from three or more European countries and were focussing on the scientific foundations of global computing. The expert report on the results of the initiative [66] states that "the Global Computing initiative successfully brought together most of the best European theoretical computer science groups. With more than 1000 peer-reviewed publications and 50 PhD theses, the scientific output was found to be very high and the results were at the forefront of the state of the art".

---

[1] AGILE, CRESCCO, DART, DBGLOBE, DEGAS, FLAGS, MIKADO, MRG, MYTHS, PEPITO, PROFUNDIS, SECURE, SOCS (see [4]).

2.2   Architectures for Mobility: The AGILE Project

The project "Architectures for Mobility" (AGILE) [2,10] had eight partners[2] (six universities, one research institution and one company) from five countries and was running from January 2002 until April 2005. It was developing an architectural approach in which mobility aspects of software can be modelled explicitly and mapped on the distribution and communication topology made available at physical levels. The approach was founded on a uniform mathematical framework based on process algebra and graph-oriented techniques that support sound methodological principles, formal analysis, and refinement across levels of development.

The AGILE project produced more than 180 scientific publications and - in addition to the cooperation with ATX - established cooperations with 10 other companies. A description of first results is given in [10], an informal overview can be found in the AGILE brochure at [2]. Main results comprise an extension of the program design language CommUnity in order to support the design of mobile components [48], an extension of UML, called Mobile UML, to model systems with mobility [14,57], two extensions of KLAIM for modelling mobile open systems [15] and for addressing quantitative aspects [31] as well as temporal logics and formalisms for specifying properties of mobile systems (e.g. the modal logic MoMo [41]), software engineering (e.g. on property driven software development and on combining agents and components [13,55]), analysis, verification and refinement techniques (e.g. [46,53]), and many foundational results (e.g. on tile systems [21]). Moreover, the AGILE methods have been applied to several case studies including the GSM handover protocol and a multi-user-dungeon game. Several tools were developed for helping the software engineer to model mobile systems, to write better software, and to analyse properties of software (e.g. the HAL modelchecker [45], for an overview see the tools list at [2]).

2.3   A Framework for Network-Aware Programming

A cornerstone of the AGILE project was the experimental programming language KLAIM (**K**ernel **L**anguage for **A**gents **I**nteraction and **M**obility) and its framework for network aware programming [15]. KLAIM has already been defined before AGILE [29] and was also an important ingredient of the MIKADO project. The KLAIM framework was developed by Rocco De Nicola (at that time professor at Università di Firenze) and his research group in cooperation with colleagues from ISTI and Università di Pisa.

KLAIM. KLAIM is specifically designed to model and to program distributed concurrent applications with code mobility. It is inspired by the Linda coordination model [26,49]; it relies on the concept of tuple space to store data and on

---

[2] The AGILE partners were LMU München (coordinator), Università di Pisa, Università di Firenze, ISTI Pisa, ATX Software SA, Universidade de Lisboa, University of Warsaw (from August 2002), and University of Leicester (from January 2003).

pattern matching for retrieving data. Concurrency is based on a basic process calculus with process invocation and CCS-like parallel composition and action prefixing; name restriction as in the π-calculus is available on the level of nets. Distribution is modeled by hierarchically structuring concurrency: a KLAIM program is a net which consists of a parallel composition of nodes; each node has a name (called site) and contains a single tuple space and possibly several concurrent processes in execution. The processes are the active computational units. They may run concurrently either at the same node or at different nodes and can perform different actions which in turn manage the tuple spaces, provide code mobility and permit to create new network nodes.

Syntax and Semantics of KLAIM. More formally, a KLAIM net can be either a single *node* or a composition of nets N_1 and N_2, $N_1 \parallel N_2$. A *node* is a triple $s ::_\rho C$ where s is a *site*, i.e. a name for a locality, C is the *component* that is located at s, and ρ defines an *allocation environment*. A *site* can be thought of as a globally valid identifier for a node. Sites are considered to be first-order data which can be created dynamically and shared using the tuple space. A *component* consists of a parallel composition $P|\langle t_1 \rangle|...|\langle t_n \rangle$ of a process P and tuples $\langle t_1 \rangle, ..., \langle t_n \rangle$. An *allocation environment* is a (partial) function from (locality) variables to sites. $[s/l]$ denotes the environment that maps the variable l to the site s. The distinguished variable *self* refers to the current execution site.

The four basic actions $out(t)@l$, $eval(Q)@l$, $read(T)@l$, and $in(T)@l$ correspond to the Linda operations to generate a tuple t (**out**) at the site denoted by l, spawn a process Q (**eval**), read a tuple matching the pattern T (**read**), and consume a tuple matching T (**in**) [26]. In KLAIM, the actions have locality variables as a postfix, which denote the sites the actions address. In addition to the operations borrowed from Linda, the $newloc(u)$ action is used to create a fresh site; the locality variable u refers to that fresh site in the prefixed process. The latter action is not postfixed with an address because it always acts locally.

The KLAIM semantics is given in terms of a structural congruence, rules for pattern matching, and a reduction relation $\rightarrowtail$ over the nets. Figure 1 shows a few structural operational rules; for the complete semantics see [15]. In rule (In) σ

$$(\text{Out}) \frac{\rho(l) = s' \quad [\![t]\!]_\rho = et}{s ::_\rho out(t)@l.P \parallel s' ::_{\rho'} P' \rightarrowtail s ::_\rho P \parallel s' ::_{\rho'} P' \parallel s' ::_{\rho'} \langle et \rangle}$$

$$(\text{Eval}) \frac{\rho(l) = s'}{s ::_\rho eval(Q)@l.P \parallel s' ::_{\rho'} P' \rightarrowtail s ::_\rho P \parallel s' ::_{\rho'} P'|Q}$$

$$(\text{In}) \frac{\rho(l) = s' \quad match([\![T]\!]_\rho, t) = \sigma}{s ::_\rho in(T)@l.P \parallel s' ::_{\rho'} \langle t \rangle \rightarrowtail s ::_\rho P\sigma \parallel s' ::_{\rho'} nil}$$

$$(\text{New}) \frac{s' \notin S}{S \vdash s ::_\rho newloc(u).P \rightarrowtail S \cup \{s'\} \vdash s ::_\rho P[s'/u] \parallel s' ::_{\rho[s'/self]} nil}$$

Fig. 1. A few rules of KLAIM

is a substitution, in rule (New) S stands for the set of all currently existing sites and $S \vdash N$ expresses that all sites occurring in the net N are elements of S.

Extensions of KLAIM. KLAIM has several extensions that support particular programming and modelling styles.

MetaKLAIM is an extension of KLAIM to permit meta-programming activities such as linking of code fragments. It integrates an extension of SML for multi-stage programming, called MetaML, with KLAIM and exploits an expressive type system to dynamically enforce security policies [47]. STOcKLAIM [40] is a stochastic extension of (the core calculus cKLAIM of) KLAIM for modelling quantitative and qualitative aspects of mobile systems. The key idea is to measure action durations in a stochastic way by adding continuous random variables with exponential distributions to the actions. The Kaos language [31] enriches KLAIM actions with attributes for specifying quality of service properties and access rights. Quality of service costs are described as abstract costs, formally given as elements of a constraint semiring [18]. X-KLAIM is a programming language that extends KLAIM with high-level constructs and strong mobility [16].

Logics and Type Systems for KLAIM. KLAIM is equipped with type systems that express and ensure security policies. A capability-based static type system guarantees the control of access rights and a dynamic type system enables to program the acquisition of dynamic privileges, e.g. for controlling the access of host resources by possibly malicious mobile processes (see [15,41], Sect. 4).

For reasoning about KLAIM and STOcKLAIM programs appropriate modal logics ([15], Sect. 3 and [41]) and stochastic logics [36] have been developed. The first logic is inspired by the Hennessy-Milner logic [51] and the μ-calculus [54] and permits to specify and verify dynamic properties of networks such as resource management and mobility aspects of concurrent processes. The modal logic is accompanied by the KlaiML framework for analysing the properties of KLAIM systems. Temporal properties of processes are typically expressed as $\langle \mathcal{A} \rangle \Phi$ by means of the diamond operator $\langle \rangle$ indexed with a set $\mathcal{A}$ of so-called label predicates, i.e. predicates that specify finite or infinite sets of KLAIM actions. A net N satisfies $\langle \mathcal{A} \rangle \Phi$ if there exists an action a in $\mathcal{A}$ and a net N' such that by performing a, N reduces to N' and N' satisfies the formula Φ.

A second modal logic, called MoMo [41], is not so closely related to KLAIM. It abstracts from the specific KLAIM actions and instead models resource production and consumption by state predicates and can express nominal properties for handling names and mobility properties for controlling mobile processes. The logics for reasoning on STOcKLAIM processes are the temporal stochastic logics MOSL (Mobile Stochastic Logic) and $MOSL^+$ [36]. The latter is inspired by MoMo and can be seen as an action-based variant of the continuous stochastic logic CSL [11]. $MOSL^+$ formulas express stochastic performance and dependability properties such as the likelihood of resource consumption and production.

Tools for Interpreting and Analysing KLAIM. Several tools support interpreting and analysing KLAIM models. Klava (KLAIM in JAVA) [17] is a JAVA package implementing all the functionalities for the run-time systems of KLAIM. Also the logics for KLAIM come with tools. The KLAIML prover supports reachability analysis and satisfiability checking of properties [15]. Similarly, the reasoning tool SAM [36] for MOSL$^+$ supports simulating STOcKLAIM specifications, analysing their reachability graphs and checking the satisfiability of MOSL$^+$ formulas.

3   Service-Oriented Systems

In 2004 the Future Emerging Technology unit launched a follow up call on Global Computing for deepening and consolidating the results of the first Global Computing Initiative (see Sect. 3.1). With its focus on service-oriented computing, SENSORIA (see Sect. 3.2) was one of the three funded Integrated Projects. Process calculi were a main strand of research in SENSORIA. They served as a semantic basis for programming and modelling the dynamic aspects of service-oriented systems and for analysing their properties (see Sect. 3.3).

3.1   The Global Computing Initiative II

In the 6th framework programme of the European Commission, the Future Emerging Technology unit launched a follow-up action of the first Global Computing Initiative. The call IST-2004-2.3.4.2(v) on Global Computing was focussing on "computational infrastructures available globally and able to provide uniform services with variable guarantees for communication, co-operation and mobility, resource usage, security policies and mechanisms, etc., with particular regard to exploiting their universal scale and the programmability of their services." Moreover, the call asked for large projects, so-called Integrated Projects, and for a "research approach aiming at substantial integration between theory, systems building and experimentation, following a foundational approach typical of computer science research."

As a result, in 2005 three Integrated Projects were funded: AEOLUS [1] on "algorithmic principles for building efficient overlay computers", MOBIUS [5] on "proof-carrying code for Java on mobile devices", and SENSORIA [7] on "software engineering for service-oriented overlay computers."

3.2   Modelling and Engineering Service-Oriented Systems: The SENSORIA Project

The SENSORIA project [70,73] was a joint initiative of researchers from four projects of the first Global Computing Initiative[3]. SENSORIA had 19 partners[4] (14 universities, one research institution, and four companies) from seven countries and was running from October 2005 until February 2010. The aim of the SENSORIA project was to develop a comprehensive approach to the engineering of service-oriented software systems where foundational theories, techniques and methods were fully integrated in a pragmatic software engineering approach.

The SENSORIA project produced more than 650 scientific publications and more than 25 software tools; based on SENSORIA results, three spin-off companies were founded. The main results are collected in [73], an informal overview of the results is given in the SENSORIA brochure at [7]. The results of SENSORIA include semantically well-defined modelling and programming concepts (including the SENSORIA Reference Modelling Language SRML and UML extensions for service-oriented systems), calculi for service-oriented computing, calculi and methods for negotiations, planning, and reconfiguration as well as qualitative and quantitative analysis techniques and tools, and methods for model-driven development and reverse engineering. The SENSORIA methods have been applied to case studies in the service-intensive areas of e-business, automotive systems, e-learning, and telecommunications.

3.3   A Family of Core Process Calculi for Service-Oriented Systems

Process calculi for service specification and analysis were a main strand of research in SENSORIA. They served as a semantic basis for programming and modelling dynamic aspects of services and service-oriented systems and for analysing qualitative and quantitative properties of services. In cooperation with colleagues from Bologna, Lisboa, and Pisa, Rocco De Nicola and his research group were leading and coordinating the SENSORIA research on calculi for service-oriented computing.

Several calculi have been developed and studied. The core calculi aim at a foundational understanding of the service-oriented computing paradigm whereas the other calculi (such as λ^{req} [12], CC-Pi [22], and PEPA [25]) focus on particular issues such as service discovery, negotiation, composition, transactions, or performance modelling. The core calculi support complementary aspects of

---

[3] AGILE, DEGAS, MIKADO, PROFUNDIS.

[4] The SENSORIA partners were LMU München (coordinator), Università di Trento, University of Leicester, University of Warsaw, TU Demark at Lyngby, Università di Pisa, Università di Firenze, Università di Bologna, ISTI Pisa, Universidade de Lisboa, ATX Software SA (ATX II Technologies SA, from October 2006), Telecom Italia S.p.A., Imperial College London, University College London, FAST GmbH (Cirquent GmbH, from 2008), S & N AG Paderborn, Budapest University of Technology and Economics, and MIP Business School of Politecnico di Milano (from March 2007).

service-oriented computing [24,71]. The SENSORIA core calculi are SCC [19], COWS [65], SOCK [50] and three SCC extensions CaSPIS [20], SSCC [56], and CC [68]. MarCaSPiS [38] is a Markovian extension of CaSPiS.

A characteristics of service-oriented computing is the way how a service client and the service provider communicate. In contrast to, e.g., the call mechanism of object-oriented programming, a client does not call its partner only once but both communication partners engage in a conversation during which they interact several times. There are two types of conversations: a session instantiates implicitly a private channel between client and server which is then used for the communication; in a correlation-based communication, the link between client and server is determined by so-called correlation values which are explicitly included in the exchanged messages. We can classify the core calculi according to their type of communication: SCC and its extensions are session-based, whereas COWS and SOCK use correlations.

SCC is a minimalistic calculus following the slogan "everything is a service"; sessions are dyadic conversations between exactly two communication partners. The three other calculi extend SCC by a mechanism for inter-session communication: CaSPIS is dataflow-oriented and (similar to Orc [62]) uses pipelines for passing data between different sessions; SSCC uses streams for inter-session communication whereas CC focusses on multi-party conversations between several communication partners such that conversation partners can be dynamically added and dismissed. Both COWS and SOCK are inspired by WS-BPEL but they differ in their form of correlation. COWS uses memoryless correlation based on pattern matching whereas correlation in SOCK depends on the state of so-called correlation variables and thus is memoryful.

The key notions of the session-oriented calculi are service definition, service invocation and session. In particular, the session-oriented calculi SCC, CaSPIS, and SSCC support explicit modelling of sessions both on the client and on the service side, and provide mechanisms for session naming and scoping, by relying on the constructs of π-calculus [61]. Here we use CaSPIS to describe the basic service interactions for establishing a session in more detail (see [24]). For comparison we show also the corresponding rules of (the μ-fragment of) COWS which use pattern matching for identifying the communication partners (see [65]).

A service definition in CaSPIS takes the form $s.P$, where s is a service name, and P the body of the service. A client of a service is written $\overline{s}.Q$. Synchronisation of $s.P$ and $\overline{s}.Q$ causes the activation of a new session, identified by a fresh name r that can be viewed as a private, synchronous channel binding caller and callee. A session naturally comes with two sides, written $r \triangleright P$ and $r \triangleright Q$, with r bound above them by (νr) (see rule (Sync) below). Values produced by P can be consumed by Q, and vice-versa. Figure 2 shows three basic rules of the operational semantics of CaSPIS: service definition, service invocation and synchronisation.

In COWS a correlation is dyadic and indicated by two endpoints where an endpoint is a pair $p \bullet o$ consisting of a communication partner name p and an operation name o. A service invocation by client is atomic and has the form $n!e$

$$(\text{Def})\frac{r \notin \text{fn}(P)}{s.P \xrightarrow{s(r)} r \triangleright P} \qquad (\text{Call})\frac{r \notin \text{fn}(Q)}{\bar{s}.Q \xrightarrow{\bar{s}(r)} r \triangleright Q}$$

$$(\text{Sync})\frac{P_1 \xrightarrow{s(r)} P_2 \quad Q_1 \xrightarrow{\bar{s}(r)} Q_2}{P_1|Q_1 \xrightarrow{\tau} (\nu r)(P_2|Q_2)}$$

Fig. 2. Basic rules of CaSPIS

where n is an endpoint $p \bullet o$ and e is a tuple of expressions possibly containing variables. The invocation can take place if all variables of the argument expression are instantiated (by fully evaluating e with the result v, see rule (Inv) of Fig. 3). A receive activity of a server has the form $n?w$ where n is an endpoint $p \bullet o$ and w is a tuple of variables and values (see rule (Rec) of Fig. 3). For a communication (see rule (Com) of Fig. 3), client and server are correlated by performing matching of invocation and receive activities.

$$(\text{Inv})\frac{[\![e]\!] = v}{n!e \xrightarrow{n \triangleleft v} 0} \qquad (\text{Rec}) \ n?w.s \xrightarrow{n \triangleright w} s$$

$$(\text{Com})\frac{s_1 \xrightarrow{n \triangleright w} s_1' \quad s_2 \xrightarrow{n \triangleleft v} s_2' \quad match(w,v) = \sigma}{s_1|s_2 \xrightarrow{\sigma} s_1'|s_2'}$$

Fig. 3. Basic rules of COWS

3.4 Analysis Techniques, Logics and Case Studies

Static analysis techniques have been developed for all three session-oriented core calculi CaSPIS, SSCC, and CC. In particular, CaSPIS has a type system for control flow and client progress [8], CC a type system for conversation fidelity and progress [8], and SSCC a type system for protocol compatibility for SSCC [56].

SocL [44] is an action and state-based branching time temporal logic for expressing properties of COWS specifications. The CMC/UMC modelchecker [44] supports the analysis of COWS models by an on-the-fly model checking algorithm for SocL formulas; it has been applied to many SENSORIA case studies.

The stochastic temporal logic SoSL [39] is a variant of MOSL^{+} [36]; it supports reasoning on quantitative properties of service-oriented systems expressed in MarCaSPIS. For the automated analysis of SoSL formulas an existing state-based stochastic modelchecker is used.

All core calculi have been applied for modelling and analysing properties of the SENSORIA case studies (from the automotive, finance, telecommunication, and eUniversity domains) [67].

4   Collective Autonomic Systems

In 2009 "Self-Awareness in Autonomic Systems" was the topic of a call of the Future Emerging Technology unit in the 7th framework programme of the European Commission (see Sect. 4.1). The ASCENS project – one of four funded projects – developed a comprehensive engineering approach for engineering distributed autonomic systems, so-called autonomic ensembles (see Sect. 4.2). A central result of ASCENS is the Service Component Ensemble Language (SCEL) and its framework for programming and reasoning on ensembles of autonomic components (see Sect. 4.3).

4.1   Self-Awareness in Autonomic Systems

In the 7th framework programme for ICT of the European Commission, the Future Emerging Technology unit launched several calls for projects in the area of computing and communication paradigms. The action ICT-2009.8.5 addressed the topic "Self-Awareness in Autonomic Systems" and called for "new concepts, architectures, foundations and technologies" for computing and communication systems "that are able to optimise overall performance and resource usage in response to changing conditions, adapting to both context (such as user behaviour) and internal changes (such as topology)."

In 2010 four projects were funded: ASCENS [3] on "autonomic service-component ensembles", Recognition on "relevance and cognition for self-awareness in a content-centric internet", SAPERE on "self-aware pervasive service ecosystems", and EPiCS on "engineering proprioception in computing systems."

4.2   Autonomic Service-Component Ensembles: The ASCENS Project

Ensembles are distributed software-intensive systems that can operate in open-ended environments, adapt to changing environments or requirements, and handle failures of individual nodes [52]. The idea for the ASCENS project started with discussions at several workshops of the Interlink project [69] where leading international experts had identified the new paradigm of ensemble computing systems and the development of self-organising systems as important challenges and trends for software-intensive systems [52]. Consequently, the aim of the ASCENS project [75] was to develop a comprehensive approach to engineer autonomic ensembles. The ASCENS project had 17 partners[5] (11 universities,

---

[5] The ASCENS partners were LMU München (coordinator), Università di Pisa, Università di Firenze, Fraunhofer FIRST (now Fraunhofer FOKUS), VERIMAG Laboratory, Università di Modena e Reggio Emilia, Université Libre de Bruxelles, Ecole Polytechnique Fédérale de Lausanne, Volkswagen AG, Lero - University of Limerick, Zimory GmbH, and ISTI Pisa, and from July 2011 IMT Lucca, Mobsya, and Charles University Prague.

four research institutions, and two companies) from seven countries and was running from October 2010 until March 2015.

The ASCENS project produced more than 300 scientific publications - among them 8 best paper awards - and more than 25 software products and prototypes. ASCENS achieved both pragmatic and formal results (for a collection of main results see [74], for an informal overview see the ASCENS brochure at [3]). The pragmatic results comprise a process model for systems development called the Ensemble Development Life Cycle (EDLC), engineering techniques and tools for collective autonomic systems as well as case studies on autonomic robot swarms, autonomic cloud computing platforms, and autonomic e-mobility support. The foundational theories and methods developed in ASCENS support languages and verification for collective autonomic systems, modelling and theory for adaptive and self-aware systems, validation and verification of complex controlled systems, monitoring and dynamic adaptation of autonomic systems, both at design and at runtime.

4.3   The SCEL Framework for Ensemble Computing

A central result of ASCENS is the Service Component Ensemble Language (SCEL) [37] and its framework for programming and reasoning on ensembles of autonomic components. SCEL and its runtime environment were developed by Rocco De Nicola and his research group in cooperation with colleagues from ISTI and Pisa.

SCEL is a generic, high-level language for modelling autonomic systems. It provides programmers with a complete set of linguistic abstractions for programming the behaviour of components and the formation of ensembles, and for controlling the interaction among them. These abstractions permit autonomic systems to be described in terms of behaviours, knowledge and aggregations, by complying with specific policies, and to support programming context-awareness, self-awareness and adaptation.

Parameterised SCEL. SCEL can be seen as a generalisation and further development of KLAIM with a number of important new features. A SCEL system can be either a single component or a composition of systems S_1 and S_2 denoted by $S_1 \parallel S_2$. This is similar to a KLAIM net which is structured into a parallel composition of nodes. A SCEL component $\mathcal{J}[\mathcal{K}, \Pi, P]$ consists of four subparts (see Fig. 4): an interface $\mathcal{I}$ for publishing and making available structural and behavioural information about the component itself in the form of attributes, a knowledge repository $\mathcal{K}$ managing application data, internal status data (supporting self-awareness) and environmental data (supporting context-awareness), a set of policies Π regulating the interaction within the component and with other components, and process P (which can be composed by several processes). In particular, policies specify the authorisation requirements for communication such as quality of service or security requirements.

Thus a SCEL component is more elaborated and software engineering-oriented than a KLAIM node whose tuple space can be seen as a particular instance

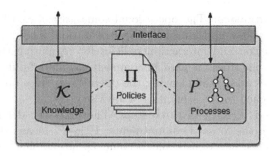

Fig. 4. SCEL component [37]

of a component's knowledge repository and whose site corresponds to the value of the identifier attribute of the component. Moreover, KLAIM offers no choice of policy; instead it adheres to a fixed (interleaving) policy.

Processes in SCEL are built with the usual CCS-like operators *nil*, action prefixing and non-deterministic choice. In addition, there is process invocation and - worth emphasising - a generalised parallel combinator the semantics of which is not only parameterised but can also be dynamically given by the current policy.

The actions of processes in SCEL are similar to those of KLAIM but instead of addressing a single node, SCEL actions can single out dynamically ensembles of communication partners by using predicates over their attributes, thus permitting a sort of attribute-based communication. The SCEL actions $get(T)@e$, $qry(T)@e$ and $put(t)@e$ are used to manage the shared knowledge repositories identified by e where e is either a component name n or a predicate p; T denotes patterns for selecting knowledge items t in the repositories. Component names are used for point-to-point communication, while the predicate enables a group-oriented "ensemble" communication. The set of components satisfying predicate p are considered as the ensemble with which the process performing the action intends to interact. The point-to-point communication action $get(T)@n$ corresponds to the KLAIM *in* for withdrawing information items, $qry(T)@n$ corresponds to the KLAIM *read* for retrieving items, and $put(t)@n$ corresponds to the KLAIM *out* for adding items. A main difference to KLAIM is the group communication where $get(T)@p$ and $qry(T)@p$ choose nondeterministically one item from a component interface satisfying the predicate p whereas $put(t)@p$ stores t in the repositories of all components satisfying p. Action $new(\mathcal{I}, \mathcal{K}, \Pi, P)$ creates a new component $\mathcal{I}[\mathcal{K}, \Pi, P]$ with process P. This corresponds in KLAIM to a composed action $newloc(u).eval(P)@u....$ which creates a new node with process P. Action $fresh(n)$ realises name restriction. It introduces a scope restriction for the name n so that this name is guaranteed to be different from any other name previously used. It has no directly corresponding action in KLAIM but a similar effect as $(\nu n)N$.

Operational Semantics. The operational semantics of SCEL is parametric in the notions of policy and knowledge representation. This allows the use of different authorisation and interaction policies for regulating the execution of actions (including the rules for parallel composition) and of different formats of knowledge representation while leaving the operational rules untouched (for an early similar approach to the semantics of Java see [27]).

The semantics is defined in three steps. The first step defines the semantics of processes in the form of commitments: $P \downarrow_\alpha P'$ means that process "P can commit to perform action α and become P' after doing so." The second step specifies a labelled transition system for SCEL systems which is parametric w.r.t. the process semantics and two predicates ($\succ$ and $\vdash$) expressing interaction patterns and authorisation policies. There are particular system labels to indicate the intention of a component to perform a (repository access) action or the agreement with the execution of such an action depending on the current policy. The final operational semantics consists of unlabelled reductions that rely on the conditions and labels checked in the second step.

We describe briefly the semantics for creating a new component and for group communication concerning *put* for which we need the rules shown in Fig. 5 (see [37] for the full operational semantics of SCEL).

$$(\text{pr-sys}) \frac{P \downarrow_\alpha P' \quad \Pi, \mathcal{I} : \alpha \succ \lambda, \sigma, \Pi'}{\mathcal{I}[\mathcal{K}, \Pi, P] \xrightarrow{\lambda} \mathcal{I}[\mathcal{K}, \Pi', P'\sigma]}$$

$$(\text{newc}) \frac{C \xrightarrow{\mathcal{I}:new(\mathcal{J},\mathcal{K},\Pi,Q)} C' \quad \mathcal{I}.\pi \vdash \mathcal{I} : new(\mathcal{J},\mathcal{K},\Pi,Q), \Pi'}{C \xrightarrow{\tau} C'[\Pi'/\bullet] \parallel \mathcal{J}[\mathcal{K}, \Pi, Q]}$$

$$(\text{accput}) \frac{\Pi \vdash \mathcal{I} : t \,\tilde{\triangleright}\, \mathcal{J}, \Pi' \quad \mathcal{K} \oplus t = \mathcal{K}'}{\mathcal{J}[\mathcal{K}, \Pi, Q] \xrightarrow{\mathcal{I}:t \,\tilde{\triangleright}\, \mathcal{J}[\Pi'/\mathcal{J}.\pi]} \mathcal{J}[\mathcal{K}', \Pi', Q]}$$

$$(\text{grput}) \frac{S_1 \xrightarrow{\mathcal{I}:t \triangleright p} S_1' \quad S_2 \xrightarrow{\mathcal{I}:t \,\tilde{\triangleright}\, \mathcal{J}} S_2' \quad \mathcal{J} \models p \quad \mathcal{I}.\pi \vdash \mathcal{I} : t \,\tilde{\triangleright}\, \mathcal{J}, \Pi'}{S_1 \parallel S_2 \xrightarrow{\mathcal{I}[\Pi'/\mathcal{I}.\pi]:t \triangleright p} S_1' \parallel S_2'}$$

$$(\text{engrput}) \frac{S \xrightarrow{\mathcal{I}:t \triangleright p} S' \quad (\mathcal{J} \not\models p \ \vee \ \Pi \nvdash \mathcal{I} : t \,\tilde{\triangleright}\, \mathcal{J}, \Pi' \ \vee \ \mathcal{I}.\pi \nvdash \mathcal{I} : t \,\tilde{\triangleright}\, \mathcal{J}, \Pi')}{S \parallel \mathcal{J}[\mathcal{K}, \Pi, Q] \xrightarrow{\mathcal{I}:t \triangleright p} S' \parallel \mathcal{J}[\mathcal{K}, \Pi, Q]}$$

$$(\text{put}) \frac{S \xrightarrow{\mathcal{I}:t \triangleright p} S'}{(\nu\bar{n})S \rightarrowtail (\nu\bar{n})S'[\mathcal{I}.\pi/\bullet]}$$

Fig. 5. A few rules of SCEL

Rule (pr-sys) in Fig. 5 stems from [42]; it is a specialisation of the corresponding rule in [37] omitting the case of action *fresh(n)*. The purpose of this rule is to lift process actions to the component level. If a process commitment $P \downarrow_\alpha P'$ is given and if the interaction predicate $\Pi, \mathcal{I} : \alpha \succ \lambda, \sigma, \Pi'$ generates, under policy Π and interface $\mathcal{I}$, from process action α the system label λ, substitution σ and policy Π', then the component $\mathcal{I}[\mathcal{K}, \Pi, P]$ can perform λ and becomes $\mathcal{I}[\mathcal{K}, \Pi', P'\sigma]$. A specific interaction predicate for component creation and *put* action is defined by

$$\Pi, \mathcal{I} : new(\mathcal{J}, \mathcal{K}, \Pi, Q) \succ \mathcal{I} : new(\mathcal{J}, \mathcal{K}, \Pi, [\![Q]\!]_\mathcal{I}), \{\}, \Pi \tag{1}$$

$$\frac{[\![t]\!]_\mathcal{I} = t' \quad [\![e]\!]_\mathcal{I} = \gamma}{\Pi, \mathcal{I} : put(t)@e \succ \mathcal{I} : t' \triangleright \gamma, \{\}, \Pi} \tag{2}$$

where $[\![\cdot]\!]$ denotes the evaluation of terms w.r.t. interface $\mathcal{I}$. Note that this interaction predicate yields the empty substitution and does not change policies.

In case (1), the system label $\mathcal{I} : new(\mathcal{J}, \mathcal{K}, \Pi, [\![Q]\!]_\mathcal{I})$ expresses the willingness of component $\mathcal{I}$ to create the new component. Rule (pr-sys) generates a transition with this label from the commitment $(new(\mathcal{J}, \mathcal{K}, \Pi, Q).P') \downarrow_{new(\mathcal{J}, \mathcal{K}, \Pi, Q)} P'$. In the next step rule (newc) can be applied if the policy $\mathcal{I}.\pi$ of $\mathcal{I}$ authorises the creation of the new component which is expressed by the authorisation predicate $\mathcal{I}.\pi \vdash \mathcal{I} : new(\mathcal{J}, \mathcal{K}, \Pi, Q), \Pi'$. This leads to the internal computation step τ for component C which adds the new component in parallel and additionally realises, in accordance with the authorisation predicate, a possible change of C's policy to Π'. Internal computation steps can be propagated from components to systems and finally moved to unlabelled system transitions (involving a name restriction) with two further rules not shown here.

In case (2) the system label $\mathcal{I} : t' \triangleright \gamma$ denotes the intention of component $\mathcal{I}$ to add item t' to the repositories determined by γ. Rule (pr-sys) generates a transition with this label from the commitment $(put(t)@e.P') \downarrow_{put(t)@e} P'$. Now we take into account rule (accput) which generates a transition with system label $\mathcal{I} : t \triangleright \mathcal{J}[\Pi'/\mathcal{J}.\pi]$ expressing that component $\mathcal{J}$ is ready to add an item t to its knowledge base $\mathcal{K}$ and updating its policy $\mathcal{J}.\pi$ to Π' (provided the authorisation predicate $\Pi \vdash \mathcal{I} : t \triangleright \mathcal{J}, \Pi'$ is satisfied). The intention to put an item and willingness to accept an item are combined in rule (grput). This rule generates a transition for a composed system $S_1 \parallel S_2$ where S_1 is intending to transfer an item to all components satisfying predicate p and S_2 is ready for acceptance where the target component $\mathcal{J}$ satisfies the predicate. Since we are dealing with group communication for *put*, the resulting system transition from $S_1 \parallel S_2$ to $S_1' \parallel S_2'$ is again labelled by expressing the intention of $\mathcal{I}$ to send the item (while updating its policy). Rule (engrput) is a congruence rule that combines a system S willing to transfer an item t with a component that is not involved in this action. "By repeatedly applying rules (grput) and (engrput) it is possible ... that a component produces an item which is added to the repository of all ensemble components that simultaneously are willing to receive the item." Finally an unlabelled system transition, denoted by $\rightarrowtail$ can be inferred from rule (put).

SCEL Instantiations, Runtime, Analysis Tools, and Case Studies. The first full instantiation of SCEL uses tuple spaces as knowledge representation mechanism and the language FACPL ([74], Sect. 4) as policy language. FACPL is a language for defining access control, resource usage and adaptation policies; it is inspired by the XACML [63] standard for access control. StocS ([74], Sect. 7) is a stochastic extension of SCEL where all repository operations have probabilistic behaviour. The run-time environment jRESP ([74], Sect. 6) of SCEL supports the development of autonomic and adaptive systems according to the SCEL paradigm. It provides an interpreter, has been integrated with FACPL, and offers a simulation environment and a statistical modelchecker. SCEL has also been integrated with the SPIN modelchecker and the Maude-based modelchecker MISSCEL (see [74], Sect. 6).

SCEL has been applied to all three main ASCENS case studies (on swarm robotics, cloud computing, and e-mobility). Moreover, SCEL has been used to model self-expression [23] and different adaptation patterns [28].

5 Conclusion

This paper gives a short review of process calculi and languages that are able to capture the essential dynamic features of mobile, service-oriented and collective autonomic systems and to provide a semantic basis for analysing properties of such systems. These calculi and languages have been developed and studied by Rocco De Nicola and his students and co-workers within the three European projects AGILE, SENSORIA, and ASCENS during the years 2002–2015.

Process-algebraic research of modern programming language features is not complete with these results but continues to be very active. Rocco is a perfect role model for this research. For instance, the results of ASCENS were further developed by Rocco and his colleagues in the project QUANTICOL [6] for quantitatively modelling collective adaptive systems. The language CAS-SCEL - renamed to CARMA in [58] (Collective Adaptive Resource-sharing Markovian Agents) - focusses on quantitative evaluation and verification and offers constructs for "expressing timed and probabilistic behaviour of components which operate in collectives" [6]. The novel basic process calculus AbC [9] can be seen as the minimal subset of SCEL which focusses on attribute-based communication. In addition, Rocco was one of the chairs of the track "Rigorous Engineering of Collective Adaptive Systems" of the ISOLA 2018 conference where process-algebraic methods played again a major role.

References

1. AEOLUS: Algorithmic principles for building efficient overlay computers. EU 6th Framework Programme, Integrated Project, 2005-09-01–2009-08-31, Grant 15964. https://cordis.europa.eu/project/rcn/80615/. Accessed 06 January 2019

2. AGILE: architectures for mobility. EU 5th Framework Programme, Global Computing Initiative, 2002-01-01–2005-04-30, Contract IST-2001-32747. https://cordis.europa.eu/project/rcn/60315/factsheet/en. http://www.pst.ifi.lmu.de/Forschung/projekte/agile/. Accessed 06 Jan 2019

3. ASCENS: Autonomic component ensembles. EU 7th Framework Programme, Integrated Project, 2010-10-01–2015-03-31, Grant 257414. http://www.ascens-ist.eu/. https://cordis.europa.eu/project/rcn/95141/. Accessed 06 Jan 2019

4. Global computing: co-operation of autonomous and mobile entities in dynamic environments - IST-2001-6.2.2, Cordis Database, European Commission. https://cordis.europa.eu/programme/rcn/7974/en. Accessed 13 Jan 2019

5. MOBIUS: Mobility, ubiquity and security for small devices. EU 6th Framework Programme, Integrated Project, 2010-10-01–2009-08-31, Grant 015905. http://software.imdea.org/gbarthe/mobius/. https://cordis.europa.eu/project/rcn/80614/. Accessed 06 Jan 2019

6. QUANTICOL: A quantitative approach to management and design of collective and adaptive behaviours. EU 7th Framework Programme, Fundamentals of Collective Adaptive Systems, 2013-04-01–2017-03-31, Contract 600708. http://blog.inf.ed.ac.uk/quanticol/. https://cordis.europa.eu/project/rcn/106237/. Accessed 17 Jan 2019

7. SENSORIA: Software engineering for service-oriented overlay computers. EU 6th Framework Programme, Integrated Project, 2005-09-01–2010-02-28, Grant Id: 16004. http://www.sensoria-ist.eu/. https://cordis.europa.eu/project/rcn/80616/. Accessed 06 Jan 2019

8. Acciai, L., Bodei, C., Boreale, M., Bruni, R., Vieira, H.T.: Static analysis techniques for session-oriented calculi. In: Wirsing and Hölzl [73], pp. 214–231 (2011)

9. Alrahman, Y.A., De Nicola, R., Loreti, M., Tiezzi, F., Vigo, R.: A calculus for attribute-based communication. In: Wainwright, R.L., Corchado, J.M., Bechini, A., Hong, J. (eds.) SAC 2015, pp. 1840–1845. ACM (2015)

10. Andrade, L., et al.: AGILE: software architecture for mobility. In: Wirsing, M., Pattinson, D., Hennicker, R. (eds.) WADT 2002. LNCS, vol. 2755, pp. 1–33. Springer, Heidelberg (2003). https://doi.org/10.1007/978-3-540-40020-2_1

11. Baier, C., Katoen, J.-P., Hermanns, H.: Approximative symbolic model checking of continuous-time Markov chains. In: Baeten, J.C.M., Mauw, S. (eds.) CONCUR 1999. LNCS, vol. 1664, pp. 146–161. Springer, Heidelberg (1999). https://doi.org/10.1007/3-540-48320-9_12

12. Bartoletti, M., Degano, P., Ferrari, G.L., Zunino, R.: Call-by-contract for service discovery, orchestration and recovery. In: Wirsing and Hölzl [73], pp. 232–261 (2011)

13. Baumeister, H., Knapp, A., Wirsing, M.: Property-driven development. In: SEFM 2004, pp. 96–102. IEEE Computer Society (2004)

14. Baumeister, H., Koch, N., Kosiuczenko, P., Stevens, P., Wirsing, M.: UML for global computing. In: Priami [64], pp. 1–24 (2003)

15. Bettini, L., et al.: The Klaim project: theory and practice. In: Priami [64], pp. 88–150 (2003)

16. Bettini, L., De Nicola, R.: Mobile distributed programming in X-KLAIM. In: Bernardo, M., Bogliolo, A. (eds.) SFM-Moby 2005. LNCS, vol. 3465, pp. 29–68. Springer, Heidelberg (2005). https://doi.org/10.1007/11419822_2

17. Bettini, L., De Nicola, R., Pugliese, R.: Klava: a Java package for distributed and mobile applications. Softw. Pract. Exper. **32**(14), 1365–1394 (2002)

18. Bistarelli, S., Montanari, U., Rossi, F.: Semiring-based constraint satisfaction and optimization. J. ACM **44**(2), 201–236 (1997)

19. Boreale, M., et al.: SCC: a service centered calculus. In: Bravetti, M., Núñez, M., Zavattaro, G. (eds.) WS-FM 2006. LNCS, vol. 4184, pp. 38–57. Springer, Heidelberg (2006). https://doi.org/10.1007/11841197_3

20. Boreale, M., Bruni, R., De Nicola, R., Loreti, M.: Sessions and pipelines for structured service programming. In: Barthe, G., de Boer, F.S. (eds.) FMOODS 2008. LNCS, vol. 5051, pp. 19–38. Springer, Heidelberg (2008). https://doi.org/10.1007/978-3-540-68863-1_3

21. Bruni, R., Montanari, U., Sassone, V.: Observational congruences for dynamically reconfigurable tile systems. Theor. Comput. Sci. **335**(2–3), 331–372 (2005)

22. Buscemi, M.G., Montanari, U.: CC-PI: a constraint language for service negotiation and composition. In: Wirsing and Hölzl [73], pp. 262–281 (2011)

23. Cabri, G., et al.: Self-expression and dynamic attribute-based ensembles in SCEL. In: Margaria and Steffen [59], pp. 147–163 (2014)

24. Caires, L., De Nicola, R., Pugliese, R., Vasconcelos, V.T., Zavattaro, G.: Core calculi for service-oriented computing. In: Wirsing and Hölzl [73], pp. 153–188 (2011)

25. Cappello, I., et al.: Quantitative analysis of services. In: Wirsing and Hölzl [73], pp. 522–540 (2011)

26. Carriero, N., Gelernter, D.: Linda in context. Commun. ACM **32**, 444–458 (1989)

27. Cenciarelli, P., Knapp, A., Reus, B., Wirsing, M.: From sequential to multi-threaded Java: an event-based operational semantics. In: Johnson, M. (ed.) AMAST 1997. LNCS, vol. 1349, pp. 75–90. Springer, Heidelberg (1997). https://doi.org/10.1007/BFb0000464

28. Cesari, L., De Nicola, R., Pugliese, R., Puviani, M., Tiezzi, F., Zambonelli, F.: Formalising adaptation patterns for autonomic ensembles. In: Fiadeiro, J.L., Liu, Z., Xue, J. (eds.) FACS 2013. LNCS, vol. 8348, pp. 100–118. Springer, Cham (2014). https://doi.org/10.1007/978-3-319-07602-7_8

29. De Nicola, R., Ferrari, G.L., Pugliese, R.: KLAIM: a kernel language for agents interaction and mobility. IEEE TSE **24**, 315–330 (1998)

30. De Nicola, R.: Testing equivalences and fully abstract models for communicating systems. Ph.D. thesis, University of Edinburgh, UK (1986)

31. De Nicola, R., Ferrari, G., Montanari, U., Pugliese, R., Tuosto, E.: A formal basis for reasoning on programmable QoS. In: Dershowitz, N. (ed.) Verification: Theory and Practice. LNCS, vol. 2772, pp. 436–479. Springer, Heidelberg (2003). https://doi.org/10.1007/978-3-540-39910-0_21

32. de Nicola, R., Hennessy, M.C.B.: Testing equivalences for processes. In: Diaz, J. (ed.) ICALP 1983. LNCS, vol. 154, pp. 548–560. Springer, Heidelberg (1983). https://doi.org/10.1007/BFb0036936

33. De Nicola, R., Hennicker, R.: A homage to Martin Wirsing. In: Software, Services, and Systems [34], pp. 1–12 (2015)

34. De Nicola, R., Hennicker, R. (eds.): Software, Services, and Systems. LNCS, vol. 8950. Springer, Heidelberg (2015). https://doi.org/10.1007/978-3-319-15545-6

35. De Nicola, R., Jähnichen, S., Wirsing, M.: Rigorous engineering of collective adaptive systems - introduction to the 2nd track edition. In: Margaria and Steffen [60], pp. 3–12 (2018)

36. De Nicola, R., Katoen, J., Latella, D., Loreti, M., Massink, M.: Model checking mobile stochastic logic. Theor. Comput. Sci. **382**(1), 42–70 (2007)

37. De Nicola, R., et al.: The SCEL language: design, implementation, verification. In: Wirsing et al. [74], pp. 3–71 (2011)

38. De Nicola, R., Latella, D., Loreti, M., Massink, M.: MarCaSPiS: a Markovian extension of a calculus for services. Electr. Notes Theor. Comput. Sci. **229**(4), 11–26 (2009)

39. De Nicola, R., Latella, D., Loreti, M., Massink, M.: Sosl: a service-oriented stochastic logic. In: Wirsing and Hölzl [73], pp. 447–466 (2011)

40. De Nicola, R., Latella, D., Massink, M.: Formal modeling and quantitative analysis of KLAIM-based mobile systems. In: Haddad, H., Liebrock, L.M., Omicini, A., Wainwright, R.L. (eds.) ACM Symposium on Applied Computing (SAC), pp. 428–435. ACM (2005)

41. De Nicola, R., Loreti, M.: MoMo: a modal logic for reasoning about mobility. In: de Boer, F.S., Bonsangue, M.M., Graf, S., de Roever, W.-P. (eds.) FMCO 2004. LNCS, vol. 3657, pp. 95–119. Springer, Heidelberg (2005). https://doi.org/10.1007/11561163_5

42. De Nicola, R., Loreti, M., Pugliese, R., Tiezzi, F.: A formal approach to autonomic systems programming: the SCEL language. TAAS **9**(2), 7:1–7:29 (2014)

43. De Nicola, R., Vaandrager, F.W.: Three logics for branching bisimulation (extended abstract). In: LICS, pp. 118–129 (1990)

44. Fantechi, A., Gnesi, S., Lapadula, A., Mazzanti, F., Pugliese, R., Tiezzi, F.: A model checking approach for verifying COWS specifications. In: Fiadeiro, J.L., Inverardi, P. (eds.) FASE 2008. LNCS, vol. 4961, pp. 230–245. Springer, Heidelberg (2008). https://doi.org/10.1007/978-3-540-78743-3_17

45. Ferrari, G.L., Gnesi, S., Montanari, U., Pistore, M.: A model-checking verification environment for mobile processes. ACM Trans. Softw. Eng. Methodol. **12**(4), 440–473 (2003)

46. Ferrari, G.L., Gnesi, S., Montanari, U., Raggi, R., Trentanni, G., Tuosto, E.: Verification on the web of mobile systems. In: Augusto, J.C., Ultes-Nitsche, U. (eds.) VVEIS 2004, pp. 72–74. INSTICC Press (2004)

47. Ferrari, G.L., Moggi, E., Pugliese, R.: MetaKlaim: a type safe multi-stage language for global computing. Math. Struct. Comput. Sci. **14**(3), 367–395 (2004)

48. Fiadeiro, J.L., Lopes, A.: CommUnity on the move: architectures for distribution and mobility. In: de Boer, F.S., Bonsangue, M.M., Graf, S., de Roever, W.-P. (eds.) FMCO 2003. LNCS, vol. 3188, pp. 177–196. Springer, Heidelberg (2004). https://doi.org/10.1007/978-3-540-30101-1_8

49. Gelernter, D.: Generative communication in Linda. TOPLAS **7**, 80–112 (1985)

50. Guidi, C.: Formalizing languages for service-oriented computing. Ph.D. thesis, Universita di Bologna (2007)

51. Hennessy, M., Milner, R.: Algebraic laws for nondeterminism and concurrency. J. ACM **32**(1), 137–161 (1985)

52. Hölzl, M.M., Rauschmayer, A., Wirsing, M.: Engineering of software-intensive systems: state of the art and research challenges. In: Wirsing et al. [69], pp. 1–44 (2008)

53. Knapp, A., Merz, S., Wirsing, M., Zappe, J.: Specification and refinement of mobile systems in MTLA and mobile UML. Theor. Comput. Sci. **351**(2), 184–202 (2006)

54. Kozen, D.: Results on the propositional μ-calculus. Theor. Comput. Sci. **27**, 333–354 (1983)

55. Krutisch, R., Meier, P., Wirsing, M.: The AgentComponent approach, combining agents, and components. In: Schillo, M., Klusch, M., Müller, J., Tianfield, H. (eds.) MATES 2003. LNCS (LNAI), vol. 2831, pp. 1–12. Springer, Heidelberg (2003). https://doi.org/10.1007/978-3-540-39869-1_1

56. Lanese, I., Martins, F., Vasconcelos, V.T., Ravara, A.: Disciplining orchestration and conversation in service-oriented computing. In: SEFM 2007, pp. 305–314. IEEE Computer Society (2007)

57. Latella, D., Massink, M., Baumeister, H., Wirsing, M.: Mobile UML statecharts with localities. In: Priami, C., Quaglia, P. (eds.) GC 2004. LNCS, vol. 3267, pp. 34–58. Springer, Heidelberg (2005). https://doi.org/10.1007/978-3-540-31794-4_3

58. Loreti, M., Hillston, J.: Modelling and analysis of collective adaptive systems with CARMA and its tools. In: Bernardo, M., De Nicola, R., Hillston, J. (eds.) SFM 2016. LNCS, vol. 9700, pp. 83–119. Springer, Cham (2016). https://doi.org/10.1007/978-3-319-34096-8_4

59. Margaria, T., Steffen, B. (eds.): ISoLA 2014. LNCS, vol. 8802. Springer, Heidelberg (2014)

60. Margaria, T., Steffen, B. (eds.): ISoLA 2018, Proceedings, Part III. LNCS, vol. 11246. Springer, Heidelberg (2018). https://doi.org/10.1007/978-3-030-03424-5

61. Milner, R.: Communicating and Mobile Systems: the π-Calculus. Cambridge University Press, Cambridge (1999)

62. Misra, J., Cook, W.R.: Computation orchestration. Softw. Syst. Model. **6**(1), 83–110 (2007)

63. OASIS: eXtensible Access Control Markup Language (XACML) version 3.0, January 2013. http://docs.oasis-open.org/xacml/3.0/xacml-3.0-core-spec-os-en.pdf. Accessed 22 Jan 2019

64. Priami, C. (ed.): GC 2003. Lecture Notes in Computer Science, vol. 2874. Springer, Heidelberg (2003). https://doi.org/10.1007/b94264

65. Pugliese, R., Tiezzi, F.: A calculus for orchestration of web services. J. Appl. Log. **10**(1), 2–31 (2007)

66. Sestini, F., Hogenhout, W.: A report on the FET global computing initiative. European Commission, DG Information Society, Future and Emerging Technologies (2005)

67. ter Beek, M.H.: SENSORIA results applied to the case studies. In: Wirsing and Hölzl [73], pp. 655–677 (2011)

68. Vieira, H.T., Caires, L., Seco, J.C.: The conversation calculus: a model of service-oriented computation. In: Drossopoulou, S. (ed.) ESOP 2008. LNCS, vol. 4960, pp. 269–283. Springer, Heidelberg (2008). https://doi.org/10.1007/978-3-540-78739-6_21

69. Wirsing, M., Banâtre, J., Hölzl, M.M., Rauschmayer, A. (eds.): Software-Intensive Systems and New Computing Paradigms - Challenges and Visions. LNCS, vol. 5380. Springer, Heidelberg (2008). https://doi.org/10.1007/978-3-540-89437-7

70. Wirsing, M., et al.: Semantic-based development of service-oriented systems. In: Najm, E., Pradat-Peyre, J.-F., Donzeau-Gouge, V.V. (eds.) FORTE 2006. LNCS, vol. 4229, pp. 24–45. Springer, Heidelberg (2006). https://doi.org/10.1007/11888116_3

71. Wirsing, M., et al.: SENSORIA process calculi for service-oriented computing. In: Montanari, U., Sannella, D., Bruni, R. (eds.) TGC 2006. LNCS, vol. 4661, pp. 30–50. Springer, Heidelberg (2007). https://doi.org/10.1007/978-3-540-75336-0_3

72. Wirsing, M., De Nicola, R., Hölzl, M.M.: Introduction to 'rigorous engineering of autonomic ensembles'- track introduction. In: Margaria and Steffen [59], pp. 96–98 (2014)
73. Wirsing, M., Hölzl, M.M. (eds.): Rigorous Software Engineering for Service-Oriented Systems - Results of the SENSORIA Project on Software Engineering for Service-Oriented Computing. LNCS, vol. 6582. Springer, Heidelberg (2011). https://doi.org/10.1007/978-3-642-20401-2
74. Wirsing, M., Hölzl, M.M., Koch, N., Mayer, P. (eds.): Software Engineering for Collective Autonomic Systems - The ASCENS Approach. LNCS, vol. 8998. Springer, Heidelberg (2015). https://doi.org/10.1007/978-3-319-16310-9
75. Wirsing, M., Hölzl, M., Tribastone, M., Zambonelli, F.: ASCENS: engineering autonomic service-component ensembles. In: Beckert, B., Damiani, F., de Boer, F.S., Bonsangue, M.M. (eds.) FMCO 2011. LNCS, vol. 7542, pp. 1–24. Springer, Heidelberg (2013). https://doi.org/10.1007/978-3-642-35887-6_1

Autonomous Systems – An Architectural Characterization

Joseph Sifakis[(✉)]

Verimag Laboratory, Univ. Grenoble Alpes, Bâtiment IMAG,
700 avenue Centrale, 38401 St Martin d'Hères, France
joseph.sifakis@imag.fr

Abstract. The concept of autonomy is key to the IoT vision promising increasing integration of smart services and systems minimizing human intervention. This vision challenges our capability to build complex open trustworthy autonomous systems. We lack a rigorous common semantic framework for autonomous systems. It is remarkable that the debate about autonomous vehicles focuses almost exclusively on AI and learning techniques while it ignores many other equally important autonomous system design issues.

Autonomous systems involve agents and objects coordinated in some common environment so that their collective behavior meets a set of global goals. We propose a general computational model combining a system architecture model and an agent model. The architecture model allows expression of dynamic reconfigurable multi-mode coordination between components. The agent model consists of five interacting modules implementing each one a characteristic function: Perception, Reflection, Goal management, Planning and Self-adaptation. It determines a concept of autonomic complexity accounting for the specific difficulty to build autonomous systems.

We emphasize that the main characteristic of autonomous systems is their ability to handle knowledge and adaptively respond to environment changes. We advocate that autonomy should be associated with functionality and not with specific techniques. Machine learning is essential for autonomy although it can meet only a small portion of the needs implied by autonomous system design.

We conclude that autonomy is a kind of broad intelligence. Building trustworthy and optimal autonomous systems goes far beyond the AI challenge.

Keywords: Autonomous systems · Architecture · Trustworthiness

1 The Concept of Autonomy

The concept of autonomy is key to the IoT vision promising increasing integration of smart services and systems to achieve global goals such as optimal resource management and enhanced quality of life, with minimal human intervention.

This vision challenges our capability to build complex open trustworthy autonomous systems. In particular, we need an as much as possible, rigorous definition of autonomy. Is there a general reference model that could provide a basis for evaluating system autonomy? What are the technical solutions for enhancing a system's

© Springer Nature Switzerland AG 2019
M. Boreale et al. (Eds.): De Nicola-Festschrift, LNCS 11665, pp. 388–410, 2019.
https://doi.org/10.1007/978-3-030-21485-2_21

autonomy? For each enhancement, is it possible to estimate the implied technical difficulties and risks? These are very important questions for autonomous systems engineering.

Currently, the profusion of concepts and terms related to autonomy reflects the lack of a common semantic framework. It is remarkable that the technical discussion about autonomous vehicles focuses almost exclusively on AI and learning techniques while it ignores many other equally important autonomous system design issues.

An autonomous system consists of components of predefined types, agents and objects sharing some common environment and coordinated so that the collective behavior of the components meets given global goals.

- Objects are physical dynamic systems. Their states that can change either by agent actions or internally.
- Agents are reactive systems. They have the ability to monitor the objects and act on their state, either alone or in some coordinated manner. Each agent pursues specific goals that may dynamically change depending on the state of its environment.
- The environment provides infrastructure and mechanisms implementing coordination rules that govern the interaction between components. These determine in particular the connectivity between agents as well as the observability/ controllability of the objects.

Autonomous system design aims to determine the behavior of the system agents pursuing each one its own specific goals so that the collective behavior of the system including its agents and objects meets the global system goals.

We propose a technical definition of autonomy based on a general computational model consisting of an agent architecture model and a system architecture model:

- The agent architecture model involves five modules, each one dealing with one fundamental aspect of autonomy: Perception, Refection, Goal management, Planning and Self-adaptation. It specifies the coordination between these features in order to achieve autonomous behavior. It also implicitly defines some abstract partial order relation for comparing the autonomy level of agents pursuing identical goals.
- The system architecture model specifies coordination between system agents and their effect on the objects. We need such a model to explicate how an agent perceives its environment and elaborates its control strategy.

We progressively introduce the concept of autonomy through a comparison between five automated systems: a thermostat, an automatic train shuttle, a chess-playing robot, a soccer-playing robot and a robocar.

1.1 Agent Environment

All the above systems automatically perform some mission characterized by their respective goals. They integrate agents continuously interacting with their environment through sensors and actuators. The sensors provide stimuli to the agent; the actuators receive commands from the agent and change accordingly the state of its environment.

All agents receive inputs and produce outputs so that their I/O relation meets their specific goals. They are real-time controllers monitoring state changes of the controlled environment and producing adequate responses. Nonetheless, there are significant differences regarding the complexity and intricacy of their environments and their goals with associated decision process.

The environment of a thermostat is simply a room and a heating device. Stimuli are the temperature of the room and the state of the heater.

For the automatic shuttle, the environment includes the cars composing the shuttle with their equipment and passengers. Stimuli take the form of numeric information about the position and speed of the cars and the state of various equipment and peripherals.

For the chess robot, the environment is a chessboard with pawns and the adversary robot. Stimuli are the configuration of the pawns on the chessboard extracted from static images provided by the robot camera.

For the soccer robot, the environment consists of all other players, the ball, the goalposts and lines delimiting regions of the field. Stimuli are extracted in real time from dynamic images; they include the position and speed of players and ball.

Finally for the robocar, the environment is more involved as it includes vehicles and obstacles in its vicinity as well as traffic control and communication equipment. The perceived environment state is the configuration of other robocars and obstacles with their dynamic attributes and the state of traffic control and communication equipment. The environment state is built from data provided by different types of sensors adequately treated and interpreted.

1.2 Agent Goals and Plan Generation

As explained, agents behave as controllers acting on their environment to achieve their specific goals. The agent environment can be modeled as a state machine with two types of actions: controllable actions triggered by the agent; and uncontrollable actions that are internal state changes of the environment. Without getting into technical details, given a set of goals and an agent environment model, there are methods (semi-algorithms) for the computation of plans. Figure 1 illustrates their principle for given environment and goals. In the considered example, the goals require that the generated plans avoid the state Bad and eventually reach the state Target. The plan generation method consists in finding a subgraph of the environment state graph that is closed with respect to uncontrollable actions (dashed arrows) and does not contain state Bad; furthermore, by adequately triggering controllable actions (solid arrows) the state Target can be reached.

In general, environment models are infinite and the generated plans for given goals are infinite trees with alternating controllable and uncontrollable actions. When the environment model is finite, algorithms are used to compute a maximal controller including all the plans meeting the goals [1].

For infinite or complex environments, it is not possible to generate an explicit a controller. The existence of plans cannot be theoretically guaranteed. It depends on the type of goals and the controllability/observability relations.

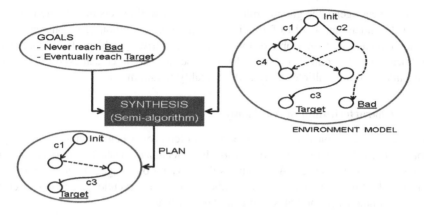

Fig. 1. Plan generation from goals and the environment model

In practice, for given goals, finite-horizon plans are computed on line from the agent's environment model. To cope with complexity, heuristics are used as well as precomputed plan skeletons. Furthermore, adequately choosing at design time the controllability/observability relation can significantly simplify on line plan generation. For instance, for simple safety goals e.g. avoiding harmful states, a finite horizon exploration from the current state may suffice.

Going back to the considered examples, the thermostat has an explicit controller that is a simple two-mode automaton switching between On and Off modes when temperature reaches minimal and maximal values, respectively.

The shuttle has a more involved decision process. Usually an explicit controller ensures safety properties, while commands computed on line ensure adaptation to load variation and comfort optimization.

For the chess robot, there is no explicitly precomputed controller. Depending on the current configuration of the chessboard, the robotic agent chooses between a set of strategies optimizing criteria implied by the rules of the game. Each strategy corresponds to a sub-goal from a hierarchically structured set of goals. To accelerate plan generation, precomputed knowledge is often used e.g. patterns of plans and associated methods.

Similarly, for the soccer robot, plans are computed on line from the agent's environment model and its current configuration. Here a significant difference is the dynamic nature of the game as the controller is subject to hard real-time constraints. The game involves interaction between dynamically changing sets of agents (players). Although the game rules are well-defined, their dynamicity makes the outcome less predictable. The decision process generates plans from a dynamically changing environment model. It should adequately combine defense and attack strategies to win a game within 90 min. Knowledge is instrumental for plan generation; it consists in using precomputed patterns and learning techniques for parameter estimation.

For the robocar, the controller is even much more complex. In contrast to the previous examples, the environment involves a dynamically and unpredictably changing number of agents and objects in particular due to agent mobility. While for chess or soccer agents the gaming rules are static and well-understood, traffic rules are context-dependent and hard to formalize [2]. Rigorous definition of a coherent set of individual goals for an ensemble of robocars is a non-trivial problem. Individual goals of robocars may be conflicting and a global consensus should be achieved in real-time taking into account multiple safety and optimality requirements.

1.3   A Characterization of Autonomy

The discussed examples illustrate important differences when moving from simple automation to full autonomy. They also show technical obstacles to overcome in autonomous systems design. Autonomy is the capacity of an agent to achieve a set of coordinated goals by its own means (without human intervention) adapting to environment variations. It combines five complementary aspects:

- Perception e.g. interpretation of stimuli, removing ambiguity/vagueness from complex input data and determining relevant information;
- Reflection e.g. building/updating a faithful environment run-time model;
- Goal management e.g. choosing among possible goals the most appropriate ones for a given configuration of the environment model;
- Planning to achieve chosen goals resulting in actuation of devices that affect the environment;
- Self-adaptation e.g. the ability to adjust behavior through learning and reasoning and to change dynamically the goal management and planning processes.

Note that the first two aspects deal with agent's situational awareness while the third and the forth aspect deal with adaptation of decision. These four aspects are orthogonal. Self-adaptation ensures adequacy of decisions based on predefined or on line acquired knowledge.

The above characterization, which we refine in the following section, gives a clear insight about the very nature of the concept of autonomy. An autonomous agent needs to some extent each one of these five functions.

The level of autonomy of a system characterizes the relation between machine-empowered vs. human-assisted autonomy. Figure 2 illustrates this relation in a five-dimensional space. Improving autonomy for some aspect consists in replacing human intervention by autonomous steering. Full autonomy means that the function for each aspect is machine empowered.

An illustration of this concept is provided by the five autonomy levels for cars defined by the SAE, shown in Table 1. Level 5 corresponds to full autonomy while lower levels require increasing assistance of the driver.

Note that a thermostat is an automated agent that is not autonomous as it does not use anyone of these functions. Its decision process is implemented by an explicit controller for a fixed set of goals. Furthermore, it has a fully observable/controllable environment providing stimuli that need no interpretation.

Automated agents are often integrated in complex processes where autonomy is ensured by human operators. For instance, PLCs ensure production automation while qualified staff performs supervision and overall coordination.

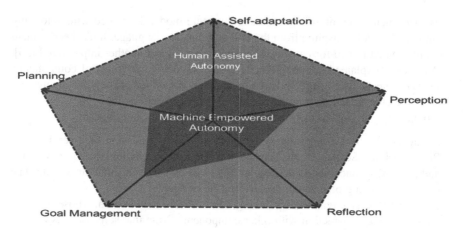

Fig. 2. Human assisted vs. machine empowered autonomy.

Table 1. SAE autonomy levels (https://en.wikipedia.org/wiki/Self-driving_car)

	SAE autonomy levels
Level 0	No automation
Level 1	Driver assistance required ("hands on")
	The driver still needs to maintain full situational awareness and control of the vehicle e.g. cruise control
Level 2	Partial automation option available ("hands off")
	Autopilot manages both speed and steering under certain conditions, e.g. highway driving
Level 3	Conditional Automation ("eyes off")
	The car, rather than the driver, takes over actively monitoring the environment when the system is engaged. However, human drivers must be prepared to respond to a "request to intervene"
Level 4	High automation ("mind off")
	Self driving is supported only in limited areas (geofenced) or under special circumstances, like traffic jams
Level 5	Full automation ("steering wheel optional")
	No human intervention is required e.g. a robotic taxi

2   A Computational Model for Autonomous Systems

2.1   A System Architecture Model

In order explain how an autonomous agent behaves, we need an adequate holistic model of its environment including other agents and objects. The model should in particular, propose concepts and principles accounting for the complex structure of the agent's environment and intricate coordination mechanisms.

We succinctly present an expressive architecture model developed with autonomy in mind. The model is inspired from the BIP coordination language. It has been studied and implemented in two formalisms, one declarative [3] and another imperative [4, 5].

As already explained, an autonomous system involves two kinds of components: agents and objects. The agents have computational capabilities. They can change the states of the objects and coordinate to enforce global system goals.

Components are instances of predefined types of agents and objects:

- An agent type is a computing system characterizing a mission or a service, e.g. Player, Arbiter, Sender, etc. Its semantics is a transition relation labeled with events and associated functions. Functions are triggered by the events that are atomic state changes involving other components, objects or agents.
- An object type is a dynamic system e.g. electromechanical system, whose state can change through interaction with other components. Note that some objects may be passive such as a pawn or a static obstacle.

We consider that a system model is a collection of architecture motifs, simply called motifs.

A motif is a "world" where live dynamically changing sets of agents and objects. It is equipped with a map represented by a graph specified by sets of nodes and edges. Nodes represent abstract coordinates in some reference space. The connectivity relation between the nodes of a map may admit a physical or a logical interpretation. For a lift or a shuttle, the map is a simple linear structure: the nodes are floors or stations, respectively. In the chess game, the map is an array representing the chessboard.

The position of an agent a or of an object o is given by a partial address function @: @(a) and @(o) is the node of the map where a and o are located, respectively.

For example, an address function can define the distribution of pawns over the chessboard. The function changes when pawns move; it is undefined for pawns not placed on the board. For the soccer game, the map is a three-dimensional array representing the field with some granularity grain. The only mobile object is the ball while all the agents are mobile.

Finally, for robocars we need several maps to model the system. Figure 3 depicts a model consisting of two motifs with their corresponding maps. A Road Chunk Map accounts for the spatial configuration of robocars and of relevant objects, typically obstacles. Other logical maps are necessary to specify coordination structure between robocars; for instance, to form platoons or to describe connectivity of communication infrastructure used by cars.

The dynamics of the system described by a motif is a transition relation between configurations. A configuration is the set of the states of its components as well as their corresponding addresses on the map. Configurations change when events occur as the result of agent coordination: by execution of interactions rules or of configuration rules.

Interaction Rules. An interaction is an atomic state change of a non-empty set of synchronizing agents that may also affect the state of objects. When the set is a singleton, the interaction is simply an action. We use rules in the form of guarded commands to describe interactions: the guard involves state variables of the synchronizing components and the command is a sequence of operations on their states. The

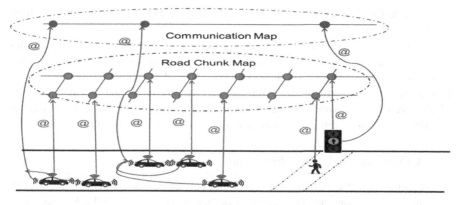

Fig. 3. Modeling principle for robocars with two motifs

rules are parametric which requires iteration over types of components. For example the rule

for all a, a':vehicle, if [distance(@(a),@(a'))<l] then exchange(a.speed, a'.speed).

says that when two vehicles *a* and *a'* are close enough they exchange their speeds.

The model provides primitives encompassing strong or weak synchronization and interactions of arbitrary arity.

Configuration Rules. Configuration rules allow the expression of three independent types of dynamism: component dynamism, component mobility, and map dynamism. They are guarded commands consisting of guards (conditions on state variables of components) and sequences of specific reconfiguration operations.

Typical operations are *create/delete* for components and *add/remove* for elements of maps. For instance, the operation *create(a:messenger,@(a)=n)* creates an agent named *a* of type messenger at address *n*. The operation *delete(o:pawn)* removes the pawn named *o*.

Agent mobility is modeled by rules modifying the address function of components. For example, the execution of the rule

for all a:mobile if @(a)=n and @-1(n+1)=empty then @(a):=n+1

consists in moving forward agents of type mobile by one space of the map.

The proposed model is minimal and expressive. Each motif is a dynamic reconfigurable architecture, an ensemble of agents and objects governed by specific coordination rules.

Note that an agent may belong to more than one motif. Furthermore, components can migrate from one motif to another using reconfiguration commands.

For instance, the model of a soccer game involves at least two motifs.

The Attack motif ensures coordination rules that aim at getting inside the adversary's defense and finally score a goal. The Defense motif ensures coordination rules that aim at slowing down an offense to disrupt the pace and/or numerical advantage of an attack and finally get possession of the ball. Players can dynamically migrate from one motif to the other.

The model for an automated highway involves several motifs. All vehicles belonging to a Road Chunk motif are subject to general traffic coordination rules. A Platoon motif groups and coordinates an ensemble of vehicles cruising at the same speed and closely following a leader vehicle. An Overtake motif involves an overtaking vehicle and vehicles moving in the same direction in its vicinity. Finally, a Communication motif groups vehicles sharing a common communication infrastructure.

2.2 A Computational Model for Agents

We present the agent computational model that puts emphasis on architectural aspects following the same line as [7]. It consists of four main modules and a Repository as depicted in Fig. 4.

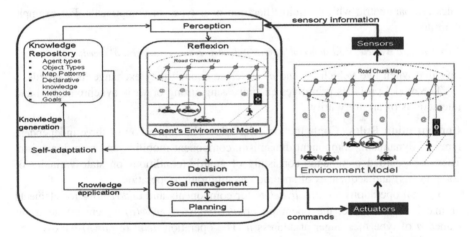

Fig. 4. The general architecture of the computational model for agents

The Knowledge Repository. The Knowledge Repository contains different kinds of knowledge used by the other modules for (1) the interpretation of sensory information; (2) building the environment model of the agent; (3) goal management and subsequent goal planning.

Some of the Repository knowledge is developed at design time and some is produced and stored at run time.

Design time knowledge specifies basic components of the agent's environment, their main observability/controllability features as well as key properties and methods related to system goals. It includes in particular:

- A list of all the relevant types of agents and objects and their corresponding behavioral specification with the admitted coordination patterns e.g. interaction types and reconfiguration commands;

- A list of predefined maps and coordination patterns used to build the agent's environment model;
- A list of the goals pursued by the agent as sets of properties of two types: (1) critical properties requiring that some condition is never violated; (2) best-effort properties dealing with resource management e.g. finding tradeoffs between performance and resource utilization.
- A list of methods used to enrich the knowledge about the environment model and so to produce additional knowledge at run time e.g. monitoring and learning techniques.

Run time knowledge is generated on line from monitors, learning and analysis techniques. It includes in particular:

- Properties of the agent model that may be generated by application of analysis techniques or inferred by application of reasoning techniques;
- Knowledge produced by monitors of the agent's behavior e.g. detecting failures or intrusion;
- Knowledge produced by application of learning techniques, in particular to remove ambiguity about the environment configuration or to estimate parameters characterizing the dynamic behavior of the environment e.g. worst-case and average execution times.

This presentation leaves open important questions about the nature of knowledge and the different forms it can take [2]. We discuss below some issues relevant for agent design.

We consider that knowledge is "truthful" information that is used in some specific context to understand/predict a situation or to solve a problem. Truthfulness cannot always be asserted in a rigorous manner. Mathematical knowledge has definitely the highest degree of truthfulness, e.g. knowledge extracted from programs using analysis tools. At the other extreme, empirical knowledge although not theoretically substantiated, proves to be very useful in practice. The most widely used knowledge is empirical e.g. common sense knowledge, but also knowledge from machine learning.

Additionally, knowledge may be declarative or procedural, regarding the form it can take.

Declarative knowledge is a relation (property) involving entities of a domain. In the Repository, can be stored: (1) logic formulas inferred from a set of axioms; (2) valid system properties extracted from a system model e.g. system invariants; (3) architecture patterns enforcing given properties.

Procedural knowledge takes the form of an executable description such as algorithms, behavioral description of components and various analysis techniques.

The Knowledge Repository contains all these types knowledge. Utilizing them effectively is essential for ensuring agent's self-adaptation and autonomy.

The Perception Module. The Perception module extracts relevant information from the various stimuli provided by sensors. For this purpose, it makes use of learning techniques or of analysis and recognition processes. The extracted information is linked to knowledge of the Repository. It concerns

- the type and possibly the identity of each sensed agent or object;
- the state of the so identified components;
- the type of the external environment characterized as a set of motifs with maps and associated coordination features.

For instance, the Perception module of a soccer agent provides, for each identified component of the environment, its position and speed in the field map. The Perception module of a robocar provides the types of the components in the vicinity with their associated attributes. Some attributes connect the components to motifs and their corresponding maps.

The Reflection Module. The Reflection module uses information provided by the Perception module in order to build/update a model of the agent's environment. For some agents, the environment model - number of components, map, coordination rules - does not change over lifetime e.g. chessboard robot, soccer robot. Thus, sensory information determines mainly the state of components e.g. their position in the maps and interactions.

Agents with dynamically changing environment e.g. robocars, are initially equipped with some environment model that is dynamically updated e.g. by creating/deleting motifs. For this to be feasible, the stimuli should provide information about architectural changes of the environment. Furthermore, the detected changes should correspond to patterns stored in the Knowledge Repository.

Reflection module extensively uses design-time knowledge of the Repository to build a complete behavioral model of its perceived environment. Nonetheless, to preserve faithfulness and freshness of the model, stimuli interpretation should be precise enough and performed within acceptable delay.

Performance of this module is critical for mobile agents subject to real-time constraints. How fast the agent's environment model can track changes of the real environment? Additionally, for distributed multi-agents systems, there is an inherent uncertainty about the global system states and thus a risk of discrepancy between environment models of different agents [7].

Note that each agent builds a partial model of the system environment reflecting its knowledge about its "neighborhood" that can be observed. In a distributed system, there is no global model of the system environment.

The Decision Module. The Decision module is decomposed into two cooperating submodules: a Goal Manager handling the actual agent's goals and a Planner generating plans that implement particular goals.

The module manages a set of goals both critical and best effort. It assigns higher priority to critical goals according to their importance.

Often goal management boils down to solving an optimization problem. It consists in translating goals into utility function policies: a goal is characterized as the desired set of feasible states for which the objective function is optimized subject to a set of constraints [9].

For a selected goal, the Planner computes from the environment model a corresponding plan. To cope with the exploding complexity of the planning process, various heuristics and precomputed patterns from the Knowledge Repository may be used.

The generated plans involve commands for interaction with other agents or reconfiguration of their environment provided by the system architecture model. The allowed coordination patterns with other components of the environment are specified in their definition stored in the Knowledge Repository. Note that interactions may involve exchange of knowledge between interacting agents e.g. changing methods or goals.

The Self-adaption Module. The Self-adaptation module supervises and coordinates all the other modules. It continuously reassesses the coherency of the exchanged information, creates new knowledge and provides directives to the Goal manager.

The module applies existing knowledge or generates new knowledge by combining reasoning and run-time analysis techniques to detect significant changes in the environment that require responsive adaptation. For instance, it applies monitoring or analysis techniques to the environment model to detect critical situations; it also can use learning techniques to estimate parameters or detect abnormal situations.

The adaptation directives to the Goal Manager concern:

(1) Change of parameters affecting the choice of the managed goals, especially estimates of dynamic characteristics of the environment components;
(2) Change of the set of the managed goals (adding or removing a goal), in response to some exceptional event in the environment or to an explicit requirement through interaction with another agent.

3   Autonomous System Design Complexity Issues

An interesting technical question is how to adequately choose the autonomy level for risk-benefit optimization in system design. Four main factors determine this choice.

The first is the required degree of trustworthiness. For critical complex systems, semi-autonomy seems to be the realistic choice under the current state of the art e.g. ADAS cars.

The other factors are three independent types of complexity discussed below: autonomic complexity, design complexity and implementation complexity.

3.1   Autonomic Complexity

We need a concept of complexity accounting for the specific difficulty to build autonomous systems. The following factors related to the fundamental aspects of autonomy, capture autonomic complexity.

1. Complexity of perception characterizes the difficulty to interpret stimuli provided by the environment and to timely generate corresponding inputs for the agent environment model. It has various sources such as stimuli ambiguity (admitting different interpretations) or vagueness (fuzzy or noisy stimuli). Additionally, complexity is aggravated with the volume of stimuli data to be analyzed in order to extract relevant input information.

2. Lack of observability/controllability which implies partial knowledge of the agent's environment and consequently limitations for building a faithful run time model by the Reflection module. This affects the ability to build plans and act on the environment.
3. Complexity of goal management which is the complexity of the process of choosing amongst a set of goals a maximal subset of compatible goals characterizing a strategy for which a consistent plan is generated. The selection process may involve both qualitative criteria such as priorities and quantitative criteria such as optimization of physical quantities.
4. Complexity of planning which directly depends on the type of goals and the complexity of the agent's environment model. As explained goals may be as simple as non-violation of a constraint and more complicated such as reachability of a condition or achieving optimality over a given time period.
5. Complexity of adaptation which is directly related to uncertainty about the agent's environment. Sources of uncertainty are multiple, including time-varying load, dynamic change due to mobility, bursty events, and most critical events such as failures and attacks. The Self-adaptation module generates objectives to cope with such situations involving imperfect knowledge and lack of predictability [2, 5]. This can be achieved to some extent, using knowledge, e.g. [8].

Obviously, reduced observability is a source of uncertainty. Nonetheless, uncertainty is not completely resolved by simply enhancing observability [2].

Note that for agents not directly interacting with a physical environment, autonomy simply means to cope with the complexity of goals and limited uncertainty e.g. an encoder adapting to varying load to avoid frame skipping. For a chess robot, only complexity of goals and planning are relevant; its environment is fully observable/controllable without uncertainty and the stimuli are non-ambiguous. For robocars, all types of complexity are relevant.

3.2   Design Complexity and Its Relationship to Autonomy

System design complexity characterizes the difficulty to build a system out of components – autonomous or not. It is conceptualized in a two-dimensional space [2].

One dimension represents reactive complexity [10] of the agents constituting a system. The other dimension represents the complexity of the architectures used to coordinate the agents.

Although design complexity is independent from autonomic complexity, it is interesting to understand how the demand for autonomy affects system design choices.

Reactive Complexity. Reactive complexity characterizes the intricacy of the interaction between an agent and its environment. It is independent from space complexity or time complexity measuring the quantity of computational resources needed by an agent. We discuss below a classification of agents according to their reactive complexity (Fig. 5).

- The simplest agents are **transformational agents** where the relation of the input to the output is sufficient to characterize their behavior. Computation is performed in batch mode without reference to any operating environment. Such agents are often software systems oblivious to real-time constraints, with simple well-defined environments. Adaptation consists in using precomputed knowledge to cope with inherent complexity of decision problems, e.g. intelligent resource orchestration in data centers, intelligent personal assistant, game playing agent.

- **Streaming agents** compute functions on streams of data. For a given input stream of values, they compute a corresponding output stream. The output value at some time t depends on the history of input values received by t. The goals for streamers deal with functional correctness and specific time-dependent properties such as latency. Data-flow systems are usually composed of streamers. Adaptation is essential to cope with load unpredictability and meet latency constraints, see for example [11].

- **Embedded agents** continuously interact with a physical environment to ensure global properties. They are mixed HW/SW systems where real-time behavior and dynamic properties are essential for correctness. Autonomous behavior is required when their mission involves high-level goals and complex environments, in particular to adaptively manage computational resources and meet critical goals. Embedded agents are integrated in industrial systems, transport systems and all kinds of devices.

  Note that the model of embedded agents should account for the behavior of their internal environment including computational resources (see discussion below).

- **A cyber physical agent** is an embedded agent integrating in its internal environment objects that are exclusively under its control. Its behavior involves both discrete and continuous variables representing the state of the integrated objects.

The environment model of such an agent should be refined to distinguish between internal and external environment as shown in Fig. 6. The Perception module gets sensory information from both the external and the internal environment model. The Reflection module builds/updates the two models corresponding to the two environments. The decision process is applied to the product of the environment models to generate plans with commands acting on both environments.

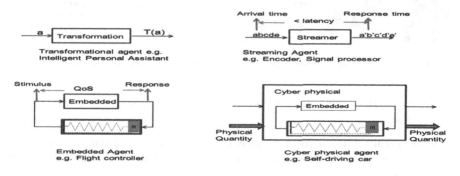

Fig. 5. Classification of agents according to their reactive complexity

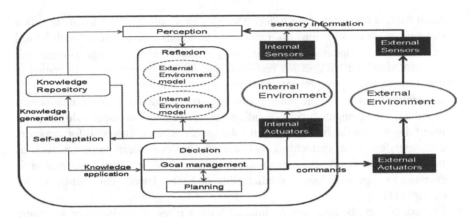

Fig. 6. Computational model for cyber physical agent

Cyber physical systems seek a tight integration between computers and their physical environment. They are essential for building complex autonomous systems e.g. self-driving cars.

Architecture Complexity. The proposed system architecture model provides a basis for classifying system architectures according to their degree of dynamism, from static to self-organizing architectures as shown in Fig. 7.

System Architecture Model	Motifs	Single motif	Many motifs	Dynamic motifs
	Interactions	No agent interaction (actions on objects)	Static interactions	Parametric interactions
	Reconfiguration — Dynamic agents		NO	YES
	Dynamic objects		NO	YES
	Mobility (dynamic @)		NO	YES
	Dynamic map		NO	YES
System Goals		Single fixed goal	Many structured goals	Many conflicting goals	Dynamic goals
Implementation	Agent	Software	Hardware/ Software	Cyber physical
	Architecture	Centralized	Decentralized	Distributed

Fig. 7. Complexity variation with respect to architecture, goals and implementation

We enumerate some representative cases below for increasing complexity of coordination.

1. **Static architectures** involve a given number of agents and objects, with fixed coordinates e.g. a smart building with fixed microcontrollers and electromechanical equipment.

2. **Parametric architectures** can have arbitrary initially known numbers of "pluggable" components for fixed coordination patterns e.g. token ring architecture, an array computer.

3. **Dynamic architectures** are parametric architectures with dynamic creation/deletion of agents or objects, e.g. array architecture for the Game of Life, client-server architecture.

4. **Mobile architectures** are dynamic architectures where also the coordinates of objects and agents can change dynamically, e.g. swarm robotic system. Additionally, they may involve dynamic change of maps when mobile agents explore a space and progressively build a model of their environment.

5. **Self-organizing architectures** are mobile architectures with many dynamically changing motifs e.g. for robocars, soccer playing robots. Self-organization reflects the ability of agents to migrate between motifs that are a kind of coordination modes. It is essential for adaption to changing system dynamics. The coordination rules of each motif correspond to sets of goals that must be met by the system.

All these types of architectures can be formalized as operators taking as arguments arbitrary numbers of instances of agent and objects types [3–5]. We badly need theory for studying their properties in a compositional manner.

Knowing the properties of the types of objects and agents involved, is it possible to infer global system properties? A more ambitious avenue is to develop theory for correctness by construction [6]: how to combine basic architecture patterns with well-established properties in order to build complex architectures that preserve the properties. These are largely open hard problems that urgently need exploration.

Figure 8 illustrates design complexity for different types of systems depending on the reactive complexity of their agents and their architectural complexity. Note the separation between services and systems. Services use streamers and transformational agents. IoT systems with advanced autonomy features, require mobile or self-organizing architectures and integrate embedded or cyber physical agents. Self-organization is important for such systems with many conflicting goals. Nonetheless, contrary to common opinion, self-organization is not an intrinsic property of autonomous systems. An ordinary distributed system involving agents with explicit controllers communicating by exchange of non-ambiguous messages is self-organizing if it has multiple coordination modes. Similar arguments are applicable for other "self"-prefixed properties commonly considered as characteristic properties of autonomous systems.

3.3   Implementation Complexity

Implementation is the process that leads to the realization of the designed system model. The latter can admit different implementations depending on the available computational resources and their organization. In rigorous approaches, the outcome of the implementation process is another model accounting for the physical distribution of agents and features of infrastructure implementing the model coordination mechanisms [12].

Fig. 8. Design complexity

We discuss below main choices for the implementation architecture depending on how/where the decisions are made and how/where the information is shared between the coordinating agents. We distinguish three main types of implementation architecture.

1. **Centralized architecture** where the agents are not geographically distributed. They coordinate through a shared memory that stores the data of a common Knowledge Repository as well as the data representing the state of a common environment model. In other words, each agent directly modifies/reads a shared data structure representing the motifs with their maps and the associated addressing functions. Such an implementation presents the advantage of the overall coherency of decision and coordination. Nonetheless, access conflicts may affect performance. A typical example is a blackboard architecture equipped with a common knowledge base, iteratively updated by agents starting with a problem specification and ending with a solution.

2. **Decentralized architecture** where agents are geographically distributed and there is no central storage. Every agent makes decisions based on local knowledge and the resulting system behavior is the aggregate response. Nonetheless, agents can coordinate through local memory depending on the topology of the environment maps. A typical example are stigmergic systems where mobile independent agents e.g. ants, robots, use their common environment to for coordination purposes [13].

3. **Distributed architecture** where there are no shared data storages. Each agent handles its own data and makes decisions according to its own goals. Coordination between agents is exclusively through asynchronous message passing. A key issue for such systems is coherency of coordination between components to achieve global goals. These are an emerging property of the collective behavior of the agents.

Distributed autonomous agent systems are today a vast and active research field because of multiple applications in various domains from blockchain protocols to complex autonomous transportation systems.

4   Trustworthy Autonomous Systems – From Correctness at Design Time to Autonomic Correctness

Systems Engineering comes to a turning point moving from small-size centralized non-evolvable automated systems with predictable environments, to large distributed evolvable autonomous systems with non-predicable dynamically changing environments.

Is it possible to build trustworthy autonomous systems? As autonomous systems are often critical, this is the object of a considerable and sometimes heated debate [15]. As explained in [2], the trend for autonomous systems renders obsolete current critical systems engineering techniques and standards, such as ISO26262 and DO178B, requiring conclusive trustworthiness evidence based on some rigorous design methodology.

It is remarkable that currently cars with autonomy features are self-certified by their manufacturers, contrary to most industrial products that are certified by independent authorities. Furthermore, some carmakers consider that successfully passing an extremely large number of test cases is a sufficient evidence of trustworthiness.

Trustworthiness is a transversal design issue. It is not limited to purely functional correctness. A system is deemed trustworthy if it behaves as expected despite design errors, hardware failures and any kind of harmful interaction with its human and physical environment, including misuse, attacks, disturbances and any kind of unpredictable events [6].

We briefly discuss how the rigorous model-based approach for guaranteeing trustworthiness can be in principle, extended to autonomous systems and the implied technical difficulties.

Currently, model-based approaches for achieving trustworthiness involve two steps.

The first step aims at providing guarantees that some abstract system model representing the system's nominal behavior satisfies critical system goals. The nominal behavior model usually assumes that system environment is fully reliable and to some extent predictable. The second step deals with possible violations of these assumptions for a given implementation.

Building autonomous system models accounting for nominal behavior requires strong expertise on both modeling and algorithmic aspects. Algorithms describe how individual goals of agents contribute to achieving global system goals. Their design is a non-trivial problem because they are distributed or decentralized. Furthermore, they pursue jointly critical and best effort goals for dynamically changing environments. They allow the management of critical resources (space, time, memory, energy) by optimizing performance and additionally respecting smoothness conditions. Typical examples are collision avoidance algorithms for vehicles (cars, aircraft) that manage the available space respecting requirements on speed and avoiding collision with obstacles.

Other examples are mixed criticality systems involving critical and non-critical features.

Modeling deals with agent nominal behavior description and coordination. Agent nominal behavior assumes that both the sensors and the Perception function are flawless and that sensory information is correctly interpreted into predefined concepts. It focuses on Reflection and Decision and in particular on their dynamic aspects.

Following our approach, the coordination is described as the composition of motifs each one corresponding to a system mode and solving a specific coordination problem. Model correctness can be inferred in principle, by proving that the motifs are correct with respect to their coordination goals and that they are composable [6].

Providing guarantees for complex autonomous systems faces several limitations [2]. One is the decomposition and formalization of high-level goals in terms of concrete requirements verifiable on the system behavioral model. A second limitation concerns our ability to build faithful system models, especially when they involve cyber physical components. The third limitation is that machine-learning techniques do not lend themselves to behavioral modeling and should be treated as "black boxes".

The second step aims at ensuring trustworthiness for a given implementation taking into account deviations from nominal behavior e.g. possible harmful events such as failures and security threats. It starts from the characterization of trustworthy states for nominal behavior provided by the first step (Fig. 9). It involves a more or less exhaustive analysis to identify all kind of harmful events and their possible effect. Then, for each harmful event, specific techniques are used to ensure resilience e.g. typically redundancy-based techniques. This practically means that the occurrence of a single harmful event does not (immediately) compromise system trustworthiness. It leads to some non-fatal state from which using DIR (Detection, Isolation, Recovery) mechanisms it is possible to bring the system back to a trustworthy state [14].

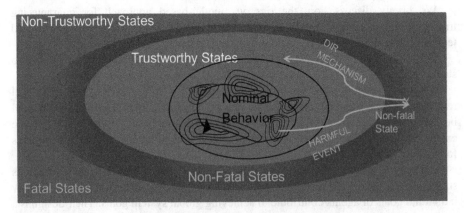

Fig. 9. Recovery from non-fatal states

This approach has been successfully applied to small, centralized critical systems. It is costly and leads to overprovisioned systems [6] as it consists in estimating independently, for each type of harmful event and associated DIR mechanism, worst-case situations and statically reserving the needed resources to cope with them. Its application to autonomous systems is even more difficult as the characterization of the effect of harmful events depends on complex environmental conditions. Such a characterization cannot be enumerative and exhaustive; it should be symbolic and conservative, the result of a global model-based analysis.

Complexity of environmental conditions is illustrated by the pre-crash failure typology shown in Fig. 10. For example, "Vehicle failure" needs further detailed and complex analysis to identify recovery policies, depending on the conditions under which this event occurs.

1 Vehicle Failure	19 Vehicle(s) Drifting – Same Direction
2 Control Loss With Prior Vehicle Action	20 Vehicle(s) Making a Maneuver – Opposite Direction
3 Control Loss Without Prior Vehicle Action	23 Lead Vehicle Accelerating
4 Running Red Light	
5 Running Stop Sign	24 Lead Vehicle Moving at Lower Constant Speed
6 Road Edge Departure With Prior Vehicle Maneuver	25 Lead Vehicle Decelerating
7 Road Edge Departure Without Prior Vehicle Maneuver	26 Lead Vehicle Stopped
8 Road Edge Departure While Backing Up	27 Left Turn Across Path From Opposite Directions at Signalized Junctions
9 Animal Crash With Prior Vehicle Maneuver	28 Vehicle Turning Right at Signalized Junctions
10 Animal Crash Without Prior Vehicle Maneuver	29 Left Turn Across Path From Opposite Directions at Non-Signalized Junctions
11 Pedestrian Crash With Prior Vehicle Maneuver	30 Straight Crossing Paths at Non-Signalized Junctions
12 Pedestrian Crash Without Prior Vehicle Maneuver	31 Vehicle(s) Turning at Non-Signalized Junctions
13 Pedalcyclist Crash With Prior Vehicle Maneuver	32 Evasive Action With Prior Vehicle Maneuver
14 Pedalcyclist Crash Without Prior Vehicle Maneuver	33 Evasive Action Without Prior Vehicle Maneuver
15 Backing Up Into Another Vehicle	34 Non-Collision Incident
16 Vehicle(s) Turning – Same Direction	35 Object Crash With Prior Vehicle Maneuver
17 Vehicle(s) Parking – Same Direction	36 Object Crash Without Prior Vehicle Maneuver
18 Vehicle(s) Changing Lanes – Same Direction	37 Other

Fig. 10. Pre-crash scenario typology covering 99.4% of all light-vehicle crashes for 5,942,000 cases, DOT HS 810 767, April 2017

For autonomous systems, a key idea is to replace the individual DIR mechanisms developed at design time, by adaptive mechanisms managing system resources globally to achieve, first of all critical goals and plan best-effort goals according to resource availability. Such an approach would avoid overprovisioning of traditional approaches and would close the existing gap between critical and best-effort systems engineering [6].

Moving from correctness at design time to autonomic correctness requires not only cutting-edge theory but also finding adequate tradeoffs between quality of control and performance. The adaptive DIR process involves complex decision methods that may affect the ability to react promptly for timely recovery.

To conclude, the proposed computational model for autonomous systems can provide a basis for studying model-based autonomous system design. Nonetheless, we are far from ensuring that the conditions are in place to develop rigorous design flows.

5 Discussion

The main characteristic of autonomous systems is their ability to handle knowledge about their situation and adaptively respond to environment changes. The identified aspects of autonomy have some similarity with types of awareness exhibited by human mind [7].

Closing the gap between artificial and human autonomy encounters several difficult to overcome barriers.

A first barrier is that human mind understands goals in terms of high-level concepts. It is not trivial to link concepts to massive information collected by sensors or to commands of actuators. The Perception process should be robust and reliable for dynamically changing environment conditions.

Similarly, there is a big distance between directives such as "deviate from the reference trajectory to avoid the obstacle" and their implementation in terms of concrete goals from which corresponding plans are effectively computed [2].

A second barrier is that situation awareness of humans is largely rooted in common sense reasoning. Our mind has built and continuously maintains since our birth, a complex semantic model of both our external and internal environments. It is practically impossible to elicit all the knowledge encompassed by such a model. No need to understand Newton's laws to expect that apple fall out of trees, that parents are older than their children are, etc. The important question is how close computers can get to a solution of this problem.

As humans have innate knowledge, we can equip an agent at design time with built-in knowledge and a faithful model of its initial environment. Then the agent's Reflection function should: (1) have access to a huge Knowledge Repository involving all common concepts and their relations; and (2) be able to consistently update the environment model by matching the perceived information to predefined knowledge patterns.

A third barrier for computers is matching human self-adaptation and the capacity: to supervise the state of acquired knowledge; to understand never encountered situations; and to create new goals. Goal creation and handling is a grand challenge of autonomy. How to assign individual goals to agents so that they all together concur to the achievement of given global system goals?

The paper provides a technical characterization of autonomy as the combination of five basic and independent features. It clearly separates aspects that are essential for autonomic behavior from other general systems engineering aspects. In that respect, it differs from other approaches using a large number of poorly understood "self"-prefixed terms: Self-configuration, Self-healing, Self-optimization, Self-protection, Self-regulation, Self-learning, Self-awareness, Self-organization, Self-creation, Self-management, Self-description [16–18]. Such characterizations based on technically non-substantiated terms obscure the debate about the very nature of autonomy. It should be noticed that any ordinary fault-tolerant system with massive redundancy is to some extent Self-Configuring, Self-Healing and Self-Protecting.

A main conclusion is that autonomy should be associated with functionality and not with specific techniques. Machine learning is essential for removing ambiguity from complex stimuli and coping with uncertainty of unpredictable environments. Nonetheless, it can be used to meet only a small portion of the needs implied by autonomous system design. Furthermore, it is not the only way to build perceptors and controllers.

Autonomy is a kind of broad intelligence. Intelligence is not just automation of decisions even if this requires the computation of strategies with exploding complexity. Our characterization of autonomy as the combination of five different types of abilities shows a big difference between an autonomous vehicle and a game playing robot. The situation awareness required for the robot is minimal. The stimuli and the environment models are trivial to interpret and build. The rules of the game are well-understood and can be directly related to goals.

Computers would exhibit intelligence when they can handle knowledge (create and use knowledge) in order to cope with the ever changing reality, as humans do. Building trustworthy and optimal autonomous systems goes for far beyond the current AI challenge.

References

1. Maler, O., Pnueli, A., Sifakis, J.: On the synthesis of discrete controllers for timed systems. In: Mayr, E.W., Puech, C. (eds.) STACS 1995. LNCS, vol. 900, pp. 229–242. Springer, Heidelberg (1995). https://doi.org/10.1007/3-540-59042-0_76
2. Sifakis, J.: System design in the era of IoT—meeting the autonomy challenge, invited paper. In: MetRiD 2018, EPTCS, vol. 272, pp. 1–22 (2018). https://doi.org/10.4204/eptcs.272.1
3. De Nicola, R., Maggi, A., Sifakis, J.: DReAM: dynamic reconfigurable architecture modeling. In: Margaria, T., Steffen, B. (eds.) ISoLA 2018. LNCS, vol. 11246, pp. 13–31. Springer, Cham (2018). https://doi.org/10.1007/978-3-030-03424-5_2
4. El Ballouli, R., Bensalem, S., Bozga, M., Sifakis, J.: Four exercises in programming dynamic reconfigurable systems: methodology and solution in DR-BIP. In: Margaria, T., Steffen, B. (eds.) ISoLA 2018. LNCS, vol. 11246, pp. 304–320. Springer, Cham (2018). https://doi.org/10.1007/978-3-030-03424-5_20
5. El Ballouli, R., Bensalem, S., Bozga, M., Sifakis, J.: Programming dynamic reconfigurable systems. In: FACS 2018, pp. 118–136 (2018)
6. Sifakis, J.: Rigorous system design. Found. Trends Electron. Des. Autom. 6(4), 293–362 (2012)
7. Lewis, P.R., et al.: Architectural aspects of self-aware and self-expressive computing systems: from psychology to engineering. IEEE Comput. 48(8), 62–70 (2015)
8. Bensalem, S., Bozga, M., Quilbeuf, J., Sifakis, J.: Optimized distributed implementation of multiparty interactions with restriction. Sci. Comput. Program. 98(2), 293–316 (2015)
9. Maggio, M., et al.: Self-adaptation for individual self-aware computing systems. In: Kounev, S., Kephart, J., Milenkoski, A., Zhu, X. (eds.) Self-Aware Computing Systems, pp. 375–399. Springer, Cham (2017). https://doi.org/10.1007/978-3-319-47474-8_12
10. Efroni, S., Harel, D., Cohen, I.R.: Reactive animation: realistic modeling of complex dynamic systems. Computer 38, 38–47 (2005)
11. Combaz, J., Fernandez, J.-C., Sifakis, J., Strus, L.: Symbolic quality control for multimedia applications. Real-Time J. 40(1), 1–43 (2008)
12. Basu, A., et al.: Rigorous component-based system design using the BIP framework. IEEE Softw. 28(3), 41–48 (2011)

13. Nouyan, S., Gross, R., Bonani, M., Mondada, F., Dorigo, M.: Teamwork in self-organized robot colonies. IEEE Trans. Evol. Comput. **13**(4), 695–711 (2009)
14. Zolghadri, A.: Advanced model-based FDIR techniques for aerospace systems: today challenges and opportunities. Progr. Aerosp. Sci. **53**, 18–29 (2012)
15. Shalev-Shwartz, S., Shammah, S., Shashua, A.: On a formal model of safe and scalable self-driving cars. Mobileye (2017). arXiv:1708.06374v5 [cs.RO]
16. Wikipedia. https://en.wikipedia.org/wiki/Autonomic_computing
17. Kephart, J., Walsh, W.: An artificial intelligence perspective on autonomic computing policies. In: Proceedings of the Fifth IEEE International Workshop on Policies for Distributed Systems and Networks (POLICY 2004) (2004)
18. An architectural blueprint for autonomic computing. White paper, 3rd edn. IBM, June 2005

Fluidware: An Approach Towards Adaptive and Scalable Programming of the IoT

Giancarlo Fortino[1], Barbara Re[2], Mirko Viroli[3(✉)], and Franco Zambonelli[4]

[1] Università della Calabria, Rende, Italy
`giancarlo.fortino@unical.it`
[2] Università di Camerino, Camerino, Italy
`barbara.re@unicam.it`
[3] Alma Mater Studiorum – Università di Bologna, Cesena, Italy
`mirko.viroli@unibo.it`
[4] Università di Modena e Reggio Emilia, Modena, Italy
`franco.zambonelli@unimore.it`

Abstract. The objective of this paper is to present the vision and structure of Fluidware, an approach towards an innovative programming model to ease the development of flexible and robust large-scale IoT services and applications. The key distinctive idea of Fluidware is to abstract collectives of devices of the IoT fabric as sources, digesters, and targets of distributed "flows" of contextualized events, carrying information about data produced and actuating commands. Accordingly, programming of services and applications relies on declarative specification of "funnel processes" to channel, elaborate, and re-direct such flows in a fully-distributed way, as a means to coordinate the activities of devices and realize services and applications. The potential applicability of Fluidware and its expected advantages are exemplified via a case study scenario in the area of ambient assisted living.

Keywords: Internet of Things · Distributed programming · Middleware · Adaptive systems

1 Introduction

This article focuses on future "Internet of Things" (IoT) environments in which our everyday objects, and our domestic and urban environments, will be densely enriched with sensing, computational, and actuating capabilities [4,29]. Such "IoT fabric" can potentially become a very powerful infrastructure that, if properly programmed, can provide a variety of smart IoT services and IoT applications (intended as coherent suites of services): they can work both at the personal and at the community level, and can help us better interact with the cyber-physical world and the objects in it. However, unveiling the true potentials of large-scale IoT deployments requires novel and dedicated models and programming abstractions [7,44].

© Springer Nature Switzerland AG 2019
M. Boreale et al. (Eds.): De Nicola-Festschrift, LNCS 11665, pp. 411–427, 2019.
https://doi.org/10.1007/978-3-030-21485-2_22

Programming services and applications for the IoT fabric may involve the composition and coordination of a multitude of heterogeneous devices, possibly dispersed over a wide and/or articulated area—e.g., from smart houses, buildings and hospitals, to whole factories or even smart cities. However, this scenario embeds many sources of complexity: the potential high number and density of deployed devices; the high frequency of computational events to occur and be managed; the need to self-adapt to short-/medium-/long-term changes and faults; the need to operate on top of a dynamically evolving infrastructure comprising IoT/edge/cloud devices and resources; the need of promptly (often in quasi real-time) reacting to sophisticated space-time situations; and the potential of running complex, goal-oriented orchestrations of distributed activities across devices of heterogeneous computational power (from tiny devices to cloud servers).

The above issues can make it very hard to develop and deploy dependable services and applications exhibiting predictable behavior, especially when using traditional service composition approaches that would require explicit handling of a multitude of possible exceptions and alternate scenarios. Accordingly, there is compulsory need of novel programming approaches that make it possible to abstract from mundane complexity details and rather rely on high-level constructs enabling to express the potentials of the IoT fabric in full.

To address such issues, we envision a novel programming model for IoT services and applications (along with the associated supporting platform, engineering methodology and tools) conceived to ease the development of flexible and robust large-scale IoT services and applications. Starting from previous findings in the areas of attribute-based coordination [1,2,20], field-based coordination [28,40], collective adaptive systems [3,34], and stream computing and aggregate computing [5,7], the proposed "Fluidware" framework will address the complexity of building modern, large-scale IoT systems, by a full-fledged engineering approach revolving around a new notion of distributed programming.

Our approach relies on the idea to abstract collectives of devices of the IoT fabric (sensors, actuators, and other edge/cloud devices) as sources, digesters, and targets of distributed flows of contextualized events, carrying information about data produced and manipulated over time. Accordingly, programming services and applications implies specifying "funnel processes" to channel, elaborate, and re-direct such flows in a fully-distributed way, as a means to coordinate the activities of devices and realize services and applications.

Funnel processes can be specified in a declarative way, in terms of how they consume and produce events over space and time. They can be associated to distributed and contextualized streams (i.e., flows) of events in terms of advanced pattern-matching and filtering mechanisms based on semantics of data and space-time conditions on their production. Thus, the specification of funnel processes totally abstracts from the actual devices to which events belong: it can be such to include a limited number of local streams from a limited number of devices, but also a large-number of devices spread over a large-scale, enabling to define scale-independent computational activities inherently addressing self-adaptation to contextual conditions, and smoothly fitting various computing/network infrastructures. Indeed, a proper supporting platform/middleware [32] will need to be put in place to take care of the actual deployment of funnel processes, of their allocation at the level of IoT devices and/or edge/cloud computers [35], of their optimized execution, and of their transparent replication and distribution to opportunistically cover large-scale areas.

Overall, the Fluidware approach, once fully developed, will support the bottom-up construction of complex IoT applications through a correctness-guaranteed stack of software components, incrementally encompassing basic building blocks of stream/event manipulation, libraries for distributed coordination, and reusable IoT services.

In order to present the key ideas of the Fluidware approach, the remainder of this article is organized as follows: Sect. 2 defines an application context on ambient assisted living, Sect. 3 consequently derives challenges for novel programming approaches, Sect. 4 sketches the Fluidware programming model and how it would address those challenges, Sect. 5 defines the path towards the full development of Fluidware and the research activities required, Sect. 6 discusses related work in the area, and finally Sect. 7 summarizes contributions of the paper and on-going developments.

2 A Case Study Scenario

As a reference to ground discussion, we consider an Ambient Assisted Living (AAL) scenario which we call the "Fluidware house", where the full potential of the IoT is exploited to improve Mark's daily life.

"Mark is a 65 years old retired person, married with no children. He had an ischemic stroke with paralysis of the right upper and lower limbs 14 months ago. Mark was discharged from the rehabilitation center three months after the stroke, and then he continued to rehabilitate at home. Once his socio-health situation was evaluated, the psychiatrist and social services have suggested Mark and his wife to move to a Fluidware house, more suited to the needs of the family."

In a Fluidware house, we assume that all the rooms are densely enriched with connected sensors and actuators: light and heat controllers, gas and smoke detectors, presence and motion sensors, pressure sensors located on the sittings, electric energy consume sensors, and so on. While the environment is monitored, the person is constantly controlled by wearable sensors that are able to detect vital signs (e.g. heart rate and respiration, activity level and posture). In such a scenario, IoT devices can be exploited to realize a variety of different services to support care activities of individuals, to help individuals and their family members in their everyday self-managed health-care activities, and to control the overall conditions of the house.

"Mark's day begins at 8 am. After waking up, he is able to get out of bed with the help of his wife. Mark is able to walk short distances with orthosis and a stick support and can reach quite easily the bathroom where he can wash in a bathtub with a rising platform, always with the help of a caregiver. The morning is the part of the day dedicated to rehabilitation aimed primarily at preventing complications due to hypomobility of limbs and to increase physical performance. During this phase, as for the rest of the day, it is very important to measure vital parameters through a wearable system of sensors."

In this situation, the Fluidware house will use sensors to monitor the activities carried out, which are then involved in the assessment of the condition of normality/abnormalities. The normal condition implies that at least one sensor registers the presence of the person through the recognition of a movement. Terms of inactivity (e.g. TV watching, sleeping) are considered normal if they involve the use of furniture such as chairs or bed with a pressure sensor that detects the use. Abnormality conditions can depend on prolonged inactivity or on alarms related to wearable sensors data exceeding thresholds.

"The afternoon is the time for relax and the presence of a caregiver within the home is not essential."

Here, the environmental sensors (e.g. luminosity, temperature, humidity, gas) monitor the conditions inside the house. The supplied data are used by Fluidware service to automatically adjust the environment conditions, optimizing the use of energy in the rooms where Mark won't typically move to.

"After lunch, Mark's wife leaves her husband alone in the house. Mark gets up from his chair and with the help of the stick goes into the bathroom to wash his hands. The floor is slippery and he falls. Having mobility problems, he is no longer able to stand up alone."

In the unpleasant situation of a fall, we can have the intervention of several sensors. The wearable sensors in place are able to detect the posture (vertical or horizontal) and the acceleration along three axes [22]. This is particularly useful to determine emergency conditions such as the occurrence of a fall [23]. Presence sensors are able to detect both walking movements in the selected detection zone and respond to them accordingly. Moreover, motion sensors respond to the tiniest movements using extremely high resolution and precision sensors detecting the movement of arms and fingers. The condition of horizontal position and the detection of a downward acceleration are considered fundamental situations because they are considered an abnormality. If, over a short period of time, the sensors do not detect a new acceleration upwards and if the person remains in a horizontal position without moving, the Fluidware emergency service can say, with a certain degree of certainty, that the person has fallen. The overall coordination of emergency service involving the different caregivers can be also implemented exploiting Fluidware potentialities.

"Each day, Mark's doctor receives summary information about Mark's activity and vital parameters both on its PC and its smartphone. She can check them, compare them with those of previous days or weeks to analyze trends, and can then even command changes in the configuration of the house or of the care program."

All the information provided by the several sensors deployed in the house get automatically aggregated, filtered, and channeled to the cloud. Moreover, in the discussed scenario considering a lot of information exchange taking place it is worth to notice the need to address privacy/security issues. Additional processes living in the cloud take care of redirecting general information and events to Mark's doctor.

3   Challenges

The key motivations for Fluidware are to address a number of issues that currently hinder the possibility to easily develop complex and large-scale IoT systems and applications. The case study scenario we considered helps us identify the following challenges:

Device Independence. Current IoT approaches are highly device-dependent, assuming the existence of specific types of devices in specific locations. However, the heterogeneity of devices, their ephemerality, and the impossibility to individually control all devices in an environment, require programming approaches enabling services to be programmed and expressed in device-independent terms.

In fact, Mark's house seamlessly manages the co-existence of different types of devices (e.g. motion, environment and medical sensors) in different environments and with heterogeneous characteristics (e.g. kitchen, bedroom, and bathroom introduces their own space constraints).

Scalability. IoT services may involve individual sensors and actuators, or compose and coordinate a limited number of local devices, but also exploit a multitude of cooperating devices distributed over a wide area. An approach for programming and deploying IoT services should adopt the same basic model for small and for large-scale services, and should not lose in effectiveness when scaling.

As Mark's house is densely enriched with connected IoT devices, cooperating to provide services, scalability is required for a number of reasons: Mark's personal condition can quickly change, asking for prompt change also in the environment as an increasing need of monitoring Mark's daily routine; novel IoT devices can be added into the house to provide applications that impose additional traffic overhead. As a result, there is need to handle a growing amount of data in order to automatically manage high quality information on health and environment status.

Adaptivity. IoT systems are called to operate in very dynamic environments. Devices can be faulty, mobile, or become unreachable. Yet, IoT services and applications must adaptively react and be highly available to serve reliably despite contingencies.

The house is a live dynamic environment, where devices change their sensing and actuating capability as a result of the changing condition of Mark's personal status. Different types of change need to be supported: there are situations not known a priori that are partially-repeatable, unpredictable, and emergent, while others are more structured, repeatable and predictable; overall, there is need to be able to support both a self-adaptive management of daily routines and adaptation in the sense of human-controlled (re-)configuration.

Seamless Integration of Devices, Edge, and Cloud Levels. The overall IoT fabric will include a multitude of distributed devices, edge computers that can act as "local clouds" for the devices in a locality, and general cloud resources. To effectively exploit the IoT fabric, there is thus need of supporting both direct device-to-device interactions, edge computation, and cloud resources, all within the same design and programming abstraction.

Effectively monitoring and controlling Mark's house means supporting different types of integration: direct device-to-device interactions will be needed in order to implement local alarms (e.g. exceeding a temperature threshold), edge computation to locally enact complex situation recognition (e.g. fall detection), and cloud resources to store historical information and interact with external stakeholders (e.g. caregivers and doctors).

Interoperability and Security. Enabling interoperability among heterogeneous devices and ensuring security of IoT systems and services are key challenges to enable the widespread diffusion of IoT services.

Interoperability [21] needs to be guaranteed in order to share information between devices in the house (e.g. the daily routine involve several objects dedicated to understand normal and emergency situation), as well as between the house and external environment (e.g. to interact with the hospital in case of emergency), which requires to consider the multitude of standards applicable to assistive technologies as well as the security and privacy issues concerning the personal nature of the scenario.

4   The Fluidware Approach

The Fluidware approach considers IoT-enriched environments densely populated with a variety of IoT devices (overall forming the "IoT fabric"), acting as sensors or actuators or both. Sensing devices generate "contextualized streams" of data representing events about something that is happening somewhere in the environment. Actuating devices receive "contextualized command streams" related to how they should affect the environment, and people within, over time.

4.1   Funnel Processes

The key idea of Fluidware is that IoT services and applications can be realized by transformations of widely-distributed streams of events, which we also call "event flows" (or simply "flows"), involving collectives of devices. This is achieved by means of an abstraction of "funnel process", acting as digester and producer of "event flows", elaborating/sending/(re)distributing them over the network of distributed IoT devices or over the edge/cloud (see Fig. 1).

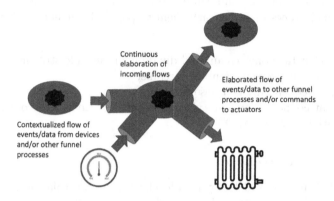

Fig. 1. A general abstract representation of funnel processes exploited locally.

Funnel processes will be specified in a declarative way independently of their actual allocation and distribution (managed by the Fluidware middleware). Their specification will be such to define which flow to connect to, depending on contextual/spatio-temporal and semantic matching (e.g., from "in room X now" to "where average temperature has been greater than 25 Celsius degrees in the last 5 min"). Thus, a funnel specification will totally abstract from the actual devices that are sources, manipulators, or targets for events: it can be such to include a limited number of local events from a limited number of devices, but also a large-number of devices spread over a large-scale. This enables to define scale-independent computational activities, inherently independent of external conditions and smoothly fitting various computing/network infrastructures. Most specifically, an event flow is manipulated computationally to produce a new flow, by a combination of mechanisms typical of stream processing frameworks and of self-adaptive and self-organizing systems, such as fully-distributed and resilient aggregation, spreading, persistence, and so on [39].

In particular, we envision the definition of a library of primitive funnel templates, including:

- *filters*, that select only the events that match certain criteria, expressed via conditions on attributes concerning event source, location, time, content, and so on [20];
- *aggregators*, that cluster events into groups (based on correlations on their attributes), and correspondingly create new events for each group (creating average values over time or space, reunifying complex multi-event situations into alert events, and so on);

– *transmuters*, that manipulate the content of events leaving their overall structure unchanged (resetting content, applying increments, mapping and so on);
– *relocators*, that move source/location/time of events (to specify space-time relocation policies for event streams).

Then, special operators and combinators will be used to compose and interconnect funnel processes and attach them to physical elements of various kind, such as;

– *splitters*, that take one stream and divide it in multiple streams;
– *mergers*, that conversely combine streams;
– *pipes*, that sequentially compose funnels;
– *hooks*, that connect funnels to virtualized devices (macro sensors/actuators/computational resources [9]).

4.2 Deployment Scenarios

At the implementation and deployment level, the Fluidware platform/middleware will take care of creating actual distributed processes, and connecting them to the actual flows of events and the physical devices supporting them, to realize funnel process specifications. Such processes can be deployed on any IoT device with enough resources to support their execution. Opportunistically, funnel processes can be deployed at the level of edge computers associated to some specific location and having access to all devices in that location [37], or even at the level of some centralized cloud.

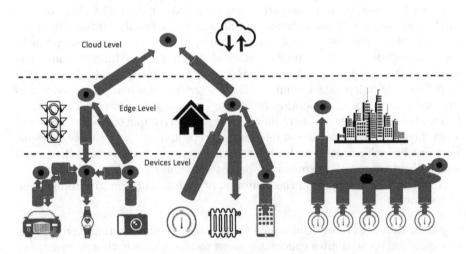

Fig. 2. Overview of the Fluidware approach.

Clearly, when allocated to individual devices, a process can pre-digest and elaborate the data sensed by that device before forwarding it to some other devices or to some collection point. However, it can also be seamlessly used to spread and re-distribute events to nearby devices, and itself contribute absorbing and possibly aggregating events coming from nearby devices. This can be used to realize composite services with a direct device-to-device coordination. This scenario is represented in the left part of Fig. 2.

In addition, a funnel process to be connected to an event flow spread over a multitude of devices, and/or a wide area, can be realized by initially replicating and distributing multiple actual processes, all logically part of the same distributed funnel process. Such aggregations can be used to realize services and applications in the large-scale by reasoning at the level of collectives of devices and, in the end, to promote scale-independent and device-independent computations, along the lines of field-based coordination and aggregate computing approaches [7, 10, 28]. The right part of Fig. 2 represents such a scenario.

On the other hand, when acting at the edge level, funnel processes can be used to collect the events provided by devices at a specific location (e.g., a room, a building, or a plaza), and elaborate them to produce flows of commands to the local actuators, and possibly forwarding streams of data to the cloud. Finally, nothing prevents one from associating funnel processes to some cloud servers to realize some sorts of centralized services, either explicitly within funnel process deployment specification [30], or implicitly as an opportunistic choice at the platform level. This scenario is represented in the central part of Fig. 2.

We emphasize that, building on previous experience on formal models of distributed and adaptive business processes [16, 17] and in distributed field-based coordination [7, 45], the Fluidware approach is meant to support a formalized description of funnel processes supporting static and behavioral property verification, independently of where the approach acts at the level of individual devices or at the edge/cloud level, and independently of whether it is used to implement traditional composition of services or rather in-the-large collective distributed coordination.

4.3   Addressing the Challenges

Let us now analyze how Fluidware has the potential to effectively address the challenges identified in Sect. 3.

Device Independence. In Fluidware, whole collectives of IoT devices are abstracted as producers (or consumers, for actuators) of distributed streams of contextualized events, thus making system programming dependent on the availability of specific patterns of events, not on the specific identity of the devices producing or consuming them.

With reference to the case study, a filter funnel can be put in place to get events tagged with a specific "biometric" attribute [20], and can be composed (by a pipe) to a relocator to make such data be available for monitoring from a remote station owned by doctors. This will be specified without any a-priori knowledge of which sensors produced such biometric data.

Scalability. In Fluidware, funnel processes can be used to access individual streams, as well as – with the same model – to aggregate, compose and control distributed flows of events generated by myriads of devices, thus seamlessly enabling small-scale service composition and large-scale services based on collective behaviors.

With reference to the case study, a filter funnel can be put in place to get events tagged with a specific "temperature" attribute, and can be composed (by a pipe) to an aggregator to extract a stream of average values of temperature, where each event is produced each minute. This will be specified without any a-priori knowledge of the dislocation and number of sensors in place: aggregation will be transparently executed by the sensors themselves by en-route combination of values [39].

Adaptivity. In Fluidware, funnel processes are not statically tied to specific IoT devices, but are dynamically bound to any flows of events matching contextual and semantic characteristics. Thus, they can operate by dynamically re-connecting to different sets of devices, simply depending on their characteristics, whenever needed to react to contingencies.

With reference to the case study, a composition of funnels can be put in place to send periodic information about the house and Mark's general status to doctors. However, as soon as some physiological data exceed safety ranges for a sufficient amount of time, those funnels start matching different streams of data, and automatically reconfigure to send fine-grained samples of all available physiological data to the doctors [9].

Seamless Integration of Devices, Edge, and Cloud Levels. In Fluidware funnel processes may be playing the role of re-directing streams of data to the edge, where further processes may digest them and re-direct them to realize composite edge services, or they can be used to re-direct streams to the cloud.

With reference to the case study, funnels like aggregators, used to perform some situation recognition across a possibly large set of devices, are specified in a way that makes it possible to carry their process on in different ways, selected depending on the available resources, or even possibly dynamically switching to address contingencies: in a fully distributed way by cooperation of devices, by having those devices simply sending their data to some cloud resource, or even by having local edge devices computing local aggregates which are sent to the cloud for further aggregation [41].

Interoperability and Security. Concerning interoperability, the possibility in Fluidware to program services in a device-independent way promotes interoperability, and just requires devices to host a Fluidware local proxy, or – in the case of very lightweight IoT devices – to directly communicate via standard IoT protocols with Fluidware edge devices. Concerning security, Fluidware can rely on existing security solutions, but can also integrate recent research approaches to trust computing for the IoT and wireless sensor networks [24].

Mark's house is intrinsically open and secure. First, when new kinds of sensors are deployed, they automatically become part of the Fluidware ecosystem:

they either have a lightweight Fluidware software agent on board that carries on all computational activities in cooperation with others, or they simply send their data using standard protocols to the nearest fully-featured Fuildware edge device (each room could have one installed in it). Additionally, Fluidware continuously run processes of trust monitoring and control to detect malevolent devices and progressively make them ignored by others to prevent unwanted perturbation of the overall house—as suggested in [12].

5   The Path Towards Fluidware

The road-map of research activities needed to fully develop Fluidware includes:

1. development of the Fluidware model and associated programming abstractions, suitable for defining and composing services and systems possibly involving a large-number of IoT devices distributed over a large area;
2. development of a prototype platform (i.e., a middleware and associated services) to support deployment and execution of IoT systems according to the Fluidware model;
3. development of an engineering methodology to guide developers in the analysis and design of Fluidware-based complex IoT service systems, and associated tools to support validation before deployment;
4. testing on IoT case studies, specifically in the area of smart healthcare and AAL.

5.1   Programming Model

From the development and programming viewpoint, it can be expected that IoT services and IoT applications will be mostly up to expert system developers. Yet, the Fluidware declarative approach will also enable local managers of a location (and, to some limited extent, end users) to be able to directly personalize the behavior of such applications with simple forms of user-level programming of funnel processes, for instance, in a similar way to "if this then that" approaches [18] or by selecting specific funnel processes and services from libraries of reusable specifications.

To formalize the Fluidware operational model and implement its basic programming interface, the following activities are to be undertaken.

- Developing the operational model of funnel processes, to serve as a blueprint for implementation of the platform, for defining composition techniques, and to check well-formedness of specifications and properties. It will need to include development of a core calculus, operational semantics, and by-construction proofs of self-stabilization and safe encapsulation.
- Implementing a library to provide the core mechanisms devised in the model, to specify and compose processes, as an interface towards the platform and existing simulators. The adoption of modern techniques can be envisaged to smoothly integrate with mainstream programming and functional-oriented declarative approaches, e.g., by the features of the Scala language as in [14].

5.2   Middleware

Fluidware can be supported by a middleware capable of instantiating local proxies of funnel processes and launch them in execution into the proper location [25,26,32], and to relocating them as needed. To promote scalability and flexibility, the platform will support interactions and coordination at three levels (as from Fig. 2): *direct device-to-device level* (e.g., for field-based coordination), with funnel processes directly instantiated on sets of devices, and with events flowing, aggregating and re-distributing from device to device; *edge level*, with funnel processes dynamically allocated on edge computers (i.e., cloudlets or fog computers), to digest streams of events, implement local coordinated services, and possibly to connect multiple edges to realize inter-edge coordination; *cloud level*, for centralized monitoring, coordination, and storage.

The activities to develop the Fluidware middleware platform will address three related objectives.

- To define a mapping from Fluidware programming specifications into a set of distributed components to be deployed atop the Fluidware platform. Mapping will be based on a model-driven development [13] and will distinguish abstract platform-independent specifications from deployable platform-dependent components.
- To implement a distributed engine for supporting the execution of Fluidware systems and services. It will be organized as a three-layered (devices, edges, and cloud) super-peer architecture. Platform-dependent components can be dynamically activated and re-configured in IoT devices, edge servers and/or cloud platforms.
- To analyze interoperability and security issues. Such an activity will define guidelines for enabling devices to connect to the Fluidware platform, and will analyze how a trust-oriented distributed infrastructure for inter-component security can be integrated within it.

5.3   Engineering Methodology

The Fluidware approach will also require the definition of new conceptual abstractions to reason about complex IoT services and applications and their requirements. In addition, it will call for the identification of specific methodological guidelines to drive the development process, to be necessarily accompanied by Fluidware-specific tools to support the activities of the development process, and to provide correctness guarantees [27,44].

Accordingly, there is need of synthesizing from the previously identified activities in order to make the basic engineering instruments available supporting the analysis, design and implementation of complex IoT systems and services with Fluidware. To this end, the following activities need to be implemented.

- Identify the key conceptual abstractions which the analysis and design of Fluidware systems and services should rely on, and on this basis it will define guidelines for analysis, design, implementation, testing, and adaptation of Fluidware services and systems.

– Identify and prototype a set of tools in support of the development of Fluidware systems and services. These will include *(i)* basic support to verify service behavior against specifications (by model-checking or static analysis) [19]; and *(ii)* a large-scale simulator to verify overall system behaviors [13]. Prototyping of such tools will be based on extending/adapting existing techniques, tools, and simulators.

5.4 Application Studies

Fluidware is a general-purpose approach, suitable for developing IoT services and applications in a variety of emerging scenarios, such as smart homes, smart cities, traffic control systems, energy control systems, and smart production systems. To keep focus without losing generality, it may be proper to focus on a specific challenge related to the ageing society: AAL [18]. This will enable putting the Fluidware approach at work in real-world problems, to guide its development strategies, and to assess the effectiveness of the approach. In particular, we intend to test AAL applications both at the scale of a real-life domestic indoor testbed and of a large-scale simulated urban scenario. The domestic testbed will be aimed at verifying ease and expressiveness of programmability of Fluidware, as well as the effectiveness of the platform and its adaptability properties. The large-scale simulated scenario will be useful to verify Fluidware scalability and flexibility.

Given the safety-critical nature of the described scenario, many services related to e.g., the health condition of patients or the ambient conditions of the house, may be required to continuously send information to be analyzed to different actors (from doctors to caregivers). Thus, any approach for developing services and applications should more properly conceive sensors and actuators as producers and consumers of continuous flows of events, rather than as loci of services to be invoked as often happens through conventional cloud-based (virtualization) approaches.

6   Related Work

The Fluidware computational model definitely owns to methods proposing the simplification of distributed programming by abstracting from individual networked devices, and working at the level of their collective behaviors, such as TOTA [28], SCEL [20], SAPERE [45], or DECCO [10]. These also include space-time models for the universal manipulation of field data structures diffused in space and evolving with time, such as spatial [36] and aggregate computing [7]. Fluidware, with its concept of funnel processes, will advance such approaches by enabling the seamless modeling of small-scale composite services as well as large-scale collective services, and by supporting the integration of semi-decentralized approaches with fully distributed ones. Also, by exploiting the lessons of process algebras [15] and formal approaches [8], Fluidware can add a process layer which *(i)* internally carries on stream computation, and *(ii)* externally defines life-cycle aspects such as funnel process generation, space-time extension, interaction with environment, and de-allocation. By taking inspiration from frameworks to automatically split data processing behavior for cloud- and cluster-style execution (e.g., Spark [43], and Flink [11]), Fluidware will enrich traditional collective and aggregate approaches to distributed programming by considering a transition from handling collective "fields" of data to the notion of distributed stream of events, thus addressing also non-functional aspects concerning the control of dynamic aspects of event generation and diffusion.

Some recent approaches to programming IoT services propose new computational abstractions as building blocks of IoT services, such as the micro-services of Osmotic computing [31,38], the core processors of EdgeIoT [37], or the deployment units of the Elastic Computing [30]. These approaches share with Fluidware the idea of enabling the adaptive deployment of such building blocks at the level of both cloud or edge computers, and possibly at the level of IoT devices. However, Fluidware will enrich that with an operational semantics addressing dynamically multi-layered architectures, with the possibility of also acting in collective terms at the level of devices to enforce large-scale adaptive service composition, like the Opportunistic IoT Services approach based on aggregate computing [13].

Concerning middleware, a variety of platforms have been proposed to support the deployment and execution of IoT services and applications (see [32] for a survey) and including solutions to adaptively handle interoperability [6,21], context-dependency [33], and adaptivity [42,45]. Similarly to them, the Fluidware platform will promote interoperability (thanks to device-independence of the funnel process abstraction), adaptivity (due to the flexible deployment of funnel processes) and context-dependency (events digested by funnel processes are inherently contextual). However, it will also provide solutions for the collective execution and coordination of funnel processes on the large-scale.

Concerning software engineering, it is recognized that the development of IoT systems and applications may require not only the extension of existing methods [27] but also novel methodologies and tools [25,44]. However, actual methodologies and tools specifically suited to future IoT scenarios are lacking, Fluidware will fill this gap by producing novel software engineering guidelines that – although studied in the context of Fluidware – can be of general help towards the development of complex and large-scale IoT applications. Also, it will produce tools (novel or extensions of existing ones) in support of the verification of IoT system behavior, and that can be of general use in the context of large-scale distributed systems.

7 Conclusions

In this article, we have presented the vision of Fluidware, an innovative approach for the development of IoT services and applications, conceived, to ease the development of flexible and robust large-scale IoT services and applications. To summarize, we can list the key innovations that Fluidware promises to bring about.

- Its funnel process abstraction goes significantly beyond the state-of-the-art in computational models for distributed and collective systems, allowing to declaratively express distributed processes managing contextualized streams of events in a way that is effectively scale-independent, device-independent, and independent of the temporal availability of specific devices, thus being adaptive to changes and contingencies.
- The interplay between Fluidware model and platform will fully provide utility-driven exploitation of infrastructure, enabling execution of funnel processes along the entire IoT device/edge/cloud stack, hence supporting scenarios where devices opportunistically exploit P2P interactions, edge devices, or cloud resources, either to improve performance, save energy, or speed-up the sense-to-react feedback.
- The definition of novel software engineering abstractions, methodologies, and tools to support activities performed to develop Fluidware applications, can shed new lights into the general software engineering issues associated to the development of complex IoT systems and services in general, independently of Fluidware.

Currently, we are in the process of developing the presented ideas, in the hope of being able, with Fluidware, to actually deliver its identified potentials.

References

1. Alrahman, Y.A., De Nicola, R., Garbi, G., Loreti, M.: A distributed coordination infrastructure for attribute-based interaction. In: Baier, C., Caires, L. (eds.) FORTE 2018. LNCS, vol. 10854, pp. 1–20. Springer, Cham (2018). https://doi.org/10.1007/978-3-319-92612-4_1
2. Alrahman, Y.A., De Nicola, R., Loreti, M., Tiezzi, F., Vigo, R.: A calculus for attribute-based communication. In: Proceedings of the 30th Annual ACM Symposium on Applied Computing, pp. 1840–1845. ACM (2015)
3. Andrikopoulos, V., Bucchiarone, A., Gómez Sáez, S., Karastoyanova, D., Mezzina, C.A.: Towards modeling and execution of collective adaptive systems. In: Lomuscio, A.R., Nepal, S., Patrizi, F., Benatallah, B., Brandić, I. (eds.) ICSOC 2013. LNCS, vol. 8377, pp. 69–81. Springer, Cham (2014). https://doi.org/10.1007/978-3-319-06859-6_7
4. Atzori, L., Iera, A., Morabito, G.: The internet of things: a survey. Comput. Netw. **54**(15), 2787–2805 (2010)
5. Audrito, G., Viroli, M., Damiani, F., Pianini, D., Beal, J.: A higher-order calculus of computational fields. ACM Trans. Comput. Log. **20**(1), 5:1–5:55 (2019). http://doi.acm.org/10.1145/3285956
6. Ayala, I., Amor, M., Fuentes, L.: The sol agent platform: enabling group communication and interoperability of self-configuring agents in the internet of things. JAISE **7**(2), 243–269 (2015)
7. Beal, J., Pianini, D., Viroli, M.: Aggregate programming for the internet of things. IEEE Comput. **48**(9), 22–30 (2015)
8. Belzner, L., Hölzl, M., Koch, N., Wirsing, M.: Collective autonomic systems: towards engineering principles and their foundations. In: Steffen, B. (ed.) Transactions on Foundations for Mastering Change I. LNCS, vol. 9960, pp. 180–200. Springer, Cham (2016). https://doi.org/10.1007/978-3-319-46508-1_10

9. Bicocchi, N., Mamei, M., Zambonelli, F.: Self-organizing virtual macro sensors. TAAS **7**(1), 2:1–2:28 (2012)
10. Bures, T., Plasil, F., Kit, M., Tuma, P., Hoch, N.: Software abstractions for component interaction in the internet of things. IEEE Comput. **49**(12), 50–59 (2016)
11. Carbone, P., Katsifodimos, A., Ewen, S., Markl, V., Haridi, S., Tzoumas, K.: Apache flink: stream and batch processing in a single engine. In: Bulletin of the IEEE Computer Society Technical Committee on Data Engineering, vol. 36, no. 4 (2015)
12. Casadei, R., Alessandro, A., Viroli, M.: Towards attack-resistant aggregate computing using trust mechanisms. Sci. Comput. Program. **167**, 114–137 (2018)
13. Casadei, R., Fortino, G., Pianini, D., Russo, W., Savaglio, C., Viroli, M.: Modelling and simulation of opportunistic IoT services with aggregate computing. Future Gener. Comput. Syst. **91**, 252–262 (2019)
14. Casadei, R., Viroli, M.: Towards aggregate programming in Scala. In: Proceedings of the 1st Workshop on Programming Models and Languages for Distributed Computing, pp. 5:1–5:7. ACM (2016)
15. Choe, Y., Lee, M.: Algebraic method to model secure IoT. In: Karagiannis, D., Mayr, H., Mylopoulos, J. (eds.) Domain-Specific Conceptual Modeling, pp. 335–355. Springer, Cham (2016). https://doi.org/10.1007/978-3-319-39417-6_15
16. Cognini, R., Corradini, F., Polini, A., Re, B.: Extending feature models to express variability in business process models. In: Persson, A., Stirna, J. (eds.) CAiSE 2015. LNBIP, vol. 215, pp. 245–256. Springer, Cham (2015). https://doi.org/10.1007/978-3-319-19243-7_24
17. Cognini, R., Corradini, F., Polini, A., Re, B.: Business process feature model: an approach to deal with variability of business processes. Domain-Specific Conceptual Modeling, pp. 171–194. Springer, Cham (2016). https://doi.org/10.1007/978-3-319-39417-6_8
18. Corno, F., De Russis, L., Roffarello, A.M.: A semantic web approach to simplifying trigger-action programming in the IoT. Computer **50**(11), 18–24 (2017)
19. Corradini, F., Fornari, F., Polini, A., Re, B., Tiezzi, F., Vandin, A.: BProVe: a formal verification framework for business process models. In: Proceedings of the 32nd International Conference on Automated Software Engineering, pp. 217–228. IEEE Computer Society (2017)
20. De Nicola, R., et al.: The SCEL language: design, implementation, verification. In: Wirsing, M., Hölzl, M., Koch, N., Mayer, P. (eds.) Software Engineering for Collective Autonomic Systems. LNCS, vol. 8998, pp. 3–71. Springer, Cham (2015). https://doi.org/10.1007/978-3-319-16310-9_1
21. Fortino, G., et al.: Towards multi-layer interoperability of heterogeneous iot platforms: the INTER-IoT approach. In: Gravina, R., Palau, C.E., Manso, M., Liotta, A., Fortino, G. (eds.) Integration, Interconnection, and Interoperability of IoT Systems. IT, pp. 199–232. Springer, Cham (2018). https://doi.org/10.1007/978-3-319-61300-0_10
22. Fortino, G., Giannantonio, R., Gravina, R., Kuryloski, P., Jafari, R.: Enabling effective programming and flexible management of efficient body sensor network applications. IEEE Trans. Hum. Mach. Syst. **43**(1), 115–133 (2013)
23. Fortino, G., Gravina, R.: Fall-mobileguard: a smart real-time fall detection system. In: Proceedings of the 10th International Conference on Body Area Networks. ICST (2015)
24. Fortino, G., Messina, F., Rosaci, D., Sarnè, G.M.L.: Using trust and local reputation for group formation in the cloud of things. Future Gener. Comput. Syst. **89**, 804–815 (2018)

25. Fortino, G., Russo, W., Savaglio, C., Shen, W., Zhou, M.: Agent-oriented cooperative smart objects: from IoT system design to implementation. IEEE Trans. Syst. Man Cybern. Syst. **48**(11), 1939–1956 (2018)
26. Galzarano, S., Giannantonio, R., Liotta, A., Fortino, G.: A task-oriented framework for networked wearable computing. IEEE Trans. Autom. Sci. Eng. **13**(2), 621–638 (2016)
27. Jacobson, I., Spence, I., Ng, P.W.: Is there a single method for the internet of things? Queue **15**(3), 20 (2017)
28. Mamei, M., Zambonelli, F.: Programming pervasive and mobile computing applications: the TOTA approach. ACM Trans. Softw. Eng. Methodol. **18**(4), 15:1–15:56 (2009)
29. Miorandi, D., Sicari, S., De Pellegrini, F., Chlamtac, I.: Internet of things: vision, applications and research challenges. Ad Hoc Netw. **10**(7), 1497–1516 (2012)
30. Moldovan, D., Copil, G., Dustdar, S.: Elastic systems: towards cyber-physical ecosystems of people, processes, and things. Comput. Stand. Interfaces **57**, 76–82 (2018)
31. Nardelli, M., Nastic, S., Dustdar, S., Villari, M., Ranjan, R.: Osmotic flow: osmotic computing+ IoT workflow. IEEE Cloud Comput. **4**(2), 68–75 (2017)
32. Palade, A., Cabrera, C., White, G., Razzaque, M.A., Clarke, S.: Middleware for internet of things: a quantitative evaluation in small scale, pp. 1–6. IEEE (2017)
33. Perera, C., Zaslavsky, A., Christen, P., Georgakopoulos, D.: Context aware computing for the internet of things: a survey. IEEE Commun. Surv. Tutor. **16**(1), 414–454 (2014)
34. Pournaras, E.: Overlay service computing - modular and reconfigurable collective adaptive systems. Scalable Comput. Pract. Exp. **16**(3), 249–270 (2015). http:// www.scpe.org/index.php/scpe/article/view/1100
35. Rausch, T., Dustdar, S., Ranjan, R.: Osmotic message-oriented middleware for the internet of things. IEEE Cloud Comput. **5**(2), 17–25 (2018)
36. Shekhar, S., Feiner, S.K., Aref, W.G.: Spatial computing. Commun. ACM **59**(1), 72–81 (2016)
37. Sun, X., Ansari, N.: EdgeIoT: mobile edge computing for the internet of things. IEEE Commun. Mag. **54**(12), 22–29 (2016)
38. Villari, M., Fazio, M., Dustdar, S., Rana, O., Ranjan, R.: Osmotic computing: a new paradigm for edge/cloud integration. IEEE Cloud Comput. **3**(6), 76–83 (2016)
39. Viroli, M., Audrito, G., Beal, J., Damiani, F., Pianini, D.: Engineering resilient collective adaptive systems by self-stabilisation. ACM Trans. Model. Comput. Simul. **28**(2), 1–28 (2018)
40. Viroli, M., Casadei, M., Montagna, S., Zambonelli, F.: Spatial coordination of pervasive services through chemical-inspired tuple spaces. ACM Trans. Auton. Adapt. Syst. **6**(2), 14:1–14:24 (2011). http://doi.acm.org/10.1145/1968513.1968517
41. Viroli, M., Casadei, R., Pianini, D.: On execution platforms for large-scale aggregate computing. In: Proceedings of the International Joint Conference on Pervasive and Ubiquitous Computing, pp. 1321–1326. ACM (2016)
42. Vlacheas, P., et al.: Enabling smart cities through a cognitive management framework for the internet of things. IEEE Commun. Mag. **51**(6), 102–111 (2013)
43. Zaharia, M., et al.: Apache Spark: a unified engine for big data processing. Commun. ACM **59**(11), 56–65 (2016)
44. Zambonelli, F.: Key abstractions for IoT-oriented software engineering. IEEE Softw. **34**(1), 38–45 (2017)
45. Zambonelli, F., et al.: Developing pervasive multi-agent systems with nature-inspired coordination. Pervasive Mob. Comput. **17**, 236–252 (2015)

HEADREST: A Specification Language for RESTful APIs

Vasco T. Vasconcelos[1], Francisco Martins[2(✉)], Antónia Lopes[1], and Nuno Burnay[1]

[1] LASIGE and Faculdade de Ciências, Universidade de Lisboa, Lisbon, Portugal
[2] LASIGE and Universidade dos Açores, Ponta Delgada, Portugal
fmartins@acm.org

Abstract. Representational State Transfer (REST), an architectural style providing an abstract model of the web, is by far the most popular platform to build web applications. Developing such applications require well-documented interfaces. However, and despite important initiatives such as the Open API Specification, the support for interface description is currently quite limited, focusing essentially on simple syntactic aspects. In this paper we present HeadREST, a dependently-typed language that allows describing semantic aspects of interfaces in a style reminiscent of Hoare triples.

Keywords: REST · Web services · Description language

1 Introduction

Software services are not just a mechanism to compose software functionalities, but, in the present case, it was also the motto to bring together once again two groups of researchers, notably De Nicolas's and Vasconcelos' teams.

It all restarted in 2005, under the auspices of Sensoria, Software Engineering for Service-oriented Overlay Computers [15], a project revolving around the idea of service as a basis for service-oriented computing. In 2006 we authored together "SCC: A Service Centered Calculus" [3], a paper that laid down the foundations for describing the dynamic behaviour of services in terms of a process calculus. SCC introduces the notions of *service definition*, which provides for service behaviours, and of *service invocation*, which consumes instances of services. The communication between both ends of a service interaction happens in the context of a *session*. Inside this, processes send and receive messages isolated from other ongoing service interactions. A system is the parallel composition of service definitions, invocations, and ongoing sessions.

Following to this work, we concentrated on the problems of composing and orchestrating services, introducing SSCC [11]. This new calculus puts forward

---

An early version of this paper was presented at the 24th International Conference on Types for Proofs and Programs, in June 2018.

© Springer Nature Switzerland AG 2019
M. Boreale et al. (Eds.): De Nicola-Festschrift, LNCS 11665, pp. 428–434, 2019.
https://doi.org/10.1007/978-3-030-21485-2_23

a *stream* construct to play the role of a service orchestrator. In the following year, De Nicola and his team proposed CaSPiS that also features intra- and inter-session communication by using *streams* and *pipelines* [4]. CaSPiS further allows for reasoning about session cancellation and termination, scenarios in which processes may abandon or terminate their current sessions.

The explosive growth of the Web, and the adoption of services as one of the pillars for building distributed applications over the Web, continued to draw our attention to service-oriented computing. This time we decided to focus on RESTful web services. Confident is a research project on the formal description of RESTful web services using type technology [5].

Following the original spirit of REST [7], and in stark contrast to the philosophy of SOAP [9], state of the art service description systems use mainly natural language. While these descriptions may occasionally suit programmers, they are not adequate for machine consumption. Machine checkable service descriptions lie at the basis of static verification of RESTful-based applications, help in enforcing service fidelity, and in the construction and evolution of complex distributed applications.

2   Context and Related Work

Representation State Transfer (REST) is an architectural style proposed as an abstract model of the web architecture. At its core lies the concept of *resource* [7]. According to Fielding and Taylor, a resource is a temporally varying membership function $M_R(t)$, mapping time t to a set of entities which are deemed equivalent [8]. The entities in the set $M_R(t)$ are *resource representations* and *resource identifiers*. REST uses a resource identifier to identify the particular resource involved in an interaction between components. Representations of resources are transferred between components in REST interactions; components perform actions on a resource by using a representation to capture the current or intended state of that resource.

In our running example—a simple contact management system—contacts are resources that admit (among others) a representation defined in terms of a nickname, a name, an email address, and a postal address. Figure 1 shows an example of two contacts. One of the contacts bears two different identifiers: me and owner (the owner of all contacts). Both contacts have JSON and XML representations that also differ in the amount of information included.

Systems that conform to the constraints of the REST architecture are called *RESTful*. A RESTful system can be seen as a set of resources together with the actions that can be performed on these. A RESTful API can be abstracted as a set of resource identifiers together with the actions that can be performed on each resource via that identifier.

REST systems typically communicate over HTTP and interface with external systems as web resources identified by URIs. The actions in this case include GET, POST, PUT, DELETE. In systems that communicate over HTTP, additional information can be sent in the *request* for the execution of the action.

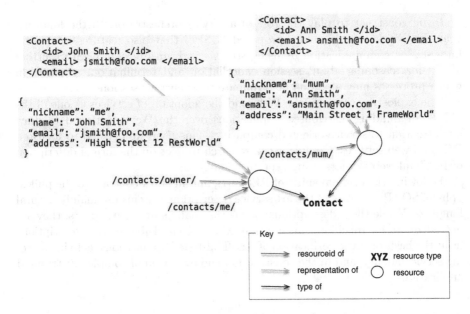

Fig. 1. Two resources in a contact management REST service.

This comes in the form of parameters embedded in the URL, headers, and body. Results always include a *response*. The table below shows four actions in the contact management system, together with their URIs and a textual description.

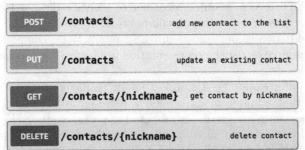

Different *interface description languages* (IDLs) have been purposely designed to support the formal description of REST APIs. The most representative ones are probably Open API Specification [12] (originally called Swagger), the RESTful API Modeling Language [13] (RAML), and API Blueprint [1]. These IDLs allow a detailed description of the syntactic aspects of the data transferred in REST interactions and are associated to a large number of tools, in particular for documentation generation, client code generation in different programming languages, and for test generation. Focused on the structure of the data exchanged, they ignore important semantic aspects, such as the ability to relate different parts of the same data, to relate the input against the state of the service, and to relate the output against the input. For instance, in the case of the contact management system, none of IDLs discussed here allow expressing facts such as that, in the creation of a new contact, the nickname must be shorter than the full name or that the name should be unique across all names known to the system. Similarly, these languages do not allow expressing that the type of representation transmitted in the response to a GET action depends on the value of a given query parameter.

3 HEADREST

Our approach to the description of RESTful APIs relies on two key ideas:

- *Types* to express properties of server states and of data exchanged in client-server interactions and
- *Pre- and post-conditions* to express the relationship between data sent in requests and that obtained in responses, as well as the resulting state changes in servers.

These ideas are embodied in HEADREST, a language built on the two fundamental concepts of DMinor [2]:

- *Refinement types*, x:T where e, consisting of values x of type T that satisfy property e and
- A *predicate*, e in T, which returns true or false depending on whether the value of expression e is or is not of type T.

HEADREST allows to describe properties of data and to observe state changes in server through a collection of *assertions*. Assertions take the form of Hoare triples [10] and are of the form

$$\{\phi\} \ (a \ t) \ \{\psi\}$$

where a is an action (GET, POST, PUT, or DELETE), t is an *URI template* (e.g., /contacts/{i}), and ϕ and ψ are boolean expressions. Formula ϕ, called the *precondition*, addresses the state in which the action is performed as well as the data transmitted in the request, whereas ψ, the *postcondition*, addresses the state resulting from the execution of the action together with the values transmitted in the response. The assertion reads

If a request for the execution of action a over an expansion of URI template t carries data satisfying formula ϕ and the action is performed in a state satisfying ϕ, then the data transmitted in the response satisfies formula ψ and so does the state resulting from the execution of the action.

A simple contact management system includes different (abstract) resources, which HEADREST captures as *new types*. Resources are introduced as follows.

```
resource Contact
```

Each resource may be associated to zero or more *representations*, each of which is given a particular type. The type system of HEADREST is structural, yet the language provides for *type abbreviations* in order to ease the writing of complex API descriptions. The syntax below introduces an identifier (`NameAndEmail`) for an object type, intended to represent resource `Contact`. `NameAndEmail` is an object composed of a `name` (a string of 3–15 lower and uppercase letter) and an `email` (a string containing the symbol ©).

```
type NameAndEmail = {
  name: (x: string where matches(x, ^[a-zA-Z]{3,15}$)),
  email: (x: string where contains(x, "@"))
}
```

Equipped with the declaration of a new resource (`Contact`) and a name for one of the representations of the resource (`NameAndEmail`), one can write a few assertions describing the behaviour of the API. One that describes a successful contact creation could be written as

```
{request in {body: NameAndEmail} &&
 ∀c: Contact. ∀r: NameAndEmail.
     r repof c ⇒ request.body.name ≠ r.name
}
POST /contacts
{response.code == 200 &&
 response in {body: NameAndEmail, header: {Location: URI}} &&
 request.body == response.body &&
 ∃c: Contact. response.body repof c &&
             response.header.Location uriof c
}
```

where `request` and `response` are builtin identifiers, and predicates `repof` and `uriof` describe values associated to resources as described in Sect. 2 (cf., Fig. 1).

The precondition first establishes that `request` contains a field named `body` of type `NameAndEmail`, and then asks the new contact `name` (provided in the `body` of the `request`) to be unique across all contacts and their representations, hence the double quantification (first on resources and then on their representations). In such a case, the postcondition signals success (`code 200`) and states that `response` includes a representation (in field `body`) that is exactly what was sent in the request. Furthermore, the response includes an URI (in field `header.Location`) of the newly created `Contact` resource `c`.

A different assertion for the same pair action-URI describes the *conflict* story: if the name of the new contact is known to the server, then this signals conflict (`code 409`).

```
{request in {body: NameAndEmail} &&
 ∃c: Contact. ∃r: NameAndEmail.
     r repof c ⇒ request.body.name == r.name
}
POST /contacts
{response.code == 409}
```

We have used HeadREST to describe different APIs, including a part of GitLab (800 lines of spec code). We have developed an Eclipse plugin to validate the good formation of HeadREST specifications [5], a tool to automatically test REST APIs against specifications [6], and a tool to generate server stubs and client SDKs from HeadREST specifications [14].

4 Conclusion

In this short abstract we informally present HeadREST, a language designed to support the entire application lifecycle based on REST APIs. We briefly discuss the language via a very simple example that illustrates the challenges of describing REST APIs and the expressiveness of our specification language.

Equipped with such an API description, we build tools that (a) validate the good formation of HeadREST specifications, (b) generate server stubs and client SDKs from HeadREST specifications, and (c) that automatically test REST APIs against specifications.

We intend to explore the specification of security issues in REST context, in particular, how to use the HeadREST language to ensure compliance with authentication and confidentiality requirements.

Acknowledgments. This work was supported by the Foundation for Science and Technology (FCT) through project CONFIDENT (PTDC/EEI-CTP/4503/2014) and the LASIGE research unit (UID/CEC/00408/2019).

References

1. API blueprint. https://apiblueprint.org/. Retrieved 7 Jan 2019
2. Bierman, G.M., Gordon, A.D., Hritcu, C., Langworthy, D.E.: Semantic subtyping with an SMT solver. J. Funct. Program. **22**(1), 31–105 (2012)
3. Boreale, M., et al.: SCC: a service centered calculus. In: Bravetti, M., Núñez, M., Zavattaro, G. (eds.) WS-FM 2006. LNCS, vol. 4184, pp. 38–57. Springer, Heidelberg (2006). https://doi.org/10.1007/11841197_3
4. Boreale, M., Bruni, R., De Nicola, R., Loreti, M.: CaSPiS: a calculus of sessions, pipelines and services. Math. Struct. Comput. Sci. **25**(3), 666–709 (2015)
5. Confident, a toolchain for the construction and evolution of REST APIs. http://rss.di.fc.ul.pt/tools/confident. Retrieved 7 Jan 2019
6. Ferreira, F.: Automatic test generation for RESTful APIs. Master's thesis, Faculty of Sciences, University of Lisbon (2017)
7. Fielding, R.T.: Architectural styles and the design of network-based software architectures. Ph.D. thesis, University of California, Irvine (2000)
8. Fielding, R.T., Taylor, R.N.: Principled design of the modern web architecture. ACM Trans. Internet Technol. **2**(2), 115–150 (2002)
9. HTTP Working Group: SOAP: Simple object access protocol. https://tools.ietf.org/html/draft-box-http-soap-00. Retrieved 31 Jan 2019
10. Hoare, C.A.R.: An axiomatic basis for computer programming. Commun. ACM **12**(10), 576–580 (1969)

11. Lanese, I., Martins, F., Vasconcelos, V.T., Ravara, A.: Disciplining orchestration and conversation in service-oriented computing. In: Proceeedings of the Fifth IEEE International Conference on Software Engineering and Formal Methods (SEFM 2007), pp. 305–314 (2007)
12. Open API Initiative. https://www.openapis.org. Retrieved 7 Jan 2019
13. RESTful API Modeling Language. https://raml.org. Retrieved 7 Jan 2019
14. Santos, T.: Code generation for RESTful APIs in headREST. Master's thesis, Faculty of Sciences, University of Lisbon (2018)
15. Sensoria: Software Engineering for Service-Oriented Overlay Computers. http://sensoria.fast.de/. Retrieved 31 Jan 2019

Security

Revealing the Trajectories of KLAIM Tuples, Statically

Chiara Bodei[1], Pierpaolo Degano[1], Gian-Luigi Ferrari[1],
and Letterio Galletta[2]

[1] Dipartimento di Informatica, Università di Pisa, Pisa, Italy
[2] IMT Institute for Advanced Studies Lucca, Lucca, Italy
letterio.galletta@imtlucca.it

Abstract. KLAIM (Kernel Language for Agents Interaction and Mobility) has been devised to design distributed applications composed by many components deployed over the nodes of a distributed infrastructure and to offer programmers primitive constructs for communicating, distributing and retrieving data. Data could be sensitive and some nodes could not be secure. As a consequence it is important to track data in their traversal of the network. To this aim, we propose a Control Flow Analysis that over-approximates the behaviour of KLAIM processes and tracks how tuple data can move in the network.

1 Introduction

Premise. About twenty years ago Rocco De Nicola contributed to the introduction of KLAIM, a Kernel Language for Agents Interaction and Mobility – as the name suggests – designed for specifying the behaviour of distributed and coordinated processes at a suitable level of abstraction. As it is often the case, this line of work changed with the times, by always evolving to deal with the challenges posed by the new programming paradigms. Starting by our common interest in languages and process algebras, we decided to honour Rocco on his 65th birthday and our long friendship, by working on KLAIM and exploiting our previous experience with static analysis techniques.

Contribution. Modern distributed systems are extremely difficult to model, specify and verify because they are inherently concurrent, asynchronous, and non deterministic. Furthermore, computing nodes in a distributed system are loosely coupled and exhibit a high level of autonomy. These features provide several benefits. For instance, scaling is simplified since each computing node can be scaled independently from the other nodes. Moreover, decoupling enables the design of new mechanisms for orchestrating the overall behaviour. Designing secure and

The first three authors have been partially supported by Università di Pisa PRA_2018_66 *DECLWARE: Metodologie dichiarative per la progettazione e il deployment di applicazioni*; the last author by IMT project *PAI VeriOSS*.

© Springer Nature Switzerland AG 2019
M. Boreale et al. (Eds.): De Nicola-Festschrift, LNCS 11665, pp. 437–454, 2019.
https://doi.org/10.1007/978-3-030-21485-2_24

safe distributed systems is of paramount importance given the vast attack surface presented by them. We cannot address these issues without a solid formal model of system security offering advantages of two different kinds. On the one hand such a model permits to evaluate *a priori* how to prevent security breaches and, on the other hand, it provides the machinery for identifying the techniques one might adopt to achieve the goal of securing distributed systems.

In previous works [3–5], we proposed a *Security by Design* development methodology, consisting of a kernel programming language to describe both the structure of the system and its interactive capabilities. The kernel language is equipped with a suitable *static analysis* that approximates the evolution of the system by providing an *abstract model* of behaviour. These abstractions allow predicting how (abstract) data may flow inside the system. Hence, designers can detect *a priori* the occurrence of unsafe data and possible security breaches, inspecting the "abstract simulation" and intervene as early as possible during the design phase. This methodology has been extended in [6] by introducing a *data path analysis* that supports tracking of the propagation of data, thus identifying their possible trajectories among the computing nodes.

In this paper we apply our methodology to support the design of distributed systems modelled using KLAIM, *Kernel Language for Agents Interaction and Mobility* [11]. This language has been specifically devised to design distributed applications made up of several loosely coupled components deployed over the nodes of a distributed infrastructure. The KLAIM programming model relies on tuples and tuple spaces to coordinate component communications and data management. The language builds on Linda's notion of *generative communication* through a single shared tuple space [17] and generalises it with multiple tuple spaces.

A distinguishing feature of the KLAIM model is the so-called *network awareness*. It indicates the ability of the software components of a distributed application to directly manage a sufficient amount of knowledge about the network environment where they are currently deployed. This capability allows components to have a highly dynamic behaviour and manage unpredictable changes of the network environment over time. Crucial to network awareness are *localities* associated with the network nodes, which are a first order feature of KLAIM.

In this paper we introduce a *control flow analysis* that extends the one proposed in [5,6], and that handles network awareness and coordination via multiple tuple spaces. Our static analysis can be used to detect where and how data are manipulated and how messages flow among the nodes of a KLAIM network. More in detail, the results of the analysis enable us to reason about

- the path in the KLAIM network through which (a value in) a tuple of a specific node reaches another one; and about
- which transformations are applied to a selected datum along those paths.

The proposed analysis permits to identify possible security breaches in the data workflow of a distributed application. For instance, it may keep the safe paths that data inside a tuple can traverse apart from those that pass through a possible untrusted node.

Plan of the Paper. The next section briefly recalls the main aspects of KLAIM. Section 3 illustrates a simple example that is used along the paper. Section 4 defines the static analysis and shows how to inspect its results for checking specific properties. The last section concludes.

2   KLAIM: A Kernel Language for Agents Interaction and Mobility

KLAIM [11] has been specifically devised to design distributed applications consisting of several components (both stationary and mobile) deployed over the nodes of a distributed infrastructure. Its programming model relies on a unique interface (i.e. set of operations) supporting component communications and data management.

The basic building blocks of KLAIM for guaranteeing network awareness are the *locations*. They are the linguistic abstraction to manage addresses (i.e. network references) of nodes and are referred to through identifiers. Locations can be exchanged among the computational components and obey to sophisticated scoping rules. They provide the naming mechanism to identify network resources and to represent the notion of administrative domain: computations at a given location are under the control of a specific authority. In this way, locations provide a natural abstraction to structure and support programming of spatially distributed applications.

KLAIM has multiple distributed tuple spaces. A tuple space is a multiset of tuples. Tuples are *anonymous* sequences of data items and are retrieved from tuple spaces by means of an *associative selection*. Interprocess communication occurs through *asynchronous* exchange of tuples via tuple spaces: there is no need for producers (i.e. senders) and consumers (i.e. receivers) of a tuple to synchronise.

The obtained communication model has a number of properties that make it appealing for distributed computing in general (see, e.g., [7,9,15,18]). It supports *time uncoupling* (data life time is independent of the producer process life time), *destination uncoupling* (the producer of a datum needs not to know the future use or the final destination of that datum) and *space uncoupling* (programmers need to know a single interface only to operate over the tuple spaces, regardless of the node where the action will take place).

2.1   Syntax and Semantics

In this section, we introduce a dialect of KLAIM in the style of a process calculus whose syntax is presented in Table 1. The set of *locations Loc* consists of three disjoint entities:

- the absolute locations $\ell \in \mathscr{L}$;
- the symbolic locations $p \in LSym$;
- the location variables $u \in LVars$.

Table 1. KLAIM syntax

NETS:		TUPLES:
$N ::= \ell ::_\rho P$	(computational node)	$t ::= \langle tf_1, \ldots, tf_r \rangle \quad r \geq 1$
$\mid \ell :: \langle t \rangle$	(located tuple, t closed)	TUPLE FIELDS:
$\mid N_1 \parallel N_2$	(net composition)	$tf ::= E \mid l$
PROCESSES:		LOCATIONS: $l \in Loc$
$P ::= \mathbf{nil}$	(null process)	$l ::= \ell \in \mathscr{L}$
$\mid \mathbf{out}(t)@l.P$	(output)	$p \in LSym$
$\mid \mathbf{in}(t)@l.P$	(input)	$u \in LVars$
$\mid \mathbf{read}(t)@l.P$	(read)	EXPRESSIONS $E \in \mathscr{E}$:
$\mid P_1 \mid P_2$	(parallel composition)	$E ::= v \in Values$
$\mid X$	(process variable)	$x \in Vars$
$\mid A$	(process invocation)	$f(E_1, \ldots, E_r)$

Absolute locations are used to denote network addresses, through names already assigned to absolute addresses of network components. Symbolic locations, instead, provide the mechanism to support symbolic addressing. They are keywords that refer to specific entities of which the currently running code is a part. The entity referred to by these keywords thus depends on the execution context. For instance, the symbolic location *self* will always refers to the current absolute address of the current execution environment. Since locations are denotable entities we also need location variables.

NETS are finite collections of nodes where processes and data can be placed. A *computational node* takes the form $\ell ::_\rho P$, where ρ is an *allocation environment* and P is a process. Since processes may refer to location variables or symbolic locations, the allocation environment acts as a *name solver* that binds locations variables and symbolic locations to absolute locations. TUPLES are sequences of fields, i.e. of expressions and of locations. The precise syntax of EXPRESSIONS is deliberately not specified; it is just assumed that they contain, at least, *basic values V*, and *value variables*, ranged over by x. The tuple space of a node consists of all the tuples that do not contain variables and that are located there (we will sometimes refer to them as evaluated tuples). We will use $[\![t]\!]$ to denote the result of evaluating the expression t, possibly applying also the allocation environment ρ.

PROCESSES are the active computational units of KLAIM. Their syntax is standard. Recursive behaviours are modelled via process definitions. For that we assume a set of *process identifiers*, ranged over by A. A process definition has the standard form $A \triangleq P$, but we additionally assume each identifier A has a *single* defining equation. The actions processes perform provide the programming abstractions that support data management. Three primitive behaviours are provided: adding (**out**), withdrawing (**in**) and reading (**read**) a tuple to/from a tuple space. Input and output actions are *mutators*: their execution modifies the

Table 2. Structural congruence

(Com)	$N_1 \parallel N_2 \equiv N_2 \parallel N_1$	(Assoc)	$(N_1 \parallel N_2) \parallel N_3 \equiv N_1 \parallel (N_2 \parallel N_3)$
(Abs)	$\ell :: P \equiv \ell :: (P\mid\textbf{nil})$	(PrInv)	$\ell :: A \equiv \ell :: P \quad if\ A \triangleq P$
(Clone)	$\ell :: (P_1\mid P_2) \equiv \ell :: P_1 \parallel \ell :: P_2$		

tuple space. The read action is an *observer*: it checks the availability and takes note of the content of a certain tuple without removing it from the tuple space. Actions are tagged with the (possibly remote) location where they will take place. Note that, in principle, each network node can provide its own implementation of the action interface. This feature can be suitably exploited to sustain different policies for data handling as done, e.g. in METAKLAIM [16].

Names occurring in processes and nets can be *bound*. For example, the action prefix $\textbf{in}(u)@l.P$ binds u in P, which is the scope of the bindings made by the action. A name that is not bound is *free*. The sets of free and bound names of a process/net term are defined in the standard way. As usual, we say that two terms are α-*equivalent*, written $\equiv_\alpha$, if one can be obtained from the other by renaming bound names. Hereafter, we shall work with terms whose bound names are all distinct and different from the free ones.

A *pattern-matching* mechanism is used for associatively selecting (evaluated) tuples from tuple spaces. Intuitively, a tuple matches against an evaluated one if both have the same number of fields and corresponding fields do match; two values (locations) match only if they are identical, while variables match any value of the same type. A successful matching returns a substitution associating the variables contained in the fields of the tuples with the values contained in the corresponding fields of the evaluated tuple. We will use σ to range over *substitutions*. As usual, substitution application may require α-conversion to avoid capturing of free names.

We will use the notation $match([\![\,t\,]\!], et) = \sigma$ to indicate that σ is the substitution resulting from the pattern matching of tuple t with the evaluated tuple et.

The operational semantics is given in terms of a structural congruence $\equiv$ and of a reduction relation $\rightarrowtail$ over nets. The *structural congruence* is defined as the smallest congruence relation over nets that satisfies the laws in Table 2. These relate nets that intuitively behave the same, stating that $\parallel$ is commutative and associative, that the null process can always be safely removed/added, that a process identifier can be replaced with the body of its definition, and that it is always possible to transform a parallel of co-located processes into a parallel over nodes. Indeed, rule (STRUCT) says that all structural congruent nets can make the same reduction steps.

The *reduction relation* is the least relation induced by the rules in Table 3. All the rules for (possibly remote) process actions require the target node to exist. In addition, the rule (IN) requires the chosen datum to occur in the target node. Moreover, the rule says that action $\textbf{in}(u)@l'$ looks for any name ℓ'' at ℓ'

Table 3. Operational semantics of KLAIM

(OUT)	$$\dfrac{\rho(l) = l' \qquad [\![t]\!] = et}{l :: \mathbf{out}(t)@l'.P \parallel l' :: P' \succ\!\!\longrightarrow l :: P \parallel l' :: P' \parallel l' :: \langle et \rangle}$$
(IN)	$$\dfrac{\rho(l) = l' \qquad match([\![t]\!], et) = \sigma}{l :: \mathbf{in}(t)@l'.P \parallel l' :: \langle et \rangle \succ\!\!\longrightarrow l :: P\sigma \parallel l' :: \mathbf{nil}}$$
(READ)	$$\dfrac{\rho(l) = l' \qquad match([\![t]\!], et) = \sigma}{l :: \mathbf{read}(t)@l'.P \parallel l' :: \langle et \rangle \succ\!\!\longrightarrow l :: P\sigma \parallel l' :: \langle et \rangle}$$
(PAR)	$$\dfrac{N_1 \succ\!\!\longrightarrow N_1'}{N_1 \parallel N_2 \succ\!\!\longrightarrow N \vdash_1' \parallel N_2}$$
(STRUCT)	$$\dfrac{N \equiv N_1 \qquad N_1 \succ\!\!\longrightarrow N_2 \qquad N_2 \equiv N'}{N \succ\!\!\longrightarrow N'}$$

that is then used to replace the free occurrences of u in the continuation of the process performing the input, while action $\mathbf{in}(\ell'')@\ell'$ looks exactly for the name ℓ'' at ℓ'; in both cases, the matched datum is consumed. With abuse of notation, we use **nil** to replace the consumed data.

Rule (PAR) says that if part of a net makes a reduction step, the whole net reduces accordingly. Process interaction is asynchronous: no synchronisation takes place between sender and receiver processes (only existence of target nodes is checked). Moreover, communication is anonymous, because data do not include the name of the sender, and associative, because data are accessed via pattern matching.

3   Example: A Microservice Architecture

Microservices have been recently introduced as a software architecture pattern used to build distributed applications composed of small, independent and highly decoupled services. A microservice is equipped with a dedicated data storage support (e.g. a data base) and provides basic (simple) services by computing certain functionalities (e.g. querying a database). A microservice-based application usually takes the form of a structured protocol composed by multiple phases. Each phase is implemented by a specific microservice. Microservices interact by exchanging messages. Since all the components of the software architecture are microservices, the overall behaviour is derived by the coordination of its components via message exchange. As an example, the Netflix service uses around 700 microservices to control each of its many parts.

Microservice software architectures present many security challenges, not new, since they apply to the Service-Oriented paradigm. However, they become

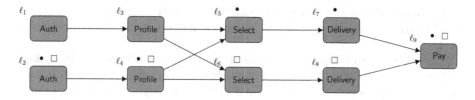

Fig. 1. A network of microservices. The same datum following the trajectory with bullets • is at risk, while it is safe along the trajectory with boxes □.

even more challenging in this context since service requests are routed among the multiple independent services. For instance, it may happen that a single microservice controlled by a malicious entity may corrupt the coordination of the service requests and therefore the overall behaviour of the application is compromised.

We outline the main features of the design of a (simplified) *Microservice Application* for delivering digital artefacts or contents (e.g. movies) to registered users. The underlying structured protocol basically consists of several stages. The first provides an authentication/authorisation facility. Registered users may select one or more products to buy. In the second phase, the selected item is sent to the users. Finally, the user pays, which requires the execution of an entire sub-protocol, involving also a digital bank. In a monolithic architecture this will be implemented as a stateful application. This is not the case with microservices since one has to route the requests to multiple independent services. Figure 1 illustrates the structure of the application together with the underlying workflow of messages. We comment on the architecture:

- The AUTH microservice provides facilities for authenticating registered user; it also grants her/him some specific interactions;
- The PROFILE microservice determines user's profile taking into account all what was stored by the application about the registered users;
- The SELECT microservice supports the user in making the choice, possibly suggesting the user the items she/he will like;
- The DELIVER microservice sends the required digital artefact to the user;
- The PAY microservice deduces the monthly fee from the user's account.

We assume that each stage of the application is split over and implemented by groups of microservices. For instance, the AUTH service is distributed over a pair of microservices independent from each other. This also implies that the application has multiple entry points to control users' access. Similarly multiple PROFILE microservices will be dedicated to manage user requests by providing the suitable context of user preferences. Note that each PROFILE micro service may be built over different database schemata storing different data. This sort of decentralised governance is applied to all the stages of the application. Figure 1 also illustrates a possible workflow of service requests with indicators of risk level.

The software architecture briefly discussed above is rendered here by making each microservice a KLAIM node. For simplicity, we will focus on the coordination among the microservices via tuple-based messaging. With an abuse of notation we will freely exploit certain suitable processes without showing their detailed implementation. The main processes of the AUTH microservice level are given below:

$$H \triangleq \mathbf{in}(usr, psw, req)@\mathsf{self}.\mathbf{out}(usr, psw)@\mathsf{self}.\mathbf{in}(usr, token)@\mathsf{self}.$$
$$\{\mathbf{for}\ l \in Policy(usr, token)$$
$$\mathbf{out}(usr, req, token)@l\}.H$$
$$C \triangleq \mathbf{in}(usr, psw)@\mathsf{self}.I.\mathbf{out}(usr, Check(usr, psw))@\mathsf{self}C$$

The handler process H receives the authentication request, obtained by sensing in the tuple space the tuple (usr, psw, req), activates one of the processes checking user credentials by emitting in the tuple space the tuple (usr, psw) and finally generates the authentication token by inspecting the tuple space. The authorisation token is made available by the checking user credential process. We abstract from the detailed description of checking user credential process C. We simply assume that the process is activated by the presence of the tuple (usr, psw) in the tuple space and yields as result the tuple $(usr, token)$, where the value $token$ is the authorisation information associated to the specific user usr. The authorisation token is computed, after having executed some internal activities I, by applying the function $Check$, which takes as input the values usr, psw, making clear that the authorisation token strictly depends on the user information. The result of the authentication is then forwarded to the PROFILE microservices hosted in the locations l, depending on a certain $Policy$ function that implements the workflow of messages in accordance with the multistage pattern of the application.

To conclude the description of the authorisation stage, we present the KLAIM nodes that realise the AUTH microservices.

$$AUTH \triangleq (l_1 ::_{\rho_1} H \mid C \mid T_1) \parallel (l_2 ::_{\rho_2} H \mid C \mid T_2)$$

The authorisation microservices consist of two KLAIM nodes located at l_1 and l_2 respectively. Intuitively, registered users can open more than one session of the application at the same time and, therefore, using more than one microservice of the application at the same time. Each node hosts the handler processes H and the process C checking user credentials as discussed above together with the local tuple spaces, represented by the suitable process T_1 and T_2. Each microservice stores and manages its own data within the local tuple space. It is worth noting the exploitation of tuple spaces to coordinate the behaviour of the processes deployed in the nodes.

We now move our attention to the PROFILE stage that computes the personal data associated to the specific registered user. Note that the user's profile depends on the location where the microservice is located, because, in a microservice-based architecture, each microservice owns and controls its own database that is not shared with others to avoid conflicts. The main processes of the PROFILE stage are given below

$$D \triangleq \mathbf{in}(usr, req, token)@\mathsf{self}.\mathbf{out}(usr, \mathsf{self}, token)@\mathsf{self}.$$
$$\qquad \mathbf{in}(usr, profile)@\mathsf{self}.\mathbf{out}(usr, token, req, profile)@next.D$$
$$P \triangleq \mathbf{in}(usr, u, token).@\mathsf{self}.I.\mathbf{out}(usr, UserProfile(usr, u))@\mathsf{self}.P$$

The driver process D receives the user request, obtained by sensing in the tuple space the tuple $(usr, req, token)$. Note that each user request is tagged with the authorisation token to identify the specific user's session. The driver activates the process that has the task of calculating the user's profile by emitting in the tuple space the tuple $(usr, profile)$. Finally, the next step in the workflow begins with the generation of the tuple $(usr, token, req, profile)$ and its transmission to the remote node identified by the symbolic location $next$ (that will be instantiated by the allocation environment of the nodes where processes will be deployed). The behaviour of the process P is straightforward. We only emphasise the role of the function $UsrProfile$. This function abstracts the activity of computing user's profile taking into account the information available locally. This feature also implies a certain amount of autonomy of the microservice. The awareness of the locality where information is taken transforms the tuple space into a bounded context: each local tuple space may have its own understanding of what a "user" is (e.g. maybe in a certain tuple space the "user" is characterised by several tuples while in a different tuple space a single tuple is enough).

The KLAIM nodes that implement the PROFILE stage are the following

$$PROFILE \triangleq (l_3 ::_{\rho_3} D \mid P \mid T_3) \parallel (l_4 ::_{\rho_4} D \mid P \mid T_4)$$

Each node hosts the drive processes D and the process P computing user's profile as discussed above, together with the local tuple spaces, represented by the suitable processes T_3 and T_4.

This third stage of the application is characterised by the SELECT microservice. Two processes drive the behaviour of the microservice. Both processes are activated by sensing in the tuple space the tuple $(usr, token, req, profile)$. The first process S_1 prompts a list of suggestions based on the user's profile taking advantage of the information made available by the auxiliary process C_S, with the obvious meaning. We only comment on the function $CheckProfile$ that abstracts the activities for computing the list of suggestions, according to the user's request and profile. The second process S_2 simply shows to the user her/his requests of the session at hand.

$$S_1 \triangleq \mathbf{in}(usr, token, req, profile)@\mathsf{self}.\mathbf{out}(usr, req, profile)@\mathsf{self}.$$
$$\qquad \mathbf{in}(usr, suggestion)@\mathsf{self}.\mathbf{out}(usr, token, req, suggestion)@\mathsf{self}.S_1$$
$$C_S \triangleq \mathbf{in}(usr, req, profile)@\mathsf{self}.\mathbf{out}(usr, CheckProfile(req, profile))$$
$$S_2 \triangleq \mathbf{in}(usr, token, req, profile)@\mathsf{self}.\mathbf{out}(usr, token, req)@\mathsf{self}.S_2$$

The KLAIM nodes that implement the SELECT stage are the followings

$$SELECT \triangleq (l_5 ::_{\rho_5} S_1 \mid S_2 \mid C_S \mid F \mid T_5) \parallel (l_6 ::_{\rho_6} S_1 \mid S_2 \mid C_S \mid F \mid T_6)$$

Each node hosts the drive processes S_1, S_2, the auxiliary process C_S discussed above, and the process F, the detailed description of which omitted here. This process takes the user's confirmation, sends the user digital rights for the purchase (via the DELIVERY microservice) and activates the payment microservice.

4   Control Flow Analysis

Below, we first introduce regular tree grammars that will be used to abstractly represent KLAIM data; then we present our control flow analysis; and finally we show that the results of the analysis can be used to check how data are manipulated and how they traverse the network of processes.

4.1   Abstract Representation of Data

In the following we represent the data populating and traversing a net of KLAIM processes in an abstract form. Since a system is designed to be continuously active and may contain feedback loops, data can grow unboundedly, while we insist on having finite representation. We resort then to set of regular trees and we associate with data regular tree grammars [8] as *finite* abstractions. The leaves of a tree in the language of a regular grammar represent basic values v and locations ℓ. Instead, its nodes represent functions applied to data, tuple constructions and transfer from the tuple space of a specific computational node to another one. A brief survey on regular tree grammars follows.

A *regular tree grammar* is a quadruple $\widehat{G} = (\mathbb{N}, \mathbb{T}, Z, R)$ where

- $\mathbb{N}$ is a set of non-terminals (with rank 0),
- $\mathbb{T}$ is a ranked alphabet, whose symbols have an associated arity,
- $Z \in \mathbb{N}$ is the starting non-terminal,
- R is a set of productions of the form $A \to t$, where t is a tree composed from symbols in $\mathbb{N} \cup \mathbb{T}$ according to their arities.

In the following we denote the language generated by a given grammar $\widehat{G}$ with $Lang(\widehat{G})$.

Given a net of processes, the grammars we use will have the alphabet $\mathbb{T}$ consisting of the following set of ranked symbols

- ℓ (with arity 0) for each $\ell \in \mathscr{L}$
- v^ℓ (with arity 0) for each value $v \in Value$ and $\ell \in \mathscr{L}$
- t^ℓ (with arity r) to represent a tuple with arity r in $\ell \in \mathscr{L}$
- f^ℓ (with arity r) for each function f in $\ell \in \mathscr{L}$ with arity r
- s^ℓ (with arity 1) to represent an output from $\ell \in \mathscr{L}$

The non-terminals $\mathbb{N}$ of our grammars include a symbol for each terminal, and carry the label of the relevant computational node. Just for readability we shall capitalize the ranked symbols above and use them as non-terminals, i.e. L^ℓ, V^ℓ, T^ℓ, F^ℓ, and S^ℓ. When irrelevant, we shall omit the labels ℓ, and we shall use a capital letter for a generic non-terminal. For example, a r-tuple is abstractly

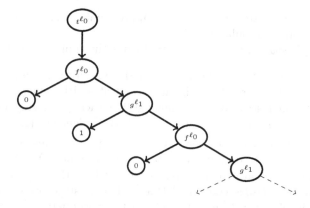

Fig. 2. An infinite abstract tree

represented by a grammar with the production $T^\ell \to t^\ell(A_1, ..., A_r)$ and the productions for A_i, that generates the tree rooted in t^ℓ and children generated by $A_1, ..., A_r$.

It is convenient introducing some notation. For brevity and when not ambiguous, we will simply write $\hat{v} = (Z, R)$ for the grammar $\widehat{G} = (\mathbb{N}, \mathbb{T}, Z, R)$ with starting non-terminal Z and regular productions in R, without explicitly listing the terminals and the non-terminals. Then, we denote with $\mathbb{R}$ the set of all possible productions over $\mathbb{N}$ and $\mathbb{T}$.

As an example of a possible infinite abstract tree, consider two computational nodes P_{ℓ_0} and P_{ℓ_1} and two binary functions f and h. Suppose that P_{ℓ_0} applies f to 0 and to a value taken in the tuple space of P_{ℓ_1}. Similarly, P_{ℓ_1} applies h to 1 and the value taken in the tuple space of P_{ℓ_0}. The resulting value in the tuple space of P_{ℓ_0} is abstracted as the set of binary trees of unbounded depth. The following grammar represents them all (an element of its language is in Fig. 2):

$$(T^{\ell_0}, \{T^{\ell_0} \to t^{\ell_0}(F^{\ell_0}), F^{\ell_0} \to f^{\ell_0}(I_0^{\ell_0}, G^{\ell_1}), I_0^{\ell_0} \to 0, G^{\ell_1} \to g^{\ell_1}(I_1^{\ell_1}, F^{\ell_0}), I_1^{\ell_1} \to 1\})$$

Now we are ready to introduce the *abstract terms* that belong to the set

$$\widehat{\mathcal{V}} = 2^{\mathbb{N} \times \mathbb{R}}$$

4.2   Specification of the Analysis

The result or *estimate* of our CFA is a pair $(\Sigma_\ell, \Theta_\ell)$ for tuple fields tf, a triple $(\Sigma_\ell, \Theta_\ell, \kappa)$ for processes P, and a triple (Σ, Θ, κ) for nets of processes. The components of an estimate are the following *abstract domains* (we omit labels ℓ for brevity):

– *abstract enviroment* $\Sigma : (LVar \cup Vars) \to \widehat{\mathcal{V}}$ is an abstract environment that associates symbolic locations and variables with a set of abstract values;

– *abstract data collection* $\Theta : \mathscr{L} \to \widehat{\mathscr{V}}$ approximates the values that a node hosted at ℓ can manipulate;
– *abstract tuple space* $\kappa : \mathscr{L} \to \widehat{\mathscr{V}}$ approximates the tuple space of a node.

The syntax directed rules of Tables 4 and 5 specify when an analysis estimate is valid and they are almost in the format of AFPL, which is a logic used to specify static analyses and which allows systematically deriving analysis algorithms [20]. For each tuple t (and its fields tf), the judgement $(\Sigma_\ell, \Theta_\ell) \models_\ell^\rho t : \vartheta$ (and $(\Sigma_\ell, \Theta_\ell) \models_\ell^\rho tf : \vartheta$) expresses that $\vartheta \in 2^{\widehat{\mathscr{V}}}$ approximates the set of tuples that t (tf) may evaluate to, given the abstract environment Σ_ℓ. An actual location and a value evaluate to the set ϑ, provided that their abstract representations belong to ϑ (rules (Loc) and (Val)). This abstract representation is a grammar made of a non-terminal symbol whose production generates a tree with a single node. For example, the abstract value for an actual location ℓ' is $(L^\ell, \{L^\ell \to \ell'\})$ that represents a grammar with the initial symbol is L^ℓ that only generates the tree ℓ'. The rule (L-sym) takes care of symbolic locations and resolves them through ρ. The rules (L-var) and (E-var) for variables require the binding for them to be included in ϑ. The rule (E-fun) analyses the application of an r-ary function f to produce the set ϑ. To do that (i) for each term E_i, it finds the sets ϑ_i, and (ii) for all sequences of r values (Z_i, R_i) in ϑ_i, it checks if ϑ includes the grammars with distinct symbol F^ℓ generating the trees rooted in f^ℓ with subtrees generated by Z_i. The rule (Tuple) is similar. Note that in all the rules above, we require that the abstract data collection $\Theta(\ell)$ includes all the abstract values in ϑ.

Table 4. Analysis of tuples $(\Sigma_\ell, \Theta_\ell) \models_\ell^\rho t : \vartheta$ and of tuple fields $(\Sigma_\ell, \Theta_\ell) \models_\ell^\rho tf : \vartheta$.

(Loc)
$$\frac{(L^\ell, \{L^\ell \to \ell'\}) \in \vartheta \subseteq \Theta_\ell}{(\Sigma_\ell, \Theta_\ell) \models_\ell^\rho \ell' : \vartheta}$$

(L-sym)
$$\frac{(L^\ell, \{L^\ell \to \rho(p)\}) \in \vartheta \subseteq \Theta_\ell}{(\Sigma_\ell, \Theta_\ell) \models_\ell^\rho p : \vartheta}$$

(L-var)
$$\frac{\Sigma_\ell(u) \subseteq \vartheta \subseteq \Theta_\ell}{(\Sigma_\ell, \Theta_\ell) \models_\ell^\rho u : \vartheta}$$

(Val)
$$\frac{(V^\ell, \{V^\ell \to v^\ell\}) \in \vartheta \subseteq \Theta_\ell}{(\Sigma_\ell, \Theta_\ell) \models_\ell^\rho v : \vartheta}$$

(E-var)
$$\frac{\Sigma_\ell(x) \subseteq \vartheta \subseteq \Theta_\ell}{(\Sigma_\ell, \Theta_\ell) \models_\ell^\rho x : \vartheta}$$

(Fun)
$$\frac{\bigwedge_{i=1}^{r} (\Sigma_\ell, \Theta_\ell) \models_\ell^\rho E_i : \vartheta_i \wedge}{\forall (Z_1, R_1), \cdots, (Z_r, R_r) : \bigwedge_{i=1}^{r} (Z_i, R_i) \in \vartheta_i \Rightarrow (F^\ell, \{F^\ell \to f^\ell(Z_1, \cdots, Z_r)\} \cup \bigcup_{i=1}^{r} R_i) \in \vartheta \subseteq \Theta_\ell}{(\Sigma_\ell, \Theta_\ell) \models_\ell^\rho f(E_1, \cdots, E_r) : \vartheta}$$

(Tuple)
$$\frac{\bigwedge_{i=1}^{r} (\Sigma_\ell, \Theta_\ell) \models_\ell^\rho tf_i : \vartheta_i \wedge}{\forall (Z_1, R_1), \cdots, (Z_r, R_r) : \bigwedge_{i=1}^{r} (Z_i, R_i) \in \vartheta_i \Rightarrow (T^\ell, \{T^\ell \to t^\ell(Z_1, \cdots, Z_r)\} \cup \bigcup_{i=1}^{r} R_i) \in \vartheta \subseteq \Theta_\ell}{(\Sigma_\ell, \Theta_\ell) \models_\ell^\rho \langle tf_1, \cdots, tf_r \rangle : \vartheta}$$

Some further auxiliary definitions may help keeping the logical specification of the analysis of nets and processes less intricate. In particular, they simplify handling the grammars and extracting the needed information from them. The function *put* constructs a grammar that records that a tuple, approximated by (Z, R), may be inserted in the tuple space of the computational node at ℓ. The function @ takes a set of grammars ϑ and returns the set of actual locations in those grammars with starting symbol L. The function *get* recursively visits a grammar to find a tuple that has been acquired by a process at ℓ; its base cases exhibit, if any, the tuple built by a process at ℓ' approximated by the grammar with starting symbol $T^{\ell'}$.

Definition 1 (Auxiliary definitions for the analysis).
Let P be a process, ℓ be an absolute location, and (Z, R) be an abstract value in the following three auxiliary functions.

- $put(\ell, (Z, R)) = (S^\ell, \{S^\ell \to s^\ell(Z)\} \cup R)$
- $\widehat{@}\vartheta = \{\ell \mid (L^\ell, \{L^\ell \to \ell\}) \in \vartheta\}$

$$
-\begin{cases}
get((S^\ell, \{S^\ell \to s^\ell(T^{\ell'}), T^{\ell'} \to t^{\ell'}(Z_1, \ldots, Z_r)\} \cup R)) = \\
\qquad \langle (S^\ell, \{S^\ell \to s^\ell(Z_1)\} \cup R_1), \ldots, (S^\ell, \{S^\ell \to s^\ell(Z_r)\} \cup R_r)\rangle \\
\qquad\qquad\qquad\qquad \textit{where } R_i \textit{ are the productions concerning } Z_i \\
get((S^\ell, \{S^\ell \to s^\ell(S_0^{\ell'})\} \cup R)) = get((S_0^{\ell'}, R)) \\
get((A, R)) = \langle\rangle \qquad \textit{if } A \neq S^\ell
\end{cases}
$$

The specification of the analysis of nets $(\Sigma, \Theta, \kappa) \models N$, and of processes $(\Sigma_\ell, \Theta_\ell, \kappa) \models_\ell^\rho P$ is in Table 5. The rules (N-node) and (N-tuple) lift a process and a tuple in a specific location where they have been analysed; note that the approximation of the tuple is included in the abstract tuple space of the node ℓ. The rule (N-par) says that the estimate of the parallel composition is also valid for the components.

The remaining rules are for processes. The rules for the inactive node (N-nil) and for parallel composition (N-par) are standard, as well as those for process definition and invocation, where to save notation, we assumed that each variable X is uniquely bound to the body P. The rule (P-out) (i) approximates the tuple t with ϑ and the symbolic location l with ϑ'; and (ii) for all grammar $\hat{v}$ in ϑ and for all locations ℓ' extracted from ϑ', it checks if the tuple space approximation $\kappa(\ell')$ contains a grammar that records that the (approximation $\hat{v}$ of the) tuple t has been inserted by the node ℓ; and finally that P has a valid approximation.

The rule (P-in) for input and read is the most complex, with a premise made of two conjuncts that imply three. The first conjunct of the condition finds the approximation ϑ of the symbolic location l. The second one extracts the actual locations ℓ' possibly bound to l and looks for the grammars approximating the tuples in the space of those locations. If there are any (non-empty) such tuples $\hat{v}_1, \cdots, \hat{v}_r$ and if a component tf_i of the input/read tuple is an actual location ℓ'', then ℓ'' must also occur in the same position in the approximation, i.e. in $\hat{v}_i$. This statically implements pattern matching on tuple, but on locations only. The first

Table 5. Analysis of nets $(\Sigma, \Theta, \kappa) \models N$, and of processes $(\Sigma_\ell, \Theta_\ell, \kappa) \models_\ell^\rho P$.

(N-NODE)
$$\frac{(\Sigma_\ell, \Theta_\ell, \kappa) \models_\ell^\rho P}{(\Sigma, \Theta, \kappa) \models \ell ::_\rho P}$$

(N-TUPLE)
$$\frac{(\Sigma_\ell, \Theta_\ell) \models_\ell^\rho t : \vartheta \wedge \vartheta \subseteq \kappa(\ell)}{(\Sigma, \Theta, \kappa) \models \ell :: t}$$

(N-PAR)
$$\frac{(\Sigma, \Theta, \kappa) \models N_1 \wedge (\Sigma, \Theta, \kappa) \models N_2}{(\Sigma, \Theta, \kappa) \models N_1 \parallel N_2}$$

(P-NIL)
$$\frac{}{(\Sigma_\ell, \Theta_\ell, \kappa) \models_\ell^\rho \mathbf{nil}}$$

(P-PAR)
$$\frac{(\Sigma_\ell, \Theta_\ell, \kappa) \models_\ell^\rho P_1 \wedge (\Sigma_\ell, \Theta_\ell, \kappa) \models_\ell^\rho P_2}{(\Sigma_\ell, \Theta_\ell, \kappa) \models_\ell^\rho P_1 \mid P_2}$$

(P-DEF)
$$\frac{(\Sigma_\ell, \Theta_\ell, \kappa) \models_\ell^\rho P}{(\Sigma_\ell, \Theta_\ell, \kappa) \models_\ell^\rho A} \quad \text{if } A \triangleq P$$

(P-VAR)
$$\frac{}{(\Sigma_\ell, \Theta_\ell, \kappa) \models_\ell^\rho A}$$

(P-OUT)
$$\frac{(\Sigma_\ell, \Theta_\ell) \models_\ell^\rho t : \vartheta \wedge (\Sigma_\ell, \Theta_\ell) \models_\ell^\rho l : \vartheta' \wedge \left(\forall \hat{v} \in \vartheta, \forall \ell' \in \hat{@}\vartheta' \Rightarrow put(\ell, \hat{v}) \in \kappa(\ell')\right) \wedge (\Sigma_\ell, \Theta_\ell, \kappa) \models_\ell^\rho P}{(\Sigma_\ell, \Theta_\ell, \kappa) \models_\ell^\rho \mathbf{out}(t)@l.P}$$

(P-IN/READ)
$$(\Sigma_\ell, \Theta_\ell) \models_\ell^\rho l : \vartheta \wedge \forall \ell' \in \hat{@}\vartheta. \forall \hat{v} \in \kappa(\ell'). \left(get(\hat{v}) = \langle \hat{v}_1, \ldots, \hat{v}_r \rangle \wedge (\bigwedge_{i=1}^{r} tf_i \in \mathscr{L} \Rightarrow tf_i \,\widehat{in}\, \hat{v}_i)\right) \Rightarrow$$
$$\left(\bigwedge_{i=1}^{r} tf_i \in (LVar \cup Vars) \Rightarrow \hat{v}_i \in \Sigma_\ell(tf_i) \wedge \bigwedge_{i=1}^{r} tf_i \in \mathscr{E} \setminus Vars \Rightarrow (\Sigma_\ell, \Theta_\ell) \models_\ell^\rho tf_i : \vartheta_i \wedge (\Sigma_\ell, \Theta_\ell, \kappa) \models_\ell^\rho P\right)$$
$$\overline{(\Sigma_\ell, \Theta_\ell, \kappa) \models_\ell^\rho \mathbf{in}(\langle tf_1, \ldots, tf_r \rangle)@l.P / \mathbf{read}(\langle tf_1, \ldots, tf_r \rangle)@l}$$

conjunct of the conclusion of the implication requires that abstract environment includes the abstract values for each identifier and location variables occurring in the read tuple. The second and the third conjuncts require that the analysis validates the other elements of the tuple and the continuation P.

4.3 Checking Data Manipulation and Trajectories

We now illustrate how the outcome of the analysis can be used to detect where and how data are manipulated and how messages flow in a system. More precisely, the results of the analysis enable us to reason about (i) the path in the network through which (a value in) a tuple of a specific node reaches another one, and about (ii) which transformations are applied to a selected datum along those paths.

In our example of Sect. 3 a designer could be interested in imposing a policy that forbids serving a request coming from a certain geographic area while the user is associated with a different area by the profile. This situation occurs, e.g. when the user is travelling, the microservices reside in different areas and the user connects to the closest such microservice. Suppose that the two AUTH microservices serve each a different region. In our terms, one has to check whether a certain request authorised in ℓ_2 does not reach the SELECT microservice in ℓ_5. For brevity, we consider below only the parts of the analysis that check this property, while we do not consider data manipulations.

From now onwards, assume that all the symbolic names l have been bound to the corresponding absolute locations by the environments. The analysis of AUTH requires that the following holds

$$(\Sigma_\ell, \Theta_\ell, \kappa) \models_{\ell_2}^{\rho_2} \mathsf{H}$$

One has to analyse first $\mathbf{in}(usr, psw, req)@\ell_2$. We skip this step and for simplicity assume that the following holds, where (Z_i, R_i) are suitable tree grammars

$$(\Sigma_{\ell_2}, \Theta_{\ell_2}) \models^{\rho_2}_{\ell_2} req : \vartheta = \{(Z_1, R_1) \dots (Z_n, R_n)\}$$

The process H terminates by sending the relevant tuple to ℓ_4 and its analysis

$$(\Sigma_{\ell}, \Theta_{\ell}, \kappa) \models^{\rho_2}_{\ell_2} \mathbf{out}(usr, req, token)@\ell_4.H$$

enriches the grammars $\{(Z'_1, R'_1) \dots (Z'_k, R'_k)\}$ of the tuple with the information about this transit, performed by the function put, yielding $\{(S^{\ell_2}, \{S^{\ell_2} \to s^{\ell_2}(Z'_1)\} \cup R'_1) \dots (S^{\ell_2}, \{S^{\ell_2} \to s^{\ell_2}(Z'_k)\} \cup R'_k)\}$.

Now the analysis of SELECT requires that of its actions, but we only concentrate on

$$(\Sigma_{\ell}, \Theta_{\ell}, \kappa) \models^{\rho_4}_{\ell_4} \mathbf{out}(usr, token, req, suggestion)@\ell_5.S_2$$

Again, the output tuple is enriched with the information represented by s^{ℓ_4}.

Before discussing how to use the analysis results of this example, we define the following notions, formalising the inspection of results. We start by defining a function that, given an abstract value $\hat{v}$ (i.e. a tree grammar) returns a finite set of finite sequences of labels, ending with either a value in $Value$ or a location in $\mathscr{L}$. Below we assume as given a network N and the result of its analysis.

Definition 2 (Extracting trajectories). *Let $\hat{v}$ be a tree grammar, the set of trajectories of the values and locations represented by $\hat{v}$ is*

$$TRJ(\hat{v}) = {}^{\emptyset}trj^{\emptyset}(\hat{v})$$

where ${}^{I}trj^{J}$ is inductively defined on the shape of $\hat{v}$ as follows

- ${}^{I}trj^{J}(A^{\ell}, \{A^{\ell} \to c^{\ell}(Z_1, \dots, Z_r)\} \cup R) = \bigcup_{i=1, Z_i \notin I}^{r} \{\ell \cdot {}^{I'}trj^{J \cup A}((Z_i, R_i))\}$

- ${}^{I}trj^{J}(L^{\ell}, \{L^{\ell} \to \ell'\}) = \ell \cdot \ell'$

- ${}^{I}trj^{J}(V^{\ell}, \{V^{\ell} \to v^{\ell}\}) = \ell \cdot v$

and

- $\ell \cdot X = \{\ell \cdot x \mid x \in X\}$
- $I' = \begin{cases} I \cup A & \text{if } A \notin J \\ I & \text{otherwise} \end{cases}$

As expected, the auxiliary function ${}^{I}trj^{J}$ extracts a trajectory from an abstract value, by accumulating on each sequence the location of a traversed node. The trajectories are kept finite because the sets I and J keep track of the visited nodes, which are not visited more than twice.

Now we define when a value or a label does not traverse a node that the designer considers malicious, and thus that trajectory violates the policy.

Definition 3 (Datum reaches). *A datum $d \in Value \cup \mathscr{L}$ reaches a node ℓ_k without passing through a node ℓ if and only if*

$$\forall \hat{v} \in \Theta_{\ell_k}.\ \ell_0 \cdots \ell_k \cdot d \in TRJ(\hat{v}) \ \Rightarrow \ \forall j.\ell \neq \ell_j$$

We turn our attention to data manipulations. In particular, we describe how a designer can check where data originates and which functions transform them.

Definition 4 (Data manipulation). *A datum $d \in Value \cup \mathscr{L}$, originated from the node with label ℓ_0, is an* ingredient *of a node ℓ_k if and only if*

$$\exists \hat{v} \in \Theta_{\ell_k}.\ \ell_0 \cdots \ell_k \cdot d \in TRJ(\hat{v})$$

Furthermore, a function f may manipulate *a value v reaching a node ℓ_k if and only if there exists an abstract value $(A, R) \in \Theta_{\ell_k}$ such that R contains a production $F^{\ell'} \rightarrow f^{\ell'}(R_1, \ldots, R_n)$, for some ℓ'.*

The first part of the above definition is straightforward since inspecting the Θ_{ℓ_k} suffices to understand if a value may be stored in the tuple space of the node ℓ_k. The second part checks if the function f may be applied in any node along the path traversed by the value v. Again, this information can be extracted from the grammars inside Θ_{ℓ_k}.

Back to our example, applying the function TRJ to an element $\hat{v}$ of Θ_{ℓ_5} gives the trajectory $\ell_2 \cdot \ell_4 \cdot \ell_5 \cdot v$. The requirement that a user can only access a service within his geographic area is therefore detected.

5   Conclusions

We have introduced a static analysis, technically a contol flow analysis, for a variant of KLAIM that provides an abstract simulation model that tracks the propagation of tuples and identifies their possible trajectories within a KLAIM net. We have illustrated our approach on a microservice-based software architecture, showing that one can detect when a datum can safely traverse a path in the network, and when passing through a specific node may be dangerous. Our variant of KLAIM includes no primitive mechanism for code mobility, e.g. the **eval** action, which however can be managed with some additional technicalities. As future work, we intend to study when nodes continue to behave in a reasonable way even in the presence of not completely reliable data, by linking our approach to that in [21]. There, the authors use the Quality Calculus to program software components with a sort of backup plan in case of partly unreliable communication or data. Finally, we plan to consider one of the available implementations of the KLAIM model, e.g. [1,2], to instrument them with our static analysis and to perform experimental evaluation on some case studies.

Related Work. Several verification techniques have been defined for KLAIM and its variants. An important effort has been devoted to exploit behavioural type systems for security [12,14,19]. By exploiting static and dynamic checks, type checking guarantees that only those processes are allowed to proceed, the intentions of which match the rights granted to them. An expressive language extension, METAKLAIM [16] integrates METAML (an extension of SML for multi-stage programming) and KLAIM, to permit interleaving of meta-programming activities (such as assembly and linking of code fragments), dynamic checking of security policies at administrative boundaries, and traditional computational activities. METAKLAIM exploits a powerful type system (including polymorphic types *á la* system F) to deal with highly parameterised mobile components and to enforce security policies dynamically: types are metadata that are extracted from code at run-time and are used to express trustiness guarantees. The dynamic type checking ensures that the trustiness guarantees of wide area network applications are maintained also when computations interoperate with potentially untrusted components.

A framework based on temporal logic [10] has been developed for specifying and verifying dynamic properties of mobile processes specified in KLAIM. This framework provides support for establishing deadlock freedom and liveness properties as well as security properties such as resource access and information disclosure. A different approach to control accesses to tuple spaces and mobility of processes is introduced in [13]. Like ours, this approach is based on Flow Logic (so also enabling to design a fully static type system) and considers a version of KLAIM slightly different from ours. The abstract domains differ, because theirs contain tuples only made by localities, while ours also have values. Since access control is of interest, their domains also record possible policies and violations.

References

1. Bettini, L., De Nicola, R., Pugliese, R.: KLAVA: a Java package for distributed and mobile applications. Softw. Pract. Exper. **32**(14), 1365–1394 (2002)
2. Bettini, L., De Nicola, R., Pugliese, R., Ferrari, G.L.: Interactive mobile agents in X-Klaim. In: Proceedings of 7th Workshop on Enabling Technologies (WETICE 1998), Infrastructure for Collaborative Enterprises, pp. 110–117. IEEE Computer Society (1998)
3. Bodei, C., Degano, P., Ferrari, G.L., Galletta, L.: A step towards checking security in IoT. In: Proceedings of ICE 2016, EPTCS, vol. 223, pp. 128–142 (2016)
4. Bodei, C., Degano, P., Ferrari, G.-L., Galletta, L.: Where do your IoT ingredients come from? In: Lluch Lafuente, A., Proença, J. (eds.) COORDINATION 2016. LNCS, vol. 9686, pp. 35–50. Springer, Cham (2016). https://doi.org/10.1007/978-3-319-39519-7_3
5. Bodei, C., Degano, P., Ferrari, G.L., Galletta, L.: Tracing where IoT data are collected and aggregated. Log. Methods Comput. Sci. **13**(3), 1–38 (2017)
6. Bodei, C., Galletta, L.: Tracking data trajectories in IoT. In: Mori, P., Furnell, S., Camp, O. (eds.) Proceedings of the 5th International Conference on Information Systems Security and Privacy, ICISSP, vol. 1, pp. 572–579. SCITEPRESS (2019). https://doi.org/10.5220/0007578305720579, ISBN 978-989-758-359-9

7. Castellani, S., Ciancarini, P., Rossi, D.: The ShaPE of ShaDE: a coordination system. Technical report UBLCS 96-5, Dip. di Scienze dell'Informazione, Univ. Bologna (1996)

8. Comon, H., et al.: Tree automata techniques and applications. http://www.grappa.univ-lille3.fr/tata (2007). Released 12 Oct 2007

9. Davies, N., Wade, S., Friday, A., Blair, G.: L^{2}imbo: a tuple space based platform for adaptive mobile applications. In: Rolia, J., Slonim, J., Botsford, J. (eds.) ICODP/ICDP. IFIPAICT, pp. 291–302. Springer, Boston (1997). https://doi.org/10.1007/978-0-387-35188-9_22

10. De Nicola, R., Loreti, M.: A modal logic for mobile agents. ACM Trans. Comput. Log. **5**(1), 79–128 (2004)

11. De Nicola, R., Ferrari, G.L., Pugliese, R.: KLAIM: a kernel language for agents interaction and mobility. IEEE Trans. Softw. Eng. **24**(5), 315–330 (1998)

12. De Nicola, R., Ferrari, G.L., Pugliese, R., Venneri, B.: Types for access control. Theor. Comput. Sci. **240**(1), 215–254 (2000)

13. De Nicola, R., et al.: From flow logic to static type systems for coordination languages. Sci. Comput. Program. **75**(6), 376–397 (2010)

14. De Nicola, R., Gorla, D., Pugliese, R.: Confining data and processes in global computing applications. Sci. Comput. Program. **63**(1), 57–87 (2006)

15. Deugo, D.: Choosing a mobile agent messaging model. In: ISADS, pp. 278–286. IEEE (2001)

16. Ferrari, G.L., Moggi, E., Pugliese, R.: MetaKlaim: a type safe multi-stage language for global computing. Math. Struct. Comput. Sci. **14**(3), 367–395 (2004)

17. Gelernter, D.: Generative communication in Linda. ACM Trans. Program. Lang. Syst. **7**(1), 80–112 (1985)

18. Gelernter, D.: Multiple tuple spaces in Linda. In: Odijk, E., Rem, M., Syre, J.-C. (eds.) PARLE 1989. LNCS, vol. 366, pp. 20–27. Springer, Heidelberg (1989). https://doi.org/10.1007/3-540-51285-3_30

19. Gorla, D., Pugliese, R.: Dynamic management of capabilities in a network aware coordination language. J. Log. Algebraic Program. **78**(8), 665–689 (2009)

20. Nielson, F., Nielson, H.R., Seidl, H.: A succinct solver for ALFP. Nordic J. Comput. **9**(4), 335–372 (2002)

21. Nielson, H.R., Nielson, F., Vigo, R.: A calculus of quality for robustness against unreliable communication. J. Log. Algebraic Meth. Program. **84**(5), 611–639 (2015)

Lightweight Information Flow

Flemming Nielson$^{(\boxtimes)}$ and Hanne Riis Nielson

Department of Mathematics and Computer Science,
Technical University of Denmark, 2800 Kgs., Lyngby, Denmark
`fnie@dtu.dk, hrni@dtu.dk`

Abstract. We develop a *type system* for identifying the information flow between variables in a program in the Guarded Commands language. First we characterise the types of information flow that may arise between variables in a non-deterministic program: *explicit, implicit, bypassing, correlated* or *sanitised*. Next we allow to specify security policies in a number of traditional ways based on mandatory access control: defining a *security lattice*, working with *components* or *decentralised labels*, both as pertains to *confidentiality* and *integrity*. Offending information flows are those identified by the type system and that violate the security policy; a program is *sufficiently secure* if it contains only acceptable information flows.

1 Introduction

Motivation. Much of the work of Rocco De Nicola has been within the general area of process algebras [5]. This is a fascinating area containing a wide range of fundamental ideas and many deep developments on topics such as semantics, equivalences (including testing equivalences [3,10] and bisimulations [1,12]) and model checking [11] to name just some of the key ones.

Some of the work of Rocco De Nicola has been on type systems ensuring various desirable properties of systems, including security properties [7,8]. In order to make these developments accessible to the wider computer science and computer engineering communities it is essential to choose the primitives of the process algebras at an appropriate level of abstraction. The work on *Klaim* (a Kernel Language for Agents Interaction and Mobility) [2,6,9] incorporates a choice that is sufficiently abstract to allow a rich theory and prototype systems to be developed, while at the same time being sufficiently concrete to appeal to a wide variety of researchers, engineers, programmers and students.

Contribution. In this paper we define a type system for identifying the security vulnerabilities that may arise in non-deterministic programs.

The traditional approach is to define a type system that intends to ensure that there are absolutely no security violations in well-typed programs. Non-interference results, or generalisations of these, then provide guarantees about the soundness of the type system. However, this does not close the loophole that security vulnerabilities may exist below the level of formalisation, as when

© Springer Nature Switzerland AG 2019
M. Boreale et al. (Eds.): De Nicola-Festschrift, LNCS 11665, pp. 455–470, 2019.
https://doi.org/10.1007/978-3-030-21485-2_25

timing attacks can still be performed on systems only achieving non-termination-sensitive security, nor that minor amounts of quantitative leakage might be acceptable in practice.

Our approach is to define a type system that intends merely to identify the security vulnerabilities that may still be present in well-typed programs. The aim is to do so in a manner that appeals to a wide variety of researchers, engineers, programmers and students, also outside the area of language based security. The acceptability of the security vulnerabilities should then be assessed as part of a code review.

The first step is to characterise the types of information flow that may arise between variables in non-deterministic programs: they may be *explicit* (as in assignments), *implicit* (as in conditional choices), *bypassing* (when one conditional choice may bypass another), *correlated* (when variables are modified in the same conditional branches that could have been bypassed) or *sanitised* (when the flow is regarded as permissible regardless of the security policy).

The next step is to admit security policies in a number of traditional ways based on mandatory access control: explicitly defining a *security lattice*, working with *components* or *decentralised labels*, both as pertains to permissions (often used for *confidentiality*) and restrictions (often used for *integrity*). This step is fairly standard.

The final step is to develop a *type system* for identifying the information flow between variables in a program in the Guarded Commands language. Offending information flows are those identified by the type system and that violate the security policy. A program is secure if it contains no information flows or only acceptable ones (like the sanitised ones); in the absence of any information flow we may establish a non-interference result but we would be more interested in being able to quantify the amount of leakage so as to provide guidance to engineers and programmers as part of a code review. The type system has been implemented and is available for experimentation at http://FormalMethods.dk/if4fun and makes use of heuristics for satisfiability of boolean expressions in Guarded Commands.

2   Guarded Commands for Security

We shall base our development on Dijkstra's language of Guarded Commands [15] extended with arrays and a security primitive (san, to be explained shortly). The conditional takes the form if $b_1 \rightarrow C_1$ [] ... [] $b_k \rightarrow C_k$ fi; as an example, to express that C_1 should be executed when b holds and that otherwise C_2 should be executed, we shall write if $b \rightarrow C_1$ [] $\neg b \rightarrow C_2$ fi. The iteration construct takes the form do $b_1 \rightarrow C_1$ [] ... [] $b_k \rightarrow C_k$ od; as an example, to express that C should be executed as long as b holds, we shall write do $b \rightarrow C$ od.

An example program is shown in the righthand half of Fig. 1; it non-deterministically updates the entries of arrays A and E, of lengths A# and E#, respectively. (It can be seen as an interleaved version of the parallel composition of two programs handling each of the arrays, as shown in the lefthand half of Fig. 1, but this is not part of the Guarded Commands language.)

```
par
   a:=0;
   do san(a)<san(A#)  →
      A[a]:=A[a]+27;
      a:=a+1
   od
[]
   e:=0;
   do san(e)<san(E#)  →
      E[e]:=E[e]+12;
      e:=e+1
   od
rap
```

```
a:=0;
e:=0;
do san(a)<san(A#)  →
   A[a]:=A[a]+27;
   a:=a+1
[] san(e)<san(E#)  →
   E[e]:=E[e]+12;
   e:=e+1
od
```

Fig. 1. Two arrays being simultaneously updated. On the left we pretend it happens in parallel, on the right we pretend it happens interleaved. Only the program on the right is within Guarded Commands for Security as studied here.

Syntax. The syntax of the commands C and guarded commands GC of the Guarded Commands for Security language are mutually recursively defined using the following BNF notation:

$$C ::= x := a \mid A[a_1] := a_2 \mid \textbf{skip} \mid C_1 ; C_2 \mid \textbf{if } GC \textbf{ fi} \mid \textbf{do } GC \textbf{ od}$$
$$GC ::= b \rightarrow C \mid GC_1 \; [] \; GC_2$$

We make use of arithmetic expressions a (used in $x := a$ and $A[a_1] := a_2$) and boolean expressions b (used as a guard for when to execute a command C as in $b \rightarrow C$) given by

$$a ::= n \mid s \mid x \mid A[a_1] \mid A\# \mid a_1 + a_2 \mid a_1 - a_2 \mid a_1 * a_2 \mid \textbf{san } a_1$$
$$b ::= \textbf{true} \mid a_1 = a_2 \mid a_1 > a_2 \mid a_1 \geq a_2 \mid b_1 \wedge b_2 \mid b_2 \mid \neg b_1$$

where numbers n, strings s, variables x and arrays A are left unspecified. The **san** construct will be used to bypass the security policy and will be explained in Sect. 3.

Semantics. We shall present the key ideas behind giving an operational semantics for Guarded Commands.

A command will be interpreted relative to a memory σ that assigns values (say integers) to all variables and array entries in the command of interest. More precisely, for each array A of length $A\#$ the memory will provide values for $A[0] \cdots A[A\#]$ as well as for $A\#$.

An arithmetic expression a is then evaluated with respect to a memory σ and we obtain a value $\mathcal{A}[\![a]\!]\sigma$ as result. Evaluation is undefined if the arithmetic expression accesses a variable or array entry for which the memory does not assign a value. Also, the value of **san** a_1 is the same as the value of a_1.

A boolean expression b is also evaluated with respect to a memory σ and we obtain a truth value $\mathcal{B}[\![b]\!]\sigma$ as result. Evaluation is undefined if one of the constituent arithmetic expressions is undefined.

We then define an operational semantics for interpreting commands (and guarded commands) and list some of the key axioms and rules:

$$\frac{\sigma(x) \text{ and } \mathcal{A}[\![a]\!]\sigma \text{ are defined}}{(x := a, \sigma) \to \sigma[x \mapsto \mathcal{A}[\![a]\!]\sigma]}$$

$$\frac{(C_1, \sigma) \to (C_1', \sigma')}{(C_1\,; C_2, \sigma) \to (C_1'\,; C_2, \sigma')} \qquad \frac{(C_1, \sigma) \to \sigma'}{(C_1\,; C_2, \sigma) \to (C_2, \sigma')}$$

$$\frac{\mathcal{B}[\![b_i]\!]\sigma \text{ is true}}{(\texttt{if } b_1 \to C_1 \; [] \; \cdots \; [] \; b_n \to C_n \; \texttt{fi}, \sigma) \to (C_i, \sigma)}$$

$$\frac{\mathcal{B}[\![b_i]\!]\sigma \text{ is true}}{(\texttt{do } \cdots \; [] \; b_i \to C_i \; [] \; \cdots \; \texttt{od}, \sigma) \to (C_i\,; \texttt{do } \cdots \; [] \; b_i \to C_i \; [] \; \cdots \; \texttt{od}, \sigma)}$$

$$\frac{\text{all of } \mathcal{B}[\![b_i]\!]\sigma \text{ are false}}{(\texttt{do } b_1 \to C_1 \; [] \; \cdots \; [] \; b_n \to C_n \; \texttt{od}, \sigma) \to \sigma}$$

In particular, this semantics is purely non-deterministic and does not make use of a scheduler. (If needed, we would model a scheduler by explicitly modifying the guards in guarded commands. Doing so would influence the results of the information flow type system. This would be our way of modelling an attacker that might collude with a scheduler.)

3   Types of Information Flow

We now introduce the types of information flow in non-deterministic programs. These are not only between variables as we also have array entries and array lengths. We therefore use the term *data container* to stand for any one of variable, array entry or length. The notions of explicit, implicit and sanitised flows are standard [13,14] whereas our treatment of bypassing flows grew out of [21] and our focus on correlation flows is more novel.

Explicit Flows. In the command y := x there is a direct and explicit flow from x to y. We write this as $x \to^E y$ to indicate that it is an explicit flow.

In general, *explicit* flows arise whenever a data container is used to compute the value of a data container.

A slightly more complex example is the command y := x; z := y where there are direct explicit flows from x to y and from y to z. The flow from x to z is an *indirect* flow, and in general we use indirect to indicate that we exploit the transitive nature of the flow relation. As for the type of flow we shall say that the indirect flow is also explicit.

Implicit Flows. In the guarded command x = 0 → y := 0 there is a direct and implicit flow from x to y. We write this as x →^{I} y to indicate that it is an implicit flow.

In general, *implicit* flows arise whenever a data container is modified inside the body of a command governed by a boolean condition containing some data container.

The command if x = 0 → y := 0 [] ¬(x = 0) → y := 1 fi ; z := y has a direct implicit flow from x to y and a direct explicit flow from y to z. The flow from x to z is an indirect flow and as for the type of flow we shall say that the indirect flow is implicit (since x is not directly copied into z).

Bypassing Flows. In y := 0 ; if x = 0 → skip [] true → y := 1 fi there are no explicit flows from x to y and also no implicit flows. However, it is still the case that the final value of y might reveal something about x if one is able to run the program many times and observe the different non-deterministic outcomes. We write this as x →^{B} y to indicate that it is a bypassing flow.

In general, *bypassing* flows arise whenever two conditions can be simultaneously true and more than one branch can be taken; in this case there is a bypassing flow from the data containers in the condition of one branch to the data containers modified in the command of the other.

In the command x := z ; y := 0 ; if x = 0 → skip [] true → y := 1 fi there is a direct explicit flow from z to x and a direct bypassing flow from x to y. The flow from z to y is an indirect flow and as for the type of flow we shall say that the indirect flow is a bypassing one.

Correlation Flows. Bypassing flows capture some of the power of non-determinism but not all of it. In if true → y := 0 ; x := 0 [] true → y := 1 ; x := 1 fi there are no explicit, implicit or bypassing flows. Yet, if y was intended to be a private key (albeit a short one) and x is a public variable, then clearly we can learn something about y from knowing x. We write this as x →^{C} y and y →^{C} x to indicate that it is a possible correlation flow between x and y.

In general, *correlation* flows arise whenever two conditions can be simultaneously true and the choice of branch is resolved non-deterministically; in this case there is a correlation flow between the data containers modified in each branch.

In if true → y := 0 ; x := 0 [] true → y := 1 ; x := 1 fi ; z := x there is a direct explicit flow from x to z and a correlation flow from y to x. The flow from y to z is an indirect flow and as for the type of flow we shall say that the indirect flow is a correlation one.

Sanitised Flows. Returning to the non-deterministic program in Fig. 1 there would seem to be bypassing flows from A# to E[] and similarly from E# to A[]. We might consider these flows to be absolutely unproblematic and a traditional approach is to use *sanitisation* for this; in our case this means using the san construct of Guarded Commands for Security as illustrated in Fig. 1.

Rather than *neglecting* the direct bypassing flows from A# to E[] and from E# to A[] we shall mark these as sanitised flows (that can be disregarded later as part of a code review) and we write A# $\to^S$ B[] and B# $\to^S$ A[].

In general, *sanitised* flows arise whenever at least one sanitisation step is involved in the flow. In line with previous decisions, if a sequence of flows involve a sanitised flow we shall regard the overall flow as a sanitised one.

Representation of Flows. We shall take the point of view that some types of flows are more worrying than others and that we only need to record the most worrying one. We order the explicit (E), implicit (I), bypassing (B), correlation (C) and sanitised (S) flows linearly by S < C < B < I < E. We then use max and min for the corresponding least upper bound and greatest lower bound operations.

A *flow relation* is a partial map from pairs of data containers to {E, I, B, C, S}, and we use F to range over flow relations and τ to range over types of flows. (This is isomorphic to a total map from pairs of data containers to {$\bot$, E, I, B, C, S} where $\bot$ < S < C < B < I < E and thus gives rise to a pointwise definition of a partial order $\leq$ between flow relations.)

We write $\delta_1 \to^\tau \delta_2$ for the flow relation that is undefined everywhere, except that the pair (δ_1, δ_2) is mapped to τ.

Extending this notation to sets of data containers we write $\Delta_1 \rightrightarrows^\tau \Delta_2$ for the flow relation that is undefined everywhere, except that a pair $(\delta_1, \delta_2) \in \Delta_1 \times \Delta_2$ is mapped to τ.

As a special case, {} $\rightrightarrows^\tau$ {} denotes the flow relation that is undefined everywhere (regardless of the choice of τ).

4   Security Policies

The key motivation behind our development is to classify data containers according to a security domain, and to consider it secure to transfer data as expressed by an ordering on the elements of the security domain (see [17] for a general introduction).

A *security domain* L is a finite and non-empty set equipped with a preorder $\sqsubseteq$; this is a relation over L that is reflexive and transitive. The preorder indicates the direction in which it is secure to move data along; we shall use this approach regardless of whether we deal with confidentiality or integrity or mixtures or modifications of these. In the literature, the security domain is often required to be a (complete) lattice and hence is called a *security lattice*, but we do not need this assumption for our approach.

A *security association* $\mathcal{L}$ is a mapping from the set of data containers of interest into the security domain. Clearly security policies can be combined using cartesian products and hence be built in a compositional manner.

A *security policy* consists of a security domain and a security association.

An information flow $\delta_1 \to^\tau \delta_2$ is secure with respect to the security policy whenever $\mathcal{L}(\delta_1) \sqsubseteq \mathcal{L}(\delta_2)$. An information flow $\delta_1 \to^\tau \delta_2$ with $\mathcal{L}(\delta_1) \not\sqsubseteq \mathcal{L}(\delta_2)$ constitutes a security violation at level τ.

Fig. 2. Illustrating restriction ordering ($\subseteq$) versus the permission ordering ($\supseteq$).

Components. Describing the security domain explicitly becomes cumbersome once the security domain grows in size. We therefore consider ways of expressing the intended security lattice in more succinct ways following the approach standard in Mandatory Access Control [17].

Define a finite and nonempty set C of *security categories*. A *security component* then is a set of security categories and the *security domain* $L = \mathsf{PowerSet}(\mathsf{C})$ is the set of all such security components. This security domain is indeed a (complete) lattice.

Whenever the security categories are considered to be *restrictions* that can be gained but cannot be lost, the security domain will be ordered by the subset ordering (taking $\sqsubseteq$ to be $\subseteq$). This is often the case for integrity policies.

Whenever the security categories are considered to be *permissions* that can be lost but cannot be gained, the security domain will be ordered by the superset ordering (taking $\sqsubseteq$ to be $\supseteq$). This is often the case for confidentiality policies.

The *security domain* is then specified by listing the finite and nonempty set of security categories and indicating whether to use the ordering for restrictions or for permissions.

In both cases we retain the important principle that data may flow along the preorder of the security domain. Determining which choice of ordering to go for depends on determining whether or not it is considered to be secure to gain or lose security categories along flows.

We shall write $\{*\}$ for the security component consisting of all security categories. In case of the restriction ordering, the least element then is $\{\,\}$ and the greatest element is $\{*\}$, whereas in the case of the permission ordering, the least element is $\{*\}$ and the greatest element is $\{\,\}$. This is illustrated in Fig. 2.

Decentralised Labels. The security perspective of components was of a rather global nature. To accommodate that different security principals might have different views on information flow, that all should be respected, we develop a notion of decentralised labels – motivated by the Decentralised Label Model of Myers and Liskov [18] and some of its adaptations [19, 22] – while staying fully within the lattice-based approach.

Define a finite and nonempty set P of *security principals*. A *decentralised label* then is a total mapping from P to $\mathsf{PowerSet}(\mathsf{P})$ and the *security domain* $L = (\mathsf{P} \to \mathsf{PowerSet}(\mathsf{P}))$ is the set of all such mappings. This security domain is indeed a (complete) lattice.

As in the previous section there are two ways of considering the labels: as restrictions that can be gained but cannot be lost, or as permissions that can be lost but cannot be gained.

Whenever the labels are considered to be *restrictions* that can be gained but cannot be lost, the security domain will be ordered as $\ell_1 \sqsubseteq \ell_2$ if and only if $\forall R \in \mathsf{R} : \ell_1(R) \subseteq \ell_2(R)$. This is often the case for integrity policies.

Whenever the security categories are considered to be *permissions* that can be lost but cannot be gained, the security domain will be ordered as $\ell_1 \sqsubseteq \ell_2$ if and only if $\forall R \in \mathsf{R} : \ell_1(R) \supseteq \ell_2(R)$. This is often the case for confidentiality policies.

The *security domain* is then specified by listing the finite and nonempty set of security categories and indicating whether to use the ordering for restrictions or for permissions.

In both cases we retain the important principle that data may flow along the preorder of the security domain. Determining which choice of ordering to go for depends on determining whether or not it is considered to be secure to gain or lose security categories along flows.

We shall allow to write $*$ for the list of all the security principals in P. In case of the restriction ordering, the least element then is $[* \mapsto \{\,\}]$ and the greatest element is $[* \mapsto \{*\}]$, whereas in the case of the permission ordering, the least element is $[* \mapsto \{*\}]$ and the greatest element is $[* \mapsto \{\,\}]$.

5   Information Flow Type System

We are now ready to develop the analysis for over-approximating the set of flows that may occur in a program. This takes the form of an inference system for defining a judgement $\vdash C : F$ associating the command C with the flow F and similarly for guarded commands. It may be seen as a generalisation of the approach of [24] to a non-deterministic language.

We shall use $\mathbf{fv}(a)$ to denote those data containers that occur in a outside any **san** construct and use $\mathbf{sv}(a)$ to denote those data containers that occur in a inside one or more **san** constructs. Similarly for $\mathbf{fv}(b)$ and $\mathbf{sv}(b)$. Finally, we shall use $\mathbf{mv}(C)$ to denote those data containers that may be modified within the command C; this generally represents an over-approximation of those modified in any execution.

Simple Assignments. For a simple assignment to a variable we need to record a flow from the data containers in the arithmetic expression to the variable being modified. These flows will be explicit unless the data container in question occurs inside at least one **san** construct. This motivates the following axiom scheme.

$$\vdash x := a : \frac{(\mathbf{fv}(a) \rightrightarrows^{\mathsf{E}} \{x\}) \oplus}{(\mathbf{sv}(a) \rightrightarrows^{\mathsf{S}} \{x\})}$$

The operation $\oplus$ is defined by

$$(F_1 \oplus F_2)(\delta_1, \delta_2) = \max\{F_1(\delta_1, \delta_2), F_2(\delta_1, \delta_2)\}$$

and incorporates the idea that whenever we have a choice between two different types of flow between two data containers we should always choose the most worrying one. (In case any of the $F_i(\delta_1, \delta_2)$ being undefined we revert to the isomorphic representation using total maps explained earlier and this amounts to disregarding such cases.)

This definition can also be seen as a pointwise addition of matrices where max plays the role of addition. It is immediate that both $F \oplus (\{\} \rightrightarrows^\tau \{\})$ and $(\{\} \rightrightarrows^\tau \{\}) \oplus F$ equal F.

Assignments to Arrays. For assignment to arrays we take the point of view that the data containers inside the index give rise to implicit rather than explicit flows. This is based on the consideration that for an array A having 5 elements the command if $a_1 = 1 \rightarrow$ A[1] := a_2 [] $\cdots$ [] $a_1 = 5 \rightarrow$ A[5] := a_2 fi is equivalent to the program A[a_1] := a_2. This motivates the following axiom scheme.

$$\vdash A[a_1] := a_2 : \begin{array}{l} (\mathsf{fv}(a_2) \rightrightarrows^{\mathsf{E}} \{A[]\}) \oplus \\ (\mathsf{fv}(a_1) \rightrightarrows^{\mathsf{I}} \{A[]\}) \oplus \\ (\mathsf{sv}(a_1) \cup \mathsf{sv}(a_2) \rightrightarrows^{\mathsf{S}} \{A[]\}) \end{array}$$

Skip. The axiom for skip is immediate: $\vdash$ skip $: (\{\} \rightrightarrows^{\mathsf{E}} \{\})$.

Sequencing. For sequential composition $C_1 ; C_2$ we need to compose the flows arising from C_1 and C_2. However, as our designation of the set of data containers modified represents an over-approximation, and as we have not required information flows to contain explicit flows from a data container to itself, we need to take care to also include the flows from each of the components.

$$\frac{\vdash C_1 : F_1 \qquad \vdash C_2 : F_2}{\vdash C_1 ; C_2 : (F_1 \otimes F_2) \oplus F_1 \oplus F_2}$$

The operation $\otimes$ is defined by

$$(F_1 \otimes F_2)(\delta_1, \delta_2) = \max\left\{\min\left\{\begin{array}{l} F_1(\delta_1, \delta), \\ F_2(\delta, \delta_2) \end{array}\right\} \mid \delta \text{ is a data container}\right\}$$

and incorporates the following two ideas: (1) If we have flows $\delta_1 \rightarrow^{\tau_1} \delta_2$ and $\delta_2 \rightarrow^{\tau_2} \delta_3$ then we also have a flow $\delta_1 \rightarrow^\tau \delta_3$ where τ is the least worrying of the two flows, i.e. $\tau = \min\{\tau_1, \tau_2\}$. (2) If additionally there is another scenario where we have flows $\delta_1 \rightarrow^{\tau_1'} \delta_2'$ and $\delta_2' \rightarrow^{\tau_2'} \delta_3$ then we want τ to be the most worrying of the two candidates $\min\{\tau_1, \tau_2\}$ and $\min\{\tau_1', \tau_2'\}$, i.e. $\tau = \max\{\min\{\tau_1, \tau_2\}, \min\{\tau_1', \tau_2'\}\}$.

This definition can also be seen as a matrix multiplication where max plays the role of addition and min plays the role of multiplication. It is immediate that both $F \otimes (\{\} \rightrightarrows^\tau \{\})$ and $(\{\} \rightrightarrows^\tau \{\}) \otimes F$ equal $\{\} \rightrightarrows^\tau \{\}$.

Conditional. For conditional most of the work is left to the analysis of the guarded command inside.

$$\frac{\vdash GC : F}{\vdash \mathtt{if}\ GC\ \mathtt{fi} : F}$$

Iteration. In the case of iteration we need to take the transitive closure to reflect the iterative nature.

$$\frac{\vdash GC : F}{\vdash \mathtt{do}\ GC\ \mathtt{od} : F^{\circledast}}$$

The operation $\circledast$ is defined by

$$F^{\circledast}(\delta_{\triangleright}, \delta_{\blacktriangleleft}) = \max \left\{ \min \left\{ \begin{array}{c} F(\delta_0, \delta_1), \\ \cdots, \\ F(\delta_{n-1}, \delta_n) \end{array} \right\} \ \middle| \ \begin{array}{l} \delta_0, \cdots, \delta_n \text{ are data containers,} \\ n > 0, \delta_0 = \delta_{\triangleright}, \delta_n = \delta_{\blacktriangleleft} \end{array} \right\}$$

and incorporates the idea that the iteration can be performed any number of times. The definition can also be seen as a form of transitive closure of a matrix.

Guarded Commands. For a guarded command $b_i \to C_i$ we need to record the implicit flow from the condition b_i to the command C_i as well as incorporate the flows arising from C_i. Some of the implicit flows will actually be sanitised flows in case the data container inside b_i occurs within at least one **san** construct. In the context of a guarded command $b_1 \to C_1\ []\ \cdots\ []\ b_n \to C_n$ with multiple choices these considerations account for the first line of the flow constructed in the rule below.

$$\frac{\vdash C_1 : F_1 \qquad \cdots \qquad \vdash C_n : F_n}{\vdash \begin{array}{c} b_1 \to C_1 \\ [] \cdots [] \\ b_n \to C_n \end{array} : \bigoplus_{i \leq n} \left(\begin{array}{c} \big(\mathbf{fv}(b_i) \rightrightarrows^{\mathsf{I}} \mathbf{mv}(C_i)\big) \oplus \big(\mathbf{sv}(b_i) \rightrightarrows^{\mathsf{S}} \mathbf{mv}(C_i)\big) \oplus F_i \oplus \\ \bigoplus_{j \in \mathbf{cosat}(i)} \big(\mathbf{fv}(b_j) \rightrightarrows^{\mathsf{B}} \mathbf{mv}(C_i)\big) \oplus \big(\mathbf{sv}(b_j) \rightrightarrows^{\mathsf{S}} \mathbf{mv}(C_i)\big) \\ \oplus \big(\mathbf{mv}(C_i) \rightrightarrows^{\mathsf{C}} \mathbf{mv}(C_i)\big) \end{array} \right)}$$

The remaining two lines take care of the additional complications arising in a non-deterministic language where more than one choice is possible. To express this we shall assume that '$j \in \mathbf{cosat}(i)$' over-approximates when $b_j \wedge b_i$ might be satisfiable for *different* choices of j and i, i.e. if $b_j \wedge b_i$ is satisfiable and $j \neq i$ then '$j \in \mathbf{cosat}(i)$' must be true. Whenever '$j \in \mathbf{cosat}(i)$' we create the bypassing flows possible, taking care of those that will actually be sanitised flows instead, and we create the correlation flows between all data containers modified in either body.

Offending Flows. Given a security policy $(\boldsymbol{L}, \mathcal{L})$ we can now obtain those flows that violate the security policy by means of the following rule.

$$\frac{\vdash C : F}{(\boldsymbol{L}, \mathcal{L}) \vdash C : F'} \quad \text{where } F'(\delta_1, \delta_2) = \begin{cases} F(\delta_1, \delta_2) & \text{if } \mathcal{L}(\delta_1) \not\sqsubseteq \mathcal{L}(\delta_2) \\ \text{undefined} & \text{otherwise} \end{cases}$$

A command C is said to be *offending at level* τ with respect to a security policy $(\boldsymbol{L}, \mathcal{L})$ whenever $(\boldsymbol{L}, \mathcal{L}) \vdash C : F$ and $F(\delta_1, \delta_2) \geq \tau$ for some (δ_1, δ_2). In practice, commands offending only at level S should be considered sufficiently secure if the code review reveals that the **san** construct has been used with due care.

Example 1. Consider again the program shown in the righthand half of Fig. 1 and suppose that the security domain $\boldsymbol{L} = \{\mathsf{cc}, \mathsf{aa}, \mathsf{ee}\}$ is ordered by $\mathsf{cc} \sqsubseteq \mathsf{aa}$ and $\mathsf{cc} \sqsubseteq \mathsf{ee}$. (You may read cc as clean, aa as Amazon and ee as eBay.)

If the security association has $\mathcal{L}(\mathsf{a}) = \mathsf{aa}$, $\mathcal{L}(\mathsf{e}) = \mathsf{ee}$, $\mathcal{L}(\mathsf{A}[\,]) = \mathsf{aa}$, $\mathcal{L}(\mathsf{E}[\,]) = \mathsf{ee}$, $\mathcal{L}(\mathsf{A}\#) = \mathsf{aa}$ and $\mathcal{L}(\mathsf{E}\#) = \mathsf{ee}$ then the only offending flows are sanitised. So the program is only offending at level S and should be considered sufficiently secure.

If the security association has $\mathcal{L}(\mathsf{a}) = \mathsf{cc}$, $\mathcal{L}(\mathsf{e}) = \mathsf{cc}$, $\mathcal{L}(\mathsf{A}[\,]) = \mathsf{aa}$, $\mathcal{L}(\mathsf{E}[\,]) = \mathsf{ee}$, $\mathcal{L}(\mathsf{A}\#) = \mathsf{cc}$ and $\mathcal{L}(\mathsf{E}\#) = \mathsf{cc}$ then we get the offending correlation flows $\mathsf{A}[\,] \rightarrow^{\mathsf{C}} \mathsf{a}$ and $\mathsf{E}[\,] \rightarrow^{\mathsf{C}} \mathsf{e}$ as well as offending sanitised flows. So the program is offending at level C which upon closer inspections might be considered not to be problematic.

Discussion of Soundness. There are other and more subtle ways in which information may flow than has been covered by our security analysis. The word *covert channel* is used to describe such phenomena. As an example, the program

$$\mathsf{y} := 0 \,; \mathsf{x}' := \mathsf{x} \,; \mathsf{do}\ \mathsf{x}' > 0 \rightarrow \mathsf{x}' := \mathsf{x}' - 1 \,[]\, \mathsf{x}' < 0 \rightarrow \mathsf{x}' := \mathsf{x}' + 1\ \mathsf{od}$$

always terminates. It has no flows of any kind from x to y but if we can observe the *execution time* it reveals some information about the absolute value of x. Similar examples can be constructed where the computation on x will only terminate successfully for some values of x and otherwise enter a loop or a stuck configuration. If we can observe the *non-termination* it also reveals some information about the value of x.

The above discussion may be construed to say that our type system is not sound. (But this holds for most published type systems for security: it is usually not too hard to find a finer semantics that allows observations disregarded when the type system was constructed.) This means that an engineer and programmer taking part in a code review must maintain a perspective on whether the covert channels not covered by the type system provide grounds for rejecting code exhibiting no offending flows.

Nonetheless it would be desirable to ensure the robustness of the type system against shortcomings other than the deliberate decision to ignore the covert channels mentioned above.

For this we would like to explore a quantitative approach based on entropy. The basic assumption is that we have joint probability distributions available to characterise how sets of data containers take their values. Shannon's *entropy* is then the expected value of information contained in each observation. An important derived concept is that of *conditional entropy*: the portion of the entropy of a data container that is independent from another data container.

There are two extreme cases of the conditional entropy. One extreme case is where the data containers are aliases for the same entity or are modified in exactly the same way. The other extreme case is where the data containers are truly independent. The consideration of correlation flows were intended as an indicator of the first extreme case mentioned – but we are not close to be able to establish a result along these lines.

We find the quantitative approach more appealing than merely establishing a non-interference result [16,23,24] that guarantees how data containers of certain security classifications cannot influence data containers of another security classification. Using the developments in [20, Section 5.5] we may establish the following result. Suppose that $(\boldsymbol{L}, \mathcal{L}) \vdash C : \{\} \Rightarrow^S \{\}$ and $(C, \sigma_1) \rightarrow^* \sigma_1'$ and $(C, \sigma_2) \rightarrow^* \sigma_2'$; if $\forall y : \mathcal{L}(y) \sqsubseteq \mathcal{L}(x) \Rightarrow \sigma_1(y) = \sigma_2(y)$ we have $\sigma_1'(x) = \sigma_2'(x)$. However, $(\boldsymbol{L}, \mathcal{L}) \vdash C : \{\} \Rightarrow^S \{\}$ is likely to fail for non-deterministic programs since the nature of non-determinism is to open up for bypassing and correlation flows.

6   Algorithmic Issues

The type system is syntax-directed and easy to implement except for finding efficient ways to deal with transitive closure and satisfiability.

Transitive Closure. For an efficient construction of $F^\circledast$ using *dynamic programming* let us define

$$F^{[0]} = F \qquad F^{[n+1]} = F \oplus (F^{[n]} \otimes F^{[n]})$$

This is intended to ensure that $F^{[m]}$ correctly summarises the effect of all paths of length between 1 and 2^m.

Proposition 1. *If there are at most N data containers in the program considered then $F^\circledast = F^{[M]}$ where $M = \lceil log_2 N \rceil$.*

Proof. We may prove by induction that

$$F^{[m]}(\delta_\circ, \delta_\bullet) = \max \left\{ \min \left\{ \begin{array}{c} F(\delta_0, \delta_1), \\ \cdots, \\ F(\delta_{n-1}, \delta_n) \end{array} \right\} \;\middle|\; \begin{array}{l} \delta_0, \cdots, \delta_n \text{ are data containers,} \\ 1 \leq n \leq 2^m, \delta_0 = \delta_\circ, \delta_n = \delta_\bullet \end{array} \right\}$$

and it then suffices to realise that we only need to consider paths of length between 1 and $N \leq 2^M$.

It is immediate that $F^\circledast(\delta_\circ, \delta_\bullet)$ is greater than or equal to $F^{[M]}(\delta_\circ, \delta_\bullet)$. If they are not equal there must be a sequence of data containers $\delta_\circ = \delta_0 = \cdots = \delta_n = \delta_\bullet$ with $n > N$ such that $\min\{F(\delta_0, \delta_1), \cdots, F(\delta_{n-1}, \delta_n)\}$ is not less than or equal to $F^{[M]}(\delta_\circ, \delta_\bullet)$. We proceed by contradiction and without loss of generality we may assume that n is as small as possible.

There must be a data container that occurs more than once in $\delta_\circ = \delta_0 = \cdots = \delta_n = \delta_\bullet$ so consider the reduced sequence obtained by omitting all data containers between the first and the last occurrence and retaining just one occurrence of the data container in question. The reduced sequence will provide a value τ of the $\min\{\cdots\}$ formula such that $\min\{F(\delta_0, \delta_1), \cdots, F(\delta_{n-1}, \delta_n)\}$ is less than or equal to τ, that is again less than or equal to $F^{[M]}(\delta_\circ, \delta_\bullet)$. This provides the desired contradiction.

Over-Approximating Satisfiability Using a DAG Construction. We next develop a heuristics for over-approximating whether or not two boolean expressions might be jointly satisfiable. Since the system at http://FormalMethods.dk/if4fun may be downloaded to personal devices and run locally we prefer this approach rather than recasting the problem as an SMT problem (Satisfaction Modulo Theories) that requires access to a solver such as Z3 [4].

Recall that we considered a construct $b_1 \to C_1 \; [] \; \cdots \; [] \; b_n \to C_n$ and used the notation '$j \in \mathbf{cosat}(i)$' to over-approximate whether or not b_i and b_j can be jointly satisfied (for different choices of i and j). We shall define

$$(j \in \mathbf{cosat}(i)) = \big(\mathbf{sat}(b_i \wedge b_j) \wedge j \neq i\big)$$

and now explain our heuristics $\mathbf{sat}(\cdot)$ in Fig. 3 for over-approximating satisfiability.

```
function sat(b)
    convert b to disjunctive normal form V_i  b^i_1∧···∧b^i_{n_i} ;
    global := false;
    iterating through all i do
        local := true;
        build the ordered DAG for b^i_1∧···∧b^i_{n_i} ;
        if the DAG contains a marked node ¬t where also t is marked
            then local := false;
        if the DAG contains marked nodes t_1 o_1 t_2 and t_1 o_2 t_2
            with (o_1,o_2) ∈ E then local := false;
        global := global ∨ local;
    return global
```

Fig. 3. Algorithm for $\mathbf{sat}(b)$.

As a preparation we need to extend the syntax to use $<$ and $\leq$ (on top of $=$, $>$ and $\geq$) and to use $\vee$ (on top of $\wedge$ and $\neg$). Recall that a boolean expression is a *literal* when it has no occurrences of $\wedge$ or $\vee$ and at most one occurrence of $\neg$.

The first step in Fig. 3 is to translate b into disjunctive normal form; this is where $\vee$ may get introduced. The result is an equivalent formula

$$\bigvee_i b^i_1 \wedge \cdots \wedge b^i_{n_i}$$

where each b^i_j is a literal.

Iterating through each conjunction of literals $b^i_1 \wedge \cdots \wedge b^i_{n_i}$ the algorithm of Fig. 3 first constructs an ordered DAG (directed acyclic graph), and next inspects the ordered DAG to over-approximate satisfiability, as detailed below.

Constructing the Ordered DAG. To increase the amount of sharing in the ordered DAG we need to keep track of the 'transposed variants' of the arithmetic and relational operators:

$$\mathcal{T} = \{(+,+),(*,*),(<,>),(\leq,\geq),(=,=),(\geq,\leq),(<,>)\}$$

This takes care of characterising both those operators that are commutative (like $+$) and those that can be 'transposed' (like $a_1 < a_2$ may be transposed to $a_2 > a_1$). In general, whenever $(o_1, o_2) \in \mathcal{T}$ it must be the case that $t_1 \, o_1 \, t_2$ is equivalent to $t_2 \, o_2 \, t_1$.

Given a conjunction of literals we construct an ordered DAG by a bottom-up traversal over the parse tree. Leaves will be numbers n, strings s, variables x, arrays A, and true; internal nodes will be $[\,]$, $\#$, $+$, $-$, $*$, san, $<$, $\leq$, $=$, $>$, $\geq$ and $\neg$. Some of the nodes will be marked, and internal nodes will retain the order of their subgraphs.

When we encounter a potential new leaf in the bottom-up traversal over the parse tree of $b_1^i \wedge \cdots \wedge b_{n_i}^i$, we reuse the node in the DAG if it is already there, otherwise we construct a new leaf.

When we encounter a potential new internal node $t_1 \, o_1 \, t_2$, we reuse the node in the DAG if it is already there, otherwise we proceed as follows. If $(o_1, o_2) \in \mathcal{T}$ and there already is a node in the DAG for $t_2 \, o_2 \, t_1$, we use that node in the DAG, otherwise we construct the node $t_1 \, o_1 \, t_2$.

Once we encounter the root of one of the b_j^i we *mark* the node.

Inspecting the Ordered DAG. To detect cases where satisfiability fails we need to keep track of pairs of relational operators that exclude each other:

$$\mathcal{E} = \{(<,=),(<,\geq),(<,>),(\leq,>),(=,<),(=,>),(\geq,<),(>,<),(>,\leq),(>,=)\}$$

In general, whenever $(o_1, o_2) \in \mathcal{E}$ it must be the case that $a_1 \, o_1 \, a_2$ and $a_1 \, o_2 \, a_2$ are not jointly satisfiable for any choices of a_1 and a_2.

We can then establish the over-approximating nature of our heuristics.

Proposition 2. *If the boolean formula b is satisfiable then the algorithm* **sat**(b) *returns true.*

Proof. If the ordered DAG for a conjunction of literals contains a marked node t that has an ancestor $\neg t$ that is also marked, then clearly the conjunction of literals is not satisfiable. Similarly, if the ordered DAG for a conjunction of literals contains nodes t_1 and t_2 that have marked ancestors $t_1 \, o_1 \, t_2$ and $t_1 \, o_2 \, t_2$ with $(o_1, o_2) \in \mathcal{E}$, then the conjunction of literals is not satisfiable.

This shows that the resulting value of local for each iteration only reports false when the conjunction of literals is not satisfiable. It follows that the overall algorithm only reports false if none of the conjuncts of the disjunctive normal form are satisfiable.

We may conclude that '$j \in$ **cosat**(i)' is a correct over-approximation of joint satisfiability of b_i and b_j (for distinct i and j) from $b_1 \to C_1 \,[] \cdots [] \, b_n \to C_n$.

7 Conclusion

We developed a type system for identifying the offending information flow between data containers in a program in the Guarded Commands language. It was based on classifying flows as being explicit, implicit, bypassing, correlated or sanitised and on having general security policies incorporating multi-level security, components and decentralised labels; the bypassing and correlation flows were motivated by the need to deal with non-determinism. These developments are incorporated in the demonstration tool at http://FormalMethods.dk/if4fun; to allow it to be run on personal devices we make use of a heuristics for satisfiability of boolean expressions in Guarded Commands.

The approach taken in this paper has been inspired by working with engineers from safety critical software and observing how they react to incorporating security into their workflow. Ultimately this means leaving the decision of the acceptability of offending flows to the engineers and programmers taking part in a code review. The type support is intended to provide support for these decisions based on its classification of flows into the categories considered here.

References

1. Bernardo, M., De Nicola, R., Loreti, M.: Revisiting bisimilarity and its modal logic for nondeterministic and probabilistic processes. Acta Inf. **52**(1), 61–106 (2015)
2. Bettini, L., De Nicola, R., Pugliese, R.: XKlaim and Klava: programming mobile code. Electr. Notes Theor. Comput. Sci. **62**, 24–37 (2001)
3. Boreale, M., De Nicola, R.: Testing equivalence for mobile processes. Inf. Comput. **120**(2), 279–303 (1995)
4. de Moura, L., Bjørner, N.: Z3: an efficient SMT solver. In: Ramakrishnan, C.R., Rehof, J. (eds.) TACAS 2008. LNCS, vol. 4963, pp. 337–340. Springer, Heidelberg (2008). https://doi.org/10.1007/978-3-540-78800-3_24
5. De Nicola, R.: Testing equivalences and fully abstract models for communicating systems. Ph.D. thesis, University of Edinburgh, UK (1986)
6. De Nicola, R., Ferrari, G.L., Pugliese, R.: KLAIM: a kernel language for agents interaction and mobility. IEEE Trans. Softw. Eng **24**(5), 315–330 (1998)
7. De Nicola, R., Ferrari, G.L., Pugliese, R., Venneri, B.: Types for access control. Theor. Comput. Sci. **240**(1), 215–254 (2000)
8. De Nicola, R., et al.: From flow logic to static type systems for coordination languages. Sci. Comput. Program. **75**(6), 376–397 (2010)
9. De Nicola, R., Gorla, D., Pugliese, R.: On the expressive power of Klaim-based calculi. Theor. Comput. Sci. **356**(3), 387–421 (2006)
10. De Nicola, R., Hennessy, M.: Testing equivalences for processes. Theor. Comput. Sci. **34**, 83–133 (1984)
11. De Nicola, R., Katoen, J.-P., Latella, D., Loreti, M., Massink, M.: Model checking mobile stochastic logic. Theor. Comput. Sci. **382**(1), 42–70 (2007)
12. De Nicola, R., Vaandrager, F.W.: Three logics for branching bisimulation. J. ACM **42**(2), 458–487 (1995)
13. Denning, D.E.: A lattice model of secure information flow. Commun. ACM **19**(5), 236–243 (1976)
14. Denning, D.E., Denning, P.J.: Certification of programs for secure information flow. Commun. ACM **20**(7), 504–513 (1977)
15. Dijkstra, E.W.: Guarded commands, nondeterminacy and formal derivation of programs. Commun. ACM **18**(8), 453–457 (1975)

16. Goguen, J.A., Meseguer, J.: Security policies and security models. In: 1982 IEEE Symposium on Security and Privacy, Oakland, CA, USA, 26–28 April 1982, pp. 11–20. IEEE Computer Society (1982)
17. Gollmann, D.: Computer Security, 3rd edn. Wiley, Hoboken (2011)
18. Myers, A.C., Liskov, B.: Protecting privacy using the decentralized label model. ACM Trans. Softw. Eng. Methodol. 9(4), 410–442 (2000)
19. Flemming Nielson and Hanne Riis Nielson: Atomistic Galois insertions for flow sensitive integrity. Comput. Lang. Syst. Struct. **50**, 82–107 (2017)
20. Nielson, F., Nielson, H.R.: Formal Methods: An Appetizer. Springer, Cham (2019)
21. Nielson, F., Nielson, H.R., Vasilikos, P.: Information flow for timed automata. In: Aceto, L., Bacci, G., Bacci, G., Ingólfsdóttir, A., Legay, A., Mardare, R. (eds.) Models, Algorithms, Logics and Tools. LNCS, vol. 10460, pp. 3–21. Springer, Cham (2017). https://doi.org/10.1007/978-3-319-63121-9_1
22. Nielson, H.R., Nielson, F.: Content dependent information flow control. J. Log. Algebr. Meth. Program. **87**, 6–32 (2017)
23. Volpano, D.M., Irvine, C.E.: Secure flow typing. Comput. Secur. **16**(2), 137–144 (1997)
24. Volpano, D.M., Irvine, C.E., Smith, G.: A sound type system for secure flow analysis. J. Comput. Secur. **4**(2/3), 167–188 (1996)

A Framework for Provenance-Preserving History Distribution and Incremental Reduction

Alberto Lluch Lafuente[(✉)]

Technical University of Denmark, Kongens Lyngby, Denmark
albl@dtu.dk

Abstract. Provenance properties help asses the level of trust on the integrity of resources and events. One of the problems of interest is to find the right balance between the expressive power of the provenance specification language and the amount of historical information that needs to be remembered for each resource or event. This gives rise to possibly conflicting objectives relevant to integrity, privacy, and performance. Related problems are how to reduce historical information in a way that the provenance properties of interest are preserved, that is suitable for a distributed setting, and that relies on an incremental construction. We investigate these problems in a simple model of computation where resources/events and their dependencies form an acyclic directed graph, and computation steps consist of addition of new resources and of provenance-based queries. The model is agnostic with respect to the actual provenance specification language. We present then a framework, parametric on such language, for distributing, and incrementally constructing reduced histories in a sound and complete way. In the resulting model of computation, reduced histories are computed incrementally and queries are tested locally on reduced histories. We study different choices for instantiating the framework with concrete provenance specification languages, and their corresponding provenance-preserving history reduction techniques.

Keywords: Provenance · Integrity · Concurrency theory · Temporal logics · Minimisation

1 Introduction

Integrity is one of the key security goals in information security. Integrity techniques aim at assessing and controlling the level of trust of resources and events. Information about the history of a resource or event, e.g. who created it, how was it derived from other resources or events, etc., is often called *provenance* or *lineage*, and can be of great support for integrity mechanisms. This paper

This work has been supported by the EU H2020-SU-ICT-03-2018 Project No. 830929 CyberSec4Europe (cybersec4europe.eu).

M. Boreale et al. (Eds.): De Nicola-Festschrift, LNCS 11665, pp. 471–486, 2019.
https://doi.org/10.1007/978-3-030-21485-2_26

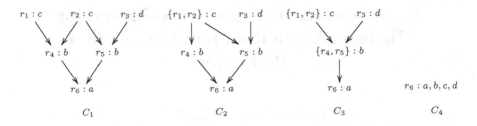

Fig. 1. Four configurations: C_1, C_2, C_3 and C_4

is motivated by the need to efficiently check integrity properties of resources or events based on their history. A typical scenario of interest are distributed ledgers where transactions and their casual dependencies form an acyclic graph, and where one would need to assess the integrity of a transaction t based on the transactions it depends on: *Is there any suspicious transaction t' in the history of t? Is there a trustworthy transaction between t and t' that would provide some guarantees on the solidity of t?* Another typical scenario of interest are repositories of linked data: *Was data item x freshly created? Or was x produced by combining trustworthy data items y and z? Are y and z related, e.g. derived from disjoint sources?*

Provenance and Expressivity: Examples. Several languages can be used to express properties of the history of resources or events. In the area of databases, for example, provenance query languages have been studied for a long time, giving rise to variations of SQL and languages for graphs (see e.g. [3,5,6,16] and the references therein). In this paper we take a different perspective based on models and techniques from the area of concurrency theory. From now on, we will talk about resources without the implication that we focus on data items or that we rule out events. We will start illustrating some basic choices for a provenance query language based on well-known models from concurrency theory with the examples of Fig. 1. The figure illustrates four different configurations, where resources $r_1, r_2, \{r_1, r_2\} \ldots$ are annotated with their atomic observable properties $(a, b, c, \ldots)$, and are related to each other with arrows ($r \to r'$ denotes that r is a direct ancestor of r').

Four natural options for a provenance query language arise if one considers histories as *sets*, *strings*, *trees*, or *graphs* over the observable properties. Typically, those options would provide an increasing observation power: a string language would allow to observe the *order* of properties in the history, a tree language would in addition allow to observe the *merging* of resources, and a graph-based language would in addition allow to observe the *forking* of resources, and in general the entire structure of the history. To illustrate this, assume a scenario where the observable properties $a, b, c \ldots$ of resources denote the agents that created the resources, respectively Alice, Bob, Charlie, ... In such scenario, examples of provenance properties in the above mentioned cases could be:

(P1) *Was the resource of interest influenced by Alice, Bob, Charlie, and Dave?*

(P2) *Was the resource of interest created by Alice and influenced by Charlie through Bob or by Dave through Bob?*

(P3) *Was the resource of interest created by Alice and influenced by resources created by Charlie and Dave that then Bob combined?*

(P4) *Was the resource of interest created by Alice and influenced by resources created by Bob, which in turn depended on the same resource created by Charlie?*

Let us now illustrate the effect of the expressive power of the provenance language on a concrete example, namely the history of r_6 in the configurations in Fig. 1. An example of a set-based language would be a specification language to check atomic observables of r_6 and its entire genealogy (its direct and indirect ancestors). In this case, the observable history of r_6 would be the same in all four configurations. Indeed we could see C_4 as the minimised history of r_6 in C_1–C_3, where all ancestors have been collapsed into r_6. Examples of string-based languages could be based on any language to check the linear histories of resources (from the resource backwards through ancestors), for example based on regular expressions or linear-time logic (LTL) over sets of observables. In this case, the observable history of r_6 would be the same in C_1–C_3 (i.e. the set of strings $\{\{a\}\{b\}\{c\}, \{a\}\{b\}\{d\}\}$) but different in C_4 (i.e. the set of strings $\{\{a, b, c\}\}$). Similarly as before we could see C_3 as the minimised history of r_6 in C_1–C_2, where resources r_1, r_2 and r_4, r_5 have been collapsed. An example of a tree language could be computation-tree logic (CTL), interpreted on the transition system obtained from the (backwards) reachable subgraph starting from the resource of interest. In this case, C_1–C_2 would be indistiguishable but distinguishable from C_3, essentially since r_4 and r_5 have different dependencies. Similarly as before we could see C_2 as the minimised history of r_6 in C_1, where resources r_1, r_2 have been collapsed. Finally, we could decide to observe the full graphical structure of the history. In that case, all four configurations would be distinguishable and there would be no room for reductions.

Reductions, Distribution and Incrementality. As we have seen, the choice of the provenance language implicitly induces a notion of abstract history. Such abstraction can be exploited to reduce concrete histories, i.e. represent them in a more compact way. For example, C_1 in Fig. 1 can be reduced to C_2 if we consider computation trees up to bisimulation, to C_3 if we consider linear histories (trace equivalence), and C_4 if we are interested just in the set of reachable properties. In many scenarios such configurations are continuously growing as new resources or events are added. Being able to build new reduced histories *incrementally* is desirable for the sake of scalability. As an orthogonal aspect, it may not be feasible or desirable in some situations to implement configurations as *global* structures. It may indeed be convenient or even mandatory to implement them as a *distributed* structure, which, on the other hand, may pose challenges in terms of communication or performance when checking provenance properties. Distributing local histories can help address some of those issues. Figures 2, 3 and 4 illustrate distributed representations of the local histories (based on trees,

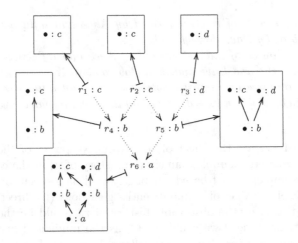

Fig. 2. Distributed configurations with minimised tree-based histories

strings and sets, respectively) for configuration C_1 of Fig. 1. In the figures, each resource is mapped via $\mapsto$ arrows to its local history (enclosed in a square box).

Research Questions and Contribution. The main research question under consideration in this paper is: *Can we define a framework that is parametric with respect to the provenance-specification language $\mathcal{L}$ and that allows us to distribute and compress the history of resources in way that is (1) sound and complete w.r.t. to $\mathcal{L}$; and (2) incremental, i.e. possibly exploiting the already computed compressed histories?* We answer to the above research question by investigating this problem in a simple model of computation where new resources (with their dependencies) can be added, and can be subject to provenance queries (Sect. 2). We present in Sect. 3 a framework for history distribution and incremental reduction that is parametric with respect to the actual provenance specification language $\mathcal{L}$, and we study in Sect. 4 several choices for $\mathcal{L}$, and the corresponding provenance-preserving history reduction techniques. Section 5 concludes the paper.

A Tribute to Rocco De Nicola. This paper is a contribution to the Festschrift that celebrates Rocco De Nicola's 65th birthday. I have had the pleasure and the honour to work closely with Rocco for several years, an experience that has inspired both my professional career and my personal life. This paper contains several elements related to Rocco's scientific contribution to models, languages and applications of concurrency theory. First, the model of programmable configurations in Sect. 2 has been inspired by coordination models investigated by Rocco (see [9] for a survey of Rocco's work in this field), in particular locality-centred process calculi [8] and attribute-based interactions [2,11]. Such works have motivated me to look for an unconventional model of coordination, based on provenance. Second, the consideration of modal logics as provenance languages, and history reductions based on semantic equivalences relate to Rocco's contributions to those fields [7,10,12–14]. Even if Sect. 4 does not directly apply Rocco's own contributions, his search for generalisations and establishing relations between semantic equivalences and logics have motivated the search for a general framework (Sect. 3) where different semantic notions of provenance could fit. Last, the application domain of information security is very dear to Rocco and has been present in his work in several occasions, from the access and information flow control features of KLAIM [8] to his white paper on the future of Cybersecurity in Italy [18].

2 A Simple Model of Programmable Global Configurations

Configurations. Let $\mathcal{R}$ denote a universe of resource identifiers (resources, for short) that we range over by $r, r_1, \ldots$. A *(global) configuration* in our model is essentially a directed acyclic graph with resources as nodes. Resources have associated values in some domain $\mathcal{V}$ and are labelled over a set Σ of atomic observable properties on those values, through a function $\pi : \mathcal{V} \to 2^\Sigma$.

Definition 1 (configuration). *A configuration is a tuple $\langle R, v, L, < \rangle$ where R is the set of nodes/resources, $v : R \to \mathcal{V}$ is a mapping of resources to their actual values, $L : R \to 2^\Sigma$ is a mapping of resources to observable properties, $< \subseteq R \times R$ is the set of edges/dependencies, and such that $<$ is acyclic.*

Figure 1 illustrates four configurations, where values are not included. We denote the set of all configurations by $\mathcal{C}$. For a configuration C we will often use R, v, L, and $<$, assuming implicitly that $C = \langle R, v, L, < \rangle$ when clear from the context. Note that $r < r'$ is illustrated as an edge $r \to r'$. Function $pre_C^* : R \to 2^R$ denotes the genealogy of a resource in C (its direct and indirect ancestors, including itself), i.e. $pre_C^*(r) = \{r' \in R \mid r' = r \text{ or } \exists r'' \in R.r'' < r \land r' \in pre_C^*(r'')\}$. With $C_{|r}$ we will denote the sub-configuration of C formed just by r and its predecessors (i.e. the subgraph of $<$ backwards-reachable from r), formally $C_{|r} = \langle pre_C^*(r), v_{|pre_C^*(r)}, L_{|pre_C^*(r)}, <_{|r} \rangle$ such that $r' <_{|r} r''$ iff $r' < r''$ and $\{r', r''\} \subseteq pre_C^*(r)$.

Provenance Properties. We use $\mathcal{L}$ to denote the provenance specification language, and $\phi \in \mathcal{L}$ to range over provenance properties. Given a configuration $C = \langle R, v, L, < \rangle$ and a resource r, we use $r, C \models \phi$ to denote that r satisfies ϕ in C. The actual semantics of $\models$ depends on the choice of $\mathcal{L}$. For a query language $\mathcal{L}$ we will consider satisfaction relations $\models \subseteq \mathcal{M} \times \mathcal{L}$ for several model domains beyond $\mathcal{R} \times \mathcal{C}$. For two model domains $\mathcal{M}_1$ and $\mathcal{M}_2$, the relation $\equiv_\mathcal{L} \subseteq \mathcal{M}_1 \times \mathcal{M}_2$ is defined in the usual way, i.e. $M_1 \equiv_\mathcal{L} M_2$ whenever for all $\phi \in \mathcal{L}$ we have that $M_1 \models \phi$ iff $M_2 \models \phi$. We restrict to our attention to languages $\mathcal{L}$ that are able to observe atomic properties, and not actual values. The actual information observable on resources is defined by function π, that can be understood as a privacy-protecting function, hiding actual information about resources and just exposing information needed to assess their integrity.

Global Computations. Computations in our model of *programmable configurations* are of the form

$$C \xrightarrow{\lambda \triangleright \rho} C'$$

denoting that configuration C reacts to action λ by transforming into C' and producing ρ.

We consider first a simple model of *internal* computations with two actions out and rd, respectively used to add fresh resources (and their explicit dependencies), and to retrieve them with provenance-based queries.

More in detail, a computation based on action $\mathsf{out}(R' < u)$ adds a fresh resource r with value u, and dependencies on a subset $R' \subseteq R$ of the current set of resources R.

$$\frac{r \notin R \qquad R' \subseteq R}{\langle R, v, L, < \rangle \xrightarrow{\mathsf{out}(R' < u) \triangleright r} \langle R \cup \{r\}, v \cup \{v \mapsto u\}, L \cup \{r \mapsto \pi(u)\}, < \cup \bigcup_{r' \in R'} \{r' < r\}\rangle}$$

Computations based on rd actions return a resource r whose history satisfies the provenance property ϕ, provided one such resource exists:

$$\frac{r \in R \qquad r, \langle R, v, L, < \rangle \models \phi}{\langle R, v, L, < \rangle \xrightarrow{\mathsf{rd}(\phi) \triangleright r} \langle R, v, L, < \rangle}$$

Internal computations expose actual resources as part of the interactions and demand causal dependencies to be specified *explicitly*. In many situations resources need to be hidden, and causal dependencies need to be *implicitly* computed. To deal with this we introduce *external* computations in our model of programmable configurations with two actions: put and get.

In particular, $\mathsf{put}(f(\phi_1, .., \phi_n))$ is an action that, given a function $f : \mathcal{V}^* \to \mathcal{V}$ and n provenance formulas $\phi_1, .., \phi_n$ adds a new resource obtained by applying f to the values of resources $r_1, .., r_n$, respectively satisfying $\phi_1, .., \phi_n$ and storing the corresponding dependencies. Such operation can be easily defined as a combination of internal computations:

$$\frac{C \xrightarrow{\mathsf{rd}(\phi_i) \triangleright r_i} C \text{ for } i \in \{1, .., n\} \qquad C \xrightarrow{\mathsf{out}(\{r_1, .., r_n\} < f(v(r_i), .., v(r_n))) \triangleright r} C'}{C \xrightarrow{\mathsf{put}(f(\phi_1, .., \phi_n)) \triangleright f(v(r_i), .., v(r_n))} C'}$$

The query operation is very much like rd but it returns the value of the resource instead of the resource identifier itself:

$$\frac{C \xrightarrow{\mathsf{rd}(\phi) \triangleright r} C}{C \xrightarrow{\mathsf{query}(\phi) \triangleright v(r)} C}$$

3   Distributed Configurations with Abstract Histories

We now introduce *distributed configurations* where the history of each resource is localised and possibly reduced into some abstract history, from a domain $\mathcal{H}$ of abstract histories, for which the satisfaction relation $\models\,\subseteq\mathcal{H}\times\mathcal{L}$ is defined.

Definition 2 (distributed configurations). *A* distributed configuration *is a tuple* $\langle R, v, L, h\rangle$ *where R is a set of resources, $v : R \to \mathcal{V}$ is a mapping of resources to their actual values, $L : R \to 2^{\Sigma}$ maps resources into their observable properties, and $h : R \to \mathcal{H}$ is a function that maps each resource to its own abstract history.*

Figures 2, 3 and 4 illustrate three examples of distributed configurations where, respectively, the domain of abstract histories are (implicitly) trees, strings, and sets of atomic properties, as we shall explain in detail in Sect. 4. Abstract histories are enclosed in square boxes, and the mapping h is denoted with $\mapsto$ arrows. Dotted arrows are used to represent the original dependencies. We denote the set of all distributed configurations by $\mathcal{D}$.

Let $\alpha : \mathcal{R} \times \mathcal{C} \to \mathcal{H}$ be a function that maps concrete histories (i.e. pairs of resources and configurations) into abstract histories. We say that α is $\mathcal{L}$-*preserving* if and only if for all configurations $C = \langle R, v, L, <\rangle \in \mathcal{C}$, all resources $r \in R$ it holds $r, C \equiv_{\mathcal{L}} \alpha(r, C)$. We will assume that all languages $\mathcal{L}$ of interest are such that $r, C \equiv_{\mathcal{L}} r, C_{|r}$, i.e. their formulas allow to observe just the history of events.

History abstraction functions can be lifted to a mapping from global configurations to distributed configurations.

Definition 3 (history distribution function). *Let $C = \langle R, v, L, <\rangle$ be a configuration and $\alpha : 2^{\mathcal{R}\times\mathcal{R}} \to \mathcal{H}$ be a history abstraction function. Then, $\alpha(C)$ is the distributed configuration* $\langle R, v, L, \{r \mapsto \alpha(r, C_{|r}) \mid r \in R\}\rangle$.

Note that for the trivial case when $\mathcal{H}$ is $\mathcal{R} \times \mathcal{C}$, there is a trivial choice for α, namely the function $\lambda r, C = (\{r\}, C_{|r})$ that would map each resource to just own history. Other, more interesting cases could be mapping each resource into a Σ-labelled transition system, finite-state automaton over Σ or just a subset of Σ, as suggested in Figs. 2, 3 and 4, respectively. These cases will be discussed in detail in Sect. 4.

Another component of our framework are *history update functions* of the form $\oplus : \mathcal{R} \times 2^{\Sigma} \times 2^{\mathcal{H}} \to \mathcal{H}$. These are functions that, given a resource r, its observations A, and a set H of abstract histories (typically, the direct ancestors of r), produce an abstract history for r.

We say that $\oplus$ *is $\mathcal{L}$-preserving for α* if and only if for all configurations $C = \langle R, c, L, <\rangle \in \mathcal{C}$, all resources $r \in R$ and all provenance formulas $\phi \in \mathcal{L}$ it holds

$$\alpha(r, C_{|r}) \equiv_{\mathcal{L}} (r, L(r)) \oplus \{\alpha(r', C_{|r'}) \mid r' < r\}$$

that is, abstract histories obtained globally are $\mathcal{L}$-equivalent to abstract histories computed incrementally with $\oplus$.

Distributed Computations. The semantics for distributed configurations is similar to that of global configurations, but based on local histories. In particular, a adding resource with out is now defined by rule

$$\dfrac{r \notin R \qquad R' \subseteq R}{\langle R, v, L, h \rangle \xrightarrow{\;\mathsf{out}(R' < u) \rhd r\;} \langle R \cup \{r\}, v \cup \{r \mapsto u\}, L \cup \{r \mapsto \pi(u)\}, h \cup \{r \mapsto (r, \pi(u)) \oplus \bigcup_{r' \in R'} h(r')\} \rangle}$$

In words: a configuration is enriched by adding a fresh resource r and computing its local, abstract history incrementally, based on the local, abstract history of its ancestors. Note that the computation is not entirely decentralised, as the preconditions still require global information, but part of that information (set R') is in any case required to compute the history of r incrementally.

Internal queries, instead, rely only on local information:

$$\dfrac{r \in R \qquad h(r) \models \phi}{\langle R, v, L, h \rangle \xrightarrow{\;\mathsf{rd}(\phi) \rhd r\;} \langle R, v, L, h \rangle}$$

External computations with put and query are defined using the same combinations of rd and out operations with rules

$$\dfrac{D \xrightarrow{\;\mathsf{rd}(\phi_i) \rhd r_i\;} D \text{ for } i \in \{1, .., n\} \qquad D \xrightarrow{\;\mathsf{out}(r_1, .., r_n < f(v(r_i), .., v(r_n))) \rhd r\;} D'}{D \xrightarrow{\;\mathsf{put}(f(\phi_1, .., \phi_n)) \rhd f(v(r_i), .., v(r_n))\;} D'}$$

and

$$\dfrac{D \xrightarrow{\;\mathsf{rd}(\phi) \rhd r\;} D}{D \xrightarrow{\;\mathsf{query}(\phi) \rhd v(r)\;} D}$$

respectively.

Provenance-Preserving Result. We define now a relation $\approx \; \subseteq \; \mathcal{C} \times \mathcal{D}$ that relates global configurations and distributed configurations over the same set of resources such that the concrete and abstract history of each resource is $\mathcal{L}$-equivalent.

Definition 4 (distribution relation). *The relation* $\approx \; \subseteq \; \mathcal{C} \times \mathcal{D}$ *is the set of all pairs* $(\langle R, v, L, < \rangle, \langle R, v, L, h \rangle)$ *such that* $\forall r \in R.\ r, C \equiv_{\mathcal{L}} h(r)$.

Note that if α is $\mathcal{L}$-preserving then, trivially, $C \approx \alpha(C)$ for all configurations $C \in \mathcal{C}$. The main property of our framework is that, if α is $\mathcal{L}$-preserving and $\oplus$ is $\mathcal{L}$-preserving for α, then $\approx$ is a bisimulation. As a consequence a global configuration C and its distributed version $\alpha(C)$ behave equivalently.

Theorem 1 (bisimilar distribution). *Let* α *be a history reduction function and* $\oplus$ *be a history update function such that (i)* α *is* $\mathcal{L}$-*preserving and (ii)* $\oplus$ *is* $\mathcal{L}$-*preserving for* α, *then* $\approx$.

Proof Sketch. To prove that $\approx$ is a bisimulation we have to show that for every $C \in \mathcal{C}$ and every $D \in \mathcal{D}$ such that $C \approx D$ the following properties hold:

1. if $C \xrightarrow{\lambda \triangleright r} C'$ then $\exists D' \in \mathcal{D}.D \xrightarrow{\lambda \triangleright r} D'$ and $C' \approx D'$.
2. if $D \xrightarrow{\lambda \triangleright r} D'$ then $\exists C' \in \mathcal{C}.C \xrightarrow{\lambda \triangleright r} C'$ and $C' \approx D'$.

We prove property (1) by considering the cases for λ separately:

$[\lambda = \mathsf{out}(r_1, .., r_n < u)]$ Let $C = \langle R, v, L, < \rangle$. By definition of $\approx$, we know that $D = \langle R, v, L, h \rangle$ for some h such that $\forall r \in R.\ r, C \equiv_\mathcal{L} h(r)$.
The new global configuration

$$C' = \langle R \cup \{r\}, v \cup \{r \mapsto u\}, L \cup \{r \mapsto \pi(u)\}, < \bigcup_{i \in \{1..n\}} \{r_i < r\}\rangle$$

differs from C only in the addition of r, its properties and its dependencies. Clearly D can make the same choice for λ by selecting the same r, thus resulting in

$$D' = \langle R \cup \{r\}, v \cup \{r \mapsto u\}, L \cup \{r \mapsto \pi(u)\}, h \cup \{r \mapsto r \oplus h(r_1), .., h(r_n)\}\rangle$$

To show that $C' \approx D'$ we just need to prove that for the newly added resource r it holds

$$r, C' \equiv_\mathcal{L} (r, L(r)) \oplus h(r_1), .., h(r_n)$$

since the above property holds for all other resources as mentioned above. We proceed as follows:

$$\begin{array}{ll}
r, C' & \\
\equiv_\mathcal{L} & (\mathcal{L} \text{ observes histories only}) \\
r, C'_{|r} & \\
\equiv_\mathcal{L} & (\alpha \text{ is } \mathcal{L}\text{-preserving}) \\
\alpha(r, C'_{|r}) & \\
\equiv_\mathcal{L} & (\oplus \text{ is } \mathcal{L}\text{-preserving for } \alpha) \\
(r, L(r)) \oplus \alpha(r_1, C'_{|r_1}), .., \alpha(r_1, C'_{|r_1}) & \\
\equiv_\mathcal{L} & (C'_{|r_i} = C_{|r_i} \text{ for } i = 1..n) \\
(r, L(r)) \oplus \alpha(r_1, C_{|r_1}), .., \alpha(r_1, C_{|r_1}) & \\
\equiv_\mathcal{L} & (\oplus \text{ is } \mathcal{L}\text{-preserving for } \alpha) \\
(r, L(r)) \oplus h(r_1), .., h(r_n) &
\end{array}$$

We can conclude that $C' \approx D'$.

$[\lambda = \mathsf{rd}(\phi)]$ Note that in this case $C' = C$. From $C \xrightarrow{\mathsf{rd}(\phi) \triangleright r} C$ we know that $r, C \models \phi$. Since $C \approx D$ we know that $r, C \equiv_\mathcal{L} h(r)$ and hence it holds $h(r) \models \phi$. We have thus the computation step $D \xrightarrow{\mathsf{rd}(\phi) \triangleright r} D$. Trivially choosing D' to be D concludes our argument.

$[\lambda = \mathsf{put}(f(\phi_1, .., \phi_n))$ and $\lambda = \mathsf{query}(\phi)]$ These are actually derived operations, obtained by composition of the above two ones.

To prove property (2) we proceed similarly. $\qquad\qquad\qquad\qquad\qquad\qquad \square$

4   Instantiating the Framework

We instantiate the framework in a set of examples, respectively based on interpreting histories as trees (thus observing merging, order, and atomic properties of resources), strings (thus observing order and atomic properties of resources only) and sets (thus just observing atomic properties of resources). Each instance consists of a specific choice for the domain $\mathcal{H}$ of abstract histories, the provenance language $\mathcal{L}$, the history reduction function α, and the incremental history update function $\oplus$. It is not the aim of this section to show the most efficient option for each case or to provide a comprehensive overview of all possibilities. Instead, we aim at illustrating the framework with well-known models computation from the area of concurrency theory and related ones.

4.1   Tree-Based Provenance

As abstract histories we will consider finite trees over Σ, compactly represented as transition systems. We recall that a state-labelled transition system (a Kripke structure) is a tuple $\langle S, I, \rightarrow, AP, M \rangle$ such that S is a set of states, $I \subseteq S$ is set of initial states, $\rightarrow \subseteq S \times S$ is a transition relation, AP is a set of atomic propositions and $M : S \rightarrow AP$ is a mapping from states into subsets of atomic propositions. Transition systems compactly represent trees in the same manner of graphs: the trees of a transition system are obtained by unfolding the transition system.

Let $\mathcal{H}$ be $\mathcal{T}$, the set of all transition systems with resources as states, dependencies as transitions, Σ as atomic propositions and L as state labelling function. In particular, $TS(C, r) = \langle R, \{r\}, <^{-1}, \Sigma, L \rangle$ denotes the transition system representing the history of r in C, where r is the initial state and the transition relation is the inverse of the predecessor relation.[1]

A natural choice for $\mathcal{L}$ is then any logic to predicate over trees in a transition system. We choose CTL for our illustration purposes. For $\phi \in$ CTL we define the satisfaction relation for resources indirectly via a transformation of the history into its transition system representation:

$$r, C \models \phi \text{ iff } TS(C, r) \models \phi$$

In our example, the property (P3) *Was the resource of interest created by Alice and influenced by resources created by Charlie and Dave that then Bob combined?* can be expressed in CTL as $a \wedge \mathbf{EF}(b \wedge \mathbf{EF}c \wedge \mathbf{EF}d)$.

Let $bmin : \mathcal{T} \rightarrow \mathcal{T}$ be a bisimulation-minimisation algorithm that transforms a transition system T into a smallest bisimilar one $bmin(T)$. Let α be defined as $\alpha(r, C) = bmin(TS(r, C_{|r}))$, that is the function that first transforms a history into a transition system and then minimises it. Clearly, α is $\mathcal{L}$-preserving since bisimilar transition systems are CTL-equivalent.

---

[1] Note that we do not introduce self-loop transitions in leaf states/resources. This allows formulae to observe whether a resource has dependencies. Alternatively, loops could have been introduced as usual in CTL semantics. In that case, the ability to observe absence of dependencies can be obtained with a dedicated predicate.

For incremental history construction we define the following function $\oplus$

$$(r, A) \oplus \biguplus_{i \in \{1..n\}} \langle R_i, r_i, \rightarrow_i, \Sigma, L_i \rangle$$
$$= bmin((\{r\} \biguplus_{i \in \{1..n\}} R_i, \{r\}, \biguplus_{i \in \{1..n\}} \{r \rightarrow r_i\} \uplus \rightarrow_i, \Sigma, \{r \mapsto A\} \biguplus_{i \in \{1..n\}} L_i))$$

In words: we first build a new transition system that has r as initial state, and has a transition from r to the initial state r_i of each of the n transitions systems that represent abstract histories (that we assume disjoint to avoid the cumbersome notation of introducing fresh renamings). Such transition system is then minimised. We need to prove that $\oplus$ is CTL-preserving for $bmin$.

Lemma 1. *The incremental history construction function $\oplus$ is CTL-preserving for bmin.*

Proof Sketch. We need to prove

$$bmin(TS(r, C_{|r})) \equiv_{\mathsf{CTL}} (r, L(r)) \oplus \{bmin(TS(r', C_{|r'})) \mid r' < r\}$$

we proceed as follows

$$bmin(TS(r, C_{|r}))$$
$$\equiv_{\mathsf{CTL}} \text{ bisimulation preserves CTL}$$
$$TS(r, C_{|r})$$
$$\equiv_{\mathsf{CTL}} (*)$$
$$(r, L(r)) \oplus \{TS(r', C_{|r'}) \mid r' < r\}$$
$$\equiv_{\mathsf{CTL}} \text{ bisimulation preserves CTL}$$
$$(r, L(r)) \oplus \{bmin(TS(r', C_{|r'})) \mid r' < r\}$$

The main idea behind (*) is that $(r, L(r)) \oplus \{TS(r', C_{|r'}) \mid r' < r\}$ essentially corresponds to an unfolding of $TS(r, C_{|r})$ into a tree-shaped transition system, and that unfolding of transitions systems preserves bisimulation and hence CTL.
□

Instantiating Theorem 1 in the above described setting provides the desired result: if we choose CTL as provenance query language we can distribute and incrementally compute histories without loosing information by resorting to bisimulation minimisation algorithms. Figure 2 illustrates a distributed representation of the transition system based local histories for configuration C_1 of Fig. 1. In the figure, the initial state of each transition system is its unique root.

4.2   Linear Provenance

We consider now abstract histories as sets of finite strings over 2^Σ. A natural way to compactly represent a set of strings is with a non-deterministic finite automaton (NFA). Recall that an NFA is a tuple $\langle Q, q_0, F, A, \rightarrow \rangle$, where Q is a set of states, $q_0 \in Q$ is an initial state, $F \subseteq Q$ is a final set of states, A is

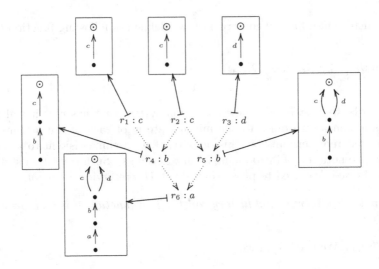

Fig. 3. Distributed configurations with minimised string-based histories

an alphabet of symbols, and $\to\,\subseteq 2^{S\times\Sigma\times S}$ is a transition relation. Let us denote with $\mathfrak{L}(B)$ the language of the NFA B.

In particular, for a configuration C and a resource r, its abstract history can be defined as the automaton $NFA(C, r) = \langle R \uplus \circ, r, \{\circ\}, 2^{\Sigma}, \to\rangle$ where $\to$ is the set of transitions $\{r' \xrightarrow{L(r')} r'' \mid r'' < r'\} \cup \{r' \xrightarrow{L(r')} \circ \mid \neg\exists r''.r'' < r'\}$. In words, the set of states of the automaton are the resources of C plus the unique final state $\circ$, and transitions correspond to the observable properties in the departing resource of the transition.

Let $\mathcal{A}$ denote the set of all such NFAs and let $\mathcal{H}$ be $\mathcal{A}$. A natural choice for $\mathcal{L}$ is then any language for finite strings, for example regular expressions. For a regular expression ϕ we define the satisfaction relation for resources indirectly via a transformation of the history into its NFA representation:

$$r, C \models \phi \text{ iff } \mathfrak{L}(NFA(C, r)) \subseteq \mathfrak{L}(\phi)$$

in words, the history of a resource r in C satisfies the property ϕ if, for each original ancestor r', the path from r to r' is accepted by ϕ.

In our example, the property (P2) *Was the resource of interest created by Alice and influenced by Charlie through Bob, or by Dave through Bob?* can be formalised by the regular expression $\{a\}(.^*\{b\}.^*\{c\} + .^*\{b\}.^*\{d\})$.

Let $min : \mathcal{A} \to \mathcal{A}$ be an NFA minimisation algorithm that transforms an NFA into the smallest NFA accepting the same language. Let α be defined as $\alpha(r, C) = min(NFA(r, C_{|r}))$, that is the function that first translates a concrete history into an NFA and then minimises it. Clearly, α is $\mathcal{L}$-preserving since NFA minimisation preserve regular language equivalence.

For incremental history construction we define the following function $\oplus$.

$$r \oplus \uplus_{i \in \{1..n\}} \langle R_i, r_i, \rightarrow_i, \Sigma, L \rangle$$
$$= min(\langle \{r\} \uplus_{i \in \{1..n\}} R_i, r_i, \uplus_{i \in \{1..n\}} \{r \rightarrow r_i\} \uplus \rightarrow_i, \Sigma, L \rangle)$$

In words: we first build an NFA that has r as initial state, and has a transition from r to the initial state r_i of each of the n NFAs that represent abstract histories. The resulting NFA is then minimised with min. Proving that $\oplus$ is $\mathcal{L}$-preserving for α can be done along the lines of Lemma 1.

Instantiating Theorem 1 allows us to use a provenance query language based NFA so to distribute and incrementally compute reduced histories based on NFA minimisation, without loosing information. Figure 3 illustrates a distributed representation of the NFA-based local history for configuration C_1 of Fig. 1. In the figure, the initial state of each automaton is its unique root.

4.3   Set-Based Provenance

Let $\mathcal{H}$ be 2^{Σ}, i.e. abstract histories are just subsets of Σ representing which properties the resource has or has been influenced by. For a configuration C and a resource r we can interpret the history of r with the following function inf to compute the influencing properties of r:

$$inf(r, C) = L(r) \odot \{inf(r') \mid r' < r\}$$

The function is parametric on a function $\odot$ to combine properties of resources with the influencing properties of its ancestors. Taking $h \odot H$ to be $h \cup \bigcup H$ would provide all properties that r *or any* of its ancestors has. If instead we take $h \odot H$ to be $h \cap \bigcap H$ we would consider the influencing properties as those that r *and all* of its ancestors have.

A natural choice for the provenance language $\mathcal{L}$ could be just propositional logic over Σ

$$r, C \models \phi \text{ iff } inf(r) \models \phi$$

The example property (P1) *Was the resource of interest influenced by Alice, Bob, Charlie, and Dave?* would be just the proposition $a \wedge b \wedge c \wedge d$.

We can now do two trivial choices for α and $\otimes$. First, let α be the function inf, which is trivially $\mathcal{L}$-preserving. Second, the incremental history construction function $\oplus$ is defined based on $\otimes$:

$$r \oplus \{A_1, .., A_n\} = L(r) \cdot \{A_1, .., A_n\}$$

which can easily be show to be $\mathcal{L}$-preserving for α. We can then instantiate Theorem 1 to obtain the desired result: we can distribute and incrementally compute histories on the above described mechanism without loosing information. Figure 4 illustrates a distributed representation of the local histories for configuration C_1 of Fig. 1, where $\cdot$ is based on set union.

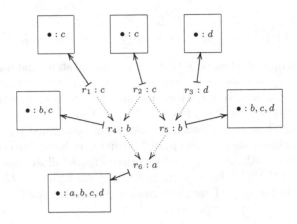

Fig. 4. Distributed configurations set-based histories

5 Conclusion

We have presented a basic framework to support provenance-based computations, with incremental history distribution and reduction. The main components of the framework are an abstract domain of histories $\mathcal{H}$, a provenance specification language $\mathcal{L}$, and two functions: α for history reduction, and $\oplus$ for incremental history construction, that are required to be sound and complete with respect to $\mathcal{L}$. We have illustrated the framework with a basic model of programmable configurations, and notions of abstract histories based on well-understood models of computation and information flow.

The approach we have presented can lead to deeper investigations in the future. First, in the examples we have used to illustrate our approach we have not considered efficiency as an issue. Efficient algorithms for minimisation of histories that exploit their acyclic structure could be to be identified. For example, in the case of bisimulations a partition refinement algorithm based on [17] could easily exploit the acyclic structure in the strategy to select the candidate partitions subject to a partition check. The basic model of computation we have used to illustrate the approach could lead to novel coordination languages, taking inspiration from locality-centred [8] and provenance-tracking [4] coordination languages, one could design a provenance-oriented coordination language where interactions depended on provenance properties. An interesting variant of the instances we have seen could be to consider histories up to stuttering. In the case of computation trees and bisimulations we could consider the corresponding notions of stuttering bisimulation minimisation algorithms [14,15]. For linear provenance, it would be also interesting to investigate provenance queries based on testing equivalences [1,10] or LTL variants.

References

1. Aceto, L., De Nicola, R., Fantechi, A.: Testing equivalences for event structures. In: Zilli, M.V. (ed.) Mathematical Models for the Semantics of Parallelism. LNCS, vol. 280, pp. 1–20. Springer, Heidelberg (1987). https://doi.org/10.1007/3-540-18419-8_9

2. Abd Alrahman, Y., De Nicola, R., Loreti, M.: On the power of attribute-based communication. In: Albert, E., Lanese, I. (eds.) FORTE 2016. LNCS, vol. 9688, pp. 1–18. Springer, Cham (2016). https://doi.org/10.1007/978-3-319-39570-8_1

3. Altintas, I., Wang, J., Crawl, D., Li, W.: Challenges and approaches for distributed workflow-driven analysis of large-scale biological data: vision paper. In: Srivastava, D., Ari, I. (eds.) Proceedings of the 2012 Joint EDBT/ICDT Workshops, Berlin, Germany, 30 March 2012, pp. 73–78. ACM (2012). https://doi.org/10.1145/2320765.2320791

4. Bodei, C., Degano, P., Ferrari, G.L., Galletta, L.: Tracing where IoT data are collected and aggregated. Log. Methods Comput. Sci. **13**(3) (2017). https://doi.org/10.23638/LMCS-13(3:5)2017

5. Chavan, A., Huang, S., Deshpande, A., Elmore, A.J., Madden, S., Parameswaran, A.G.: Towards a unified query language for provenance and versioning. In: Missier, P., Zhao, J. (eds.) 7th USENIX Workshop on the Theory and Practice of Provenance, TaPP 2015, Edinburgh, Scotland, UK, 8–9 July 2015. USENIX Association (2015). https://www.usenix.org/conference/tapp15/workshop-program/presentation/chavan

6. Davidson, S.B., Freire, J.: Provenance and scientific workflows: challenges and opportunities. In: Wang, J.T. (ed.) Proceedings of the ACM SIGMOD International Conference on Management of Data, SIGMOD 2008, Vancouver, BC, Canada, 10–12 June 2008, pp. 1345–1350. ACM (2008). https://doi.org/10.1145/1376616.1376772

7. De Nicola, R.: Extensional equivalences for transition systems. Acta Inf. **24**(2), 211–237 (1987). https://doi.org/10.1007/BF00264365

8. De Nicola, R., Ferrari, G.L., Pugliese, R.: KLAIM: a kernel language for agents interaction and mobility. IEEE Trans. Softw. Eng. **24**(5), 315–330 (1998). https://doi.org/10.1109/32.685256

9. De Nicola, R., Ferrari, G.L., Pugliese, R., Tiezzi, F.: A formal approach to the engineering of domain-specific distributed systems. In: Serugendo, G.D.M., Loreti, M. (eds.) COORDINATION 2018. LNCS, vol. 10852, pp. 110–141. Springer, Cham (2018). https://doi.org/10.1007/978-3-319-92408-3_5

10. De Nicola, R., Hennessy, M.: Testing equivalences for processes. Theor. Comput. Sci. **34**, 83–133 (1984). https://doi.org/10.1016/0304-3975(84)90113-0

11. De Nicola, R., Loreti, M., Pugliese, R., Tiezzi, F.: A formal approach to autonomic systems programming: the SCEL language. TAAS **9**(2), 7:1–7:29 (2014). https://doi.org/10.1145/2619998

12. De Nicola, R., Montanari, U., Vaandrager, F.: Back and forth bisimulations. In: Baeten, J.C.M., Klop, J.W. (eds.) CONCUR 1990. LNCS, vol. 458, pp. 152–165. Springer, Heidelberg (1990). https://doi.org/10.1007/BFb0039058

13. De Nicola, R., Vaandrager, F.: Action versus state based logics for transition systems. In: Guessarian, I. (ed.) LITP 1990. LNCS, vol. 469, pp. 407–419. Springer, Heidelberg (1990). https://doi.org/10.1007/3-540-53479-2_17

14. De Nicola, R., Vaandrager, F.W.: Three logics for branching bisimulation. J. ACM **42**(2), 458–487 (1995). https://doi.org/10.1145/201019.201032

15. Groote, J.F., Vaandrager, F.: An efficient algorithm for branching bisimulation and stuttering equivalence. In: Paterson, M.S. (ed.) ICALP 1990. LNCS, vol. 443, pp. 626–638. Springer, Heidelberg (1990). https://doi.org/10.1007/BFb0032063
16. Holland, D.A., Braun, U.J., Maclean, D., Muniswamy-Reddy, K.K., Seltzer, M.I.: Choosing a data model and query language for provenance. In: Freire, J., Koop, D. (eds.) IPAW 2008. LNCS, vol. 5272. Springer, Heidelberg (2008)
17. Paige, R., Tarjan, R.E.: Three partition refinement algorithms. SIAM J. Comput. 16(6), 973–989 (1987). https://doi.org/10.1137/0216062
18. Baldoni, R., De Nicola, R., Prinetto, P.: The future of cybersecurity in Italy: strategic focus areas. Laboratorio Nazionale di Cybersecurity, CINI - Consorzio Interuniversitario Nazionale per l'Informatica (2018). https://www.consorzio-cini.it/index.php/it/labcs-home/libro-bianco

Utility-Preserving Privacy Mechanisms for Counting Queries

Natasha Fernandes[1], Kacem Lefki[2], and Catuscia Palamidessi[1(✉)]

[1] Inria, Palaiseau, France
`catuscia@lix.polytechnique.fr`
[2] University of Paris Saclay, Orsay, France

Abstract. Differential privacy (DP) and local differential privacy (LPD) are frameworks to protect sensitive information in data collections. They are both based on obfuscation. In DP the noise is added to the result of queries on the dataset, whereas in LPD the noise is added directly on the individual records, before being collected. The main advantage of LPD with respect to DP is that it does not need to assume a trusted third party. The main disadvantage is that the trade-off between privacy and utility is usually worse than in DP, and typically to retrieve reasonably good statistics from the locally sanitized data it is necessary to have a huge collection of them. In this paper, we focus on the problem of estimating counting queries from collections of noisy answers, and we propose a variant of LDP based on the addition of geometric noise. Our main result is that the geometric noise has a better statistical utility than other LPD mechanisms from the literature.

1 Introduction

With the ever-increasing use of internet-connected devices, personal data are collected in larger and larger amounts, and then stored and manipulated for the most diverse purposes. Undeniably, the big-data technology provides enormous benefits to industry, individuals and society. On the other hand, however, the collection and manipulation of personal data raises alarming privacy issues. Not surprisingly, therefore, the investigation of mechanisms to protect privacy has become a very active field of research.

Differential privacy (DP) [3] and local differential privacy (LDP) [2] represent the cutting-edge of research on privacy. DP aims at protecting the individuals' data while allowing to answer queries on the aggregate information, and it achieves this goal by adding controlled noise to the query outcome. LDP is a distributed variant in which the data are sanitized at the user's end before being collected. One of the main reason of their success is that DP and LPD are *compositional*, i.e., robust to attacks based on combining the information from different sources. Furthermore LPD has the additional advantage that there is no need to assume that the entities collecting and storing data are trusted, because they can only see, stock and analyze the already sanitized data.

© Springer Nature Switzerland AG 2019
M. Boreale et al. (Eds.): De Nicola-Festschrift, LNCS 11665, pp. 487–495, 2019.
https://doi.org/10.1007/978-3-030-21485-2_27

LDP is having a considerable impact, especially now that large companies such as Apple and Google have adopted it for collecting their customers's data for statistical purposes.

In this paper we consider the problem of *statistical utility*, namely how precisely can we retrieve the original distribution from the collection of noisy data. Reconstruct the original distribution is important in order to make precise statistical analyses.

The notion of d-privacy has been advocated in a recent work [1] as a variant of LDP able to provide a good trade-off between privacy and statistical utility. In this paper, we consider a particular d-private mechanism: the geometric noise distribution. We explore its properties and we show that indeed, in terms of trade-off privacy-utility, it compares favorably to the typical LPD mechanism, the k-Randomized-Responses (kRR) [2].

2   Preliminaries

In this section we recall some basic notions. We will consider only finite sets and discrete mechanisms. Given a set $\mathcal{X}$, a probability distribution p on $\mathcal{X}$ is a function $p : \mathcal{X} \to \mathbb{R}$ such that $\forall x \in \mathcal{X}\, p(x) \geq 0$ and $\sum_x p(x) = 1$. We denote by $Distr(\mathcal{X})$ the set of all possible distributions on $\mathcal{X}$. We use p_x to denote $p(x)$.

2.1   Differential Privacy

Let D, D' denote collections of data (datasets), $\mathcal{D}$ the set of all datasets of interest, and let $\sim$ represent the *adjacency relation* between datasets. Namely, $D \sim D'$ means that D and D' differ only for the value of a single record. Given a query $f : \mathcal{D} \to \mathcal{X}$, a mechanism $\mathcal{K}$ for f is a probabilistic function which, for every D, gives a *reported answer* $y \in \mathcal{Y}$ with a certain probability distribution that depends on the *true answer* to the query. Let $P[\mathcal{K}(D) = y]$ denote the probability that $\mathcal{K}$ applied to D reports the answer y. We say that $\mathcal{K}$ satisfies ε-DP, where ε is a non-negative real number denoting the level of privacy, if for every pairs of adjacent datasets $D \sim D'$, and for every $y \in \mathcal{Y}$, we have:

$$P[\mathcal{K}(D) = y] \leq e^{\varepsilon}\, P[\mathcal{K}(D') = y]. \tag{1}$$

2.2   Local Differential Privacy and Randomized Responses

In LDP the idea is that the mechanism obfuscates directly the value of the data rather than the answer to a query. In this setting, let $\mathcal{X}$ denote the set of all possible values for the data. A mechanism $\mathcal{K}$ is a probabilistic function which, for every $x \in \mathcal{X}$, returns a *reported value* $y \in \mathcal{X}$ with a certain probability distribution that depends on the *true value* x. Let $P[\mathcal{K}(x) = y]$ be the probability that $\mathcal{K}$ applied to x reports y. $\mathcal{K}$ provides ε-LPD if for all $x, x', y \in \mathcal{X}$ we have:

$$P[\mathcal{K}(x) = y] \leq e^{\varepsilon}\, P[\mathcal{K}(x') = y]. \tag{2}$$

A typical mechanism to implement LDP is the Randomized Responses (kRR), where k represents the size of $\mathcal{X}$. In its simplest variant it is defined as follows:

$$P[k\text{RR}(x) = y] = \begin{cases} \frac{e^\varepsilon}{k-1+e^\varepsilon} & y = x \\[2mm] \frac{e^\varepsilon}{k-1+e^\varepsilon} & y \neq x \end{cases} \tag{3}$$

2.3 d-privacy

In d-privacy, like in LDP, mechanism obfuscates directly the value of the data. The main difference is that the domain X is assumed to be a metric space, namely be endowed with a notion of distance $d : \mathcal{X} \times \mathcal{X} \to \mathbb{R}^{\geq 0}$, where $\mathbb{R}^{\geq 0}$ is the set of non-negative real numbers.

A mechanism $\mathcal{K}$ provides ε-d-privacy if for every $x, x', y \in \mathcal{X}$ we have:

$$P[\mathcal{K}(x) = y] \leq e^{\varepsilon\, d(x,x')}\, P[\mathcal{K}(x') = y]. \tag{4}$$

2.4 Generalized Counting Queries

In DP, a counting query is a function $f : \mathcal{D} \to [0, n]$ such that $f(D)$ gives the number of records in D that satisfy a certain property. ($[0, n]$ denotes the set of integers between 0 and n.) In this paper, we will adopt a more general notion of counting query, suitable for LPD. Namely, we assume that $f : \mathcal{X} \to [0, n]$ associates a number $f(x) \in [0, n]$ to each element of $x \in X$. The idea is that each $x \in X$ represents a certain person, and $f(x)$ could return, for example, the age (in years), or the number of children, or the monthly salary (in Euros), etc.

A mechanism $\mathcal{K}$ for f, in this context, associates to each value $i \in [0, n]$ a value $j \in [0, n]$ chosen randomly according to a probability distribution. We denote by C_{ij} the probability that $\mathcal{K}(i) = j$. Note that C_{ij} represent the conditional probability of i given j, hence the values C_{ij} form a stochastic matrix C (where C_{ij} is the element at the intersection of the i-th row and j-th column). From now on for notational simplicity we will use C rather than $\mathcal{K}$.

2.5 Geometric Mechanism

In the following, for simplicity we use α to indicate $e^{-\varepsilon}$, where ε is the level of privacy. Note that $0 < \alpha \leq 1$. The geometric mechanism (for a counting query) is represented by an infinite matrix C with rows indexed by $[0, n]$ and columns indexed by $\mathbb{Z}$ (the set of integers), and whose elements are given by:

$$C_{ij} = \frac{1 - \alpha}{\alpha}^{|i-j|} \tag{5}$$

In order to avoid dealing with an infinite output domain, we consider the *truncated* version of a mechanism. The idea is that the probability mass of the negative element is *remapped* in 0, and the probability mass of the elements greater than n is *remapped* in n. The *truncated geometric mechanism* will be denoted by G and it is defined as:

$$
G_{ij} = \begin{cases} \frac{1}{1+\alpha}\alpha^i & j = 0 \\ \frac{1-\alpha}{1+\alpha}\alpha^{|i-j|} & 0 < j < n \\ \frac{1}{1+\alpha}\alpha^{|i-n|} & j = n \end{cases}
\tag{6}
$$

The truncated geometric is ε-d-private:

Proposition 1. *[4] If $\mathcal{X}$ is the domain $[0,n]$ and d is the difference between integers, then G is a d-private mechanism on $\mathcal{X}$.*

The following is another important property of the truncated geometric:

Proposition 2. *[4] The matrix G is invertible.*

3   Reconstructing the Original Distribution from a Collection of Noisy Data

Assume that we have a collection of N noisy data representing the result of the independent application of the geometric mechanism to the data of a certain population. Each datum (as well as each noisy datum) is a number in $[0,n]$. Let $\pi \in Distr([0,n])$ be the prior distribution on the original data. The set of original data is generated by a sequence of random variables $X_1, X_2, \ldots, X_N$ independent and identically distributed (i.i.d.), according to π. To each of the $X_1, X_2, \ldots, X_N$ we apply the geometric mechanism G, thus obtaining a sequence of random variables $Y_1, Y_2, \ldots, Y_N$. Let $q \in Distr([0,n])$ be the *empirical* distribution determined by $Y_1, Y_2, \ldots, Y_N$. I.e., q_j is obtained by counting the frequencies of the value j in $Y_1, Y_2, \ldots, Y_N$. Namely, $q_j = |\{h | Y_h = i\}|/N$.

The task we consider here is how best to reconstruct the original distribution π from q. To this purpose, we consider the following iterative procedure, which is inspired by the Bayes theorem. In the definition of this procedure, p represents an arbitrary probability distribution with full support.

Definition 1. *Let $\{p^{(k)}\}_k$ be the sequence defined inductively as follows:*

$$p^{(0)} = p$$

$$p_i^{(k+1)} = \sum_j q_j \frac{p_i^{(k)}\alpha^{|i-j|}}{\sum_h p_h^{(k)}\alpha^{|h-j|}}$$

The interest of the above definition relies in the following result:

Theorem 1. *[4] Let $\{p^{(k)}\}_k$ be the sequence of distributions constructed according to Definition 1. Then:*

1. *The sequence converges, i.e., $\lim_{k\to\infty} p^{(k)}$ exists.*
2. *$\lim_{k\to\infty} p^{(k)}$ is the Maximum Likelihood Estimator (MLE) of π given q.*

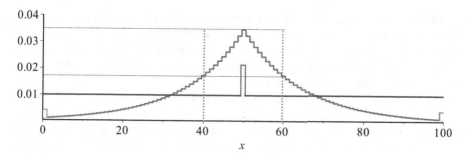

Fig. 1. The distribution generated by the kRR and the truncated geometric mechanisms applied to $x = 50$. The values of the privacy parameters ε's are $\ln 2$ and $\ln 2/10$, respectively.

We will denote by p^* the limit of the sequence $\{p^{(k)}\}_k$, i.e., $p^* \overset{\text{def}}{=} \lim_{k \to \infty} p^{(k)}$. Theorem 1(2) means that for all possible distributions p', the probability that the distribution induced from the noisy data (sanitized with G) is q when the prior is p^* is higher than or equal to the same probability when the prior is p'.

Furthermore, p^* can be characterized using G. For a distribution p and a matrix C, let pC be the product of p and C. Namely, $(pC)_j = \sum_i p_i C_{ij}$.

Proposition 3. *[4] If $r = q\,G^{-1}$ is a probability distribution, then $p^* = r$.*

4   Comparison Between the Geometric and Randomized Response Mechanisms

In this section we compare the truncated geometric and the kRR mechanisms from the point of view of the trade-off between privacy and statistical utility.

In order to make a fair comparison, we first need to calibrate the privacy parameters of these mechanisms so that they represent the same level of privacy. Indeed, although both are expressed in terms of a parameter ε, they do not have the same meaning: the first satisfies ε-d-privacy, while the second satisfies ε-LPD.

To demonstrate, consider the kRR mechanism with parameter $\varepsilon = \ln 2$ operating over integer-valued input and output domains with range $[0, 100]$. The privacy guarantee provided by this mechanism is given by the upper bound $\varepsilon^{\ln 2} = 2$, representing the maximum likelihood ratio between any possible reported value and the true value. This upper bound is realised for every pair of different values in the input and output domains. By comparison, the truncated geometric mechanism with the same $\varepsilon = \ln 2$ would provide such an upper bound 2 only for values immediately adjacent to the true one. For values further away, the bound is smaller (making more distance values less likely). If we want to provide the same upper bound 2 on the entire domain, then we would have to set ε to a value 100 times smaller, namely $\ln 2/100$, which would result in a very flat curve, making the true value almost indistinguishable from a large part of the other values.

However, we argue that it is not necessary to inject so much noise, as this destroys the utility-by-design of the geometric mechanism. As a compromise we will require the upper bound 2 on a restricted subset of elements, for instance those in a radius 10 from the true value. This can be achieved by setting ε to $\ln 2/10$. Figure 1 illustrates the situation.

As for statistical utility, intuitively it should account for how well we can approximate statistics on the original data by using only the collected noisy data. This can be formalized in terms of the distance between the original distribution and the most likely one given the noisy data, which can be estimated by applying the IBU (Definition 1). As for the notion of distance, we propose to use the Kantorovich metric (based on the standard distance between natural numbers as the ground distance). As argued in [1], in fact, this metric is related to a large class of statistical functions. We recall the definition of the Kantorovich distance:

Definition 2. *Let $(\mathcal{X}, d)$ be a metric space and let $\mu, \mu' \in Distr(\mathcal{X})$. The Kantorovich distance based on d between μ and μ' is defined as follows:*

$$K_d(\mu, mu') = \max_{g \in \mathcal{G}} \mid \sum_{x \in \mathcal{X}} g(x)\mu(x) - \sum_{x \in \mathcal{X}} g(x)\mu'(x)$$

where $\mathcal{G}$ is the set of the Lipshitz functions on $\mathcal{X}$, namely $g \in \mathcal{G}$ if and only if $\forall x, x' \in \mathcal{X} \mid f(x) - f(x') \mid \leq d(x, x')$.

4.1 Experimental Results

We now present the results of experiments designed to assess the statistical utility of each of these mechanisms using the IBU method outlined in Sect. 3.

As above, we assume integer-valued inputs and outputs in the range $[0, 100]$. We constructed two different mechanisms to output noisy values: a truncated geometric mechanism parametrised by $\varepsilon = \ln2/10$ and a kRR mechanism parametrised by $\varepsilon = \ln2$.

We ran our experiments on 2 sets of data. The first set consisted of samples of size 1000, 10000, 50000 and 100000 drawn from a binomial distribution. The second set consisted of the same sample sizes drawn from a "4-point" distribution (i.e. a random distribution over 4 'points' in the output range). For each of the 8 samples we conducted 20 experiments using the following method:

1. Obfuscate the sample using each of the (geometric and kRR) mechanisms to produce 2 obfuscated sets.
2. Convert each set into an empirical distribution over outputs using the frequency counts of elements in each set.
3. Run IBU for 5000 iterations over each empirical distribution to compute the maximum likelihood estimate (MLE) for the true distribution.
4. Compare the Kantorovich distance between the MLE and the true distribution as an estimate of the error caused by the obfuscation.

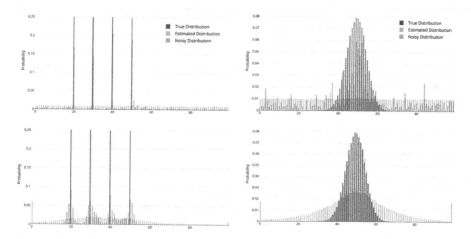

Fig. 2. IBU reconstruction of MLE (orange) distributions from noisy (green) distributions based on 100k samples drawn from '4-point' (left) and binomial (right) distributions. The blue graphs indicate the true distribution. The top distributions were obfuscated by kRR, and the bottom by the geometric mechanism. Reconstruction for the kRR is much better for the point distribution, but the opposite is true for the geometric mechanism. (Color figure online)

In Fig. 2 we present some sample runs of IBU for each mechanism and distribution. Interestingly, the reconstructed distribution for kRR is much better for the '4-point' sample than for the binomial sample. Conversely, the reconstructed distribution for the geometric mechanism is much closer to the binomial sample.

However, the computed Kantorovich distances at the 5000 iteration point for each run tell a different story. These results are shown in Fig. 3. We computed the Kantorovich distance between the estimated distribution and the true distribution, providing an approximation of the distance between the true distribution and the distribution resulting from obfuscation. We can see that the average Kantorovich distances for the geometric mechanism are significantly lower (up to 5 times) than the corresponding distances for the kRR mechanism. We conjecture that this is because the errors caused by kRR are randomly distributed over the entire output space, which directly affects the Kantorovich distance since it depends on the ground distance between points. This means that for statistical applications in which the ground distance is important, the geometric mechanism is still preferred to the kRR mechanism.

Another interesting observation we make is in the convergence rates for the IBU method when applied to the different distributions. This is graphed in Fig. 4. For each iteration of IBU we computed the 'log likelihood' function

$$L(\Theta) = \sum_{y} q_y \log(\Theta \cdot M_y)$$

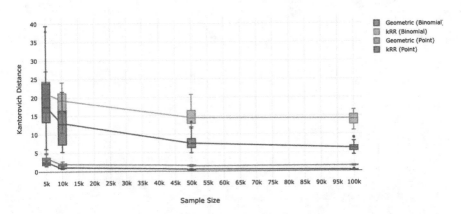

Fig. 3. Kantorovich distances between true and estimated distributions at IBU convergence for the geometric and kRR mechanisms. Distances were computed over 20 experiments for each of the 4 sample sizes indicated. This shows the distributions produced by the geometric mechanism are much closer to the true distribution than for the kRR.

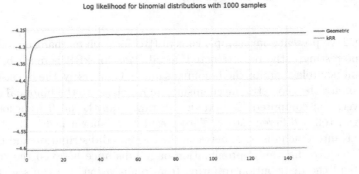

Fig. 4. Log likelihood function against number of iterations for the geometric and kRR mechanisms. This graph shows how fast each output distribution converges to the MLE for one particular (representative) run of the IBU. We observe that the geometric mechanism converges quickly whereas convergence for the kRR is almost flat.

where Θ is the current estimated distribution, q_y is the empirical distribution and M is the mechanism represented as a channel matrix.[1] The log likelihood function indicates how close the current estimate is to the true MLE. The results for one particular run are shown in Fig. 4. We can see that the geometric mechanism converges to a close approximation of the MLE within 10 iterations, whereas the convergence for kRR is linear and almost flat. This may also explain the better performance of the kRR output on the '4-point' sample, since there were far

---

[1] The notation $\Theta \cdot M_y$ indicates the dot product of Θ with the yth column of M.

fewer 'skyscrapers' in the original distribution to estimate. The shape of the geometric mechanism seemed to favour the more 'natural' shape of the binomial distribution sample.

5   Conclusion

In this paper, we have investigated the properties of the truncated geometric mechanism in relation to the reconstruction from noisy data of the original distribution on the real data. We have provided an iterative algorithm to approximate the original distribution, and we have given a characterization of the fixed point in terms of the inverse of the matrix. Finally, we have compared the trade-off between privacy and utility of the truncated geometric mechanism and of the kRRs, obtaining favorable results.

Acknowledgements. The work of Catuscia Palamidessi has been partially supported by the ANR project REPAS.

References

1. Alvim, M.S., Chatzikokolakis, K., Palamidessi, C., Pazii, A.: Local differential privacy on metric spaces: optimizing the trade-off with utility. In: 31st IEEE Computer Security Foundations Symposium, CSF 2018, Oxford, United Kingdom, 9–12 July 2018, pp. 262–267. IEEE Computer Society (2018)
2. Duchi, J.C., Jordan, M.I., Wainwright, M.J.: Local privacy and statistical Minimax rates. In: Proceedings of the 54th Annual IEEE Symposium on Foundations of Computer Science (FOCS), pp. 429–438. IEEE Computer Society (2013)
3. Dwork, C., McSherry, F., Nissim, K., Smith, A.: Calibrating noise to sensitivity in private data analysis. In: Halevi, S., Rabin, T. (eds.) TCC 2006. LNCS, vol. 3876, pp. 265–284. Springer, Heidelberg (2006). https://doi.org/10.1007/11681878_14
4. Kacem, L., Palamidessi, C.: Geometric noise for locally private counting queries. In: Proceedings of the 13th Workshop on Programming Languages and Analysis for Security, PLAS 2018, pp. 13–16. ACM, New York (2018)

Author Index

Printed in the United States
By Bookmasters